THE POLITICS OF TERROR

Erica Chenoweth and Pauline Moore

Oxford University Press is a department of the University of Oxford. It furthers
the University's objective of excellence in research, scholarship, and education
by publishing worldwide. Oxford is a registered trade mark of Oxford University
Press in the UK and certain other countries.

Published in the United States of America by Oxford University Press
198 Madison Avenue, New York, NY 10016, United States of America.

© [2018] by Oxford University Press

Library of Congress Cataloging-in-Publication Data

CIP data on file at the Library of Congress
ISBN: 978-0-19-979566-6

9 8 7 6 5 4 3 2 1

Printed by LSC Communications, United States of America

For those who have suffered
political violence in all of its forms.

BRIEF CONTENTS

CONTENTS

Part II: Explaining Terrorist Behavior

PART III: COUNTERING TERRORISM

ACKNOWLEDGMENTS

Winston Churchill once described writing a book as an adventure, and this one has been no exception. I first want to thank Jennifer Carpenter at Oxford University Press, who first approached me with the idea. In the end, I benefited tremendously from the opportunity to think through a systematic map of the field of terrorism studies, and I am hopeful that the book is useful to anyone trying to better understand terror and political violence more generally. I also thank Jennifer for agreeing to allow Pauline Moore to join the project. Pauline's contributions to this book have produced a much finer result than I could have accomplished on my own. Matthew Rohal and Scott Bledsoe have been extremely helpful during the process as well, and I thank them both.

I must also thank several people whose work on this book was absolutely vital. It is no exaggeration to say that without the diligent help of Allyson Hodges, this project would not have reached its completion. I thank Allyson for her dedication to the work, which included her sorting out the permissions, copyediting the text, formatting references, and contributing to the glossary—all under pressure! I also thank Moe Otaru and Christine Lazcano for their assistance in preparing the glossary.

Additionally, the structure and organization of this book is largely based on courses I have taught at multiple institutions over the years. Because of this, I must acknowledge the many students who have tolerated various drafts of the syllabus out of which this book emerged. Thanks to students who took *Politics of Terrorism* while I taught at Wesleyan University, and thanks to students at the University of Denver who have taken *International Terrorism* since. Several students stand out for special thanks because of their eagerness to continue to talk about and study terrorism and counterterrorism long after the courses ended. These include Joel Day, Elizabeth McClellan, Nicholas Miller, Evan Perkoski, Damian Privitera, Rachel Tecott, and Elizabeth Weisman,.

I also acknowledge many of my intellectual heroes and mentors in this field, including Victor Asal, Mia Bloom, Dan Byman, Audrey Kurth Cronin, Richard English, Page Fortna, John Horgan, Richard Jackson, Gary LaFree, Ami Pedahzur, David Rapoport, Louise Richardson, Jessica Stern, Stephen Walt, Barbara Walter, Leonard Weinberg, and the incomparable Martha Crenshaw. Their pioneering work has inspired much of my continued interest in the field. I am also incredibly lucky to enjoy a supportive network of co-authors and collaborators through the National Consortium for the Study of Terrorism and Responses to Terrorism (START). Special thanks go to Laura Dugan. Besides being one of the smartest and most capable people

I know, Laura has exercised great patience with me as my attentions have been diverted away from our ongoing research collaborations and onto projects like this one. I'm also grateful to Zoe Marks, whose encouragement and enthusiasm helped us to push the book over the finish line.

Next, I am deeply grateful to my colleagues at the University of Denver, who are so supportive, engaging, and encouraging. Special thanks go to my colleagues at the Sie Center, including Deborah Avant, Marie Berry, Rachel Epstein, Cullen Hendrix, Jill Hereau, Oliver Kaplan, Julia Macdonald, Liz McKinney, Tricia Olsen, Tim Sisk, and Rachel Stevens. There is no greater academic team than the one I'm honored to enjoy here at the Korbel School.

I would also like to thank Randall G. Bowdish, Victor J. Hinojosa, Ronald Krebs, Zachariah Mampilly, Paul R. Pillar, Timothy J. Ruback, David A. Siegel, Liubomir K. Topaloff, Joseph K. Young, Rebecca Best, Christopher K. Butler, Donald Haider-Markel, Christine Mele, James Todhunter, Joe Weinberg, Michael Jensen, Jason Ward, Andrea Malji, and Tyler R. White for reviewing and providing invaluable feedback on the proposal and manuscript. Of course, all omissions and errors in the final product remain our own.

Finally, I am deeply grateful to those in my community who keep me afloat. My thanks and love go to Kathe, Angi, Nadia, Courtney, Melody, Sarah, Matt, Tami, Lisa, and all of the others with whom I am honored to walk, shoulder to shoulder, every day. I thank Allison for her love, support, and optimism, as well as Stephanie and Tyler, Elizabeth and Adam, Juniper, Whitney Sue, and Warren for making each day joyful. I am indebted to Andrea, Phil, Christopher, and Miranda for their love and friendship, and I thank my nephews Will and Sam for their wonder and passion for learning. Finally, my unending gratitude goes to my parents Marianne and Richard for instilling in me the values of curiosity and discipline while cheering me on, every step of the way.

Erica Chenoweth
Denver, CO

I did not expect to stumble into writing a book on terrorism during my first year of graduate school. But when an offer to help Erica with the details of an upcoming book project turned into a chance to write it with her, the opportunity was difficult to pass up. I am thankful for her trust in me, and for her continued mentorship. It has been an invaluable experience.

Despite being in the early stages of my academic career, there are still many people to thank for making my contribution to this book possible. I acknowledge especially the vibrant and intellectually engaging environment of the University of Denver's Korbel School, which is my academic home. Deborah Avant is a constant source of wisdom and encouragement, and an exceptional mentor. Cullen Hendrix, Oliver Kaplan, Rachel Epstein, Marie Berry, and Tricia Olsen are also wonderful teachers and inspirations. My fellow grad students at the University of Denver are an enduring source of feedback and intellectual development. I look forward to the continued company of Jonathan Pinckney, Kyleanne Hunter, Kara Kingma, and Chris Shay in this grad school adventure, and owe a debt to Joel Day and Sarah Bakhtiari for showing me how to succeed. I am fortunate to be surrounded by such brilliant colleagues and friends.

I owe an enormous debt of gratitude to my family. My parents, Monique and Yves, have been my most fervent advocates since day one, and opened many doors throughout the years. For all that they have given me, I will be forever grateful. My sister Claire's wit and steadfastness are an inspiration to always persevere in the face of challenge, no matter the ups and downs. I also thank Don, Barb, and Cathy for supporting me in countless ways through the various stages of graduate school and this project. My debt to them is likely one that I will never fully repay.

Isaac has seen this project through from the beginning, and told me in no uncertain terms that this was not an opportunity to be taken for granted or bungled. I thank him for his constant support, enthusiasm, and intellectual curiosity, and perhaps most of all for teaching me the importance of balance in life and work. He and our incredible girls, Sophia and Sonya, are my foundation.

Pauline Moore
San Clemente, CA

PREFACE

This book has three primary aims: (1) to demystify terrorism by encouraging readers to think analytically about it; (2) to provide a comprehensive view of the cumulative knowledge obtained through the past few decades of terrorism research; and (3) to integrate core theories and concepts from terrorism studies—and conflict studies more generally—with trends and case studies of terrorism and responses to terrorism. In other words, this book will not tell readers *what* to think about terrorism, but rather *how* scholars, analysts, and observers think about terrorism systemically. To this end, the book introduces readers to the major analytical approaches used to study terrorism, while acquainting them with the historical evolution or domestic and international terrorism.

Instead of treating terrorism as an isolated or exceptional phenomenon, this book treats it as one of many types of political behavior, encouraging readers to study terrorism through typical social science lenses used to understand patterns of violence.

1)   A puzzle-driven book

Rather than being case-study or topic-focused, chapters in this book are puzzle-focused. Every chapter identifies an empirical or theoretical puzzle related to terrorism, lays out competing explanations for each question, and uses evidence to demonstrate which (if any) of the theories has the most empirical support. Puzzles range from the causes of terrorism (Chapters 2–7) to why some terrorist groups use women operatives while others predominantly use men (Chapter 12). Asking " 'why' questions" allows readers to explore and compare the wide range of potential explanations and tools experts use to approach the study of terrorism. It also encourages readers to think of terrorism analytically and systematically, rather than viewing different terrorist groups or elements of terrorist behavior in isolation from one another.

2)   Introduction of leading conflict theories and evidence

The book begins by introducing each of the leading analytical approaches available to contemporary scholars of terrorism. Many of these theoretical approaches are drawn from (or apply to) conflict more generally. This allows readers to take a comparative focus on many different groups, goals, ideologies, behaviors, countries, and time periods—but always linking these back to the cumulative knowledge scholars have gained over time both regarding terrorism and the uses of violence more generally.

Multiple terror groups, country case studies, or chapters receive boxes in each chapter. This approach makes the chapters provocative and analytical, raising questions that often take on more general forms, such as why some terror groups use certain tactics (e.g., suicide bombing) while others do not.

We designed the book to encourage further investigation, rather than purporting to provide definitive chapter-length treatments of a topic. In providing the basic information and scholarly works necessary to comprehend descriptive differences across countries, the book invites readers to compare select cases, but with the intention of pursuing further exploration. To this end, each section also provides a few suggested readings on each thematic chapter.

3) *Linking social science approaches to terrorism to the real world*

Although each chapter carefully integrates the logic of inquiry by identifying theories and bringing to bear multiple forms of evidence to evaluate these theories, the chapters also contain real-world scenarios that demonstrate the relevance of the various approaches. This allows readers to see how to use social science tools to generate unique insights into about how terror groups behave—and which types of policies can be most effective in reducing terrorism. It also encourages readers to use the tools gained in this book to think analytically about contemporary events. At the conclusion of each chapter, we provide several discussion questions, some of which encourage readers to look for recent examples of the phenomena discussed in the chapter in current headlines.

READING THE BOOK

The book contains three substantive sections, which focus on analyzing terrorism, understanding the behavior of terror groups, and countering terrorism. Each chapter opens with a list of learning objectives, which readers could keep in mind as they proceed through the material. Concepts defined in the glossary are designated throughout the text with bold print, and call-out boxes invite readers to delve into particular discussions with more detail. Although we introduce critical approaches to terrorism and the study of terrorism, the primary emphasis in this book is on the empirical study of terrorism. As a result, there are many opportunities to compare theory with evidence or to critique different approaches and evidence. Each chapter concludes with a set of discussion questions as well as recommended readings germane to the chapter's topic. The glossary provides readers with brief definitions of terms and brief descriptions of the different groups discussed throughout the book.

We encourage readers to contest the material in this book, rather than taking it for granted. Terrorism is a necessarily controversial topic, and this book is by no means the last word on the subject. Instead, it aims to provide readers with the tools available to examine terrorism analytically so that they can synthesize their comprehension, evaluate the evidence, and draw their own conclusions.

PART I

ANALYZING TERRORISM

This section introduces terrorism studies as a discipline, with an emphasis on methods and methodology, and the importance of theory and evidence. We begin Chapter 1 by laying out the justification for studying terror in the first place. We present terrorism as a contested, controversial concept, with changing meanings over time, and we introduce the many competing views of how terrorism is defined. We conclude by introducing four historical scenarios that may or may not be considered terrorism and offer a consensus conceptual definition that allows us to evaluate which of the four scenarios is terrorism.

The remaining chapters in this section address the most common question in terrorism studies: why and where does terror occur? Each chapter identifies a theoretical approach that attempts to answer this question. In each of these chapters, we identify the core assumptions and examples used to develop the theoretical approach. We also identify the observable implications of the theory (i.e. "If the strategic model is correct, we should expect groups to use terror when. . . .") and the practical implications. We then discuss flaws in the approach, including examples from history that do not conform to the theory discussed. We conclude each chapter with several case study boxes, along with provocative discussion questions. Chapter 2 identifies the strategic approach, which is by far the most common approach in the literature, while Chapter 3 discusses the organizational approach, the primary competitor to the strategic model. Chapter 4 introduces psychological approaches, while Chapter 5 focuses on ideological approaches. Chapter 6 discusses structural approaches, and Chapter 7 concludes Part I with a discussion of critical approaches.

CHAPTER 1

INTRODUCING TERRORISM

Learning Objectives

After reading this chapter, readers should be able to:

- Understand the relative lethality of terrorism compared with other violent threats and lethal hazards.
- Describe evidence suggesting terrorism is a relevant contemporary problem.
- Explain why terrorism is an essentially contested concept.
- Provide a conceptual definition of terrorism.
- Summarize remaining controversies about their own definition.
- Review different episodes of dissident activity and understand which episodes constitute terrorist violence and which ones do not.

> "Today's terrorists can strike at any place, at any time, and with virtually any weapon."
>
> —PRESIDENT GEORGE W. BUSH,
> PROPOSAL TO CREATE THE US DEPARTMENT OF
> HOMELAND SECURITY, JUNE 2002

> "If Al Qaeda operatives are as determined and inventive as assumed, they should be here by now. If they are not yet here, they must not be trying very hard or must be far less dedicated, diabolical, and competent than the common image would suggest."
>
> —JOHN MUELLER (2006, P. 3)

INTRODUCING TERRORISM: A CONTESTED, CONTROVERSIAL TERM

Terrorism is a notoriously controversial phenomenon. Defining, studying, and writing about terrorism are, themselves, political acts. As a subject of inquiry, terrorism is variously oversimplified, deeply contested, or dismissed as an analytically useless concept. In this volume, we suggest that in spite of these oft-valid critiques, it is possible to approach terrorism using established social science tools. Our aim is to bring these tools to bear on the subject in a way that demystifies terrorism. To do this, we present competing viewpoints about what terrorism is, what prevailing controversies dominate the study of terrorism, and how different analytical approaches can shed light into why some people use violence to achieve political goals. By equipping our readers with knowledge about the landscape of the field, our hope is that they will feel comfortable drawing their own conclusions about the study of terrorism and its critics.

The perspectives we explore in this volume see terrorism as an example of many different types of human behavior. Some see terrorism as war by other means (Chapter 2). Others see terrorism as an example of a byproduct of organizational competition and rivalry (Chapter 3). Some see terrorism as the outcome of pathological disorders in people who shroud their violent ideation in political causes (Chapter 4). Some see terrorism as an ideology unto itself—a particular imperative motivated by extremist beliefs (Chapter 5). Others see terrorism as politicized crime—an adverse behavior driven by substandard living conditions in the developing world (Chapter 6). Still others see terrorism as entirely subjective, a meaningless concept evoked to delegitimize and demonize people who are seen as threatening the status quo (Chapter 7).

Given these many perspectives on terrorism, the field provides ample material upon which to generate and evaluate terrorism from a variety of political science perspectives. But first, we should justify any effort to systematically study this contested and controversial topic.

WHY SHOULD WE ATTEMPT TO STUDY TERRORISM?

Despite what you might think from watching the nightly news, terrorism is extremely rare. In the United States in 2012, there were only thirteen terrorist incidents, only two of which resulted in fatalities.[1] In a country with a population of over 312 million people at the time, this amounts to one terrorist attack for every 0.0000000415601023 people. Even in India—the

---

[1] These figures come from the Global Terrorism Database (GTD), available at http://www.start.umd.edu/gtd. See Dugan and LaFree 2007 for a description.

world's most populous democracy with 1.22 billion people—the **Global Terrorism Database** records only 609 terrorist attacks in 2012. That's one attack per 0.0000004991803279 people. During the time of **the Thugs**—a cult-like group operating throughout India from the thirteenth through nine-teenth centuries and considered by many to be the deadliest terrorist group of all time—estimates of the group's total fatalities range from about 830 people to about 1,660 people per year (Rapaport 1984). Although that is a considerable figure, it is actually quite modest compared with the number of people killed annually in civil wars, international wars, communal conflict, government repression, or state terror (Figure 1.1).

In fact, terrorist attacks kill very few people even compared with fairly con-ventional hazards. If you are an American, you are more likely to die from drowning in your bathtub or from a vending machine crushing you than from a terrorist attack. You are many times likelier to die in a car accident, from preventable disease related to smoking, heart disease, obesity-related ill-ness, or a variety of other causes than to die in a terrorist attack (see Table 1.1).

In terms of world politics, terror attacks are responsible for a tiny frac-tion of the damage created by other large-scale conflicts. Many scholars have argued that terrorism is a mere nuisance in international politics—so incon-sequential in strategic terms that foreign policy decision makers ought to ignore it entirely (Mueller 2006). Others argue that terrorism always has been

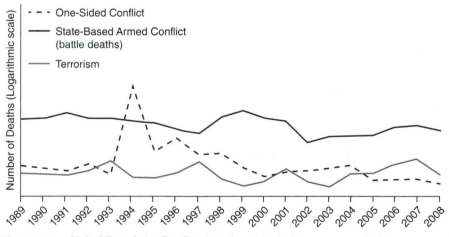

Figure 1.1 Global Trends in Conflict Deaths, 1989–2008

Source: Human Security Report Project 2012; GTD.

Note that "One-sided Conflict" refers to deaths perpetrated by an armed actor (often a state) against an unarmed group. "State-Based Armed Conflict (battle deaths)" refers to fatalities caused by war-fighting between two or more armed actors. The number of fatalities is transformed to a logarithmic scale for ease of comparison and interpretation.

TABLE 1.1 How Dangerous Is Terrorism?

Cause of Death	Times more likely to kill an American compared to a terrorist attack
Heart disease	35,079
Cancer	33,842
Alcohol-related death	4,706
Car accident	1,048
Risky sexual behavior	452
Fall	353
Starvation	187
Drowning	87
Railway accident	13
Accidental suffocation in bed	12
Lethal force by a law enforcement officer	8
Accidental electrocution	8
Hot weather	6

and always will be a normal feature of political life, that policymakers ought to accept a certain amount of terrorism as "routine," and that states ought to work together to prevent the most devastating possibilities (such as terrorists acquiring a weapon of mass destruction, or WMD) while containing the rest (Hoffman 2006). From a strategic perspective, caring too much about terrorism may actually help terrorist groups to achieve part of their aims. After all, the main mechanism through which terrorism might work is by terrorizing the population. As such, the more people pay attention to terrorism and the more it interrupts our daily lives, the more terrorists achieve their aims. Some cynical observers even suggest that policymakers and analysts deliberately exploit the threat of terrorism to distract the public from other more pressing concerns (Foster 2017).

Given this global ambivalence to terrorism as a real threat, why should any student read an entire textbook on the subject? We think there are at least eight good reasons to acquaint oneself with concepts, theories, controversies, and empirical evidence related to terrorism.

#1: Terrorism Is Real, and It Kills

The first reason is the most mundane: notwithstanding the critics described in Chapter 7, terrorism is an observable political and violent tactic that has been part of human history as long as we've been recording it. Although the concept and definition of terrorism is controversial (as we discuss in detail below), the very existence of terrorism as a political practice necessitates a more nuanced understanding of the phenomenon. Terrorism is a tactical choice that kills over ten thousand people—and injures tens of thousands more—on average each year. Most victims of terrorism bear little direct responsibility in their deaths other than being in the wrong place at the wrong time. And because acts of terrorism are based on the decisions of human beings motivated by political aims, many of these deaths and injuries are entirely preventable.

#2: Terrorism Is on the Rise

Trends indicate that global terrorism is on the rise. In 2000, the GTD recorded two thousand terrorist attacks worldwide. In 2012, that number had quadrupled to about 8,500. Moreover, the lethality of terrorist attacks is increasing. Over half of those 8,500 attacks in 2012 killed between one to ten people. Strikingly, the current decade features a higher frequency and lethality of terrorist attacks than any prior decade since 1970.[2] According to the GTD, in 2012, the **Taliban** in Afghanistan was the deadliest terrorist group, killing 1,842 people; **Boko Haram** was the second deadliest group in 2012 having killed 1,132 people in Nigeria, followed by **Al Qaeda** in Iraq, the **Communist Party of India (Maoist), Al Shabab** in Somalia and Kenya, **Al Qaeda in the Arabian Peninsula** in Yemen, and the **Pakistani Taliban**. This suggests that although terrorism has been a strategic nuisance in the past, it is becoming more of a global strategic reality in current times. That said, the distribution of terrorism is uneven worldwide. As shown in Figure 1.4, terrorist attacks happen in some places more than others at different times. This uneven distribution over time and place can often be symptomatic of larger social or political problems in each region.

In Chapter 6, we will learn about how structural approaches to studying terrorism can shed light into why some countries and regions experience so much terrorism, while others do not.

#3: Terrorism Can Be Extremely Disruptive

Although often modest in terms of the immediate impacts, sometimes terrorism can be extremely disruptive to a country's economic, political, and social arrangements. After killing more than three thousand people in a single day, the terror attacks on September 11, 2001 resulted in a near week-long shutdown of the New York Stock Exchange, a sharp drop in tourism to New York City, heightened aviation security throughout the world, retributional attacks against Muslim immigrants in the United States, the establishment of a new government cabinet (the Department of Homeland Security), and the invasion of Afghanistan. Waves of terrorism have had major consequences on the tourism industries of Israel, Turkey, Pakistan, India, Ireland, the United Kingdom, Nigeria, Algeria, Italy, Egypt, Indonesia, and Kenya, among other countries. In Israel and Turkey, terrorist attacks preceding national elections

---

[2] The Global Terrorism Database only records attacks after 1970.

have led citizens to shift their votes in support of more hawkish politicians (Berrebi and Klor 2008). Terrorist attacks against Shia pilgrims in Iraq have deepened sectarian divisions in that country, whereas tit-for-tat attacks between Israelis and Palestinians have undermined all serious efforts at achieving peace between the two peoples. Terrorism creates fear in the populations it

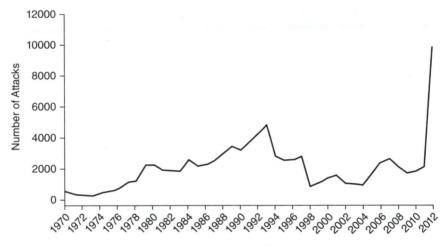

Figure 1.2   Global Trends in Terrorist Attacks, 1970–2012

Source: GTD

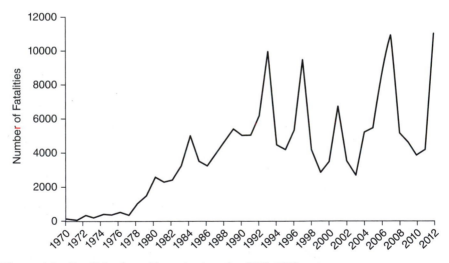

Figure 1.3   Fatalities from Terrorist Attacks, 1970–2012

Source: GTD

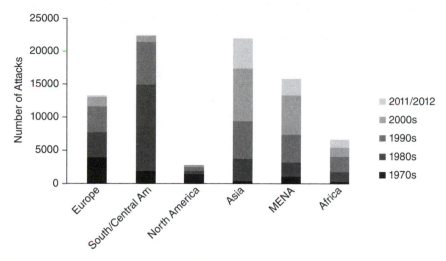

Figure 1.4 Regional Distribution of Terrorist Attacks, by Decade

Source: GTD

targets, creating longer-term psychological consequences as well (Pat-Horenczyk 2005). As such, even if terrorism is rare and results in relatively few deaths and injuries, its economic, political, social, and psychological effects extend far beyond the attacks themselves. In Chapter 2, we will learn several explanations for why terrorists view such destruction as necessary and effective.

#4: Terrorism Is Important to the Public

In public opinion polls around the globe, respondents express concern about terrorism as a critical issue. In a 2007 Pew poll of forty-seven countries, sixteen countries saw a majority or plurality of respondents reporting that terrorism was a very big problem (Pew Global Attitude Project 2007). An average of 64 percent of respondents said terrorism was a very or moderately big problem in their county. Only 14 percent said terrorism was not a problem at all. Concern was high in a diverse range of countries facing highly varying numbers of terrorist attacks, such as Morocco, Bangladesh, Lebanon, Pakistan, Israel, India, Turkey, Italy, Spain, France, Peru, and Japan. In the United States, 82 percent of respondents claimed that terrorism is a very big or moderately big problem, with more than two-thirds saying that responding to terrorism is a very important foreign policy goal. Only 4 percent of Americans thought it was not important. These numbers suggest that even if terrorism is objectively unimportant in terms of fatalities, disruption, and global politics, subjectively it is quite important to people in the world today. As a result, readers would do well to embrace the analytic tools necessary to support well-reasoned and proportional responses to terrorism—a theme to which we return in Chapter 7.

#5: Terrorism Can Provoke Overreactions by States

Although terrorist attacks rarely bring down governments, the way governments respond to terrorism can be extremely consequential. For example, in 1992, President Alberto Fujimori of Peru claimed the continuing threat of terrorism by **Sendero Luminoso (Shining Path)** as the justification for a presidential coup in which he shut down Congress, suspended the constitution, purged the judiciary, and consolidated authoritarian rule until he was deposed by a popular uprising in 2000. In Egypt, the Sisi government has used the threat of terrorism as a justification to imprison various dissidents— including liberal activists, Muslim Brotherhood adherents, Al Jazeera journalists, and other political opponents. The war in Afghanistan, which began in October 2001, may be another example of a state overreacting to terrorism. In this conflict, although the United States government did ultimately destroy the core Al Qaeda operatives responsible for 9/11, it did so at exceptional cost. The terrorist attacks on 9/11, which killed nineteen Al Qaeda hijackers and reportedly cost less than $200,000 to plan and execute, has led to a 17-year war that has resulted in the deaths of over 104,000 Afghans, 2,335 American troops, and more than one thousand troops from other coalition countries, with tens of thousands injured. The fear of experiencing another 9/11 reportedly motivated US President George W. Bush to launch a preventive war against Saddam Hussein's Iraq, resulting in an eight-and-a-half year war that resulted in the deaths of 500,000 Iraqis, 4,486 American troops, hundreds of additional deaths and casualties incurred by US allies, and hundreds of thousands injured (Bush 2010). Both wars together have cost American taxpayers between $4 and $6 trillion (Londoño 2013) and likely generated new grievances against the United States and its allies that did not exist before. Despite these costs, President Obama in his 2014 address to cadets at West Point argued that terrorist attacks on American interests at home and abroad remained the single most important threat faced by the United States (Obama 2014). In Chapter 2, we will learn about the strategic logic of terrorism, whereby relatively weak actors attempt to maximize their political influence and lure states into responding to terror in ways that often harm civilians and benefit the terrorists. And in Chapter 7, we will learn about the ways in which state overreactions often exacerbate and obscure legitimate grievances among those the terrorists purport to represent. In sum, states seem to have difficulty developing responses to terrorism that are proportional to the threat of terrorism itself—a situation that informed publics may be able to improve.

#6: Terrorism Can Lead to Large-Scale War

As terrorist groups increase their capacity, participation, and control over territory or ideological space, they can become much more stable fixtures in the political life of a country. In the early 1980s, Sikh militants began launching terrorist attacks in Punjab in an effort to bring about self-determination for Khalistan. As the Khalistan movement became more adept and more powerful, it provoked a violent government counter-reaction during the infamous **Operation Blue Star** massacre at Amritsar. During this incident in 1984, Prime Minister Indira Gandhi authorized the siege and assault of the Darbar Sahib, a holy Sikh temple known popularly as the Golden Temple, which pro-Khalistan militants were using for weapons storage. The assault cost the lives of hundreds of Sikh militants, including militant leader **Jarnail Singh Bhindranwale,** and Indian soldiers. In retaliation for this heavy-handed assault, **Indira Gandhi's** Sikh bodyguards assassinated her on October 31, 1984, precipitating mass riots against Sikhs, an era of increased government suppression of Sikhs in Punjab, and resurgence of large-scale pro-Khalistan **insurgency** within Punjab that lasted until 1997 and claimed thousands of lives. Similarly, in 2014, **Al Qaeda in Iraq,** a terrorist group that attacked Shia Iraqis throughout Iraq's Sunni-dominated northwest, morphed into **ISIS**, a full-blown insurgency establishing political and operational control over major cities within Iraq and Syria and inspiring or directing terror attacks in many countries around the world. As such, in some places, terrorist attacks may be a sign of a larger-scale conflict that may be brewing. In an even more consequential example, India and Pakistan nearly went to war in 1999 (and again in 2001) over unresolved conflicts relating to the incursion of Kashmiri militants into India—including an attack on the Indian Parliament in New Delhi in December 2001. The crises involved the most consequential nuclear stand-off in recent history (Cronin 2009: 162). Clearly, terrorist violence can lead to the escalation of crises in incredibly consequential ways. Later in this chapter, we discuss the relationships between terror groups and other kinds of political actors—and the ways in which these relationships increase or decrease violence.

#7: Terrorism Can Be Symptomatic of Larger Social and Political Ills

Terrorism does not occur (or persist) in a political vacuum. Instead, it occurs in the broader context of political crises of state authority and legitimacy, institutional dysfunction, ethnic discrimination, or other deeper sociopolitical problems. Terrorism represents the most extreme or radical tactic among a broader repertoire of contentious politics. For example, **Umkhonto we Sizwe** (Zulu for "spear of the nation"), the armed wing of the **African National Congress**, emerged on the fringes of larger mobilization by black South Africans subjected to vicious repression by the white minority apartheid regime. Bombings and summary executions by Umkhonto we Sizwe, although utterly abhorrent, were symptomatic of illegitimate and violent racial hierarchies that the group sought to rectify using terror. Thus terrorism can often be an important indicator of enduring sociopolitical conflict that requires a country's sustained resources and attention to resolve. Countries with sustained terrorism problems probably have a number of other underlying institutional, political, social, or economic problems as well. We explore such problems in Chapters 6 and 7.

#8: Terrorists Can Become Governments

On rare occasions, groups that rely on terrorism have overthrown incumbent governments, moved into ungoverned territory, or otherwise established uncontested rule over a given population. In 1948, **Irgun**—a Zionist nationalist group operating in British Mandate Palestine—successfully drove out the British Empire through a sustained campaign of spectacular attacks and produced Israel's first Prime Minister, Menachim Begin (see Chapter 2). Beginning in 1970, **Yassir Arafat**, the controversial head of the **Palestine Liberation Organization** (PLO), condoned or ordered numerous armed attacks against Israeli targets. Although labeling the PLO as a terrorist group is controversial to some, it is notable that Arafat became the first head of the Palestinian Authority (PA) when the 1993 **Oslo Accords** established the PA's territorial and political autonomy from Israel. By 1962, the **National Liberation Front** of Algeria (the **FLN**) had successfully combined terrorism tactics with other forms of political organizing to end French colonial rule, ultimately becoming the dominant ruling power in the newly-independent Algeria. Similarly, a number of members of the **Kosovo Liberation Army**, which at times used terrorist tactics to pursue its goal of secession from Serbia, are now representatives in the Republic of Kosovo's national government. And of course, the **Islamic Resistance Movement,** or **Hamas**, was founded in 1987 and has routinely launched attacks against Israel. In 2006, however, Hamas won the majority of parliamentary seats in elections in the Gaza Strip, becoming the ruling government there in 2007. As a result of its status as the legitimately elected government of Palestinians in Gaza, many major powers (including Russia, Turkey, China, Iran, and most countries in the Arab world) do not consider Hamas a terrorist organization, although the United States, the European Union, Israel, Japan, Canada, Jordan, and Egypt continue to do so. And in 1996, the Taliban overran Afghanistan and declared itself the ruling government of Afghanistan—a declaration that Pakistan, Saudi Arabia, and the United Arab Emirates recognized while the rest of the world did not. But even when their right to rule is contested, the fact that some political entities move from terrorist group to government suggests that those branded as criminals and outlaws during one season may be representing their countries in international forums during the next.

These eight realities suggest that although terrorism may not be the deadliest force in the world, its uses and misuses are significant enough that the public ought to devote thorough and considered thought to it. In this book, we aim to provide ways for readers to systematically make sense of terrorism—and responses to terrorism—using the major conceptual and theoretical approaches that scholars and experts who study terrorism (and conflict more generally) have themselves adopted . The justification for this is to provide readers with the tools they need to answer key questions—like why some groups use indiscriminate targeting while others are more discriminating (Chapter 8), why some groups use suicide bombing while others do not (Chapter 9), why some terrorist groups provide social services to their populations (Chapter 10), why some states sponsor terrorist groups (Chapter 11), why so many terrorists are men (Chapter 12), why some counterterrorism policies appear to fail while others succeed (Chapter 13), and why terrorist groups end (Chapter 15). The more familiar readers are with these analytic tools, the more they will be equipped to understand terrorist violence when it occurs, to keep in mind proportional responses, and to be self-critical of their own assumptions and emotional responses to this form of violence.

A VERY BRIEF HISTORY OF THE CONCEPT OF TERRORISM

In the ancient world, there were a number of groups that contemporary analysts (rightly or wrongly) consider terrorist groups. The **Sicarii**, for example, were an extremist offshoot of the Jewish Zealots movement to expel Roman occupation from Judea. Operating from about 63–73 AD, the Sicarii would conceal daggers beneath their cloaks, stab Romans or Roman collaborators in crowded places, and then fade back into the crowd to escape the attack undiscovered. Although these acts no doubt inspired fear among Roman sympathizers, they often resulted in mass punishment by the Romans against the entire Jewish population. Although the Zealots-Sicarii campaign did grow into a more generalized Jewish revolt, it failed to provoke a general popular uprising. The revolt was ultimately crushed when the Romans seized the fortress at Masada, only to find that its inhabitants had burned down the food stocks and committed mass suicide.

Another well-known group, the **Assassins**, was a cohort of Nizari Ismailis (a sect of Shia Islam) that formed in the late eleventh century and existed until the fifteenth century. The group targeted political and religious rivals with the aim of establishing a Nizari Islamic state within Persia. They would often kill their rivals in public to create spectacles, so as to maximize the psychological impacts on their enemies. Although they would typically use daggers dipped in poison to assassinate their victims, unlike the Sicarii they often submitted themselves to immediate martyrdom with the belief that such acts would guarantee them admission to paradise in the afterlife. The Arabic term *hashashin*, used by the groups's rivals, was a term literally meaning "user of hashish." However, the group's members were rumored by Europeans in the Middle Ages to have eaten hashish during rituals before killings, giving the term a more derogatory connotation. Europeans reinterpreted the name hashashin as meaning outcasts or rabble, the usage from which the English word "assassin" has its origin. The Assassins were virtually wiped out by the Mongol Raids of the fourteenth century, with the last documented members dying in the mid-fifteenth century.

Some consider the Thugs, a group operating in India, as the longest-lasting terrorist group on record. They lasted from about 1290 through the mid-nineteenth century and were responsible for killing between five hundred thousand and one million people during that six hundred-year period (Rapaport 1984). The thugs would travel around India in gangs, joining caravans of travelers whom they would beguile and befriend. When indicated by religious ritual, they would then execute these travelers through strangling, both to prolong the pain of death and to avoid spilling blood—a key requirement of their particular religious doctrine. The British Empire ultimately destroyed the Thugs after launching a concerted campaign against Thugee that involved amnesty and protection for informants, special police forces and tribunals, and harsh penalties including capital punishment for suspected Thugs. Although many consider the Thugs a terrorist group, some are skeptical that their goals were truly political in nature. In fact, some consider them more of a cult than a terror group, since the motives for their ritualistic killings seem to rely on sacred duty. Others suggest that despite their exceptional death toll and survival over the centuries, the Thugs' motives were primarily criminal in nature, calling into question whether or not they would qualify as a terrorist group by contemporary standards (Dash 2005).

Despite a history enduring across millennia, the word "terrorism" did not exist in ancient times. Although contemporary usage of the words "assassin" and "thug" are derived precisely from these groups, the word "terrorist" actually has its origins in the French Revolution. Popularized by Maximilien Robespierre and his followers, proponents of the so-called **Reign of Terror** viewed violence as a necessary phase of consolidation, reconfiguration, and purging of monarchist elements. The goal of this terrorism was to create a new, different, and improved society, thereby allowing its perpetrators to justify to themselves the grizzly acts of violence that resulted in forty thousand deaths. In this sense, usage of the word "terrorist" in late eighteenth century France was different from the contemporary usage in two distinct ways—a terrorist was a state agent, and terrorism was a virtuous activity. Maximilien Robespierre, the leader of the new Jacobin order, famously touted the importance of virtue, "without which terror is evil," while justifying terror, "without which virtue is helpless. . . . Terror is nothing but justice, prompt, severe and inflexible; it is therefore an emanation of virtue'" [quoted in Hoffman 2006, p. 3]. Notably, however, the concept connoted legitimate, state-directed terror against disloyal citizens, largely viewed as justified until Robespierre's own followers revolted against him and subjected him to the same fate he had imposed on his opponents—the lethal strike of the guillotine.

Following the Reign of Terror, critics of Robespierre's methods began to reinterpret the word "terrorist." Edmund Burke, the English philosopher and harsh critic of the French Revolution, began to invoke the word "terrorist" as a negative term, referring to Robespierre's Jacobins as "thousands of those Hell hounds called Terrorists" committing grave crimes against "the people" (quoted in Hoffman 2006, p. 4). Since this usage in 1798, the negative, criminal and illegitimate connotation of terrorism has remained in place, although many commentators and observers have alternated usage between state and nonstate actors.

For example, in the mid-late-nineteenth century, various anarchist groups in France and Italy debated and popularized the concept of **propaganda of the deed,** wherein clandestine groups could contest entrenched authority by acts of violence rather than by narrative or criticism alone. These debates inspired some other groups to use violence as a way to dislodge ruling elites from power, including nihilist groups like **Narodnaya Volya** (People's Will), a Russian populist network that was highly active from the late nineteenth century through the early twentieth century. Narodnaya Volya was responsible for killing at least one head of state every year at the turn of the century, including Russian Tsar Alexander II in a famed 1881 suicide bombing. The network also inspired many other groups and individuals during the time to commit terrorist acts. Leon Czolgosz was one of These. He was inspired by anarchism to assassinate American President William McKinley in 1901. Another victim of this particular wave of terrorist attacks was Archduke Francis Ferdinand, assassinated with his wife Sophie in Sarajevo on June 28, 1914 by a Serb ultra-nationalist named Gavrilo Princip. Princip's group Mlada Bosna was also inspired by the global anarchist movement of the time. Readers familiar with world history will know that this incident precipitated a series of diplomatic crises between Austria-Hungary—to whose throne Archduke Ferdinand was heir—Serbia, and their respective allies that resulted in the First World War.

At the time, terrorism referred mainly to revolutionary violence, committed against states by nonstate actors. It was deliberate, organized, yet highly discriminate violence, targeting government officials and avoiding unnecessary casualties among ordinary civilians. Although both its proponents and its critics often acknowledged the moral ambiguity of the means of violence, terrorists used violence to inspire others to rise up against the state. Many critics, including Marxist revolutionary Leon Trotsky, condemned this particular approach, arguing that such provocative acts were counter-productive and instead generated even more state repression against the people: "The anarchist prophets of the 'propaganda by the deed' can argue all they want about the elevating and stimulating influence of terrorist acts on the masses. . . . Theoretical considerations and political experience prove otherwise." (quoted in Gage 2009, p. 263).

Within several decades, the meaning had reverted back to Edmund Burke's formulation—that terrorism was a criminal act by states against their own populations. In the 1930s, however, the word was applied more commonly to leaders of totalitarian systems in existence in several places around the world. If one used the word "terrorist" in the 1930s, the term would bring to mind Adolph Hitler or Benito Mussolini. Characteristics

TABLE 1.2 The Meanings of "Terrorism" Across Two Centuries

Period	Perpetrator	Normative Frame	Example
Reign of Terror (1793–1794)	State	Legitimate	Jacobins
Post-French Revolution (1798)	State	Criminal	Jacobins
Late nineteenth century	Nonstate actors	Ambiguous	Narodnaya Volya
1930s	State	Criminal	Hitler's Germany
1940s–1960s	Nonstate actors	Ambiguous	Palestinian and Algerian self-determination movements
1960s–1990s	Nonstate actors	Criminal / Radical	ETA, IRA, LTTE, Shining Path, Red Brigades, Baader-Meinhof Gang
1980s–present	State-sponsored actors	Criminal	Hizballah
1990s–present	Nonstate actors	Criminal / Religious	Al Qaeda, Boko Haram, Al Shabab, AQAP, ISIS

of terrorism during this time included an abuse of power by governments against their own citizens, involving the routine deployment of death squads, the use of informers and collaborators to maximize fear among the population, and routine purges to compel obedience to the system. Acknowledging the rationale for using state terror, Hitler conceded that "Ruling people in the conquered regions is, I might say, of course a psychological problem. One cannot rule by force alone. . . . For, in the long run, government systems are not held together by the pressure of force, but rather by the belief in the quality and the truthfulness with which they represent and promote the interests of the people" (Hitler 1940, p. 388). Examples of "terrorist states" might include Nazi Germany, Fascist Italy, and Stalinist Russia; Argentina, Chile, and Greece during 1970s; and elected governments in El Salvador, Guatemala, Columbia, and Peru since the mid-1980s.

After World War Two, terrorism took on the meaning that is closest to its contemporary usage. Beginning with the post-colonial independence movements in the post-war period, terrorism reassumed its revolutionary, nonstate connotations. Highlighting the moral ambiguity of the use of terrorism to achieve self-determination, the use of the term "freedom fighters" became popular within the international community. At times and in some cases, terrorism was somewhat glorified, various international bodies affirming the right of national movements to defend themselves against violence by their own governments in the Additional Protocol 1 of the Geneva Convention of

IS TERRORISM DEFINED BY MEANS, ENDS, BOTH, OR NEITHER?

In 1974, Yassir Arafat, leader of the Palestine Liberation Organization, made a famous speech to the United Nations General Assembly in which he declared:

> The difference between the revolutionary and the terrorist lies in the reason for which each fights. For whoever stands by a just cause and fights for the freedom and liberation of his land from the invaders, the settlers and the colonialists cannot possibly be called terrorist, otherwise the American people in their struggle for liberation from the British colonialists would have been terrorists; the European resistance against the Nazis would be terrorism, the struggle of the Asian, African and Latin American peoples would also be terrorism, and many of you who are in this Assembly hall were considered terrorists (Arafat 1974).

Here, we can see the moral ambiguity of terrorism—Arafat claims that violence is illegitimate if its ends are illegitimate, but justified if the ends are justified. Moreover, he argues that the negative term "terrorism" is only used to describe groups with illegitimate ends, whereas the term "revolutionary" describes groups with legitimate ones.

Contrast Arafat's perspective with that of US Senator Henry Jackson (D-WA), who stated:

> The idea that one person's "terrorist" is another's "freedom fighter" cannot be sanctioned. Freedom fighters or revolutionaries don't blow up buses containing non-combatants; terrorist murderers do. Freedom fighters don't set out to capture and slaughter schoolchildren; terrorist murderers do. . . . It is a disgrace that democracies would allow the treasured word "freedom" to be associated with acts of terrorists (quoted in Ganor 2002, p. 293).

Here, Jackson is arguing that the ends of freedom are incompatible with the means of terrorism. He suggests that any moral claim to support freedom as an end goal is undermined by the use of to achieve it.

DISCUSSION QUESTION

- *In Chapter 7, we will explore **normative** approaches to the study of terrorism. In the meantime, which of these two perspectives is most convincing? Why? How might critics take issue with your argument?*

1949, (Act 1, C4), passed in 1977. This passage invokes a sense of legitimacy around guerrilla warfare, which often includes terrorist violence, viewing it as legitimate if the ultimate ends are just.

During the 1960s and 1970s, popular usage of the conception of terrorism as ascribed to nonstate actors with violent means and revolutionary goals extended to include various nationalist and ethnic separatist groups (such as the **Irish Republican Army (IRA)**, the **Liberation Tigers of Tamil Eelam**, and **Euskadi Ta Askatasuna** (Basque Fatherland and Liberty, or ETA), as well as radical, Marxist-motivated groups (such as the **Red Brigades** in Italy, the **Baader-Meinhof Gang** in West Germany, the **Japanese Red Army** in Japan, and the **Weather Underground** in the United States).

Politically motivated suicide bombings during the early 1980s brought focus to **state-sponsored terrorism**, especially as applied to states in the Middle East (Iran, Libya, Iraq, and Syria). With this kind of terrorism, nonstate actors would perform terrorist attacks as proxies for state actors. This might allow states some plausible deniability, since their own agents were not necessarily conducting the attacks. Instead, they were delegating terrorist attacks to clandestine groups or individuals whom they could fund, train, or arm to commit violent acts against their mutual enemies. Epitomizing this practice was the Marine Corps barracks bombing in Beirut, Lebanon in 1983. In this case, an Iranian-backed group organized a truck bombing that killed 247 servicemen who were acting as peacekeeping forces under UN authorization.

Of course, today, many observers talk of a **"new terrorism,"** which marks a distinct departure from terrorists of the past. Although terrorists are still widely defined as nonstate actors pursuing either revolutionary or revisionist goals, Bruce Hoffman considers contemporary terrorism "new" in three key ways: (1) it is transnational in that the grievances and the attacks themselves extend beyond national borders; (2) terrorists can access technologies that make highly lethal terrorist acts easier to commit; and (3) it is intensely religious in character (2006).

First, Hoffman suggests that new terrorist groups tend to have transnational reach. **Domestic terrorism** typically refers to terrorist incidents that start and end within a sovereign country. For example, Irish Republican Army attacks in London would be considered domestic terrorism, since the conflict was internal to the United Kingdom. **Transnational terrorism** refers to terrorism that involves perpetrators and targets from different sovereign countries. The 9/11 attacks are perhaps the best-known examples of transnational terrorism, having involved primarily Saudi hijackers attacking civilians of many different nationalities within the United States. In a more complex example, in 2012 Hizballah attacked a bus full of Israeli tourists vacationing in Bulgaria. This constitutes a transnational attack because it involves Iranian-backed perpetrators from Lebanon attacking Israeli civilians in Bulgaria.

Some critique Hoffman's claim that the transnational dimensions of the "new" terrorism are all that new. Martha Crenshaw writes that different waves of terrorism prior to 9/11 also featured high levels of cross-border collaboration and inspiration (2003). For instance, the IRA collaborated with ETA, as did the **Popular Front for the Liberation of Palestine**, the Japanese Red Army, and the West German **Red Army Faction.**

However, Crenshaw generally agrees with Hoffman's other character-izations of the new terrorism. New terrorist groups have access to consid-erably more lethal technologies, such as automatic weapons, weapons of mass destruction, potent explosives that are easy to make out of household materials, and even drones. As demonstrated in Figure 1.3, terrorist attacks are increasingly lethal in part due to heavy reliance on explosives and sui-cide attacks.

Third, the new terrorism is characterized by groups subscribing to extremist interpretations of different religious traditions. The majority of nonstate terror attacks today are perpetrated by groups adhering to various Islamic fundamentalist or revisionist beliefs. Outside of North Africa, the Arab world, and South Asia, where Islam is the dominant religion, other terrorists have been motivated by various other religions. Jewish extremists, such as Yigal Amir, who was opposed to Israeli Prime Minister Yitzak Rabin's rapprochement with Palestinians, assassinated Rabin in 1995. Baruch Goldstein, a physician who adhered to an ultra-nationalist Jewish ideology promulgated by Rabbi **Meir Kahane**, killed twenty-nine Palestinians and wounded another 125 in the massacre of the Cave of the Patriarchs in Hebron in 1994. The **Ku Klux Klan (KKK)** has used distor-tions of Christianity to justify killings in the United States. Finally, **Timo-thy McVeigh**'s bombing of the Oklahoma City federal building in April 1995 epitomizes the capacity of the new terrorists, whose access to highly lethal materials allows even single individuals to cause enormous damage. McVeigh was loosely affiliated with the **Christian Patriot** identity, which emphasizes conspiratorial, anti-government, white supremacist, anti-Se-mitic, and racist views.

Although ancient terrorist groups, such as the Zealots-Sicarii, the Thugs, and the Assassins also had religious motivations, their technologies of vio-lence (public knifing of Romans and Roman sympathizers, ritualistic stran-gling of sacrificial victims, and public assassinations of political enemies with daggers dipped in poison, respectively) limited the lethality of these groups. Today, groups with religious motivations are the most lethal. More-over, although all terrorist groups—and waves of terrorism—come to an end, religious terrorist groups tend to outlast their secular counterparts. This suggests that the current wave of "new terrorism" may be a particularly long-lasting one.

How Do Government Officials Define Terrorism?

The definition of terrorism is important for political, social, and legal reasons. However, despite its prevalence, there is little consensus among policymak-ers about what terrorism actually is. Consider six different legal definitions of terrorism that various official entities have developed (Box 1.2).

BOX 1.2

A SAMPLE OF OFFICIAL DEFINITIONS OF TERRORISM

EXERCISE: As you review the following selection of official definitions, pay attention to which elements are common to each definition. Also note which attributes of each definition are exceptional to that particular definition. What surprises you about certain definitions? What are the practical implications of the differences across definitions? How might each entity use its definition to pursue its own political goals?

From the United Nations Convention:

The Comprehensive Convention on International Terrorism is a proposed treaty which intends to criminalize all forms of international terrorism and deny terrorists, their financiers, and supporters access to funds, arms, and safe havens. The definition of the crime of terrorism that has been on the negotiating table of the Convention since 2002 reads as follows:

"1. Any person commits an offence within the meaning of this Convention if that person, by any means, unlawfully and intentionally, causes:

(a) Death or serious bodily injury to any person; or

(b) Serious damage to public or private property, including a place of public use, a State or government facility, a public transportation system, an infrastructure facility or the environment; or

(c) Damage to property, places, facilities, or systems referred to in paragraph 1(b) of this article, resulting or likely to result in major economic loss,

when the purpose of the conduct, by its nature or context, is to intimidate a population, or to compel a Government or an international organization to do or abstain from doing any act."

Source: United Nations General Assembly, Report of the Ad Hoc Committee established by General Assembly resolution 51/201 of 17 December 1996, Sixth Session (28 January ,1 February 2002), Annex IV, art. 18.

From the African Union:

The Algiers Convention was adopted by the Organization of African Unity (now called the African Union) in 1999. It defines terrorism as follows:

(a) Any act which is a violation of the criminal laws of a State Party and which may endanger the life, physical integrity or freedom of, or cause serious injury or death to, any person, any number or group of persons or causes or may cause damage to public or private property, natural resources, environmental or cultural heritage and is calculated or intended to:

(i) intimidate, put in fear, force, coerce or induce any government, body, institution, the general public or any segment thereof, to do or abstain from doing any act, or to adopt or abandon a particular standpoint, or to act according to certain principles; or

(ii) disrupt any public service, the delivery of any essential service to the public or to create a public emergency; or

(iii) create general insurrection in a State.

(b) any promotion, sponsoring, contribution to, command, aid, incitement, encouragement, attempt, threat, conspiracy, organizing, or procurement of any person, with the intent to commit any act referred to in paragraph (a) (i) to (iii)."

Source: Organization of African Unity Convention on the Prevention and Combatting of Terrorism, 14 July 1999, available at https://treaties.un.org/doc/db/Terrorism/OAU-english.pdf, last accessed 21 December 2016.

From the US Department of Justice/Federal Bureau of Investigation (FBI):

18 U.S.C. § 2331 defines "international terrorism" and "domestic terrorism" for purposes of Chapter 113B of the Code, entitled "Terrorism":

"International terrorism" means activities with the following three characteristics:

- Involve violent acts dangerous to human life that violate federal or state law;
- Appear to be intended (i) to intimidate or coerce a civilian population; (ii) to influence the policy of a government by intimidation or coercion; (iii) to affect the conduct of a government by mass destruction, assassination, or kidnapping; and
- Occur primarily outside the territorial jurisdiction of the U.S., or transcend national boundaries in terms of the means by which they are accomplished, the persons they appear intended to intimidate or coerce, or the locale in which their perpetrators operate or seek asylum.

"Domestic terrorism" means activities with the following three characteristics:

- Involve acts dangerous to human life that violate federal or state law;
- Appear to be intended (i) to intimidate or coerce a civilian population; (ii) to influence the policy of a government by intimidation or coercion; (iii) to affect the conduct of a government by mass destruction, assassination, or kidnapping; and
- Occur primarily within the territorial jurisdiction of the U.S.

18 U.S.C. § 2332b defines the term "federal crime of terrorism" as an offense that:

- Is calculated to influence or affect the conduct of government by intimidation or coercion, or to retaliate against government conduct; and

Continued

BOX 1.2

A SAMPLE OF OFFICIAL DEFINITIONS OF TERRORISM
(Continued)

- Is a violation of one of several listed statutes, including § 930(c) (relating to killing or attempted killing during an attack on a federal facility with a dangerous weapon); and §1114 (relating to killing or attempted killing of officers and employees of the U.S.).

Source: Definitions of Terrorism in the US Code (www.fbi.gov/about-us/investigate/ terrorism/terrorism-definition)

From the US State Department:

(1) The term "international terrorism" means terrorism involving citizens of the territory of more than one country;

(2) The term "terrorism" means premeditated, politically motivated violence perpetrated against non-combatant targets by subnational groups or clandestine agents; and

(3) The term "terrorist group" means any group practicing, or which has significant subgroups which practice, international terrorism.

Source: US Department of State, Country Reports on Terrorism 2013 (www.state.gov/j/ ct/rls/crt/2013/225328.htm)

From the US Department of Defense:

The Department of Defense Dictionary of Military Terms defines terrorism as:

"The calculated use of unlawful violence or threat of unlawful violence to inculcate fear; intended to coerce or to intimidate governments or societies in the pursuit of goals that are generally political, religious, or ideological."

Source: Department of Defense Dictionary of Military and Associated Terms. Joint Publication 1–02. 8 November 2010 (as amended through 15 March 2014). (www.dtic. mil/doctrine/new_pubs/jp1_02.pdf)

From the European Council Framework Decision of 13 June 2002 on combating terrorism (32002F0475):

"Article 1

Terrorist offences and fundamental rights and principles

1. Each Member State shall take the necessary measures to ensure that the intentional acts referred to below in points (a) to (i), as defined as offences under national law, which, given their nature

or context, may seriously damage a country or an international organization where committed with the aim of:

- seriously intimidating a population, or
- unduly compelling a Government or international organisation to perform or abstain from performing any act, or
- seriously destabilising or destroying the fundamental political, constitutional, economic or social structures of a country or an international organisation,
- shall be deemed to be terrorist offences:

(a) attacks upon a person's life which may cause death;
(b) attacks upon the physical integrity of a person;
(c) kidnapping or hostage taking;
(d) causing extensive destruction to a Government or public facility, a transport system, an infrastructure facility, including an information system, a fixed platform located on the continental shelf, a public place or private property likely to endanger human life or result in major economic loss;
(e) seizure of aircraft, ships or other means of public or goods transport;
(f) manufacture, possession, acquisition, transport, supply or use of weapons, explosives or of nuclear, biological or chemical weapons, as well as research into, and development of, biological and chemical weapons;
(g) release of dangerous substances, or causing fires, floods or explosions the effect of which is to endanger human life;
(h) interfering with or disrupting the supply of water, power or any other fundamental natural resource the effect of which is to endanger human life;
(i) threatening to commit any of the acts listed in (a) to (h).

2. This Framework Decision shall not have the effect of altering the obligation to respect fundamental rights and fundamental legal principles as enshrined in Article 6 of the Treaty on European Union."

From Saudi Arabia's Penal Law for Crimes of Terrorism and its Financing (the "terrorism law"), passed on January 31, 2014 to take effect on 1 February 2014:

"Any act carried out by an offender in furtherance of an individual or collective project, directly or indirectly, intended to disturb the public order of the state, or to shake the security of society, or the stability of the state, or to expose its national unity to danger, or to suspend the basic law of governance or some of its articles, or to insult the reputation of the state or its position, or to inflict damage upon one of its public utilities or its natural resources, or to attempt to force a governmental authority to carry out or prevent it from carrying out an action, or to threaten to carry out acts that lead to the named purposes or incite [these acts]."

The differences across these official definitions are striking. Saudi Arabia's definition is extremely sweeping and general—so much so that Saudi authorities could use it to suppress nonviolent dissent. The FBI's definition is slightly more limiting, referencing the threat or use of violence as a necessary criterion. The EU has adopted an operational definition, identifying certain criminal acts as terrorism when committed to further political aims. Both the US Departments of State and Defense, by contrast, each maintain succinct definitions that emphasize the premeditated and political nature of terrorist acts. Unlike the US Department of Defense, which does not specify the nature of terrorism targets, the Department of State limits its definition to attacks targeting noncombatants.

The United Nations' Convention appeals more to the laws of war. In line with the EU and US definitions (with the exception of the US State Department variation), the proposed UN conceptualization of terrorism emphasizes the coercive nature of such acts, which are perpetrated to intimidate a broader population. Importantly, no official UN definition of terrorism exists to this day, due in large part to insistence by some states that any definition should preserve the right to violent struggle in the case of foreign occupation.

However, notice the one element that each of these definitions shares in common—adopting irregular means by which to bring about a political outcome. This is precisely the source of the controversy surrounding the definition of terrorism. Many critics say that terrorism is a totally subjective and politicized term—that governments apply it to political opponents, while allowing political allies (and the state itself) to get away with murder. In reality, critics suggest, violence is committed by a multitude of different actors, and states themselves are the most prolific perpetrators of violence, with the result that terrorism is a term used only to describe people of whose politics one disapproves. This helps to explain why there is no international legal definition of terrorism—governments are ill-suited to formulate a definition precisely because of the political interests at play.

HOW DO SCHOLARS DEFINE TERRORISM?

Some of the official definitions do share in common several attributes that may be useful to distinguish terrorism analytically from other forms of political dissent—in particular, the focus on violence or the threat of violence helps to exclude otherwise nonviolent dissent from the definition of terrorism. In fact, scholars have learned that a focus on the legitimacy or illegitimacy of the ends provides very little analytical leverage because of the inherent subjectivity and contested nature of legitimacy. Instead, scholars generally try to focus on the observed characteristics of the means, rather than the legitimacy of the ends, in their definitions of terrorism.

Violence. Violence is an act of force that imposes physical harm on another person. Almost all scholarly definitions of terrorism involve the use or threat of violence. As such, a simple "disturbance" to public order does not constitute a terrorist attack. Instead, terrorists are those who use violence or explicitly threaten violence against their opponents.

Perpetrators. Most scholars accept the contemporary usage of the word terrorism as an act perpetrated by nonstate actors. Although states certainly do use terror on occasion, terrorists are explicitly thought to be nonstate actors. This means that nonstate groups like Al Qaeda are terrorist groups, whereas state agents who terrorize civilians in Afghanistan are not, even if they rely on similar methods of violence to consolidate control.

Targets. To qualify as terrorism, most scholars agree that the violence intentionally targets noncombatants. Noncombatants are people who are not part of an active combat force, meaning that civilians, journalists, civilian officials, and even uniformed military forces engaged in non-combat activities qualify as noncombatants. The latter point is controversial, with some scholars arguing that uniformed military and police never qualify as noncombatants, even during peacetime. Attacking such targets is usually considered guerrilla warfare rather than terrorism, whereas attacking civilians (including civilian employees in the government) would be considered terrorism by most scholars.

Wider Psychological Effect. So far, the definition focuses on violence by nonstate actors against civilians. However, these criteria could include a variety of forms of violence, including personally-motivated homicide. Most scholars suggest that terrorist violence creates or is intended to create fear in a wider population beyond the targets themselves. In that sense, terrorism has a highly symbolic character—the immediate targets are not necessarily the ultimate audience of the violence. Instead, terrorists target noncombatants to signal their political demands to wider populations and their governments. The 9/11 attacks on the Twin Towers and the Pentagon were meant to signal a declaration of war on Western political, economic, and military influence in the Gulf, rather than murderous hatred for the individual victims themselves.

Political Goals. Politics is the process of determining who gets what, where, how, and when. Politics is also a key characteristic that distinguishes terrorism from criminal violence, mafioso violence, or **narco-terrorism**. Most scholars argue that terrorism has explicitly political goals—such as control of a particular territory, removal of an incumbent government, establishment of a new country, or defeat of a political rival. Terrorism may indeed also have social goals—such as aims to make one religious sect more powerful than another—but these are always linked to political purposes. Criminal, mafioso, or drug-related violence may indeed involve violence against noncombatants that can be highly intimidating and symbolic, but generally the purposes are economic rather than political, per se. Moreover, such violence may result in control over a particular territory or manipulation of election outcomes, but it is not necessarily intended to produce such outcomes.

BOX 1.3
A CONSENSUS SCHOLARLY DEFINITION OF TERRORISM?

In 2011, Alex Schmid compiled a consensus definition of terrorism based on a review of hundreds of scholarly works on the subject. As a result, he produced a series of twelve attributes that reflect a scholarly consensus about what terrorism is.

1. *Terrorism refers, on the one hand, to a doctrine about the presumed effectiveness of a special form or tactic of fear-generating, coercive political violence and, on the other hand, to a conspiratorial practice of calculated, demonstrative, direct violent action without legal or moral restraints, targeting mainly civilians and non-combatants, performed for its propagandistic and psychological effects on various audiences and conflict parties;*

2. Terrorism as a tactic is employed in *three main contexts*: (i) illegal state repression, (ii) propagandistic agitation by nonstate actors in times of peace or outside zones of conflict and (iii) as an illicit tactic of irregular warfare employed by state- and nonstate actors;

3. The physical *violence* or threat thereof employed by terrorist actors involves single-phase acts of lethal violence (such as bombings and armed assaults), dual-phased life-threatening incidents (like kidnapping, hijacking and other forms of hostage-taking for coercive bargaining) as well as multi-phased sequences of actions (such as in disappearances involving kidnapping, secret detention, torture and murder).

4. The public(-ized) terrorist victimization initiates *threat-based communication processes* whereby, on the one hand, conditional demands are made to individuals, groups, governments, societies or sections thereof, and, on the other hand, the support of specific constituencies (based on ties of ethnicity, religion, political affiliation, and the like) is sought by the terrorist perpetrators;

5. At the origin of terrorism stands *terror*—instilled fear, dread, panic or mere anxiety- spread among those identifying, or sharing similarities, with the direct victims, generated by some of the modalities of the terrorist act—its shocking brutality, lack of discrimination, dramatic or symbolic quality and disregard of the rules of warfare and the rules of punishment;

6. The main direct *victims* of terrorist attacks are in general not any armed forces but are *usually civilians, non-combatants, or other innocent and defenseless persons* who bear no direct responsibility for the conflict that gave rise to acts of terrorism;

7. The *direct victims are not the ultimate target* (as in a classical assassination where victim and target coincide) but serve as message generators, more or less unwittingly helped by the news values of the mass media, to reach various audiences and conflict parties that identify either with the victims' plight or the terrorists' professed cause;

8. Sources of terrorist violence can be individual *perpetrators*, small groups, diffuse transnational networks as well as state actors or state-sponsored clandestine agents (such as death squads and hit teams);

9. While showing similarities with methods employed by organized crime as well as those found in war crimes, terrorist violence is *predominantly political*—usually in its motivation but nearly always in its societal repercussions;

10. The immediate *intent* of acts of terrorism is to terrorize, intimidate, antagonize, disorientate, destabilize, coerce, compel, demoralize or provoke a target population or conflict party in the hope of achieving from the resulting insecurity a favorable power outcome, e.g. obtaining publicity, extorting ransom money, submission to terrorist demands and/or mobilizing or immobilizing sectors of the public;

11. The *motivations* to engage in terrorism cover a broad range, including redress for alleged grievances, personal or vicarious revenge, collective punishment, revolution, national liberation and the promotion of diverse ideological, political, social, national, or religious causes and objectives;

12. Acts of terrorism rarely stand alone but form part of a *campaign* of violence which alone can, due to the serial character of acts of violence and threats of more to come, create a pervasive climate of fear that enables the terrorists to manipulate the political process (entire passage reprinted from Schmid (2011, pp. 86–87; italics in original).

DISCUSSION QUESTION

- *Are you satisfied with this consensus definition? Which elements of the definition are easy to observe? Which elements may add ambiguity?*

CONCEPTUAL CONTROVERSIES

Conceptualizing and defining terrorism is not straightforward, and the search for a universal definition is an elusive goal. Below we briefly present a few of the ongoing scholarly debates over the conceptualization of the term, particularly as it relates to other forms of conflict.

Terrorism as Synonymous with Insurgency

Clearly, the use of coercive violence transcends terrorism. Actually, a lot of the violence we see in civil wars is coercive in nature. Why, then, is some of the violence that occurs in the context of a civil war considered terrorism, while other instances of violence are not?

In many of the newspaper articles covering violent conflicts, the word terrorist is used interchangeably with the word rebel, or insurgent. The same goes for the use of "terrorism" and "insurgency." Take the conflict in Iraq as an example. The expansion of ISIS into various parts of the country has been accompanied by reports of gruesome violence against civilians, reminding us of the relevance of terrorism as a tactic. But it also begs the question— is ISIS best viewed as a terrorist group, or an insurgent organization? Like many other entities widely regarded as terrorist organizations, such as Al Qaeda, and groups often described as insurgents, ISIS employs a variety of forms of political violence, of which terrorism is only one form.

Across the globe, groups conventionally referred to as terrorists are engaged in insurgencies that aim to overthrow local regimes. Without a doubt, their activities feature classic terrorist tactics: attacks against civilians to serve political ends, and designed to instill fear across a broader population. At the same time, these groups wage battles more in line with guerrilla warfare, or insurgency: assassination campaigns, sabotage, and hit-and-run attacks against opponent security forces. In short, many groups have relied on a combination of tactics that fit within the scholarly interpretations of both terrorism and insurgency.

Interestingly, isolated campaigns of terrorism that are detached from wider conflicts are increasingly rare. In fact, Michael Findley and Joseph Young have shown that most terrorist attacks occur during civil wars, and in areas where localized conflict is ongoing. The high rates of terrorist attacks in places such as Yemen, Syria, and Iraq in 2014 confirm this trend—each of these countries is in the midst of a broader civil conflict.

Terrorism as a War Crime Committed During Peacetime

Yet some scholars contend that the key distinction between terrorism and other forms of political violence lies in the difference between attacks that occur during times of peace, and those that occur during wartime. For example, in 1992 Alex Schmid proposed a definition of terrorism as the peacetime equivalent of war crimes (see Schmid 2011). The goal of offering up this conceptualization was to broaden international agreement over a definition of the term and the unacceptability of terrorist methods, all the while narrowing down what could rightfully be considered terrorism. Notably, the Supreme Court of India adopted Schmid's definition of terrorism in 2003 (Supreme Court of India Criminal Appelate Jurisdiction Criminal Appeal No. 1285 of 2003). However, few scholars have adopted this definition precisely because they see that many violent acts that most people consider terrorist violence actually do occur during wartime.

States as Terrorists

Some see terrorism as primarily "act"-based, meaning that many different actors—including states—use violence against civilians to elicit fear in a broader population for political ends. Indeed, some have argued that limiting the primary perpetrators of terrorism to nonstate actors is arbitrary and problematic (Wilkinson 1981). They think the definition of terrorism should be based on the actions themselves rather than on the identity of the perpetrators.

Critical theorists in particular argue that mainstream terrorism research is overwhelmingly state-centric in its various approaches, and that the result has been the constant reproduction of a limited set of assumptions and narratives regarding the causes, nature, and responses to terrorism in a way that apologizes for state terrorism while delegitimizing the claims of nonstate actors using violence (see Chapter 7). Notably, this school of thought is critical of the "terrorist" label as a pejorative, rather than analytical, term. Ultimately, these scholars maintain that the term itself conveys political judgment about the legitimacy of the group labeled as such, as well as its actions (Jackson, et al. 2011). Rather than employ the term to delegitimize some actors while legitimizing others, critical theorists view terrorism fundamentally as a tactic of political violence used by both state and nonstate actors, in times of both war and peace.

Other scholars, on the other hand, argue that it is useful to distinguish between state violence and nonstate violence for various reasons (Wilkinson 1981). First, states have much greater capacity to inflict harm through violence, and, in a sense, states are states precisely because they have the monopoly on the use of force. Second, there are other terms—state terror, repression, genocide, democide, and politicide—to describe the sorts of terror campaigns that states wage against their own populations (English 2009). It is possible to identify and analyze nonstate terror acts without condoning or downplaying the very real existence of state violence.

That said, distinguishing states from nonstate actors is not always straightforward. For example, as we will see in Chapter 11, many states directly or indirectly support terror groups, complicating the distinction between them. Moreover, terrorism often occurs in the context of state collapse, where the lines between states, **pro-government militias**, terrorist groups, and **proto-states** are blurry. For example, many people consider the **Islamic State** a terrorist group, while others would argue that because the group exercises a monopoly of force over specific territories within Syria and Iraq, where the respective governments had essentially collapsed, it is more of a proto-state. The difficulty in distinguishing state from nonstate actors adds additional complexity to an already much contested concept.

Terrorism as Clandestine Violence

Some scholars have made the argument that dissidents only qualify as terrorists when they use violence in areas outside of their controlled territory in a clandestine manner (de la Calle and Sanchez-Cuenca 2011). Whereas terrorist groups operate primarily underground according to this definition, insurgent groups are able to set up camps and bases, establish roadblocks, and eventually exert some form of control over the local population. They have territorial control and do not act clandestinely.

Importantly, both terrorist groups and insurgent groups challenge their opponent's monopoly over violence. Luis de la Calle and Ignacio Sanchez-Cuenca (2011) explain that insurgents challenge the state's sovereignty by segmenting and fragmenting it in order to gain territorial control. Terrorist groups cannot do this. Because they are clandestine and control no territory, terrorist groups lack conventional military capabilities and therefore rely exclusively on spectacular violence to inflict harm. The types of violent attacks launched by terrorist groups—bombings, kidnappings, assassinations—do not require large investments in manpower or weaponry. As such, a small number of individuals can easily operate in areas of government control—for example in urban environments. Of course, these groups would rather seize territory and wage a more conventional battle against their opponents. But because of the constraints that they face, they rely on terrorism to achieve their goals.

To summarize, this argument contends that dissidents only qualify as terrorists when they act beyond their areas of control. The ensuing logic thus implies that, as groups shift from clandestine activities to open territorial control, their tactics change as well. Bombings and kidnappings become ambushes, small-scale battles, and the seizure of villages, and terrorists become insurgents.

Although this distinction has some descriptive appeal, some have criticized it for adding conceptual confusion. If we fully accepted this definition, then no attacks committed by groups with territorial control could be considered terrorism—an implication that would qualify ISIS's beheadings, crucifixions, and stake-burnings as terror attacks only when they occur outside of its bases in Iraq and Syria. Inside those bases, these same episodes would not be considered terrorism. Moreover, since the ability of dissidents to seize territorial control is largely dependent on the capacity of the state to maintain its monopoly, the distinction between terrorists and insurgents may be totally determined by the capacity of the state rather than the nature of the violence and the actions of the groups themselves. For instance, strong states (in which insurgencies would be unlikely to develop) would always face terrorism, whereas weak states (where clandestinity is unnecessary) would always face insurgencies. As a result of this conceptual problem, few scholars have adopted this definition.

The Terror-Crime Nexus

The contemporary era is rife with examples of terrorist groups and criminal networks that converge through alliances (such as the Albanian mafia and the Kosovo Liberation Army) or that transform from terror groups to criminal networks (like **Abu Sayyef** in the Philippines or the **FARC** in Colombia) (Makarenko 2004). Moreover, where state authority has collapsed entirely, terror groups and criminal networks can often converge into quasi-state authorities, as did various warlords in Afghanistan after the expulsion of the Soviet Union's military in 1989 or Al Shabab in Somalia today—a phenomenon Makarenko calls a "black hole" phenomenon (2004, p. 138).

After the end of the Cold War, some terrorism scholars began to argue that the distinction between terrorism and organized crime was increasingly murky. For one thing, Makarenko suggests that as funding from foreign powers began to evaporate, many cash-strapped terror groups began to turn to illicit markets—such as money laundering, extortion, kidnappings with ransoms, drug trafficking, counterfeit documents—to finance their operations (2004). Hence crime has been an operational necessity for some terror groups. Moreover, many criminal groups have seen terror as tactically useful to protect their own markets. For instance, the Italian Mafia has used terror tactics to attempt to intimidate the Italian government into abandoning legislation that interfered with its operations. In this case, the Mafia maintained an ultimate profit motive but adopted terror as an operational technique to secure it. Thus Makarenko suggests that terror groups and organized criminal networks exist on a continuum, with the two categories distinguished by whether their ultimate motivations are profit-driven or politics-driven (2004, p. 131). Although this approach is not without its critics (Ballina 2011), most terrorism scholars assume this distinction. We revisit the topic of the **terror-crime nexus** in Chapter 6.

In the meantime, like Makarenko (2004), most terrorism scholars look to the ultimate motivation of the violence—rather than the operational motivation for it—as a way to distinguish terrorism from organized crime. In so doing, they acknowledge that terror groups often use criminal enterprises and illicit activities to finance their activities on behalf of a larger political objective—even if that political objective is delegitimized and contested by their opponents and observers.

Not all crime is terrorism. But all terrorism is, by definition, political crime.

OUR DEFINITION FOR THIS BOOK (AND COMMON QUESTIONS RELATED TO IT)

For the purposes of this text, we draw on Schmid's (2011) consensus approach to adopt a fairly typical scholarly definition. We define terrorism as the intentional use or threat of force by a nonstate actor to evoke fear in a population to affect a political outcome. Although imperfect in the various ways already discussed, we simply present this definition here to clarify to our readers what we mean when we say terrorism or terror. Several clarifications are in order.

Does Property Damage Count as Terrorism?

According to our definition, it depends. If the property damage threatens the victim with further violence, such as the bombing of a home with a message that further attacks will occur unless the victim capitulates to the terrorists' demands, most analysts would consider this terrorism. If the property damage involves the burning of one's draft card, as happened during the Vietnam War among opponents of the war, most analysts would not consider this terrorism. Notice here that the property damage is symbolic and functional but does not threaten violence against the political opponents of the act. The reason these criteria are controversial is that they leave open a large gray area dependent on the subjective interpretation of the symbolic nature of the act. Take the case of burning down resorts built in forested area. In 1998, the **Earth Liberation Front (ELF)** claimed responsibility for an arson that burned down five buildings and four chairlifts at the Vail Mountain Ski Resort in Vail, Colorado. The group claimed that this act was merely an act of self-defense meant to protect the environment from further "violence," but that it was not meant to terrify or threaten human beings. Despite these stated intentions, however, the act may indeed have terrified and threatened those who owned the resort, those who worked at the resort, and those who visited the resort. As a result, the political effect of the act—determined entirely by the way that the victims interpret the act—often determines de facto whether the act qualifies as a terrorist attack. In the case of the ELF, the suspects accused of committing the arson were tried and convicted of terrorism-related charges.

What Makes a Terror Group a Terror Group?

If a political organization commits a terror act once, does it forever maintain the label terrorist group? Probably not. Many different types of non-state actors (rebel groups, insurgent organizations, political organizations, or even political parties) have committed acts of terror. Richard Jackson argues that terrorism is not a single causally coherent phenomenon, nor is it an ideology or form of politics in itself (2007). Terrorism is a tool employed at specific times, for specific periods of time, by specific actors and for specific political goals. It is but one option in a menu of modes of political contention. While groups specializing in only terror sometimes form, these are extremely rare, and exceedingly so today. Typically, those groups that do limit themselves to terrorist activity are highly unstable and fleeting in terms of length of existence. As we discussed above, most terrorism occurs in the context of broader conflicts, in which the use of terror is one strategy among other more routine forms of contentious action, such as nonviolent protest, violent insurgency, or full-blown civil war. Indeed, the terrorist label should rarely be ascribed as a fixed label—the majority of terrorists choose to abandon the tactic in their struggle to achieve political aims (Cronin 2009).

Interestingly, terrorism scholars have cited no fewer than four recognized "terrorists" who went on to win the Nobel Peace Prize: Menachim Begin, Sean McBride, Nelson Mandela, and Yassir Arafat (Zulaika and Douglass 1996). In a similar vein, the US and EU governments frequently differ on their categorization of groups as terrorist organizations. Table 1.3 lists some examples.

How Can One Tell the Difference Between a State Actor and a Nonstate Actor?

Both states and nonstate actors can use terror as a tactic. But finding a convincing way to distinguish between nonstate and state terrorism is more difficult than it seems for several reasons. First, all states are somewhat permissive, intentionally or unintentionally, to terrorist groups. Second, because of the global nature of finance and illegal monetary transactions, it is difficult to distinguish from whom money and other resources originate. Third, as noted above, when a terrorist group occupies territory left behind by a collapsing state and declares itself a state, it can be difficult to decide when the group ceases as a nonstate actor and begins as a state. Many terrorism scholars acknowledge these facts and then do the best they can to make distinctions between state and nonstate groups. Other more critical scholars find them to be distractions, arguing that arbitrary distinctions between state and nonstate groups obscure the more important problems of violence more generally, regardless of the perpetrator (see Chapter 7).

Throughout this text, when we refer to terrorism, we are excluding state terror, such as that perpetrated by Nazi Germany or other cases in which large-scale genocide occurred, unless we specify otherwise. We include proto-states, like Islamic State, the Taliban, or the Kosovo Liberation Army,

TABLE 1.3 Variation in terrorist group designations between EU and United States

	Listed as Terrorist Organization	
	EU	United States
Al Aqsa Foundation	✓	
Great Eastern Islamic Raiders' Front	✓	
Indian Mujahideen		✓
Holy Land Foundation for Relief and Development	✓	
Haqqani Network		✓
Revolutionary Organization 17 November		✓

as nonstate actors simply because so few countries recognized them as sovereign entities after they claimed statehood. This limits the definition of terrorism to those nonstate groups that challenge the state's monopoly on force, and may even seek to undermine, divide, or overthrow the host state itself.

In contemporary usage, there is an important distinction between state terror and terrorism. Whereas the former is perpetrated by governments, the latter is perpetrated by nonstate actors. This distinction is important because it precludes area bombing, such as the fire-bombing of Japanese cities during World War II or the dropping of nuclear weapons on Hiroshima and Nagasaki in 1945. Generally, when states rely on such methods to compel a foreign power to change its behavior, analysts refer to this as coercive diplomacy or war crimes. When states rely on such methods to compel their own citizens to behave in certain ways, analysts generally refer to this behavior as state terror. As such, states certainly rely on terror to achieve political goals at times. However, throughout this text we treat state behavior as analytically distinct from terrorism unless otherwise indicated. Critical theorists, on the other hand, argue that state terror (or state terrorism) is a much more pressing concern than the use of terrorism by nonstate actors.

What Is the Difference Between Civilian Victimization During Civil War and Terrorism?

Civilian victimization is a method of violence intended to consolidate control over a particular territory during civil war. In a sense, this form of violence is directed against particular people rather than as a symbolic act meant to send a message to a wider population. Differentiating between acts of terrorism and civilian victimization is one area where it may be useful to return to Luis de la Calle and Sanchez-Cuenca's definition (2011), which we briefly reviewed above. In this case, acts of violence against civilians are considered terrorism when they are committed in areas outside of the perpetrators' zone of control. When insurgents commit atrocities against local populations in areas under their control, it is considered civilian victimization. The activities of Sendero Luminoso in Peru provide an example. Able to control certain swaths of Peru's mountainous countryside, Sendero insurgents subjected local rural populations—in particular those in the Huallaga Valley—to intense violence in order to consolidate their power in specific areas. These instances of violence are largely characterized as civilian victimization. Sendero's bombing campaigns in Peru's capital city of Lima, on the other hand, are best interpreted as acts of terrorism in that they occurred in areas outside of insurgent zones of control, and served to intimidate a broader population.

EXERCISE

Take a look at the four scenarios in Box 1.4.

BOX 1.4

WHICH, IF ANY, OF THESE REAL HISTORICAL EVENTS IS "TERRORISM"?

1. A group of anti-government protestors destroys both public and private property during a premeditated assault.

2. A suicide bomber rams a truck full of explosives into a military barracks full of troops assigned to a multilateral peacekeeping mission, while the troops lay sleeping at night.

3. An organized criminal group assassinates a member of a rival gang.

4. Two people hijack an airplane demanding political change, with hostages released the same day unharmed.

DISCUSSION QUESTIONS

- *Which, if any, of these four scenarios would you categorize as a terror attack? Why would you say so?*

- *Did you have any difficulty distinguishing which of these were terror attacks and which ones were not? Why?*

Discussion

Our definition of terrorism focuses on acts of violence perpetrated by non-state actors against civilians, intended to intimidate a broader population in order to achieve political goals. With this in mind, let's use the table below to determine which of the four scenarios from Box 1.4 can be categorized as terrorist attacks.

TABLE 1.4 Evaluation of scenarios

	Political	Violent	Nonstate Actor	Noncombatant Target	Psychological Effect
1. Boston Tea Party	✓	✗	✓	✓	✗
2. Marine Corps Barracks Attack, Lebanon	✓	✓	✓	✓	✓
3. Cosa Nostra Assassination	✗	✓	✓	✓	✗
4. Air Malta 830 Hijacking	✓	✓	✓	✓	✓

If an act of terrorism is to meet all of our criteria listed above, only two of the scenarios can be considered as acts of terrorism: scenario 2 (1983 Marine Corps Barracks bombing in Beirut, Lebanon) and scenario 4 (Air Malta Flight 830 hijacking in 1997). Let's discuss each scenario in turn.

- The Boston Tea Party: not terrorism.
- The 1983 Marine Corps Barracks bombing in Beirut: terrorism
- A Cosa Nostra assassination of a rival gang member: not terrorism
- Air Malta Flight 830 hijacking in 1997: terrorism

Why Are Scenarios 1 and 3 Not Considered Acts of Terrorism?

As a form of political violence, an act of terrorism requires that the act itself be political in nature. Put simply, the act of violence must be an attempt to influence who gets what, where, and why, and as mentioned above, aim to impact a large number of people. These broad caveats clearly eliminate scenario 3. The killings depicted here—a **Cosa Nostra** assassination of a rival gang member—are limited to a single act not representative of a broader agenda. Although the violence may have indeed "sent a message" to other rivals, there was no larger public audience to influence, and the goals of the killer were not political, religious, or ideological. The profit motive is the important distinction here. The aim remained limited to killing or intimidating rivals threatening the business of one gang, and the ultimate goal of the act was likely to achieve economic ends.

Though the case of the **Boston Tea Party** (scenario 1) leaves more room for debate, we do not consider this an act of terrorism according to our standard definition. There are two main reasons for this. First, we take the position that the act of sabotage (destroying a shipment of tea) was symbolic and functional, but did not necessarily threaten future violence against the British Crown. Second, the goal of the Sons of Liberty was not to create fear among a general population, but rather to demonstrate to the British government the intense dissatisfaction felt against the Tea Act. Unlike acts of terrorism, the target of violence and the target of influence in this case are one and the same: the British Crown. Commonly viewed as the first act of the American Revolution, the incident is also best viewed as an act of political protest.

Why Are Scenarios 2 and 4 Considered Acts of Terrorism?

In the case of the **1983 bombings of the Marine Corps barracks** in Lebanon, the target of violence were the sleeping Marines assigned to an international peacekeeping mission. Some consider this example controversial because the targets were uniformed military personnel.

Under many circumstances, this would disqualify this incident as terrorism; scholars would generally consider attacks on uniformed police and military acts of guerrilla warfare rather than terrorism per se. However, the key distinction here is that the military personnel were not combatants—they were not deployed to Lebanon to engage in acts of war, and at the time of the attack they were sleeping in their beds. The targets of influence were the national governments of countries taking part in the mission, viewed by extremists as foreign occupiers. The political goal of the terrorists, members of an obscure nonstate group calling itself Islamic Jihad, was to force the withdrawal of the international peacekeeping force from Lebanon.

Finally, the 1997 **hijacking of Air Malta 830** bound from Valetta, Malta to Istanbul also meets all of the criteria included in our definition of an act of terrorism. Even though not one shot was fired over the course of the incident and all hostages were released unharmed, the act nonetheless remains terrorist in nature. The hijackers threatened to inflict violence on the plane's pilots and intimidated passengers into submission. Although these threats involved fake weapons and bombs, the two hijackers were eventually convicted of terrorism and served prison sentences for their actions. It was revealed later that the two men had simply not wanted to return to Turkey, claiming that they diverted the plane to Germany because of Germany's reputation for press freedoms and its receptiveness to those claiming to be oppressed.

SUMMARY

In this chapter, we demonstrated that terrorism is a proportionately modest threat compared to other forms of violence as well as more mundane hazards. However, we then provided a number of reasons why readers should take terrorism seriously as a topic. We then provided a very brief overview of the evolution of terrorism as a concept over various historical periods. We evaluated several reasons why terrorism is so difficult to define and provided competing definitions from various government institutions. Finally, we presented our own modest scholarly definition and outlined the remaining controversies with various definitions.

Discussion Questions

1. Why is terrorism so difficult to define?
2. How might some scholars critique this textbook's definition of terrorism?

3. Given this textbook's definition of terrorism, do you think the Thugs and Sicarii qualify as terrorist groups?

4. Why do you think so many people worry about terrorism, given its relative unimportance compared with other threats?

5. How would you know if a violent attack was meant to have a wider psychological effect (thereby distinguishing it from other forms of violence)? What kind of evidence would you need to establish this intent?

6. Can a state be a terrorist?

7. Since at least 1993, the US and Israel have designated the Islamic Resistance Movement (Hamas) as a terrorist organization due to the group's persistent use of suicide bombing and rocket attacks against Israel. In municipal elections in 2006, Palestinian voters in the Gaza Strip elected Hamas as the leading political party in the Palestinian Authority in the Gaza Strip. Given its status as the elected representative of Gaza voters and the de facto governing authority of the Gaza Strip, can Hamas still be considered a terrorist organization?

8. Consider the following two photographs. Which of these two public figures do you think is more universally recognizable? Why do you think this is the case?

Photo 1.1 Stephen Harper, the former Prime Minister of Canada (a major ally and northern neighbor of the United States)

Photo 1.2   Osama bin Laden, leader of Al Qaeda from 1998–2011

KEY TAKEAWAYS

- The threat of terrorism is relatively miniscule compared with other violent threats and lethal hazards.
- That said, there are many reasons why terrorism is still an extraordinarily relevant problem.
- Terrorism is a fundamentally contested concept, creating many practical, policy, and scholarly controversies about how to handle it.
- For the purposes of this book, we define terrorism as the intentional use or threat of force by a nonstate actor to evoke fear in a population to affect a political outcome.
- Not all dissident activity is terrorism, and the distinctions between dissident activity and terrorism are often extremely subjective.
- Not all criminal activity is terrorism, although many terrorists engage in illicit activities to support their operations while maintaining political goals.

SUGGESTED FURTHER READINGS

Asal, Victor, Luis De La Calle, Michael Findley, and Joseph Young. 2012. "Killing Civilians or Holding Territory? How to Think About Terrorism." *International Studies Review* 14 (3): 475–497. doi:10.1111/j.1468-2486.2011.01127.x.

Claridge, David. 1996. "State Terrorism? Applying a Definitional Model." *Terrorism and Political Violence* 8 (3): 47–63. doi:10.1080/09546559608427363.

Donahue, Thomas J. 2013. "Terrorism, Moral Conceptions, and Moral Innocence." *The Philosophical Forum* 44 (4): 413–435. doi:10.1111/phil.12021.

Ganor, Boaz. 2002. "Defining Terrorism: Is One Man's Terrorist another Man's Freedom Fighter?" *Police Practice and Research* 3 (4): 287–304. doi:10.1080/1561426 022000032060.

Harmon, Christopher C. 1992. "Terrorism: A Matter for Moral Judgement." *Terrorism and Political Violence* 4 (1): 1–21. doi:10.1080/09546559208427135.

Hoffman, Bruce. 2006. *Inside Terrorism*. 1st ed. New York: Columbia University Press.

Jagger, Alison M. 2005. "What Is Terrorism, Why Is It Wrong, And Could It Ever Be Morally Permissible?." *Journal of Social Philosophy* 36 (2): 202–217. doi:10.1111/j.1467-9833.2005.00267.x.

Meisels, Tamar, and Ted Honderich. 2010. "Can Terrorism Ever Be Justified?." In *Debating Terrorism and Counterterrorism*, edited by Stuart Gottlieb, Washington, DC: CQ Press.

Merari, Ariel. 1993. "Terrorism as A Strategy of Insurgency." *Terrorism and Political Violence* 5 (4): 213–251. doi:10.1080/09546559308427227.

Mueller, John. 2006. "Is There Still A Terrorist Threat?: The Myth of the Omnipresent Enemy." *Foreign Affairs* 85 (5): 2–8. doi:10.2307/20032065.

Mueller, John E. 2006. *Overblown: How Politicians and the Terrorism Industry Inflate National Security Threats, and Why We Believe Them*, 1st ed. New York: Free Press.

Orr, Allan. 2012. "Terrorism: A Philosophical Discourse." *Journal of Applied Security Research* 7 (1): 93–106. doi:10.1080/19361610.2011.604022.

Rapaport, David. 1984. "Fear and Trembling: Terrorism in Three Religious Traditions." *American Political Science Review* 78 (3): 658–677. doi:10.2307/1961835.

Rapin, Ami-Jacques. 2011. "What Is Terrorism?" *Behavioral Sciences of Terrorism and Political Aggression* 3 (3): 161–175. doi:10.1080/19434472.2010.512155.

Sandler, Todd. 2011. "New Frontiers of Terrorism Research: An Introduction." *Journal of Peace Research* 48 (3): 279–286. doi:10.1177/0022343311399131.

Schmid, Alex P., ed. 2011. *The Routledge Handbook of Terrorism Research*. 1st ed. New York: Routledge.

Shughart, William F. 2006. "An Analytical History of Terrorism, 1945–2000." *Public Choice* 128 (1–2): 7–39. doi:10.1007/s11127-006-9043-y.

Wilkinson, Paul. 1981. "Can a State Be 'Terrorist'?" *International Affairs (Royal Institute of International Affairs 1944-)* 57 (3): 467–472. doi:10.2307/2619580.

CHAPTER 2

THE STRATEGIC APPROACH

Learning Objectives

After reading this chapter, readers should be able to:

- Explain the strategic approach in their own words.
- Summarize the main assertions and expectations of the strategic approach
- Describe examples of terrorist groups that appeared to behave in accordance with the strategic approach's expectations.
- Explain the major shortcomings of the strategic approach.
- Critique the strategic approach by describing several examples of terrorist groups whose behavior has contradicted the strategic approach's expectations.

> "When a tendency toward violence evolves, it is always strategic. Organisms are selected to deploy violence only in circumstances where the expected benefits outweigh the expected costs."
>
> —STEVEN PINKER (2011, P. 33)

> "[T]he method of martyrdom operation [is] the most successful way of inflicting damage against the opponent and least costly to the Mujahedin in terms of casualties."
>
> —AYMAN AL ZAWAHIRI (AL QAEDA'S SECOND IN COMMAND), 2001
> (CITED IN PAPE 2005, P. 124)

INTRODUCING THE STRATEGIC APPROACH

The strategic approach follows from **rationalist perspectives** on international relations, which assume that people generally behave in ways that benefit their own interests. In the study of terrorism, scholars typically refer to this approach as the strategic approach, the **rational choice** approach, the

rationalist model, or **instrumental** approaches. Some also refer to this as a **bargaining** approach, since it assumes that political outcomes are the result of rational decisions by two or more actors, each of whom is seeking to achieve its own ends (see Enders and Sandler 2006). Essentially, each political interaction is a **game**, where each actor—whether terror group, government, or some other actor—brings to bear its own best guess regarding how it can achieve its political goals (see, for example, Bueno de Mesquita and Dickson 2007 and Lake 2002).

It is appropriate to study the strategic approach first, since most terrorism scholars adopt the strategic approach explicitly or implicitly in their research. Those that adopt different approaches (like those described in Chapters 3 through 7) are often doing so in a way that directly or indirectly challenges the strategic approach.

By making a few simple assumptions, proponents of the strategic approach can explain most terrorist violence in an exceptionally **parsimonious** way. Contrary to sentimental views that terrorists must be "crazy" or "irrational" to use violence in the way they do, or charges that most terrorists are ideological fanatics, proponents of the strategic approach assume that the choice to use terrorism is calculated, purposeful, and often entirely rational in the sense that it helps political actors to get what they want at a reasonably low cost to themselves. Many people find this approach intellectually satisfying in that it produces clear observable implications that are common across many different cases—whether the behavior we are trying to explain comes from Al Qaeda, the Baader Meinhof Gang, or Aum Shinrikyo.

Rationality is a process by which individuals or groups with set objectives examine available alternatives for achieving their objectives. Rational actors then select the alternative that will maximize their **expected utility** with regard to those objectives. For example, if a group had the set objective of controlling a specific territory, the group would evaluate its own strengths and weaknesses, the opponent's strengths and weaknesses, and the available ways that the group could establish control over the territory (e.g., through protest, through armed insurgency, or through terrorist violence). Conversely, the opponent would do the same with regard to how to maximize its own interest. Both the group and the opponent would calculate the costs, risks, and benefits to using each available alternative. Ultimately, those groups that view terrorism as the most efficient way to get what they want while navigating through an **uncertain information environment** about their opponents' responses are the most likely to use it.

Of course, human beings are not supercomputers. We are incapable of accessing infinite sources of information, nor are we capable of processing information as dispassionately as rational choice perspectives suggest. Certainly, emotions, psychology, and cognitive limitations often lead us to make choices that run counter to our preferences. The noted political scientist Herbert Simon calls this **bounded rationality**—or the observation that human beings cannot make pure rational choice decisions because of

imperfect information and cognitive and emotional barriers to emotionless reasoning (1982). With these caveats in mind, proponents of bounded rationality emphasize that despite our human limitations, the attempt to make self-interested choices and to find the least costly alternatives for pursuing self-interest is a generalizable pattern among human behavior.

Proponents of this approach generally argue that whenever we see terrorism, it is generally the outcome of rational choice decision games, even if those processes are totally informal. As such, proponents of the strategic approach view the decision to use terrorism as akin to a decision to invest in a promising stock, to vote for a political party most likely to benefit one's own interests, or to pursue a college degree as the most efficient path to greater prosperity.

Importantly, proponents of the strategic approach do not argue that such choices always yield the expected outcomes. Sometimes terrorism backfires, just like the value of the stock that you bought unexpectedly plummets, your preferred political party does not fully champion your interests, or your college degree doesn't immediately result in your dream job. Of course, there is a vast amount of uncertainty as well as a great number of unforeseen factors that might affect the outcomes in ways that rational actors do not anticipate. The key for the strategic approach is that rational actors make a reasonably calculated assessment at the outset based on projections that their chosen method will be the most productive way to arrive at their set objectives vis-à-vis their opponents' choices.

However, the strategic approach does suggest that if terrorism proves to be an inefficient way to pursue political goals, groups will learn from this experience and re-evaluate their choices. In somewhat more technical terms, rational actors constantly scan their environment for new information that they can use to update and maximize their choices. They also tend to consider their opponents' preferences and likely moves when arriving at their decisions. Repeated experiences or interactions with the opponent showing that terrorism is too costly or highly ineffective should change the information environment. Therefore, the **strategic interactions** between terrorists and their opponents should yield new information that affects the **cost-benefit calculation** regarding the use of terrorism as an expedient method. Ultimately if terrorism doesn't produce results, over time groups should stop using it and start using a more efficient method of change. Such methods may be strongly influenced by the nature of their political, social, and economic environments—a set of factors covered in more detail in Chapter 6.

Finally, the strategic approach sees terrorism as a tool or instrument of achieving political ends rather than seeing terrorist violence as an end in itself. Terrorism is simply a means to achieving an end; the final goal does not necessarily dictate that political actors use terrorism. Kydd and Walter argue that there are five key strategies of terrorism; people may use terrorism as a means of **intimidation** to control a social group, **spoiling** a peace process, **outbidding** a political rival for influence, provoking a political opponent into overreacting, or waging a war of **attrition** against a bitter enemy (2006). At times, we might see the ultimate objectives—such as justice for underrepresented ethnic groups—as fairly benign or even wholly legitimate. Proponents of the strategic approach make no explicit moral judgments about the righteousness of the decision to use terrorism or the objectives sought by the groups, although some argue that the implicit focus on terrorism as a **negative externality** betrays a pro-state normative bias (see Chapter 7). Regardless, the strategic approach simply implies that terrorism becomes the most effective and efficient way to achieve these ends, regardless of what they are.

ASSUMPTIONS OF THE STRATEGIC APPROACH

The strategic approach has widespread appeal in part because of the simplicity and elegance of its core assumptions. In fact, the core assumptions are deliberate oversimplifications precisely because human behavior can be so complex. By simplifying it, scholars can use fairly straightforward and transparent **formal models** by which to produce elegant and unique theoretical insights with clear observable (and testable) implications. Such insights are often counterintuitive—like the fact that terrorists sometimes deliberately provoke massive repression as a way to achieve their goals (Lake 2002). For instance, Kydd and Walter argue that the Basque Fatherland and Liberty (ETA) group sought to provoke an overreaction by Spanish security forces so that Basques would recognize the tyranny of Spanish rule and mobilize against it (2006, p. 70). As Woodworth notes, "Nothing radicalizes a people faster than the unleashing of undisciplined security forces on its towns and villages" (2001, p. 7). When analysts can estimate the likely value that different actors place on achieving various preferences, they can generate predictions about the actors' future choices. Such approaches often appeal to policymakers precisely because they distill complex policy problems into simple representations that yield a very clear set of ideal policy responses, along with estimated likelihood of success. Rational actor assumptions are therefore not meant to line up with reality *per se*; instead, proponents use them to lay out clear, falsifiable observable implications, and to provide a set of general principles about how human beings behave. Let's take a closer look at these assumptions.

Outcomes Result from Strategic Interactions. First, every act is directed at an audience: either the government, would-be sympathizers or constituents, or hardcore members of the terror group (Bueno de Mesquita and Dickson 2007). Political outcomes depend both on an actor's own actions as well as the actions of the target audience. A rational actor therefore considers not only its own preferences, but also the preferences and objectives of its primary audience; groups therefore make the decision to use terrorism based on a best-guess judgment regarding how that choice will increase the chances of their success given the way they anticipate other actors will react to that choice. For example, if a group aims to establish territorial independence, the primary audience may be the opponent government. Although the group can assume that the government prefers maintaining the territorial status quo, the group might also look for signs that that government prefers peace to continued violence as well as signals of the government's capacity to obtain its most-preferred outcome. If the government prefers peace to violence but has little capacity to enforce the peace, then a group might calculate that terrorism is a rational option for forcing the government to negotiate to avoid its least-preferred outcome of continuous violence. Overall, then, the terrorists' choice of attrition, intimidation, spoiling, outbidding, or provocation depends on the target audiences' preferences just as much as the terrorists.'

Agnosticism About Preferences. Crucially, the strategic approach takes preferences as given. The approach assumes actors have preferences but does not question where those preferences come from. This means that proponents make no judgment as to the morality, ethics, appropriateness, or "soundness" of an actor's stated preferences. In fact, what might sound like an insane objective to one person might seem entirely sane and reasonable to another. This key assumption allows proponents of the strategic approach to account for the behavior of terrorist groups with a wide variety of goals, beliefs, and ideologies in any context.

For example, one challenge to the strategic approach has been suicide bombing—a practice that many observers consider totally irrational. Many people find it difficult to understand suicide bombing as a rational activity, since the perpetrators of the act die in the process and therefore cannot themselves realize a political goal—or even witness the achievement of their goals in the longer term. Those defending the rational choice perspective would argue that suicide bombing may still be a rational activity under three conditions: (1) the perpetrator calculates that her own death will benefit the political goal more than her life; (2) the perpetrator's goal is spiritual rather than secular, in that the perpetrator believes that she will derive more benefit in an afterlife by committing a suicide attack in the name of a larger cause (Pape 2005); or (3) the perpetrator's desired outcome is that her family achieves rewards in exchange for her martyrdom. On the latter point, some families of Palestinian suicide bombers during the Second Intifada received cash payments from Hamas, Palestinian Islamic Jihad, or the Iraqi government (Moghadam 2003, p. 72). Whether a researcher agrees with these values or not is beside the point. The key is that the researcher takes the terrorist group's set objectives at face value, whether those stated objectives are to control territory, provoke a revolution, save one's community and kin from state repression, achieve paradise in one's afterlife, or any other outcome.

Preferences Are Ordered. The third key assumption is that stated prefer-ences of the terrorist group are ranked in terms of level of satisfaction with the outcome. For example, let's say that your set objective was to obtain a full-time job. You would clearly prefer this as your top or **preferred outcome**. But let's assume that this particular outcome was not immediately achievable for you. Perhaps in that case, you would next prefer to obtain a part-time job to remaining unemployed—a **suboptimal outcome** but not the **least-preferred outcome**. This would make the ordering of your preferences as follows:

Preferred outcome: Full-time employment

> *Next-preferred outcome:* Part-time employment

> *Least-preferred outcome:* Unemployment

Certainly, among terrorist groups, there may also be a set of **ordered pref-erences**. For example, let us assume that the LTTE has the following prefer-ence ordering:

Preferred outcome: Secede from Sri Lanka and create an independent Tamil Ealam

> *Next-preferred outcome:* De facto and de jure autonomy within Sri Lanka

> *Least-preferred outcome:* Control no territory within Sri Lanka

As we can see, the group's optimal outcome is seceding and forming an independent country itself. But short of achieving this optimal outcome, the group also prefers achieving significant actual and legal autonomy for Tamil people within Sri Lanka over controlling no territory. This means that the group's preferences are ordered, from high to low, in terms of their level of satisfaction with the outcome.

Preferences Are Transitive. Next, the approach assumes that the ordered ranking of the stated preferences of the terrorist group are **transitive**, mean-ing that if the preferred outcome is greater than the next-preferred outcome, and the next-preferred outcome is ranked higher than the least-preferred outcome, then the preferred outcome is also greater than the least-preferred outcome. Returning to the example above, because

Preferred outcome: Secede from Sri Lanka and create an independent Tamil Ealam

> *Next-preferred outcome:* De facto and de jure autonomy within Sri Lanka

> *Least-preferred outcome:* Control no territory within Sri Lanka;

it follows that

Preferred outcome: Secede from Sri Lanka and create an independent Tamil Ealam

> *Least-preferred outcome:* Control no territory within Sri Lanka

Because we know that the LTTE prefers secession and independence to de facto and de jure autonomy, and we know that the LTTE prefers de facto and de jure autonomy to no territorial control, we can furthermore conclude that the LTTE prefers secession and independence to no territorial control.

Preferences Are Stable Over Time. Fifth, proponents assume that these ordered and transitive preferences remain stable over time. In other words, if the Tamil Tigers say that secession is their ultimate goal and that they prefer it to both autonomy and lack of autonomy, this preference ordering should stay the same over the group's life cycle. This assumption helps to provide some stability to the predictions about how the group will behave in light of changing circumstances on the ground. Although the means through which the group pursues its goals may change over time due to information updating, most proponents of the strategic approach argue that preferences and their transitive orderings stay the same.

The Unitary Actor Assumption. Finally, proponents of the strategic model assume that terrorists and terrorist groups act as **unitary actors**. This means that terrorists or terrorist groups operate as single entities. This is fairly straightforward with regard to lone wolf terrorists, where only a single person is making decisions about how to pursue their goals. In the case of Ted Kaczinski, otherwise known as the Unabomber, it is clear that having acted as an individual, he acted as a unitary or singular entity. According to the unitary actor assumption, even terrorist groups operate in the way that an individual terrorist would. This might resonate with readers based on news stories that refer to terrorist groups as a singular entity, implying that they act as a whole (e.g., "Al Qaeda attacks targets in Yemen," or "ISIS takes over the Tal Afar airport in northern Iraq"). Notice how these headlines personify the groups, referring to them in the singular even though we know that it was not all of Al Qaeda that attacked targets in Yemen, and that it was a specific division within ISIS that overtook the Tal Afar airport. This common journalistic practice reflects a common scholarly practice of downplaying the leadership structure, internal conflict, and makeup of the group's participants. At times, the strategic model views these group-level characteristics as irrelevant to the group's decision-making process (e.g., Pape 2005). Instead, the strategic model generally assumes that the group operates as a whole, with proponents of this model deliberately simplifying internal divisions or disagreements about preference ordering, and other complexities within the group. Although rational choice perspectives acknowledge that these characteristics often exist within terrorist groups, they tend to argue that the unitary actor assumption still provides a level of theoretical simplicity and empirical validity that makes it superior to more complex approaches. As we will see in Chapter 3, this argument is controversial because of the empirical reality that terror groups (and their opponents) are often deeply fragmented, conflictual, and unstable in terms of the coherence of their internal decision-making.

For instance, recent developments in rationalist scholarship have attempted to model strategic interactions among factions within terror groups (Bueno de Mesquita 2005) or among moderates and hardliners in militant organizations (Bueno de Mesquita and Dickson 2007).

Regardless of whether their assumptions are empirically valid, however, proponents of the strategic approach argue that taken together they provide an internally consistent theoretical framework through which to explain terrorist violence.

OBSERVABLE IMPLICATIONS OF THE STRATEGIC APPROACH

Although many proponents of the strategic approach arrive at their assertions through equilibria discovered through formal models, one major benefit to this framework is its ability to generate clear, unique, and falsifiable implications that we can test against empirical evidence. Although there are many types of evidence that could be available to test each implication, such evidence is not always readily available. In some cases, scholars have already tested such implications; in other cases, the implications are yet to be systematically tested. Let's consider them one by one.

Terrorists Evaluate the Expected Responses of their Adversaries. The strategic approach sees interactions between actors, their opponents, and the broader audience as an interest-maximization game. As a result, this approach suggests that terrorists should carefully consider how their adversaries will respond to different types of attacks—as well as whether the group's perceived constituents will view the attack favorably or unfavorably—prior to authorizing the attack. If terror groups are rational, they should take these considerations into account when developing their plans, and they should make adjustments to their plans when they expect too costly a political response. For instance, with regard to the expected impact of attacks on a group's constituents, Jacob Shapiro indicates some evidence of strategic thinking along these lines (2013). For instance, in a letter to the head of a Ramadi cell of Al Qaeda in Iraq, AQI's leadership writes: " 'Stop the killing of people unless they are spying, military, or police officers. We have to find a secure method because if we continue using the same method, people will start fighting us in the streets' " (quoted in Shapiro 2013, p. 48). With regard to the expected behavior of the United States in response to Al Qaeda operations, Osama bin Laden once said, " 'All that we have to do is to send two mujahedeen to the furthest point east to raise a piece of cloth on which is written Al Qaeda, in order to make generals race there to cause America to suffer human, economic, and political losses without their achieving anything of note other than some benefits for their private corporations' " (quoted in CNN, 2004). Here we can see that bin Laden is invoking the logic of provocation to justify plans for small-scale Al Qaeda attacks expected to produce large political payoffs relative to the United States.

Further evidence in support of this observable implication might include qualitative evidence—such as internal communications within terror groups or speeches made by their leaders—during the planning phase of different attacks demonstrating that they take the expected responses of opponents and supporters into account. With regard to Islamic fundamentalism, the **Harmony Program**, an archive housed at the Combating Terrorism Center at West Point, publishes documents recovered from Al Qaeda and other jihadi groups during US military operations. Shapiro and others have evaluated many of these documents as well as internal documents from the Party of the Socialist Revolutionaries in Russia, the Ulster Volunteer Force and the Irish Republican Army in Northern Ireland, and Fatah and Hamas in Palestine (2013).

Coercive Effectiveness. Perhaps the most powerful empirical implication of the strategic model is that terrorism should often help political groups to maximize the return on their preferences. This is often called **coercive effectiveness**—the ability to coerce an opponent into making concessions. Overall, the strategic approach suggests that people use terrorist violence because it makes them more likely (than other alternatives) to get some or all of what they want relative to the anticipated opponents' response. If this is true, then we should expect to see terrorist violence outperform other methods of social change in achieving political objectives (or in achieving significant political concessions).

How do terrorists achieve such concessions? Generally, the logic of this argument suggests that targeting noncombatants constitutes a **costly signal** that demonstrates the resolve of the terrorist group as well as its capacity to do harm to the opponent unless the opponent complies with the terrorists' demands. Because terrorists attack **soft targets** by definition, these attacks signal to the population that (1) civilians are vulnerable to lethal attacks at any time; (2) their government is incapable of protecting civilians; (3) the terrorist group is so committed to its cause that it is willing to inflict massive amounts of harm on the civilian population; and (4) the only way to make the terrorist violence stop is to capitulate. Having ascertained that the terrorists will not back down, the argument goes, civilians demand that their governments make concessions to resolve the conflict.

Evidence that would support this observable implication might include quantitative evidence that terrorist violence has been more effective than other forms of political action in similar contexts. For example, Jakana Thomas analyzed the results of terrorism used by rebel groups during the course of African civil wars between 1989 and 2010 (2014). She found that increases in terrorist attacks by these armed groups were consistently correlated with concessions, such as getting a seat at the negotiating table. Reed Wood and Jason Kathman arrive at similar conclusions, finding that when insurgents victimize civilians at moderate levels during civil wars, the conflicts are more likely to end with negotiated settlements than government victory over the rebels (2014).

Additional evidence that would support this observable implication might include public opinion polling data or quasi-experimental evidence that civilians threatened with terrorist violence tend to favor capitulation or negotiation with terrorist groups.

Terrorism as a Last Resort. A second empirical implication is that aggrieved groups should evaluate and dismiss a variety of different tactics before turning to terrorism. Precisely because terrorism is a costly signal—often with very high risks—we would expect groups to use terrorist violence only after they have fully exhausted other less costly alternatives. There are certainly a wide variety of alternatives available to groups seeking political change. In democracies, groups can redress their grievances through legal channels, through numerous forms of political, social, and economic protest, through voting, through championing particular political candidates for election, through organizing one's own political, social, or economic cooperatives, or through practicing civil disobedience (see Chapter 6). Even in highly repressive countries, groups have alternatives to terrorist violence, including forming parallel or alternative institutions, engaging in everyday forms of resistance like shirking, foot-dragging, and feigned incompetence, engaging in clandestine forms of noncooperation, and protest. All of these methods of seeking change have certain costs, risks, and payoffs—indeed, in many situations, they may be highly risky and costly—but they are alternatives to using terrorist violence, which is often a considerably more costly behavior.

Evidence that would support this particular implication might include qualitative evidence—from memoirs, interviews, or recovered documents— that terrorist groups considered and evaluated other less costly methods of social change before turning to terrorism. Quantitative evidence that terrorist groups attempted many other less costly methods of social change (e.g., nonviolent alternatives) before turning to terrorism could also be useful here, as would any discussions in memoirs by terrorists or interviews of terrorists of how they "had no choice" but to use terrorism, since other potential alternatives were cut off, removed, or costlier than terrorism.

Terrorists Are Often Willing to Compromise. As a result of the preference ordering assumption, proponents of the strategic model generally assume that terrorist groups and their opponents prefer achieving their next-preferred outcome to their least-preferred one. As a consequence, the result of the game might be a **suboptimal outcome** for both the terrorists and their opponents, but both prefer this suboptimal outcome to achieving nothing. Few interactions between terrorists and governments are thus truly **zero-sum games**, or all-or-nothing conflicts. Instead, there are often opportunities for **bargaining** and negotiation depending on the opponent's preference ordering as well as the level of capability and resolve of both sides.

For example, let's say that the Sri Lankan government is absolutely unwilling to allow Tamil Eelam to become an independent country, considering the status quo territorial integrity of Sri Lanka to be a vital national interest, but that it also concluded that outright defeat of the Tamil Tigers was impossible. Let's also assume that the militarily inferior Tamil Tiger force concluded that there was no way that it could successfully achieve secession from Sri Lanka, but that it preferred some territorial autonomy to complete defeat. This scenario is hypothetical because this particular conflict and the respective sides' preference orderings were much more varied and complex. But let's just consider it for a moment as an illustration of why some terrorist groups—despite stating extreme goals—might nevertheless be willing to compromise:

Tamil Tiger's preference ordering:

Secede from Sri Lanka & create an independent Tamil Ealam

> De facto and de jure autonomy within Sri Lanka

> Suffer defeat and control no territory within Sri Lanka

Sri Lanka's preference ordering:

Defeat Tamil insurgency

> Allow for de facto autonomy and face much-reduced Tamil violence

> Face continued Tamil insurgency

> Tamil secession

We can see from this illustration that, according to the strategic model, both sides would be willing to negotiate an outcome where both would settle for a suboptimal outcome rather than holding out for their most-preferred outcome. This may be why the LTTE in 2002 dropped its demand for secession and claimed that it would be satisfied with regional autonomy—a shift that led to numerous attempted negotiations. Ultimately these attempts to negotiate all ended in failure and the Sri Lankan government defeated the LTTE in 2009. Contrary to mainstream views that terrorists are irrational fanatics, therefore, proponents of the strategic approach argue that even extremist terrorist groups are willing to compromise on their optimal preferences to avoid their worst-case outcome.

Evidence in support of this observable implication might include quantitative evidence on how many terrorist groups negotiated with governments over time and space. As we have seen from the work of Thomas (2014) and Wood and Kathman (2014), there is some quantitative data to support the notion that terrorism yields a higher probability of concessions and political settlements than armed insurgency alone, suggesting that these groups are willing to compromise as well. Further evidence might include quantitative data on the types of concessions achieved by terrorist groups over time and space, compared with the type of demands these groups articulated at the outset. Or it might include historical evidence on "hard cases" where seemingly fanatical terrorist groups compromised on core demands to achieve lesser concessions deemed acceptable by the group (see, for instance, Krause 2013 and Bueno de Mesquita 2005).

Terrorists Should Generally Claim Operationally Successful Attacks. The strategic model argues that groups use terrorism to maximize the return on their political preferences. This means that terrorists should be generally eager to claim responsibility for the attacks that are operationally successful (i.e., the attack itself was completed as intended). The reason is that their attacks are costly signals meant to demonstrate their capacity to inflict harm as well as their resolve to win. As a consequence, claiming responsibility for their attacks has **reputational effects** that bolster their credibility on both counts. It is no surprise, for instance, that the Pakistani Taliban claimed responsibility for the June 2014 offensive against the Jinnah International Airport in Karachi, Pakistan, in which thirty-six people died (the ten attackers as well as twenty-six airport and Pakistani security personnel). The attack was fairly bold and spectacular in its execution, demonstrating that the Pakistani Taliban was capable of launching highly disruptive and sustained attacks within the country. As such, claiming the attack no doubt signaled the group's growing capacity and resolve to the Pakistani government and public while sowing doubts in the public's mind as to the Pakistani government's ability to destroy the group.

Evidence in support of this observable implication might include quantitative evidence showing that terrorist groups tend to claim responsibility for most terrorist attacks—especially operationally successful ones—while disavowing operationally blundered terrorist attacks. For instance, an article by Max Abrahms and Justin Conrad (2017) argues that leaders of terror groups tend to claim attacks directed toward government installations because of their ability to use such attacks to reinforce their capacity to inflict future harm. Conversely, leaders of terror groups tend to avoid credit-taking for attacks against civilians, since such actions may undermine support among their base. These findings are consistent with another study by Eric Min (2013), who argues that terror groups tend to claim credit for the most operationally costly attacks while avoiding credit-taking for attacks that may alienate potential supporters by spoiling peace processes. Additional qualitative evidence could further shed light on this theoretical implication if it indicated that the rationale behind claiming terrorist attacks was to bolster signals of the groups' credibility and resolve. Ideally scholars would glean such evidence from terrorists' memoirs, interviews, or internal documents recovered through counterterrorist raids and released to the public.

Terrorists Should Attack Their Enemies. Another crucial implication of this approach is that the target selections of the terrorist groups should themselves send clear signals to their opponents. Although terrorists often engage in indiscriminate killing of civilians, such targets are not necessarily random or unintentional. Instead, terrorists often target civilians who symbolize the governments, ethnic groups, or religions they oppose. Instead of targeting constituencies or rivals with identical preferences, which might signal internal division or conflict, the strategic approach implies that terrorist groups should generally select targets that symbolize or represent those who stand in their way of maximizing the terrorists' preferences. For example, although the Al Qaeda attacks on the World Trade Center in New York killed civilians indiscriminately, Al Qaeda operatives carefully selected these targets (as well as the Pentagon and, allegedly, the US Capitol) to signal Al Qaeda's grievances toward US policies in the Muslim world.

Further evidence in support of this observable implication might include quantitative evidence (including summary statistics) showing that most terrorist attacks target civilians on the opponents' side. One could also demonstrate this point by uncovering qualitative evidence—from memoirs, interviews, or recovered documents—indicating that terrorist groups deliberately select the targets of their attacks to send signals to their opponents about their coercive potential.

Terrorists Should Learn from Successes and Failures. If terrorist groups are solely self-interested actors attempting to achieve their goals using the most efficient methods available, then they should also be quite practiced in self-survey, self-evaluation, and self-correction. Indeed, as with any other rational, unitary actor, terrorist groups should be willing to adapt to new information—including information related to their own performance—in ways that cause them to re-evaluate their strategies. When certain tactics are successful, we should expect groups to replicate them and rely on them continuously. For example, where suicide bombings are thought to be effective operational techniques, we should expect to see them diffuse rapidly both within the groups that innovated the tactics and across groups that collaborate with them. Suicide bombings have diffused across groups such as the Pakistani Taliban and the Islamic Movement of Uzbekistan, who have collaborated on occasion and now share a similar tactical repertoire based on perceived operational success. We should also expect other groups to emulate and adopt methods seen to succeed elsewhere—a process commonly called a **demonstration effect**. For example, Boko Haram, a jihadist group in Nigeria, has adopted suicide terrorism as a particular tactic with which to establish zones of control in Nigeria. The group has clearly articulated its source of inspiration as other jihadist groups who have used the tactic—particularly other Al Qaeda-affiliated groups.

When certain tactics are exceedingly unsuccessful, we should expect terrorist groups to discard them. Political assassinations, as were commonly used by anarchist groups during the late nineteenth and early twentieth centuries throughout Europe and North America, have gone out of style in part because contemporary heads of state have surrounded themselves with such high levels of personal security that such tactics are operationally ineffective.

It is notable that few terrorist groups today consider political assassination of government leaders—particularly heads of state—as viable courses of action.

Moreover, when terrorism itself has proven to be futile, groups should abandon it and adopt different methods of political change. For example, the Provisional IRA, which swore off violence in 2005, judged that terrorism could not advance the cause of Northern Irish Republicanism any further and opted to participate in a political process of negotiation, political party formation, and demobilization.

Evidence in support of this observable implication might include qualitative evidence—from memoirs, interviews, or recovered documents—that terrorist groups possess internal learning mechanisms through which to evaluate their progress toward achieving their goals; that they abandoned certain tactics soon after the group reached an agreement that they are unsuccessful or counterproductive; and that groups abandon terrorism and choose alternative methods of political change soon after the group reaches an agreement that terrorism is futile or counterproductive or that other methods have a superior chance of succeeding.

Terrorists Generally Replace Ineffective Techniques with Adaptive Ones. Similar to the learning process described above, proponents of the strategic model argue that terrorist groups replace or substitute tactics that become ineffective with newer tactics that governments do not yet know how to prevent. Terrorism scholars call this the **substitution effect**, wherein terrorists effectively innovate new tactics to supplant those that have become compromised. Terrorist groups have often substituted targets to work around government interventions. In perhaps the best-known example of the substitution effect, Todd Sandler and Walter Enders found that airline hijackings—a common tactic among internationalized terrorist groups in the 1960s and 1970s—dropped significantly as airports installed metal detectors worldwide (1993). No longer able to bring Kalashnikov rifles onto airplanes, terrorist groups opted for tactics that were harder to prevent, such as hostage-takings and assassinations, which increased dramatically.

The substitution effect can take many forms beyond just tactical substitutions. Terrorists can also substitute perpetrators, targets, or locations. With regard to perpetrators, terrorist groups have substituted women or children to carry out terrorist attacks once it has become clear that security forces are more likely to stop, search, and question male members of the group. This was done during the Algerian independence movement, for example, where female fighters often perpetrated terrorist attacks where men could not. This is depicted in the feature film *The Battle of Algiers*, in which a classic scene shows three female volunteers of the Algerian National Liberation Front (FLN) moving easily through French security checkpoints to plant bombs in the French Quarter of Algiers. They were able to do this because of local customs that made male searches of Muslim women taboo, while also playing to stereotypes of femininity and docility.

Terror groups also engage in locational substitution (Enders and Sandler 2006). For instance, because of travel restrictions, improved control over terrorist financing, and different forms of surveillance, it is fairly difficult for foreign terrorist groups to send operatives to the United States. As a result, in recent years there have been very few successful foreign attacks on US soil. Instead, groups tend to target American interests and installations abroad, as with the attack on the US Embassy in Kabul in September 2011. Locational substitutions can cause serious problems, of course, for the countries in which these attacks occur. When terrorists attack US installations or businesses abroad, most of the casualties are locals rather than Americans. This was certainly the case with the bombing of the US Embassy in Kabul, wherein several Afghan visa applicants were wounded. Scholars call these effects negative externalities, or adverse impacts on a new location (in this case, Afghan nationals) that result from another location's improved defenses (in this case, the United States).

Evidence in support of this observable implication might include quantitative evidence of tactical substitutions following the introduction of an effective defense measure. We have already seen evidence of this from the Enders and Sandler study (1993). In a more recent example, in response to a wave of suicide bombings within Israel, the Israeli government began to build a concrete barrier (called a "fence" by many Israelis, and called a "wall" by many Palestinians) around the West Bank and the Gaza Strip. Mostly completed by 2004, the barrier reduced suicide bombings dramatically, although rocket fire from the Gaza Strip into southern Israel subsequently increased (Figure 2.1).

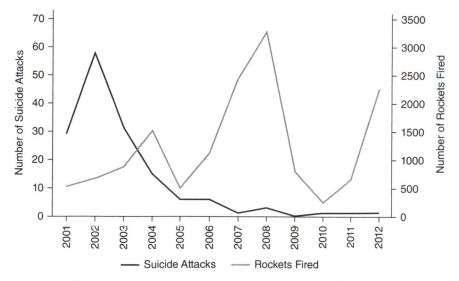

Figure 2.1 Suicide Attacks and Rockets Fired, Israel and the Palestinian Territories, 2001–2012

TABLE 2.1 Examples of Armed Groups using Child Soldiers

Group Name	Country
Revolutionary Armed Forces of Colombia (FARC)	Colombia
National Liberation Army (ELN)	Colombia
Liberation Tigers of Tamil Eelam (LTTE)	Sri Lanka
Lord's Resistance Army (LRA)	Uganda

Moreover, some have argued that groups sometimes use child soldiers as substitutes when adult combatants are unavailable. In its 2004 Global Report on the Use of Child Soldiers, the Coalition to Stop the Use of Child Soldiers noted nine documented cases of Palestinian minors engaging in terrorist attacks against Israel (and thousands elsewhere, but mainly in ongoing civil wars). Yet in 2008, the Coalition to Stop the Use of Child Soldiers reported a likely decrease in the use of child soldiers globally, thanks to conditions outlined in peace agreements in Afghanistan, Burundi, Democratic Republic of the Congo, Liberia, and elsewhere. Nonetheless, many tens of thousands of child soldiers continued to be recruited into conflict. The report identifies several well-known examples of groups using child soldiers (Table 2.1). All of these groups have used terrorist violence at times, although they fought larger-scale insurgencies as well.

Further evidence in support of this implication might include quantitative evidence of locational substitutions following the introduction of an effective defense measure, or quantitative evidence of increases in terrorist attacks in Country B following the introduction of an effective defense measure in Country A. Qualitative evidence—from terrorists' memoirs, internal documents, or records—may also reveal useful insight as to whether their targeting choices were related to substitution dynamics.

PRACTICAL IMPLICATIONS OF THE STRATEGIC APPROACH

One source of the strategic approach's widespread appeal comes from its straightforward practical implications. The model yields clear guidance depending on the terrorists' strategy. In general, if terrorists are pursuing a spoiling strategy, governments can make groups stop using terrorism by imposing high costs on the use of terrorism, while never rewarding terrorism (Walter and Kydd 2006). This explains the logic of many government policies not to negotiate with terrorists. As Thomas notes, when governments reward terror groups by allowing them a seat at the negotiating table, they provide incentives for other groups to use terrorism (2014).

Moreover, if the terrorists are pursuing a strategy of intimidation or attrition, then governments should credibly demonstrate that they can and will capture, detain, or kill people who use terrorism; simply put, the perceived risks and costs would then become too high to make terrorist violence a viable option (Kydd and Walter 2006). This may be the logic behind the United States' strategy of engaging in high spending on defensive measures related to "homeland security" while engaging in a continued campaign of targeted assassination against Al Qaeda operatives in Afghanistan, Pakistan, Yemen, and elsewhere. The aim is to demonstrate the futility of planning and attempting terrorist attacks against the United States, while demonstrating the certainty of death to those who would otherwise resort to terrorism. The combined outcome of this strategy is to make the costs prohibitively high relative to the expected benefits of engaging in terrorism against the United States.

As one can see, the logic of the strategic model can sometimes result in draconian and normatively troubling implications. For suicide terrorists, whose calculation leads them to view their own deaths as preferable to living struggle, proponents of the strategic model suggest that the costs of this behavior can be imposed as a **collective punishment** against the suicide terrorists' family to deter future suicide terrorism. During the Second Intifada, for instance, the Israeli government engaged in home demolitions, deliberately targeting the homes of suicide bombers' families. The aim was to signal to potential suicide bombers that even if they themselves enjoyed paradise in their afterlife, their families would pay for their crimes, thus altering the interest calculation for would-be bombers. Indeed, a study by Afraim Benmelech, Claude Berrebi, and Esteban Klor suggests that this strategy may have reduced the number of suicide bombings, making it a fairly effective **deterrence** strategy (2010).

On the other hand, if the terror group is pursuing a strategy of **provocation**, where the aim of the violence is to provoke the government to overreact, then the clear policy implication is to avoid overreaction (Lake 2002). This was the cornerstone of the Obama Administration's approach to fighting Al Qaeda, which involved "targeted" interventions such as drone strikes and assassinations of Al Qaeda leaders and key support personnel, rather than turning to larger-scale military operations.

Finally, if a terror group is engaged in **outbidding** vis-à-vis other factions, a government should react by either trying to unify and consolidate the various factions into a single oppositional group, or by rewarding moderate or nonviolent factions with concessions while denying any concessions to the factions employing terror (Kydd and Walter 2006, p. 78).

CRITIQUES OF THE STRATEGIC APPROACH

As with any academic approach, the strategic approach has a number of critics. In fact, most of the remaining approaches in this text developed as direct challenges to the strategic approach, with their proponents offering correctives and alternative explanations they say better approximate empirical realities on the ground. Here we will briefly examine a few of the key critiques of the strategic approach, beginning with critiques of the model's assumptions, followed by critiques of the model's empirical and policy implications. Chapters 3 through 7 will comprehensively present alternative approaches meant to address these shortcomings.

Terrorist Groups Are Rarely Unitary Actors. One common critique is of the unitary actor assumption. This critique emerges from the observation that many terrorist groups seem rife with internal conflict, power struggles, leadership and succession challenges, recruitment issues, and various other management challenges that greatly influence the ways in which these groups operate. Of course, the unitary actor assumption may apply more clearly to lone wolf terrorists, but most scholars and policymakers are more concerned with terror groups because they are much more lethal and enduring than lone wolves. While some rationalist scholars admit that terror groups are not monolithic (Bueno de Mesquita and Dickson 2007; Bapat and Best 2014), many maintain the unitary actor assumption for simplicity (e.g., Pape 2005). Critics claim that the unitary actor assumption causes the strategic model to miss important aspects of the incentives and capacity of groups, at certain times, to commit terrorist attacks. For example, it may be that terrorist groups cohere and fragment over time, leading to splits and splinters that may strongly influence attack patterns that the strategic model cannot capture (Pearlman 2009). Because the strategic model assumes that terrorist groups operate as single entities, it is perhaps not well-equipped to explain variation in the timing of terrorist attacks.

Furthermore, terrorist groups are rarely just terrorist groups. They often belong to larger collaborative networks (such as various jihadi groups that have pledged allegiance to ISIS) or insurgencies (such as the Shining Path in Peru). Sometimes they attach themselves to political parties, as with the IRA and Sinn Fein in Northern Ireland or Hamas in the Palestinian Territories. As with Hizballah or the Pakistani Taliban at different times, sometimes terror groups provide numerous social services to including welfare and health care. In fact, they often do this where local governments do not. Sometimes terrorist violence constitutes only a fraction of their larger political activities (Flanigan 2008). The unitary actor assumption limits the analysis to exclude these other organizational functions, which may also alter the incentives and opportunity to use terrorism.

Preferences Are Rarely Stable Over Time. Some critics assert that terrorists do not possess stable preferences. Instead, they argue, terrorists' stated preferences shift quite often. As Max Abrahms points out, Al Qaeda's goals have shifted considerably over time (2008). Al Qaeda's main focus was initially on defensive jihad in the Balkans and in Afghanistan, but the goals shifted in the mid-late-1990s to focus on attacking the United States. After the US invasions of Afghanistan and Iraq in 2001 and 2003, respectively, Al Qaeda has focused less on attacking the West and more on exploiting local conflicts and shoring up support in weak states such as Pakistan, Syria, Iraq, and Yemen. The French group Action Directe is another example of a group with seemingly shifting preferences, ranging from countering Israeli influence to opposing nuclear proliferation and anything else that seemed fashionable among leftists at the time.

Terrorism Is Relatively Ineffective. Importantly, few scholars argue that terrorism is a particularly effective tactic. In fact, terrorism has an extremely poor record as a coercive method, almost always failing to produce the overall political results sought by terrorist actors. In an influential study, Max Abrahms suggests that terrorist groups have achieved their stated goals only about 7 percent of the time (2006). This is an exceedingly poor rate of coercive success, especially when one compares the strategic success rates of terrorism to that of large-scale insurgency (at about 25 percent success) or even mass-based nonviolent resistance (at about 52 percent success), according to a comparative study by Erica Chenoweth and Maria Stephan (2011).

Moreover, the implication's fundamental mechanism about civilian response to terrorism is flawed. Rather than making civilians more likely to support concessions toward terrorist groups, terrorism tends to move publics to the right, supporting far more hawkish and far less conciliatory attitudes toward terrorists and the populations that support them (Berrebi and Klor 2008). Voters who already possess conservative beliefs also tend to become much more sensitive to terror attacks over time, gradually reducing their support for extending basic liberties to the population from which the terror groups emerge (Peffley, Hutchison, and Shamir 2015). In other words, terrorists often succeed in terrorizing civilian populations, but that rarely translates into civilian amenability to conceding to terrorists' demands.

That said, proponents of the strategic method argue that terrorist groups have succeeded in achieving concessions (Thomas 2014; Wood and Kathman 2014) or increasing short-term recruitment and other tactical successes (Krause 2013). Because many groups are satisfied with avoiding their least-preferred outcome, the strategic approach can account for such moderate outcomes. Moreover, proponents of the strategic approach argue that terrorists pursuing a provocation strategy often *prefer* to drive polities to the right so that the target government overreacts. In the Israeli case, for instance, Berrebi and Klor suggest that Palestinian groups deliberately increase their attacks against Israeli civilians in the months and weeks leading up to an election to terrify the Israeli population into electing more hawkish politicians who will pursue a more (counterproductive) coercive strategy against the Palestinian population (2008).

Terrorism Is Sometimes a First Resort. Some critics of the strategic model contest the claim that terrorist groups truly "try everything" before turning to terrorism (Abrahms 2008). Instead, they argue, many groups appear to adopt terrorism at the outset or before making genuine attempts to try other methods to pursue their political goals. Al Qaeda members, for example, did not attempt to lobby the US Congress to alter American foreign policy, protest American military bases in the Muslim world, or entreat American citizens to elect more dovish politicians before launching into a campaign of terrorist violence against the United States. Even the IRA, whose members claimed that they had "no other choice" but to use terrorism, undermined the progress of a mass-based civil rights movement that was highly active (and arguably effective) in putting the Northern Ireland conflict on the international agenda.

That said, proponents of the strategic approach suggest that terrorism can still be a rational choice, even if it is a first resort. Terrorism would only be irrational if actors fail to adapt and continue to use terrorism once it has proven to be an ineffective method for achieving some gains—or if they ignore better alternatives in favor of using terrorism. Proponents of this approach argue that terrorism can be a rational first resort when few obvious alternatives exist, such as in closed systems where other channels of political influence are blocked (see Chapter 6). Moreover, if terrorists are pursuing a spoiling strategy, then the strategic model can account for incidents when groups turn to terror even as their more moderate constituents are succeeding.

Terrorists Are Often Unwilling to Compromise. Some critics claim that terrorists often engage in all-or-nothing behavior, eschewing credible opportunities to negotiate terms that would improve their own status quo. Several Sunni jihadi groups, for example, seem particularly unwilling to compromise—especially since their goal is to essentially eliminate all "nonbelievers" and establish a uniform caliphate. Reports of ISIS' brutality against Sunni Muslims who seem too secular or who want to co-govern ISIS-conquered territories speak to this unwillingness to compromise. In a more secular example, the 1998 Good Friday Accords, a monumental agreement between the British government, Republican, and Loyalist groups, created devolution, self-rule, and significant autonomy in Northern Ireland. This was a greater set of concessions to the Republican cause than the British government had ever been willing to provide. Yet the Real IRA, a radical offshoot of the Official IRA, attempted to act as a spoiler to the Accords. On August 15, 1998, the group detonated a car bomb in Omagh that killed twenty-nine people and injured over two hundred others, making it the deadliest single attack during the entire conflict. The group launched the attack explicitly to reject and disrupt the IRA's declared ceasefire and maintain the armed struggle posture, exhibiting an unwillingness to settle for any concessions short of full reunification between Northern Ireland and Ireland.

As noted above, some rationalist approaches can nevertheless explain the tendency of terrorist groups to hold out for greater concessions (Bueno de

Mesquita 2005; Greenhill and Major 2007)—even if the group was mistaken in its calculation that it could generate concessions by spoiling the peace. The key is that the group adapts to new information as it becomes available, which the Real IRA did when it called for a ceasefire on October 8, 1998 in response to its marginalization after the Omagh bombing.

Terrorists Usually Avoid Claiming Attacks. One empirical pattern is particularly puzzling for the strategic approach: that terrorist groups rarely claim terrorist attacks. From 1970–1997, only about half of the terrorist attacks in the Global Terrorism Database were claimed by a terrorist group. Since 1998, this figure has decreased substantially, with only 14 percent of attacks documented in the Global Terrorism Database credibly claimed by a terrorist group (GTD). If the strategic approach is correct, the dearth of claims of terrorist attacks is strange indeed. Proponents of the strategic model generally explain this anomaly by arguing that many of the attacks were not operational successes, hence few groups would want to brag about them (Abrahms and Conrad 2017). Others argue that groups use certain "calling cards" during attacks, such as Al Qaeda's tendency to launch simultaneous suicide bombings, so that audiences know that Al Qaeda is responsible without Al Qaeda needing to claim the attack. Other strategic reasons for avoiding claims of attacks might relate to a groups' desire to remain underground; due to heightened surveillance in the Internet age, claims of responsibility might allow governments to better detect the group's members and location.

Terrorists Often Attack Each Other. The reality is that terrorists often spend considerable time and energy attacking targets—such as rival groups, political parties, or even their own constituents—other than their own stated audiences. For example, the Red Brigades' (BR's) stated enemy was the Italian government, which the BR viewed as hopelessly corrupted by capitalist, imperialist forces. However, the BR consistently targeted other leftist groups, Italian Communist Party leaders, and rival organizations it viewed as "selling out" to imperialists and capitalists despite shared goals with such groups. Hamas and Fatah fought a bloody internecine conflict in the Palestinian Territories in the mid-2000s, ultimately resulting in Hamas' violent expulsion of Fatah from the Gaza Strip in 2007. In another example, the Tamil Tigers reportedly killed thousands of Tamils they had accused of collaborating with the Sinhalese. And Al Qaeda in Iraq's (AQI's) brutality against Sunnis in Iraq's Anbar province became so intolerable that it precipitated the so-called Sunni Awakening, resulting in the temporary defeat of AQI in 2007. Although inter- and intra-group terrorist attack patterns may reflect outbidding logics, these tendencies reveal serious inferential complications when it comes to inferring terrorists' strategies. Can terrorists simultaneously pursue outbidding, attrition, provocation, and intimidation strategies? Can they shift in and out of different strategies? If so, then the policy implications become much less straightforward and, at times, contradictory.

Terrorists Sometimes Seem Impervious to Lessons about Their Own Successes and Failures. In a 2008 article, Max Abrahms argues that some terrorist groups seem to "toil along in futility" long after terrorism could be effective. For instance, despite the fact that most Marxist groups abandoned armed struggle in the 1980s and 1990s, there remained second- and third-generation Marxist terrorist groups around the world well into the 2000s. The Red Brigades Fighting Communist Party (BR-PCC), for example, were still engaging in lethal attacks in 2002, when they assassinated economist Marco Biagi in Bologna, Italy, because of his work on a controversial labor reform plan. Many observers argue that such attacks are difficult to explain from a strategic perspective because they have such little ability to influence or produce larger political outcomes. Moreover, waves of suicide terrorism committed against Israel during the Second Intifada did nothing to advance the cause of Palestinian self-determination. Instead, these attacks led Israel to construct a security barrier that effectively imposed unilateral borders on the West Bank and Gaza Strip, at times leading to seemingly permanent (albeit illegal) Israeli land appropriations.

Purely Military Strategies Distract from Legitimate Grievances. A cliché within counterterrorism scholarship is that few protracted terrorist conflicts have purely military solutions. Instead, political, social, and economic solutions are often required in order to fully remove the motivations and incentives to use terrorist violence. Critical approaches to terrorism and counterterrorism are particularly troubled by the unwillingness of governments to explore the root causes of terrorism before reacting to the perpetrators (see Chapter 7). In some cases, terrorism occurs as part of larger social or political movements that can—at times—have legitimate grievances about discrimination, lack of political, economic, or social rights, or government repression. Strategic approaches are, by nature, fairly amoral and totally agnostic as to the origins of the terrorists' preferences. The focus is entirely on the tactic of terrorism— where it comes from and how to stop it—rather than the reasons why people are willing to engage in such an extreme method of fighting in the first place.

But many are concerned with the strategic approach's lack of attention to moral concerns about its implications. For example, in the case of Sri Lanka, massive and indiscriminate government repression against the Tamil population, which resulted in countless human rights abuses, failed to deter LTTE attacks. Only outright military defeat of the LTTE, constituting the killing of tens of thousands of LTTE operatives and many innocent Tamil civilians, ended LTTE terror attacks (and the Sri Lankan civil war). Although the strategic approach might have implicated such massive government repression to be optimal under the circumstances, those concerned with human rights, fairness, and justice would question whether the model's dispassionate focus on utility-maximization actually makes it *immoral* rather than *amoral*. See Chapter 7 for a more thorough discussion of these critiques.

Assumptions and Methodologies Are Too Abstract and Detached. Some scholars critique rationalist approaches because of their oversimplification and emphasis on prediction. The strategic choices represented by formal models are so abstract that some critics question whether *any* historical cases could empirically validate them (Neumann and Smith 2005). Some claim that the tendency to test formal models with quantitative data necessarily obscures the historical context involved in the dynamics of violence, concealing useful patterns and insights (Jackson, et al. 2011). In the search for general patterns of cause and effect, often identified through correlations in large-scale observational datasets, proponents of the strategic approach may fail to capture important variation in the behavior of different groups. Moreover, in selecting different qualitative historical examples by which to validate their predictive models, proponents of the strategic approach might inadvertently focus on cases that illustrate the logic of their arguments, rather than cases that diverge from them (Ashworth, et al. 2008). This reveals a tendency toward an important **selection bias** of cases that tend to confirm or reinforce prior assumptions, rather than complicating or correcting them. In a deeper epistemological critique, **critical terrorism studies** scholars question the entire **positivist** project represented by the strategic approach and some of its theoretical contenders, which focus on establishing clear-cut relations between cause and effect for the purposes of prediction (and, implicitly, interdiction) (see Chapter 7).

Discerning the Strategies of Terrorism Is Not Straightforward. Even if terror groups do adopt a singular, consistent strategy, it is notable that the strategies of terrorism are not easy to infer. Whether a group is pursuing attrition or provocation as a strategy, for instance, may not always be self-evident from the behaviors the group exhibits. As a result, governments may make serious errors about which strategy a terror group is pursuing. For example, the United States may have thought that Al Qaeda was pursuing strategies of intimidation and attrition against it, leading the United States to pursue a repressive strategy meant to increase the costs of terrorism. Despite the United States' continued effort to degrade Al Qaeda through a decade-long targeted assassination program, Al Qaeda persists. In fact, second-generation jihadi groups such as ISIS have reconstituted themselves and pose a greater threat to US allies than Al Qaeda ever did. Some may argue that Al Qaeda was actually pursuing a provocation strategy, but such conclusions may only be obvious after the damage is done. Moreover, Al Qaeda may have been pursuing an attrition and intimidation strategy, while inadvertently provoking an overreaction in a way that benefited it relative to the United States.

The inability to sufficiently gauge the strategies of terrorism casts doubt on the utility of the strategic approach, particular with regard to the predictive power it claims to have. Alternately, it may be that terrorists are not motivated just by cost-benefit calculations; rather, they may be motivated by their political, economic, or social environments, socio-organizational dynamics, extremist ideologies, or even psychological conditions that make purely rational choice perspectives unlikely to yield much value. These alternative explanations are the subjects of Chapters 3 through 7.

BOX 2.1

A CASE STUDY OF THE JEWISH NATIONAL MOVEMENT AGAINST THE BRITISH EMPIRE, 1931–1947

Today, most discussions around terrorism in the Middle East revolve around jihadi groups. Yet not that long ago, it was the actions of Jewish terrorists in Palestine that captured global attention. The Jewish nationalist movement provides a useful example of a terrorist group that was highly strategic in its behavior. In fact, Jewish terrorists were able to frustrate British security forces in the Middle East so much as to critically erode the imperial power's ability to control Palestine, eventually forcing Great Britain to abandon the Palestinian Mandate in September 1947.

This short case study illustrates through a concrete example six of the seven observable implications of the strategic model of terrorism presented in this chapter. We'll look at how the Jewish National Movement demonstrated each of the following behaviors:

- Coercive effectiveness;
- Using terrorism as a last resort;
- Holding stable political goals;
- Claiming attacks for political effect;
- Attacking only the opponent; and
- Quitting terrorism after having achieved its goals (success).

Toward the end of the nineteenth century, a rise in modern European nationalism precipitated the marginalization and persecution of much of the continent's Jewish population, which in turn revived and politicized the Zionist movement dedicated to re-creating a Jewish homeland in the ancient lands of Israel. For the British, this translated into an obligation to help create a Jewish state on a portion of previously Ottoman lands (British-controlled Palestine), while simultaneously supporting the formation of independent Arab states on these same areas. Britain's inability to reconcile these two contradictory missions led to intense fighting between Jewish nationalists and Palestinian Arabs.

During the Second World War, the Zionist movement—which had heretofore focused exclusively on carrying out violent actions against Palestinian Arabs—became divided over the issue of cooperation with Britain in the war effort. While two Zionist factions, the **Haganah** and the **Irgun**, were willing to do so to a certain degree, a few dissidents within the movement considered this a betrayal given that British policy toward Palestine ultimately proposed the creation of only an Arab state (and not a separate Jewish state). The Holocaust further changed the Zionist calculus, reinforcing the moral case for a Jewish homeland—and a militarized defense of it.

In October 1945, Jewish underground groups launched an insurgency against British rule, coordinating a series of attacks on oil refineries, railways, and police boats. While the Haganah used violence principally as a pressure tactic to coerce the British into changing their policy on Jewish immigration into Palestine, the Irgun was more committed to an "all-out" nationalist war. The Irgun did not believe that the British would change their policies and therefore needed to be forced out of Palestine through violence. In July 1946, after the Irgun blew up the British administration headquarters building in Jerusalem killing ninety-two people, the Haganah renounced armed operations. The Irgun quickly escalated its violent activity, carrying out 286 attacks and killing more than one thousand people from 1945 to 1946.

ארגון צבאי לאומי

IRGUN ZWAÏ LEUMI BE-EREZ JISRAËL
ORGANISATION MILITAIRE NATIONALE JUIVE D'EREZ JISRAËL
JEWISH NATIONAL MILITARY ORGANISATION OF EREZ JISRAËL
An Irgun poster for distribution in Central Europe.

Photo 2.1 Historic poster of the Irgun, made for distribution in Central Europe, ca. 1931–1938. It depicts "Erez Yisrael" in the borders proposed in the Balfour Declaration.

On the tactical front, the Irgun used innovative terrorist tactics to sow chaos throughout Palestine, making the country ungovernable for the British. In addition, the armed struggle was expanded to Europe, and an anti-British propaganda campaign was launched to serve the terrorists' cause in the United States. The logic was that every Irgun attack that the British were unable to prevent would strike a blow to the empire's prestige while promoting the Irgun's image and message. As such, claiming responsibility for successful attacks was routine.

As the fight wore on, British military advantages were offset one by one by the terrorists' tactical innovations. For example, as the British improved the local road networks and added to their vast fleet of vehicles to enhance movement throughout the territory, the Irgun began to rely on improvised explosive device (IEDs), blowing up British military vehicles to reduce their opponent's

Continued

65

A CASE STUDY OF THE JEWISH NATIONAL MOVEMENT AGAINST THE BRITISH EMPIRE, 1931–1947 *(Continued)*

mobility. When the British passed death sentences on convicted terrorists, their own personnel were abducted by the Irgun and held for ransom. Gradually, Britain's control over Palestine eroded, and in September 1947 the British government deemed Palestine ungovernable. A terrorist group had essentially succeeded in forcing the British out of their declared homeland.

In its decision to wage a violent campaign against British forces in Palestine, the Irgun effectively dismissed the nonviolent policies and strategies of the Yishuv and the World Zionist Organization. The events of World War II convinced the Irgun leadership that the only way to achieve a Jewish state was by attacking British forces, eventually forcing them to leave. The coercive effectiveness of the Irgun's terrorist tactics is clearly depicted in the story told above. The violence, which lasted from 1945 through much of 1947, succeeded in coercing the British out of Palestine. Tactically, the Irgun was able to evolve in response to changes in British military strategy, and largely refrained from attacking Jews and targets not associated with their British opponent. As mentioned previously, the Irgun claimed responsibility for their successful attacks as a means of exposing British weakness. Furthermore, the goals of the Jewish nationalist movement remained consistent until 1947: removal of the British occupying forces as a means of establishing a Jewish state. Once this goal was achieved, the Irgun refrained from inciting further violence against the British, although there were mass expulsions of Palestinian Arabs from the land. In fact, once the establishment of the State of Israel was proclaimed on May 13, 1948, all military organizations—including the Irgun—were absorbed into the Israeli Defense Forces.

SUMMARY

In this chapter, we introduced and evaluated the strategic approach to explaining terrorism. We looked at the theory's underlying assumptions, assertions, observable implications, and policy implications. We reviewed several critiques of the theory and presented some evidence demonstrating why the approach remains controversial. We also reviewed the Irgun as a case of a terrorist group that closely aligns with the behavior the strategic approach expects to see.

Discussion Questions

1. Is terrorism a rational behavior? Why or why not?

2. How would you know a "rational terrorist" from an "irrational" one?

3. In April 2014, Boko Haram kidnapped more than two hundred schoolgirls in northern Nigeria. How would you explain this incident using the strategic approach?

4. What types of behaviors would exemplify attrition, outbidding, intimidation, provocation, and spoiling strategies among terror groups? How would you know each strategy when you saw it?

5. Watch the feature film *The Battle of Algiers*. Which elements of the strategic approach are consistent with the depiction of the FLN's use of terrorism against French colonial power? Which elements of the strategic approach do you find inconsistent with this depiction?

6. Do you think that Irgun was a rational terrorist group? Are there any alternative explanations for Irgun's behavior?

KEY TAKEAWAYS

- The strategic approach argues that terrorism is a rational activity. It suggests a series of predictable patterns of behavior among terrorist groups.

- Bargaining models see terror groups and their adversaries as engaging in a strategic interaction. Where terror groups may employ strategies of attrition, spoiling, intimidation, outbidding, or provocation, their opponents anticipate those expected strategies and respond in the way that maximizes their own preferences as well.

- Critics argue that the strategic model is simplistic and unrealistic, obscuring many important motivations and dynamics of terror groups.

- Some groups seem to behave in ways that contradict the expectations of the strategic approach. For instance, some groups continue to use terrorism even when it is unsuccessful or when other options appear to be available. Others seem to adopt particular behaviors—such as changing their goals, attacking their rivals, avoiding claiming attacks, or refusing to compromise—that contradict the strategic approach.

SUGGESTED FURTHER READINGS

Abrahms, Max. 2004. "Are Terrorists Really Rational? The Palestinian Example." *Orbis* 4: 533–549.

Abrahms, Max. 2006. "Why Terrorism Does Not Work." *International Security* 31 (2): 42–78. doi:10.1162/isec.2006.31.2.42.

Abrahms, Max. 2008. "What Terrorists Really Want: Terrorist Motives and Counterterrorism Strategy." *International Security* 32 (4): 78–105. doi:10.1162/isec.2008.32.4.78.

Abrahms, Max. 2012. "The Political Effectiveness of Terrorism Revisited." *Comparative Political Studies* 45 (3): 366–393. doi:10.1177/0010414011433104.

Abrahms, Max. 2013. "The Credibility Paradox: Violence as a Double-Edged Sword in International Politics." *International Studies Quarterly* 57 (4): 660–671. doi:10.1111/isqu.12098.

Abrahms, Max, and Justin Conrad. 2017. "The Strategic Logic of Credit Claiming: A New Theory on Anonymous Terrorist Attacks." *Security Studies* 26(2): 279–304.

Berrebi, Claude, and Esteban Klor. 2008. "Are Voters Sensitive to Terrorism? Direct Evidence from the Israeli Electorate." *American Political Science Review* 102 (3): 279–301. doi:10.2139/ssrn.1003908.

Bueno De Mesquita, Ethan. 2005. "Conciliation, Counterterrorism, and Patterns of Terrorist Violence." *International Organization* 59 (1): 145–176. doi:10.1017/s0020818305050022.

Bueno De Mesquita, Ethan, and Eric S. Dickson. 2007. "The Propaganda of the Deed: Terrorism, Counterterrorism, and Mobilization." *American Journal of Political Science* 51 (2): 364–381. doi:10.1111/j.1540-5907.2007.00256.x

Caplan, Bryan. 2006. "Terrorism: The Relevance of the Rational Choice Model." *Public Choice* 128 (1–2): 91–107. doi:10.1007/s11127-006-9046-8.

Clauset, A., L. Heger, M. Young, and K. S. Gleditsch. 2010. "The Strategic Calculus of Terrorism: Substitution and Competition in The Israel-Palestine Conflict." *Cooperation and Conflict* 45 (1): 6–33. doi:10.1177/0010836709347113.

Crenshaw, Martha. 2001. "Theories of Terrorism: Instrumental and Organizational Approaches," in David Rapaport, ed., *Inside Terrorist Organizations*, revised edition. London: Frank Cass.

Dershowitz, Alan. 2002. *Why Terrorism Works: Understanding the Threat, Responding to the Challenge.* New Haven: Yale University Press.

Enders, Walter, and Todd Sandler. 1993. "The Effectiveness of Anti-Terrorism Policies: A Vector-Autoregression-Intervention Analysis." *American Political Science Review* 87 (4): 829–844.

English, Richard. 2016. *Does Terrorism Work? A History.* Oxford: Oxford University Press.

Feinstein, Jonathan S., and Edward H. Kaplan. 2010. "Analysis of a Strategic Terror Organization." *The Journal of Conflict Resolution* 54 (2): 281–302. doi:10.1177/0022002709355438.

Fromkin, David. 1975. "The Strategy of Terrorism." *Foreign Affairs* 53 (4): 683: 698. doi:10.2307/20039540.

Krause, Peter. 2013. "The Political Effectiveness of Non-State Violence: A Two-Level Framework to Transform a Deceptive Debate." *Security Studies* 22 (2): 259–294. doi:10.1080/09636412.2013.786914.

Kydd, Andrew H., and Barbara F. Walter. 2006. "The Strategies of Terrorism." *International Security* 31 (1): 49–80. doi:10.1162/isec.2006.31.1.49

Lake, David A. 2002. "Rational Extremism: Understanding Terrorism in the Twenty-First Century." *Dialogue IO* 1(01): 15–29.

Neumann, Peter R., and Michael LR Smith. 2005. "Strategic Terrorism: The Framework and Its Fallacies." *The Journal of Strategic Studies* 28 (4): 571–595. doi:10.1080/01402390500300923.

Pape, Robert A. 2005. *Dying to Win: The Strategic Logic of Suicide Terrorism.* 1st ed. New York: Random House.

Peffley, Mark, Marc L. Hutchison, and Michal Shamir. 2015. "The Impact of Persistent Terrorism on Political Tolerance: Israel, 1980 to 2011." *American Political Science Review* 109 (4): 817–832.

Thomas, Jakana. 2014. "Rewarding Bad Behavior: How Governments Respond to Terrorism in Civil War." *American Journal of Political Science* 58 (4): 804–818. doi:10.1111/ajps.12113.

Wood, Reed M., and Jacob D. Kathman. 2014. "Too Much of a Bad Thing? Civilian Victimization and Bargaining in Civil War." *British Journal of Political Science* 44 (3): 685–706. doi:10.1017/S000712341300001x.

Woodworth, Paddy. 2001. "Why Do They Kill: The Basque Conflict in Spain?." *World Policy Journal* 18 (1): 1–12. doi:10.1215/07402775-2001-2002.

CHAPTER 3

THE ORGANIZATIONAL APPROACH

Learning Objectives

After reading this chapter, readers should be able to:

- Explain the organizational approach in their own words.
- Summarize the main assertions and expectations of the organizational approach.
- Critique the organizational approach by describing its main shortcomings.
- Describe several examples of terrorist groups that appeared to behave in accordance with the organizational approach's expectations.
- Describe several examples of terrorist groups that appeared to behave in ways that contradict the organizational approach's expectations.
- Distinguish between the strategic and organizational approaches.

> "[T]he preponderance of evidence is that people participate in terrorist organizations for the social solidarity, not for their political return."
>
> —MAX ABRAHMS 2008, P. 94

> "[W]e had some very heinous and counterproductive activities being carried out that the leadership didn't punish because they had to maintain the hearts and minds within the organization."
>
> —DAVID ERVINE, FORMER ULSTER VOLUNTEER
> FORCE BOMB-MAKER, 2006, QUOTED
> IN SHAPIRO 2013, P. 45

INTRODUCING THE ORGANIZATIONAL APPROACH

The organizational approach follows from **social perspectives** on international relations by starting from the assumption that we cannot make sense of human behavior without taking into account the social environment in which people operate. The organizational model suggests that if we want to understand group behavior, we must look at how these groups relate to other groups in their environments rather than only looking at how they relate to their opponents. Therefore, proponents of this approach tend to emphasize group rivalries, inter-group alliances, and other linkages *between* social organizations while also examining characteristics *within* organizations, such as group structure, leadership, and membership. In the study of terrorism, scholars typically refer to this approach as the **organizational model**, the socio-organizational approach, the **social network** approach, or **social movement organization** (SMO) approach.

This perspective directly challenges rationalist, unitary assumptions by focusing explicitly on the **relational** dimensions of human behavior. The approach assumes that people generally prioritize their own status in their immediate social environments above longer-term political goals, and that the internal authority and legitimacy of social organizations can be highly fragmented and contested. Rivalries with other groups and internal conflicts over leadership and strategy often make such groups behave in ways that contradict the predictions of both the strategic and structural approaches (Chapter 6).

This argument follows in the tradition of theories of social organizations and social movements developed in sociology, which assume that the main purposes of socio-political organizations is to survive rather than to achieve strategic success per se. Contrary to the strategic approach, this model suggests that political organizations are primarily interested in maintaining themselves and are therefore primarily concerned with outperforming competitor organizations, resolving internal conflicts, and maintaining a steady stream of recruits—organizational tasks that some scholars refer to as **process goals**. These motives create incentives for groups to engage in tactical innovations (such as terrorism) to increase their chances of achieving these process goals. Some scholars have even identified particular terrorist tactics, like suicide bombing, as tactical innovations aimed at obtaining support from the constituencies the groups purport to represent and enhancing group attractiveness to potential recruits (Bloom 2004). According to the organizational approach, terrorism is less related to rationalist motives or structural opportunities to use violence, and more related to pressures emerging from the density and intensity of the organizational environment in which different social organizations operate. We should therefore expect to see numerous types of violence: **inter-group violence**, where terror groups attack violent groups representing the opponent's constituency; and **intra-group violence** (sometimes called outbidding), where terror groups escalate violence to compete with (or directly attack) other groups operating within their own constituencies. Importantly, according to the organizational approach the violence is meant to send a message—that the organization perpetrating the violence is the best representative of the population it purports to represent, and that it will destroy other organizations that attempt to compete with it.

According to this approach, the relationship between the terror group and its opponent is not **dyadic,** nor is the life cycle of different terror groups linear. Instead, a conflict environment is better construed as a **dynamic system**, with ever-changing social relationships that are interdependent with one another. This is why we often see **splinter groups** emerging out of terror groups, as well as terror organizations reformulating themselves into **second- and third-generation groups** over time and space. As a result, organizational approaches are quite amenable to **social network analysis**, which attempts to map out the different inter-relationships among different actors involved in a conflict and uses characteristics of the associations between these groups (e.g., the degree of conflict or cooperation between them, the intensity of a rivalry, or the centrality of a relationship) as key factors explaining terror group behavior.

Like strategic approaches, organizational approaches allow that terrorism is a game between different political actors seeking to maximize their preferences. For the strategic approach the primary players of the game are the group, the opponent, and the broader public audience. For the organizational approach, the primary players of the game are the group's leaders, followers, rivals, and potential sympathizers.

The organizational perspective has a number of core strengths. First, the observation that inter-organizational rivalries account for a good deal of the violence we see resonates when one examines the organizational landscape of many ongoing conflicts. Especially in protracted conflicts, it is rarely the case that the conflict is limited to one terror group fighting against a government. Typically the organizational environment is much more diverse, featuring a number of nonviolent contentious organizations, social movements, interest groups, and political parties, alongside more militant and radical groups that combine both violent and nonviolent methods of contention, as well as some groups that rely primarily on terror attacks to promote their aims. This approach also accords with revelations that many terror groups are rife with internal conflicts, personality conflicts, and petty rivalries among members. The complexity of most conflicts gives the organizational approach some intuitive appeal.

Second, the organizational approach helps to explain the timing of different waves of terrorism. As opposed to using the static measures employed in structural models, organizational models emphasize more dynamic shifts in the year-to-year organizational environment. For example, one important implication of prior social movement research is that tactical innovations—such as the escalation to terrorist violence—should occur at the end of a protest cycle. Sidney Tarrow and Donatella Della Porta conducted research on the rise and fall of the Red Brigades in Italy and found that violence emerged among left-wing radical groups only after participation in popular mobilization, strikes, and other nonviolent activities began to decline (Tarrow 1989; Della Porta 1995). Preliminary evidence on the ETA in Spain corroborates this finding (Sánchez-Cuenca and Aguilar 2009), suggesting that ETA adopted terrorism as a way to outbid other nonviolent and violent Basque separatist groups recruiting from the same shrinking pool of potential members.

Third, the organizational approach helps to explain why terrorism is common in places where people would not otherwise expect terrorism to occur (e.g., some established democracies). Historically, democracies have tended to produce more protest cycles than authoritarian regimes, meaning that they have much richer and denser organizational environments than classic authoritarian regimes. Whereas some democracies, like France, the UK, and Spain, are routine targets of terrorist violence, others—like the Nordic countries and Japan—have been relatively immune from terrorism. Yet Sweden, Norway, Denmark, and Japan also have relatively low levels of mobilization in general, with far fewer protests and strikes than countries like France, the UK, and Spain.

ASSUMPTIONS OF THE ORGANIZATIONAL APPROACH

The organizational approach helps to explain several of the puzzles emerging out of the strategic model, such as the tendency of terrorist groups to attack one another, the tendency of groups to outlive their usefulness and to switch goals, and the internal turmoil that seems to beset many terror groups. Let's take a closer look at the assumptions behind the organizational approach.

Preference for Organizational Survival Above All Else. Unlike the strategic approach, which assumes an organization's preferences, the organizational approach assumes that every political organization has one overarching preference that guides its behavior—the survival of the organization itself. This means that the ultimate priority for the political organization is to maintain itself, such that the organization tends to focus on tasks related to its continuance more than tasks related to strategic success. Organizations therefore tend to emphasize recruitment, maintaining a popular public image (particularly among those it purports to represent), finding prestigious donors and supporters, gaining attention and media coverage, eliminating rivals, and overcoming internal divisions. Aside from group survival, however, the organizational approach assumes that second- or third-order preferences—such as what the ultimate political goals of the group are—are highly contested within political organizations. So are decisions about tactical choices. In fact, this contestation over preferences and methods is often the source of internal conflicts or inter-group conflicts that can divert the organizations from achieving both political efficacy and group survival in the long term.

Organizations Are Not Unitary Actors. Instead of assuming that organizations are unitary, proponents of this approach contend that organizations tend towards **fragmentation** and fracture. This is particularly due to the fact that political organizations—political parties, interest groups, community organizations, social movements, and even terrorist groups— are comprised of numerous individuals with wide variance in terms of their own preferences. In reality, there is often a considerable amount of disagreement over the ultimate goals (i.e., ends) of the organization, with constant conflict between those arguing for moderate goals and those arguing for radical goals, and ongoing contention over the methods (i.e., means) through which the organization should be pursuing change. As a result, ends and means are often contested and such organizations are often fragmented. Some members of the organization push to use more moderate methods, such as political organizing, forming a political party, or using negotiations backed by international diplomacy to pursue their goals. Others within the organization may argue that the organization must use armed struggle—either guerrilla warfare or terrorism or both— to pursue change. For example, in 1969, the Weather Underground (WUO) split off from the Students for a Democratic Society (SDS)—a nonviolent leftist movement calling for workers' rights, the end of racism, and the end of the Vietnam War. The WUO, also called "The Weathermen," was a faction of the broader movement that believed that the SDS was not radical enough in its goals or its methods. The WUO set the revolutionary overthrow of the US government as its main goal, and it adopted armed struggle as its primary method. The Weathermen commenced to bomb government buildings over the next decade, suspecting that these actions would inspire and provoke a mass insurrection. This insurrection never came, and by the mid-1980s, most members of the WUO had either been arrested in the field or had turned themselves in to federal authorities having grown weary of life on the run.

To illustrate the diversity of actors in many conflict environments, Table 3.1 illustrates the distribution of preferences around ends and means among a sample of Republican groups in Northern Ireland.

Here were can see that even among Republican groups, there is a wide amount of room for disagreement among actors with similar broad claims. This disagreement often makes for serious inter-group conflict. For example, among radicals such as the Provisional Irish Republican Army (PIRA) and

TABLE 3.1 Differing Perspectives on Ends and Means in the Conflict over Northern Ireland

		Ends	
		Moderates	**Radicals**
Means	**Moderates**	Civil rights for Catholics in Northern Ireland through nonviolent mass mobilization (NICRA)	Full reunification with Ireland through political action (Sinn Fein; 32 County Sovereignty Movement)
	Radicals	Devolution and autonomy through armed action (Provisional Irish Republican Army after 1997)	Full reunification with Ireland through armed action (Provisional IRA through early 1990s; Continuity Irish Republican Army; Real Irish Republican Army)

the Real Irish Republican Army (RIRA), there was a lethal rivalry wherein the RIRA split off from the PIRA in 1997. The RIRA accused the "Provos" of "selling out" on the movement for agreeing to compromise on the issue of full reunification with Ireland and agreeing to lay down arms as part of the Good Friday Accords. At that point, the RIRA scaled up its violence so as to distinguish itself from the PIRA in the public mind. In an attempt to resurrect the armed struggle, the RIRA detonated a car bomb in Omagh, a predominantly Catholic city in Northern Ireland, on August 15, 1998. Although the RIRA issued several warnings to police prior to the detonation, the botched placement of the car bomb resulted in a grisly explosion that killed 29 people and injured hundreds more.

Organizations Must Consistently Manage Internal Conflict. The conflict between the PIRA and the RIRA is typical of many different conflicts where terror groups are active. In fact, because the organizations prefer survival above all else, and because they navigate numerous internal disagreements about ends and means, terror groups are in a perpetual state of instability. As a result of disagreements regarding ends and means, organizations are constantly shifting in terms of their internal power structures, while individuals within the organization jockey for power and influence. Sometimes, some members may act independently of the organization, actively taking the initiative (or even disobeying or defying authority figures within the organization) to pursue their own agendas. Many organizations fragment or produce **splinter factions**, which may behave in more radical ways than their erstwhile comrades. For instance, the RIRA's attack in Omagh was the single deadliest incident of the twenty-five years of **The Troubles**.

Terror groups are therefore characterized by near-constant internal paranoia, with group leaders attempting to avoid internal collapse or fragmentation by enforcing hierarchies through routine purges, strict financial management and accounting, discipline, indoctrination, and control. Terror groups often use violence to eliminate internal dissenters or to incorporate them into the group's structure. Leaders' constant need to prove to lower-level radicals that their leadership remains robust and committed to the cause often results in the leaders authorizing high-profile terror attacks. Heightened tension within a terror organization—or conflicts over the internal power structure of an organization—may therefore be strong predictors of increased violence.

Organizations Must Consistently Manage External Competitors. In addition to preventing internal collapse, terror groups often compete with external competitors for recruits, resources, and influence. This is most obviously true with regard to inter-group violence, such as the violence that occurred between Republican and Loyalist terror groups in Northern Ireland. Given that the PIRA and the Ulster Defense Force (UDF) were on opposing ends of the ideological spectrum, with the PIRA endorsing reunification with Ireland and the UDF demanding that Northern Ireland remain part of the UK, it is not especially surprising that these groups frequently attacked one another. The organizational approach suggests that terror groups often react to opposing groups by matching their violence or brutality so as to maintain the spotlight. Left-wing and right-wing groups in Italy similarly attacked one another during the 1970s and 1980s, referring to the use of violence as a "strategy of tension" meant to balance the impacts of violence by the opposing group.

But bitter rivalries often characterize the relations between various terror groups even if they share similar goals. ETA, for instance, pursued eliminationist strategies against other Basque separatist groups, killing many different separatist factions who would not pledge allegiance to ETA. The same was true of the LTTE, which killed thousands in its attempt to wipe out Tamil factions who were attempting to maintain independence from the LTTE.

Social Concerns, Rather than Political Concerns, Are the Primary Motivators of Recruits to Terror Groups. Unlike the structural approach, which assumes that recruits to terror groups join them because of political, economic, or social grievances (see Chapter 6), the organizational approach tends to assume that people join terror groups because of the social benefits of doing so. In an influential article, Max Abrahms suggests that most recruits to terror organizations are primarily motivated by an intense desire to belong to a meaningful collective entity, to bond strongly with others, and to use social relations to strengthen one's own sense of identity (2008). Individuals with social motivations will often demonstrate a very strong connection to others within the terror group, while also exhibiting a paradoxical suspicion and skepticism toward the group's leadership. Because such individuals wish to maintain social bonds above all else, they will see internal divisions as greatly threatening to their own personal interest in the organization's survival. As such, recruits to terror groups often seek out like-minded members with whom to form their own groups in the event of the dissolution of the main organization. This dynamic may create a self-fulfilling prophecy, however, as factions within the organization build the confidence and capacity to split off from the main group and form their own groups. A good illustration of this point is the ever-changing cycle of alliance-formation and splintering that characterized various armed groups in Afghanistan. As Christia (2012) notes, a defining feature of the Afghan civil conflict of the 1990s was the total fragmentation of the different militant groups into small factions, which constantly switched sides and formed ad-hoc alliances in an attempt to create a balance of power in the conflict. This pattern of behavior made ceasefires impossible to maintain and prolonged the conflict. And as Evan Perkoski (2015) notes, factions that split because of disagreements over the use of tactics tend to be even more violent and durable than their "parent" organizations.

Organizational Cultures, Subcultures, and Tactical Repertoires Shape Groups' Behavior. Terror groups tend to coalesce around certain belief systems, including those that rationalize their use of violence, in ways that reinforce their identities as groups. They also tend to specialize in their own unique brands of violence, which leads them to develop internal routines regarding training, planning, recruiting, and preparation. Groups tend to stick to particular types of tactics—like IED attacks, suicide bombings, or hostage-taking—which shape (and are shaped by) the organizational culture of the group. For example, the Weather Underground in the United States adopted a subculture of underground Marxism-inspired revolutionary identity that rejected most Western political and societal institutions and norms as bourgeois. They adopted a common nomenclature used among cadres, upended norms of monogamy by engaging in promiscuous sex within the group, rejected patriarchal and racial power hierarchies within the group, and used illicit drugs. In operations, the group primarily relied on bombings of unoccupied federal buildings (or their perceived collaborators) along with issuing communiqués rationalizing their attacks. Such routines and practices created a unique identity within the group that its members sought to preserve above and beyond their larger political project.

Because tactical innovations may disrupt the identity and common routines of the group, terrorist organizations rarely innovate new techniques on their own (see Horowitz 2010). This can help to explain why some terror groups fail to develop new tactics, even after their opponent governments begin to successfully defend against or contain them.

OBSERVABLE IMPLICATIONS OF THE ORGANIZATIONAL APPROACH

Many proponents of the organizational approach have arrived at their conclusions by examining the behavior of specific terror groups or specific conflict environments over time. Let's consider the observable implications of this model, as well as the types of evidence one might seek out to test them.

Contexts with High Organizational Density (and Competition) Experience the Highest Frequency and Intensity of Terrorist Attacks. The organizational explanation posits that terrorist violence occurs on the margins of popular protest and other repertoires of contention. According to this view, groups and individuals resort to terrorism as a way to amplify their voices in a competitive environment of seemingly powerful rivals.

Take, for example, Figure 3.1, which illustrates a very simple network of actors within a conflict environment. In this hypothetical scenario, there is a broad-based social movement pursuing a particular goal in opposition to the rest of the population. Notice that there are three terror groups roughly "affiliated" with the social movement's goals, and notice that only one of those terror groups shares a direct link to that social movement (perhaps the group volunteered to be a "self-defense force" or "armed wing," despite the broader movement's preference to operate nonviolently). As depicted by the arrows, the three terror groups may have different views as to the necessary means and ends of the conflict, and therefore have organized themselves into three factions. As such, they are necessarily in competition with one another for influence, attention, and resources. In addition to attacks against the opponent's counter-movement, the arrows depict intra-group violence between two of these groups. Notice also that the opposing population's counter-movement has an armed wing, as well as another group that has emerged outside of the movement. These two groups may attack the terror groups on the opposing side as well as the social movement from which one of these groups emerged.

Figure 3.1 is an oversimplification of a conflict environment. In reality, there are often many more actors who are related in various ways that shift over time. But what becomes clear from Figure 3.1 is the organizational approach's main intellectual emphasis: violence can multiply itself in contexts where numerous different armed factions operate. In fact, the organizational approach assumes that the fierceness of the competition among different actors within a given context is a powerful predictor of patterns of political violence.

Evidence in support of this observable implication might include quantitative evidence demonstrating that the lethality and frequency of terror attacks increase alongside other contentious activities, such as protests, strikes, or mass civil disobedience. For example, Chenoweth (2010) finds that countries with denser interest group sectors experience the emergence of higher

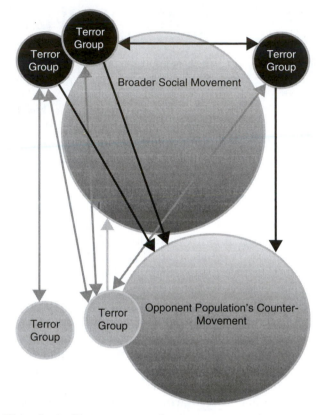

Figure 3.1 Hypothetical intra-group and inter-group attack patterns among terror groups emerging from within opposing social movements.

numbers of terrorist groups, while Moore, et al. (2011) find that higher levels of dissident protest activity are associated with higher numbers of terrorist attacks. Other quantitative evidence that would support this observable implication might demonstrate that the lethality and frequency of terror attacks increase with the onset of splinter factions, or that a higher number of distinct terror groups is associated with a higher number of attacks. An article by Findley and Young casts doubt on the latter implication, finding that the number of terror groups is not correlated with the number of attacks (2012).

Violence Escalates during Group Leadership Crises. In a 2009 article, Wendy Pearlman argues that organizational cohesion and fragmentation are the primary drivers of nonviolent and violent behavior, respectively. Political organizations that maintain internal cohesion through defined and legitimate leadership, internal rules and institutions for enforcing them, and a collective vision of the future were more likely to adhere to nonviolent modes of contestation. Groups that faced crises over the legitimacy and authority of leadership, disagreement about internal rules and sanctions, and division about the vision of the future were much more likely to turn to violence. The reason, she argues, is that such moments in an organizational life cycle motivate radicals within the organization to attempt to establish their own authority and agendas, usually by using violence to suppress dissenting views and practices (Pearlman 2009). The losers of this conflict are likely to form splinter groups to carry out their own agendas.

Relations between splinter groups and their erstwhile allies may therefore develop into bitter rivalries earmarked by varying levels of violence. Furthermore, leaders under attack from within often begin to engage in higher-risk behavior, such as adopting greater levels of violence against their opponent, in order to prove to their cadre that they ought to remain in control. As such, during moments of heightened fragmentation, the organizational model expects the highest levels of lethality.

Evidence in support of this observable implication might include quantitative evidence of correspondence between leadership decapitation and a subsequent short-term increase in the lethality of the terrorist group. In fact, Max Abrahms and Philip Potter argue that targeted assassinations of leaders of terror organizations are correlated with increased lethality among such groups in the aftermath, as internal rivalries push radical leaders upward in the organization and such leaders use spectacular incidents of violence to legitimize their right to rule (2015). They also draw on additional qualitative evidence from the Al Aqsa Martyrs Brigades' attack patterns during the Second Intifada, which indicate a high correspondence between intense levels of internal conflict within an organization and high attack frequency and lethality. Additional qualitative evidence from other cases might allow scholars to confirm this mechanism as a general pattern.

Terrorist Groups Modify Their Behaviors to Outdo Their Rivals. The organizational approach expects terror groups to engage in risky and (often) counterproductive behavior to outdo their competitors. Therefore, as opposed to the strategic approach, organizational approaches suggest that most seemingly non-rational violence follows the logic of outbidding, whereby groups attempt to compete against their rivals by escalating to more violent action. Terror groups tend to escalate the level of violence—in terms of lethality or targets—when they are competing with other groups for the same political space or "market share" of popular support (Bloom 2004). For instance, Yelena Biberman and Farhan Zahid argue that two massacres of schoolchildren—one in 2014 in Peshawar by the group Tehrik-i-Taliban Pakistan (TTP) and the other in 2004 in Beslan by the Riyadus-Salikhin Battalion of Chechen Martyrs—are best explained by this logic. In analyzing each of these episodes, Biberman and Zahid discovered that the timing of these massacres corresponded with intense internal leadership struggles within the organizations as well as rivalries with other terror groups active contemporaneously. As such, outbidding within and among

BOX 3.1

THE CHANGING STRUCTURE OF THE GLOBAL JIHADI MOVEMENT

Many proponents of the organizational approach see the internal structure of terror groups as important drivers of group behavior. One common way to differentiate group structures is whether they are primarily hierarchical or decentralized—a **leaderless resistance** model (see Shaul and Rosenthal 2005 for a thorough discussion of different organizational structures). Another common typology focuses on the relationship between leaders, followers, and potential recruits—whether groups see themselves as elite vanguards of a broader population, or whether they see themselves as facilitators and protectors of a grassroots revolution already in progress.

Jessica Stern and J. M. Berger (2015) compare Al Qaeda and ISIS along these lines. Al Qaeda had its origins in the late 1980s, when Islamist rebels or mujahedeen drove the Soviet Union out of Afghanistan (with the support of US and Pakistani intelligence agencies). The conflict, which had attracted many foreign fighters, brought Osama bin Laden together with thousands of other now-experienced fighters from around the Muslim world. Many of them returned to their respective countries to fight in wars at home (as in Chechnya, Bosnia, Somalia, and elsewhere), while Al Qaeda's core leadership began to develop plans for the next global jihad. But ever since its inception, Al Qaeda's core leadership has been a highly secretive, exclusive group that adopted sophisticated security measures to prevent infiltration and betrayal. Throughout the 1990s, Al Qaeda financed or facilitated various attacks around the world—like the twin bombings against the US embassies in Tanzania and Kenya—but rarely took direct credit for them. In fact, the group even balked in claiming credit for the 9/11 attacks in the United States; the CIA intercepted a half-produced video in which senior Al Qaeda leaders discuss their preparations for the attacks. Stern and Berger argue that this is because Al Qaeda saw itself as an elite vanguard whose attacks would awaken the global Muslim community to wage violent jihad. Indeed, throughout the 2000s, aggressive counterterrorism measures significantly degraded Al Qaeda's core, causing the movement to appeal to different local affiliates to adopt the Al Qaeda name and continue waging violent jihad against the West. Adopting the Al Qaeda name came at a price; aspiring affiliates had to swear fealty to Osama bin Laden, agree to certain shared religious principles, and swear obedience to the core leadership. Affiliate groups also had to submit to some degree of management (and, at times, condemnation) by the core leadership as well (Stern and Berger 2015, p. 54; see also Shapiro 2013). Some local Al Qaeda cells responded to the call, launching attacks in Bali (2002), Madrid (2004), London (2005), and elsewhere. Islamist insurgencies already active in several countries also began to adopt the Al Qaeda name, such as the Armed Salafist Group for Preaching and Combat, which renamed itself Al Qaeda in the Islamic Maghreb (AQIM) and swore allegiance to Osama bin Laden in 2008. Jordanian militant Zarqawi, who led the Iraqi insurgency against US forces in Iraq, similarly swore allegiance to bin Laden and renamed his group Al Qaeda in Iraq (AQI) in 2005. But these affiliations came at a significant cost to Al Qaeda as well. Al Qaeda leaders often reprimanded Zarqawi for killing too many people, or for killing Muslims, in ways that Al Qaeda leaders thought would undermine their popularity among the umma (Shapiro 2013, p. 48). In other cases, Al Qaeda's affiliates were too incompetent to complete their missions. For instance, based in Yemen, Al Qaeda in the Arabian Peninsula (AQAP) attempted numerous attacks against the United States, including the failed 2009 Christmas Day bombing aboard a KLM flight from Amsterdam to Minneapolis, as well as a foiled plot to detonate a cargo plane over the United States in 2010. Moreover, most of these Al Qaeda affiliates were actively fighting insurgencies in their own contexts against local governments for their own parochial interests, meaning that they had little use for Al Qaeda's global ambitions to resist and destroy the United States' influence over the Muslim world. For instance, Al Nusra front, an Al Qaeda affiliate in Syria, could not be bothered to plot attacks against the United States at the same time as it was fighting the Russian- and Iranian-backed Syrian government under Bashar al Assad. Although Al Qaeda has inspired some successful attacks in recent years (such as the Charlie Hebdo attacks in Paris in 2015), such attacks have grown increasingly rare. Byman suggests that affiliate structures, while potentially effective in theory, are rarely effective in practice (2014). By embracing a theory of change often seen in elite revolutionary movements, Al Qaeda leaders wrongly assumed that the masses would see their attacks, hear their religious exhortations, and become compelled to initiate a coordinated fight themselves—in the precise manner envisioned by Al Qaeda's core.

Stern and Berger contrast Al Qaeda's structure with that of ISIS, which grew out of remnants of AQI with a different theory of change. In fact, some have even argued that Al Qaeda and ISIS are engaging in an outbidding war for supremacy over the global jihadist movement (Zelin 2014). For ISIS, establishing an exclusive, secretive core leadership to inspire a global rebellion was a self-defeating and ineffective strategy. Instead, the group emphasized a potent combination of deploying "ultraviolence" while simultaneously mobilizing Muslim "civil society" (Stern and Berger 2015, p. 72). Making use of the various foreign fighters drawn to the region in the context of ongoing civil wars in Syria and Iraq, the group set out to conquer swathes of land to establish an enduring territorial base, inspire and coordinate migration to the newly-conquered territory, and then expand as appropriate to satisfy further religious duties of conquest. The structure of the group, while hierarchical in its conquered territories, also relied on "blended groups of ISIS members and supporters" who would "take jobs upon themselves, including translating communiqués and propaganda into multiple languages and crafting armies of Twitter 'bots' " to amplify its impact (ibid, 2015, p. 71). As such, in addition to the thousands of foreign fighters recruited as ISIS warriors, the group deployed an incredibly sophisticated network of thousands of social media users to communicate this message, engage in hacks, and manage propaganda more broadly.

For ISIS, the primary aim was first to create a true Muslim society that would attract anyone who wished to live free of the toxicity of Western influence, while also deterring Western interference in this society. As Stern and Berger put it, ISIS's message that "you have a place here, if you want it, and we'll put you to work on this exciting new project just as soon as you show up"

Continued

BOX 3.1
THE CHANGING STRUCTURE OF THE GLOBAL
JIHADI MOVEMENT *(Continued)*

Photo 3.1 In January 2015, ISIS hacked United States Central Command and used the hijacked account to threaten US soldiers

was markedly different from Al Qaeda's (2015, p. 73). As soon as ISIS seized its territorial base in Iraq and Syria, the group established banks, schools, news publications, courts, hospitals, nursing homes, and other social services in order to complete the transition to statehood and attract a true popular following (ibid). The group also established sex slavery markets, looted and sold antiquities on the black market for funds, kidnapped and executed hostages, forcibly extracted "taxes" from its subjects, and used excessive brutality to force acquiescence to ISIS rule in conquered villages, among other abuses. Unlike Al Qaeda, ISIS was unapologetic about its killings of Muslims seen as enemies of ISIS's project. The group's emphasis on the performance value of ultraviolence meant that the group had few constraints on the type, intensity, or targets of its violence. Because of this, ISIS has not displayed much interest in managing the violence used by its fighters. Once established, the new state could then direct attacks abroad using its own human capital without requiring the considerable oversight costs Byman (2014) describes. Or, if threatened and dispersed by militarized responses to the group, ISIS could send its followers into Western countries, after which the group could exploit its global network of now-trained supporters to attack opponents. For instance, ISIS took credit for a massacre in Paris in November 2015, during which several jihadis who had trained in ISIS-held territory returned to Europe to conduct deadly coordinated attacks. Similarly, the group welcomed self-proclaimed affiliates in other regions without requiring obedience to a central authority. Boko Haram, also known as ISIS-West Africa, has been the deadliest of these affiliates, killing thousands throughout Nigeria. The Islamic State in the Sinai Peninsula, which is thought to be responsible for the bombing of a Russian airliner over Egypt's Sinai desert, is another notable self-proclaimed affiliate. Operations by ISIS-trained or ISIS-inspired affiliates in Tunis, Istanbul, Ankara, Dhaka, Jakarta, San Bernadino, Orlando, Brussels, Nice, Tipo-Tipo, Kabul, Baghdad, Peshawar, Jalalabad, Sydney, Melbourne, and Berlin demonstrate the global reach of ISIS's well-equipped network. But unlike Al Qaeda, ISIS eschewed the model of the elite vanguard in favor of the notion of popular revolution.

DISCUSSION QUESTIONS

- *Al Qaeda and ISIS both have affiliate groups around the world. What is the difference between the types of affiliates claimed by each group?*
- *Al Qaeda adopted an elite vanguard structure, whereas ISIS adopted a popular revolutionary structure. Which is more difficult to combat and contain? Why?*

militant organizations helped to explain these brutal and seemingly mindless attacks (2016).

Further evidence in support of this observable implication might include archival evidence from terrorist memoirs or captured documents indicating a choice to escalate violence against civilians based upon a desire to undercut other terror groups, social movements, or political rivals. Additional supportive evidence would include quantitative evidence indicating that terrorist groups sharing broadly similar goals escalate attacks against civilians in a tit-for-tat pattern during a fairly compressed period of time, particularly when they experience leadership vacuums.

Terrorist Groups Attack Competitors as well as Stated Enemies. Because terror groups see themselves as engaged in a life-and-death struggle for organizational survival, they should view other political organizations operating in the same context as engaged in a zero-sum game for recruits, resources, attention, and influence. As a result, the organizational approach expects terror groups to spend much of their time and resources attacking these competitors rather than just directing attacks at their stated opponents. In the Palestinian Territories, for example, Hamas and Fatah engaged in major gun battles in the Gaza Strip following Hamas' victory in municipal elections in 2006, as Hamas attempted to drive its remaining political rivals out of Gaza. In Peru, Abimael Guzmán's faction of Sendero Luminoso ("Shining Path") was notorious for attacking other leftists whom he viewed as "sell-outs" to the Maoist cause. This bloody behavior led to the deaths of hundreds of leftist activists and politicians accused of corrupting Sendero Luminoso's attempted revolution. The organizational approach expects a great deal of similar **internecine violence**, particularly in protracted conflicts.

Evidence in support of this observable implication might include archival evidence from terrorist memoirs or captured documents indicating a high degree of concern about and preoccupation with the advancements of other terror groups, social movements, or political rivals rather than solely preoccupation with the group's stated enemy. Additional supportive evidence would include quantitative evidence indicating that terrorist groups sharing broadly similar goals attacked one another.

Terrorist Groups Do Not Always Claim Operationally Successful Attacks. Whereas the strategic approach would expect terror groups to claim attacks as a way to demonstrate their capability and resolve to their opponents, the organizational approach would expect groups to assess the social and political popularity of such attacks prior to claiming them. For instance, Mia Bloom argues that following terror attacks by different Palestinian groups during the Second Intifada, the groups first waited to see how Palestinian public opinion responded to the attacks before claiming them (2005). If opinions were generally positive, the groups would claim the attacks, seeing them as opportunities to elevate their status and prestige ahead of other groups. Indeed, she cites cases where multiple groups claimed highly popular attacks, seeking to amplify their status from them (ibid). However, if the Palestinian public rejected an attack as too barbarous or counterproductive, the groups would avoid claiming the attacks even if they had hit their marks. Indeed, Bloom shows that many groups (including the PIRA in Northern Ireland) actively avoided engaging in suicide bombing in order to avoid alienating potential recruits, supporters, and donors. As such, the organizational approach offers an explanation for why some terror groups would avoid claiming attacks that were otherwise tactically successful.

Evidence in support of this observable implication might include historical evidence from a number of different cases demonstrating a correlation between negative public opinion and a drop in credit-taking for terror attacks. Indeed, Abrahms and Conrad (2017) find that terror groups' leaders often avoid public credit-taking for attacks against civilians, which may undermine their popularity and potential recruitment bases. Additional evidence that might support this implication is archival evidence from terrorist memoirs or recovered documents indicating that groups eschewed taking credit for specific attacks out of concern for public image vis-à-vis rivals, and that groups justified taking credit for other attacks by referencing the popularity benefits.

Once Having Adopted Unique Tactical Repertoires, Terrorist Groups have Difficulty Abandoning Them. The strategic model assumes that popular attacks will replicate themselves, whereas unpopular tactics will decline. This is because organizations have no real attachment to particular tactics other than their efficacy in yielding progress toward strategic goals. The organizational approach, on the other hand, suggests that organizations often stick to unproductive tactics for a couple of reasons.

First, there are significant organizational barriers to tactical innovation. The more a terror group identifies itself by its tactics, the more tied to these tactics the group may become. For example, Hamas' rocket attacks against Israel have yielded few (if any) strategic benefits toward Palestinian self-determination. However, Hamas may strongly identify the firing of rockets into Israeli territory as one of its tactical identifiers or "calling cards"—it has become an essential part of Hamas' **tactical repertoire**. As a result, abandoning this tactic would require it to abandon one of the few unique brands that distinguishes it from other Palestinian armed groups. Therefore, terror groups often persist in using counterproductive tactics if they view these tactics as signaling that their "brands" remain prominent on the political scene.

Second, the adoption of new tactics is costly. Organizations have finite resources, which they invest in activities that allow them to distinguish themselves from competitors. They also develop routines and expertise around specific tactics that require time, experience, and operational consistency. For example, if a terror group invests in training its members to wage urban guerrilla warfare against its opponents, then it will tend to accumulate weapons and other materials that will allow it to engage in a limited set of tactics related to that repertoire. It will develop internal procedures and mechanisms for assessing and improving the effectiveness of these tactics. As a result, if the group survives, over the course of several years, the group will likely improve its efficacy at urban guerrilla attacks. However, in light of these organizational investments, routines, procedures, and operational expertise, switching to suicide bombing is not necessarily easy for a group to do.

As such, evidence in support of this observable implication might include social network analyses showing a homogenization of tactical choices among groups linked to the same network, and tactical diversity among groups located outside of established networks. For instance, Michael Horowitz finds that most terror groups do not adopt suicide bombing as a tactic because of these organizational constraints. Instead, he argues that two types of groups tend to adopt suicide terrorism: (1) new groups who have no such organizational barriers in place to prevent them from adopting the tactic; and (2) organizations with direct links to other groups that use suicide terrorism, suggesting that they do not have to invest any resources into developing this tactic themselves (2010). Horowitz finds that older groups and groups that form outside of established networks of suicide terror groups are highly unlikely to adopt this technique. Once again, we see that organizational context matters in determining both the adoption and abandonment of different tactics.

Additional confirming evidence would include quantitative evidence demonstrating the persistent use of seemingly counterproductive tactics or qualitative, archival evidence through terrorist memoirs or recovered documents that terror groups have well-established organizational routines that make it difficult for them to innovate new tactics. Useful evidence would be signs that the group engages in internal arguments and debates about adopting different tactics but maintains its current course because of concerns about branding, allocation of resources, or the costliness of tactical innovation.

Terrorist Groups Endure After their Stated Goals are Moot, or They Change Their Stated Goals over Time. The African National Congress (ANC), a South African anti-apartheid organization that developed an armed wing called Umkhonto we Sizwe (Zulu for "Spear of the Nation"), was known to use the saying "A luta continua, vitória e cérta" or "The struggle continues; victory is certain." However, once mass popular mobilization, boycotts against white businesses, international pressure, and political action against the apartheid regime sidelined Umkhonto we Sizwe, armed struggle became unnecessary to end legal apartheid. Nevertheless, some members of the organizations insisted on maintaining armed action even after it was clear that the apartheid system was coming to an end. Critics of this view quipped that the organization's motto should become "The struggle is certain; victory continues" (Barrell 2014). This anecdote well illustrates a key implication of the organizational approach—that organizations will hang on to violent tactics much longer than is needed to produce the essential political change.

Alternately, some organizations that achieve their original goals may shift their attention to achieving new political goals over time, in order to avoid the organization's dissolution. For example, Jessica Stern argues that Al Qaeda amounted to a "protean enemy" with so many abstract goals that its leaders could not possibly expect to achieve them (2003). At times, Al Qaeda seemed primarily concerned with defending Muslims in different war zones (as in Bosnia, Chechnya, and the Philippines). At other times, it seemed preoccupied with expelling American troops from Saudi Arabia and ending Western influence over Arab leaders. Occasionally Osama bin Laden would call for attacks against Israel, but the ultimate goal of such attacks was unclear. Indeed, some members of Al Qaeda themselves expressed frustration with the group's lack of consistent, actionable aims. Other organizations, such as Action Directe in France, Revolutionary Struggle in Greece, and the Pakistani Taliban have displayed a similar inconsistency in articulating their strategic goals (Abrahms 2008).

Evidence in support of this observable implication might include additional historical evidence of the persistence of many terror groups after their goals have been achieved, or that groups experience serious internal crises as their operations come to a close—including the split of the group into factions who reinterpret and re-state the group's goals. Quantitative evidence supporting this implication might include data suggesting that terror attacks become most lethal and frequent toward the end of a conflict—particularly during settlement negotiations—as terror groups act as spoilers to prolong the conflict to justify their own existence. In fact, Tarrow (1989) finds evidence to confirm the latter implication in his study on protest, mobilization, and violence in the Italian case. Specifically, he finds that violence tended to occur once protest began to decline, leading hardliners to radicalize their methods to compete for a declining share of possible recruits.

Terrorist Groups Avoid or Disrupt Negotiations. One of the enduring puzzles of the strategic approach is that terror groups tend to avoid compromising with their adversaries, even when political settlements might win them greater concessions than protracted conflict could. The organizational approach provides a clear explanation for why. Very simply, political settlements threaten the continued survival of the group. If a conflict ends, the group's *raison d'être* evaporates. As a consequence, we should expect terror groups to avoid negotiations—even when governments offer them—and we should also expect to see terror groups try to spoil peace accords by escalating violence immediately before and during their negotiations. Moreover, we should expect to see such activity pay off, in the sense that using terrorism during negotiations should either disrupt or postpone peace. For example, as the Colombian government engaged in earnest negotiations with the FARC in the spring of 2016, another leftist group fighting the Colombian government for decades, **Ejército de Liberación Nacional (ELN)**, began to ramp up its presence in contested areas.

Quantitative research suggests that this argument has merits. For instance, Michael Findley and Joseph Young (2015) find that terrorism prolongs armed conflict. Moreover, incidences of terror attacks during peace negotiations make recurrence of civil conflict more likely even after political settlements have come into effect.

Further evidence might include internal documents from terror groups that demonstrate the spoiling logic at play in decisions to escalate violence in the context of peace negotiations with rival groups—particularly if the documents express concern about the long-term survival of the group as the main motivation for such violence.

Recruits to Terrorist Groups Proffer Social Rather than Political Explanations for Joining the Group. If the organizational approach is correct, recruits to terror groups should be less concerned about the political aims of the group, and more concerned with the social benefits of belonging to a group. Moreover, they should tend to seek out these social benefits continually, even after their own groups have collapsed.

Evidence in support of this observable implication might include survey or interview evidence that members of terror organizations joined the group through inspiration of members of their personal network, because of a desire to "be somebody" or obtain notoriety, because of a desire to elevate their status to obtain other social benefits (e.g., marriage, community leadership, family respect, or control), or because of a desire to prevent the rise of a rival group. For example, in 2012, Vera Mironova, Loubna Mrie, and Sam Whitt conducted a survey of fighters associated with the Free Syrian Army and different armed Islamist groups engaged in fighting in Syria. They asked

BOX 3.2

HOW ORGANIZATIONAL FACTORS LIMIT OR PROMOTE TACTICAL INNOVATION

In an influential article, Michael Horowitz explains that tactical innovations are always costly for an organization to adopt. They require new training and new resources within the organization. For example, if a group begins to use suicide bombing, training regimens might change from firearms practice, evading capture, or handling interrogations to ideological training, bomb-handling, and hand-to-hand combat. Recruitment techniques also change from attracting adventurous risk-takers to attracting true believers and vulnerable youth (2010). Hence, innovating new tactics requires organizational investments and cultural changes that may disrupt accepted routines and threaten the survival of the organization.

In fact, Horowitz, Perkoski, and Potter (forthcoming) find that most militant organizations tend to use the same tactics over and over. For instance, as mentioned above, since the mid-2000s, Hamas has engaged in a routine practice of firing rockets from its stronghold in Gaza into southern Israel on a fairly regular basis. These rocket attacks have caused very few fatalities among Israelis in recent years. The Israeli government has developed a sophisticated defense system—including bomb shelters, sirens and other alarms, and a missile defense shield—to protect Israeli civilians against rockets fired from the Gaza Strip by Hamas. Yet since Hamas expelled Fatah from the Gaza Strip in 2007, it has few local competitors motivating it to innovate new tactics. Moreover, Hamas's firing of rockets exemplifies an organizational routine—something the group does at a fairly consistent pace because of easy access to materials, widespread know-how within the group regarding how to fire these weapons, and, perhaps, an organizational incapacity and unwillingness to innovate new techniques.

When groups do expand their tactical repertoires, they do so in response to competition with other terror groups combined with severe government repression. For example, from the late 1960s through the 1970s, the PFLP engaged in high-profile airline hijackings and attacks, targeting El Al flights from within Europe and the United States. Airline hijackings were the PFLP's modus operandi. In the 1980s, after airline security improved, the group turned to other methods, like hijacking buses, assassinations, and roadside bombings. During the Second Intifada, the group turned to suicide bombings, much like other Palestinian militant groups active at that time. Horowitz, Perkoski, and Potter (forthcoming) argue that such diversification of tactics likely occurred in response to pressure from both increasing Israeli government repression and an incredibly competitive sector of Palestinian nationalist groups—including Al Aqsa Martyrs Brigades, Hamas, the DFLP, PIJ, and others. Moghadam (2013) further argues that such innovations are as likely to come from the bottom up—primarily from new members recruited to groups because of their novel tactical expertise or from middle managers wishing to prove their worthiness to the group's leadership—as from the top down. In reality, the PFLP had a vast amount of resources upon which to innovate these new techniques. These resources included an influx of local recruits eager to join into an armed movement fighting renewed Israeli military operations during the Second Intifada, as well as transnational connections with groups that could transfer know-how to the PFLP, thereby reducing the costs of tactical innovation (Horowitz 2010).

DISCUSSION QUESTIONS

- *Think of three terrorist groups. Just pick the first three that come to your mind.*
- *(1) Which tactic(s) do you associate them with?*
- *(2) Have the group's tactics changed over time, or have they remained roughly the same? If they have changed tactics over time, what factors led to that change?*

why different rebels joined these groups. Although these groups are associated with a larger insurgency against Bashar al-Assad's government in Syria, the responses illustrate the diverse motivations for why people join armed groups in general. Unsurprisingly, most respondents claimed that their primary motivations were to take revenge against Assad's forces, to defend their community, and to defeat Assad—all clearly political goals. However, more than half of the respondents also claimed that they joined because they felt inspired by people in the group. Just under half of the respondents claimed they joined because their friends joined. Nearly 17% claimed that family pressure was a significant factor impacting their decision to join, with nearly 10 percent claiming that they wanted people to respect them (Mironova, Mrie, and Whitt 2014). Note that the latter motivations have very little to do with politics—they are entirely social in nature, and they clearly evoke the sense that these recruits are strongly motivated by a desire to belong to a meaningful group, that these motivations emerge from various pressures within their immediate social environments, and that personal notoriety has a role to play in influencing this choice.

Additional evidence might include archival data (through terrorist memoirs, recovered documents, surveys, or otherwise) indicating that recruits to terrorist organizations are strongly motivated by the desire to belong to a group, or indicating that after a terror groups ends, its members tend to join other terror groups rather than voluntarily demobilizing.

PRACTICAL IMPLICATIONS OF THE ORGANIZATIONAL APPROACH

The organizational perspective suggests that government repression rarely reduces terrorism. Instead, repression likely has no effect on terror attacks (or may even increase terrorist violence). This is because the opponent government is only one of many conflict actors affecting terror groups' behavior in an incredibly dense and fragmented conflict sector. Indeed, frequently the government opponent is not even the most important actor involved the conflict (from the group's point of view). Instead, terrorism tends to endure until the groups destroy one another or simply die out.

As such, governments wishing to contain or reduce terrorism adopt strategies that accelerate this process. As opposed to the strategic model, where an effective counterterrorism approach would depend on an accurate strike to destroy the groups outright using massive force, the organizational approach would suggest a counterterrorism strategy meant to fragment terror groups while degrading their capacity to do damage. For instance, sowing divisions within terror groups, which may have an escalatory effect in the short-term, may ultimately reduce the capacity of various groups so much that they can do little damage to the public. Alternatively, providing clear benefits to members that exit terror groups can accelerate their demise. The latter two approaches require a high level of human intelligence, including infiltration within the groups (Cronin 2009).

A third (and more troubling) policy implication is that governments should do what they can to contain all forms of contention. If terrorism emerges in environments where other forms of contention occur at high levels, then it follows that governments would seek to limit these other forms of contention to prevent terrorism. This policy implication raises a host of normative problems, the most alarming of which is that governments would limit freedoms of assembly, expression, and protest in the name of countering terrorism. Moreover, since many terror groups emerge as splinter groups within broader social movements, a disturbing implication would be the possibility that governments might use this fact as a justification for monitoring or infiltrating nonviolent social movements because of their oppositional views, rather than their violent behavior. This practice might essentially undermine rights to privacy and free conscience as well as rights to assembly and expression. A well-known example of overreach in this regard was the US government's COINTELPRO program, which was designed to root out left-wing political opposition groups. Through this program, the US government actively infiltrated and subverted nonviolent organizations, harassed and intimidated activists (including Martin Luther King Jr.), and even killed a number of black activists accused of armed revolution against the United States government. Ultimately, most of the targets of the COINTEL-PRO program were nonviolent dissidents singled out for their beliefs rather than the threat that they might engage in any violent activities.

Therefore, analysts must keep in mind that terror groups that emerge out of broader social movements typically form as factions within and competitors to these movements rather than as representatives of the movement. Nearly always, radicals who are drawn to terror groups are not the same as moderates drawn to social movements engaged in nonviolent dissent, meaning that the vast majority of participants in social movements would not engage in armed action. A great deal of sophistication is often required to distinguish radicals from moderates within conflict environments; according to the organizational approach, it is always a mistake to lump them together.

CRITIQUES OF THE ORGANIZATIONAL APPROACH

The organizational approach has three major shortcomings frequently noted in the literature.

Mixed or Limited Empirical Support. Scholars who have tested the occurrence of outbidding or competitive dynamics among terrorist groups have found mixed support for this phenomenon. Chenoweth (2010) finds a higher number of terrorist attacks and more new terrorist groups emerging in countries with pre-existing terrorist groups that are ideologically diverse, particularly in emerging or intermediate-level democracies. Young and Findley (2012), on the other hand, find no support for outbidding dynamics when they examine cross-national patterns of terrorist attacks from 1970 to 2004. These two studies, however, only examine competition among terrorist groups and do not take into account how terrorist groups might be responding to organizational and political pressure from nonviolent and conventional political actors. Studies that do incorporate other dissident behavior are supportive of competitive organizational dynamics (Moore, et al. 2011), but the persistent absence of cross-national, time-series data means that scholars have not been able to fully establish these patterns across cases. Thus empirical support for competitive organizational dynamics is not yet fully established, and further testing is necessary to identify the conditions under which they operate.

The Organizational Approach Predicts Too Much Terrorism. If the contentions of the organizational argument were true, then we would see a lot more terrorism than we do. For one thing, terrorism does not emerge everywhere mobilization occurs. Most people who engage in dissent do so nonviolently, even when the organizational environment is dense and competitive. Moreover, once terrorism does emerge as a tactical innovation, the model's logic suggests that we should observe ever-increasing escalation of terrorist violence. Instead, we see ebbs and flows, indicating that some groups tend to exercise at least some restraint even while they compete with other groups for power.

Indeterminate Outcomes. The assumptions behind organizational arguments sometimes predict opposing or contradictory outcomes. For example, the approach can explain the lethality of violence based on both competition and cooperation among terror groups. On its surface, the approach predicts that fragmented terror groups in competition with one another may be especially lethal because of the escalatory dynamics produced by such rivalries.

This certainly seems to resonate with the lethal spirals of violence created during inter-group tensions among different jihadi groups in Pakistan. Such rivalries have produced some of the most lethal attacks in Pakistani history, including the December 2014 attack on a school resulting in the death or injury of hundreds of children (Biberman and Zahid 2016). However, some proponents of the organizational approach argue that lethality increases when terror groups actually cooperate with one another. For instance, Victor Asal and Karl Rethemeyer's work on terrorist networks suggests that the most lethal groups are those that cooperate with other like-minded groups (2010). And an important article published by Michael Horowitz and Philip Potter demonstrates that terrorist groups are most lethal when they are highly embedded in terror networks (2014). Horowitz and Potter suggest that cooperation, not competition, increases lethality because groups in alliance with one another greatly heighten their capacity (in terms of weapons, money, and members) to carry out high-impact attacks. There are also lower barriers to tactical adaptation, meaning that groups that ally with other groups have access to a more diverse tactical repertoire than others. Therefore, they can do more damage. In short, the problem here is that the organizational approach itself predicts that terrorist group competition and terrorist group cooperation *both* increase lethality. This leaves us with a fundamental problem of indeterminacy: the same assumptions produce opposing predictions, meaning that the organizational approach itself is difficult to falsify.

SUMMARY

The organizational approach departs from the strategic model by bringing the internal dynamics and external relationships of terror groups into the mix. This approach focuses on the group's internal cohesion and relative position among a diverse set of conflict actors as the major sources of its behavior. We have seen a few examples of how the organizational model applies to various groups. Although this approach has a good deal of explanatory appeal, we have also addressed some of the empirical and normative critiques of this approach.

Several important puzzles remain. Most importantly, the organizational explanation does not help us to understand why some people mobilize by using violence while others either mobilize nonviolently or do not mobilize at all. Why is it, for example, that the Weather Underground remained such a small splinter group without inspiring participation from the larger Students for a Democratic Society? Why did only a small cadre of members emerge from a larger movement with similar goals and interests? In other words, what explains the division between moderates and radicals within movements? We turn to these key puzzles in Chapters 4 and 5, which examine psychological and ideological approaches respectively. Moreover, the organizational approach often focuses on the nature of competing terror groups as the main source of their respective behaviors. But why do some countries develop competitive sectors of terror groups in the first place? Chapter 6 addresses the structural factors that motivate and facilitate the rise of protracted conflicts involving terrorist violence.

Discussion Questions

1. What are the key differences between the strategic and organizational approaches? Which of these approaches do you find more convincing? Why?

2. Is it possible to explain terrorist group behavior using *both* the strategic and organizational models? Why or why not?

3. In December of 2014, the Pakistani Taliban attacked a school, killing hundreds of children and wounding hundreds more. How would you explain this attack using the organizational approach? What types of internal and external conditions would you look for in order to make an organizational argument?

4. If you watched *The Battle of Algiers* after reading Chapter 2, which elements of the organizational approach do you notice at work in the FLN's behavior?

5. Is it ethically justified for a government to infiltrate a nonviolent organization to identify potential terrorists operating within it? Why or why not?

KEY TAKEAWAYS

- The organizational approach argues that most behaviors of terrorist groups can best be understood by looking at the internal structures and dynamics of groups. This approach assumes that people join terrorist groups for primarily social, rather than political, reasons.

- The organizational approach emphasizes outbidding, fragmentation, and competition as primary sources of violence escalation.

- The organizational approach generally expects that terrorist violence will be highest when there are multiple rival organizations operating in the same place at the same time; when an organization is suffering a leadership vacuum; during peace negotiations; and when groups splinter due to strategic disagreements. It also expects that groups will have difficulty changing or diversifying the tactics that define their "brand;" that groups will directly attack their rivals, even when they share similar political goals; that groups will not always claim terror attacks; and that groups will endure after their goals are moot.

- Some groups seem to behave in ways that contradict the expectations of the organizational approach. For instance, some groups seem to be more lethal when they cooperate with other groups than when they compete. Moreover, the organizational approach tends to over-predict terrorist violence and receives only mixed empirical support across cases.

SUGGESTED FURTHER READINGS

Abrahms, Max. 2008. "What Terrorists Really Want: Terrorist Motives and Counterterrorism Strategy." *International Security* 32 (4): 78–105. doi:10.1162/isec.2008.32.4.78.

Abrahms, Max and Philip B. K. Potter. 2015. "Explaining Terrorism: Leadership Deficits and Militant Group Tactics." *International Organization* 69 (2): 311–342. doi:10.1017/s0020818314000411.

Asal, Victor, and R. Karl Rethemeyer. 2008. "The Nature of the Beast: Organizational Structures and The Lethality of Terrorist Attacks." *The Journal of Politics* 70 (2): 437–449. doi:10.1017/s0022381608080419.

Bloom, Mia M. 2004. "Palestinian Suicide Bombing: Public Support, Market Share, and Outbidding." *Political Science Quarterly* 119 (1): 61–88. doi:10.2307/20202305.

Bloom, Mia M. 2005. *Dying to Kill: The Allure of Suicide Terror.* New York: Columbia University Press.

Byman, Daniel. 2014. "Buddies or Burdens? Understanding the Al Qaeda Relationship with its Affiliate Organizations." *Security Studies* 23 (3): 431–470. Doi:10.1080/09636412.2014.935228.

Chenoweth, Erica, Nicholas Miller, Elizabeth McClellan, Hillel Frisch, Paul Staniland, and Max Abrahms. 2009. "What Makes Terrorists Tick." *International Security* 33 (4): 180–202. doi:10.1162/isec.2009.33.4.180.

Chenoweth, Erica. 2010. "Democratic Competition and Terrorist Activity." *The Journal of Politics* 72 (1): 16–30. doi:10.1017/s0022381609990442.

Crenshaw, Martha. 2001. "The Causes of Terrorism: Instrumental and Organizational Approaches," in David Rapaport, ed., *Inside Terrorist Organizations*, revised edition. London: Routledge.

Della Porta, Donatella. 1995. "Left-Wing Terrorism in Italy," in Martha Crenshaw, ed., *Terrorism in Context.* University Park, PA: Pennsylvania State University Press.

Dugan, Laura, and Gary LaFree. 2007. "Introducing the Global Terrorism Database." *Terrorism and Political Violence* 19: 181–2004.

Findley, Michael G., and Joseph K. Young. 2012. "More Combatant Groups, More Terror?: Empirical Tests of an Outbidding Logic." *Terrorism and Political Violence* 24 (5): 706–721. doi:10.1080/09546553.2011.639415.

Flanigan, Shawn Teresa. 2008. "Nonprofit Service Provision by Insurgent Organizations: The Cases of Hizballah and The Tamil Tigers." *Studies in Conflict & Terrorism* 31 (6): 499–519. doi:10.1080/10576100802065103.

Heger, Lindsay, Danielle Jung, and Wendy H. Wong. 2012. "Organizing for Resistance: How Group Structure Impacts the Character of Violence." *Terrorism and Political Violence* 24 (5): 743–768. doi:10.1080/09546553.2011.642908.

Hoffman, Aaron M. 2010. "Voice and Silence: Why Groups Take Credit for Acts of Terror." *Journal of Peace Research* 47 (5): 615–626. doi:10.1177/0022343310376439.

Horowitz, Michael C., and Philip B.K. Potter. 2014. "Allying to Kill: Terrorist Intergroup Cooperation and the Consequences for Lethality." *Journal of Conflict Resolution*, 58 (2): 199–225. doi:10.1177/0022002712468726.

Jones, David Martin, Ann Lane, and Paul Schulte. 2010. *Terrorism, Security and the Power of Informal Networks*. Cheltenham: Edward Elgar.

Kennedy, Jonathan, and Gabriel Weimann. 2011. "The Strength of Weak Terrorist Ties." *Terrorism and Political Violence* 23 (2): 201–212. doi:10.1080/09546553.2010.52 1087.

Kilberg, Joshua. 2012. "A Basic Model Explaining Terrorist Group Organizational Structure." *Studies in Conflict & Terrorism* 35 (11): 810–830. doi:10.1080/1057610x. 2012.720240.

McCormick, Gordon H. 2003. "Terrorist Decision Making." *Annual Review of Political Science* 6 (1): 473–507. doi:10.1146/annurev.polisci.6.121901.085601.

Moore, Will H., Ryan Bakker, and Daniel W Hill. 2011. "How Much Terror? Dissidents, Governments, Institutions and the Cross-National Study of Terror Attacks." (December 28) *SSRN Electronic Journal*. unpublished paper available at http://papers.ssrn.com/sol3/papers.cfm?abstract_id=1977262. doi:10.2139/ssrn.1977262.

Morrison, John F. 2013. *The Origins and Rise of Dissident Irish Republicanism: The Role and Impact of Organizational Splits*. New York: Bloomsbury Academic.

Oots, Kent L. 1986. *A Political Organization Approach to Transnational Terrorism*. New York: Greenwood Press.

Pearlman, Wendy. 2009. "Spoiling Inside and Out: Internal Political Contestation and The Middle East Peace Process." *International Security* 33 (3): 79–109. doi:10.1162/isec. 2009.33.3.79.

Perkoski, Evan. 2015. "Organizational Fragmentation and the Trajectory of Militant Splinter Groups" (January 1, 2015). *Dissertations available from ProQuest*. Paper AAI10003874. http://repository.upenn.edu/dissertations/AAI10003874.

Sageman, Marc. 2004. *Understanding Terror Networks*. Philadelphia: University of Pennsylvania Press.

Sánchez-Cuenca, Ignacio, and Paloma Aguilar. 2009. "Terrorist Violence and Popular Mobilization: The Case of the Spanish Transition to Democracy." *Politics & Society* 37 (3): 428–453. doi:10.1177/0032329209338927.

Shapiro, Jacob N. 2013. *The Terrorist's Dilemma: Managing Violent Covert Organizations*. Princeton: Princeton University Press.

Smith, Allison G. 2008. "The Implicit Motives of Terrorist Groups: How The Needs for Affiliation and Power Translate into Death and Destruction." *Political Psychology* 29 (1): 55–75. doi:10.1111/j.1467-9221.2007.00612.x.

Turner, Mark. 2003. "The Management of Violence in a Conflict Organization: The Case of the Abu Sayyaf." *Public Organization Review* 3 (4): 387–401. doi:10.1023/b:porj.0000004816.29771.0f.

Zirakzadeh, Cyrus Ernesto. 2002. "From Revolutionary Dreams to Organizational Fragmentation: Disputes over Violence within ETA and Sendero Luminoso." *Terrorism and Political Violence* 14 (4): 66–92. doi:10.1080/714005641.

CHAPTER 4

THE PSYCHOLOGICAL APPROACH

Learning Objectives

After reading this chapter, readers should be able to:

- Explain the psychological approach in their own words;
- Summarize the main assertions and expectations of the various psychological theories explored;
- Describe and critique examples of how psychological factors (at the individual and group levels) have been used to explain terrorism;
- Compare and contrast the psychological, organizational, and strategic approaches;
- Describe how psychological approaches might inform or misinform counterterrorism policy.

> "We often think of terrorists as crazies... Their actions seem to make no sense at all. But terrorists, by and large, are not insane at all. Their primary shared characteristic is their normalcy, insofar as we understand the term."
> —LOUISE RICHARDSON (2006, P. 14)

> "Terror consists of mostly useless cruelties perpetrated by frightened people in order to reassure themselves."
> —FRIEDRICH ENGELS IN A LETTER TO KARL MARX, 1870

INTRODUCING THE PSYCHOLOGICAL APPROACH

Psychological approaches attempt to explain why people are inclined towards specific types of behavior, (i.e., to use terrorism). These theories are essentially bottom-up approaches to the phenomenon that try to understand why individuals might gravitate towards committing outrageous attacks against innocent civilians, or commit so deeply to a goal that often appears unlikely to be achieved in the first place. As Marc Sedgwick observed, psychological approaches to terrorism represent attempts to understand individual **radicalization**, or "what goes on before the bomb goes off" (2010, p. 479). Insofar as the concept of radicalization can be conceptualized as both a state of mind or a particular behavior, it is perhaps best understood as a process through which people become persuaded that violent activity is justified, and eventually determine to engage in the violence personally.

Psychological or behavioral approaches to terrorism help to explain the enduring puzzle that, despite our ability to understand the rational (Chapter 3) or socio-organizational impetus for violence (Chapter 4), the fact remains that a relatively small number of individuals—among hundreds of thousands in virtually identical positions—turn to terrorism. As Brian Crozier remarked, "it takes a rebel to rebel" (1960, p. 9). Therefore, this approach begins with the assumption that individual factors must be at work to explain why some people turn to such extreme forms of violence while others with similar grievances do not. Rather than looking exclusively at terror groups as rational, unitary actors, psychological approaches tend to operate at the individual level of analysis, meaning that they are often concerned with how particular people arrive at terrorist behavior. How, for example, do people like Ted Kaczynski come to be "lone wolf" terrorists? Rather than looking to strategic decisions (Chapter 2) or inter-group rivalry (Chapter 3), psychological theories look to an impressive host of emotions: romanticizing risk; feeding a self-destructive urge for "success" through martyrdom; falling victim to the influence of charismatic leaders; the power of rage over reason; blind ambition; frenzied revenge or spite, to name a few (Victoroff 2005). That said, because different individual pathways of radicalization are so personalized, idiosyncratic, and varied, the psychological approach is more appropriate as an explanatory approach than a predictive one.

Whereas some psychological approaches do attempt to classify terrorists as crazed fanatics (see below), others deliberately eschew pathologizing terrorists. Therefore, psychological approaches to terrorism do not necessarily argue that terrorist behavior results from specific psychopathological conditions per se. Instead, some argue that the political decision to join a terrorist organization is influenced—and in some cases is determined by—subconscious or latent psychological motives (Crenshaw 1986, p. 386). In this sense **psychological traits**—not pathological disorders—might explain why some individuals become terrorists. Traits are the distinguishing qualities, attributes, and habitual behavioral patterns that describe a person's nature. Some common personality traits, for example, may include bravery, perfectionism, extraversion, laziness, enthusiasm, stubbornness, or close-mindedness. Some common character trait descriptors may include "brave" or "pious" or "caring" or kind" or "ambitious" or "stubborn." In psychological terms, scholars typically think about personality traits as behavioral characteristics that define an individual. The unique combination of personality traits we each possess defines us as individuals.

In this chapter, we review the leading theories about the degree to which the roots of terrorist behavior are the products of **individual** and/or **group psychological** forces. The first set of psychological approaches focuses on the individual level of analysis, meaning that they attempt to differentiate the personal traits of people who use terrorism from those who do not. The second set of approaches focuses on the psychology of groups, meaning that they take group-level dynamics into consideration to explain terrorist behavior, albeit from a psychological perspective (in contrast to the group-level explanations that we presented in Chapter 3). An ongoing controversy within psychological approaches relates to the degree to which terrorist behaviors are **innate versus acquired**—that is, whether terrorists are born or made. As you will see, a wide range of theories emerges from the field of psychology, each of which inform the various approaches that we will discuss.

IS TERRORISM A PERSONALITY DISORDER?

Some argue that terrorism is an adverse behavior with its origins in the central nervous system (Victoroff 2005, p. 16), which may yield identifiable pathologies that set terrorists apart from other people.

Narcissistic Rage Theory. The narcissistic rage theory focuses on the early, formative years of the terrorist persona. Ultimately, such theories emphasize the presence of personality disturbances, some caused by events experienced during the terrorist's childhood, to explain violent behavior in later life stages. Consider, as a starting point, the example of a highly narcissistic child who harbors a tendency towards extreme self-aggrandizement, and who is not neutralized by reality. According to certain psychologists, this unchecked "grandiose self" produces highly anti-social individuals who exhibit traits such as arrogance and a general lack of regard for others. Similarly, when an individual is unable to integrate difficult feelings, specific defenses are mobilized to overcome what the individual perceives as an unbearable and highly disappointing situation. These conditions of helpless and narcissistic defeatism can lead to intense reactions of rage and a desire to destroy the source of narcissistic injury.

An example of the narcissism-aggression hypothesis to explain terrorism is found in the work of Jerrold M. Post, whose theory links defense mechanisms such as "splitting" to terrorist behavior. Splitting – the tendency to view events or people as either all bad or all good—is found "in individuals with narcissistic and borderline personality disturbances," whose personality development is influenced by narcissistic injury during childhood (Post 1998, p. 27). Post's principal argument is that individuals are drawn to the path of terrorism specifically in order to commit acts of violence, and their psychologically-grounded logic and rhetoric becomes the justification for the violent acts that they commit. In other words, people become terrorists because they want to use violence. To support this claim,

Post points to the commonalities that exist in the "us vs. them" rhetoric of various terrorists, despite the diversity in their causes.

The influence of narcissism-based psychological explanations for terrorism has decreased significantly in more recent research. Many of these early theories generated little empirical support, likely because they were and continue to be difficult to test. Isolating such a specific psychological mechanism in individuals presents obvious challenges, and there is really no way of knowing whether a narcissistic personality or some other kind of mental disorder led a person to commit an act of violence. It remains undetermined whether the prevalence of narcissistic traits among terrorists exceeds that of the general population (Victoroff 2005, p. 24). Ultimately, the conclusions regarding narcissism may be more impressionistic than empirical.

Moreover, the narcissistic rage hypothesis yields few effective counterterrorism options, other than interdiction or other forms of coercion. If a terrorist only attains some form of self-significance through the act of becoming a terrorist, or joining a terrorist group, then she cannot be made to give up terrorism. To do so would be to lose her very reason for being. We deal more specifically with the policy implications of psychological approaches to understanding terrorism at the end of this chapter.

Paranoia Theory. Echoing the work of psychoanalyst Heinz Kohut (1972, 1978), paranoia theory posits that a recurring feature of terrorist psychology is projection—a behavior Victoroff describes as "an infantile defense that assigns intolerable internal feelings to an external object" that may occur in a person who has "grown up with a damaged self-concept" after she "idealizes the good self and splits out the bad self" (2005, p. 24). While not necessarily psychotic, the paranoid psychology of the terrorist enflames her with suspicions of the other that are used to justify acts of extreme violence, usually in the name of self-defense.

Paranoia theory and the narcissistic rage theory of terrorism described above have important similarities. Ideas of being persecuted and perceptions of a grandiose self provide protection against inadequacy or shame brought on by some kind of early-life trauma. Recall our description of Post's "splitting" mechanism, whereby an important feature of the terrorist mentality is the differentiation between the good and bad self. This reaction is associated with an adult persistence of the infantile phase called the "paranoid-schizoid position" (Robins and Post 1997). Post's paranoia theory inflames the terrorist with suspicions that justify the act of violence as self-defense—he is eager to destroy what he believes represents his devalued and disowned "self" (Victoroff 2005, p. 25). This sense of paranoia may help to explain why terrorists target individuals who do not appear to pose an imminent threat, at least to the outside observer.

Post's theory of paranoia has been criticized for a variety of shortcomings. Nowhere in his studies, for example, does he present a specific definition of what paranoia is, or what such a trait might look like in an individual.

Another criticism comes from Marc Sageman's (2004) finding that nine out of ten Muslim terrorist biographies revealed no evidence of paranoia. None of the mujahedin he evaluated made any mention of a painful split self, nor did any of them live a life of patterned paranoia prior to becoming terrorists (Sageman 2004, p. 88–89).

Moreover, there are certainly far more people with narcissistic or paranoid personality disorders than there are terrorists with those disorders. But the impracticalities of deriving accurate psychological profiles of terrorists and would-be terrorists compared with other people make it difficult to test such approaches without subjecting such studies to an important selection bias, where terrorist subjects are not compared against others in the general population.

Besides, there is reason to doubt that terrorists are pathologically different from others, aggressive or not. As Martha Crenshaw has said, the outstanding common feature of most terrorists is their normalcy (1981, p. 390).

Novelty-Seeking. Another possibility explored by psychological approaches to terrorism is that the trait of novelty-seeking among individuals may be associated with choices to engage in terrorism. This approach suggests that notoriety and adventure-seeking are often key motivators of highly risky or adverse behavior. Terrorist planning and executing is certainly out-of-the-ordinary and indisputably "thrilling," and some scholars have suggested that political violence may satiate certain innate, perhaps genetically determined needs for high-level stimulation and risk (Victoroff 2005, p. 28).

For instance, in a recent study, Simon Cottee and Keith Hayward (2011) draw on militants' memoirs to suggest that terrorist activity characteristically involves high levels of violence, danger, and sacrifice—but also risk, excitement, and drama. A core existential motive for engaging in terrorism, in their view, is the desire for excitement found in certain individuals: "to do violence is to experience a euphoric sense of transcendence, of being outside the self and thrust into the present in a way that is like a drug. Ordinary life, with its banal routines and civilized constraints, does not permit this kind of pure, elemental experience. . ." (p. 967).

The romance of risk, for example, may explain why so many young men and women are leaving for Syria and Iraq to join a variety of rebel groups. In 2015, researchers of the Lebanon-based Quantum Communications collected televised interviews with forty-nine fighters in Iraq and Syria. After analyzing fighters' statements using a psycho-contextual analytical technique to identify the motivating forces and personal characteristics of each interviewee, the researchers concluded that a number of them had traveled to the conflict zone primarily as thrill-seekers. This category of fighter is described in the report as "filled with energy and drive. . . They want to prove their potential/power by accomplishing an arduous task or surviving a harrowing adventure. They are mostly in it for the opportunity to engage in action while enjoying a certain level of impunity for their acts" (Quantum 2015, p. 5). Approximately 33 percent of those identified as thrill-seekers were Westerners.

Humiliation-Revenge. An important set of factors that has been linked to individual radicalization is the need to respond to grievances, either at a personal level (for someone, for instance, who has experienced the death of a loved one at the hands of security forces), or at a more collective group level. For example, Anne Speckhard and Khapta Akhmedova note that all of the "Black Widow" terrorists in Chechnya included in their study had experienced personal trauma or witnessed family members beaten by Russian security forces (2006). Indeed, Russian and international press actually named this group "Black Widows" after it became clear that many of them were acting in revenge for the deaths of their husbands, sons, and brothers. From 2000 to 2005, Chechen female terrorists have been involved in more than 80 percent of the suicide attacks attributed to Chechen rebels. Through interviews with surviving hostages of suicide attacks, as well as family members and close associates of these so-called Black Widows, Speckhard and Akhmedova were able to discern no serious personality disorders in their sample of female suicide bombers. They were, however, able to conclude that all of the individuals had experienced deep personal trauma and exhibited symptoms of post-traumatic stress disorder and other dissociative phenomena. The study authors conclude that psychological trauma was likely one of the deepest leading motivational factors that spurred the radicalization of each bomber and drew her to embracing terrorism. Furthermore, they argued that the adoption of the jihadist ideology worked to meet the needs inherent both within the Chechen tradition of seeking revenge for the killing of a family members, as well as in definitions of general traumatic stress theory (ibid).

Some scholars have also argued that radicalization and the embrace of terrorism have been acts of revenge for hurts—both real and imagined—perpetrated against their parents' generations. Post, for example, demonstrates how the generational transmission of hatred shaped terrorist identity for social-revolutionary terrorists and nationalist-separatist terrorists in the 1970s. One member of the German terrorist group Red Army Faction, for example, described his targets and victims as "the corrupt old men who gave us Auschwitz and Hiroshima" (Post 2010, p. 16).

What may become apparent in the discussion of the humiliation-revenge hypothesis is the strong impact of grievances on individual radicalization. Yet prominent scholars of terrorism such as Walter Laqueur have warned against upholding the general perception that addressing or accommodating grievances is the most efficient counterterrorism policy for such individuals. Indeed, while most people share a variety of grievances related to nationalism, identity, violent experiences, or social injustices, very few actually employ terrorism in response (see Chapters 5 and 6).

Therefore, a primary concern for critics of individual-level approaches to studying terrorist behavior is the fact that personal psychological conditions or traits may be necessary yet insufficient explanations for terrorist behavior. Unlike psychological approaches to studying political phenomena more generally, it is impossible to do randomized controlled experiments on terror groups compared to others in the population. Therefore, the field tends to suffer from an important selection bias in that researchers tend to identify incidents like childhood trauma as common among terrorists. That said, countless other people in society may have experienced childhood trauma without becoming terrorists—and researchers generally do not study such people to evaluate the differences between terrorists and non-terrorists.

Moreover, although individual-level psychological approaches may accurately explain why some people tend to gravitate toward aggression, they do not necessarily describe why such aggression would manifest as terrorism as opposed to, say, nonpolitical criminal behavior.

WHAT TRAITS DO TERRORISTS HAVE IN COMMON?

Another school of thought within the psychological approach has argued that terrorist behavior is not a function of pathology, but rather can be the result of the intersection of various traits common to most humans. John Horgan (2008, p. 84–85), for example, found that people who are more open to terrorist recruitment and radicalization tend to:

- Feel angry, alienated, or disenfranchised;
- Believe that their current political involvement does not give them the power to effect real change;
- Identify with perceived victims of the social injustice they are fighting;
- Feel the need to take action rather than just talking out the problem; and
- Believe that engaging in violence against the state is not immoral.

Note that this approach centers on emotions, beliefs, and identities that may affect any person, rather than on disorders that may categorically set terrorists apart from others. Several strands of political psychology seek to understand how these traits combine and intersect to produce terrorist behavior in individuals.

Social Identity Theory. This theory posits that a person's own sense of self-identity is highly dependent upon her membership in a group. Moreover, the groups to which people belong are important sources of self-esteem, self-image, and pride (Tajfel 1974). For example, political psychologist Jeanne N. Knutson (1981) argued that the political terrorist consciously assumes a negative identity, one that involves a vindictive rejection of the role regarded as desirable by members of the wider community. A study carried out by Knutson and published after her death concluded that the violent acts of terrorists "stem from feelings of rage and hopelessness engendered by the belief that society permits no other access to information-dissemination and policy-formation processes" (Knutson 1984, p. 287). For young people, the turn to political violence in a desperate search for identity may materialize as lone wolf acts of terrorism, or through joining a particular group. Identity-starved joiners are believed to be motivated by a desire to embrace the tutelage of a charismatic leader—a form of choosing a love object resembling a parent (Victoroff 2005).

Identity theories of terrorism are also reminiscent of the argument set forth by Frantz Fanon (1965), who posited that violence against the "germs of rot" of colonial oppression is a mechanism through which individuals can cleanse their self-identities and their bodies from internalized colonial repression. Menachem Begin, too, reflected this mode of thinking in his book *The Revolt*, where he declared that "we fight, therefore we are" (Begin 1977, p. 26).

Post's splitting mechanism in the narcissistic rage thesis strongly resembles psychological explanations for terrorism that are based on social identity theory. But there is a key distinction between the two psychological mechanisms. In the former, the attachment to an "us versus them" mentality is the direct result of a particular type of psychological injury incurred during childhood that produces narcissistic wounds. Individuals with these personality traits split into mentalities of "me" and "not me." This split personality idealizes the "grandiose" self, and splits out and projects onto others all of the hated and devalued weakness caused by the early childhood trauma (Post 1998, p. 27). By contrast, in social identity theory, the need to belong to a clearly defined group is what motivates an individual to commit acts of violence, and this need does not rest on the occurrence of some kind of early childhood trauma.

More recent identity theories of terrorism outline the role of different forms of identity in motivating specific categories of terrorism. For instance, Schwartz, Dunkel, and Waterman (2009) suggest that terrorist behavior represents the confluence of cultural, social, and personal identity. In the case of religious or ethnically motivated terror groups, their student found cultural identities strongly based in collectivism and in fundamentalist adherence to religious or cultural principles; social identities founded on sharp contrasts between their own group (the in-group) and groups perceived as threats (the out-group); and personal identities of terrorists that were foreclosed, authoritarian, and at times even aimless. They argue that the interaction of these three forms of identity leads to greater propensities for terrorism (ibid).

A variant of social identity theory is the *quest for significance*. A number of early psychological studies identified the quest for personal significance as a fundamental human motivation and driver of individual behavior (Frankl 2000). The quest for meaning is often central to what psychologists refer to as "authentic happiness," and can be attained by attaching oneself to a larger cause (Seligman 2002). When an individual is threatened with personal insignificance, she might thus attach herself to a larger social group, and act to defend that particular group's view of the world. Kruglanski and Orehek (2011) extend this logic to suggest that individuals who define themselves according to their membership in a particular group might be more supportive of violence against out-groups, and use violent tactics such as terrorism on behalf of the group in order to gain personal significance.

The authors tested this theory using surveys conducted in fourteen Muslim countries, and found some preliminary support for the dynamics described above (Kruglanski and Orehek 2011). Survey respondents who identified primarily with either their nation or their religion—i.e., those individuals who identified primarily with collective goals—were more likely to show support for terrorism. Those who identified first and foremost as individuals, on the other hand, were significantly less likely to do so. Of course, the survey alone was unable to demonstrate whether the quest for personal significance itself played a particularly strong role in individuals' identification with collective goals, and in shaping subsequent support for terrorism. The fact that the quest for personal significance is present in almost all individuals across all cultures, but that only a small minority of people in the world actually supports terrorism, casts some doubt on the generalizability of the study's findings, as well as on the study's causal inference. Indeed, personal significance can be gained from a variety of accomplishments and group memberships, the overwhelming majority of which are nonviolent.

Importantly, the quest for significance framework does suggest potential ways to reduce terrorism. Creating alternative opportunities for individuals to gain personal significance, such as providing increased support for individuals' personal aspirations, or enhancing social mobility, might induce people to embrace alternatives to violence. At the level of groups, reducing perceived injustices through diplomacy or negotiation might also lessen the need to use violence as a means of achieving one's objectives.

Cognitive Theory. Social cognitive theory directly rejects rationalist assumptions about the ability to collect and integrate knowledge dispassionately (Chapter 2). Instead, this approach holds that a person's acquired knowledge relates to how they have observed the behavior of others within their social interactions, experiences, or other external influences. When people witness certain types of behavior and the consequences of that behavior, they remember the sequence of events and use the information to guide and shape their own future behaviors. In contrast to the strategic approach (Chapter 2), however, these behaviors may not be easy to predict or generalize, since perceptions can vary so widely across individuals. Martha Crenshaw puts it this way: "the actions of terrorists are based on a subjective interpretation of the world rather than objective reality. Perceptions of the political and social environment are filtered through beliefs and attitudes that reflect experiences and memories" (Crenshaw 1988, p. 12).

Crenshaw also suggests that the principles of cognitive theory can apply as much to groups and organizations as to individuals. Terrorist groups may adapt their tactics in direct response to the experiences of other groups, and to the memories of particularly dramatic and devastating attacks. But cognitive theories argue that the global diffusion of specific attack patterns and increasing levels of devastation are not the product of rational, calculated decisions on the part of terrorists. Instead, they are based on the subjective interpretation of the world in which they find themselves. For example, the attacks of 9/11 have been construed as an example of "propaganda by deed" with global repercussions. Since the attacks in New York and Washington, DC, numerous grassroots jihadi cells and networks have attempted to emulate Al Qaeda's violence (Torres et al. 2008). Moreover, the successful 1983 suicide attacks on US Marines barracks in Beirut by Hizballah invoked a powerful message to other groups such as Al Qaeda that terrorism was effective in forcing US forces to withdraw from Middle Eastern countries, even though the decision to withdraw from Lebanon may have resulted from a host of factors unrelated to the attacks themselves. Ultimately, cognitive theories argue that individuals do not only learn behaviors through trial and error, but by replicating the actions of others—even if this thought process is subject to significant cognitive deficits.

Are terrorists different from ordinary people in this regard? Psychiatrists have found two common cognitive or processing deficits to be present in highly aggressive individuals: (1) the inability to generate non-aggressive solutions to conflicts; and (2) a perceptual hypersensitivity to hostile or aggressive cues in their surrounding environments—particularly interpersonal cues.

Closely linked with social cognition theory are the concepts of **cognitive distortion** and **attribution error**. Cognitive distortions are exaggerated or irrational thought patterns that perpetuate false beliefs, such as the tendency to suppress or ignore information that contradicts our prior beliefs. A common cognitive distortion linked to terrorist behavior is overgeneralization—that is, the supposed harm caused by an identified enemy that spreads to encompass the entire population. Attributions, in turn, are inferences that people draw about the causes of their own behavior or the behavior of others. In some cases, due to faulty logical processes, biased media influence, or other factors, attributions may occur on the basis of appearance alone. Physical features such as skin color or gender, combined with one's own beliefs of what those features might imply, are one of the most common ways impressions of others are formed (Stout 2002, p. 135).

Combined, arguments that draw on both cognitive distortion and attribution error suggest that people joining terrorist groups—like other humans—hold cognitive biases that inaccurately attribute evil motives to those that they perceive as oppressors. Consider as an example the Red Brigades terrorist group, which was active in Italy during the 1970s and 1980s. The group's Marxist ideology construed all visible representations of capitalism as evil and representative of the Italian government's betrayal of the Marxist imperative to abolish the bourgeoisie. As such, private businesses with no affiliation to the government were considered legitimate targets of terror attacks because the group attributed them with what they believed to be capitalist oppression.

BOX 4.1

DYLANN ROOF AND THE QUESTION OF SANITY: PATHOLOGICAL OR ORDINARY?

On the evening of June 17, 2015, Dylann Roof walked into a prayer service at the Emanuel African Methodist Episcopal Church in downtown Charleston, South Carolina and murdered nine African Americans. Facebook images of Roof found after the attack depicted the twenty-one year old wearing a jacket decorated with two emblems popular among American white supremacists: the flags of the former Rhodesia, and apartheid-era South Africa. He had a criminal record consisting of two prior arrests.

In the aftermath of the attack, investigators linked Roof to a website called *The Last Rhodesian*. The site included what appeared to be an unsigned manifesto containing Roof's opinions of "blacks," "Jews," "Hispanics," and "East Asians," as well as a cache of photos of himself posing with weapons and a Confederate flag. Roof's seized computer showed that he had communicated with other white supremacists online.

After his arrest, Roof admitted to having committed the attack, stating that his intent was to "start a race war." Though few details emerged about Roof's mental state before he committed the mass murder, media reports began to debate whether he was mentally sane.

Some of the individual-level psychological traits that we have discussed so far in this chapter might be useful in explaining why Roof was capable of such violence. On the one hand, he could have been affected by some kind of pathological disorder or serious mental illness, such as schizophrenia, delusions, or other psychoses, and not known what he was doing at the time of the attack. On the other hand, he may have had a personality or antisocial disorder and exhibited paranoia and a severe lack of empathy towards his victims, but knew exactly what he was doing. In fact, a court-appointed psychiatrist who evaluated Roof in jail during November 2016 stated that he suffered from "Social Anxiety Disorder, a Mixed Substance Abuse Disorder, a Schizoid Anxiety Disorder, depression by history, and a possible Autistic Spectrum Disorder" (Sack 2017). Roof's deep hatred for blacks and other minorities and the proclamation to his victims that "you rape our women, and you're taking over our country" (Sanchez and Foster 2015) may also be suggestive of narcissistic rage. Of course, such comments also indicate a racist ideology regardless of whether Roof had a personality or antisocial disorder.

Indeed, terrorists and mass shooters come in a variety of forms—some may be depressed, others enraged and vengeful about personal slights, and still others paranoid. Some may be **sociopaths** who do not suffer from serious mental illness, and are thus unlikely to be identified or helped by the mental health system until after they commit an act of violence. Others may not be mentally ill at all.

The variation that exists in the minds of terrorists begs the question of whether seeking to link terrorism to psychological disorders and mental illness is actually useful, especially when it comes to prescribing policy solutions. If most terrorists are not mentally ill, then implementing sweeping measures aimed at overhauling the mental-health system in order to curb mass shootings and other forms of violence could be counterproductive. Most of the terrorists and individuals who have committed mass shootings in the past would fall under the radar of screenings focused on identifying persons with mental illnesses. Even worse, efforts at addressing mental illness to stem violence could stigmatize the mentally ill, and work to deter them from seeking treatment. Moreover, seeing incidents like the Charleston shooting as an isolated mass murder involving a mentally ill perpetrator may deflect attention from endemic social problems of racism and white supremacy.

Photo 4.1   Dylann Roof

GROUP-BASED PSYCHOLOGICAL EXPLANATIONS

Some psychological theories of terrorism turn to **group psychology** to explain terrorist behavior. The primary difference here is that group-based explanations look to forces internal to the group—such as ideological indoctrination, repetitive training, peer pressures, and the effects of social networks more broadly—to understand both individual and collective radicalization. Clark McCauley and Sophia Moskalenko, for instance, point to the "power of love" in influencing individual propensities to join a terrorist organization. Trust, they argue, may define the pool of individuals from which a terrorist group may attempt to recruit, but love will often determine who actually joins. Devotion to friends or comrades can lead to the formation of cliques of individuals who join terrorist organizations together. Members of the Red Army Faction (RAF), for example, were drawn into the organization by devotion to friends. Most RAF terrorists joined radical groups through personal connections with people or relatives (McCauley and Moskalenko 2008). According to studies of the organization, there was an astonishing number of couples and siblings among the ranks of the RAF (Della Porta 1995, p. 168; Wasmund 1986, p. 204).

More recent studies conclude that real-world social networks, friendships, and small-group dynamics are the decisive influence in radicalizing British young men and making them travel to fight for a number of armed groups in Syria. In fact, terrorism scholar Peter Neumann suggests that jihadist propaganda videos such as those put out by the Islamic State (ISIS) are not causing young people to join terrorist organizations (McVeigh 2014). More typically, "there is a pre-existing friendship," and travel to fight in Syria is the result of small group dynamics and peer pressure, and "the feeling that one wants to be with one's friends" (Peter Neumann, as quoted in McVeigh 2014).

Once a block of individuals joins a radical group, their devotion to one another other is likely to increase further as common goals and threats enhance cohesion. The powerful cohesion, in turn, leads to further isolation from other elements of society and forces an otherwise visible group to go underground. The combination of isolation and external threat makes group dynamics more powerful in the underground cell than in the otherwise "open" radical group that preceded it. In short, such theories contend that once group dynamics take over, individual motivations for terrorism become secondary to collective dynamics as the key explanatory variable for violence. For many terrorists that belong to a group, the survival of the group is paramount because of the sense of identity and purpose it provides to its members (McCauley and Moskalenko 2008).

These group-level theories are thus particularly useful when it comes to explaining shifts in the radical behavior of groups over time. Indeed, the same study by McCauley and Moskalenko (2008) shows that when individuals form groups and isolate themselves, there tends to be an extremity shift in their views. A common reaction is to find an out-group to play the role of the villain who threatens the group's survival. These dynamics can help to explain how once-peaceful activist groups can slide towards more radical beliefs and behaviors.

An important subset of group-based psychological theories of terrorism is linked to the concept of **groupthink**, a psychological phenomenon that occurs within a group of people in which the desire for conformity in the group results in a somewhat irrational and at times dysfunctional decision-making outcome (Janis 1972). Members of the group attempt to minimize conflict and reach a consensus decision without critical evaluation of alternatives, and thus actively suppress dissenting viewpoints and isolate themselves from external influence.

Importantly, such processes of irrational radicalization driven by groupthink do not occur randomly. In a case study of the Weather Underground (colloquially called "the Weatherman"), a terrorist group active in the US from 1969 to the late 1970s, Tsintsadze-Maass and Maas demonstrate how specific antecedent conditions made the group susceptible to groupthink, and ultimately to the adoption of counterproductive policies of marked by intense violence (2014). Figure 4.1 illustrates these dynamics.

Despite originally advocating for nonviolent civil action as a means of effecting change, the Weather Underground became a violent organization. The group formed in the late 1960s under the context of a highly contentious social environment, and its isolation began with its split from the Students for a Democratic Society (SDS), an iconic youth activist organization with nation-wide membership. As the organization issued increasingly radical statements and moved further underground, its insulation deepened. Its members came from homogenous social backgrounds, while leaders dominated group politics as well as quotidian activities within the collective. The group viewed their adversaries in the US government in terms of extreme stereotypes, and its members held deep convictions of the morality that characterized their cause and subsequent actions. In the end, the groupthink mentality led to the group's self-destruction. Members ignored the desirability of alternatives to violence, and refused to reevaluate their strategy despite strong evidence of its counterproductivity (Tsintsadze-Maass and Maas 2014).

As applied to understanding terrorism, groupthink theories stress that nonrational radicalization occurs when groups begin and sustain terrorist campaigns despite clear evidence of their futility, and when they justify this ineffective behavior by adjusting their rhetoric to fit any undesired results. At the level of the group, certain social psychological factors influence the propensity for nonrational radicalization, causing members to interpret clear failures as successes, and to reject and punish any impulses by other group members to reevaluate a failing strategy.

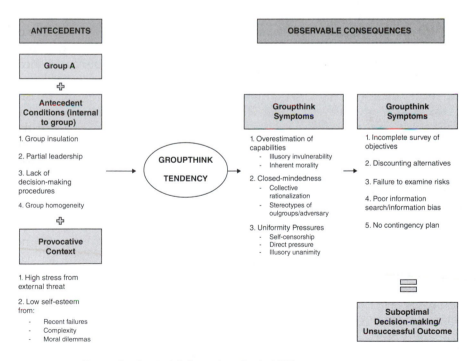

Figure 4.1 Groupthink Model (based on Janis 1973)

Several scholars suggest that group dynamics lead to terrorism when the collective identity subsumes the individual identity. In this case, the tight fusion that exists within the group appears to provide the necessary justification for actions, stripping away the sense of responsibility from individual group members (Post, Sprinzak and Denny 2003). In their interviews of incarcerated Middle Eastern terrorists, Post, Sprinzak, and Denny noted that sentiments of "pride and shame as expressed by the individual were reflections of group actions, not individual actions, feelings, or experiences (2003, p. 176). Having been consumed by an overarching sense of the collective, individual terrorists were frequently unable to distinguish between personal goals and those of the organization.

Groupthink theories should not be confused with organizational approaches to terrorism, which stress that groups prioritize organizational goals rather than political goals. Remember that from this perspective, certain group imperatives such as recruitment and fundraising drive behavior as groups face competition from rival organizations, rather than from the government (see Chapter 3). In contrast, groupthink speaks to the displacement of responsibility for a group's actions; because responsibility is fragmented across the group, group members can engage in riskier behaviors than they would individually, while simultaneously denying that they had a choice over the decision to engage in risky or adverse behavior (Milgram 1974).

Moral Disengagement. Over the course of routine socialization, people adopt moral standards that serve as guides and deterrents for conduct. Once individuals have internalized a certain level of control, they regulate their behavior according to processes of self-sanctioning. That is to say, people do things that bring them satisfaction and that contribute to their own self-worth, but they refrain from behaving in ways that would attract condemnation.

Psychologists such as Albert Bandura, who focuses on cognitive theory and personality psychology, suggest that such moral standards do not function as fixed internal regulators of conduct (1999). Instead, they only operate when they are activated, and there are specific psychological processes by which people can disengage their moral reactions from inhumane conduct. While Bandura has used these psychosocial mechanisms of **moral disengagement** to explain acts of political violence, they appear particularly applicable to explaining the slaughter in cold blood of innocent women and children in buses, department stores, and airports. Indeed, Bandura argues that "intensive psychological training in moral disengagement is needed to create the capacity to kill innocent human beings as a way of toppling rulers or regimes or of accomplishing other political goals" (Bandura 1999, p. 163). We briefly review Bandura's take on how some of these moral disengagement practices operate in the execution of inhumane acts in the subsections that follow, focusing on five specific mechanisms.

Moral justification. Moral justification for terrorist acts is founded on the notion that people can reconstrue what is otherwise immoral—or culpable—as honorable. For example, volunteers for military service are often rapidly transformed into skilled combatants, despite their prior socialization to deplore killing as morally condemnable (1998). The conversion of socialized people into dedicated combatants is not achieved by radically altering their personality structures, but rather by cognitively reconstructing the moral value of killing, so that the act is no longer construed as culpable: "through moral sanction of violent means, people see themselves as fighting ruthless oppressors who have an unquenchable appetite for conquest" (Bandura 1998, p. 164). Often, perpetrators of terrorism who hinge on a moral justification for their actions appeal to what they regard as a higher level of morality, derived principally from communal concerns. They view their constituencies as comprising the collective of people who are victimized either directly or indirectly by harmful social practices. Therefore, it is their moral imperative to put a stop to a tradition of maltreatment of their communities.

Displacement of responsibility. Another set of dissociative practices operates via the distortion of the relationship between one's actions and the effects that they cause. People are often willing to behave in harmful ways if they know that a legitimate authority will accept responsibility for the act. Under this condition, called **displaced responsibility**, people conceive of their actions as springing from the dogma of authorities, rather than from their own volition. Nazi prison guards and staff, for example, engaged in similar processes to distance themselves from personal responsibility for their inhumanities during the Holocaust (Milgram 1974).

Some radical Shi'ite clerics, for example, have gone to great lengths to produce moral justifications for violence that appears to run counter to Islamic law, such as suicide bombings or hostage taking (Kramer 1998). These efforts are likely designed to persuade the clerics themselves of the morality of such actions, but also to preserve the legitimacy of the perpetrator group in the eyes of other Muslim nations. On the one hand, they invoke utilitarian justifications for violent acts, claiming that tyrannical circumstances drive oppressed people to resort to violence against a massively more powerful opponent. On the other hand, they claim that death as a suicide bomber is no different from dying at the hands of an enemy soldier, so long as the cause for which one is dying is moral. In the case of hostage takings, clerics replaced the term "hostage" with "spies" (Bandura 1998, p. 174).

Distortion of consequences. When people choose to engage in actions that will harm others, they often minimize the injury that they cause. In some cases, this might be a case of "selective memory," where one is less able to remember the harmful effects of her actions. People are particularly prone to minimizing the harm that they have caused to others when they act alone and cannot easily displace responsibility to a higher authority (Mynatt and Herman 1975).

Along these same lines, it might also be easier to hurt others when their suffering is not visible, or when actions are physically or temporally removed from their consequences. When people can see or hear the suffering that they have caused through their actions, aroused distress and other emotions are more likely to serve as self-restraining influences. Ultimately, the farther removed (both mentally and physically) individuals are from the end results of their actions, the weaker the restraining power of realistic consequences. With the advent of unmanned aerial vehicles, robots, and other technology, our ways of killing people have become at once very lethal and depersonalized. Attacking from a distance gets around two of the fundamental obstacles faced during violent conflict: fear of killing, and fear of being killed. Fear is hypothesized to be one of the greatest barriers to effectiveness in battle (Daddis 2004; Sharkey 2012), and also to killing itself (Grossman 2009). With the advent of remote-controlled killing technology, killing may arguably become easier both technologically and psychologically speaking, though the level of moral risk will remain just as high.

Dehumanization of victims. The strength of self-censuring reactions like morality depends in part on how the perpetrator regards the people she is harming. To perceive another person as human is more likely to enhance empathetic reactions. Perceiving another person or group as inhuman, on the other hand, reduces self-sanctioning mechanisms. Once divested of their human qualities, potential victims are no longer perceived of as humans, but as subhuman objects such as "satanic fiends" or "savages" (Bandura 1998, p. 181). Dehumanized persons are treated much more punitively than persons who remain human in the eyes of the perpetrator of violence. Under certain conditions, individuals or small groups in positions of power shape conditions so that they become conducive to dehumanization. For instance, dehumanization is widely thought to have been a critical factor in fueling the genocide in Rwanda in 1994. By dehumanizing the opposing side into animals, vermin, or disease, killing was made easier for both Hutus and Tutsis.

Attribution of blame. One last mechanism of moral disengagement lies in the terrorist's conviction that his victims are not entirely blameless, because, by their behavior, they contribute in part to their own plight. By imputing blame to one's antagonists, the perpetrator can interpret his own violent conduct as compelled by forcible provocation. This particular mechanism is grounded in the notion that destructive interactions usually involve a series of reciprocally escalatory actions, in which neither side is ever purely faultless. A person can thus always select from a chain of contentious events an instance in which the adversary's conduct can be construed as the original instigation. Harmful behavior is a justifiable defensive reaction to belligerent provocations (Bandura 1998, p. 184).

Blame attribution is particularly salient when terror attacks take a heavy toll on civilian lives. In 1987, the Irish Republican Army (IRA) planted a bomb that killed a large number of family members attending a war memorial ceremony in a town square. The attack was blamed on the British army for having detonated the bomb prematurely with a bomb detection devise (Staff Writer 1987, p. 19). A similar incident occurred in 1983, when members of the IRA set off a bomb in Harrods department store in London without the authorization of the organization's command structure. The group blamed the police for failing to evacuate the store in time despite a call warning of the impending explosion (Staff Writer 1983).

OBSERVABLE IMPLICATIONS OF THE PSYCHOLOGICAL APPROACH

Unlike some of the other analytical approaches, psychological theories are not always amenable to yielding strong observable implications. Given the difficulty of observing psychological traits across a large number of individuals, psychological approaches are primarily explanatory, as opposed to predictive. They may be useful for understanding specific instances of terrorism committed by specific individuals, but less useful when it comes to anticipating the likelihood of future acts of terrorism, or to generalizing across a broader population.

Furthermore, many of the psychoanalytic hypotheses that we have reviewed in this chapter are not amenable to empirical testing. This is clear from the shortage of empirical studies relative to the number of published theories. Gathering detailed data on the psychologies and behavioral tendencies of a large number of individuals is prohibitive, in terms of cost, practicality, and ethics. Of the studies that do attempt to gather data on the psychological profiles of terrorists or would-be terrorists, most are based on interviews of a small handful of individuals, making findings difficult to generalize. The effect of an individual's psychological profile is also difficult to disentangle and isolate from the role of socioeconomic or other factors when it comes to explaining terrorism. For instance, was Omar Mateen driven to commit a mass shooting in a gay nightclub in Orlando as a result of his hatred for the LGBT population (an ideological explanation), or because of his personality traits (a psychological explanation)? In the absence of a written manifesto explaining his intentions and ultimate actions, it is difficult to discern what led this particular individual to commit such a gruesome act of violence.

Finally, a weakness of the psychological approach comes to light when we consider that terrorists are most often identified as such only *after* having committed their violent acts. Prior to doing so, most do not exhibit psychological traits that are significantly different from those of a non-terrorist. Many of the recent so-called "lone wolf" terror attacks in the United States, for instance, underscore the point emphasized by researchers that radicalization is a "complex psycho-social process that belies a simple explanation" (James and Pisoui 2016). It is unlikely that Dylann Roof, Omar Mateen,

Tashfeen Malik, Nidal Hasan, or Tamerlan and Dzhokhar Tsarnaev shared identical psychological profiles, or showed the same signs and symptoms of a specific personality disorder prior to their attacks.

Although full empirical testing of psychological approaches has been hampered by a lack of data, in the last decade psychologists have worked to compile more reliable data on the psychology of terrorism. For example, a 2009 report issued by the American Psychological Association suggests that psychologists are finding it to be more useful to view terrorism in terms of political and group dynamics, and that universal psychological principles—such as our subconscious fear of death and our desire for meaning and personal significance—may help to explain some aspects of terrorist actions better than others (DeAngelis 2009). The National Consortium for the Study of Terrorism and Responses to Terrorism (START) also sponsors efforts to collect data on individual extremists in the United States through its Profiles of Individual Radicalization in the United States (PIRUS) project.

In addition, recent studies such as Ariel Merari's evaluation of suicide bombers have made important headways in terms of data collection on individual terrorists, and led to more robust findings regarding the psychological profiles and personality styles of specific types of terrorists. A preliminary analysis of START's PIRUS data on Islamist, Far Left, and Far Right individuals who radicalized to violent and nonviolent extremism in the United States since World War II suggests that individuals characterized as loners or those with psychological issues were most likely to use violence. Similarly, people who experienced a drop in social standing prior to their extremist actions were more likely to use violence (Jensen et al. 2015). Eventually, such information and research practices could contribute to better identification of the observable implications of psychological approaches to terrorism.

Indeed, proponents of the psychological approach tend to argue that if one holds all other factors constant (i.e., environmental factors), we should be able to attribute variation in terrorist vs. non-terrorist behavior to different innate and learned traits. In his interview of fifteen would-be suicide bombers, for instance, Ariel Merari (2010) finds systematic differences between these individuals and a control group of non-suicide terrorists and organizers of suicide terror attacks. Holding important environmental factors constant (such as age, time spent in jail, education, marital status, and organizational affiliation), the study finds that suicide bombers are more likely than members of the control group to display some of the personality traits that we have reviewed in this chapter. Here is a summary of his findings:

- Sixty percent of suicide bombers achieved a diagnosis of Avoidant-Dependent Personality Disorder, compared to 17 percent of controls;

- Forty percent of suicide bombers displayed suicidal tendencies, compared to 0 percent of controls;

- 53 percent of suicide bombers had depressive symptoms, compared to 8 percent of controls (Merari 2010).

Merari's study is a particularly important contribution to terrorism scholarship. Unlike many terrorism scholars, he uses his findings to argue in favor of a psychological profile that distinguishes suicide bombers from others. But his findings do not necessarily offer a practical solution to countering terrorism. The manifestations of personality disorders are often subtle and unnoticeable to observers at large. Treatment for such disorders is also lengthy and unpredictable, at best. While the finding that there may be a common personality disorder among suicide terrorists advances our understanding of what a terrorist profile might look like, it may fall short of being useful for those trying to prevent terrorism.

PRACTICAL IMPLICATIONS OF THE PSYCHOLOGICAL APPROACH

Importantly, psychological approaches to understanding terrorist behavior emphasize that terrorism is here to stay for generations to come. There is no short-term solution to the problem. Once an individual finds himself in the "pressure cooker of the terrorist group" in the words of Jerrold Post (1998, p. 39), he is beyond the reach of most policies. In the long run, the approach stresses the importance of developing strategies aimed at preventing potential terrorist recruits from signing up in the first place. For terrorists whose only sense of significance stems from being a terrorist, or from being a member of a terrorist group, getting them to abandon this position once they have already joined seems futile, at best.

That said, various psychological theories provide some room for policy interventions. For example, studies that point to the link between groupthink dynamics and terrorism suggest that intervention strategies aimed at producing dissent within groups, and facilitating exit from the group, might be effective at deterring socially displaced individuals from terrorism. Such efforts would likely involve infiltrating groups at the early stages of formation, perhaps before they even turn to terrorism, to influence internal dynamics away from the harmful groupthink symptoms highlighted in Figure 4.1. Offering aggrieved individuals and groups opportunities to have their voices heard, or to negotiate specific outcomes, might also alleviate the stress that these individuals feel, and make them feel less threatened. In addition, theories that link violent behavior to a quest for personal significance suggest that providing more opportunities for social mobility and for individuals to fulfill their aspirations might lessen the extent to which some people feel the need to join a potentially violent collective.

Other practical strategies derived from a psychological understanding of terrorism focus on reducing terrorism by promoting the healing of individual terrorists' dysfunction, for instance by promoting coping strategies to assuage the existential fear of death (Stritzke et al. 2009). As we discussed in the context of Ariel Merari's study of would-be suicide bombers, and as is indicated by recent examples of terrorism in the United States, there is little doubt that some terrorists are mentally unbalanced and/or socially out of place. In fact, an increased focus on mental health is a core component of Countering Violent Extremism (CVE) programs. For example, a recent study published by START recommends that CVE initiatives find roles for family therapy, individual psychotherapy, psychiatric medications, mentoring, life skills education, and substance abuse treatment in practices to address extremism (Weine et al. 2015).

Of course, intervention strategies based on mental health assessments are limited insofar as terrorists are usually identified as such only after they have committed an act of violence. In addition, such strategies might run the risk of further stigmatizing mentally ill individuals, especially if they are not integrated into a well-embedded and multidisciplinary program that carefully draws on the expertise of other community partners including those in education, religion, law, and law enforcement. Nevertheless, research completed by organizations such as START shows that partnerships between mental health, education, and law enforcement personnel offer especially promising means of addressing the full spectrum of needs and threats that might be relevant when addressing violent extremism (Weine et al. 2015). Proactive and preventative approaches to education in particular, and increasing the extent to which mental health professionals are aware of the risks related to violent extremism, can help to identify at-risk individuals before they fall in with violent groups or commit acts of violence on their own.

Finally, other approaches to de-radicalization that are also rooted in a psychological understanding of terrorism find promise in the possibility of talking terrorists out of committing violence or joining a violent organization. John Horgan, for example, has suggested focusing not on the reasons *why* people become terrorists, but rather on *how* they do so (2008). Framing the question this way has the potential to reveal critical information about the processes of entry, involvement, and leaving an organization. For instance, how do specific leaders influence people's decisions to adopt certain roles, and how do other group members motivate others to leave? Such questions could lead to better evaluating the influence of terrorist group recruitment strategies as opposed to personal decision-making processes.

For instance, initiatives taking place in countries such as Egypt, Iraq, Saudi Arabia, and the United Kingdom seek to "soften the hearts and minds" of terrorists (American Psychological Association 2009). These programs focus on three important components: (1) holding dialogue with former terrorists about their understandings of religion and violence; (2) defusing anger and frustration by showing concern for terrorists' families; and (3) addressing the reality that detainees will often reenter societal situations that rekindle radical beliefs. A key implication of the psychological approach, however, is that programs be designed on a case-by-case basis, taking into consideration the specific contexts in which individuals were drawn to terrorism in the first place.

In conclusion, psychological approaches to understanding terrorism highlight the important role that multidisciplinary intervention strategies play in countering terrorism, in particular when it comes to addressing violent extremism and the radicalization of individuals. To some extent, this is a direct reflection of the shift in the field of terrorism studies towards a more interdisciplinary approach. Scholarship has progressed from being limited to political science and sociological methodologies to emphasizing and incorporating psychological methods and theories. The range of policy options available to communities and governments today mirrors these positive developments that characterize the contemporary study of terrorism.

CRITIQUES OF PSYCHOLOGICAL APPROACHES

As discussed at various points throughout this chapter, the psychological approach has a number of major shortcomings.

Overgeneralization of the terrorist personality. A primary critique of psychological approaches is that they tend to overgeneralize the terrorist "persona." As we've seen throughout this text, a diverse range of people with an even more diverse range of beliefs has been carrying out terrorist acts for hundreds of years. Given this variety and scope, critics of psychological theories contend that it hardly makes sense to believe that psychological principles can be derived to explain all of the entries in the record (Reich 1998; Victoroff 2005). Even the most exhaustive interview studies of terrorists carried out—of 227 left-wing West German terrorists and twenty-three right-wing extremists—reveal numerous behavioral patterns in subjects' personal histories (Reich 1998, p. 269). Some terrorists experienced loss of one or both parents at an early age, severe conflicts with authority, and frequent failure in the workplace or in school. Others exhibited what psychologists refer to as "two personality constellations," one consisting of extreme dependence on the terrorist group itself, extroversion, and stimulus seeking, and the other of hostility, suspicion, and aggression (ibid). Consider the number of explanations and theories that are included in this chapter alone. Certainly, terrorists and terrorist groups mentioned throughout the book likely reflect a number of these traits and mechanisms. But the search for specific psychological qualities that are shared by all of them—or nearly all of them—remains elusive.

Overreliance on a Reductionist Approach. Proponents of psychological explanations for terrorism have also been accused of adopting an overly reductionist approach. Indeed, the search for a specific "terrorist personality" is likely futile insofar as such a personality likely does not exist. Focusing on identifying individual terrorists on the basis of their psychological traits may be a misuse of valuable resources that could be better applied to detecting and defeating entire terrorist groups.

Difficulties in Inferring Causality. A common critique of psychological approaches is that they are unable to provide strong causal connections between terrorism and the various traits that they identify as key predictors of terrorism. To some extent, this difficulty arises because researchers tend not to have the opportunity to observe the traits of terrorists *prior* to their committing a terrorist act. Indeed, many terrorists fall under the radar of some of the most rigorous screening procedures undertaken by law enforcement professionals or members of the mental health profession. Furthermore, it is not clear whether the pathologies or traits observed among terrorists were the cause of terrorist behavior, or caused by the terrorist behavior itself. This might be particularly true when terrorists are diagnosed as suffering from post-traumatic stress disorder, a condition that may have predated the act of violence, or may have developed after the individual participated in an act of violence.

Terrorists are also unlikely to volunteer as experimental subjects, and examining their activities at a distance can lead to erroneous conclusions. Even if they are imprisoned, terrorists are likely to be reluctant to meet with a researcher whose goal is to assign him a psychological disorder or ask about sensitive details related to childhood in order to explain his behavior. It is understandable that many convicted terrorists would question any attempt to explain their motivation in psychological terms that diminish the political validity of their ideas and actions.

This particular critique may be especially salient when trying to explain cases of lone-wolf terrorism, where the attacker does not have an obvious connection to an established terror group. Consider the example of Mohamed Lahouaiej Bouhlel, who drove a truck through a crowd gathered to watch fireworks on France's national holiday in July 2016 in Nice. From a distance, this French man of Tunisian national origin may appear to have been motivated by the ongoing wave of Islamist terrorism inspired by the Islamic State in Iraq and Syria (ISIS). But Bouhlel had no preexisting jihadist connections, and did not carry any ISIS-related paraphernalia with him on the day of the attack. His neighbors described him as a "loner" who became depressed following a divorce that left behind three children (Samuel and Morgan 2016). We can therefore not be certain whether Bouhlel's act of terror was an instance of ISIS-inspired terrorism, or the culmination of some kind of personality disorder related to depression and social alienation.

When it comes to radicalization, critics contend that other explanatory models such as organizational approaches may lead to more practical observable implications. For example, organizational models of radicalization suggest that the individuals who make up a person's social network can help to predict who may be at higher risk for radicalization and recruitment into terrorism. The social networks of potential terrorists are easier to identify and evaluate, relative to the unobservable psychological traits that may be driving an individual's behavior.

Severe Data Limitations. Performing psychological analyses on large numbers of terrorists is practically infeasible, a limitation that significantly curtails the amount of data that can be used to study the psychological determinants of terrorism. The lack of data also suggests that findings from psychological studies of terrorism are difficult to generalize across populations. With relatively few exceptions (see e.g., Merari et al. 2009; Merari 2010; Jensen et al. 2015), many studies that attempt to uncover a terrorist profile turn to the evaluation of memoirs or interviews with family members, which may return biased results.

Methodologies Suffer from Selection Bias. Limitations on direct access to terrorists themselves have contributed to the relative dearth of systematic psychological research on the subject. Studies that do involve direct access to terrorists typically require researchers to gain permission to enter prisons where convicted terrorists are located. For instance, as discussed above, Ariel Merari gained access to fifteen would-be suicide bombers being held in jail for attempted attacks against Israeli targets. Before the would-be attackers would speak to him, Merari had to gain the consent of higher-ranking members of organizations such as Hamas, the Palestinian Islamic Jihad, and Fatah's al-Aqsa Martyrs Brigades. Only once participation in the study was negotiated could Merari follow through with his study (Merari 2010). However, this practice produces an important selection bias: most psychological studies are based on terrorists who have surrendered, or whom the authorities have apprehended. Given that they either failed to evade or capitulated to authorities, convicted terrorists may therefore have systematically different personality profiles than terrorists who remain at large (i.e., who have either evaded authorities or who have refused to surrender). Moreover, research attempting to assemble terrorist personality profiles based on the memoirs and writings of terrorists, interviews with their family members, and/or interviews with their associates, may also be subject to important biases. Two particularly important sources of bias may include **retrospective bias**, which involves a retelling of historical events in ways that produce favorable interpretations of one's own former choices, and **social desirability bias**, which involves presenting oneself in a way the interviewer wants to hear, rather than presenting oneself the way one actually is (Roese and Vohs 2012; Paulhus 1991).

Policy Implications are Immoral. Some researchers have raised normative concerns about psychological approaches as well. Critical terrorism scholars (Chapter 7) have argued that identifying patterns of thought or behavior associated with aggression may violate privacy and freedom of conscience for people who may share some of the same propensities for violence without ever engaging in aggressive behavior. As a consequence of policies focused on identification and interdiction of potential terrorists, critical terrorism scholars worry about **profiling**—a practice wherein authorities attempt to monitor and detect certain attributes, habits, identities, and behaviors to single out people for early interdiction.

BOX 4.2

ARE SUICIDE BOMBERS ACTUALLY SUICIDAL?

Why do certain terrorists become suicide bombers? In this short case study, let's explore some of the psychologically grounded theories of suicide terrorism (see Chapter 9 for a longer treatment of the subject).

In an article on female suicide bombers, Mia Bloom suggests that the characteristics of the typical suicide bomber are elusive (2005). Contrary to popular thinking, most of these individuals are not unbalanced sociopaths prone to suicidal or other self-destructive tendencies. In addition, they are not necessarily poor, and frequently defy characterizations as "uneducated religious fanatics" (ibid). An jihadi commander incarcerated in the Middle East, and interviewed by Jerrold Post, Ehud Sprinzak, and Laurita Denny shortly after the September 11, 2001 terrorist attacks, confirms this rejection of the sociopath-terrorist profile:

> "I am not a murderer. A murderer is someone with a psychological problem; armed actions have a goal. Even if civilians are killed, it is not because we like it or are bloodthirsty. It is a fact of life in a people's struggle. . . The group doesn't do it because it wants to kill civilians, but because the jihad must go on."

In another study of Palestinian suicide bombers in Gaza, the Gaza Community Mental Health Program determined that many Palestinian suicide bombers shared childhood trauma, often related to the humiliation of their fathers by Israeli forces. These traumatic episodes worked to alienate would-be suicide bombers from their surrounding societies, pushing them to seek retribution for humiliation. In a study of female bombers in Sri Lanka, studies have found that many women bombers were raped or sexually abused by representatives of the state or by insurgents during the 1983–2009 civil war (Hassan 2014). Acts of suicide bombing were therefore construed both as revenge for the loss of a family member and as efforts to redeem the family name following the humiliation wrought by rape.

Other studies, however, suggest that suicide terrorists may simply be suicidal. A study of seventy-five individual suicide terrorists conducted by Adam Lankford (2011) points to evidence that these individuals may have exhibited classic suicidal tendencies. In fact, many of the psychological mechanisms that we have reviewed in this chapter may themselves lead to the development of suicidal tendencies. Lankford reports that some suicide terrorists have clearly attempted to kill themselves in their earlier lives, a telltale sign of suicidal tendencies. Consider the following set of risk factors for suicide Lankford discusses (Table 4.1).

The conventional wisdom that suicide bombers are always motivated by a political cause, Lankford argues, is often based on the claims of terrorist leaders and other rank-and-file terrorists about the suicide terrorists themselves. However, by looking at their own videos, reading their own diaries and writings, and observing other videos about their behavior, Lankford concludes that most of these subjects would have committed suicide one way or another—and suicide terrorism seemed like a more honorable way out.

TABLE 4.1 Risk Factors for Suicide

Event-Based Risk Factors for Suicide	Psychological Risk-Factors for Suicide
Exposure to suicidal behavior of others	Depression
Negative precipitating event	Post-traumatic stress disorder
Loss of security	Guilt or shame
Serious illness or injury to oneself	Hopelessness
Seriously injuring/killing another	Rage
Substance abuse	
Traumatic brain injury	
Neurotransmitter imbalance	

Source: Lankford 2011

If Lankford is right, his argument could present important openings into discrediting terrorist organizations. In those cases where terrorist organizations have clearly coerced individuals with past records of suicidal tendencies or mental illness into blowing themselves up, the exploitation could be exposed. Moreover, a first step towards curbing the propensity of groups to use suicide bombings would be to change the perception of such attacks among the terrorists' constituencies. A strong message that suicide terrorism merely constitutes suicide – and not martyrdom – could delegitimatize the act in communities where suicide is taboo.

Lankford's study has received a number of critiques on both methodological and theoretical grounds. Methodologically, critics argue that reconstructing a psychological profile of an individual only by looking at secondary sources about their lives is impossible (see e.g., Lankford 2014). Moreover, generalizing from such a small number of observations is generally a dubious practice. Others suggest that Lankford's study underestimates the degree to which political, economic, social, or cultural conditions create the event- and psychology-based risk factors for suicide (Lankford 2014). We return to these factors in Chapter 6.

Moreover, some critical terrorism scholars have argued that by pathologizing terrorists, governments can conveniently discard legitimate grievances of terror groups as crazy and fanatical. Critical terrorism scholars suggest that efforts to discredit terror groups as bands of fanatics serve state interests by distracting from the underlying sources of conflict motivating people to turn to terrorism in the first place (see Chapter 7). Psychological approaches may ignore the very real economic, political, and social factors that have motivated radical action.

Nonetheless, psychological approaches to terrorism remind us that terrorism is varied and likely irreducible to any one theory or precise explanation. Researchers relying on psychological approaches should take special care to identify the individuals and groups whose behavior they are studying, and limit their explanations to those specific subjects.

SUMMARY

The psychological approach focuses first and foremost on understanding why individuals join terrorist groups or commit acts of terrorism. The approach assumes that individual-level factors must be at work to explain why certain people turn to terrorism, while others do not. Psychological theories are bottom-up approaches to understanding terrorism, and are also useful for understanding individual radicalization, or how people reach certain states of mind or are pushed towards particular patterns of behavior in which they justify violence. We have reviewed the various psychological and personality traits that terrorism scholars have linked to terrorism, as well as group psychological forces that might influence why groups turn to violence. We ended the chapter by listing some practical implications of psychological models of terrorism, and by addressing some of the critiques of the psychological approach.

Importantly, these critiques suggest that the psychological approach is unable to help us explain certain puzzles. For example, psychological theories are unable to explain why, despite the fact that the majority of individuals undergo quests for personal significance at some point in their lifetime, only a very small minority turns to terrorism in response to this mental state. Indeed, the majority of terrorists are not psychopaths or sadists, but more likely ordinary people shaped by group dynamics to do harm in the name of some cause that they see as noble. Furthermore, the reductionist nature of psychological models makes them unable to explain why certain organized groups favor terrorism, while many others do not. In the next chapter we turn to ideological approaches to terrorism, which may help to answer some of these questions.

Discussion Questions

1. How rigorous are psychological approaches to terrorism? Are they more or less powerful than other approaches we have reviewed? Can they be included alongside other explanations for terrorism, such as strategic or organizational approaches? If so, how?

2. Consider the profiles of specific terrorists included in this chapter. What specific psychological explanations might best match their actions?

3. Are psychological approaches to terrorism valuable in explaining suicide terrorism specifically?

4. Consider some recent terrorist personalities, such as "Jihadi John," the British man thought to be the person seen in several ISIS videos showing the beheadings of a number of captives in 2014 and 2015. Apply a psychological approach to explaining this particular person's path to terrorism. Then critique the approach.

KEY TAKEAWAYS

- The psychological approach focuses on identifying personality traits and characteristics that make individuals more predisposed to terrorism.

- There are a wide variety of psychological theories—at the individual and group levels—that scholars have used to explain variation in terrorist violence. This approach often emphasizes personal quests for significance motivated by various life experiences, which may lead individuals to radicalize.

- The approach has intuitive appeal because it attempts to specify the reasons why individuals—or people in particular group settings—might be driven to particularly aggressive, anti-social behaviors.

- However, critics argue that psychological approaches are often indeterminate in explaining terrorism because most people with psychological disorders are not terrorists, and most terrorists do not have any obvious (or visible) pathologies. Critics also suggest that viewing terrorists as fanatics distracts from the objective material, social, political, and economic conditions that may drive them to violence. We return to these factors in Chapter 6.

SUGGESTED FURTHER READINGS

Bandura, Albert. 1999. "Social Cognitive Theory of Personality" in *Handbook of Personality: Theory and Research,* ed. Lawrence A. Pervin and Oliver P. John. New York: Guilford, pp. 154–196.

Cottee, Simon and Keith Hayward. 2011. "Terrorist (E)Motives: The Existential Attractions of Terrorism," *Studies in Conflict & Terrorism* 34 (12): 963–986. doi:10.1080/1057610x.2011.621116.

Crenshaw, Martha. 1981. "The Causes of Terrorism." *Comparative Politics* 13 (4): 379. doi:10.2307/421717.

Crenshaw, Martha. 1986. The Psychology of Political Terrorism." *Political Psychology* 21 (2): 379–413.

Crenshaw, Martha. 1988. "The Subjective Reality of the Terrorist: Ideological and Psychological Factors in Terrorism," in *Current Perspectives on International Terrorism,* eds. Robert O. Slater and Michael Stohl. London: MacMillan Press.

DeAngelis, Tori. 2009. "Understanding Terrorism." *Monitor on Psychology, American Psychological Association* 40 (10): 60. Available online: http://www.apa.org/monitor/2009/11/terrorism.aspx. Last accessed 9-March-2017.

Fanon, Frantz, Jean-Paul Sartre, and Constance Farrington. 1965. *The Wretched of the Earth.* New York: Grove Press, Inc.

Freedman, Lawrence D., Robert Pape, and Mia Bloom. 2005. "Dying to Win: The Strategic Logic of Suicide Terrorism." *Foreign Affairs* 84 (5): 172. doi:10.2307/20031726.

Janis, Irving L. 1972. *Victims of Groupthink; A Psychological Study of Foreign-Policy Decisions and Fiascoes*. Boston: Houghton, Mifflin.

Knutson, Jeanne N. 1981. "Social and Psychodynamic Pressures Toward a Negative Identity: The case of an American Revolutionary Terrorist." *Behavioral and Quantitative Perspectives on Terrorism*. 105–150.

Knutson, Jeanne K. 1984. "Toward a United States Policy on Terrorism." *Political Psychology* 5 (2): 287–294. doi:10.2307/3791191.

Kramer, Martin. 1998. "The Moral Logic of Hizballah", in Walter Reich, ed. *Origins of Terrorism*. Johns Hopkins University Press.

Kruglanski, Arie W. and Edward Orehek. 2011. "The role of the quest for personal significance in motivating terrorism," in J. Forgas, A. Kruglanski, and K. Williams (eds.), *The Psychology of Social Conflict and Aggression*, New York: Psychology Press. 153–166.

Lankford, Adam. 2011. "Could Suicide Terrorists Actually Be Suicidal?" *Studies in Conflict & Terrorism* 34 (4): 337–366. doi:10.1080/1057610x.2011.551721.

McCauley, Clark, and Sophia Moskalenko. 2008. "Mechanisms of Political Radicalization: Pathways Toward Terrorism." *Terrorism and Political Violence* 20 (3): 415–433. doi:10.1080/09546550802073367.

Merari, Ariel. 2010. *Driven to Death: Psychological and Social Aspects of Suicide Terrorism*. Oxford: Oxford University Press.

Milgram, Stanley. 1974. *Obedience to Authority: An Experimental View*. London: Tavistock Publications.

Post, Jerrold, Ehud Sprinzak, and Laurita Denny. 2003. "The Terrorists in Their Own Words: Interviews with 35 Incarcerated Middle Eastern Terrorists." *Terrorism and Political Violence* 15 (1): 171–184. doi:10.1080/09546550312331293007.

Post, Jerrold M. 2010. "When Hatred is Bred in the Bone': The Social Psychology of Terrorism." *Annals of the New York Academy of Sciences* 1208 (1): 15–23. doi:10.1111/j.1749-6632.2010.05694.x.

Reich, Walter. 1998. *Origins of Terrorism*. Washington, DC: Woodrow Wilson Center Press.

Schwartz, Seth J, Curtis S. Dunkel and Alan S. Waterman. 2009. "Terrorism: An Identity Theory Perspective." *Studies in Conflict & Terrorism* 32 (6): 537–559. doi:10.1080/10576100902888453

Sedgwick, Mark. 2004. "Al-Qaeda and the Nature of Religious Terrorism." *Terrorism and Political Violence* 16 (4): 795–814. doi:10.1080/09546550590906098.

Sedgwick, Mark. 2010. "The Concept of Radicalization as a Source of Confusion." *Terrorism and Political Violence* 22 (4): 479–494. doi:10.1080/09546553.2010.491009.

Tajfel, Henri. 1974. "Social Identity and Intergroup Behaviour." *Social Science Information* 13 (2): 65–93. doi:10.1177/053901847401300204.

Tsintsadze-Maass, Eteri, and Richard W. Maas. 2014. "Groupthink and Terrorist Radicalization." *Terrorism and Political Violence* 26 (5): 735–758. http://dx.doi.org/10.1080/09546553.2013.805094.

Victoroff, Jeff. 2005. "The Mind of the Terrorist: A Review and Critique of Psychological Approaches." *Journal of Conflict Resolution* 49 (1): 3–42. doi:10.1177/0022002704272040.

CHAPTER 5

THE IDEOLOGICAL APPROACH

Learning Objectives

After reading this chapter, readers should be able to:

- Explain the ideological approach in their own words.
- Describe the core tenants of several terror groups' ideologies.
- Summarize and contrast the main assertions and expectations of the ideological approach with that of the psychological, organizational, and strategic approaches.
- Describe an example of a terrorist group that appeared to behave in accordance with the ideological approach's expectations.
- Describe the major shortcomings of the ideological approach. Identify several examples of terrorist groups that appeared to behave in ways that contradict the ideological approach's expectations.

> "The fundamentalist seeks to bring down a great deal more than buildings. Such people are against, to offer just a brief list, freedom of speech, a multi-party political system, universal adult suffrage, accountable government, Jews, homosexuals, women's rights, pluralism, secularism, short skits, dancing, beardlessness, evolution theory, sex. They are tyrants, not Muslims"
> —SALMAN RUSHDIE, *STEP ACROSS THIS LINE: COLLECTED NONFICTION 1992–2002.*

> "The war we fight today is more than a military conflict; it is the decisive ideological struggle of the 21st century. On one side are those who believe in the values of freedom and moderation—the right of all people to speak, and worship, and live in liberty. And on the other side are those driven by the values of tyranny and extremism— the right of a self-appointed few to impose their fanatical views on all the rest. As veterans, you have seen this kind of enemy before. They're successors to Fascists, to Nazis,

to Communists, and other totalitarians of the 20th century. And history shows what the outcome will be: This
war will be difficult; this war will be long; and this war
will end in the defeat of the terrorists and totalitarians,
and a victory for the cause of freedom and liberty."
—GEORGE W. BUSH, SPEAKING AT THE AMERICAN LEGION
NATIONAL CONVENTION, SALT LAKE CITY, UTAH, 2006

INTRODUCING THE IDEOLOGICAL APPROACH

In 2009, the US Department of Homeland Security (DHS) issued a report warning that right-wing extremists could exploit the weak US economy, returning veterans, and election of the country's first black president to recruit new members
to their cause. While there was no specific information regarding an imminent
attack, the agency warned that an extended economic downturn, high unemployment, difficulties in obtaining credit, and an influx of newly-discharged veterans could foster an environment for extremists to recruit new members who
may not have been supportive of these causes in the past. The report drew fierce
criticism from Republican lawmakers and the conservative news media, which
tagged it as an unfair assessment of legitimate critiques of the government and a
demonization of American service members. The DHS eventually retracted the
document, and the agency's Extremism and Radicalization Branch was quietly
dismantled after Homeland Security secretary Janet Napolitano issued a formal
apology to veterans and other groups. Yet these moves severely curtailed the
agency's ability to monitor and counter potential terror threats emanating from
far-right groups, and according to some critics (Nixon 2016), eased the armed
takeover of a federal wildlife refuge in Oregon by a far-right armed group in 2016.

While the agency has failed to gather the intelligence needed to fight
right-wing extremism in the United States, DHS continues to dedicate substantial resources to reducing terrorism among Muslims. Even during the
2016 siege in Oregon, the agency announced the creation of a task force to
focus on countering home grown extremists radicalized by foreign groups
such as the Islamic State, though it made no such announcement regarding
investigations of domestic antigovernment groups.

In this chapter, we turn to the **ideological approach** to studying terrorism,
which focuses on particular belief systems that motivate, incite, and rationalize violence. As we shall see, ideology is an extremely difficult concept
to study, and as the above example demonstrates, frequently falls victim to
entrenched political interests. In fact, many terrorism scholars warn against
classifying terror groups according to their ideologies, since such classification schemes can easily fall prey to political manipulation (see Chapter 7).
However, proponents of an ideological approach typically argue that while
not all extreme ideologies produce terrorism, all terrorists have an extreme
ideology. Because terrorism is a behavior and a tactic, it is really the ideologies
that motivate terrorists that require the most scholarly and policy attention.

Ideological approaches emerge from the **constructivist** school of thought in international relations, which speculates that particular beliefs, ideas, and identities are the most important factors in explaining how individuals, groups, and states behave. Constructivist scholars typically fall into two camps: **constitutive** and **regulative constructivists**. Constitutive constructivists are mainly interested in identifying where ideas and identities come from, and how such ideas and identities motivate human behavior. For example, constructivists would be very interested to know where and how the idea of sovereignty emerged and became the primary organizing principle in the international system during the seventeenth and eighteenth centuries. Or they may be interested in understanding how the adoption of nuclear capabilities—both in terms of nuclear energy and nuclear weapons—came to become such an important element in whether states identify themselves as "modern and civilized." Regulative constructivists are typically more interested in how ideas and norms shape and constrain human behavior. For example, they might be interested in how the norms of sovereignty prevent states from interfering in one another's affairs, even when it would be in their interests to do so. Or they would be very interested to know how norms against the offensive use of nuclear weapons affect states' willingness (or unwillingness) to use tactical nuclear weapons despite potential military advantages of using such weapons during war.

Within terrorism scholarship, the primary focus has been on how ideology motivates, regulates, and constrains the behavior of different actors such that some become terrorists and others do not. Importantly, there is no single terrorist ideology. As we have seen before, terrorism is a method of political action that many different actors have used across a range of ideological persuasions. Moreover, few ideologies have been immune from some groups espousing them while using terrorism.

Let's look at some of the different ideological foundations that scholars have ascribed to terror groups. This list is not meant to be exhaustive—we discuss some other ideologies in other chapters—but it gives a sampling of the range of ideologies in whose names people have perpetrated terror attacks. We divide the sampling of groups and ideologies into two sections, one focusing on secular ideologies and the other on religious ideologies. Importantly, though the terms religion and ideology overlap closely, they are also distinct insofar as not all ideologies are religious. Furthermore, there is a debate within the literature over whether there is in fact a meaningful difference between secular and religious forms of violence.

SECULAR IDEOLOGIES

Although it may surprise students of terrorism today, for the past hundred and fifty years, terrorism was mostly a secular phenomenon. Hoffman explains this as a function of the "growing popularity of various schools of radical political thought, embracing Marxist ideology (or its subsequent Leninist and Maoist interpretations), anarchism, and nihilism" in the late nineteenth and early twentieth centuries (2006, p. 84). As such ideologies became more popular, conservative and reactionary ideologies also emerged to contest and compete with those on the left. And the decline of imperial power during the mid-twentieth century ushered in a period where nationalist-separatist groups—often associating themselves with various strands on thought on the right or left—emerged as key players.

Anarchist Extremism. As discussed in Chapter 1, the late nineteenth and early twentieth centuries featured growing support for **anarchist** ideologies. Anarchism is a philosophy that advocates the removal of all forms of government, with a reorganization of society on the basis of voluntary, cooperative, nonviolent self-organization. A concurrent intellectual trend at the time was **populism**—a philosophy that speculates that ordinary people are consistently abused by a corrupt circle of establishment elites, and that by working together, the masses can overthrow these elites and create a fairer society. And, of course, several other related ideological currents—including **Marxism** and **socialism**—were beginning to win some popular support. Marx's critique of the exploitative nature of capitalism—combined with growing populist movements around the world—were integrated into the anarchist critique of government systems as well. These varieties of terrorism are also commonly referred to as left-wing or **far-left** terrorism.

Anarchist approaches are well-represented by this excerpt from the pamphlet "Le Révolté," published by Pyotr Kropotkin in 1880:

In periods of frenzied haste toward wealth, of feverish speculation and of crisis, of the sudden downfall of great industries and the ephemeral expansion of other branches of production, of scandalous fortunes amassed in a few years and dissipated as quickly, it becomes evident that the economic institutions which control production and exchange are far from giving to society the prosperity which they are supposed to guarantee. Instead of order they bring forth chaos; instead of prosperity, poverty and insecurity; instead of reconciled interests, war—a perpetual war of the exploiter against the worker, of exploiters and of workers among themselves. Human society is seen to be splitting more and more into two hostile camps, and at the same time to be subdividing into thousands of small groups waging merciless war against each other. Weary of these wars, weary of the miseries which they cause, society rushes to seek a new organization. It clamors loudly for a complete remodeling of the system of property ownership, of production, of exchange and all economic relations which spring from it. . . . Every day gives rise to a new demand. 'Reform this,' 'Reform that,' is heard from all sides. 'War, finance, taxes, courts, police, everything must be remodeled, reorganized, established on a new basis,' say the reformers. And yet all know it is impossible to make things over, to remodel anything at all because everything is interrelated; everything would have to be remade at once. And how can society be remodeled when it is divided into two openly hostile camps? To satisfy the discontented would be only to create new malcontents. . . . Such periods demand revolution. It becomes a social necessity; the situation itself is revolutionary. . . . It is through action that minorities succeed in awakening that feeling of independence and that spirit of audacity without which no revolution can come to a head. . . . Nevertheless the cautious theoreticians are angry at these madmen, they excommunicate them, they anathematize them. But the madmen win sympathy, the mass of the people secretly applaud their courage, and they find imitators. In proportion as the pioneers go to fill the jails and the penal colonies, others continue their work. Acts of illegal protest, of revolt, of vengeance, multiply. Indifference from this point on is impossible. Those who at the beginning never so much as asked what the 'madmen' wanted are compelled to think about them, to discuss their ideas, to take sides for or against. By actions which compel general attention, the new idea seeps into people's minds and wins converts. One such act may, in a few days, make more propaganda than thousands of pamphlets (Pyotr Kropotkin, "The Sprit of Revolt," first published in *Le Révolté* (Geneva 1880), translated by Arnold Roller (aka Siegfried Nacht), quoted in Laqueur 2004, p. 95–98).

Although many (if not most) anarchists promoted nonviolent means of social and political change, some groups interpreted anarchist philosophy as necessitating the violent overthrow of existing governments. Some groups, such as Narodnaya Volya ("People's Will") possessed an ideology that combined elements of socialism, populism, and anarchism. Emerging in 1879 as a revolutionary political organization in the Russian Empire, the group advocated an end to the Russian monarchy and the installation of a populist, socialist alternative. In 1881, the group assassinated Tsar Alexander II.

Marxist/Maoist Extremism. Basic tenants of Marxism include the fact that workers are fundamentally alienated from the items they produce, because the capitalist classes own both the products and the means of production (e.g., the factories, lands, and materials used for production). The capitalist class (designated as the bourgeoisie) is exploitative and dominant, leading to an ever-deepening alienation as industrialization spreads. Ultimately, the only way for the system to correct itself is for the working class (or proletariat) to revolt against the bourgeoisie, recapture the means of production, and distribute wealth equally across the classes.

In the mid-twentieth century, Marxist critiques of the capitalist international economic system had taken hold as a mainstream view among many popular movements around the world. With the rise of the Union of Socialist Soviet Republics (USSR), Marxist and quasi-Marxist groups became emboldened about the prospects for their own struggles, and often received direct support from the USSR or its satellite governments.

Of course, Marxism became key to the platforms of many legitimate political groups—such as labor organizations around the world, social movements seeking economic justice, and even formal political parties such as the Communist Party in Italy, which dominated the Italian parliament for decades. Thus Marxism and extralegal violence are by no means synonymous with one another.

That said, many groups that subscribed to Marxist beliefs interpreted this ideology as requiring the armed overthrow of the bourgeoisie by the proletariat. For example, in Italy, the **Brigatte Rosse (Red Brigades, BR)** saw the Italian Communist Party's success in electoral politics as a betrayal of the Marxist imperative to confront and dismantle existing institutions rather than cooperating with them. Created in 1970, the Red Brigades sought to overthrow the Italian government, to end Italy's membership in NATO, and create a new Italian state through revolutionary armed struggle. In 1978, the group infamously abducted and murdered former Italian prime minister Aldo Moro and dispensed of his body in an alleyway in Rome near the Communist Party of Italy's headquarters.

In Germany, the quasi-Marxist **Rote Armee Fraktion (Red Army Faction, RAF)** adapted a number of tenants of Marxism to justify its goal of overthrowing the West German government and undermining American military and economic hegemony.

This 1971 communique describes the thinking behind the RAF's adoption of a Marxist ideology:

> American imperialism is a paper tiger. . . . Victory over American imperialism has become possible because the struggle against it is now being waged in all four corners of the earth, with the result that the forces of imperialism are fragmented. . . . The concept of the urban guerrilla originated

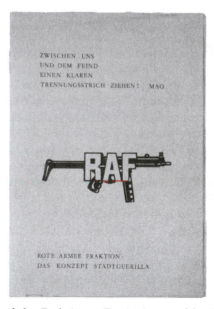

Photo 5.1 The cover of the Red Army Faction's pamphlet "The Urban Guerrilla Concept." The saying at the top translates to: "A clear line must be drawn between us and the enemy. Mao."

in Latin America. Here, the urban guerrilla can only be what he is there: the only revolutionary method of intervention available to what are on the whole weak revolutionary forces. . . .in a country whose potential for violence is as great and whose revolutionary traditions are as broken and feeble as the Federal Republic's, there will not—without revolutionary initiative—even be revolutionary orientation when conditions for revolutionary struggle are better than they are at present, which will happen as an inevitable consequence of the development of late capitalism itself. To this extent, the urban guerrilla is the logical consequence of the negation of parliamentary democracy long since perpetrated by its very own representatives; the only and inevitable response to emergency laws and the rule of the hand grenade; the readiness to fight with those same means the system has chosen to use in trying to eliminate its opponents. . . . The urban guerrilla's aim is to attack the state's apparatus of control at certain points and put them out of action, to destroy the myth of the system's omnipresence and invulnerability. . . . In our original concept, we planned to combine urban guerrilla action with grass-roots work. What we wanted was for each of us to work simultaneously within existing socialist groups at the work place and in local districts, helping to influence the discussion process, learning, gaining experience. It has become clear that this cannot be done. These groups are under such close surveillance by the political police, their meetings, timetables, and the content of their discussion we well monitored, that it is impossible to attend without being put under surveillance oneself. We have learned that individuals cannot combine legal and illegal activity (Rote Armee Fraktion (RAF), *Das Konzept Stadtguerilla*, April 1971, transl. Laqueur 2004, p. 166–168).

Maosim has a slightly different take on the process by which revolution takes place. Evolving through the writings of Mao Tsedung of China, this doctrine emphasizes the permanence of political, social, and economic revolution as well as the primacy of the peasant in bringing about and sustaining revolution. Mao's preference was for small-scale, state-owned industry as well as agricultural collectivization, which he attempted to achieve in China through several successive redistributive plans from the early 1950s through the early 1970s.

Several groups have espoused Maoism as a core ideology. For example, the **Communist Party of Nepal—Maoist** (CPN-M, also called the **United People's Front**) was founded in 1991 and advocated a system of economic and political exchange that approximated Mao's China. The group relied on peasant organization and armed action against the Nepalese monarchy to promote this system. Another such group is the **Communist Party of India—Maoist (CPI-M)**, which was formed in 2004 and is part of the broader **Naxalite-Maoist** insurgency in India. The Naxalites are a group of far-left radical communists supportive of Maoist political sentiment and ideology; they are active throughout West Bengal and the rural areas of central and eastern India. The original objective of the Naxalites was the rightful redistribution of land in India to working peasants, and it has since shifted to include the overthrow of the Indian government through a people's war. The CPI-Maoist rejects any form of engagement with what it considers to be the prevailing bourgeois democracy in India, and instead focuses its efforts on capturing political power through insurgency and the use of terrorist tactics.

Hoffman argues that the ideologies of Marxist and Maoist groups are somewhat of a double-edged sword when it comes to violence. On the one hand, groups perceive violence as necessary to awaken the masses and provoke a mass revolt that would disband sources of capitalist and imperialist domination. On the other hand, the BR, RAF, CPN-M, and CPI-M recognized or continue to recognize the potentially alienating effects of indiscriminate violence, and are thus highly selective in their use of violence. These groups typically engage in kidnapping or assassinating specific people "whom they blamed for economic exploitation or political repression in order to attract publicity and promote a Marxist-Leninist revolution" (Hoffman 2006, p. 230). They typically eschew attacking members of the broader population, focusing instead on symbolic targets as a way to awaken and inspire larger popular revolts. For example, 40 percent of targets of CPI-Maoist terror attacks are characterized as police, government, or military forces or installations. The group targets private citizens in 29 percent of its attacks (GTD 2017). In sum, the populist dimensions of the Marxist and Maoist ideologies have constrained the use of violence against the broader public precisely because these groups saw the broader public as the victims rather than the perpetrators of the capitalist system.

Fascist, Neo-Fascist, and Right-Wing Extremism. **Fascism** is an ideology characterized by the rejection of liberal democracy, communism, and anarchism as valid doctrines. Fascism calls for a militarized citizenry ruled by a powerful authoritarian leader, demands autarkic economic policies leading to social and economic self-determination, and elevates powerful national myths capable of promoting mass mobilization in defense of the nation. Fascism tends to glorify violence as a purifying force, and its proponents tend to focus on symbols of youth, masculinity, and racial supremacy to garner support.

Neo-fascism is essentially the contemporary equivalent of fascism, which emerged after World War I and reached preeminence in Germany, Spain, and Italy before World War II. Neo-fascist groups, such as the neo-Nazi group **Aryan Nations** in the United States or **Unité Radicale** in France, espouse a mix of **racial supremacy**, **xenophobia**, **nationalism**, and **militarism**. The secular dimensions of this ideology, particularly among European neo-fascists, distinguish them somewhat from neo-fascist groups in the United States, which tend to invoke and integrate liturgical influences and seek clerical sanction for their actions (Hoffman 2006, p. 237).

Fascism tends to be associated with the extreme right wing, but there are other non-fascist, secular, right-wing ideologies. For example, **the Contras—** a series of US-backed death squads in Central America—systematically

Photo 5.2   Anders Behring Brevik, an anti-Muslim white supremacist, killed seventy-seven and injured 319 in his attacks in Oslo and Utoya, Norway, on July 22, 2011. Here he is pictured in a staged photo from his fifteen hundred-page manifesto.

relied on terror against thousands of civilians to intimidate and ultimately expel the socialist Sandinista government in Nicaragua.

Racial-ethnic supremacist extremism is another variant of right-wing terrorism. Racial and ethnic supremacist beliefs see specific races and ethnic identities as innately superior to others, and groups that espouse them interpret racial superiority as leading to a natural hierarchy within society. According to such views, political and social life should reflect this hierarchy, meaning that superior races and ethnicities should rule all others.

One of the most prominent examples of a white supremacist group is the **Ku Klux Klan (KKK)**, which first emerged in about 1866. The group originally combined claims to white racial superiority with various Biblical references to formulate their racist ideology. The second generation of the KKK lasted from 1915–1944, while the contemporary third generation has been in existence since 1946. In addition to organizing lynch mobs, crossburnings, and other vigilante actions, in 1951, the KKK killed two National Association for the Advancement of Colored People (NAACP) activists in Florida. In 1963, the group bombed a church in Birmingham, Alabama, which killed four African-American girls. The group also attacked white activists who collaborated with the cause of racial justice. For example, in 1964, the group infamously abducted and murdered three civil rights workers, Chaney, Goodman, and Schwerner, in Mississippi. Supremacist groups have existed among other racial and ethnic groups as well. For example, the **Afrikaner Resistance Movement** in South Africa falls into this category.

Another contemporary example of home-grown, far-right terrorism in the US is the **Sovereign Citizen Movement**, whose adherents hold complex anti-government beliefs, such as the need to obey only the laws of one's choosing and the right to not pay taxes. The movement's subculture began to grow in earnest in the late 2000s, though its roots lie in the early 1980s. During its early years, the movement mainly attracted white supremacists and anti-Semites, reflecting its views that Jews were working behind the scenes to manipulate financial institutions and control the government. Many early proponents of the sovereign movement believed that being white was a pre-requisite to being considered a "sovereign."

Sovereign extremists have been implicated in acts of deadly violence, many of them directed against government officials. In 1997, a sovereign extremist in New Hampshire killed two police officers and two civilians. That same year, two brothers in Idaho killed a police officer who pulled them over for failing to use their turn signal. In 2010, a father and son team of sovereigns killed two police officers with an assault rifle when they were pulled over in West Memphis, Arkansas for speeding.

Whereas left-wing groups have been fairly constrained in their use of violence, extremist right-wing groups have been responsible for some particularly bloody incidents. According to Hoffman, "right-wing terrorists see themselves, if not as a revolutionary vanguard, then as a catalyst of events that will lead to the imposition of an authoritarian form of government" (2006, p. 238). For example, in August 1980, a neo-fascist group in Italy bombed the crowded rail station in Bologna during the summer holiday rush, killing eighty-four people and wounding 180 more (Hoffman 2006, p. 237).

Nationalist-Separatist Extremism. Another wave of popular ideologies that dominated the twentieth century was anti-colonialism and anti-imperialism. **Post-colonial** ideologies acknowledged the right of people to **self-determination**—as well as the right of people to use armed struggle to confront colonial or imperial powers. Thus the primary concern of nationalist-separatist groups related specifically to the territory that they wished to capture or recapture in order to exercise their self-determination. In 1961, Frantz Fanon, an Algerian doctor, wrote a treatise called *The Wretched of the Earth*, in which he argued that:

> Violence liberates people from their shortcomings and anxieties. It inculcates in them both courage and fearlessness concerning death. Violence has a therapeutic effect, purifying society of its diseases. 'Violence will purify the individuals from venom, it will redeem the colonized from inferiority complex, it will return courage to the countryman. . . .Blazing our armed revolution . . . is a healing medicine for all our people's diseases'" (Yehoshafat Harkabi, "Al Fatah's Doctrine," reprinted from the original

article published in *Adelphi Papers*, No. 53 (December 1968), Institute of Strategic Studies, London, as quoted in Laqueur 2004, p. 153).

In other words, many nationalist-separatist groups saw violence as a vital process by which oppressed peoples overcome the inferiority complex that colonial and imperial powers inculcated in them to maintain control.

Many groups with separatist or secessionist goals used this claim to justify their armed actions. For example, Fanon's writings had a major influence on **Euskadi Ta Askatasuna (Basque Fatherland and Liberty, ETA),** a militant Basque nationalist and separatist organization in northern Spain and southwestern France established in 1959 with the goal of gaining independence for the Greater Basque Country (Berberoglu 2009, p. 197). Since 1968, ETA has killed 829 people and injured thousands more.

We can see, too, that some nationalist-separatist groups draw on Marxist-socialist belief systems with which to justify their struggles and their use of arms. Take, for example, this platform statement from the **Popular Front for the Liberation of Palestine (PFLP):**

The Arab bourgeoisie has developed armies which are not prepared to sacrifice their own interests or to risk their privileges. Arab militarism has become an apparatus for oppressing revolutionary socialist movements within the Arab states, while at the same time claiming to be staunchly anti-imperialist. Under the guise of the national question, the bourgeoisie has used its armies to strengthen its bureaucratic power over the masses and to prevent the workers and peasants from acquiring political power. So far it has demanded the help of the workers and peasants without organizing them or without developing a proletarian ideology. The national bourgeoisie usually comes to power through military coups and without any activity on the part of the masses; as soon as it has captured power it reinforces its bureaucratic position. Through widespread application of terror it is able to talk about revolution while at the same time it suppresses all the revolutionary movements and arrests everyone who tries to advocate revolutionary action (quoted in Laqueur 2004, p. 149).

Notice how the quasi-Marxist inspiration for the PFLP platform leads the group to reject the interventions of elite Arab powers on behalf on Palestinian self-determination, seeing such actors as bourgeois antagonists rather than allies.

Violent nationalist-separatist groups often use terror alongside other guerrilla attacks, and rely on symbolic forms of violence primarily to generate publicity, rally support among co-ethnics, demonstrate the government's incapacity to end the group, and coerce the government into making concessions (Hoffman 2006, p. 233). As an IRA operative claimed, " 'You don't bloody well kill people for the sake of killing them.' " (quoted in Hoffman

2006, p. 239). Nevertheless, such groups see killing people as necessary for success against a militarily superior colonial opponent. For instance, in their communiqué *Freedom Struggle*, the Provisional IRA explain and justify their use of violence as a fairly moderate act when compared against the brutality of colonial rule:

> Quite frankly it suited IRA strategy to carry out selective bombings in Belfast, Derry and other towns in occupied Ulster. They see these actions as a legitimate part of war, the targets chosen being military and police barracks, outposts, customs officers, administrative and government buildings, electricity transformers and pylons, certain cinemas, hotels, clubs, dance halls, pubs, all of which provide relaxation and personal comforts for the British forces; also business targets (e.g., factories, firms, stores—sometimes under the guise of co-ops) owned in whole or part by British financiers or companies, or who in any way are a contributory factor to the well-being of Her Majesty's invading forces, and in certain instances residences of people known to harbor or be in league with espionage personnel or agents provocateurs, namely the SAS, MRF, and SIB In many ways this campaign is reminiscent of that carried out by the underground resistance in France during WWII. In all cases IRA bomb squads give adequate warning though these warnings are sometimes withheld or delayed deliberately by the British army as a counter-tactic, with view to making optimum publicity out of the injured and the dead in their propaganda war on the IRA. In no instance has the 'warning rule' been violated by the guerrilla forces in sharp contrast to the 'no warning' methods used by the unionist gangs and British army agents provocateurs (quoted in Laqueur 2004, p. 138).

Between 1972 and 2002, the IRA killed over 1,800 people—about six hundred fifty of whom were civilians.

Single-Issue Extremism. Of course, some terror groups do not possess grand narratives or worldviews. Instead, they prioritize a single policy goal or reform around which they see action as necessary. For example, the environmental movement has produced several extremist manifestations, including radical environmental protection groups as well as radical animal rights groups. **Earth First!,** a radical environmental advocacy organization founded in the United States in 1980, began with nonviolent civil disobedience actions to protest against an Oregon logging company in 1985. However, the group claimed responsibility for an arson attack on a livestock company in California in 1989 and vandalized a ski resort in Telluride, Colorado in 1991. During this incident, the group left several slogans, including "Hayduke lives"—a reference to a fictional character named George Washington Hayduke in Edward Abbey's novel *The Monkey Wrench Gang*. The story depicts a group of people who travel around the southwestern United States sabotaging construction equipment and thwarting attempts to develop land. The trial of several members and associates of this group under terrorism laws has been extremely controversial, given that the group has destroyed

BOX 5.1
LONE WOLF TERRORISM

Since the early 2000s, the phenomenon of lone-wolf terrorism has drawn increasing attention from the media and from policymakers. But because this form of terrorism bucks the common perception of terrorism as a collective, organized activity, scholarly attention to the phenomenon has not matched recent levels of public attention. Lone wolf terrorists are typically characterized as operating individually, not belonging to an organized group, and difficult for authorities to detect (Berntzen and Sandberg 2014). The focus on the individual perpetrator of violence—rather than on specific political, religious, or social goals—further suggests that lone wolf terrorism should not necessarily be viewed as a distinct, ideological category of terrorism. In fact, many lone wolf terrorists identify or sympathize with extremist ideologies such as those described in this chapter, but, by definition, are not a part of these movements. Juergensmeyer (2003), for example, has argued that many of the acts that appear to be solo ventures conducted by rogue agents, so to speak, are validated by broader ideologies.

TABLE 5.1 Examples of Lone Wolf Terrorism

Name	Location	Time Span	Fatalities/ Injuries
Theodore Kaczyinski	United States	1978–1996	3/23
David Copeland	United Kingdom	April 17–30, 1999	3/129
Anders Behring Breivik	Norway	2011	69/60
Mohamed Lahouaiej-Bouhlel	France	2016	86/434
Alexandre Bissonnette	Canada	2017	6/19

Like the definition of terrorism provided in Chapter 1, what separates the actions of a lone wolf terrorist from those of a murderer is the existence of a larger political, ideological, or social cause that informs the lone terrorist's actions. In ascribing such motivations, however, the boundaries of what constitutes lone wolf terrorism are somewhat arbitrary (Spaaij 2012). Like the example of the DHS retraction provided at the beginning of this chapter, whether an act of violence is considered lone wolf terrorism, a mass shooting, or a hate crime is often highly politicized.

As an example, consider how law enforcement officials—and popular discourse—characterized two recent acts of lone wolf terrorism in the US. On June 18, 2015, a white twenty-one-year old man named Dylann Roof opened fire and killed nine people during a prayer meeting at an African American church in Charleston, SC. Roof later stated that he had carried out the shootings in the hopes of starting a race war. In the immediate aftermath of the attack, federal

Continued

BOX 5.1
LONE WOLF TERRORISM
(Continued)

law enforcement officials and the US Department of Justice declared that they were investigating the attack as a hate crime. In contrast, On June 12, 2016, Omar Mateen, a twenty-nine-year old US-citizen of Afghan descent, killed 49 people and wounded 53 others after he opened fire in a gay night club in Orlando, FL. After the shooting began, Mateen called 911 to pledge his allegiance to ISIS, and officials instantly described the massacre as a domestic terror incident. While the media and law enforcement most often associate Mateen with lone wolf terrorism, this is not the case when it comes to describing the actions of Dylann Roof. Ultimately, the comparison of these two attacks serves to highlight how racial, ethnic, or religious biases and power structures can inform the identification of lone wolf terrorism.

Because of these and other complications tied to the phenomenon of lone wolf terrorism, some scholars question whether such acts should even be considered terrorism. After all, terrorism is predominantly a group dynamic, and collective socialization is a common precursor to individual pathways into terror (Spaaji 2010). This has complicated matters for authorities when it comes to convicting individuals of terrorism. In Norway, for example, prosecutors must prove that there was more than one plotter involved in an attack to try accused individuals as terrorists (Pantucci 2011). Others argue that the majority of lone wolf terrorists are actually mentally ill, in contrast to the majority of individuals who join terrorist groups. Marc Sageman, for example, has claimed that there are "two kinds of Lone Wolves, real lone wolves and mass murderers" (quoted in Pantucci 2011, p. 5; see also Chapter 4). While the former are often part of some type of community, real or virtual, the latter have their own personal pathologies. The difference is difficult to distinguish.

property without harming any people. In a sense, those who consider Earth First! a terrorist group demonstrate the difficulty with defining violence, let alone terrorism.

The **Animal Liberation Front (ALF),** a clandestine resistance movement with the objective of upholding animal rights, was established in 1976 in the United Kingdom. The group, which operates in about 40 countries, destroys and vandalizes farms and animal facilities, freeing animals and operating underground sanctuaries where the animals subsequently live. In 1982, the ALF sent letter bombs to all four major party leaders in the UK, including then Prime Minister Margaret Thatcher, though there were no casualties. In 2005, the US Department of Homeland Security classified the ALF as a domestic terrorist group because of the group's threats against hunters, professors using animals in laboratory research, and industrial farmers.

RELIGIOUS IDEOLOGIES

Religious groups often espouse commitment to a faith-based doctrine, which compels them to use violence as a "sacramental act or divine duty executed in direct response to some theological demand or imperative" (Hoffman 2006, p. 88). Such groups often have starkly defined in- and out-groups, along with a strong moral compulsion to eliminate outsiders to fulfill their duties. Religious terror groups often possess millennial or apocalyptic views, which seek to fundamentally change or replace the existing order rather than to correct or improve it.

While religious terrorism has so far dominated much of the landscape in the twenty-first century, David Rapaport argues that religious groups had a monopoly on terrorism prior to the nineteenth century (Hoffman 2006, p. 84). Hoffman suggests that religious terrorism made its comeback in 1979, after the Iranian Revolution ushered in a new period of Islamist empowerment coupled with new expressions of long-standing resentments against Western interference in the Islamic world. He also suggests that the end of the cold war dried up funding for both right- and left-wing groups by the world's two superpowers, and discredited many Marxist and neo-Marxist groups (ibid, p. 86). With its broad trends of globalization and secularization, the post-cold war period likewise ushered in a sense of crisis among numerous fundamentalist groups, who saw such trends as threatening their own religious beliefs, identities, and goals.

Fundamentalist Sunni Islamist Extremism. In 1948–1950, Egyptian **Sayyid Qutb** attended university at the Colorado State College of Education (now the University of Northern Colorado) in Greeley, CO in the United States. After several more educational experiences in Washington, DC and California, he described his experience with the emptiness of Western life in a critical piece called "The America I Have Seen." In it, he lays out his perceptions of Americans as materialistic, sexually promiscuous, artistically tasteless, racist, pro-Israel, and unkempt.

Upon his return to Egypt, Qutb joined the **Muslim Brotherhood**, a **Sunni** religious network that opposed the growing secular Arab nationalism that was beginning to dominate Arab governments as in Egypt. Qutb was jailed and executed in 1964 for his political activities on behalf of **Islamism**. Prior to his execution, he wrote "**Ma'alim fi al-Tariq**" (sometimes translated as "Milestones" or "Signposts"), a text that would later prove seminal to second and third-generation Muslim Brotherhood adherents throughout the Arab world. In "Milestones," Qutb argues that the global Muslim community has been replaced by a corrupt and evil system of secular values, ideas, and rules. He contends that the only release from the corrupt and evil influences that have replaced the global Muslim community is sharia law—and that sharia law must be revived and imposed by an Islamic vanguard that sees Islam as a complete moral, political, social, and legal system. Instead of consulting

SHOULD WE DISTINGUISH BETWEEN RELIGIOUS AND SECULAR TERRORISM?

One of the foremost scholars of religious terrorism, Mark Juergensmeyer, argues that what is most unique to recent acts of religious terrorism is that they replace military objectives with claims of moral justification and a sense of absolutism that transforms otherwise wordly struggles into cosmic battles (Juergensmeyer 2003). According to Juergensmeyer, three elements set religious terrorism apart from its secular variations. First, religious terrorist movements reject the compromises with secular institutions and liberal values that most mainstream religions such as Christianity, Islam, Judaism, Hinduism, or Buddhism have made. Second, they reject the notion that religion should be kept private, claiming instead that it should be allowed to intrude into public spaces. Finally, these religious movements attempt to create a new form of religiosity that rejects the modern substitutes highlighted above, namely globalization and secularization (ibid). Others, like Jessica Stern, similarly argue that religious motivations are fundamental to understanding many contemporary terror groups (2003). However, critics challenge Juergensmeyer's characterization of religious terrorism as acts of unrestrained and largely irrational violence insofar as it offers few, if any, effective policy options for countering this kind of violence.

Jeurgensemeyer's work is based on the premise that there is in fact a meaningful difference between religious violence and secular violence, and that religion tends to promote violence. But many scholars reject this claim. Cavanaugh (2009), for example, argues that the distinction between what counts as religion and what does not is overly fuzzy. Consider this brief passage from his book *The Myth of Religious Violence*: "… ideologies and institutions labeled secular can be just as absolutist, divisive, and irrational as those labeled religious. What gets labeled religious and what does not is therefore of crucial importance. The myth of religious violence tried to establish as timeless, universal, and natural a very contingent set of categories—religious and secular—that are in fact constructions of the modern West" (Cavanaugh 2009, p. 7).

Furthermore, a number of terrorist groups appear to center on what could be interpreted as both religious and ethno-nationalist ideologies. Take Hamas as an example. The group's charter calls for establishing an Islamic Palestinian state in place of Israel, and rejects all agreements made between the Palestine Liberation Organization (PLO) and Israel. While the goal of creating an explicitly Islamic state certainly highlights the religious component of Hamas' overall objectives, it likely makes little sense to characterize the group solely as religious, given its strong territorial ambitions.

Islam for guidance, he argues, this vanguard should take direct orders from Quranic scripture. In this treatise, Qutb also directs attention to the fact that corrupt Western powers tend to manipulate and oppress Muslims by installing secular, pro-Western leaders into power in Arab states, removing the ability of Muslims to realize their own aspirations of self-government, Islamic law, and pure society. The tenants that emerged from Qutb's writings are known as **Qutbism**. More generally, those who advocated for coercion to realize the implementation of an Islamist government are known as **Salafists.** And the word **jihad** can be interpreted as an internal struggle within one-self, or as a quest or struggle in the world. As a result, some observers refer to violent groups motivated by Qutb's ideology as **Salafi jihadi** groups.

Qutb's tenants resurrected themselves in the late 1980s and early 1990s as second-generation Muslim Brotherhood groups such as the **Armed Islamic Group of Algeria**, **Egyptian Islamic Jihad**, **Palestinian Islamic Jihad**, and the **Islamic Resistance Movement (Hamas)** came into the scene (among others). Moreover, in Saudi Arabia, a particular strand of Sunni Is-lamism, known as **neo-Wahhabism**, grew in popularity among the more pious elements of Saudi society. Neo-Wahhabism advocates a strict and his-torical version of Islam that calls its followers to adhere to seventh century Is-lamic practices, doctrines, and ideals. Adherents included personalities like Osama bin Laden, the co-founder of Al Qaeda.

In fact, Al Qaeda was itself the result of a fateful meeting of Egyptian militants subscribing to Qutubism, and Saudi militants subscribing to neo-Wahhabism during the anti-Soviet wars in Afghanistan in the late 1980s. As they joined in the fight against the "apostate" Soviets in Afghanistan, Sunni Muslims from around the world brought their own brands of Islamism with them. Ayman al Zawahiri, the Egyptian doctor who established Al Jihad, and Osama bin Laden, first met in Afghanistan while resisting the Soviets along-side US-backed Afghan **mujahideen**. Upon the conclusion of the Afghan campaign, bin Laden and Zawahiri returned to their respective homes, only to find dissatisfaction with the state of political life there as well. In par-ticular, as bin Laden witnessed the US invasion of Iraq to defend Kuwaiti and Saudi oil fields during the First Gulf War in 1991, he began to formulate the view that the West was indeed responsible for much the suffering of Muslim peoples around the world, and that Islamists would likely not make political progress in their own countries unless Western influence was elimi-nated from their governments. This idea was explicit in his 1998 declaration of war, in which he demanded the withdrawal of American armed forces from Saudi Arabia and the end of Western support for secular dictators in Muslim-majority countries. A secondary goal included the destruction of Israel, which bin Laden saw as both apostate in its treatment of Palestinian Muslims and a proxy of US interests.

With regard to Israel, a similar claim emerges in Hamas' Convenant, its official operational and philosophical statement released in 1993. Hamas claims that its primary goal is to prevent the expansion of Zionist forces and to provide space for Islamic peoples to live independently of them:

> World Zionism and Imperialist forces have been attempting, with smart moves and considered planning, to push the Arab countries, one after another, out of the circle of conflict with Zionism, in order, ultimately, to

isolate the Palestinian people. Egypt has already been cast out of the conflict, to a very great extent through the treacherous Camp David Accords, and she has been trying to drag other countries into similar agreements in order to push them out of the circle of conflict. Hamas is calling upon the Arab and Islamic peoples to act seriously and tirelessly in order to frustrate that dreadful scheme and to make the masses aware of the danger of copping out of the circle of struggle with Zionism. Today it is Palestine and tomorrow it may be another country or other countries. For Zionist scheming has no end, and after Palestine they will covet expansion from the Nile to the Euphrates. Only when they have completed digesting the area on which they will have laid their hand, they will look forward to more expansion, etc. Their scheme has been laid out in the Protocols of the Elders of Zion, and their present [conduct] is the best proof of what is said there (transl. and quoted in Laqueur 2004, p. 437–8).

Sunni jihadi groups tend to view all those who do not subscribe to this particular view as worthy of death. For example, one Egyptian militant was fairly unapologetic after learning he killed 9 German tourists instead of Israelis, saying that " 'infidels are all the same'" (quoted in Hoffman 2006, p. 239).

Fundamentalist Christian Extremism. A number of groups in the United States have used violence on the basis of extremist Christian beliefs. For example, the **Christian Identity** movement advances the belief that Anglo-Saxon, Nordic and Germanic peoples are the true descendants of the Biblical Israelites, that Jews are descendants of Satan, and that the white race is supreme. Proponents of this view use Biblical passages to justify white supremacy, contest the right of Jews to claim themselves as "God's chosen people," and claim that the righteous must themselves wage war to hasten the end-times described in the Book of Revelation. Like many of the groups described here, Christian Identity movement followers often publish blogs, websites, and other media where they promote such ideas. One popular movement novel, called *The Turner Diaries*, was published by William Pierce in 1978. In it, the protagonist wages war to successfully overthrow the US government and exterminate all non-white, Jewish, and gay people. Notably, Timothy McVeigh, the co-conspirator with Terry Nichol of the Oklahoma City bombing in April 1995, was a loose follower of the Christian Identity movement and apparently drew inspiration from a passage of the book that involved the bombing of an FBI building. The book has also inspired the actions of groups like **The Order**, which carried out bank robberies and murders in Washington State in 1983–1984, and of lone-wolf actors like John William King, who murdered James Byrd, an African-American, in Texas in 1998.

Anti-abortion attackers represent another single-issue group motivated by extremist Christian beliefs. Although they often possess religious overtones, several of the groups that have claimed responsibility for murders of abortion clinic doctors and staff have been singularly focused on "protecting unborn babies." Examples of such anti-abortion terrorism include the 1996 attacks on Centennial Park during the Summer Olympic Games and later attacks on an abortion clinic and a lesbian bar. The perpetrator of these attacks, Eric Rudolph, belonged to the anti-abortion group **The Army of God**, an extremist group that continues to run a website devoted to the writings and philosophy of Rudolph (see http://www.armyofgod.com/EricRudolphHomepage.html).

In 2015, Robert Lewis Dear assaulted a Planned Parenthood clinic in Colorado Springs, citing the need to do "God's work." During the trial, Dear's associates cited his deeply held Christian beliefs as a motivation for his actions. For example, in legal documents related to his 1993 divorce, his ex-wife states: "He claims to be a Christian and is extremely evangelistic, but does not follow the Bible in his actions. He says that as long as he believes he will be saved, he can do whatever he pleases. He is obsessed with the world coming to an end" (Fausset 2015).

Zionist/Jewish Extremism. Some Jewish extremist groups have committed terror attacks as well. Perhaps most notoriously, Baruch Goldstein, a follower of Rabbi Meir Kahane and the Jewish ultra-nationalist **Kach movement**, believed in the doctrine of **Kahanism**, which suggested that Arabs were enemies of the Jews and Israel, that Israel should be a Jewish theocracy, that all Jews should be educated enough about the Torah to qualify as rabbis, and that Jews should settle their historical homelands of Judea and Samaria (what Palestinians refer to as the West Bank). On February 25, 1994, the Purim holiday, Goldstein entered the Cave of the Patriarchs while Muslims prayed inside and opened fire with his military-issue weapon, massacring twenty-nine Muslim

Photo 5.3 Tombstone of Baruch Goldstein, Meir Kahane Tourist Park, Kiryat Arba, Palestinian Occupied Territories

Palestinian worshippers and wounding 125 more. Many ultra-nationalist Jewish extremists continue to celebrate Goldstein as a hero and martyr.

On November 4, 1995, Yigal Amir, another ultranationalist Jewish extremist, assassinated Israeli Prime Minister Yitzakh Rabin. Amir justified the killing on the basis that Rabin was guilty of treason because of his negotiation of the **Oslo Accords**, which allowed a degree of self-determination for Palestinians. Amir saw Rabin as illegitimate because he formed a coalition of Jews and Arabs; he saw the killing as justified because any degradation of Jews was a step backward in the return of Judea and Samaria to the Jews.

Hindu Fundamentalism. Since the election of Narendra Modi as India's prime minister in May 2014, sources suggest that groups of radical Hindu nationalists have been terrorizing the country's religious minorities. According to the Global Terrorism Database (GTD), the group **Rashtriya Swayamsevak Sangh (RSS)** perpetrated at least four attacks in 2015, killing at least one person and injuring others (GTD 2017). The group, which acts in support of their vision of a pure "Hindustan," has forced Muslims to convert to Hinduism, called for the rewriting of textbooks in India, and held training camps for teenage boys and girls to inculcate children into their cause. Hindu terrorism is often also referred to as **saffron terror**, a term that comes from Hindu nationalists' symbolic use of the yellow-ish color made of saffron.

ASSUMPTIONS OF THE IDEOLOGICAL APPROACH

The aim of ideological approaches is to identify the commonalities across different ideological orientations to understand how they motivate and constrain the use of violence by their adherents. The ability to do this accurately and compellingly rests on several core assumptions.

Taking Preferences Seriously. In contrast to the strategic approach, which remains agnostic about a terror group's preferences, the ideological approach attempts to discern where those preferences come from in the first place. What kinds of ideologies motivate, incite, and legitimate violence in ways that make terrorism a desirable and laudable method? The ideological approach is preoccupied with this question. Specifically, one's ideology shapes one's preferences and determines the range of behaviors one deems acceptable to pursue them. For example, let's assume a group becomes convinced that the capitalist class will increasingly dominate the masses unless an armed worker revolt upends the exploitative economic system. Let's also assume the group becomes convinced that its members alone comprehend the true nature of the situation. Once the group accepts both these core beliefs, one can imagine the group expressing strong preferences for both the liberation of the masses as well as an armed revolt as an acceptable means of creating change. In fact, most (if not all) terror groups claim legitimacy through interpretation of doctrines, texts, or scriptures in ways that justify their violence.

BOX 5.3

TERROR GROUP OR APOCALYPTIC CULT?

Certain terrorist groups—such as **Aum Shinrikyo** in Japan—are considered apocalyptic in their desire for mass destruction as a path towards replacing the corrupt world with a pure and new social order. More recently, officials in the Pentagon described the Islamic State of Iraq and Syria (ISIS) as an "apocalyptic" organization with an "end-of-days" strategic vision (Ackerman 2014). Members of ISIS, including an Australian preacher reported in 2015 as being one of the group's most influential recruiters, believe it is foretold that ISIS will conquer Istanbul before being beaten back by the anti-Messiah, whose eventual death will usher in the apocalypse (Wood 2015).

These apocalyptic theories of terrorism focus on one particular motivation of groups—violence is used to hasten the end of times and usher in an anticipated new world. Many theories of religious terrorism have emphasized the apocalyptic, millennial, or messianic message that drives groups to committing acts of terrorism.

Apocalyptic theories of terrorism posit that the primary aim of certain groups is to cause cataclysmic destruction. Most often, this pursuit is uniquely religious and is perhaps the most common stereotype of religiously motivated terrorism. Some apocalyptic groups have been characterized by their longings for the coming of the messiah (which would coincide with the end of the world). Other theories of millennial terrorism argue that apocalyptic imagining is a cause of terrorism in cults and New Religious Movements, but alone does not typically result in violence (Mayer 2001).

An example of an apocalyptic group is the **Gush Emunim** in Israel. In 1984, the group plotted to blow up the Muslim Dome of the Rock Shrine in Jerusalem in order to spark a nuclear and chemical confrontation between Israel and Muslim countries. The goal was to create "catastrophic messianism," disastrous consequences that would hasten the coming of the Messiah (Gregg 2014). True apocalyptic terrorism makes counterterrorism strategy particularly difficult, insofar as there is likely little that anyone can do to persuade such groups to alter their aims.

The problem with many apocalyptic explanations for religious terrorism is the narrow focus on one particular motivation. In reality, religious terrorist groups actually have other goals, some of which are more "earthly" and political in nature. Marc Sedgwick, for example, contends that the apocalyptic aims of terrorist groups are most often secondary to their more immediate, political goals (Sedgwick 2004). Even in many interpretations of non-religious terrorism, however, the apocalyptic goal of groups has been taken as a given as a result of the intensity of the violent tactics that terrorist groups employ. Indeed, Max Abrahms (2013) found that often the inherently radical and dramatic tactics of terrorism (killing many innocent civilians) do not correspond with the goals of the terrorist organization, which are most often of a more mundane, political nature. As such, terrorists undermine their very ability to coerce by employing tactics that do not match their true goals.

Agnosticism about the Unit of Analysis. Ideologies can motivate individuals, groups, communities, or societies. The ideological approach in terrorism studies typically does not specify at what level different ideas and identities are generated and sustained. Certainly it is the case that some lone wolf terrorists have highly conspiratorial and paranoid ideologies that motivate their behavior. For example, Ted Kaczynski, known more commonly as "The Unabomber," believed that the Industrial Revolution—and in particular the machines and technology emerging from it—was destroying humanity. He detailed these grievances in a published manifesto, which *The Washington Post* carried in 1995. Although his beliefs were apparently not shared widely or passionately enough for a sustained violent group to form around his claims, Kaczynski was nevertheless able to commit several acts of violence through the use of mail bombs. It is also the case that some groups, such as the Aum Shinrikyo cult in Japan, have been particularly adept at convincing large numbers of followers to adopt their beliefs. And of course, some ideologies become accepted enough that whole societies mobilize on their behalf. This was the case, for example, with the Fascism that emerged during the early 1930s throughout Europe. Although there were certainly groups that perpetrated discrete and specific acts of violence, such as the Hitler Youth, there were also broader ideological currents of anti-Semitism, nativism, and fascism that allowed the Nationalist Socialist (Nazi) Party to rise to power in Germany. Therefore, ideological motivations can occur at the individual, group, or societal levels.

Features of the Ideology Predict Whether and How a Group Becomes Violent. Many groups possess extremist views without becoming violent themselves. Ideological approaches tend to focus on a few key ideological elements thought to predispose a believer or group of believers to perpetrate violence. First, such ideologies often possess strict elements of intransigence. Proponents have depicted a cosmic, collective struggle, with clear-cut stakes (good vs. evil, life vs. death, in-group vs. out-group) where any compromise would be impossible. For example, Marc Jurgensmeyer (2003) writes that violent religious ideologies tend to focus on three key elements that define the struggle in terms of "cosmic war": that the group is on the defensive in terms of their basic identity, freedom, or dignity; that losing the struggle would be unthinkable, such that any victims are better off dead than alive in the current system; and that the struggle is nearly impossible to win in real time or in real terms. Instead, the possibility of victory rests in God's hands. However, victory will result in a better world for all. As a result of such ideological tenants, the groups' struggles become disproportionate and extremely difficult to resolve in any other way besides violence. One can easily imagine secular ideologies that depict the same cosmic war, albeit without the intervention of a deity.

Second, such ideologies often depict a faceless, collective enemy that proponents dehumanize using "othering" language, such as "dogs," "infidels," "children of Satan," etc. As Hoffman writes, "The deliberate use of such terminology to condone and justify terrorism is significant, for it further erodes constraints on violence and bloodshed by portraying the terrorists' victims as either subhuman or unworthy of living" (2006, p. 89).

Third, ideologies of terror groups often depict the struggle as requiring intense personal sacrifice, including one's own death, to achieve victory in a larger-than-life struggle. As such, proponents of such ideologies typically see violent actors as engaging in a fundamentally altruistic act, obedient to the call and responding to an intense sense of personal duty to advance a wider cause.

Among those groups that do become violent, proponents of the ideological approach tend to see patterns of terrorist violence as closely linked to the specific commands inherent in the ideology itself. For example, Hoffman argues that most left-wing terrorists do not frequently engage in truly indiscriminate killing because they see their goals as secular and limited in nature (2006, p. 88). Many religious groups, on the other hand, see their rewards in the afterlife and therefore are less likely to feel constrained in their use of violence.

Violence Is Symbolic. The ideological approach suggests that terror attacks are fundamentally performative acts rather than strategic ones. The acts themselves are symbolic, usually targeting symbols rather than the "enemy" itself. For example, at 2 A.M. on June 12, 2016, Omar Mateen walked into the Pulse gay bar in Orlando, Florida, and massacred 50 people who were dancing inside. In the weeks prior to the attack, Mateen's family and co-workers had observed him making anti-gay comments. Having decided that homosexuals were immoral and unworthy of life, Mateen chose a well-known gay bar during Gay Pride month in the United States as his target. While he must have known that this act would not eliminate homosexuality, he clearly chose this attack venue as a way to express his disgust with homosexuality.

The Perpetrator's Ideology Motivates and Justifies Violence. Proponents of the ideological approach assume that when terrorists explain their motivations and reasoning for an attack after it is over, they are telling the truth. In other words, when terrorists survive an attack and provide ideological explanations for them, proponents of the ideological approach think we should believe them. Here, we can see an explicit assumption that ideology is the true motivation of an attack, as opposed to a post-hoc justification of violence.

OBSERVABLE IMPLICATIONS OF THE IDEOLOGICAL APPROACH

These core assumptions yield multiple observable implications that, if supported by evidence, would provide strong support for the idea that ideology can help to motivate, regulate, and constrain the use of terrorist violence above and beyond strategic, organizational, structural, or psychological concerns. Most proponents of ideological approaches rely on primary sources as evidence—that is, they rely on the words and statements of the terrorists themselves to garner support for ideological arguments.

Radicalization Moves Nonviolent Believers to Become Violent Believers. Most people with extreme beliefs do not commit acts of violence. Ideological approaches assume, therefore, that a process called **radicalization** turns erstwhile nonviolent extremists into violent ones. Through such processes, different grievances and claims are cast in "larger than life" terms. Ideological claims remain not only moral imperatives, but rather they must also be expressed through violent public acts. The struggle facing the radicalized believer is one between good and evil and is often linked to notions such as conquest and failure, martyrdom and sacrifice. Ironically, many terrorists view themselves, fundamentally, as altruists.

Evidence that would support this observable implication might include:

- Qualitative evidence—from memoirs, manifests, or other internal documents—suggesting that radicalization *preceded* (rather than followed) the first act of violence. Such evidence would involve demonstrating an evolution in the group's internal discourse, wherein the group would begin to harden its positions vis-à-vis intransigence, in- vs. out-group differentiation, dehumanization, and altruistic duty.

- Qualitative evidence that terrorists rely on moral sanction (such as blessings of clergy or permission from the ideological leader of the movement) before conducting an attack.

The More Extreme the Beliefs, the More Deadly the Terrorism. Believers with less extremist views are likelier to remain nonviolent, whereas those with the most uncompromising, dehumanizing beliefs are more likely to turn to violence. In this formulation, it is a person's convictions—rather than their psychology, for instance—that motivate and justify their violence toward others. Many terrorism scholars have argued for a distinction between secular and religious terrorists in this regard. Secular terrorists, they argue, use violence to correct a concrete flaw in the political, social, or economic system. Religious terrorists, on the other hand, see themselves as transcending human systems of government, economy, and social life. Instead, they seek to please a supernatural power. Hence, the intended audiences of the violence differ; for secular terrorists, the intended audience is a public who can change the system, whereas for religious terrorists, the intended audience is a deity whom they see as sanctioning and blessing violence. Proponents of this view believe that religious terrorism, therefore, should be exceedingly violent compared with secular terrorism (Hoffman 2006, p. 87–89; 230).

Evidence that would support this observable implication might include:

- Qualitative evidence to suggest that perpetrators belonged to a preexisting organizational apparatus, which can often provide social welfare services or charity to attract followers.

- Qualitative evidence to suggest that the organization practices strict internal discipline, with many resources devoted to indoctrination rather than just operational training.
- Qualitative or quantitative evidence to suggest that the primary targets of terrorism are nonbelievers, whereas with psychological and organizational approaches the pattern should look more random.
- Quantitative evidence suggesting that attacks by religious terrorists are bloodier than attacks by secular groups, holding other factors constant.

Strategically Counterproductive Behavior. If the ideological approach is correct, then groups using terror should often do so counterproductively from a strategic perspective because of ideological imperatives to do so. They may take highly risky and potentially self-defeating actions that divert resources away from successful operations. For example, anarchists in Greece are often unable to wage sustained campaigns in part because their ideology proscribes the kind of group-level governance that would allow them to coalesce into a durable organization. Additionally, some observers have pointed out that the Islamic State often engages in highly risky and counterproductive behaviors in its campaign. For example, the group incurred significant losses to conquer the small Syrian village of Dabiq because of its interpretation of a saying by the Prophet Mohammed that Muslims would conquer the West in Dabiq (McCants 2015, p. 102). Moreover, the Islamic State has banned smoking in the areas it controls—a law sure to evoke resentment from the population there (Cockburn 2015, p. 39). In other words, a highly ideological group is less interested in winning per se, and more interested in discharging its sworn duty.

Evidence that would support this observable implication would include:

- Qualitative evidence suggesting routine operational setbacks due to an unwillingness to deviate from an ideologically-prescribed plan.
- Qualitative or quantitative evidence suggesting that the group tends to target an entire out-group, rather than specific individuals perceived as enemies.
- Qualitative evidence from terrorists' memoirs, diaries, or surveillance indicating a total indifference to or contempt for public opinion, both in terms of its target population and in terms of its own constituents.
- Qualitative evidence suggesting a stubborn refusal to accept assistance (including material or nonmaterial assistance) from nonbelievers. For example, the Islamic State refuses to cooperate with other Salafi jihadi groups that have not sworn their obedience to the Islamic State, despite the fact that entering into an alliance with such groups might expand its capacity (Byman 2016, p. 139).
- Qualitative evidence suggesting that the group sees more moderate believers as traitors or sell-outs, rather than potential allies.

Violence for Its Own Sake. Ideological approaches allow for the possibility that acts of violence have no broader purpose than the killing itself. Contrary to instrumental approaches, which see terrorist violence as having a broader political, social, or personal purpose, proponents of the ideological approach acknowledge that some groups are motivated by ideologies that mandate the extermination of particular peoples. In other words, the killing is ingrained in the ideology as part of the commitment of a true believer. As such, violence can be an end in itself.

Evidence that would support this observable implication would include:

- Qualitative evidence suggesting an ideological mandate to kill others as part of the ideology.
- Surveys indicating killing as a primary motivation of engaging in terrorism. For example, Ayla Schbley conducted a survey of Lebanese Shi'a terrorists and published the results in a 1990 study in the journal *Terrorism*. He found that none of those he sampled were motivated by the possibility that their violence would sway popular opinion or influence their own constituencies. Instead, he found that "their sole preoccupation was serving God through the fulfillment of their divinely ordained mission" (quoted in Hoffman 2006, p. 239). As such, the violence, which was dictated by a deity, served as an end in itself.

Never-Ending Terrorism. A final observable implication of this approach regards the durability of terrorist groups well beyond their own strategic or organizational purposes. Specifically, because their motivation is ideological, terrorist groups remain committed to violence until they have realized their ideological commitments. They feel compelled and duty-bound to do so. They rarely recognize the futility of their struggles, seeing each setback as part of the cosmic struggle in which they are engaged. As such, the ideological approach predicts that terrorist groups will be remarkably resilient to repression.

Evidence that would support this observable implication would include:

- Qualitative evidence—including internal group documents, manifestos, memos, or memoirs—indicating indifference to government countermeasures.
- Qualitative evidence demonstrating that a groups' resolve remains unchanged (or even increases) in the face of government countermeasures.

PRACTICAL IMPLICATIONS OF THE IDEOLOGICAL APPROACH

Overall, the ideological approach suggests that very few policy options are available to interrupt, contain, and end terrorism. The least invasive options are **counter-radicalization** and **de-radicalization**—that is, the direct countering of the ideology through persuasion, public communications, and propaganda. Here, the main thrust is to "win the war of ideas" with competing ideologies and narratives, either to directly contest extremist ideologies or to de-program those who have already succumbed to them.

For example, some have advertised the counter-narrative approach as a potentially powerful defense against the terrorist group ISIS. The organization exploits social media such as Twitter and YouTube to engage with young potential recruits, and uses a number of narrative themes such as brutality, victimhood, mercy, belonging, and utopianism, among others, to attract followers and inspire attacks. There may be ways to develop counter-narratives that expose the fallacies in the dominant self-image of ISIS. One way is to spread the stories told by ISIS defectors, who maintain that ISIS' atrocities are a far cry from Islam, and that the reality of the so-called caliphate is completely different from what is portrayed in ISIS propaganda. An example of a counterterrorism approach that draws on this concept of creating alternative narratives is the Peer-to-Peer Challenging Extremism program, in which the US State Department is involved. The initiative hosts competitions for young people to create social or digital campaigns to counter violent extremism.

Yet there are more troubling policy options available, including developing ways to identify people with ideologies that have propensities toward violence and prevent them from radicalizing. In particular, this specific approach requires invasion of privacy, primarily through surveillance, of many innocent persons so that authorities can detect would-be perpetrators well before they break any laws. Such approaches are violations of basic human rights, which guarantee freedom of conscience and freedom of thought. According to international human rights law, it is legal to think or believe anything. Practically speaking, it would be nearly impossible for a government to effectively discern which extremist views would result in violent acts, leading the government to detect many "false positives" that would expose innocent people to life-altering interference (and harassment) by the authorities. As such, human rights advocates worry that early-interdiction policies aimed at different ideologies are inherently discriminatory and unethical.

Because the ideological approach sees terror groups as motivated primarily by their beliefs rather than by their enemies' actions, the logical practical outgrowth of this view is that governments should prepare for widespread, enduring, and massive repression against those who perpetrate terrorism. Proponents believe the focus should be on eradicating the ideology as the best way to contain or prevent future violence. This leads us to the morally uncomfortable conclusion that the government response will necessarily target belief systems rather than actions—a return to some of the darkest days in global history (such as the Spanish Inquisition and the Thirty Years' War, for example), where people were detained, tortured, and killed for how they thought rather than what they did.

CRITIQUES OF THE IDEOLOGICAL APPROACH

As with any approach, the ideological approach has its detractors. Here we will briefly examine a few of the key critiques of the ideological approach, beginning with critiques of the model's assumptions, followed by critiques of the model's empirical and policy implications.

Correlation Is Not Causation. Some critics have argued that ascribing an ideology to the perpetrator of a terrorist attack—and then seeing that ideology as a motivation for the attack—is confusing correlation with causation. Even if someone is associated with an ideology, this does not mean that ideology motivated their behavior. For example, just because Timothy McVeigh was affiliated with the Christian Patriot movement it does not mean that he was motivated by the ideology espoused by that group. See, for example, the explanation he provided for the Oklahoma City bombing:

> I explain herein why I bombed the Murrah Federal Building in Oklahoma City. I explain this not for publicity, nor seeking to win an argument of right or wrong. I explain so that the record is clear as to my thinking and motivations in bombing a government installation. I chose to bomb a federal building because such an action served more purposes than other options. Foremost, the bombing was a retaliatory strike; a counter attack, for the cumulative raids (and subsequent violence and damage) that federal agents had participated in over the preceding years (including, but not limited to, Waco.) From the formation of such units as the FBI's "Hostage Rescue" and other assault teams amongst federal agencies during the '80's; culminating in the Waco incident, federal actions grew increasingly militaristic and violent, to the point where at Waco, our government—like the Chinese—was deploying tanks against its own citizens. Knowledge of these multiple and ever-more aggressive raids across the country constituted an identifiable pattern of conduct within and by the federal government and amongst its various agencies. (see enclosed) For all intents and purposes, federal agents had become "soldiers" (using military training, tactics, techniques, equipment, language, dress, organization, and mindset) and they were escalating their behavior. Therefore, this bombing was also meant as a pre-emptive (or pro-active) strike against these forces and their command and control centers within the federal building. When an aggressor force continually launches attacks from a particular base of operation, it is sound military strategy to take the fight to the enemy. Additionally, borrowing a page from US foreign policy, I decided to send a message to a government that was becoming increasingly hostile, by bombing a government building and the government employees within that building who represent that government. Bombing the Murrah Federal Building was morally and strategically equivalent to the US hitting a government building in Serbia, Iraq, or other nations. (see enclosed) Based on observations of the policies of my own government, I viewed this action as an acceptable option. From this perspective, what occurred in Oklahoma City was no different than what Americans rain on the heads of others all the time, and subsequently, my mindset was and is one of clinical detachment. (The bombing

of the Murrah building was not personal, no more than when Air Force, Army, Navy, or Marine personnel bomb or launch cruise missiles against government installations and their personnel.) (excerpted from a post at: http://www.truthinourtime.com/2010/02/19/timothy-mcveighs-manifesto/, last accessed 13 March, 2017).

Here, one sees that McVeigh is particularly outraged by the United States' militaristic domestic and foreign policy, rather than any of the typical motivations proffered by adherents to the Christian Identity movement.

A similar critique could exist for those who see Al Qaeda as primarily the product of an ideological marriage between Salafi jihadi and neo-Wahhabi Islamist groups. See Box 5.4.

Besides, most people who have extremist ideologies never become terrorists. Therefore, the ideological approach is at its best an insufficient explanation. This has led critics to propose alternative explanations for patterns of terrorist violence, which proponents of ideological approaches have a difficult time rejecting.

Ideology Is Unobservable. A second critique regards the fact that ideology is fundamentally impossible to observe and categorize. Although we can read what terrorists say and write before or after they attack, or we can sometimes observe how they behave during and after the perpetration of an attack, it is fundamentally impossible to know, truly, what they think about or believe. As a consequence, some scholars have argued that observing behaviors and practices is more productive than trying to observe ideologies per se.

Most Terrorists Are Ideologically Illiterate. Despite the fact that many terror groups develop sophisticated ideologies, terrorism researchers have discovered a consistent pattern—that very few terrorists are, themselves, aware of the ideological commitments their groups espouse. Although the leaders within such groups may be well-educated as to the core tenants of these ideologies, such an education rarely occurs among the rank-and-file of the groups. Moreover, many volunteers and recruits join such groups with very little background in the group's ideological commitments. This fact undermines a core implication of the ideological model—that terrorists should know what beliefs are motivating them.

Ideologies Are Not Monolithic. As one can see from many of the manifestos contained in this chapter, it is seldom the case that a perpetrator of a terror attack possesses one clear-cut, straightforward ideological commitment. Instead, most perpetrators espouse complex, overlapping ideologies, which borrow various strands of contemporary and historical thought. For example, some groups might be properly categorized as nationalist-separatists and left-wing (e.g. Palestine Liberation Organization, LTTE), whereas others may be classified as both religious and racially-motivated (e.g. KKK). Still others could be classified as religious and **nihilistic** (e.g. Islamic State, Aum Shinrikyo), while others could be classified as anarchist and populist

BOX 5.4

ANALYZING OSAMA BIN LADEN'S "FATWA" AGAINST THE WEST

Read the following statement, released by the so-called World Islamic Front (another name for Al Qaeda) in 1998.

"23 February 1998
Shaykh Usamah Bin-Muhammad Bin-Ladin
Ayman al-Zawahiri, amir of the Jihad Group in Egypt
Abu-Yasir Rifa'i Ahmad Taha, Egyptian Islamic Group
Shaykh Mir Hamzah, secretary of the Jamiat-ul-Ulema-e-Pakistan
Fazlur Rahman, amir of the Jihad Movement in Bangladesh

Praise be to Allah, who revealed the Book, controls the clouds, defeats factionalism, and says in His Book: "But when the forbidden months are past, then fight and slay the pagans wherever ye find them, seize them, beleaguer them, and lie in wait for them in every stratagem (of war)"; and peace be upon our Prophet, Muhammad Bin-'Abdallah, who said: I have been sent with the sword between my hands to ensure that no one but Allah is worshipped, Allah who put my livelihood under the shadow of my spear and who inflicts humiliation and scorn on those who disobey my orders.

The Arabian Peninsula has never—since Allah made it flat, created its desert, and encircled it with seas—been stormed by any forces like the crusader armies spreading in it like locusts, eating its riches and wiping out its plantations. All this is happening at a time in which nations are attacking Muslims like people fighting over a plate of food. In the light of the grave situation and the lack of support, we and you are obliged to discuss current events, and we should all agree on how to settle the matter.

No one argues today about three facts that are known to everyone; we will list them, in order to remind everyone:

First, for over seven years the United States has been occupying the lands of Islam in the holiest of places, the Arabian Peninsula, plundering its riches, dictating to its rulers, humiliating its people, terrorizing its neighbors, and turning its bases in the Peninsula into a spearhead through which to fight the neighboring Muslim peoples.

If some people have in the past argued about the fact of the occupation, all the people of the Peninsula have now acknowledged it. The best proof of this is the Americans' continuing aggression against the Iraqi people using the Peninsula as a staging post, even though all its rulers are against their territories being used to that end, but they are helpless.

Second, despite the great devastation inflicted on the Iraqi people by the crusader-Zionist alliance, and despite the huge number of those killed, which has exceeded 1 million... despite all this, the Americans are once again trying to repeat the horrific massacres, as though they are not content with the protracted blockade imposed after the ferocious war or the fragmentation and devastation.

So here they come to annihilate what is left of this people and to humiliate their Muslim neighbors.

Third, if the Americans' aims behind these wars are religious and economic, the aim is also to serve the Jews' petty state and divert attention from its occupation of Jerusalem and murder of Muslims there. The best proof of this is their eagerness to destroy Iraq, the strongest neighboring Arab state, and their endeavor to fragment all the states of the region such as Iraq, Saudi Arabia, Egypt, and Sudan into paper statelets and through their disunion and weakness to guarantee Israel's survival and the continuation of the brutal crusade occupation of the Peninsula.

All these crimes and sins committed by the Americans are a clear declaration of war on Allah, his messenger, and Muslims. And ulema have throughout Islamic history unanimously agreed that the jihad is an individual duty if the enemy destroys the Muslim countries. This was revealed by Imam Bin-Qadamah in "Al- Mughni," Imam al-Kisa'i in "Al-Bada'i," al-Qurtubi in his interpretation, and the shaykh of al-Islam in his books, where he said: "As for the fighting to repulse [an enemy], it is aimed at defending sanctity and religion, and it is a duty as agreed [by the ulema]. Nothing is more sacred than belief except repulsing an enemy who is attacking religion and life."

On that basis, and in compliance with Allah's order, we issue the following fatwa to all Muslims:

The ruling to kill the Americans and their allies—civilians and military—is an individual duty for every Muslim who can do it in any country in which it is possible to do it, in order to liberate the al-Aqsa Mosque and the holy mosque [Mecca] from their grip, and in order for their armies to move out of all the lands of Islam, defeated and unable to threaten any Muslim. This is in accordance with the words of Almighty Allah, "and fight the pagans all together as they fight you all together," and "fight them until there is no more tumult or oppression, and there prevail justice and faith in Allah."

This is in addition to the words of Almighty Allah: "And why should ye not fight in the cause of Allah and of those who, being weak, are ill-treated (and oppressed)?— women and children, whose cry is: 'Our Lord, rescue us from this town, whose people are oppressors; and raise for us from thee one who will help!'"

Continued

155

ANALYZING OSAMA BIN LADEN'S "FATWA" AGAINST THE WEST (Continued)

We—with Allah's help—call on every Muslim who believes in Allah and wishes to be rewarded to comply with Allah's order to kill the Americans and plunder their money wherever and whenever they find it. We also call on Muslim ulema, leaders, youths, and soldiers to launch the raid on Satan's U.S. troops and the devil's supporters allying with them, and to displace those who are behind them so that they may learn a lesson.

Almighty Allah said: "O ye who believe, give your response to Allah and His Apostle, when He calleth you to that which will give you life. And know that Allah cometh between a man and his heart, and that it is He to whom ye shall all be gathered."

Almighty Allah also says: "O ye who believe, what is the matter with you, that when ye are asked to go forth in the cause of Allah, ye cling so heavily to the earth! Do ye prefer the life of this world to the hereafter? But little is the comfort of this life, as compared with the hereafter. Unless ye go forth, He will punish you with a grievous penalty, and put others in your place; but Him ye would not harm in the least. For Allah hath power over all things."

Almighty Allah also says: "So lose no heart, nor fall into despair. For ye must gain mastery if ye are true in faith."

DISCUSSION QUESTIONS

- Having read this statement, to what extent do you think Al Qaeda's attacks against the United States between 1998 and 2001 were motivated by its ideology?
- What features of bin Laden's ideology are most clearly linked to motivating or justifying violence?
- What other non-ideological motivations for violence are expressed in this statement?

(Narodnaya Volya). Still others possess a wildly diverse set of beliefs, some of which may contain ideological inconsistencies or contradictions (e.g., the Totally Anti-War Group in France) or idiosyncrasies (the Unabomber). As a result, it is impossible to isolate which (if any) ideological influences truly affect the turn to violence.

Ideology Cannot Explain the Timing of Terrorist Violence. Because ideologies endure over long periods of time but terrorism occurs in fits and spurts, critics have argued that ideology is an insufficient explanation for terrorism.

The structural approach, in particular, seeks to explain why extremist ideologies resonate so much in some time periods but not others. For example, why did Qutbism appeal to so many Muslims during the historical period in which it became popular? Some scholars would argue that the nature of the political turmoil in Egypt—and the secular Egyptian government's brutal suppression of the Muslim Brotherhood—helped to explain why Qutbism began to win adherents. It was not just because of the appeal of the ideology, but also because of the domestic and geopolitical situation, that groups began to wage armed struggle using Qutbism as an inspiration.

Moreover, some groups with virtually identical ideologies engage in quite different patterns of violence. This was true during the Peruvian civil war, where segments of the radical left engaged in extraordinarily different degrees of violence. Despite similar commitments to Maoist beliefs, Guzman's sect of Sendero Luminosos (Shining Path) was notorious for its seemingly indiscriminate bloodshed, while other groups (like the **Tupac Amaru Revolutionary Movement, or MRTA**) were more restrained. In the case of Sendero Luminoso, the group began to escalate its violence in response to the opening of political opportunity before and during elections—despite the fact that its ideology remained the same. In an influential 2001 article, James Ron argues that we must take ideology in context when attempting to explain variations in the timing and pattern of violence among groups with similar ideologies.

Furthermore, there are often compelling explanations for indiscriminate violence other than the ideology of the group. Take the Armed Islamic Group (GIA) in Algeria. Established in 1993, the GIA was one of the two prominent warring Islamist insurgency movements that fought against the Algerian government during the civil war (the other was the **Islamic Salvation Front**, or **FIS**). Stathis Kalyvas writes that the GIA's notorious massacres, often described as "wanton and senseless," had an underlying grisly logic—to obtain and consolidate political and social control over the civilian population during the context of a brutal civil war (1999). James Ron likewise argues that Sendero Luminoso's most brutal strand was fighting for political hegemony over a competitive sphere of rival groups.

Ideology Cannot Explain Why Some Extremists Become Terrorists, and Others Do Not. Because so many individuals adhere to a particular ideology, but a minuscule number of people actually turn to terrorism, critics argue that ideology is insufficient to explain who actually joins a terrorist group, or who commits acts of terror. The psychological approach, in particular, is better able to explain variations in individual patterns of terrorist behavior. The critique is also extendable to level of the group. While a very large number of organized Christian, Muslim, Hindu, Jewish, and other religious groups are active throughout the world, only a very small minority of them adopt terrorist tactics to achieve their goals. As such, ideology must often be considered alongside other individual- or group-level factors in order to be significantly associated with terrorism.

Motivation and Justification Are Impossible to Differentiate. Critics of the ideological approach also point out that it is often impossible to know the true motivation for violence as opposed to post-hoc justifications for it. For example, terror groups may attempt to explain the rationale behind their attacks in the aftermath, ascribing a more noble and altruistic explanation for an attack than they conjured up during the planning stage. As Hoffman notes, in their memoirs or court documents, many terrorists cite the personal sense of excitement and "rush" they experienced in carrying out the attacks (2006, p. 247). Yet characterizing a terror attack as a primarily selfish act that satisfies a personal need for excitement or adrenaline may be too embarrassing to admit. So instead, such terrorists borrow from prevailing oppositional ideologies to justify their actions—regardless of whether such justifications are robust, intellectually consistent, or ideologically literate.

Policy Implications Are Immoral. Finally, critics of the ideological approach decry its normative implications—that to combat terrorism, government authorities must cast aside freedom of conscience and persecute people on the basis of their beliefs. By focusing on specific ideologies (like Islam) as the source of terrorism, critics say that governments needlessly deepen in-group and out-group polarization, which is both counterproductive and unethical. Because the ideological approach implies that massive profiling is required to crush all at-risk believers, human rights advocates decry such analyses for inferring the need to violate human rights, and for placing innocent people at grave risk of state violence.

SUMMARY

The ideological approach focuses on features of a terror group's ideology as yielding clues as to why it turned to terror in the first place. By examining terrorists' statements, manifestos, writings, and claims, proponents of this approach attempt to isolate the elements of groups' beliefs that draw them into violence.

To summarize the insights from Chapters 4 and 5, Table 5.2 compares the assumptions, arguments, and implications of the psychological and ideological approaches. Although Table 5.2 presents these approaches as competing with one another, some who use individual psychology to explain radicalization rely on ideology as the link that connects personal desires to violent extremist acts.

Discussion Questions

1. What is ideology? How can you tell what a person's ideology is?
2. Do you think that ISIS is motivated primarily by ideology, or something else? Can you think of any alternative explanations for ISIS's behavior?
3. Historically, right-wing terror groups have been deadlier than left-wing terror groups. Why?

TABLE 5.2 The Psychological and Ideological Approaches Compared

	Psychological Approach	Ideological Approach
Source of choice	Personal psychology	Ideology
Motivation for terrorism	To satisfy psychological impulses	To fulfill requirements of ideology
Group structure	Not assumed (fragmented and contested)	Assumed (unitary)
Primary audience	Unspecified	Nonbelievers
Patterns of terrorism	Random	Against nonbelievers and "sell-outs"
Policy implications	Early identification & interdiction.	Early identification and interdiction. Massive repression.
Observable implications	Terrorism is a constant but does not escalate because the pool of potential terrorists is relatively limited.	Terrorism does not end until group is totally destroyed.

4. Pick a group discussed in this chapter. Identify the core tenants of its ideology. Then conduct some research to identify a nonviolent group that shares similar core ideological tenants. Compare and contrast the ideologies of the two groups. By doing so, are you able to explain why one group has used terrorism while the other has not?

5. Under Secretary Janet Napolitano, the US Department of Homeland Security issued a report in 2009 stating that right-wing terrorism was the greatest threat to the United States. Republican members of Congress demanded that she retract the report, claiming that it wrongly singled out conservatives on the basis of their beliefs, amounting to an ideological witch-hunt. The report was retracted. Do you agree or disagree that the report should have been retracted? Why?

6. Is religious terrorism fundamentally different from secular terrorism? Why, or why not?

7. Are the psychological and ideological approaches compatible or incompatible with one another? What might an effective synthesis of these two approaches look like?

KEY TAKEAWAYS

- The ideological approach argues that extremist ideologies are primarily to blame for terrorist violence. This approach assumes that certain ideologies are more prone to violence than others, and that these extremist ideologies are observable in advance of the violence.

- The ideological approach emphasizes elements of intransigence, all-or-nothing cosmic war, a sense of deep personal sacrifice and duty, and collective dehumanization of a discernable out-group as primary sources of violence escalation. Moreover, ideological approaches expect to see acts of symbolic violence that are directly attributable to elements of the ideology itself (e.g. if ritual killings are embedded in the ideology, groups that subscribe to these ideologies will pattern their violence accordingly).

- Critics of ideological approaches argue that ideology is virtually impossible to observe and measure, rendering the analysis of such approaches extremely difficult. Moreover, ideological approaches tend to be unsatisfying explanations for the timing of the escalation of terrorist violence, since many ideologies persist for millennia but terrorism only features at particular moments in time. Similarly, ideological approaches are poor at explaining variation regarding which followers of certain beliefs become terrorists and which followers do not.

- Finally, ideological approaches are extremely susceptible to political manipulation, since it is easy to label all followers of particular ideologies "terrorists" when some extremists use violence on behalf of the ideology.

SUGGESTED FURTHER READINGS

Asal, Victor and R. Karl Rethemeyer. 2008. "Dilettantes, Ideologues, and the Weak: Terrorists Who Don't Kill." *Conflict Man. & Peace Sc.* 25 (3): 244–263. doi:10.1080/07388940802219000.

Ayers. Bill. 2008. *Fugitive Days: Memoirs of an Anti-War Activist.* Boston: Beacon Press.

Berberoglu, Berch. 2009. *The National Question: Nationalism, Ethnic Conflict, and Self-Determination in the Twentieth Century.* Philadelphia: Temple University Press.

Berman, Eli and David D. Laitin. 2008. "Religion, Terrorism and Public Goods: Testing The Club Model." *Journal of Public Economics* 92 (10–11): 1942–1967. doi:10.1016/j.jpubeco.2008.03.007.

Byman, Daniel. 1998. "The Logic of Ethnic Terrorism." *Studies in Conflict and Terrorism.* 21 (2): 149–169. doi:10.1080/10576109808436060.

Childs, Steven. 2011. "From Identity to Militancy: The Shi'A of Hizbollah." *Comparative Strategy* 30 (4): 363–372. doi:10.1080/01495933.2011.605026.

Cockburn, Patrick. 2015. *The Rise of the Islamic State: ISIS and the New Sunni Revolution.* London: Verso.

Conrad, Justin and Daniel Milton. 2013. "Unpacking the Connection between Terror and Islam." *Studies in Conflict & Terrorism* 36 (4): 315–336. doi:10.1080/1057610x.2013.763600.

Dees, Morris and James Corcoran. 1996. *Gathering Storm: America's Militia Threat.* New York: HarperCollins Publishers.

Dohrn, Bernardine, William Ayers, and Jeff Jones. 2006. *Sing A Battle Song: The Revolutionary Poetry, Statements, and Communiqués of the Weather Underground 1970 1974*. New York: Seven Stories Press.

Gambetta, Diego and Steffen Hertog. 2009. "Why Are There So Many Engineers Among Islamic Radicals?." *Arch. Eur. Sociol.* 50 (02): 201–230. doi:10.1017/s0003975609990129.

Gregg, Heather S. 2010. "Fighting The Jihad of The Pen: Countering Revolutionary Islam's Ideology." *Terrorism and Political Violence* 22 (2): 292–314. doi:10.1080/09546551003597584.

Hoffman, Bruce. 2006. *Inside Terrorism*, 2nd edition. New York: Columbia University Press.

Jacobs, Ron. 1997. *The Way the Wind Blew*. London: Verso.

Jones, David Martin and M. L. R. Smith. 2010. "Beyond Belief: Islamist Strategic Thinking and International Relations Theory." *Terrorism and Political Violence* 22 (2): 242–266. doi:10.1080/09546550903472286.

Juergensmeyer, Mark. 2003. *Terror in the Mind of God: The Global Rise of Religious Violence*, 2nd ed. Berkeley: University of California Press.

Kaufman, Stuart J. 2009. "Narratives and Symbols in Violent Mobilization: The Palestinian-Israeli Case." *Security Studies* 18 (3): 400–434. doi:10.1080/09636410903132938.

Kellen, Konrad. 1998. "Ideology and Rebellion: Terrorism in West Germany," in Reich, *Origins of Terrorism*, Ch. 3. Washington, DC: Woodrow Wilson Center Press.

Levitt, Matthew. 2006. *Hamas*. New Haven: Yale University Press.

Masters, Daniel. 2008. "The Origin of Terrorist Threats: Religious, Separatist, Or Something Else?." *Terrorism and Political Violence* 20 (3): 396–414. doi:10.1080/09546550802073359.

McCants, William F. 2015. *The ISIS Apocalypse: The History, Strategy, and Doomsday Vision of the Islamic State*. New York: St. Martin's Press.

Pedahzur, Ami. 2001. "Struggling with the Challenges Of Right-Wing Extremism And Terrorism Within Democratic Boundaries: A Comparative Analysis". *Studies in Conflict & Terrorism* 24 (5): 339–359. doi:10.1080/105761001750434213.

Piazza, James A. 2009. "Is Islamist Terrorism More Dangerous?: An Empirical Study Of Group Ideology, Organization, And Goal Structure." *Terrorism and Political Violence* 21 (1): 62–88. doi:10.1080/09546550802544698.

Pratt, Douglas. 2010. "Religion and Terrorism: Christian Fundamentalism and Extremism." *Terrorism and Political Violence* 22 (3): 438–456. doi:10.1080/09546551003689399.

Ranstorp, Magnus. 1996. "Terrorism in the Name of Religion." *Journal of International Affairs*, Vol. 50 (1): 41–63.

Rapoport, David C. 1984. "Fear and Trembling: Terrorism in Three Religious Traditions." *The American Political Science Review* 78 (3): 658–677. doi:10.2307/1961835.

Ron, James. 2001. "Ideology in Context: Explaining Sendero Luminoso's Tactical Escalation." *Journal of Peace Research* 38 (5): 569–592. doi:10.1177/0022343301038005002.

Sànchez-Cuenca, Ignacio. 2007. "The Dynamics of Nationalist Terrorism: ETA and the IRA." *Terrorism and Political Violence* 19 (3): 289–306. doi:10.1080/09546550701246981.

Schbley, Ayla H. 1990. "Religious Terrorists: What They Aren't Going to Tell Us." *Terrorism* 13 (3): 237–241. doi:10.1080/10576109008435834.

Snow, David A, and Scott Byrd. 2007. "Ideology, Framing Processes, and Islamic Terrorist Movements." *Mobilization* 12 (2): 119–136.

Stern, Jessica. 2003. *Terror in The Name of God*: Why Religious Militants Kill. New York: Ecco.

Stern, Jessica, and J. M Berger. 2015. *ISIS: The State of Terror*. New York: Ecco.

Warrick, Joby. 2015. *Black Flags: The Rise of ISIS*. New York: Doubleday.

Weinberg, Leonard, and Peter Merkl, eds. 2003. *Right-Wing Extremism in the Twenty-First Century*. London: Frank Cass & Co. 2003.

Weiss, Michael and Hassan Hassan. 2015. *ISIS: Inside the Army of Terror*. New York: Regan Arts.

Woodworth, Paddy. 2001. "Why Do They Kill: The Basque Conflict in Spain?". *World Policy Journal* 18 (1): 1–12. doi:10.1215/07402775-2001-2002.

CHAPTER 6

STRUCTURAL APPROACHES

Learning Objectives

After reading this chapter, readers should be able to:

- Explain the structural approach in their own words;
- Summarize the main assertions and expectations of the various structural causes explored;
- Compare and contrast the structural and strategic approaches;
- Identify and synthesize structural variables that have been used to explain terrorism;
- Critique the structural approach;
- Describe how structural approaches might inform or misinform counterterrorism policy.

> "We must address the root causes of terrorism to end it for all time. I believe putting resources into improving the lives of poor people is a better strategy than spending it on guns."
>
> —MUHAMMAD YUNUS, 2006

> "Terrorism is tempting with its tremendous possibilities. It offers a mechanical solution, as it were, in hopeless situations. . . . Absolute power corrupts and defeats its partisans no less than its opponents. A people that knows not liberty becomes accustomed to dictatorship: fighting despotism and counter-revolution, terrorism itself becomes their efficient school."
>
> —ALEXANDER BERKMAN, 1922

INTRODUCING THE STRUCTURAL APPROACH

Of the plethora of theories that exist to explain the causes of terrorism, among the most popular is the view that the **root causes** of terrorism can be found in the underlying environment and political, social, cultural, and economic structures of societies. Proponents of structural theories suggest that conditions—like geography, regime type, group grievances, or repression, to name a few—shape both the incentives and the opportunities to use terrorism (Crenshaw 1981). The goal of causal models using structural variables is to identify the dominant macro-level processes that give people the grievances and opportunities to use terrorism. Quantitative analyses tend to dominate structural analyses, since the primary

TABLE 6.1 A Sample of Structural Variables Associated with the Onset of Terrorism

Structural Causes	Principal Variables	Relationship to Terrorism	Dependent Variable Measured	Example Sources*
Democracy	Participation (voter turnout in democracies)	Negative	Transnational terrorist attacks	Li (2005)
	Political competition index (from Polity IV)	Positive	Transnational terrorist attacks	Chenoweth (2010a)
	Institutional constraints (from Polity IV)	Positive	Transnational terrorist attacks	Li (2005) Chenoweth (2010a)
	Press freedom	Positive	Transnational terrorist attacks	Li (2005)
State capacity	Government capability (population share + GDP + GDP/ energy + military manpower & expenditures)	Positive	Transnational terrorist attacks	Li and Schaub (2004) Chenoweth (2010a)
	State Failures Index Score	Positive	Number of transnational terror attacks	Piazza (2008)
Welfare provision	Total welfare spending	Negative	Transnational terrorist attacks; total terrorist attacks; origins of "significant" terror attacks	Burgoon (2006)
Economic variables	HDI; Economic inequality; GDP growth; Inflation; Unemployment	No relationship	Incidents of terrorism/ Casualty rates from terrorism	Piazza (2006)

	Economic development (GDP per capita (PPP))	Negative	Transnational terrorist attacks	Li and Schaub (2004)
	Infant mortality rate	Negative	Terrorist attacks and domestic armed conflict onset	Urdal (2006)
Demographics	Population	Positive	Incidents of terrorism/ Casualty rates from terrorism	Piazza (2006)
	Ethno-religious diversity	Positive	Incidents of terrorism/ Casualty rates from terrorism	Piazza (2006); Piazza (2008)
	Urbanization	Positive	Islamist and leftist terror attacks	Robison et al. (2006)
Global balance of power	Hegemonic capabilities	Negative	Number of international terrorist attacks	Volgy et al. (1997)
	American dominance	Positive	Terror attacks on American interests	Braithwaite & Sobek (2005)
	Political proximity to US	Positive	Number of transnational terror events	Dreher & Gassebner (2007)
Counterterrorism/ Foreign policy	Conciliatory measures	Negative	Number of terrorist attacks (Israel)	Dugan & Chenoweth (2012)
	Drone strikes	Negative	Number of terrorist attacks (Pakistan & Afghanistan)	Johnston & Sarbahi (2016)
	Interstate rivalry	Positive	Number of transnational terrorist attacks	Findley, Piazza, and Young (2012)
	Military intervention	Positive	Number of suicide terrorist attacks; Number of terrorist attacks	Pape (2005); Azam and Thelen (2010)
Counterterrorism/ Foreign policy	Physical integrity rights index	Negative	Number of domestic and international terrorist attacks	Walsh and Piazza (2010)

* For full citation list see end of chapter.

aim is to identify average patterns regarding the most common venues for terrorist violence.

Many scholars find these approaches particularly useful because they tend to produce straightforward correlations that are relatively easy to test empirically. It is much easier to operationalize and measure state- or international-level structural variables than it is to measure psychological, ideological, organizational, or strategic ones. As a result, in many models that seek to explain and predict when and where terrorism will occur, structural causes are an ideal starting point.

Needless to say, structural theories of terrorism are plentiful and vary widely. One survey of the literature on structural determinants of terror found that over 20 different factors have a robust and statistically significant relationship to terrorism (Gassebner and Leuchinger 2011). Table 6.1 provides a partial sample of these studies.

The structural approach has a great deal of intuitive appeal, because it ascribes otherwise inexplicable violent behavior to a series of tangible and measurable circumstances and conditions thought to motivate and facilitate violence. Unlike the strategic model, which is agnostic about the origins of terrorists' preferences (Chapter 2), the structural approach attempts to isolate the conditions that produce the grievances and opportunities for terrorism in the first place.

ASSUMPTIONS OF THE STRUCTURAL APPROACH

Like the strategic approach surveyed in Chapter 2, structural approaches consider terrorism a mode of political contention that results from the deliberate choice of a unitary, rational actor: the terrorist or terrorist organization. Importantly, structural approaches also take into account the environment in which the act of terrorism occurs, and investigate whether broader **political, social, and economic conditions** make terrorism comparatively more rational in one context as opposed to another. Ultimately, structural approaches to terrorism seek to answer the question: which circumstances lead to terrorism?

A framework for the analysis of settings—or structures—likely to engender terrorism establishes conceptual distinctions among different types of factors. As early as 1981, Martha Crenshaw offered two critical distinctions, the first being between **preconditions** and **precipitants.** Whereas the former identifies factors that set the stage for terrorism over the long term, the latter points to specific events that immediately precede the occurrence of terrorism. The second critical distinction made by Crenshaw divides preconditions into enabling and **permissive factors**, both of which provide opportunities for terrorism to happen, and situations that can be construed as direct motivations for actors and groups to engage in terrorism.

As will become evident throughout this chapter, structural approaches require that observers take into account the terrorist organization's perception and interpretation of the situation in order to explain its behavior. When terrorists view the **context as permissive**, terrorism becomes a viable option: the means are placed at the terrorist's disposal by the underlying environment. Circumstances, too, can provide terrorists with compelling reasons or motivations to seek political change. Frequently, there is a precipitant **condition** that snaps the terrorist's patience with the opponent, and terrorism becomes not only possible but also morally acceptable—or even morally necessary—in the mind of the terrorist.

OBSERVABLE IMPLICATIONS OF THE STRUCTURAL APPROACH: PERMISSIVE PRECONDITIONS & FACILITATING STRUCTURES

Factors considered to be permissive to terrorism exist in every society. In essence, they are those deeper systemic conditions that facilitate the presence of precipitants that more directly lead to acts of terrorism. Scholars deem such facilitating structures as **necessary but insufficient** conditions for terrorism. We break causes permissive to the occurrence of terrorism into nine facilitating structures, each of which will be discussed in turn.

Regime Type. Several possible interactions have been theorized to explain the prevalence of terrorism under different forms of government. One perspective argues that democracy reduces terrorism because democracies offer avenues for citizens to express their interests through conventional political channels, thus endorsing the nonviolent resolution of conflicts (Choi 2010). As such, one would expect to see more terrorism in authoritarian countries. Along similar lines, some link terrorism to the lack of political opportunity for expression in closed systems of government (Crenshaw 1981; Li 2005). Authoritarian governments shut off channels for political expression, leading dissenters to resort to violence for lack of other options.

Contrary to what most people might assume, however, through the mid-2000s, terrorism actually flourished primarily in democracies compared to authoritarian regimes (Chenoweth 2012). Generally speaking, the bulk of terrorist activity took place in democracies because of the strengths and limitations of this type of political system. In particular, the ease of communication, high levels of media publicity, and proportional government responses that exist within democratic regimes are facilitating factors for terrorist attacks.

The comparatively high rate of occurrence of terrorism in democracies is a proven trend. Figure 7.1 shows that over the last several decades, terrorism has tended to occur much more in democratic countries than in nondemocratic ones. In fact, not only are democracies the most frequent *targets* of terrorist attacks, they are also the most frequent *sources* of terrorist activity. Though at first glance this might seem surprising, the explanations are actually quite logical. Scholars typically cite the defense of fundamental civil liberties, press freedoms, acceptance of diverse political views and guarantees of freedom of expression, and law-abiding security forces as facilitating factors for terrorist groups to operate, plan, and carry out their attacks (Chenoweth 2012). Yet despite these trends, democracies remain extremely resilient in the face of terrorist threats (Chenoweth and Young 2017).

It is nonetheless important to note that authoritarian regimes may deliberately underreport terrorism in an effort to avoid being perceived as weak, a practice that may skew the counting of terrorist events towards democracies (Sandler 1995). Moreover, Figure 6.1 also suggests a shift in the distribution of terror attacks from consolidated democracies to partial democracies, autocracies, and occupied countries since about 2009. This shift overlaps with the decline of leftist and nationalist-separatist terrorism (which predominated in advanced democracies) and the rise of global jihadi terrorism (which predominates in Middle Eastern autocracies, partial democracies like Pakistan, and countries under military occupation by Western states like Iraq and Afghanistan).

State Capacity. A growing number of scholars and policymakers have suggested that weak, failed, and failing states pose a grave danger to

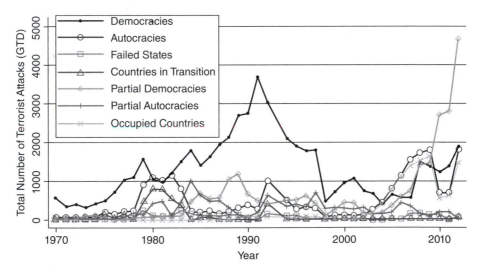

Figure 6.1 Number of Annual Terrorist Attacks by Regime Type, 1970–2012

Sources: GTD & POLITY IV Dataset

international security because they produce facilitating conditions under which terrorist groups can thrive. In fact, some studies have shown that these states overwhelmingly contribute to terrorism in terms of being targeted by terrorist attacks and hosting active terrorist groups that execute attacks abroad (Piazza 2008; See also Chapter 11). The perpetrators of transnational terrorist attacks are also more likely to be citizens of failed or failing states (ibid).

The inherent problem with failed and failing states is that they are unable to monopolize the use of force vis-à-vis other nonstate actors within their borders, and are thus incapable of projecting power. As such, failing states are often plagued by threats of secession, civil war, or other forms of large-scale violent conflict between nonstate groups and the government. Importantly, such states are also largely incapable of providing basic services to their populations, leaving room for violent nonstate groups to step in to fill the gap and gain support from an otherwise suffering local population (Idler and Forest 2015; See also Chapter 10). This pattern occurs because failed and failing states are easier for terrorist movements to penetrate, recruit from, and operate within. Unhindered by the state's credible ability to police for and deter terrorist activity, failed states provide boundless opportunity for terrorists seeking low-cost environments in which to operate. Indeed, organizing, training, recruiting, and financing are all made easy for terrorist groups operating in such states.

The emergence of extremist groups such as the **Islamic State in Iraq and Syria (ISIS),** for example, has been linked directly to situations of social breakdown caused by elite divisions, financial problems of the state, and popular unrest caused by the state's oppressive or arbitrary actions in both Syria and Iraq. In such situations, which often involve high levels of violence and disorder as well as the collapse of established institutions, more moderate groups lack the resources to establish order and find themselves at a disadvantage compared to their more radical counterparts who are able to add organizational power and discipline to their claims. This aura of discipline engendered by the most extreme of terrorist groups in otherwise chaotic environments helps to attract followers and recruits to the ranks (Yeginsu 2014).

Other scholars, however, argue that failed or failing states actually put terrorists at a disadvantage (Piazza 2008). First, terrorist groups operating in these environments might be more vulnerable to policing and repression from third-party states, due in large part to the fact that norms of sovereignty and nonintervention are weaker when it comes to weak states. Second, foreigners are highly conspicuous in failed or failing states, making clandestine operations significantly more difficult. Finally, the total chaos that usually envelopes failed states frequently negatively affects terrorists, who themselves become the targets of extortion or harassment by the state, or may be forced to take sides in intractable local conflicts.

BOX 6.1

FAILED STATES AND TERRORISM: THE CASE OF LEBANON & HIZBALLAH

Photo 6.1.   Lebanese Hizbollah women supporters chant slogans and carry a Hizbollah flag during a religious procession to mark Ashura in Beirut's southern suburbs.

The case of Hizballah in Lebanon provides a useful example of the complex ways through which state weakness attracts terrorist groups. As we will see through this brief case study, the mechanisms at play in this process are variegated and complex. What this suggests is that a state's simple lack of monopoly over the use of force may not be sufficient to explain why some weak states see terrorist organizations emerge within their borders.

When we talk about state weakness, what exactly does this imply? The traditional approach to the question suggests that a state is weak (or considered to be a "failed state") when it is unable to control its territory, fostering a vacuum of power from which violent nonstate groups can benefit. It is thus assumed that the lack of military or police control allows militant organizations to establish training bases, recruit freely, and act with general impunity.

In reality, the story is much more complex. State weakness occurs not only through absence of a monopoly over the use of force, but also through institutional weakness and a lack of legitimacy. When a state is weak, its institutions can no longer function efficiently, and are unable to penetrate civil society. State weakness is also characterized by the extent to which large segments of the population no longer identify with the state and withdraw their loyalty (Atzili 2010).

Viewed from this perspective, there are several ways through which the weakness of the Lebanese state has helped foster and sustain transnational terrorist groups—perhaps most notably Hizballah. In essence, weak states (1) provide a base for terrorist recruitment and other critical operations; (2) provide opportunities for gaining the support of local populations; and (3) attract the involvement of third parties.

Recruitment. Though globalization has likely benefitted terrorist organizations in terms of recruitment and other operational logistics, all armed groups need some degree of sanctuary to achieve their political ends. While the Internet and social media can help attract fighters from faraway locales, there is no substitute for a physical space for the training, organization, and consolidation that provides longevity to militant organizations (Atzili 2010).

When Israel withdrew from southern Lebanon in 2000, a power vacuum ensued as the Lebanese military was unable to physically control the region, and a divided government was unable to instill any semblance of political stability. In response, the already active Hizballah took responsibility for controlling territory in the south. The group benefitted from complete freedom of maneuver, not only monopolizing the legitimate use of force in the area, but also imposing itself politically. Initially, recruitment into the militant organization was organized through a process of mass mobilization along family and clan ties, which facilitated the enrollment of hundreds of volunteers (Atzili 2010). In these southern portions of the country, devout, young Shias needed little incentive to join the resistance, given that their homes and land had born the brunt of the Israeli occupation. In addition to an elaborate childhood induction process, Hizballah also deploys recruiters to every village under its area of influence. The Lebanese state does not resist these efforts.

Local Support. Active support from local populations is practically the *sine qua non* of armed groups. For a terrorist organization aspiring to govern, obtaining such local support is much easier in areas where the state is weak, or altogether absent. Importantly, weak states lack legitimacy in the eyes of their populations, not only because they no longer have a monopoly on the use of force, but also because they lack the capacity to provide basic goods and services to their people. Hizballah built its power to a significant extent on the Shia population's isolation from the absent Lebanese state.

In Lebanon today, many young Shias naturally gravitate towards an organization that has helped empower their communities and that has earned their respect through military victories over the years. After having been a member of the group for two or three years, Hizballah members receive monthly salaries and financial support for housing, their children's education, and medical needs. The group has hosted social activities and provided various public services systematically. For instance, among many other services, Hizballah has established a "Martyr's Agency" to provide for the families of fallen fighters. Its members run schools, hospitals, and mosques in the south. The group controls drinking water supplies and has established small lending banks. The list goes on. As a result, the group can rely on the local population for further recruiting, bases, and political support.

Attracting Third Parties. Weak states are also ideal targets for other states seeking to invest in proxies to carry out their dirty deeds (see Chapter 11). Often this entails the use of guerilla and terrorist methods against enemies while operating from a third country. In states such as Lebanon, the recruitment, training, and operation of proxy forces is easier than it might be in a stronger state, much in the same way that recruiting members into terrorist organizations is easier in these environments.

Continued

171

FAILED STATES AND TERRORISM: THE CASE OF LEBANON & HIZBALLAH *(Continued)*

In Lebanon, the involvement of third party states in search of proxies is exemplified through Hizballah's relationships with outside states, namely Iran and Syria. From its inception in the 1980s, Hizballah maintained tight ideological, financial, and operational ties with Iran, and a strategic alliance with Syria (Byman 2005). Iran's motives for sustaining its ties with Hizballah are relatively straightforward. Absent any opportunities for direct confrontation with its two worst enemies (the United States and Israel), a relationship with Hizballah supplied such an opportunity. During Israel's occupation of Lebanon from 1982 through 2000, Iran was able to confront and thwart its enemy through its proxy in Lebanon. Similarly, the presence of US Marines in Beirut was viewed as an opportunity to confront the United States, again via proxy.

Modernization. Modernization—a model of a progressive transition from a "pre-modern" or "traditional" to a "modern" society—has been argued to produce an interrelated set of permissive causes of terrorism (Krieger and Meierrieks 2011; Robison et al. 2006; Ross 1993). Specifically, increased complexity, ranging from the development of sophisticated public transportation networks, to enhanced communications tools, to the advent of the airplane, has created opportunities for terrorists and made people more vulnerable to their tactics.

Other arguments are based in the assessment that modernization and the introduction of market-oriented production schemes have threatened particularistic, cultural identities, or have been simply unjust in cases where the bulk or all the benefits have been siphoned off by elites (Mousseau 2005). Some have argued that modernization leads to resource competition and harms the landless and poorest sections of the rural population (Bradshaw 1987). For instance, problems related to resource scarcity in the wake of modernization led to violent rebellion in Senegal over the Casamance region, and spurred ethnic conflict between the state and Tuareg populations in Mali. Certain elements of these groups turned to tactics of terrorism to redress their grievances originally caused by projects linked to modernization efforts.

Interestingly, modernization can isolate certain groups while simultaneously providing more cost effective ways of equipping these same groups to use violence. Ultimately, this view of modernization suggests that terrorism may be more prevalent in higher income countries with high levels of inequality, which tend to experience higher rates of technological progress/modernization alongside a dissatisfied and aggrieved population.

Urbanization. Urbanization, or the mass movement of peoples from rural environments to urban areas, is somewhat linked to modernization, inasmuch as it is part of the modern trend toward aggregation and complexity. For terrorists, the movement of large numbers of people to densely packed cities has increased the number and accessibility of both targets and methods. Densely located populations provide terrorist groups with superior logistical capabilities, more recruits, and more support as compared to rural settings where populations are more widely dispersed. From a logistical standpoint, urban environments narrow the distance between terrorists and their actual targets, provide more resources (such as banks to be robbed), secure anonymity as well as a broader audience, and enhance the ease or surprise and speed with which terrorists carry out their attacks. Sympathizers come in greater numbers in cities, as do potential recruits.

Urbanization is linked to terrorism in several studies (see e.g, Sanchez-Cuenca and de la Calle 2009, de la Calle and Sanchez-Cuenca 2011). When paired with unemployment and poverty, the phenomenon has the potential to generate disaffected populations, enhancing recruitment and organizational potential for terrorist groups. According to Douglas Massey, "urbanization, rising income inequality, and increasing class segregation have produced a geographic concentration of affluence and poverty throughout the world, creating a radical change in the geographic basis of human society. As the density of poverty rises in the environment of the world's poor, so will their exposure to crime, disease, violence, and family disruption (1996, p. 395). Others have argued that water and food shortages in rural areas have crippled the farming industry in many countrysides, forcing large numbers of people into urban slums, where they become prime targets for recruitment into terrorism (Newman 2006).

In fact, the conceptualization of terrorism as "urban guerrilla warfare" largely came out of the Latin American experience of the 1960s. Examples of so-called urban guerrilla groups around the globe include the 19th of April Movement (M-19) in Colombia; Action Directe in France; the Red Army Faction in Germany, and Hamas in the Palestinian Territories. Table 6.2 provides a list of the ten most commonly attacked cities from 1970 to 2014, many of which were in Latin America.

TABLE 6.2 Cities Most Frequently Attacked by Terrorists, 1970–2014

Country	City	Total Attacks (1970–2014)
Iraq	Baghdad	5,239
Pakistan	Karachi	2,386
Peru	Lima	2,359
Northern Ireland	Belfast	2,011
Chile	Santiago	1,615
El Salvador	San Salvador	1,547
Iraq	Mosul	1,501
Somalia	Mogadishu	1,077
Colombia	Bogota	967
Turkey	Istanbul	920

Source: GTD.

Figure 6.2 shows the distribution of those attacks over time. The data also suggest that the distribution of attacks has shifted from cities in democracies or contested democracies (Belfast, San Salvador, Lima, Santiago, Istanbul) before 2001 to cities in autocracies or occupied states (Baghdad, Karachi, Mosul, Mogadishu) since the mid-2000s. This city-level data is consistent with the data presented in Figure 6.1.

Some scholars argue that violence perpetrated by insurgent groups in urban areas should be characterized as terrorism, while violence committed in rural environments—specifically those rural areas under the control of the insurgent group—is best characterized as guerrilla warfare (de la Calle and Sanchez-Cuenca 2011).

Of course, urban areas can also be ideal settings for other forms of political behavior, particularly those that arguably benefit from high visibility in order to achieve success. For example, nonviolent action—often characterized by mass protests, sit-ins, and demonstrations—frequently also takes place in (and benefits from) urban settings. Wide city boulevards and open plazas are ideal gathering places for crowds seeking to target their national governments to achieve change (Routledge 1994).

Technology. Some have also argued that technological progress contributes to the emergence of terrorism, whether through increased access to simpler and deadlier weapons technology, or through the impact of dramatic changes in communications and information technology.

Prominent terrorism scholars such as Bruce Hoffman contend that the revolution in communications technology in the 1990s dramatically changed the nature of terrorism. Satellite phones, fax machines, and laptop computers provided Al Qaeda with the flexibility to maintain its operations even while

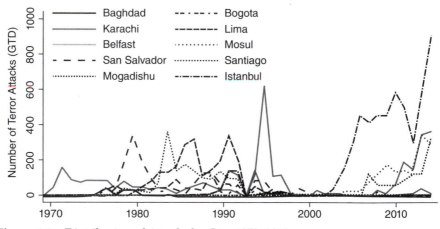

Figure 6.2 Distribution of Attacks by City, 1970–2014

Source: GTD

scattered across numerous countries, from the Sahel to Afghanistan (Hoffman 2006, p. 158–159). Ultimately, improvements in technology facilitated a global terror movement based increasingly on a loose, decentralized network of fighters that transcended the limitations of face-to-face interaction.

The Internet, too, has had a significant impact on terrorism, in particular by creating a seemingly concrete bond between individuals and a virtual community of like-minded others. Whereas recruitment to terrorism was traditionally based on face-to-face interactions (della Porta 1988), web-based communication tools have also greatly facilitated recruitment into terrorist organizations, through the wide dissemination of video propaganda, far-reaching Tweets, Facebook links, etc. While in-person connections may continue to be important to fostering the growth of terrorist movements, as well as precipitating the transformation of individuals from outsiders to dedicated members of the group, an established terrorist organization may no longer require such direct connections. Older communication technologies—such as the simple telephone—did not allow for such interactions. The risk of an isolated operative losing his sense of fanaticism was much greater than it is today, when communications technology such as video-capable smartphones, the Internet, and other web-based communications tools are for the most part ubiquitous. Because of its virtual nature, the Internet community within which terrorists connect may have an earthly counterpart, having become idealized in the mind of websurfers. Communications in chat rooms or via platforms such as Skype, Twitter, etc. may seem more egalitarian, providing arguments and messages that appeal to or inspire people from various educational or ideological backgrounds.

Rapidly developing information technologies have also been used as an offensive weapon by terrorist groups to instill fear in target audiences. The gruesome beheadings of Western aid workers and journalists by ISIS in 2014, for example, were purposefully posted to social media sites such as YouTube for the world to see (and fear) (Berger and Stern 2015). Others have pointed to the fact that evolving technologies, as well as the recruitment of more tech-savvy members into terrorist groups, have brought such organizations closer to carrying out a cyber attack capable of crippling a country's transportation or communications infrastructure (Rollins and Wilson 2007).

Of course, some skeptics suggest that the effects of the Internet on terrorism have been overstated. David Benson argues that the advantages of the Internet for terrorists are offset by the advantages of the Internet for counterterrorists. Improved surveillance capabilities, the ability to dismantle or disrupt Internet communications among terrorists and their would-be recruits through offensive cyber attacks, and global movement-tracking all assist governments attempting to thwart and investigate terror attacks (Benson 2014).

For the time being, however, terrorists have continued to prefer bombs to bytes. Too great a reliance on new technologies leaves terrorist organizations and individual group members vulnerable to sophisticated monitoring of communication and triangulation of its source. Counterterrorism operations have relied greatly on intercepts of cell phone calls to capture terrorists, and many major terrorist leaders have given up certain technologies because of such vulnerabilities. Osama bin Laden, for example, stopped using satellite phones in 1998 after one of his associate's phone records were introduced as evidence in a trial in New York. Documents found in computers seized in anti-terrorist raids have also played a major role in the conviction of terrorists, as in the trials of those responsible for the US embassy bombings in Kenya and Tanzania in 1998. And the trove of documents discovered after the 2011 raid on bin Laden's compound in Abbotabad, Pakistan revealed a great deal about Al Qaeda's remaining networks around the globe.

Advances in weapons technology—specifically improvements in the overall simplicity with which increasingly lethal weapons are fabricated—have also been construed as a facilitating factor for terrorism. Increasingly, terrorist groups have relied less and less on complicated schemes such as airline hijackings and turned more to using simple techniques to create havoc. These simple devices—termed **improvised explosive devices**, or IEDs—use flammable gas or liquids to create explosions in crowded areas and cause mass casualties. Somewhat alarmingly, such devices are very simple to put together, with all of the necessary materials easily acquired at hardware stores or gas stations.

According to the Global Terrorism Database, terrorists used explosive and/or incendiary devices in some 218 terrorist incidents in the United States between 2001 and 2015—over 71 percent of the 308 incidents in the US during that time period. One infamous IED attack in the United States was the pressure-cooker attack during the April 15, 2013 Boston Marathon that killed three people and injured hundreds of others. A pressure cooker was also used in the May 1, 2010 attempted vehicle bombing in New York City's Times Square. While police thwarted that attempted attack, the bomb's simplicity sent a chilling reminder about the ease with which motivated terrorists can assemble lethal devices. In this case, the car bomb contained propane, gasoline, and fireworks—all relatively mundane household items.

Indeed, a primary concern today is that purchases of the raw materials necessary to assemble many of the weapons of modern-day terrorists do not draw attention, and the subsequent construction of an IED or inflammatory device requires little or no training to prepare and use. In fact, simple instructions are easily found on the Internet. Even more ominously, information on the concoction of chemical, biological, radiological, and nuclear (**CBRN**) weapons is increasingly available on the Internet. Many groups throughout the world have expressed interest in acquiring such instruments of devastation (Bunn and Wier 2005).

Globalization. Some scholars have argued that a distinguishing feature of modern terrorism is the connection between sweeping political and ideological concepts and increasing levels of terrorist activity globally (Mousseau 2003). In the wake of globalization, terrorist groups have taken aim against

BOX 6.2

HACKTIVISM OR TERRORISM?

Some groups have begun to rely on cyberattacks on individual Internet sites and automated "email bombs" to coerce political opponents and attract media attention without inducing casualties. Groups like Anonymous, for instance, seek to dismantle or disable various websites and web capabilities. Typically, these types of attacks (which have included the defacement or hijacking of websites, web sit-ins, denial-of-service attacks, etc.) allow the hackers to operate anonymously and in a dispersed environment. Because such activities rarely constitute direct attacks on a person, groups like Anonymous maintain that they are "hacktivists"—not terrorists.

DISCUSSION QUESTION

- *Information warfare specialist Dorothy Denning writes: "While the vast majority of hackers may be disinclined towards violence, it would only take a few to turn cyber terrorism into reality" (2001). Do you agree with her assessment that cyber terrorism is the same as violence? Do cyber attacks that harm infrastructure without directly harming people constitute acts of terrorism? Why or why not?*

empires, colonial powers, and most recently the US-led international system (see Chapters 1 and 5).

Globalization is shorthand for an array of trends highlighting the increasing movement of people and goods, technological progress, secularization, democratization, consumerism, or the growth of market capitalism. Somewhat paradoxically, many of the deeply penetrating mechanisms of globalization are themselves exploited by terrorist groups to build their organizations and carry out their attacks.

Technological advantages aside, globalization has enabled terrorist organizations to reach across borders to attract recruits, much in the same way that businesses have been able to increase global commerce. The virtual non-existence of borders in North America and throughout Europe, for example, has allowed the smooth flow of people and weapons (Cronin 2006). Globalization has also opened new avenues for terrorist groups to fund their endeavors. More and more terrorist organizations are acquiring global financing networks that allow them to broaden their reach. Sources of financing include legal enterprises such as nonprofit organizations and charities, whose illicit activity is at times unknown to donors (see Chapter 11). Other terrorist groups receive funding through legitimate corporations that divert their profits to illegal activities (this was the case for Osama bin Laden's large network of construction companies). In what seems to be an increasing trend, terrorist organizations are becoming directly involved in illegal enterprises such as drug production and smuggling, as is the case in the Sahel region of northern Africa, where groups connected to Al Qaeda in the Islamic Maghreb (AQIM) have been linked to organized crime (Hübschle 2011). Kidnapping, bank robberies, fraud, and extortion have also been sources of revenue for terrorist organizations operating in an increasingly globalized environment. For other groups, websites are important vehicles for raising funds, as evidenced by the inclusion of links or physical addresses for contributions on many group web pages.

Importantly, some have argued that globalization and the so-called "clash of civilizations" between east and west has been an important motivating factor for terrorism, in addition to being a facilitating factor for the reasons outlined above (Huntington 1993). This set of arguments, which focuses principally on explaining the social basis of terrorism, highlights the importance of understanding the values and beliefs that legitimate the use of terrorism tactics for some groups. We will see how globalization has affected terrorist motivations below.

In summary, an increasingly globalized world has allowed terrorist organizations to exploit the same avenues of communication, coordination, and cooperation as other international actors, including states, NGOs, multinational corporations, and even individuals. And critics of globalization have also argued that the process has ostracized and atomized large numbers of people, aggravating grievances and ultimately leading to more attacks (Mousseau 2011).

American Dominance. Closely related to those arguments that link increased globalization to terrorism are those that posit that the increasing concentration of political, military, and diplomatic power in United States and allied hands has generated corresponding increases in terrorist attacks directed against the West. More specifically, periods of dominance by a state leads to increases in the amount of terrorism targeted specifically against that state by actors that perceive (and generally are) themselves as weak (Braithwaite and Sobek 2010). Some scholars contend that American dominance silences oppositional views and cuts off all possibilities for challengers to be heard. As direct military challenges to US power become more and more futile, groups will begin to employ unconventional methods to counter American dominance. Terrorism is the most extreme of these methods.

Finally, other studies have suggested that political alignment with the United States—measured in terms of voting patterns within the UN General Assembly—leads countries to become victims of more and deadlier terror (Dreher and Gassebner 2008). Consider the major terror attacks in Spain and the UK in March 2004 and July 2005 respectively. Al Qaeda and its affiliates claim that both of these attacks were in retaliation for the countries' participation in the US-led war in Iraq.

Failed Counterterrorism. The occurrence of terrorism may be affected by the very measures that seek to disrupt it. In fact, responses to terrorism, encompassed in the counterterrorism policies of states, have at times backfired inasmuch as they generated more terrorist attacks than they have curbed.

BOX 6.3

GLOBAL FIGHTER NETWORKS: DO FOREIGN FIGHTERS STRENGTHEN OR WEAKEN MILITANT ORGANIZATIONS?

Photo 6.2   Free Syrian Army soldiers during the Battle of Aleppo, 2012.

In the fall of 2013, the United Nations (UN) released a report suggesting that unprecedented numbers of foreigners were travelling to Iraq and Syria to fight with the Islamic State of Iraq and Syria and similar extremist groups in the region. As many as fifteen thousand jihadists were thought to have come from more than 80 different countries: France, Russia, the United Kingdom, and various North African countries turned out to be significant sources of re-cruits for an extremist group waging battle in a far off place.

In an increasingly globalized world, terrorist organizations have been able to take advantage of sources of recruitment, financing, and legitimacy that are geo-graphically removed from their areas of operation. Whereas terrorists were once confined to relying on the support of local populations for fighters, logistical sup-port, and legitimacy, the development of far-reaching and accessible communi-cations networks, more porous borders, and increased international flows have benefitted them as much as other types of actors in the context of globalization.

The seemingly rising occurrence of foreign fighter-heavy rebel groups (to include some terror organizations) provides an interesting lens through which to study the impact that globalization has had on militant organizations. Per-haps most relevant today is the case of foreign fighters in the context of the ongoing conflict in Syria, and the influence that these militants have had on organizations such as the Free Syrian Army (FSA), the Al Nusra Front, and ISIS. On the surface, it may appear that globalization and the influx of foreign fighters to otherwise domestic insurgent groups has worked to strengthen these organizations. Indeed, fighters from western countries in particular, but also from other Middle Eastern countries, not only reinforce the fighting ranks of Al Nusra and ISIS, but they also bring with them technological know-how, more weapons, and in some instances money. But are foreign fighters always a boon to militant organizations, or can they actually have negative impacts on the groups that they join?

Continued

BOX 6.3

GLOBAL FIGHTER NETWORKS: DO FOREIGN FIGHTERS
STRENGTHEN OR WEAKEN MILITANT ORGANIZATIONS?
(Continued)

The Importance of Local Support. Traditionally, violent groups have had to rely
on the support of local populations in order to sustain themselves through
conflict. While this may be less true for terrorist organizations, which do not
necessarily seek to control territory as part of their struggle, certain levels of
local legitimacy remain salient in order for them to gain strength and survive.

ISIS and its fighters have managed to accumulate a significant amount
of revenues from oil smuggling operations, as well as through high-profile
kidnapping-for-ransom tactics. Some sources report that oil brought in as much
as $1 million on a daily basis for the group during its peak in 2014, and as much
as $45 million may have been reaped from kidnapping ransoms (Swanson 2015).

But more local level factors have also been important to ISIS' growth and
survival. The organization has been careful not to alienate certain local populations, specifically many of the Sunni tribes that had turned on Al Qaeda in
2007/2008 when that terrorist group was fighting US forces in Iraq (Ahmed
2015). In fact, the seizure by ISIS of major Iraqi cities such as Fallujah, Ramadi,
and Mosul may have been impossible without some forms of local support.

The exceptionally large flow of foreign fighters to ISIS's ranks, however, suggests that some of the organization's critical mass of support is coming from
areas far from where the battle is actually raging. How this significant influx
of outsiders affects the fighting capacity and overall resilience of ISIS, as well as
other militant organizations that recruit or otherwise attract foreign combatants,
remains an important question. For example, the addition of foreign fighters with
no ties to local populations could have the effect of reducing the group's local
legitimacy amongst Iraqis and Syrians alike, alienating it from critical battlefield
resources. Like past and present conflicts in Chechnya, Afghanistan, Mali, and
the Balkans, foreign fighters have brought with them more radical tactics that
were otherwise nonexistent in local repertoires of contention (Bakke 2014).

Globalization, Foreign Fighters, and New Sources of Support. Thanks to advances
in mass communications technology and the rise of the Internet, local populations are no longer the sole source of human support upon which militant
organizations can rely. These dynamics have profoundly changed the nature
of substate conflict. Instead, support for one group might lie in populations
spread throughout the globe. This form of outside support has been beneficial
to ISIS thus far, which has significantly increased its fighter base and likely
also improved its overall capabilities through the recruitment of foreigners.
Young fighters from Western countries come equipped with knowledge on the
low cost, ease-of-use, and security benefits of emerging technologies. Not only
have foreign combatants boosted the group's recruitment numbers, but they
have also arguably increased the battle-savviness of ISIS as it confronts a more
technologically advanced or more mechanized opponent.

What remains unclear, however, is whether these foreign fighters will prove
to be advantageous to the long-term goals and ultimate survival of ISIS. The

group's defeat in its stronghold of Mosul in the summer of 2017 suggests perhaps not. In fact, some studies have shown that the introduction of foreign fighters to the ranks of domestic insurgent groups in places such as Chechnya and Syria has actually undermined the strength of militant organizations (Rich and Conduit 2014). The radical ideas and tactics that they frequently carry with them have fostered divisions within local militant organizations, and ultimately degraded the ability of the broader group to achieve its goals (Bakke 2014). A recent quantitative study of the effect of foreign fighters on civil conflict outcomes further finds that while foreign combatants do not directly contribute to insurgent victory over the government, their presence is associated with lower likelihoods of government victory (Chu and Braithwaite 2017).

Foreign fighters might work against ISIS's longer term goals for other reasons as well. Sarah Parkinson (2013) has found everyday ties to be critical to maintaining rebel organizations' capacity to survive through crises. Militant groups whose members are local to the area in which they are fighting can rely on existing relationships for resupply, medical care, and shelter. When the fighter base shifts to being comprised of networks of foreign fighters, however, these local ties disappear. Recognizing this, a group such as ISIS may include as part of its long-term strategy the forceful development of ties of kinship with local populations. The prevalence of forced marriages in ISIS-controlled territories both in Syria and Iraq suggests this may indeed be happening. According to reports from the town of Raqqa in Syria, for instance, local women and girls have been kidnapped and married off to ISIS foreign fighters to further integrate them into Syrian society. Ultimately, the goal has been to get foreign fighters closer to the clans in the areas that they occupy. Similar dynamics also characterize the behavior of some militants belonging to Al Qaeda in the Islamic Maghreb (AQIM), an organization that relies on fighters from different geographical origins.

Heightened levels of indiscriminate violence against civilians—perpetrated in large part by foreign fighters—could serve to undermine the strength of ISIS. In parallel, the continued influx of these foreigners could work to create divisions within the group, potentially leading to group fragmentation and even higher levels of violence. While in the short-term the presence of foreign fighters may have worked to strengthen ISIS, the long-term effects or a multinational fighter base remain somewhat in question. Some of this may depend on how well the foreign fighters are able to integrate themselves into the local context, and into local populations specifically. Nonetheless, the case of ISIS— as well as the multitude of other groups that include foreign combatants in their ranks—demonstrates that the advantages of foreigners on militant organization strength and survival are hardly assured.

In the wake of the 9/11 terrorist attacks, for instance, United States counterterrorism policies falling under the rubric of the "war on terror" have been criticized on many fronts. One such criticism is that military occupations— similar to those that occurred in Afghanistan in 2001 and then Iraq in 2003— actually trigger terrorist acts (Pape 2005). In fact, a 2006 National Intelligence Estimate released by the US government concluded that the war in Iraq had increased the threat of terrorism against the US (DNI 2006).

BOX 6.4

DRONES AND TERRORISM: COUNTERTERRORISM SUCCESS OR FAILURE IN PAKISTAN?

Photo 6.3 MQ-1 Predator Unmanned Aircraft. This unmanned aerial vehicle is used primarily by the US Air Force and the Central Intelligence Agency (CIA). Initially conceived for reconnaissance missions, it has been modified and upgraded to carry and fire hellfire missiles.

The effectiveness of drone strikes as a means of countering terrorism is the subject of an enduring debate. While some scholars maintain that the track record of drone strikes in places such as Yemen, Pakistan, and Afghanistan highlight the policy's failures, others argue that drones have done their job remarkably well. How have pundits and scholars come to such different conclusions?

Pakistan provides a useful case for analysis. From 2004 to 2014, the United States launched a total of 354 drone strikes against Al Qaeda and Taliban targets in Pakistan. The strike resulted in the confirmed deaths of about twenty-five hundred suspected terrorists.

The data demonstrate that from 2004 to about 2010, United States counterterrorism policy in Pakistan relied increasingly on the use of unmanned aerial vehicles best known as drones, to target insurgent and terrorist groups active in Pakistan. The small footprint in terms of US troops required for the deployment of such a strategy made it attractive in the eyes of policy makers and the broader public, and their accuracy relative to other tactics such as conventional airstrikes has been argued to limit civilian casualties. Proponents of the US policy point to the fact that the strikes have successfully disrupted the ability of terrorist organizations to organize and plan attacks.

The trend lines depicted in Figure 6.3 appear to suggest that drones have been effective at curbing the occurrence of terrorist attacks in Pakistan. Though the effect of drones on terrorist activity remains a relatively understudied topic in the academic world, some studies have demonstrated that drone strikes are generally associated with a reduction in the rate of terrorist attacks, a reduction in noncombatant casualty relates resulting from the strikes, and decreases in the rates of particularly lethal or intimidating tactics, such as suicide or IED bombings (Johnston and Sarbahi 2016).

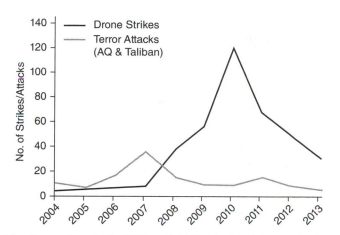

Figure 6.3 Terror Attacks by TTP and Al Qaeda & US Drone Strikes in Pakistan, 2004–2013

Sources: GTD (Tehrik-i-Talian Pakistan (the Pakistani Taliban, or TTP) and Al Qaeda attacks in Pakistan only); The *Long War Journal* statistics on drone strikes in Pakistan gathered from Pakistani news sources, wire reports (AP, Reuters), and *Long War Journal* data (available at http://www.longwarjournal.org/pakistan-strikes.php).

Drone Policy: What the Naysayers Contend. Such findings, however, leave room for criticism. Other counterterrorism measures occurring in conjunction with drone strikes, for instance, might be doing the actual work in terms of reducing the incidence of terrorism. Indeed, it may prove difficult to disaggregate the effects of Pakistani counterterrorism operations occurring on the ground from the effect of US strikes that target militant organizations. In addition, the relatively short time horizon that these studies use leave in question the long-term impacts of US drone policy.

Moreover, a common criticism of the US drone policy centers on the notion that strikes actually serve to incite more terrorism by virtue of the fact that they anger Muslim populations. Some critics have suggested, for instance, that drone strikes have done little to degrade Al Qaeda's propaganda strategy. Others contend that the strikes have fueled anti-US sentiment in areas of Pakistan that would otherwise not harbor hostile attitudes towards the United States. For each drone strike carried out, such naysayers argue, an exponentially larger number of terrorists is created (Cronin 2013).

A second set of criticisms surrounds the conjecture that killing the leader of terrorist cells—oftentimes the goal of specific drone strikes—is the best way to degrade a terrorist organization (Johnston 2012; See also Chapter 13). The evidence in support of such theories is mixed. In fact, eliminating the leader of a militant group, particularly if that group is large and well-established, has seldom precipitated its rapid demise.

An additional criticism suggests that drone strikes may only serve to displace terrorist activity. In Pakistan, drone strikes targeting militants based in rural areas close to the border with Afghanistan have prompted cross-border flows of

Continued

BOX 6.4
DRONES AND TERRORISM: COUNTERTERRORISM SUCCESS OR FAILURE IN PAKISTAN? *(Continued)*

fighters seeking refuge in Afghanistan's mountainous hideouts. Alternatively, terrorists could shift the bulk of their activity to urban environments, where drone strikes become even more controversial due to high population densities and potentials for high rates of civilian casualties (Johnston and Sarbahi 2016).

Finally, some have argued that the use of drones may go against international law, since it constitutes a violation of sovereign borders as well as extrajudicial killing of suspected terrorists who are not subject to due process prior to execution. Debate about the morality and legality of drone strikes was especially vibrant after the killing of Anwar Al Awlaki in Yemen in September 2011. Al Awlaki, a core member of Al Qaeda in the Arabian Peninsula (AQAP), was the first US citizen killed in a US drone strike, prompting a domestic debate concerning the legality of such actions. Prior to his killing, the Center for Constitutional Rights (CCR) and the American Civil Liberties Union (ACLU) had filed a lawsuit against the US government on behalf of Al Awlaki's father, requesting that his son be removed from the "kill list" maintained by the US government. The suit was dismissed, but after Al Awlaki's death, the CCR and ACLU filed a second case alleging that the killings did not follow due process. That case was also dismissed in 2014 (see CCR's description of "Al-Aulaqi v. Panetta," retrieved at http://ccrjustice.org/home/what-we-do/our-cases/al-aulaqi-v-panetta).

Photo 6.4   Anwar Al-Awlaki, a key member of Al Qaeda in the Arabian Peninsula, whom the United States killed in September 2011 in Yemen.

Photo credit: see https://commons.wikimedia.org/wiki/File:Awlaki_1008.JPG.

The Future of US Drone Strikes. The controversial nature of US drone strikes in countries such as Pakistan suggests that counterterrorism policy may come to rely less on targeted killings and more on a balanced mix of tactics. In fact, a somewhat greater reliance on Special Forces raids such as the one that led to the death of Osama bin Laden suggests that the US may be moving more towards these and other strategies as the war in Afghanistan winds down. In addition, these types of raids will likely involve the development of new bilateral partnerships to address the threat of terrorism, and strengthen existing ones. So while it is unlikely that the use of drones will be dropped altogether, the adoption of a more diverse set of counterterrorism strategies is likely to take hold.

Other counterterrorist strategies have been ineffective inasmuch as they have prompted the substitution of terrorist tactics, instead of curbing terrorism altogether. For example, as discussed in Chapter 2, scholars have found that the installation of metal detectors in airports led to a reduction in airline hijackings, but also to a subsequent increase in hostage taking events (Brandt and Sandler 2010). While this does not represent a complete failure of counterterrorism per se, counterterrorist measures have been deemed only partially effective if they serve to induce shifts in tactics used by terrorists. Nonetheless, comprehensive counterterrorist strategies that seek to lower the expected utility of all types of terrorist attacks would likely be prohibitively costly (see also Chapters 13 and 14).

OBSERVABLE IMPLICATIONS OF THE STRUCTURAL APPROACH: MOTIVATING CONDITIONS & PRECIPITANTS TO TERRORISM

Specific circumstances, too, can provide terrorists with compelling reasons or motivation to seek political change using violence. Frequently, there exist certain **precipitant conditions** that have a direct impact on the aggrieved actor(s), and terrorism becomes not only possible but also morally acceptable to the perpetrators. Indeed, socio-economic, ideological, historical, and cultural factors can all reinforce the notion that the risks of committing acts of terrorism are relatively small. These factors can provide inspiration to act, increase commitment to a group, or instill ideological justification for the use of terrorism.

Globalization and the "Clash of Civilizations." As we saw in earlier sections of this chapter, globalization serves not only to facilitate terrorism under certain circumstances, it has also been used as an underlying motivation that leads groups to use terrorism. In this respect, globalization is construed as a set of destabilizing forces that disrupt traditional patterns of activity at the global level, as well as local norms, arrangements, and understandings (Mousseau 2006). These redistributions often have the effect of widening disparities between individuals, groups, and states. The more interconnected the world becomes under the influence of globalization, the more salient these redistributions and disparities will also become.

This argument is somewhat related to arguments that contend that American dominance has attracted terrorist attacks against US interests. In fact, disentangling globalization from Americanization is not always that obvious. As a result, some of the backlash against globalization manifested in the form of terrorist attacks finds its expression in anti-Americanism, as well as broader opposition to Western cultural and economic values. In this sense, terrorism scholars have argued that increases in terrorism against American interests are perhaps best viewed as a consequence of American domination (unipolarity) and globalization (Sobek and Braithwaite 2005).

While most of the factors that we've highlighted thus far can be construed as rational explanations for terrorism, saying that globalization is a motivation for terrorism relies heavily on a cultural approach. Cultural explanations, in contrast to those that assume that specific observable factors cause terror, do not focus on political or economic factors, but rather on the notion that the values and beliefs of terrorists and their supporters are dramatically different from those of their victims. These kinds of explanations are obviously problematic in that they don't help to explain why certain elements of one culture use terrorist tactics, while others abstain from doing so.

In response to some of these criticisms, some studies have made arguments for rational-cultural explanations that build on both approaches to explaining terrorism. Michael Mousseau, for example, traces the origins of terrorism in clientelist economies not to underdevelopment per se, but rather to the social anarchy produced by globalization and the difficulties inherent in transitions to a market economy. The "clash of cultures," then, may best be construed as "market civilization versus the rest" (Mousseau 2003).

Globalization and the so-called clash of civilizations can also affect the expression of violence, for example through the increased likelihood of acts of terror designed to inflict mass casualties. While high civilian casualty tolls undermine indigenous support for terrorist groups acting locally, globalized terrorist networks that attack far from home face fewer constraints in their quest for resources, financing, and legitimacy.

Grievance-Based Explanations. Every terrorist needs a specific cause or motivation to justify the use of terror tactics both to himself and the intended audience he is attempting to influence. From this perspective, then, it is assumed that terrorism is rooted in specific economic, social, and political conditions that lead to specific overarching grievances.

For instance, many studies of terrorism have attempted to link poverty with terror, and with political violence more broadly (Lichbach 1989). The argument suggests that poverty fosters terror because it creates a sense of hopelessness, restricts educational opportunity, and produces frustration over inequality. While the logic might make sense, the bulk of studies actually find no direct relationship between poverty or unemployment, and terrorism (Piazza 2006). When absolute levels of poverty do show a positive relationship with terrorism, this is nearly always in combination with other factors. For example, poverty and low economic growth are positively correlated to instances of terrorism when identity politics, or discriminatory or exclusionary government policies are also at play. When groups perceive their status to be in decline relative to other groups, violence may erupt (this is the theory of relative depravation). **Economic grievances** such as poverty and inequality can therefore best be qualified as mobilizing and/or aggravating factors in combination with others mainly of political nature.

The ongoing Arab-Israeli conflict is a good example of how **political grievances** have led to terrorism. Indeed, some of the world's most violent terrorist acts have been committed in the name of Palestinian self-determination (or the ultimate destruction of Israel). In 1964, Palestinian terror groups coalesced to form the Palestine Liberation Organization (PLO) under the leadership of Arafat, with the mission of establishing a Palestinian state. The dispute, in essence, was over the possession of land. Palestinians consider much of the territory occupied by Israel as rightfully theirs. Other separatist groups that use terrorist tactics—such as Basque separatists in Spain, Chechens in Russia, or the Irish Republic Army in the UK—also frame their struggles largely in terms of political grievances.

Finally, another set of arguments has been made highlighting the role of **social grievances** in inciting terrorism. Some view terrorism in Latin America, for instance, as essentially a product of class conflict. Until the late 1970s and 1980s, nearly all Latin American countries were controlled by authoritarian regimes that gave little consideration to the welfare of their people. As a result, much of the continent's undereducated and impoverished population found themselves receptive to the philosophies espoused by Marxist, Leninist, and other varieties of terrorism. Indeed, the driving force behind many of Latin America's terrorist groups—such as the Sendero Luminoso in Peru and the Fuerzas Armadas Revolucionarias de Colombia (FARC)—has been the desire to reorganize society along socialist lines and carry out a wholesale redistribution of land and wealth.

Authoritarianism and Repression. As we briefly covered in our discussion of facilitating preconditions, scholars have laid out an array of different ideas about how regime type affects terrorism. To a large extent, those that posit a number of specific reasons why democracies should be more prone to terrorism emphasize linkages conceptualized as permissive or enabling preconditions. Other ideas, however, argue that regime type—specifically autocracy—can become an important precipitant of terrorism.

Indeed, authoritarian states restrict opportunities for political participation or implement discriminatory or exclusionary policies that severely disadvantage specific groups in society. It is also generally accepted that authoritarian governments engage in repression of their populations to a much greater degree than democracies (Davenport 2007). These common patterns of repressive government action against protest or other forms of organized political action compel some actors to view terrorism as justified and necessary.

When governments adopt repressive policies on certain groups to decrease the probability of rebellion, for instance, this repression decreases group resources dedicated to the fight. The repressed groups will find themselves with less ammunition, and with less people. In this sense, regime type (autocracy) serves as a constraint on groups' abilities to use terrorism. But repression affects groups in a second, perhaps more important way. Specifically, by increasing the level of disadvantages faced by certain groups, repressive governments actually create opportunities and motivation for ethnic leaders to mobilize the group as a whole for rebellion. In this instance, repression has aggravated group grievances, and perhaps directly precipitated acts of terrorism.

Belligerent Foreign Policy. In addition to setting the stage for terror attacks against deployed troops, a belligerent foreign policy posture—such as military intervention—can also motivate retaliatory terrorism (Pape 2005; Azam and Thelen 2010). In his 2009 book, David Kilcullen lays out a process he calls the "**accidental guerrilla syndrome**" (2009, p. 35). As Kilcullen describes, when militaries occupy countries in response to terrorism, they tend to anger the local population, motivating them to begin to join armed struggles against the occupier. Often this activity takes the form of guerrilla warfare, where local recruits attack military forces in the occupied country. For example, as discussed above, the United States and its NATO allies invaded Afghanistan in October 2001 to retaliate against Al Qaeda's operation on 9/11 and deprive it of a safe-haven. By the time the invasion took place, however, Al Qaeda and its affiliate groups had already used their safe havens in Afghanistan (and neighboring Pakistan) to develop a broader web of supporters and sympathizers. Moreover, many local warlords feared that NATO occupation would interfere with their own influence in the country. Therefore, NATO troops quickly began to face a large-scale insurgency from various armed Afghan factions. In some cases, Afghan warlords swore allegiance to Al Qaeda, complicating the NATO mission and fulfilling the final stage of the accidental guerrilla syndrome.

In some cases, bellicose foreign policies can also motivate retaliatory international terrorism. In more popular parlance, this process is called **blowback** (Johnson 2000). For instance, in spring 1986, the US sank two Libyan boats in the Gulf of Sirte, killing dozens of Libyan sailors. In retaliation, Libyan dictator Muammar Qaddafi called for a wave of attacks against Americans worldwide. The Libyan government allegedly supported the bombing of a Berlin nightclub on April 5, 1986, which resulted in three deaths and hundreds of injuries—mainly among off-duty American troops known to frequent

BOX 6.5

TERRORISM, THE MEDIA, AND COMMUNICATION TECHNOLOGY

Because terrorism is a form of political communication, terror groups often rely on traditional media and other communication technologies in order to maximize the psychological and political effects of their actions. Without media coverage, most terror attacks would not create fear in the broader population, thereby undermining one of its key intended effects. As you have probably noticed, terror attacks tend to draw media attention, underlining the truism "If it bleeds, it leads." Because of the attention devoted to spectacular incidents of violence, some have accused the news media of being willingly complicit in the perpetuation of terrorists' political influence. For instance, Margaret Thatcher, then Prime Minister of the United Kingdom, once referred to the media as "oxygen" for terrorists' publicity aims (1985). In fact, the United Kingdom was so intent on depriving the IRA of its sought-after publicity that the government censored news media interviews of IRA suspects between 1988 and 1994.

With the arrival of the digital age, groups using terror often exploit the use of smartphones, encryption technology, and the Internet not only to evade authorities, but also to control the pictures of themselves that different audiences see. For example, ISIS is known to publish different types of propaganda based on each targeted audience. English-language propaganda videos tend to depict grisly scenes of beheadings accompanied by threats to Western audiences, whereas films targeting would-be recruits in the Islamic world tend to feature Arabic-language depictions of a happy life where Muslims live comfortably together free from Western intervention (Stern and Berger 2015).

As with any strategic interaction, however, digital technology is a double-edged sword for terror groups. When companies that own user data cooperate with governments, such technology allows intelligence services to more carefully track and apprehend would-be terrorists or to recover key information about terror networks upon capture of such technologies (Benson 2014). This was the case for Al Qaeda, whose online chat rooms were quickly infiltrated by government agents who were (successfully) seeking intelligence. Moreover, because critics of the groups can also publish material online, terror groups cannot always assert control over their public image. ISIS learned this lesson when people living in ISIS-controlled territories began to release homemade videos depicting the brutal reality of life under ISIS, a stark contrast to ISIS's own propaganda videos (see Stern and Berger 2015).

DISCUSSION QUESTIONS

- *From a strategic perspective, does the rise of digital technologies advantage terror groups? Why, or why not?*
- *Should governments limit the coverage of terror attacks on the news media? Why or why not?*

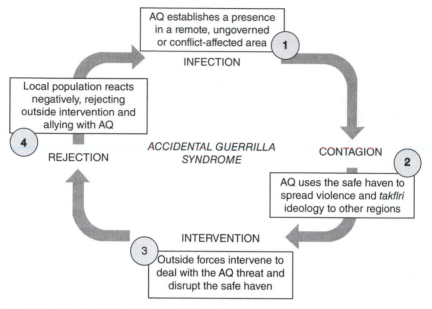

Figure 6.4 The Accidental Guerrilla Syndrome.

Source: Kilcullen 2009, p. 35.

the discotheque. In response, the United States launched airstrikes against Benghazi and Tripoli, which killed dozens of Libyans. In fact, Qaddafi himself narrowly survived the airstrikes, claiming that one of his children was killed during the bombardment. The Libyan government then retaliated against these airstrikes by supporting the hijacking of Pan Am Flight 73 in Pakistan, killing twenty people. Later, in December 1988, Libyan operatives bombed Pan Am Flight 103 over Lockerbie, Scotland, killing 270 people. A variety of other assassinations, kidnappings, and killings also appeared related to Libya's grievances regarding US bellicosity. Such instances illustrate the use of terrorism as a weapon that weak states use to attempt to coerce and punish more militarily powerful rivals (Findley, Piazza, and Young 2012).

PRACTICAL IMPLICATIONS OF STRUCTURAL EXPLANATIONS

To summarize how this multitude of preconditions and precipitating factors come together to produce terrorism, let's turn to an explanation published by Thomas Homer-Dixon on September 26, 2001 in the *Toronto Globe and Mail*:

> In the Middle East and South Asia, [terrorism's underlying factors] include a demographic explosion that has produced a huge bulge of urbanized,

young men—the most dangerous social group, according to many social scientists. They also include environmental stresses—especially shortages of cropland and freshwater – that have crippled farming in the countryside and forced immense numbers of people into squalid urban slums, where they are easy fodder for fanatics. The impact of these factors is compounded by chronic conflict (including the Israeli/Palestinian and Afghan conflicts) that have shattered economies and created vast refugee camps; by the region's corrupt, incompetent, and undemocratic governments; and by an international political and economic system that's more concerned about Realpolitik, oil supply, and the interest of global finance than about the well-being of the region's human beings.

If these underlying conditions and so-called root causes are important for understanding and explaining terrorism, they surely also have important implications for policy.

For example, if structural explanations are right, then prevention of terrorism requires more than domestic police or military responses, improved information-sharing at high levels of government, and other such forms of collaboration. Indeed, if terrorism is explained through structural conditions, then its eradication demands the need for deep structural changes within states and within the global system. It also suggests that counterterrorism efforts should be directed towards addressing underlying grievances and well as factors that enable groups to form, recruit, and sustain themselves. Academics and those involved directly in counterterrorism policy have advocated for the implementation of efforts dedicated to undermining support for terrorism in societies at risk—people facing environmental challenges and rapid urbanization; those overwhelmed by poverty; those living in protracted conflict zones or in squalor within neglected refugee camps; and those subject to the policies of repressive authoritarian governments. Structural explanations for terrorism speak to the importance of overcoming sustained global challenges and implementing increasingly good governance as a way of reducing terror.

Such reforms, however, should also pay heed to the notion that direct links between some structural factors and terrorism are tenuous at best. For example, as mentioned above, academic research suggests that the links between poverty and terrorism are inconclusive. Along the same lines, democratization is not necessarily the best solution to eradicating terrorism, in light of the fact that in some cases, democratization and democracy itself have historically fostered the phenomenon. Moreover, some scholars have found that although democracy tends to pacify populations, the process of democratization can be exceedingly bumpy and violent. Indeed, in several cases of democratic transition during the twentieth century, terrorism increased during the period of democratic consolidation (Chenoweth 2010b; Mansfield and Snyder 1995). The use of force, too, clearly should be applied with caution inasmuch as it can backfire and incite additional grievances among local populations (among its other substantial costs in blood and treasure).

Perhaps what structural approaches to terrorism best demonstrate is the need for balanced policies to confront it, ones that employ various assortments of instruments to treat such a complex phenomenon. Short-term strategies that focus on the use of military action need to be complemented by long-term policies designed to induce change in the international environment that enables terrorism. Such long-term strategies could involve greater cooperation with allies, the development of international legal instruments to deal with terrorism, and the use of economic instruments (both assistance and sanctions).

CRITIQUES OF STRUCTURAL APPROACHES

As with any other approach, structural approaches have several important limitations.

Most Structural Factors are Static. One of the major critiques of this approach is that most structural factors—such as wealth, regime type, region, terrain, and ethno-linguistic cleavages—are extremely slow to change, if they change at all. This fact has several problematic implications. First, these structural factors often stay the same year-to-year while patterns of terrorism fluctuate widely. As such, it is difficult to argue that static structural factors can explain variation in patterns of terrorist violence alone. For example, why is terrorism absent in a weak state during one year, and present the next? This fact becomes particularly important when trying to explain the timing of the escalation or de-escalation of terrorist violence.

Of course, some structural factors explicitly attempt to take into account changes in such factors as a way to overcome this problem. For example, Chenoweth (2010b) argues that sudden transitions toward (or away from) democracy are periods in which states have been vulnerable to corresponding increases in terrorist violence. Moreover, structural analyses that focus on policy decisions—like military intervention—may also better account for the timing of terrorism. However, many common structural approaches— like those focused on poverty, economic inequality, or demographic characteristics—have a much harder time with such explanations.

Structural Analyses are Too Deterministic. Like analyses of political behavior more generally, some criticize structural explanations as being ahistorical and overly deterministic (Crenshaw 1981). **Determinism** essentially argues that people are so strongly conditioned by their environments that their actions are more or less predetermined, automatic, and inevitable. Indeed, explanations focusing on the root causes of terrorism leave little, if any, room for the influence and decisions of individuals, groups, or organizational dynamics. Observationally, we know that although many countries have high levels of repression, for example, only a small number of people within those countries ever turn to terrorism. Structural explanations may therefore be useful in understanding which countries have higher propensities for terrorism, but they cannot explain why some people in similar conditions use terrorism whereas most others do not. Such approaches cannot speak to the role that power, psychology, relationships, or other factors might play in explaining the behavior of terrorist groups, let alone individual terrorists.

Furthermore, structural explanations for terrorism do not help in explaining variation across similar cases. Why, for example do some democracies experience more terrorism than others? Indeed, disaggregated studies of the phenomenon speak to the need for more nuanced explanations and explanatory variables disaggregated beyond what are typically considered structural causes.

Does Everything Cause Terrorism? When scanning the list of structural causes of terrorism in Table 6.1, one could easily conclude that anything can cause terrorism. Democracy or autocracy can cause terrorism. State weakness or state repression can cause terrorism. Conciliatory or militaristic policies can cause terrorism. With a focus on explaining terrorism—an extremely widespread yet varying phenomenon—many scholars have avoided identifying the factors that seem to make countries immune to terrorism. One exception is Mares (2011), who explains the relative absence of terrorism in East Central Europe as a result of the countries' peaceful transitions to democracy in 1989 as well as their relatively pacific foreign policies. However, these, too, are structural factors shared by many other countries with terrorist violence. Norway, for example, had experienced a peaceful transition to democracy with universal suffrage by 1913 and has since maintained a largely pacific foreign policy posture. Yet the country still experiences terrorism from extreme right-wing groups, including a large-scale terrorist attack in 2011. Thus peaceful democracy does not make countries immune from terrorism either. As a result, many structural analyses that begin by asking "what causes terrorism?" leave scholars wondering "what *does not* cause terrorism?"

Indeterminate or Counterproductive Counterterrorism Policy. Many structural analyses make designing and implementing counterterrorism policy a difficult task indeed. For example, placing undue emphasis on poverty as a root cause of terrorism can lead to the implementation of development strategies that fail to address the true reasons why some individuals might join extremist groups. Furthermore, because structural factors are so static and slow-to-change, counterterrorism policies informed by structural analysis rarely yield immediate impacts. Instead, policymakers have to see such policies as long-term investments with few visible short-term effects.

Moreover, the "everything matters" approach to studying terrorism complicates the development of effective policy solutions. When scholars point to regime type, poverty and inequality, culture, and repression as sources of terrorist violence, it is difficult to assess which types of policies to implement—particularly when such approaches might contradict one another or have unacceptable costs. For instance, under the Bush administration, many US officials believed that terrorism emanated from weak and failed states, and that the antidote to terrorism was to strengthen them. As a consequence, the US government pursued policies that involved military intervention and occupation in a failed state (Afghanistan), military invasion in an antagonistic autocratic regime (Iraq), and the shoring up of autocratic allies (e.g., Egypt) to prevent such states from becoming weaker. However, this policy approach initiated several other structural processes thought to increase terrorism: military intervention and regime transition. Hence structural approaches can often fail to make clear which types of structural factors are most influential (in which situations) to increase or decrease terrorism.

Additionally, structural factors make clear that there are policy trade-offs when it comes to combating terrorism. For instance, supporting democratic movements in authoritarian regimes might be a valid grand strategic goal, but such efforts may come at the expense of peace within that country. Moreover, targeting terrorists through military intervention may (or may not) reduce the terrorism threat, but it may also come at the expense of global stability. Therefore, when applied solely to counterterrorism, structural analyses can often obscure the bigger picture of how different policies might affect security as a whole rather than just terrorist violence.

Much as a balanced assortment of instruments must be used to address the challenges of terrorism, an assessment of its causes must too be balanced. Given the complexity of terrorism itself, its causes are also likely to be complex, multifaceted, and difficult to capture in a handful of structural variables.

A final critique of the structural approach emerges from the critical school, which we examine in the next chapter (Chapter 7). Critical approaches reject the notion that scholarly analysis or policy choices are value-free. Instead, they argue that scholars who study terrorism from an empirical perspective ignore important biases and subjective understandings that obscure their own incentives to prop up empire. In particular, they suggest that narrow focuses on structural factors like poverty reduction, political liberalization, or modernization as inherently "good" sideline other important values like self-determination, justice for oppressed peoples, and freedom from all forms of violence. Critical theorists view common "antidotes" to terrorism—such as militaristic policies, capitalism, and the expansion of Euro-centric, patriarchal systems—as far more damaging than terrorism itself (see Chapter 7).

SUMMARY

This chapter has provided an overview of the main structural factors—or root causes—of terrorism. Structural causes are found in the underlying environment and political, social, cultural, and economic structures of societies. Over the course of the chapter, we weighed the relative utility of a set of factors considered pre-conditions and precipitant factors to terrorism. We also explored several cases that demonstrate the effect that factors such as globalization, state weakness, regime type, and counterterrorism policy have had on terrorism. We presented some potential implications that structural approaches to the study of terrorism can have on counterterrorism policy, as well as several critiques of the approach.

Discussion Questions

1. What structural causes (preconditions and precipitating factors) appear to hold the most explanatory power in terms of predicting where terrorism will occur?

2. How can the structural approach be combined with the strategic approach to explain terrorism? How do these approaches differ?

3. How can structural factors explain the resurgence of the terrorist organization ISIS in Iraq in 2014?

4. What elements of democracy do you think best explain why terrorism occurs more frequently in democracies than autocracies?

5. Consider Figure 6.1 again. Why do you think terrorism has declined in democracies and increased in non-democratic regime types?

6. Based on a structural approach to terrorism, what would you include in a policy memo to the US Department of Homeland Security on how best to protect the country from terrorist attacks?

7. Explain the "accidental guerrilla syndrome" in your own words. Why would local populations be more inclined to support local terror groups than foreign invading armies?

KEY TAKEAWAYS

- The structural approach focuses on identifying the root causes—social, political, economic, environmental—that might both facilitate and motivate the use of terrorism. The structural approach tries to identify specific factors (or groups of factors) associated with the presence and absence of terrorism.

- Many structural analyses of terrorism rely on quantitative methods, since the primary aim is to understand general patterns and propensities for terrorism.

- The approach has intuitive appeal because it helps to identify broad-based conditions that might anger, frustrate, or injure people such that they view terrorism as a logical choice. As such, it seeks to help understand where terrorists' preferences come from.

- However, the structural approach is often critiqued for being overly deterministic while failing to explain important variations in patterns of terrorist behavior. Perhaps most importantly, because most structural variables are static and slow-to-change, structural explanations often fail to explain the timing of terrorist violence.

- Structural explanations often point to practical implications that require patient and long-term interventions—such as investments in education, poverty-reduction, or political liberalization. Such changes can often yield few short-term gains. And, in fact, some policies may even generate short-term increases in terrorist violence.

SUGGESTED FURTHER READINGS

Atzili, Boaz. 2010. "State Weakness and 'Vacuum of Power' in Lebanon". *Studies in Conflict & Terrorism* 33 (8): 757–782. doi: 10.1080/1057610X.2010.494172.

Azam, Jean-Paul, and Véronique Thelen. 2010. "Foreign Aid Versus Military Intervention in the War on Terror." *Journal of Conflict Resolution* 54 (2): 237–261. doi:10.1177/0022002709356051.

Bakke, Kristin M. 2014. "Help Wanted?: The Mixed Record of Foreign Fighters in Domestic Insurgencies." *International Security* 38 (4): 150–187. doi:10.1162/isec_a_00156.

Braithwaite, Alex, and David Sobek. 2005. "Victim of Success" American Dominance and International Terrorism." *Conflict Management and Peace Science* 22 (2): 135–148.

Brandt, Patrick T. and Todd Sandler. 2010. "What Do Transnational Terrorists Target? Has it Changed? Are We Safer?." *Journal of Conflict Resolution* 54 (2): 214–236. doi:10.1177/0022002709355437.

Bunn, Matthew and Anthony Wier. 2005 "The Seven Myths of Nuclear Terrorism." *Economist* 104 (681): 153–161.

Burgoon, Brian. 2006. "On Welfare and Terror: Social Welfare Policies and Political-Economic Roots of Terrorism." *Journal of Conflict Resolution* 50 (2): 176–203. doi:10.1177/0022002705284829.

Chenoweth, Erica. 2010. "Democratic Competition and Terrorist Activity." *The Journal of Politics* 72 (1): 16–30. doi:10.1017/s0022381609990442.

Crenshaw, Martha. 1981. "The Causes of Terrorism." *Comparative Politics* 13 (4): 379–399. doi:10.2307/421717.

Davenport, Christian. 2007. "State Repression and Political Order." *Annual Review of Political Science* 10 (1): 1–23.doi:10.1146/annurev.polisci.10.101405.143216.

De la Calle, Luis, and Ignacio Sánchez-Cuenca. 2011. "What We Talk About When We Talk About Terrorism." *Politics & Society* 39 (3): 451–472. doi:10.1177/0032329211415506.

Della Porta, Donatella. 1988. "Recruitment Processes in Clandestine Political Organizations: Italian Left-Wing Terrorism." *International Social Movement Research* 1: 155–169.

Dreher, Axel, and Martin Gassebner. 2008. "Does Political Proximity to the U.S. Cause Terror?" *Economics Letters* 99 (1): 27–29. doi:10.1016/j.econlet.2007.05.020.

Gassebner, Martin, and Simon Luechinger. 2011. "Lock, Stock, and Barrel: A Comprehensive Assessment of the Determinants of Terror." *Public Choice* 149 (3–4): 235–261. doi:10.1007/s11127-011-9873-0.

Hübschle, Annette. 2011. "From Theory to Practice: Exploring the Organized Crime-Terror Nexus in Sub-Saharan Africa." *Perspectives on Terrorism* 5(3–4).

Huntington, Samuel P. 1993. "The Clash of Civilizations?" *Foreign Affairs* 72 (3): 22–49. doi:10.2307/20045621.

Idler, Annette, and James J.F. Forest. 2015. "Behavioral Patterns Among (violent) Non-State Actors: A Study of Complementary Governance." *Stability: International Journal of Security and Development*, 4 (1): 1–19.

Krieger, Tim, and Daniel Meierrieks. 2011. "What Causes Terrorism?" *Public Choice* 147 (1/2): 3–27. doi:10.1007/sl1127-010-9601-1

Li, Quan and Drew Schaub. 2004. "Economic Globalization and Transnational Terrorism: A Pooled Time-Series Analysis". *Journal of Conflict Resolution* 48 (2): 230–258. doi:10.1177/0022002703262869.

Li, Quan. 2005. "Does Democracy Promote or Reduce Transnational Terrorist Incidents?" *Journal of Conflict Resolution* 49 (2): 278–297. doi:10.1177/0022002704272830.

Malet, David. 2013. *Foreign Fighters: Transnational Identity in Civic Conflicts*. Oxford: Oxford University Press.

Mousseau, Michael. 2002/2003. "Market Civilization and Its Clash with Terror." *International Security* 27 (3): 5–29.doi:10.1162/01622880260553615.

Mousseau, Michael. 2011. "Urban Poverty and Support for Islamist Terror: Survey Results of Muslims in Fourteen Countries." *Journal of Peace Research* 48 (1): 35–47. DOI: 10.1177/0022343310391724.

Newman, Edward. 2006. "Exploring the 'Root Causes' of Terrorism." *Studies in Conflict and Terrorism* 29 8): 749–772. doi:10.1080/10576100600704069.

Parkinson, Sarah Elizabeth. 2013. "Organizing Rebellion: Rethinking High-Risk Mobilization and Social Networks in War." *American Political Science Review* 107 (3): 418–432. doi:10.1017/s0003055413000208.

Piazza, James A. 2006. "Rooted in poverty? Terrorism, Poor Economic Development, and Social Cleavages." *Terrorism and Political Violence* 18 (1): 159–177. doi:10.1080/095465590944578.

Piazza, James A. 2008. "Incubators of Terror: Do Failed and Failing States Promote Transnational Terrorism?" *International Studies Quarterly* 52: 469–488. doi:10.1111/j.1468-2478.2008.00511.x.

Ross, Jeffrey Ian. 1993. "The Structural Causes of Oppositional Political Terrorism: Towards a Causal Mode.l" *Journal of Peace Research* 30 (3): 317–329.

Routledge, Paul. 1994. "Backstreets, Barricades and Blackouts: Urban Terrains of Resistance in Nepal." *Environment and Planning D: Society and Space* 12 (5): 559–578. doi:10.1068/d120559.

Sánchez-Cuenca, Ignacio, and Luis de la Calle. 2009. "Domestic Terrorism: The Hidden Side of Political Violence." *Annual Review of Political Science* 12 (1): 31–49. doi:10.1146/annurev.polisci.12.031607.094133.

Urdal, Henrik. 2006. "A Clash of Generations? Youth Gulges and Political Violence." *International Studies Quarterly* 50 (3): 607–629. doi:10.1111/j.1468-2478.2006.00416.x.

Volgy, Thomas J., Lawrence E. Imwalle, and Jeff J. Corntassel. 1997. "Structural Determinants of International Terrorism: The Effects of Hegemony and Polarity on Terrorist Activity." *International Interactions* 23 (2): 207–231. doi:10.1080/03050629708434907.

Walsh, James I., and James A. Piazza. 2010. "Why Respecting Physical Integrity Rights Reduces Terrorism." *Comparative Political Studies* 43 (5): 551–577.

CHAPTER 7

CRITICAL APPROACHES

Learning Objectives

After reading this chapter, readers should be able to:

- Compare and contrast critical approaches—including feminist, post-colonial, and Marxist variants—in their own words.

- Summarize the main assertions and expectations of the Critical Terrorism Studies (CTS) research program.

- Compare and contrast the different assumptions and implications of empirical terrorism studies and CTS.

- Explain the major shortcomings of critical approaches.

> "Everybody's worried about stopping terrorism. Well, there's a really easy way: stop participating in it.
> —NOAM CHOMSKY, 2002 (CITED IN CHOMSKY, JUNKERMAN, AND MASAKAZU 2011, P. 20)

> "One of the most significant contributions to our understanding of terrorism is the realization that terrorism is a social construct. Indeed, terrorism is not a given in the real world, but 'an interpretation of events and their presumed causes.' Such interpretation is not an unbiased attempt to depict truth; rather, it is a conscious effort to 'manipulate perceptions to promote certain interests at the expense of others.' Definitions of terrorism typically reflect the interests of those who do the defining, and in many social conflicts the government and related agencies ... are the 'primary definer' and hold de facto 'definition power.' "
>
> —RAMON SPAAIJ (2011, P. 15)

INTRODUCING CRITICAL APPROACHES

Critical approaches are primarily concerned with questioning the politics behind the production of knowledge and policy related to terrorism. In particular, **critical terrorism studies** (CTS) researchers call into question the empirical terrorism studies enterprise. They suggest that terrorism is a contested and pejorative concept, which entrenched authorities use to delegitimize the valid claims of people living under oppression. Hence the primary aim of CTS researchers is to identify, expose, and problematize existing power structures and hierarchies that lead to the persistence of oppressive systems. Moreover, CTS researchers suggest that those who attempt to study terrorism from an empirical perspective are knowingly or unwittingly participating in, reinforcing, and contributing to these existing systems of oppression by tacitly or explicitly endorsing a gendered and **state-centric** status quo. In other words, proponents of the CTS approach argue that everything we think we know about terrorism is both empirically wrong and morally misguided.

To understand CTS, we first need to understand that it embraces a different **epistemological** standpoint from empirical terrorism research. Epistemology is the study of knowledge itself—an attempt to interrogate the origins, methods and validation practices involved in developing consensus, knowledge, and belief. In other words, epistemology is concerned with studying how people come to know what they know.

As a critical epistemology, CTS has its intellectual origins in various theories popularized during the twentieth century. Marxist theorists argue that the unrestricted flow of capital has created a system of wealth inequality in which a capitalist class of bourgeoisie dominates and exploits the worker class of the proletariat. Antonio **Gramsci**'s theories on **cultural hegemony** have informed a critical discussion explaining how the ruling classes use various symbolic, linguistic, artistic, educational, and cultural institutions to sustain rules and norms that allow the state to consolidate power (Gramsci 1971). Proponents of **critical race theory** and **post-colonial theories** suggest that race and the legacy of colonialism have been fundamental organizing principles in the international system (see, for example, Bell 1980; Vitalis 2015; Fanon 1963). Colonial expansion occurred in a deeply racist way, with European and American officials claiming the right to subordinate colonial populations because on the basis of perceived racial inferiority. To accumulate power within their colonies, colonial powers created structural dependencies that rendered indigenous peoples incapable of improving their own economic, social, or political well-being. For example, in many British colonies, like India, people would develop products in high demand in Europe in exchange for exceedingly low wages. Colonial authorities would also routinely use divide-and-rule strategies, exploiting (or in some cases manufacturing) rivalries between different ethnic, social, or political groups in order to prevent the population from organizing effective rebellion against

Photo 7.1   Frantz Fanon, whose book *The Wretched of the Earth* advanced an anti-colonial philosophy emphasizing violence as a purifying process necessary to liberate oppressed peoples from imperial and colonial power. He argued that any violence by oppressed people was justified given the wrongs imposed upon them for centuries, and that the limited violence they might use for self-liberation could not possibly surpass the violence against them by the colonial powers.

Credit: https://commons.wikimedia.org/wiki/File:Frantzfanonpjwproductions.jpg

imperial rule. Despite the end of colonialism in a literal sense, critical race and post-colonial theories assume that the dominant hierarchies and exploitative practices remain intact, albeit through channels that **neo-imperial** powers can more easily deny. For example, they suggest that **neoliberal economic policies** allow powerful capitalist states to exploit natural resources and cheap labor in developing countries. The result of such exploitation is short-term wage exploitation as well as many forms of **structural violence**—including economic insecurity, poor health, ecological devastation, racial and/or ethnic discrimination, political instability, high crime rates, and other dimensions of human suffering—in the longer term as well (Galtung 1969).

How do these conditions affect terrorism? CTS proponents suggest that colonialism and racist policies more generally also affect the politics of terrorism, by conditioning both the grievances leading to violence and the ways in which the hegemonic state system interprets and responds to such acts of dissent. For instance, they suggest that most acts of violence by nonstate actors are responses to intolerable conditions brought upon people living in the **Global South** as a result of the racist and imperial policies of the **Global North**. And CTS proponents also point out that racist and colonial policies affect the production of knowledge about terrorism. For example, the primary authors of the field of terrorism studies have been white European or American scholars. This is especially true in quantitative research, which is dominated by North American scholars. Such scholars are conveniently isolated from the economic, social, and political realities of life in the Global South. Proponents of CTS argue that scholars from the Global South are routinely silenced or marginalized within the field, particularly when they critique the policies of countries in the Global North or when they adopt unconventional methods to conducting their own scholarship.

Feminism has also informed contemporary CTS scholarship. Although feminists acknowledge the important roles that class, race, and other systems of privilege and deprivation play in affecting global politics, they argue that patriarchy forms the basis of the hierarchy that dominates social, political, economic, and cultural life (Tickner 2001). Around the world, the primary actors involved in both terror attacks and counterterrorism responses are men. Some feminists argue that sex and gender inequities within societies are primary drivers of terrorism, as such inequities rob societies of the inclusive, collaborative, and cooperative capacity necessary to fully remedy social, political, and economic conflicts (Caprioli 2000; Hudson et al. 2013). And within the field of terrorism studies, most terrorism researchers are men as well. As a result of this gendered production of both practice and knowledge, feminists argue that basic assumptions about why terrorism happens (and how to stop it) are fundamentally limited to the perspectives of men (Gentry and Sjoberg 2008). Similar to critical race theory, feminists suggest that attempts to point out or remedy these inequities are typically crushed.

Each of these intellectual traditions shares in common several basic assumptions. First, the international system is characterized by systems of hierarchy, domination, and exploitation. Existing power structures tend to further develop and concentrate power, wealth, and resources into a core of "haves." They do this by dominating and exploiting a periphery of "have nots," who possess fewer and fewer rights and resources over time. The current international system concentrates power, wealth, and resources into a state-centric system, which benefits a select few at the expense of the many. Entrenched authorities seek to preserve this status quo using norms and ideologies that reify the state as the only relevant unit of the international system, while legitimizing its right to maintain its hegemony. The result of this process is a deepening of the inequalities existing within and across states.

Second, a state-centric view sees the **sovereign** state as the proper ruling authority from which public goods—including security—can flow. CTS proponents view this state-centric orientation with a great deal of skepticism because of the moral liberties afforded to states in the name of security (Jackson, et al. 2009). For example, CTS theorists routinely point out that the deaths resulting from state violence are orders of magnitude larger than the deaths resulting from terrorist attacks. In fact, they suggest that states, not nonstate actors, are the primary perpetrators of political violence. CTS researchers are also deeply concerned with the morality (or immorality) of state responses to terrorism. They argue that such methods have often wrought more damage than they prevented.

Finally, CTS proponents are deeply critical of empirical terrorism researchers for keeping the spotlight on terror groups rather than focusing on the abuses and atrocities committed by states. In fact, CTS proponents reject the **positivist** epistemology, in which scholars assert that truth is objective, knowable, and value-free more generally. They argue instead for a **post-positivist** position in which scholars, analysts, and policymakers acknowledge that knowledge is not value-free. CTS researchers assume that "Theory is always *for* someone and *for* some purpose" (Robert Cox 1981, p. 128).

ASSUMPTIONS OF THE CRITICAL APPROACH

The CTS approach includes a number of assumptions building upon the intellectual traditions of Cox, Gramsci, Foucault, and Chomsky.

Terrorism is an Inherently Subjective, Pejorative Concept. CTS rejects the notion that terrorism is an observable phenomenon that one can define or conceptualize objectively. It has no inherent meaning. Instead, they see terrorism as a subjective, socially-constructed device. The meaning of real acts of violence are sometimes labeled terrorism, and sometimes labeled something else (e.g,. mass shooting, massacre, collateral damage, self-defense). It is the labeling—and the various processes that lead to such labeling in some cases but not others—that become the object of interest for critical approaches. As a result, when a person uses the term "terrorism," one reveals more about one's own political, social, cultural, and economic position than about the act itself. Moreover, students of terrorism should approach "widely accepted knowledge" about this phenomenon with "caution," and they should see conventional wisdom as constantly "open to question" (Jackson, et al. 2009, p. 3).

Jackson et al. (2011) use a helpful analogy of a boxing match to make this point:

> In a similar process to that by which a boxing ring, an official referee, a set of rules, and the expectations of an audience transforms a fist-fight into a socially accepted sporting match, the actions and pronouncements of politicians, academics, lawyers and others transform a particular act of violence – such as a bombing or a murder – into an act of "terrorism" (ibid., p. 3).

CTS also assumes that elites choose the term terrorism to delegitimize an act of violence, while avoiding the use of the term to describe acts of violence they see as legitimate. As such, terrorism is fundamentally a pejorative device, meant to discredit and demonize the perpetrator of the violence while elevating the state's justification for acting as it will.

State-Centrism. Because CTS embraces the subjectivity of terrorism, its core curiosity is to determine who benefits from labeling acts of violence "terrorism." Here, critical approaches tend to focus on the primacy of state-centrism as the central, underlying normative system in which we live. They argue that the pejorative use of the term terrorism reinforces the legitimacy of the state to use violence and other means to amass power, while simultaneously challenging the right of nonstate actors to use violence to pursue their own goals. Critical approaches assume that sovereignty—the norm that the state has a monopoly over the legitimate use of violence—is itself a socially constructed idea that serves the interests of established states and allows elites to continue to reinforce and fortify their claims to legitimacy. Like the referee in the boxing match, politicians, the media, and other elites decide whether those engaging in violence are using terrorism or not, according to whether the violence supports or challenges the legitimacy and power of the state. Critical approaches assume that the state will seek and take extra powers when it can; it therefore tends to benefit from labeling acts as "terrorism" to expand its powers without provoking resistance from the general public.

Empirical Research on Terrorism Serves the State and Has an Interest in Perpetuating Itself. CTS is deeply skeptical of the knowledge produced by those engaged in **empirical terrorism studies**. First, those engaged in such research are cooperating—consciously or unconsciously—with the state by allowing the state's language and problems to drive their own research agendas (Jackson, et al. 2011, p. 26). For example, the **National Consortium for the Study of Terrorism and Responses to Terrorism (START)** formed as a research collective in 2004 in response to the US Department of Homeland Security's call for Centers of Excellence that could help to advance the study of terrorism from a systematic, empirical perspective. More than one hundred researchers have been involved in START-affiliated projects, resulting in the production of key resources such as the Global Terrorism Database, various databases on terrorist groups, studies of the processes of radicalization and de-radicalization, and data-driven analyses about which types of counterterrorism are more effective than others. CTS scholars suggest that this uncritical acceptance of the state's research mandates—as well as its labeling practices—implies that the state has essentially coopted empirical terrorism studies. As Jackson, et al. note, empirical terrorism researchers are "institutionally, financially, politically and ideologically tied to the state and function as an integral part of the state's apparatus of power—even if they do not always necessarily agree on what causes terrorism or how it should be dealt with and sometimes criticize state actions and policies" (ibid, p. 12–13).

Moreover, once scholars produce knowledge valuable to the state, they develop a long-term interest in retaining their influence by (1) maintaining a problem-solving orientation to their research programs; and (2) ensuring that terrorism and counterterrorism remain primary concerns for public policy and debate. As a consequence, the world has seen the rise of a "terrorism industry"—a group of scholars, analysts, pundits, media, and private secu-rity companies—whose prestige and pocketbooks thrive as a result of the prioritization of terrorism as a primary public concern. As Noam Chomsky has argued, the terrorism industry has often "acted as an arm of western state policy and an apologist for state terrorism carried out by Western states and its allies" (Jackson, et al. 2011, p. 14; Chomsky and Vitchek 2013). Within the terrorism research field, empirical terrorism scholars have elevated quan-titative, pseudoscientific methodologies over pluralistic methodologies. And the field tends to marginalize those who adopt more critical, post-positivist, socio-historical methods, either by denying them access to publication in the field's primary journals, access to conferences or workshops, or entry to in-fluential policy venues (Ilardi 2004, p. 222; Reid 2007).

More generally, critical approaches draw on Gramscian perspectives to argue that knowledge serves power, and that terrorism scholars "are embed-ded within historical-political structures which shape their values" (Jack-son, et al. 2011, p. 14). In other words, scholars who are not critical about the way in which their birthplace, upbringing, family life, and political, social, cultural, and economic influences have shaped their own worldviews are deceiving themselves. These scholars cannot possibly live up to the claims of objectivity that their positivist research methodologies purport to possess.

Problem-solving Approaches Tend to Result in Poor Research Practices.
CTS assumes that positivist research—particularly quantitative positivist research—generally results in low-quality findings. This is because such methodologies reduce their research subjects to numbers, devoid of histori-cal context and without questioning the socio-political origins of the "terror-ist" label. Because positivists believe that objective truths are fundamentally knowable and that human behavior is as stable and predictable as gravita-tional physics, they tend to adopt "what appear to be scientific language and methods" (Jackson et al. 2011, p. 19). Yet despite giving off an impression of accuracy, "traditional theory also transforms the management of social conflict into a series of technical problems, thereby obscuring the deeper political and ethical questions at the heart of managing social conflict" (ibid, p. 19). This gives empirical terrorism studies the illusion of authority.

CTS asserts that empirical researchers have failed to produce a single, agreed-upon definition of terrorism, demonstrating the inherent subjectiv-ity of the concept—as well as its vulnerability to political manipulation. Moreover, the nonstate connotation to the contemporary concept of terror-ism restricts the definition of terrorism to that which uncritically benefits the state, undermining empirical researchers' claims to scientific objectiv-ity. Proponents of this approach argue that empirical terrorism researchers rarely (if ever) truly engage with their research subjects through primary re-search, such as direct interviews, in-depth contextual analysis, or other eth-nographic methods. As a result, their conclusions are incomplete at best—or fundamentally wrong at worst. Moreover, empirical terrorism researchers privilege the study of terrorism by nonstate actors, ignoring or neglecting the study of the "more serious issue" of state terrorism—a primary concern for critical terrorism researchers (Jackson, et al. 2011, p. 14–15). In short, empirical terrorism research rarely engages in sufficient self-reflection to fully challenge it own methods, knowledge, or epistemological assumptions.

Problem-solving Approaches Privilege the Status Quo. CTS researchers assume that problem-solving approaches, which the state dictates, fundamentally favor the maintenance of the status quo. In particular, the public discourse on terrorism and counterterrorism, empirical terrorism research, and the terrorism industry more broadly accept the state-centric status quo as natural and good, whereas challenges to that status quo are unnatural and bad. Thus, CTS argues that much knowledge developed by empirical terrorism research has knowingly or unknowingly neglected the pressing concerns of inequality, injustice, patriarchy, and violence, which plague our times. Therefore, empirical terrorism research tends to see security in state-centric terms rather than in human-centric terms, and it tends to avoid examination of the underlying hierarchies, injustices, and uses of state terror that generate conflict in the first place.

Empirical Terrorism Studies Has Perpetuated Destructive Myths about Terrorism. CTS researchers point out that the result of this uncritical discourse about terrorism has been the construction and perpetuation of important myths about terrorism. The most obvious myth is that terrorism by nonstate actors constitutes an urgent, existential threat to Western civilization. A corollary of this myth is that without significant commitment to counterterrorism—in terms of popular support, lives lost, and money invested—nonstate terrorism will destroy Western states and revise the international system (Jackson, et al. 2011, p. 22). CTS researchers point out that the real threat of terrorism is significantly exaggerated. As we saw in Chapter 1, terrorism is a marginal threat to human life compared to other forms of violence, and it is a negligible source of death compared with various public health concerns. Furthermore, it is unclear whether investments in counterterrorism have decreased terrorist violence, increased it, or had no effect whatsoever. Nevertheless, the existential threat of terrorism and necessity of sustained counterterrorism have become the dominant narrative, and governments have justified many vital decisions on the basis of this threat (e.g., the US invasion of Iraq in 2003, NATO's invasion of Afghanistan in 2001, the passage of tough counterterrorism laws in Europe, and various Western governments' bombings of Islamic State positions in Iraq, Syria, Yemen, Libya, etc.).

The Study of Terrorism Is Inherently Social and Political. Finally, CTS researchers assume that politics and social context drive both the study of terrorism and the larger public discourse surrounding terrorism. To paraphrase Cox (1981), knowledge about terrorism is always created for someone. In the contemporary era, CTS researchers see the study of terrorism as

BOX 7.1

ARE ALL VICTIMS EQUAL?

On November 13, 2015, a group of Islamic State-inspired militants launched a series of coordinated attacks in Paris and the Parisian suburb of Saint Denis, killing 130 people and wounding 368 others. In the aftermath of these attacks, the hashtag #JeSuisParis went viral on social media, with millions of people worldwide expressing their sympathy and solidarity with the victims of the attack. But critics immediately noticed a double-standard in this campaign— in particular, that similarly-devastating attacks in Beirut, Istanbul, Baghdad, and Syria during the same week yielded no such response on social media, particularly in the West. This stinging omission was especially poignant given that millions of people were fleeing brutal violence in the Middle East and North Africa, but were stopped cold when they reached the borders of European states.

DISCUSSION QUESTION

- *CTS researchers would see the #JeSuisParis movement as double-standard indicative of the Euro-centric lens through which we see terrorism and its victims. Do you agree or disagree? Why?*

focused primarily on groups that oppose the Euro-centric, state-centric, capitalist, patriarchal systems characterized by liberal democratic and neoliberal economic practice. As a result, the study of terrorism has primarily focused on communist, Islamist, and nationalist-separatist groups who would revise these dominant systems. For example, during the 1970s and 1980s, terrorism research focused primarily on crushing the various Marxist-Leninist groups that existed around the world, rather than the various right-wing reactionary groups, paramilitaries, and deaths squads that often existed in tandem. Similarly, terrorism researchers in the 1980s and 1990s tended to focus on containing or stopping the violence of the IRA rather than interrogating the violence that British military and paramilitary groups and Ulster loyalists used to suppress the IRA and its supporters. And CTS researchers today decry the focus on Islamist terrorism to the neglect of domestic and international state violence against Muslim peoples around the world. For example, human rights violations during the war in Iraq and Afghanistan, extrajudicial killings of terrorist suspects in Yemen, Libya, Syria, torture scandals in Abu Ghraib and Guantanamo Bay, and the US government's rendition of suspects to countries that practice systematic torture all yielded far less mainstream academic or public scrutiny than one might expect if state terrorism were considered as interesting and important as terrorism carried out by nonstate terrorism (Weinberg and Eubank 2008, p. 191).

The generation and perpetuation of this dominant discourse about terrorism—both within academic and policy circles—is thus a political and

TABLE 7.1 Empirical and Critical Terrorism Studies Compared

	Empirical Terrorism Studies	*Critical Terrorism Studies*
Primary aim of research program	Explanation, prediction, problem-solving	Reveal politics behind knowledge
View of terrorism	Observable, predictable concept	Contested and pejorative concept, focus on origin of term
View of terrorism research	Problem-oriented	Social process constructed through language, discourse, and inter-subjective practices
Normative aim	Provide reliable answers to questions about terrorism	Emancipatory theme; disrupt patriarchal, militaristic, and Euro-centric status quo
Practices	Careful definition of terms & scope of study, empirical rigor, objectivity	Avoid uncritical use of language, methodological pluralism, critical of state and other entrenched power hierarchies; empathy
Epistemological assumptions	Knowledge and policy can be objective	Knowledge cannot be objective
Methods	Hypothesis-testing, empirical	Deconstructive, narrative, genealogical, ethnographic, historical, constructivist

social process. CTS scholars assume that the positions and institutional location of the researchers (i.e. whether they are recognized authorities on the topic, and which types of institutions they affiliate with), the types of methodologies they employ, and the intended end-users of the research (i.e., whether the work is for the government, other academics, the general public, or a different audience) all influence the result of the research. And each stage of the research process provides a different point for critical examination.

Table 7.1 summarizes the core differences in the assumptions made by empirical and critical terrorism studies.

OBSERVABLE IMPLICATIONS OF THE CRITICAL APPROACH

Most CTS researchers purposefully avoid the use of positivist methodologies to generate and support theoretical claims. That said, if CTS is right, we should expect to observe several trends over time.

Preoccupation with Nonstate Terrorism. If CTS is right, then the field of empirical terrorism studies should focus almost exclusively on terrorism by nonstate actors, rather than terrorism perpetuated by states. Existing terrorism scholarship should not focus on violence by states, like the United States' carpet-bombing of North Vietnamese villages during the Vietnam War, but rather on violence by nonstate actors who challenge the status quo system.

Evidence that would support this observable implication would include:

- Qualitative or quantitative evidence revealing that most state funding for terrorism research is directed toward topics related to nonstate terrorism.

- Qualitative or quantitative evidence revealing that academics and analysts who have achieved widespread recognition as "terrorism experts" (through citations, promotions, external funding, and representation in the mainstream media) have done so by focusing on nonstate terrorism.

- Quantitative and qualitative evidence (from Google Scholar or other citation metric systems) revealing that most highly-cited works in terrorism studies focus on nonstate terrorism, whereas studies that focus on state terrorism receive few citations.

Preoccupation with Terrorism against the West. One of the primary CTS critiques is that traditional terrorism research tends to focus on violence by groups attempting to revise the existing Euro-centric, liberal, patriarchal order. It also tends to avoid studying violence by groups supported by Western states, like the Contras in Nicaragua. In other words, the state's interest in suppressing nonstate terrorism should extend mostly to groups that oppose Western states. And academic research should tend to follow the Western states' interests in this regard, privileging scholarship on Islamic groups, which are revisionist actors, rather than right-wing groups, which are often status quo actors.

Evidence that would support this observable implication would include:

- Qualitative or quantitative evidence revealing that most state funding for terrorism research is directed toward topics related to terrorism against Western states and their allies.

- Qualitative or quantitative evidence revealing that academics and analysts who have achieved widespread recognition as "terrorism experts" (through citations, promotions, external funding, and representation in the mainstream media) have done so by focusing on terrorism against Western states and their allies.

- Quantitative and qualitative evidence (from Google Scholar or other citation metric systems) revealing that most highly-cited works in terrorism studies focus on terrorism against Western states and their allies, whereas studies that focus on terrorism in the developing world or terrorism by groups supported by Western states receive few citations.

Preoccupation with Terrorism by "Non-Western" Perpetrators. Of course, there is variation regarding who commits acts of terror in the West. The CTS school expects that public and scholarly reactions to terrorism should be much more pronounced, decisive, and unreflective when the perpetrator is perceived to be non-Western. For example, Dylann Roof, a white man inspired by racist extremist groups, walked into a predominantly black church in June 2015 and shot to death nine worshippers. He left one victim alive, instructing her to report to others what he had done and why, ostensibly to spread fear in other black Americans. By all accounts, this crime easily fit the standard definition of terrorism. However, US officials did not label this event "terrorism," opting for the term "hate crime" instead. This event contrasts with attacks by Muhammad Youssef Abdulazeez a few weeks later. Abdulazeez, who was allegedly inspired by Al Qaeda in the Arabian Peninsula and other transnational jihadist groups, attacked several servicemen in two different locations in Chattanooga, Tennessee, killing five people before law enforcement officers killed him. The twenty-four-year-old was born in Kuwait but raised in the United States and reportedly sought out information on Islamist groups and their activities on the Internet. In contrast to his handling of Roof's case, the FBI director was quick to label Abdulazeez's assault a terrorist attack.

For the CTS research program, this different treatment of perpetrators on the basis of ascribed national identities is typical of attempts to explain and prevent terrorism. As such, evidence that would support this claim might include:

- Further qualitative or quantitative evidence demonstrating a tendency to avoid labeling violent assaults by white people as terrorism, combined with a tendency to label violent assaults by non-white people as terrorism.

- Qualitative or quantitative evidence suggesting that governments direct significant funds to preventing terrorism by non-white, non-European perpetrators, rather than all perpetrators of terrorism.

Preoccupations with Terrorism Should Change over Time. Because research about in nonstate terrorism should serve specific political and social purposes, we should observe some variation over time in the interest with which researchers and other academics treat the topic. In particular, we should observe greater interest in other forms of oppositional politics—like rebellion, insurgency, or guerrilla warfare—when the meanings of such concepts are more relevant to the respective time period.

Take, for example, Figure 7.1. Here, we used Google NGRAMS to create a longitudinal graph that identifies the frequency with which English-language books used the terms "Terrorist," "Rebel," "Guerrilla," and "Insurgent" in their titles between 1800 and 2008. Unsurprisingly, the term "rebel" was the most common used to describe oppositional nonstate actors from 1800 until about 1990. Its use peaked during the US Civil War and tapered off to maintain a steady hegemony over the discourse throughout the twentieth century. Then, as the cold war ended, the term "Terrorist" became equally prominent, becoming the dominant term after 2001. In other words, 9/11— and Western states' preoccupation with delegitimizing and crushing this type of oppositional activity—may explain the rise of the term more than an objective rise in the frequency of violence by nonstate groups, per se.

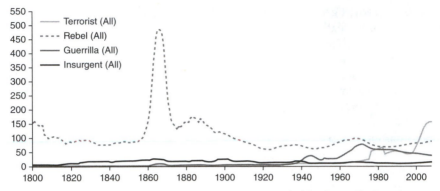

Figure 7.1 Frequency of Mentions of "Terrorist," "Rebel," "Guerrilla," and "Insurgent" in English Language Book Titles from 1800–2008

This graph helps to illustrate how academic interest in a topic may be driven by key events that attract the interest of the state—and that those objects of interest for the state may change over time in ways that allow us to observe these effects directly.

As such, evidence that would support this observable implication would include:

- Further qualitative or quantitative evidence demonstrating a decided shift in attention to terrorism by scholars after attacks on Western states.

- Qualitative or qualitative evidence suggesting that governments direct significant funds toward terrorism following major attacks on Western states.

Terrorism Scholars Should Be Preoccupied with State-Centric Approaches to Addressing Terrorism. Critical approaches assume that terrorism researchers are, themselves, part of the system that reinforces the power of the state. Although this positionality can often be unwitting on the part of terrorism scholars, the approach nevertheless expects that researchers will tend to promote state-centric solutions to terrorism in a way that reinforces existing power structures.

Evidence to support this conclusion might include an analysis of the different policy implications that scholars draw from their analyses and the ways in which they represent largely cooperative or adversarial positions regarding the state-centric status quo. Evidence in support of the critical approach would include:

- Qualitative evidence showing that the most highly-cited terrorism scholars tend to recommend state-centric policy responses to terrorism.

- Network analyses showing that scholars who promote state-centric solutions also tend to receive the greatest number of resources from government-funded agencies and that, in turn, those scholars continue to produce state-centric work.

PRACTICAL IMPLICATIONS OF THE CRITICAL APPROACH

Unlike empirical terrorism studies, CTS is a fundamentally and explicitly prescriptive approach to the subject. As a result, it is more concerned with formulating practical and intellectual implications, rather than stressing empirical implications.

The Human as the Subject of Security. First, CTS calls for scholars and decision makers to elevate concerns for human security above the security of states. Instead of responding to the interests of states, scholars should be more interested in the well-being of individuals, and of "ending the avoidable suffering of human beings" (Jackson et al. 2011, p. 40). Thus, CTS researchers jettison the assumption that state violence is legitimate because states decide what is legitimate. Instead, they promote a notion of legitimacy that focuses on whether an action (either by states or nonstate actors) improves the well-being of people (ibid). CTS researchers acknowledge that this practice will often put CTS scholars in opposition to the state. They welcome and embrace this possibility where their opposition may improve human welfare.

Terrorism as a Tactic. Second, CTS calls for a broader definition of terrorism, which defines terrorism as a tactic that states or nonstate actors use to promote fear in the broader population. They suggest that this will encourage scholars and the public to pay more attention to state terrorism, while also alleviating some of the propagandistic aspects of the definition (ibid, 32). Another potential solution would be to avoid using the term "terrorism" altogether, in light of the intransigence of its current socio-historical connotations. Instead, scholars could aim to classify certain forms of violence as "massacres," "assassinations," or "killings," thus focusing on what is objectively knowable while removing the pejorative dimensions of the subject.

Pluralistic Research Methodologies. CTS researchers reject the superiority of positivist approaches to terrorism, arguing that we cannot understand human behavior in the same way we can understand astrophysics, chemistry, or biology—and that pretending otherwise gives a false sense of authority to analysts relying on such methods. CTS researchers reject the possibility that we can generalize about terrorism, and they urge caution with regard to comparing violent groups or states existing in different historical, political, or cultural contexts. Instead terrorism scholarship should be characterized by a diverse range of methodologies, particularly those that engage in primary research. Ethnography, discourse analysis, in-depth historical analysis, narrative analysis, critical theory, interpretivist, self-reflective, artistic, symbolic, and cultural analysis can help to generate a more complete understanding of political violence. For example, they argue that by directly engaging with their subjects and listening to their own explanations of their grievances, scholars can identify the points of injustice that can be resolved to create peace. They also recommend that the field of terrorism studies diversify itself, deliberately encouraging marginalized voices to take the stage. CTS researchers therefore embrace—and seek to amplify—perspectives on terrorism from women, racial and ethnic minorities, people from the Global South, victims of terrorism, and victims of counterterrorism.

Embrace and Be Transparent about the Subjectivity of One's Perspectives. CTS researchers urge scholars, analysts, practitioners, and the public to practice self-reflection and transparency with regard to their own identities, values, and worldviews rather than attempting to demonstrate impartiality about terrorism. CTS scholars reject the notion that any subject is value-free. Instead, they encourage one another to recognize the ways in which nationality, gender, class, race, and ethnicity may have influenced their own views on terrorism and counterterrorism, and to be explicit and transparent about how they believe these identities and experiences have shaped their perspectives. This also means that CTS scholars are committed to engaging in primary research in order to better understand the perspectives and experiences of the "terrorists" themselves (Jackson et al. 2011, p. 38). In particular, CTS recommends that researchers maintain constant attention to the links between power, knowledge, and the status quo bias that prevails in the contemporary international system. Researchers must always be aware of the ways in which the dominant power structure can use or misuse terrorism and counterterrorism research to do harm in the interest of the state, rather than to improve human well-being.

Here we have the opportunity to engage in some self-reflection about our own positionality, and the way that it may have affected the writing of this book. We are white, upper-middle-class women living in Western societies with advanced education. As such, we have access to extraordinary privilege that is not available to many people around the world. Furthermore, we have both spent the majority of our lives in countries that have considered themselves under attack by transnational terrorists. We have taken courses on terrorism and political violence with syllabi featuring scholarship written largely by white, male, highly-educated, European and American scholars. It has been more than fifteen years since 9/11, and the United States still has troops in Afghanistan and Iraq to combat Al Qaeda-inspired groups as well as many others that have emerged since. In our travels, we have both encountered over a decade of inconvenient security measures to protect us from terrorism. The subject has dominated the news for the majority of our adult lives. In all of the US presidential elections in which we have voted since 2000, all presidential candidates have cited terrorism as the most important national security threat facing the United States. It is impossible to deny that this constant bombardment of information and experience has strongly influenced what we think of terrorism and how we study it. On the other hand, we live in a country that is remarkably safe for white people. We have not had to develop our views about terrorism or approaches to studying it in the context of mass violence or in the context of sustained discrimination on the basis of our race or class. The experience of relative peace is a powerful indicator of our privilege. We have been able to evaluate the subject from the perspective of biased observers, rather than biased victims.

As such, our positionality may have affected the content for this book in numerous ways; it may have influenced the overall orientation of the book as attempting to explain and understand terrorism; the collection of terror groups we chose to include in discussions (e.g., a subconscious tendency to discuss groups targeting Western countries rather than non-Western ones);

BOX 7.3

CAN A STATE BE A TERRORIST? THE US ATOMIC BOMBINGS OF HIROSHIMA AND NAGASAKI

In mid-July 1945, the United States completed its first successful detonation of an atomic bomb in New Mexico. US President Harry Truman soon made the decision to use the weapons to strike Japan. The primary purpose was to force Japan to surrender unconditionally at the lowest possible cost to the United States. Truman reasoned that demonstrating the lethal power of the atomic bomb would terrify the Japanese population and government into capitulating without a ground war on the Japanese mainland. On August 6, 1945, the United States dropped an atomic bomb on Hiroshima, killing about eighty thousand Japanese people immediately. On August 9, the United States dropped a second atomic bomb on the city of Nagasaki, killing another forty thousand people. Fearing further attacks, Japan surrendered on August 15, 1945. In the weeks and months following these attacks, hundreds of thousands died from burns, radiation sickness, and impact injuries sustained during the attacks.

The attacks on Hiroshima and Nagasaki deliberately targeted civilians with massive violence meant to provoke terror in the broader Japanese population for a political purpose.

DISCUSSION QUESTIONS

- *Is it fair to call such attacks terrorism? Why, or why not?*
- *How does the label we choose to describe the attacks on Hiroshima and Nagasaki affect: (a) the popular legitimacy of this attack? (b) the legitimacy of the perpetrator? (c) the likelihood of recurrence of such attacks?*

which methods we tend to privilege (e.g., quantitative methods over interpretive ones); and even the order in which we structured the chapters (e.g., beginning with the strategic approach and ending with the critical approach). We embrace and acknowledge that our positionality has had an influence on our perspectives on terrorism. We have attempted to be transparent in this regard, have sought to mitigate potential biases in our analysis as much as possible, and have attempted to present an inclusive view into a field often segmented into two camps: the empiricists and the critics.

Part of the process of self-reflection is to identify what one is trying to achieve through one's actions. In our case, our main goal in writing this volume is to demystify terrorism, to present contrasting views about its origins and consequences, and to encourage a more thoughtful understanding of terrorism and the politics of terrorism. We do this in an attempt to minimize the harm in the world caused by misunderstandings about both terrorism and state responses to terrorism. As a consequence, although imperfect and undoubtedly flawed, we believe our aims are consistent with the professional ethic described by CTS, which we describe next.

Embrace an Emancipatory Professional Ethic. Finally, proponents of CTS commit to a specific set of personal and professional ethics in which they attempt to do no harm and elevate the well-being of all human beings as they engage in their work. Specifically, proponents of CTS say they are committed to **emancipation**—or the constant relevance of human rights, social, economic, and political justice and equality, and an end to discrimination and violence in all forms—as the primary goal of their research program. CTS scholars actively work to challenge and influence the dominant public discourse and public policy with regard to terrorism and counterterrorism (Jackson, et al. 2011, p. 41; see also Herring 2008). In this way, CTS proponents put themselves in an explicit advocacy role.

CRITIQUES OF THE CRITICAL APPROACH

The CTS approach is not without its critics. Scholars labeled as empirical terrorism scholars by CTS proponents have responded with their own self-defenses, along with critiques of the CTS program. For many critics, the CTS program positions itself against a caricature of empirical terrorism studies, which it elevates as a straw man against whom to establish a poorly-scoped research agenda. John Horgan and Michael Boyle went so far as to write that CTS is "based on a superficial reading of the current literature that creates an image of the field of study unrecognizable to scholars working within it" (2008, p. 51). Here we outline some of the primary critiques launched against CTS by those within and without the research program.

Ill-Defined Concepts and Overly-Complex Language. Critics argue that CTS poorly defines what constitutes "critical" approaches. Because CTS adopts a deliberately adversarial position vis-à-vis the state and other dominant structures, being "critical" may simply mean being adversarial. To critics of CTS, this is an unsatisfying and potentially limiting framework. Moreover, many critics of CTS have specifically criticized the notion of "emancipation," questioning what it actually means in practice. Horgan and Boyle call this notion "maddeningly vague," arguing that "it remains unclear just who has agency in their account, how 'emancipation' would be achieved, and to what substantive normative and political goals 'emancipation' is directed" (Horgan and Boyle 2008, p. 54). On the other hand, critics also suggest that the CTS approach uses unnecessarily complex language that is incredibly inaccessible. "Emancipatory praxis," "epistemology," and "neoliberalism" are not everyday terms, nor are Gramsci and Foucault household names outside of the ivory tower. To understand the main ideas of this approach, one must be steeped in critical race theory, feminist theory, and Marxist theory, among other established intellectual traditions that remain outside of mainstream educational canon. Critics of CTS suggest that in adopting such inaccessible and unnecessarily complex theories and concepts, CTS itself prevents more widespread adoption of the research program.

Overgeneralizations and Exaggerations about the Pitfalls and Biases of Empirical Research. CTS researchers assume that empirical research tends to be uncritical, unreflective, and oriented toward serving existing power structures. However, some argue that these critiques are too far-reaching, pointing out that some empirical research directly challenges existing structures, even if it adopts the nomenclature of the hegemonic state. For instance, Alexander George used positivist methodologies to identify instances where Western governments used terrorism to advance their goals in various conflicts (1991). In his seminal book, called *Western State Terrorism*, he critiques the field for its state-centric pro-West biases and uses positivist methodologies to identify instances where Western governments used terrorism to advance their goals in various conflicts. Moreover, Paul Wilkinson—described by CTS researchers as among the main beneficiaries of the terrorism industry—himself often critiqued the field for neglecting state terrorism, penning a seminal article called "Can a State Be a Terrorist?" in the journal *International Affairs* in 1981. He includes the following revealing passage:

> It is quite apparent that the French government and higher military authorities in Algeria knowingly allowed lower-level officers in charge of interrogations to make extensive use of torture, not only to obtain information, but also to terrorise the Algerians and to make the costs of helping the FLN greater than the risks of refusing to do so. In this poisoned climate of terror and counter-terror, when torture was often used as a mean of irrational vengeance against FLN atrocities, who would be bold enough to assert that the torture was morally superior to the FLN bomb-planter in Algiers? (Wilkinson 1981, p. 467)

Similarly, Weinberg and Eubank point out that "whole libraries have been devoted to the terrorism of the Nazi dictatorship" (2008, p. 191). Moreover, countless scholars have examined government repression, civilian victimization during war, human rights violations, torture, politicide, genocide, and ethnic cleansing—often in ways that directly implicate states in criminal acts of violence toward civilians. As a result, the field is rife with exceedingly sophisticated, high-quality research on such topics, which often overlap with what CTS scholars call "state terrorism."

Horgan and Boyle also point out that the failure of empirical terrorism studies to arrive at a single definition should not be interpreted as a weakness in that field. Instead, it should be interpreted as a sign that the field has long grappled with precisely the issues that CTS says it ignores—that subjectivity, political manipulation, and bias can interfere with establishing a useful concept and definition (2008, p. 57).

Many empirical terrorism researchers have written extensively on the terrorism industry, critiquing the state and its agents for exaggerating the threat of terrorism for its own cynical gains (Mueller 2006). As Horgan and Boyle point out, George and Mueller were able to advance such criticisms while relying on positivist, empirical methods, as opposed to a CTS framework (2008, p. 58).

CTS proponents tend to argue that the field has privileged positivist empirical terrorism studies over other methodological approaches. But critics point out that terrorism studies have always been multidisciplinary and open to an exceedingly diverse set of methodological and epistemo-logical approaches. Even the START program involves prominent schol-ars in political science, economics, history, anthropology, psychology, sociology, medicine, public health, and geography—many of whom have spent their time there critiquing US government policy on terrorism and counterterrorism.

Moreover, scholars have worked to integrate voices from the Global South and to better understand terrorist groups with pro-Western agendas. There-fore, the general claim that empirical terrorism scholars have never attended much to such groups is not well substantiated. Figure 7.2 roughly illustrates this point. Here we generated a Google NGRAM that lists the number of English-language books published between 1990 and 2008 on the IRA, Al Qaeda, Hamas, ETA, and the Contras. Despite a steady interest in the IRA and ETA, we can see that interest in the jihadist groups Al Qaeda and Hamas has increased considerably following 9/11. Although there was more interest in the Contras in 1990 than in any of the Islamist groups evaluated here, that interest declined steadily through 2008 as other groups rose in priority.

Support for the notion that terrorism scholars have avoided studying the Contras is thus misplaced or exaggerated, although the graph does support the broader point within CTS that scholarly interest in particular groups often coincides with state interest in the same actors.

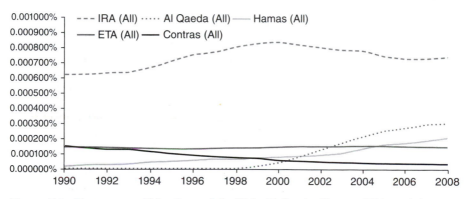

Figure 7.2 Frequency of Mentions of the IRA, Al Qaeda, Hamas, ETA, and the Contras in English Language Book Titles from 1990–2008

Furthermore, many empirical terrorism researchers agree that no research is unbiased. Instead, if empirical researchers are transparent about their biases and accountable for their choices, they can minimize the effects of bias. What's more, the notion that empirical terrorism researchers tend to be blind to their biases has yet to be demonstrated. And CTS researchers can be equally accused of motivated bias—the fact that their strongly-held beliefs about entrenched power structures blind them to evidence than may contravene these beliefs.

Overgeneralizations and Exaggerations about the Complicity of Empirical Terrorism Researchers with the Status Quo. Many empirical terrorism scholars have been surprised (and sometimes offended) to discover that CTS researchers have labeled them as complicit in state violence due to their having published "uncritical" scholarship on terrorism or counterterrorism, or due to their involvement in conducting studies funded by government sources. Many empirical terrorism researchers have arrived at results that are highly critical of dominant systems (e.g., Pape 2005, Bloom 2005), although they may not adhere to all of the normative commitments of CTS. As Weinberg and Eubank write:

> For those committed to the belief that terrorism's root causes include poverty, economic inequalities, social discrimination, and the absence of democracy, the findings have been disappointing. There are evidently exceptions here and there, but by and large, those identified as engaged in terrorist violence do not come from settings of great poverty. Nor at the individual level do terrorists come from backgrounds of poverty. Some terrorists have come from populations victimised by a government's discriminatory practices, but others have not. The advent of democracy does not seem to usher in a terrorism-free political life either—as citizens of Lebanon, Russia, Turkey, Sri Lanka, and now Iraq, can attest. Widespread poverty may have given rise to terrorism in Peru (the Shining Path), Northern Ireland, and the Palestinian territories and refugee camps. But we should remember that Germany and Japan, among the world's most prosperous countries, experienced serious terrorism problems in the 1970s and 1980s, and that the Red Brigades, Front Line, and ETA waged serious terrorist campaigns in the wealthiest regions of Italy and Spain (the Basque region) at about the same time. In other words, modifying the existing distribution of wealth, power, and status in society may be desirable in itself, but such changes rarely bear a direct causal relationship to the severity of a country's level of terrorist violence. The linkages between broad economic and social developments and terrorist violence appear to be complex. If this result seems to be a defence of the status quo, it seems the unintentional outcome of multiple "problem solving" investigations (2008, p. 193).

In other words, if multiple studies representing a diverse range of methods from numerous perspectives invalidate some of the implicit claims of CTS—such as the claim that neoliberal economic policies are linked to nonstate terrorism—this may simply be due to the fact that such policies do not lead to terrorism. Although this may be comforting news for states promoting neoliberal economic policies, this does not mean that such findings are invalid, that they will help the dominant system remain dominant, that the researchers themselves do not recognize the difficult normative stakes involved in such findings, or that they cannot conduct such studies responsibly.

Moreover, the CTS claim that different terrorism researchers have little autonomy or independence over their scholarship because they are subject to the norms and practices of their project's funders is controversial. Many empirical terrorism scholars see themselves as having a great deal of agency regarding the projects they accept, how they conduct their research, and whether the outcomes of their studies are uncritical or critical of the dominant system. Critics also argue that CTS has an overly essentialist notion of the state, seeing it as a monolithic entity. In reality, critics argue, states are nothing more than groups of people who are, themselves, capable of exercising their own agency and opposing the state when it suits their interest or conscience to do so. If states were monolithic, then how do we explain the powerful oppositional impact of defectors like Chelsea Manning and Edward Snowden?

Some empirical terrorism researchers acknowledge that much of the popular literature that has emerged about terrorism is of a very poor quality and often yields disturbing or dangerous effects on the public discourse about terrorism. But they also argue that these types of popular books and writings are wholly different from the "serious work done by real scholars in the field," much of which already integrates some of the main suggestions of CTS—like engaging in primary research or "talking to terrorists" (Horgan and Boyle 2008, p. 58). Indeed, Horgan and Boyle view the conflation of sloppy popular writings and empirical terrorism scholarship of an "aggressive" reading of the accumulated literature, which CTS scholars have wrongly conflated to set up a straw man account of the field that is easy to dismantle (Horgan and Boyle 2008, p. 61).

Redundancy. In his 2009 critique of CTS, historian Richard English suggests that CTS is a redundant research program that "is not needed to tell us that research is seldom objective or value-neutral" (p. 380). Instead, English argues, almost all empirical terrorism researchers active in the field have recognized and embraced this reality for decades. Moreover, many of the concerns of CTS—such as social justice, human well-being, and freedom—are equally interesting and motivating for most empirical terrorism researchers. As such, critics argue that CTS's claim to advancing a novel research program is an exaggerated one (Horgan and Boyle 2008, p. 51). Without advancing new knowledge—but instead focusing on constantly deconstructing others' knowledge—some critics worry that "the field will become so self-conscious that it will in effect become the study of itself" and that this "may lead to a progressive disengagement from the subject itself" (Weinberg and Eubank 2008, p. 194).

Further Segmentation of the Field. Critics of CTS suggest that by advancing such an aggressive and adversarial position vis-à-vis empirical terrorism studies, many of the valid points within CTS will not have their desired effect on the broader research program. In particular, even some CTS researchers acknowledge the risk that "the critical side of the field will remain isolated and marginalized, and as a consequence remain locked out of being able to influence policymakers or compete for research funding" (Jackson et al. 2011, p. 47).

This critique is matched with the concern that CTS is too impractical to affect political decisions. Because of its focus on the politics of knowledge and the production of knowledge, critics suggest that CTS is far too abstract, theoretical, and academic to appeal to more popular or policy audiences. Moreover, the approach offers a multitude of critiques but few practical, well-defined solutions.

Similarly, some critics worry that CTS will be marginalized because of its tolerance of lapses in academic rigor in the name of methodological pluralism.

Hypocrisy. Finally, some critics have pointed to various practices within CTS about which proponents of CTS criticize others. First, empirical terrorism researchers are often accused of having unreflective biases, but as Horgan and Boyle point out, CTS researchers are equally subject to ideological biases that affect the questions they ask and the answers they develop (2008, p. 54–55). Although CTS researchers may be more explicit than many empirical terrorism researchers about their biases, CTS has made an explicit choice about which norms and values it wishes to advance. One could thus respond that empirical terrorism researchers have also fully reflected on their choices, and arrived at different conclusions about the norms and values they wish to advance.

Second, critics have argued that CTS has similarly chosen to be policy-relevant, albeit to "a different audience, including non-governmental organizations (NGOs), civil society, [rather] than just government and security services. In other words, CTS aims to whisper into the ear of the prince, but it is just a different prince" (Horgan and Boyle 2008, p. 59). Again, CTS has made a value-based judgment, and many empirical terrorism researchers may have made such judgments for themselves and arrived at different conclusions about whom to support. Adjudicating between these two choices—and identifying which ones are "right" or "wrong"—is not as simple as CTS researchers suggest.

Third, some critics have argued that the CTS call for incorporating primary material into terrorism research is impractical. In his critique of CTS on this basis, Richard English writes that "the quite justified CTS demand that scholars focus on first-hand research must be operationalised. This demand is repeatedly made in the pages of this fine book, but the notes to the chapters themselves contain, for example, very few references to interviews conducted by the authors themselves" (2009, p. 382).

Finally, some critics point out that despite all of the pejorative and subjective meanings of the word "terrorism," CTS researchers still choose to use the term. Indeed, such researchers use the term "terrorism" to describe their own research program, and as part of the name of the main academic journal involved in publishing work on this topic (*Critical Studies on Terrorism*). Thus, calling out empirical terrorism studies for using the term in a self-serving and unreflective way strikes many critics as unsatisfactory.

SUMMARY

In this chapter, we introduced and evaluated critical approaches to the study of terrorism. We looked at the underlying assumptions, assertions, and practical implications of critical approaches. We reviewed several critiques of the theory and presented some evidence demonstrating why the approach remains controversial. We also reviewed several cases—including the 2015 Paris attacks, the 1972 Munich Olympics Massacre, and the use of atomic weapons in Hiroshima and Nagaski—as ways to demonstrate and discuss the reasons why critical terrorism scholars aim to push more self-reflective practices forward in the field.

Discussion Questions

1. In what ways do your own values, identity, and environment affect your views about terrorism?
2. Is it possible to conduct objective, dispassionate research about terrorism? Why or why not?
3. Is there a "terrorism industry"?
4. Is it possible to engage in positivist empirical research but maintain a normative commitment to emancipatory praxis? Why or why not?
5. Look up several recent trials of terrorists in the United States, the United Kingdom, and Canada. Read some details about these trials. Who are the accused? How do the publicly reported details of the trial proceedings reinforce or contest state-centric perceptions of terrorism? Are there differences across cases? Across countries? How might you explain their similarities and differences from a critical perspective?

KEY TAKEAWAYS

- Critical approaches—including feminist, post-colonial, and Marxist variants—attempt to understand terrorism from a critical epistemology. Instead of taking empirical knowledge for granted, these approaches emphasize the power structures that produce widely accepted knowledge in the first place.

- CTS approaches argue that terrorism is not an objective reality, but rather a socially-constructed, pejorative phenomenon. They suggest that most empirical terrorism studies adopt conscious or subconscious biases that reinforce state-centric, Euro-centric, patriarchal, status quo power hierarchies. They also suggest that preoccupations with terrorism tend to obscure the oft-legitimate grievances underlying dissent. They reject problem-solving approaches as producing empirically weak research that favors the status quo.

- CTS asks scholars and observers to engage in routine self-critique, acknowledge the ways that positionality creates inescapable subjectivity, and adopt an emancipatory ethic in their work. They also suggest that the field should be much more open to pluralistic methodologies—particularly with regard to creating inclusive processes and institutions to elevate voices that are marginalized in the field.

- Critics of CTS suggest that the approach misstates and overgeneralizes its critiques about empirical terrorism studies; that the approach misstates its originality; that the CTS research program is unnecessarily complex and inaccessible; that it threatens to marginalize itself further by alienating many potential allies within the field; and that proponents of the approach have failed to implement their own suggestion of creating a more inclusive and pluralistic research community.

SUGGESTED FURTHER READINGS

Barsamian, David. 2001. "The U.S. Is Leading a Terrorist State: An interview with Noam Chomsky," *Monthly Review* (1 November). Available online at http://monthlyreview.org/2001/11/01/the-united-states-is-a-leading-terrorist-state/. Last accessed 13-January-2017.

Blakeley, Ruth. 2007. "Bringing the State Back into Terrorism Studies," *European Political Science* 6 (3): 228–235. doi:10.1057/palgrave.eps.2210139.

Chomsky, Noam, John Junkerman, and Takei Masakazu. 2011. *Power and Terror: Conflict, Hegemony, and the Rule of Force*. London: Routledge.

Chomsky, Noam, and Andre Vitchek. 2013 *On Western Terrorism: From Hiroshima to Drone Warfare*. London: Pluto Press.

Donahue, Thomas J. 2013. "Terrorism, Moral Conceptions, and Moral Innocence." *The Philosophical Form* 44 (4): 413–435. doi:10.1111/phil.12021.

Egerton, Frantz, 2009. "A Case for a Critical Approach to Terrorism." *European Political Science* 8 (1): 57–67. doi:10.1057/eps.2008.47

Erlenbusch, Verena. 2014. "How (Not) to Study Terrorism." *Critical Review of International Social and Political Philosophy* 17 (4): 470–491. doi.org/10.1080/136982 30.2013.767040

English, Richard. 2009. "The Future of Terrorism Studies." *Critical Studies on Terrorism* 2 (2): 377–382. doi:10.1080/17539150903025119.

Fanon, Frantz. 1963. *The Wretched of the Earth*. New York: Grove Press.

Gunning, Jeroen. 2007. "Babies and Bathwaters: Reflecting On The Pitfalls Of Critical Terrorism Studies." *European Political Science* 6 (3): 236–243. doi:10.1057/palgrave. eps.2210144.

Gunning, Jeroen. 2007. "A Case for Critical Terrorism Studies?" *Government and Opposition*, 42 (3): 363–393. doi:10.1111/j.1477-7053.2007.00228.x

Herman, Edward S, and Gerry O'Sullivan. 1989. *The "Terrorism" Industry: The Experts and Institutions that Shape our View of Terror*. New York: Pantheon Books.

Herring, Eric. 2008. "Critical Terrorism Studies: An Activist Scholar Perspective." *Critical Studies On Terrorism* 1 (2): 197–212. doi:10.1080/17539150802187507.

Horgan, John, and Michael J. Boyle. 2008. "A Case Against 'Critical Terrorism Studies'." *Critical Studies on Terrorism* 1 (1): 51–64. doi:10.1080/17539150701848225.

Jackson, Richard. 2005. *Writing The War On Terrorism: Language, Politics and Counterterrorism*. Manchester: Manchester University Press.

Jackson, Richard. 2007. "The Core Commitments of Critical Terrorism Studies," *European Political Science* 6 (3): 244–251. doi:10.1057/palgrave.eps.2210141.

Jackson, Richard. 2007. "Constructing Enemies: 'Islamic Terrorism' in Political and Academic Discourse." *Government and Opposition* 42 (3): 394–426. doi:10.1111/ j.1477-7053.2007.00229.x.

Jackson, Richard, Marie Breen Smyth, and Jeroen Gunning, eds. 2009. *Critical Terrorism Studies: A New Research Agenda*. Hoboken: Taylor and Francis.

Jackson, Richard. 2009. "The Study of Political Terror After 11 September 2001: Problems, Challenges and Future Developments." *Political Studies Review* 7 (2): 171–184. doi:10.1111/j.1478-9299.2009.00177.x.

Jackson, Richard, Lee Jarvis, Jeroen Gunning, and Marie Breen Smyth. 2011. *Terrorism: A Critical Introduction*. London: Palgrave Macmillan.

Jaggar, Alison M. 2005. "What Is Terrorism, Why Is It Wrong, and Could It Ever Be Morally Permissible?" *Journal of Social Philosophy* 36 (2): 202–217. doi:10.1111/ j.1467-9833.2005.00267.x.

Jarvis, Lee. 2009. "The Spaces and Faces of Critical Terrorism Studies." *Security Dialogue* 40 (1): 5–27. doi:10.1177/0967010608100845.

Jaggar, Alison M. 2005. "What is Terrorism, Why is it Wrong, and Could it Ever Be Morally Permissible?" *Journal of Soc ial Philosophy* 36 (2): 202–217.

Mueller, John. 2006. *Overblown: How Politicians and the Terrorism Industry Inflate National Security Threats and Why We Believe Them*. New York, NY: Free Press.

Smyth, Marie Breen. 2007. "A Critical Research Agenda for the Study of Political Terror." *European Political Science* 6 (3): 260–267. doi:10.1057/palgrave.eps.2210138.

Stump, Jacob L., and Priya Dixit. 2013. *Critical Terrorism Studies: An Introduction to Research Methods.* Hoboken: Taylor and Francis.

Weinberg, Leonard, and William Eubank. 2008. "Problems with the Critical Studies Approach to The Study of Terrorism." *Critical Studies on Terrorism* 1 (2): 185–195. doi:10.1080/17539150802184595.

Wilkinson, Paul. 1981. "Can a State Be a 'Terrorist?'" *International Affairs* 57 (3): 467–472. doi:10.2307/2619580.

PART II

Explaining Terrorist Behavior

In Part I, we looked at six analytical approaches with distinct sets of assumptions and implications. Table I summarizes them.

In Part II, we apply these frameworks to various puzzles in the study of terrorism, which include variation in terrorist target selection (Chapter 8), suicide terrorism (Chapter 9), the provision of social services by terrorist groups (Chapter 10), state sponsorship of terrorism (Chapter 11), and variation in the prevalence of men and women in terror groups (Chapter 12). Each chapter identifies the empirical puzzle and its relevance in the real world. It then reviews how one can use the competing approaches to explain the puzzle, the prevailing evidence available to address the puzzle, and some key takeaways related to it.

TABLE I: Six Analytic Approaches Compared

	Strategic Approach	Organizational Approach	Psychological Approach	Ideological Approach	Structural Approach	Critical Approach
Source of choice	Strategic choice	Internal group dynamics	Personal psychology	Ideology	Environmental factors	Injustice
Motivation for terrorism	To pursue change and compensate for weakness	To provide incentives for members to remain; to satisfy social needs	To satisfy psychological impulses	To fulfill requirements of ideology	To pursue change in environment and compensate for weakness	Intolerable conditions imposed by more violent states
Group structure	Assumed (unitary)	Not assumed (fragmented and contested)	Not assumed (fragmented and contested)	Assumed (unitary)	Assumed (unitary)	Not assumed (unspecified)
Primary audience	Opponent government	Competitor groups	Unspecified	Nonbelievers	Opponent government	Unspecified
Patterns of terrorism	Tit for tat; substitution effect	Unpredictable; seemingly random	Random	Against nonbelievers & "sell-outs"	Contingent on motivation and opportunity	Predictable based on source of the injustice
Practical implications	Increase costs, decrease benefits of terrorism	Do not impose external pressure. Encourage exit instead.	Early identification & interdiction.	Early identification & interdiction. Massive repression.	Increase costs, decrease benefits of terrorism.	Emancipation
Observable implications	Terrorism ends when the group fails or achieves its stated aims.	Terrorism does not end until organization disintegrates.	Terrorism is a constant but does not escalate because the pool of potential terrorists is relatively limited.	Terrorism does not end until group is totally destroyed.	Terrorism happens where it is easy and does not occur when it is difficult.	Empirical terrorism research will produce findings that reinforce the state-centric status quo.

CHAPTER 8

TERRORIST TARGET SELECTION

Learning Objectives

After reading this chapter, readers should be able to:

- Enumerate the ways in which target selection might vary across terrorist groups.
- Explain how different approaches to studying terrorism address variation in the targeting decisions of groups.
- Provide examples of how terrorist groups have varied in their target selection.
- Explain how the target selection decisions of groups should inform counterterrorism policy.
- Discuss the risks involved in CBRN terrorism.

> "It is foolish to hunt the tiger when there are plenty of sheep around."
>
> —HAMAS TRAINING MANUAL

> "It is forbidden to kill those who do not fight . . . It is forbidden to combat those who are unarmed, who cause no harm, and from whom sedition is not feared, like children, women, the helpless . . ."
>
> —ABDALLAH AZZAM, AS QUOTED IN KEPEL AND
> MILELLI, 2008, P. 128

> "After the enemies with guns have been wiped out, there will still be enemies without guns; they are bound to struggle desperately against us, and we must never regard these enemies lightly."
>
> —CHAIRMAN MAO ZEDONG, REPORT TO THE SECOND
> PLENARY SESSION OF THE SEVENTH CENTRAL
> COMMITTEE OF THE COMMUNIST PARTY OF CHINA.
> MARCH 5, 1949, SELECTED WORKS, VOL. IV, P. 364.

THE PUZZLE

How do terrorist groups select the targets, venues, and locations of their attacks? Why do some terrorist groups tend to attack **discriminate** targets whereas others attack **indiscriminate** targets? Why do some choose inter-national, as opposed to domestic targets? Why do they choose to attack cer-tain countries over others? These are just some of the puzzles associated with the **targeting decisions** of terrorists. This chapter investigates how targets of terrorism have changed over time, and surveys the various ways that different approaches to studying terrorism have addressed this varia-tion. We are particularly interested in identifying the underlying drivers of terrorists' target choices. Are the actions of a terror group a response to the evolution of state counterterrorism policies; are they the result of strategic decision-making; or are they the product of ideological orientations or orga-nizational dynamics?

The University of Maryland's Global Terrorism Database (GTD) provides data on the targeting choices of groups, disaggregating terrorism targets into more than twenty categories that range from government, business, tourism, private citizens, military, police, and many in between. Figure 8.1 presents the overall distribution of terrorist target selection from 1970–2015. Note that over 53 percent of the attacks targeted civilians.

Other studies show that among 119 terrorist groups active between 2002–2012, approximately 32 percent of attacks targeted civilians (Moghadam 2015). About 16 percent of attacks during this same period targeted military installations or personnel, and over 15 percent targeted government officials. Police forces were targets in over 13 percent of terrorist attacks during this time period, with the remaining attacks constituting a wide variety of other target types (ibid).

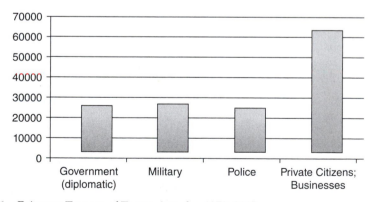

Figure 8.1 Primary Targets of Terror Attacks, 1970–2015

Source: GTD

EXPLAINING HOW AND WHY TERRORISTS CHOOSE THEIR TARGETS

Strategic approaches to understanding terrorism view terrorist groups as rational actors who engage in violence instrumentally. For this approach, terror attacks are means by which they communicate their political goals. As such, groups select their targets for attack to demonstrate their resolve and credibility and to accrue the greatest benefits to their stated cause. Proponents of this approach claim that target choices reflect terrorists' aims of posing a credible threat to their opponent. A particularly devastating attack against the civilian population of a target state, for instance, might better convince the enemy of the group's power and resolve than a smaller attack on military forces stationed abroad. This perspective is consistent with Kydd and Walter's (2006) logic that terrorism is a form of **costly signaling**, whereby weak groups use terror to demonstrate that they are credible adversaries.

Indeed, large-scale attacks on soft targets such as shopping centers, public transport, and religious institutions may spark a number of the strategic logics associated with terrorism—in particular attrition, intimidation, and provocation (Kydd and Walter 2006). A sustained campaign of attacks that kills many civilians over a period of time might persuade an opponent government of the terror group's strength and resolve, and may also provoke an overreaction marked by repressive countermeasures. For example, Kydd and Walter suggest that one might interpret the 9/11 attacks on New York's financial district that killed thousands of civilians as examples of the attrition and provocation hypotheses: "al-Qaida may have been attempting to increase the cost of US policy of stationing soldiers in Saudi Arabia . . . [and] trying to goad the United States into an extreme military response." A large-scale and highly repressive response could benefit Al Qaeda's by attracting more supporters to its cause (Walter and Kydd 2006, p. 59).

A strategic logic might also help to explain why terrorists target civilians instead of an opponent's armed forces. Unlike attacks that result in the deaths of soldiers or members of the security forces, attacks that kill civilians inspire high levels of fear among the target audience and convey a political message with a particularly resounding effect (O'Neill 2005). The image of civilians dying is generally much more powerful and remarkable than the image of attacks on members of the armed forces, who assume greater risks as part of their jobs. Through a strategic lens, the selection of civilian targets thus represents a value-maximizing solution for terrorist groups.

Other studies based on rational actor perspectives highlight the selective nature of some attacks that target civilians. In his work on the Algerian civil war, Stathis Kalyvas suggests that the massacres conducted by armed Islamist groups such as the National Liberation Front (FLN) were part of the groups' rational strategy to maximize popular support (1999). Massacres of ordinary Algerians were in fact targeted killings; insurgents selectively killed civilians in the context of fragmented and unstable rule, when many Algerians were defecting en masse toward the side of the state. Various militant groups thus employed terror strategically to punish those who supported the state and to deter other civilians from doing so. Evidence from Algeria's civil war suggests that the FLN targeted individuals who were either local opponents (especially members of the security forces, informants, etc.); people who supported rival guerrilla organizations; or former sympathizers who switched sides, refused to help the rebels, or appeared likely to switch sides (ibid). Indeed, Kalyvas suggests that completely indiscriminate massacres—those that targeted Algerians at random—would have likely backfired against the Islamist groups, pulling away popular support and further prompting civilians to support the incumbent regime.

In addition to explaining variation in the choice of discriminate over indiscriminate targets, strategic approaches offer insight into why some groups may turn to selecting international, as opposed to domestic, targets. Attacking foreign nationals is strategic for a number of reasons, even if the terror group is seeking to gain political influence in its home country. For instance, Neumayer and Plümper (2011) find that groups with domestic agendas attack foreign targets when they believe that such attacks will grant them the upper hand against domestic opponents, and earn them additional support from local peers. This logic is particularly powerful when it comes to explaining the prevalence of anti-American terrorism worldwide. Transnational terrorism against US targets is more likely to come from groups based in countries that receive significant levels of military support from the United States, or that host more US military personnel. These groups attack outside targets in order to gain a strategic advantage over the government that they oppose. Staging attacks against Americans in particular is strategically valuable if the United States retreats from the country or pulls back aid in the face of these attacks—an outcome that would ease the terrorists' political battle at home (Crenshaw 2001).

If the strategic approach were right, we would expect to see terror groups achieve their desired outcomes after attacking their intended targets. Furthermore, we should see terrorists claim responsibility over their attacks only when they expect to gain politically from doing so (Abrahms 2016). Yet recent studies across disciplines have found that escalating to terrorism and to high-casualty attacks rarely, if ever, encourages government concessions. In fact, terrorism is arguably more effective at lowering the likelihood of concessions, casting significant doubt on the plausibility of strategic explanations (Abrahms 2012; Crenshaw 2007; Jones and Libicki 2008; Cronin 2009). What's more, brutal attacks against civilians have caused splits within groups, precipitating their demise (see Chapter 15). The **Groupe Salafiste pour la Prédication et le Combat** (GSPC) in Algeria, for example, was formed after several commanders of the **Groupe Islamiste Armé** (GIA) grew concerned that brutal tactics such as beheadings were only working to alienate their Algerian constituency (Harmon 2010). Evidence shows that terrorist leaders also warn their members of the potentially counterproductive effects of indiscriminate, high-casualty attacks against civilians. For instance, **Abdullah Yusuf Azzam** of Al Qaeda and **Ernesto "Che" Guevara** repeatedly called on their foot soldiers to refrain from attacking civilians, emphasizing that indiscriminate would turn people against their movements. Other groups such as the FARC in Colombia, the PIRA in Ireland, and the PKK in Turkey have provided similar guidance. Documents found in Osama bin Laden's compound in Pakistan following his death indicate that Al Qaeda leaders frequently wrote to one another and to affiliated groups about the need to minimize civilian casualties—in particular among Muslims—to avoid marginalizing themselves from such communities (Bergen 2013).

Organizational approaches to understanding target selection focus primarily on the pressures that emerge from the groups' organizational environments. As such, these theories offer that inter-group rivalry, internal group fissures, or factors related to a group's overall capacity, such as its size, age, etc., provide the best explanations for variation in the targeting decisions of groups (Asal et al. 2009).

Some organizational theories suggest that terror groups select their targets according to their group's overall strength in terms of size. For example, Chalmers Johnson finds that smaller and relatively weak groups tend to attack undefended civilian targets because soldiers seem so invulnerable to attack (2000). On the other hand, he argues that larger groups with higher organizational capacity are more likely to choose seemingly invulnerable targets, because they perceive the playing field to be more even. Group strength opens doors for targeting a wide variety of targets, and group strength goes beyond numbers of members, funds, or weapons. For example, recent studies find that terrorist groups are likelier to stage maritime attacks when they are larger in size, control territory, and have many connections to other groups (Asal and Hastings 2015). Attacking targets at sea requires terror groups to have a unique set of skills, as well as specific materials, such as boats, large amounts of fuel, and training. Connections to other groups help to recruit a more diversified and experienced set of fighters, elicit greater access to necessary skills, and provide more materials for attacks. And control of territory may also engender the aspiration to control the waters that border this territory for both defensive and offensive operations. The LTTE, for example, formed a naval subgroup called the Sea Tigers in 1984 to smuggle supplies to its bases of operation. It also destroyed nearly thirty Sri Lankan naval vessels and civilian cargo ships (ibid).

A terror group's age might also be an important factor in explaining its target selection—in particular the continuation of specific targeting decisions (or **tactical repertoires**) that endure over time. When a group first makes the decision to employ terror to achieve its goals, it is likely to select a specific target category it deems the most opportune or strategic. In the early stages of a group's existence, violence may be a means to an end. Over time, however, violence might become an end in itself as the group becomes more

Photo 8.1 The USS *Cole* is towed away from the port city of Aden, Yemen, into open sea by the Military Sealift Command ocean-going tug USNS *Catawba*

involved in the habit and routine of killing. This dynamic helps to explain why some terrorist groups commit increasingly frequent attacks on civilian targets as they age (Asal et al. 2009). The continuation of particularly lethal attacks might also help older terrorist organizations prove that they are still relevant compared with their rivals and draw in additional recruits (Asal and Rethemeyer 2008b).

Organizational approaches also suggest that groups select their targets based on the behavior of the other political groups that operate in their environment. In particular, some studies suggest that groups turn to planning and launching mass casualty attacks against civilians in highly competitive environments. Consider the example of Al Qaeda. According to Bruce Hoffman, the extent of the group's power and popular appeal in certain parts of the world is a direct result of the devastation wreaked by the 9/11 attacks (2006). The sophistication of the attacks drew in many new recruits, and signaled the strength and prestige of the organization both to its targeted opponents in the West and to rival Islamist groups. As the number of violent organizations that exists in a particular conflict context increases, organizational theories posit that more groups target civilians to prove their worthiness over that of their competitors.

Other organizational approaches underscore the fact that terror groups consciously learn from one another when it comes to tactics as well as target selection. Right-wing groups in Germany, for example, emulated the targeting choices of left-wing terrorist organizations in the hopes of linking their movements to a clearer purpose and more attainable goal (Hoffman 2006, p. 238). These groups were also envious of the attention, status, and tactical victories of left-wing groups. Their survival and continued relevance thus depended on innovation when it came to target selection. These dynamics help to explain why right-wing groups turned to a more lethally discriminate campaign of terrorism in the 1980s, one that was more in line with left-wing patterns of attacks. They turned to assassinating prominent Jews and communists and political leaders, all in an attempt to "bring neo-Nazi terrorism up to the level of that carried out by the radical Left" (Hasselbach, as quoted in Hoffman 2006, p. 239).

Cooperation between terrorists might also lead to groups diversify their targets (Horowitz et al. 2017). By building relationships with other groups, terrorists learn and adopt new tactics (Horowitz 2010), which may be geared towards different types of targets. An alliance with another group may also alter their reliance on discriminate or selective forms of violence. On average, a more varied tactical repertoire also leads to a wider variety of targets. The adoption of suicide terrorism, for instance, increases the propensity of terrorist groups to attack both hard targets (those associated with the state, such as security forces) and soft targets (such as population centers), as opposed to targeting only one of these categories (Horowitz et al. 2017). Moreover, studies show that tactical diversification on the part of terrorist groups increases the number of targets that a state must defend, as well as the methods that the state uses to defend them (Wilkinson 2014). Therefore, the adoption of new counterterrorism measures by a government is an observable implication of terrorist tactical diversification that alters the groups' target selection.

Finally, organizational approaches might help to understand some of the more obscure or understudied targeting decisions of terrorist groups. For example, why do some groups sometimes target their own members with violence? A straightforward answer to this question is that terror groups often adopt violence as a way to punish indiscipline, insubordination, disloyalty, or betrayal within the group. For instance, the IRA punished suspected informants with violence (Monaghan 2004). But a less direct explanation for internal violence focuses on internal rifts within the organization, particularly threats to a group's leadership. Many terror groups are comprised of ambitious yet inexperienced members who call for immediate and spectacular action. At times, this new generation may ultimately assassinate senior commanders they see as weak, indecisive, unimaginative, or corrupt. In turn, terror group leaders who feel threatened from within and may use both internal and external violence to ensure their own security and survival. An example is the choice of some terror groups to target children. Drawing on terrorist-led school massacres that occurred Peshawar, Pakistan and Beslan, North Ossetia (Russia) in 2014 and 2004, respectively, Biberman and Zahid (2016) suggest that decisions to target children are a product of internal rifts within terrorist groups, and external factors that threaten the groups' existence. More specifically, internal divisions lead to the emergence of an outbidding mechanism between group members—in particular ambitious commanders-to-be—who take drastic steps to prove their worth over internal rivals. Moreover, groups who are under serious pressure from the state and on the brink of extinction shift their ambitions to survival, leading them to pursue particularly shocking tactics that attract media attention—such as the targeting of children. In short, dramatic acts of violence such as the massacre of school children, but also the targeting of civilians more generally, often result from a lack of stable leadership, which encourages the younger, inexperienced generation of group members to prove their commitment to a cause via hyper-violence (Abrahms and Potter 2015).

If socio-organizational approaches are correct, we would expect to see the timing of shifts in targeting strategies to coincide with intra- or inter-organizational dynamics. Change in leadership, for example, would prompt groups to move away from or towards targeting civilians. Alternatively, the splitting of an organization into two groups might lead to the adoption of different targeting choices. If the two resulting groups engage in a competition to outbid one another, an observable implication could be heightened attacks against civilians, designed to signal one side's relevance over another.

However, a potential weakness of organizational approaches is that many dynamics that occur internally within groups are difficult to observe from the outside. Furthermore, organizational dynamics may be relatively static in nature, failing to explain why groups change their targeting strategies during periods of organizational stability or cohesion.

In addition, some organizational theories produce contradictory implications. For example, while some suggest that large, highly capable groups should be more likely to attack hard targets, such as members of the armed forces, others suggest that large, highly capable groups are actually more likely to target civilians. Moreover, as we saw in the case of explanations that seek to link cooperation among groups to tactical diversification, these theories are indeterminate when it comes to predicting whether groups with many relationships will turn increasingly towards hard or soft targets. Finally, if theories that stress the role of internal rivalries in predicting target selection are correct, we should see far more groups than we actually do engage in hyper-violent forms of behavior against highly sensitive targets, such as children. In reality, though a number of groups experience internal divisions within their ranks, massacres of children by terror groups remain mercifully rare.

Ideological explanations of terrorist target selection contend that ideology, or group beliefs, demarcate the range of targets the group perceives as legitimate. As discussed in Chapter 5, founding members often codify the value systems and identities of groups and formalize them into manifestos. Group ideologies change subtly over time and are thus most appropriate for understanding variation in target selection across groups, as opposed to within groups over time.

The dominant beliefs of a particular terrorist group may supply terrorists with an initial motive for action and provide a lens through which to interpret events and the actions of others. Targets seen as legitimate for the group are those deemed guilty of transgressing the terrorists' moral framework. An ideology allows terrorists to justify their violence by displacing responsibility onto their victims, whom they hold responsible for the grievances that led them to violence in the first place (Drake 1998). Scholars suspect that groups whose ideological leanings possess exclusivist narratives are less likely to discriminate in their selection of targets, as they view entire populations who are "on the other side" as legitimate targets (Asal and Rethemeyer 2008a).

Figure 8.2 presents a simple cross-tabulation of terrorist target selection and ideology for a number of groups active in Western Europe from 1965 to 2005.

These summary statistics provide preliminary support for several hypotheses derived by ideological approaches. For instance, nationalist-separatist groups are most likely to target members of the security services, particularly military and police forces. Such groups view these targets as active supporters of what they consider to be a "foreign" occupier. In Spain, the Basque

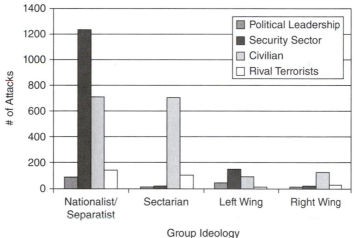

Figure 8.2 Target Selection by Ideological Classification in Western Europe, 1965–2005

Source: Wright 2013 (data are from Domestic Terrorist Victims (DTV); de la Calle and Sanchez-Cuenca 2011 and Terrorism in Western Europe: Event Data (TWEED); Engene 2007)

separatist group ETA, for example, frequently targeted the Guardia Civil (a national paramilitary-style police force), the national police, and the military as their primary targets (see Figure 8.3). Law enforcement, members of the Spanish armed forces, and government installations collectively made up as much as much as 44 percent of all ETA attacks between 1970 and 2011 (see also Llera, Mata and Irwin 1993).

But there are other reasons that ideology might restrict the range of acceptable terrorism targets. In the case of left-wing terrorism, for instance, Maoist influence specifies the list of enemies towards which groups should direct violence: "all those with imperialism—the warlords, the bureaucrats, the comprador class, the big Landlord class and the reactionary section of the intelligentsia attached to them" (Mao Zedong 1926, p. 19). As the case of the Red Brigades in Italy demonstrates, one of the main targets of left-wing groups has been government installations and members of the police forces. These patterns reflect groups' ultimate aim of bringing down the state as well as a desire to minimize damage to the poor and working class. Another primary target of terror attacks staged by the Red Brigades was business, which reflected the group's goals of overthrowing the capitalist political and economic system. The Red Army Faction (RAF) in Germany, which generally framed their objective as the destruction of international capitalism and imperialism as a whole, chose to target US military facilities and other perceived symbols of US imperialism.

Consider also the 1969 terrorist attack by the **Tupamaros-West Berlin (TW)**, a precursor to the RAF, in West Berlin. Hoffman (2006) writes that the group wanted to stage an attack that would attract attention to their cause, which was to publicize the plight of the Palestinian people and

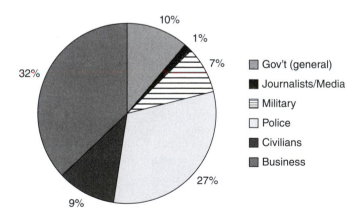

Figure 8.3   ETA Attacks by Target Type, 1970–2011

Source: GTD

demonstrate the West German left's solidarity with Palestinians. Its members attempted to bomb the Jewish Community Center in Berlin on the anniversary of Kristallnacht during Hitler's reign. By striking this specific target on this particular date, the group sought to draw a deliberate parallel between Israeli oppression of Palestinians and Nazi persecution of the Jews (Hoffman 2006, p. 232). Though the bomb never exploded, the story nevertheless made news headlines around the world, suggesting that the decision to strike this particular target was an effective one for raising attention for the TW.

Sectarian and extremist right-wing groups are both more likely than other groups to target civilians, as well as the members of other violent groups. Right-wing organizations typically use terror to protect the existing status quo, and at times they claim that their actions are intended to protect the state from subversion. Empirical evidence also suggests that right-wing groups are likely to target members of nationalist or left-wing groups active in the same political context in an attempt to undermine rivals. For example, a paramilitary organization active in Colombia during the 1980s called **Death to Kidnappers** frequently targeted communist insurgents from the **April 19th Movement** or the **FARC**, as well as their supporters, to protect the economic interests of drug cartels and Colombian politicians. Bruce Hoffman likens right-wing terrorism to "mindless 'street' violence" and draws attention to the high number of unsophisticated attacks that target immigrants, refugees, and other foreigners that these groups perpetrate (2006, p. 236). In Europe today, the pattern of right-wing attacks remains largely unchanged from its origins in the 1970s. Most instances of right-wing terrorism in the region involve

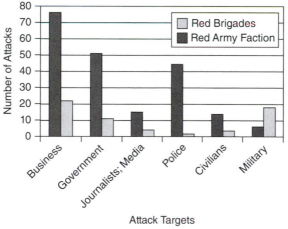

Figure 8.4   Target Selection of the Red Brigades & the Red Army Faction

Source: GTD

attacks on refugee shelters, immigrant workers' hostels, anarchist houses, political party offices, guest workers, Arab and African immigrants, and Jewish-owned businesses.

Finally, ideological approaches help to explain the targeting decisions of religious groups, and why attacks launched by these groups are often more lethal than attacks by secular groups. Religion can serve as a powerful legitimizing force for widespread violence against a broad range of nonbelievers as targets that their beliefs oblige them to target (Hoffman 2006). A key difference between secular and religious groups is that the latter often perform for a supernatural audience (God) as opposed to an earthly one (Asal and Rethemeyer 2008a). This difference allows for an almost open-ended category of opponents: "for the religious terrorist, violence is a sacramental act or divine duty, executed in direct response to some theological demand or imperative and justified by scripture" (Hoffman 1999, p. VII). By comparison, nationalist, leftist, or even right-wing groups appear more responsive to the risk that widespread and indiscriminate violence might undercut their claims to legitimacy in the eyes of their supporters.

Furthermore, religion might construe a powerful sense of being part of a "cosmic war," where viewing the enemy as "the other" is strongly enforced (Juergensmeyer 2003, p. 149). This tendency to draw a clear dividing line between their members and "others" sets religious terror groups apart from others in important ways, and is particularly useful when it comes to explaining extraordinary, indiscriminate violence against civilians such as the 9/11 attacks. Using Al Qaeda as an example, Wiktorowicz and Kaltner (2003) suggest that some religious groups rationalize violence against civilian targets by making references to civilian support for the governments that the group opposes. Such groups label their victims as heretics or "infidels," declaring them unfit to continue living. The incentive to kill large numbers of civilians is high (Cronin 2004); the more "others" killed, the better. Consider the reaction of the leader of an Egyptian terror cell after hearing that an attack staged by his group killed nine German tourists instead of the intended Jewish tourist targets. He professed no remorse, replying in a matter-of-fact way that "infidels are all the same" (Hoffman 2006, p. 239).

There are, however, significant problems with relying on religion or other ideologies to explain the targeting decisions of terror groups. In particular, group ideologies are often static, and can therefore not explain why groups shift their targeting choices at different points in time. Consider, for example, the fact that the LTTE transitioned toward targeting civilians after focusing most of its attacks on members of the Sri Lankan military and police forces. The group's singular adherence to Hinduism cannot explain this shift in targeting strategy. Instead, the decision to target civilians was more likely a response to the LTTE's weakened position vis-à-vis the

Sri Lankan state in 2007. Faced with impending defeat, LTTE leaders may have turned to attacking civilians in desperation or to signal the group's continued resolve. Similarly, an Islamist ideology did not cause the al-Aqsa Martyrs Brigade to begin targeting Israeli civilians during the Second Intifada (2000–2005). Instead, as Israeli Defense Forces either killed or arrested a number of the group's leaders, rank-and-file militants began to engage in more lethal attacks that the group's erstwhile leadership had believed to be counterproductive (Abrahms and Potter 2015). The fact that the group has been motivated by a stable set of religious and ethnonationalist beliefs since its inception cannot explain this shift in targeting strategy.

As we reviewed in Chapter 4, psychological approaches focus primarily on individual decisions to engage in terrorism. As such, turning our attention to the psychological state of individual terrorist leaders may help to explain why certain groups choose certain targets. Consider as an example the charismatic leaders of certain cults, such as Shoko Asahara of Aum Shinrikyo, which launched a sarin gas attack on the Tokyo subway in 1995, killing twelve people and severely injuring fifty others. Some studies attribute the decision to select an indiscriminate target (Japanese civilians) as the result of Asahara's mental instability (Akimoto 2006). In particular, psychiatrists diagnosed him as a pathological liar, which allowed him to portray himself as a true believer in the eyes of his followers. Furthermore, this particular personality disorder imbued Asahara with unusual imaginative power and made him particularly skilled when it came to appealing to people's minds and attracting attention (ibid). It is also possible that Asahara's reportedly delusional mental state caused him to outline a doomsday prophecy, which he sought to precipitate through a fantastical attack against Japanese civilians.

Psychological explanations may be particularly useful when it comes to explaining how lone wolf terrorists select their targets. Unpredictable or unstable mental processes, or a lack of mental capacity, may motivate mentally ill individuals to commit acts of violence, but impede them from choosing targets that match their preferred political outcomes (Becker 2014). In reality, however, most lone wolf terrorists probably exist somewhere in the continuum of complete mental stability and total mental psychopathy. As such, it is difficult to generalize about the effects of psychological factors across all lone wolf (or other) terrorists.

Group-level traits such as the presence of groupthink, discussed in Chapter 4, may also explain why groups select specific targets, such as civilians. Recall that groupthink occurs when the group is under severe pressure from outside forces and its desire for conformity leads to dysfunctional or counterproductive decision-making procedures. Terror groups under the influence of groupthink may be less likely to select strategically obvious targets for attack, and more likely to engage in counterproductive attacks such as killing large numbers of civilians.

Finally, psychological approaches might suggest that terrorists select certain targets because of the expected psychological impact that their attack will have on their intended audience. For some scholars, groups such as Aum Shinrikyo or Al Qaeda choose to perpetrate mass casualty attacks on civilians to cause social paralysis. Terrorists thus choose to stage horrific attacks on unsuspecting or seemingly random targets because of the psychological trauma that these events induce (Post 2002). Studies show that psychological suffering is much more prevalent than physical injury in the wake of a terrorist attack (Stith et al. 2003). Compared to other types of traumatic events, such as natural disasters, terrorist events result in more severe psychological damage because of a perceived lack of control among victims and the divisions they tend to sow within the targeted society. The rise in violence against Muslim Americans in the aftermath of the September 11, 2001 attacks is an example of the socio-psychological damage terrorism can cause (Human Rights Watch 2002).

While anecdotal evidence may help to reveal the potential utility of psychological approaches to explaining terrorist target selection patterns, it is difficult to rigorously test these theories to generalize across terrorist groups. Short of obtaining detailed information on a large number of individual terrorist leaders or lone wolf terrorists, it is difficult to determine when and how psychology may indeed play a role in the targeting decisions of groups or individuals. That said, psychological approaches may be more valuable when it comes to explaining why some groups decide to stage large-scale, mass casualty attacks against civilians. For instance, explicit reference to the widespread trauma by a terrorist group's leader or other members could provide convincing evidence that a particular target was chosen for psychological effect. Similarly, manifestos or recordings left in the wake of lone wolf terror attacks may help to determine whether the desire to induce a certain level of psychological trauma motivated the selection of a particular location for attack.

Structural approaches to explaining variation in target selection focus on the underlying society-wide factors that might motivate groups to select specific targets. For example, a variable that may affect the targeting decisions of a large number of groups is the behavior of a dominant power in the international system. Policies of powerful states across the globe might help to explain why terrorist groups shift from attacking domestic to international targets, as we discussed earlier in the context of strategic approaches to target selection. The study by Neumayer and Plümper (2011) demonstrates how the distribution of aid (a structural factor) drives otherwise internally-focused terrorist groups to attack transnational targets (e.g., symbols of American imperialism).

Consider the example of terror groups active in Saudi Arabia. Following Iraq's invasion of Kuwait in 1990, the United States temporarily stationed a large number of troops in the country. While the numbers decreased soon after Iraq's retreat, the United States continued to deliver large amounts of weapons to the Saudi regime throughout the 1990s. Prior to 1995, there were no recorded attacks on American by Saudi terrorists. Then, from 1995 to 2000, Saudi terrorists killed forty-three Americans, making Saudi Arabia one of the top producers of anti-American terror attacks even before the September 11 attacks (Neumayer and Plümper 2011). The structural approach would suggest that the increase in terror attacks against US targets was a direct result of the continued presence of US troops on Saudi soil, which many there viewed as an illegitimate foreign occupation.

Some studies focus on the role of geography to understand target selection by terrorist groups. For example, capital cities and other large population centers are common targets of terror attacks (Nemeth et al. 2014). Similarly, transnational terrorist attacks are more likely to target areas with high levels of economic activity (Findley et al. 2015). Civilians are more likely to be targets of terrorist attacks in populated urban areas, since the state cannot provide all of them with equal levels of protection. Police forces, on

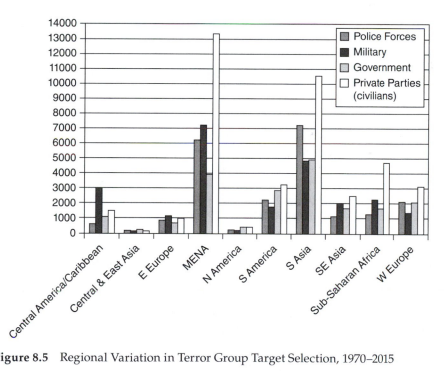

Figure 8.5 Regional Variation in Terror Group Target Selection, 1970–2015

Source: GTD

the other hand, are less likely to be targeted in urban environments since they are better protected there. They may, however, be more vulnerable to attack when they leave their urban bases for rural areas (Hinkkainen and Pickering 2017).

Regime type may also be an important structural factor that influences patterns of terrorism target selection. As we saw in Chapter 6, a number of studies address the relationship between democracy and terrorism, some of them focusing specifically on democratic states as targets of terrorism. Some groups justify attacking the civilians of democratic states by reasoning that since an elected government reflects the will of the people, civilians and government forces are equally legitimate targets (Goodwin 2006). Civilians of democratic states are also seen as benefiting from the policies of the governments that are the ultimate target of terrorist groups (ibid). Moreover, word of an attack on civilians can spread especially fast in democracies because of their well-developed and relatively unrestricted mass media outlets. Terror attacks are therefore better publicized in democratic contexts.

Other structural factors, such as the condition of a national economy, or state repressive actions, also impact the targeting decisions of terrorist groups. Stephen Nemeth (2010) finds that public support for a government—proxied by economic performance and levels of repression—influences the extent to which terrorist groups target civilians. When a country benefits from favorable economic conditions and the government demonstrates respect for the physical integrity rights of its citizens, it is costly for terrorist groups to stage attacks against civilians. Civilian targeting might further push popular support toward the side of the government and weaken the popularity of the terrorist group. But when a government represses its population and economic conditions become unfavorable, attacks against civilians may be less politically costly for terror groups. If this argument is correct, we should expect to see excessive attacks on soft targets when economic conditions deteriorate and when the government increases domestic repression. A number of groups cite poor economic conditions, or unfair revenue distribution schemes, as justification for attacks against civilians. The **Free Aceh Movement (GAM)** in Indonesia cites exploitation of the Aceh region as motivation for their attacks, while the **Movement for the Emancipation of the Niger Delta (MEND)** employs a rhetoric of redistribution and economic inequality in defense of their violent activities (Ross 2004; Nemeth 2010).

Of course, direct connections between poor economic conditions and terrorism are difficult to establish. Practically all states face unfavorable economic conditions now and then, yet not all states are victims of terror attacks during such times. And like ideology, many structural factors do not vary sufficiently over time to explain shifts in targeting, or why groups may attack particular combinations of targets. Structural factors are therefore unreliable in explaining or predicting the timing of shifts in target selection strategies.

What's more, structural factors cannot explain why groups operating under similar structural conditions—such as Western democracy—choose different types of targets. For example, the Red Brigades in Italy primarily attacked businesses, while Germany's Red Army Faction relied mostly on attacks against military targets.

More dynamic structural factors such as state counterterrorism practices may better explain target selection. For example, the installation of metal detectors in airports in 1973 reduced airline hijackings but led to increases in kidnappings of government officials by terror groups (Santifort et al. 2013). Counterterrorism officials around the world responded to this targeting shift by fortifying embassies, which in turn led terrorist groups to focus on assassinations of government officials while they were at large (Enders and Sandler 1993). After 9/11 and following the onset of the Global War on Terrorism, the installation of locks on cockpit doors and direct US military interventions led terror groups to rely on simpler forms of attack such as bombings, which primarily targeted private parties. The effects hold true for both domestic and transnational terrorism, though targeting shifts tend to originate at the domestic level and then spill over to affect patterns of transnational terrorism (Santifort et al. 1993). In sum, as targets become increasingly difficult to attack due to enhanced counterterrorism measures, terrorists gravitate to targeting soft targets, or civilians.

Finally, **critical explanations** of terrorist target selection would question first and foremost the terrorist label that is applied to oppositional groups. Recall from Chapter 7 that critical terrorism studies rejects the notion that terrorism objectively exists as such and view the term as a primarily pejorative device intended to delegitimize the claims of the group. In the view of critical scholars, a variety of state and nonstate actors employ terror as a tactic, and thus it is inappropriate to set apart nonstate terrorism as a isolated phenomenon (Jackson 2007). Terrorism occurs in the context of wider political struggles in which other contentious tactics are also prominent (Tilly 2004). The targeting strategies of groups further highlight this argument. If terrorism is a strategy of contention that specifically targets civilians or noncombatants (Schmid 2004), then any act of violence that targets members of a state military should not be considered terrorism. Yet many groups that do target military forces are considered terror groups. To name a few, ETA in Spain, the Red Army Faction in Germany, Al Qaeda globally, and Hamas in the Palestinian Territories all fall into this category. Critical terrorism scholars would likely argue that widespread variation in the targeting patterns of terrorist attacks calls into question empirical efforts to study terrorism as an objective phenomenon.

Moreover, critical terrorism scholars typically point out that government violence that targets civilians is not different from attacks on civilian orchestrated by nonstate actors. Focusing on the targeting choices of only a subset of actors—nonstate groups—but not others, detracts from understanding the underlying causes of a conflict.

That said, empirical terrorism scholars often do take into account the broader social, economic, and political context of terror, contrary to what some critical terrorism scholars may argue. Many recent studies address the conceptual fuzziness that exists between terrorism, insurgency, and civil war (e.g., Fortna 2015; Findley and Young 2012), recognizing that groups that stick to only one strategy (insurgency, terrorism, or something else) are rare. What's more, these studies suggest that there are important differences between groups that completely renounce the use of terrorism, and those that do employ it—an insight that validates the importance of including terrorism as a unique category of contention in the study of political violence.

PRACTICAL IMPLICATIONS

The findings on terrorist target selection are diverse, and in many cases over-determined, especially when it comes to explaining certain outcomes such as the targeting of civilians. For example, evaluations of how certain structural variables such as regime type affect the targeting decisions of groups yield contradictory findings. While some studies suggest that regime openness is linked to a reduce likelihood of attacks against civilians, others find that terrorist groups are actually more likely to target civilians in democratic states. Similarly, organizational approaches suggest that both small and large groups are likely to attack civilians over hard targets such as state security forces, and that rivalrous relations between groups but also strong connections among groups are likely to prompt terrorists to attack civilians. These ambiguities make it difficult to isolate government policies that reduce terror attacks in all cases.

Nevertheless, dynamic models that take into account the relationship between terrorist target selection and changes in government measures do have important policy implications. The hardening of specific locations seen as potential venues for future terrorist attacks—like airplanes, religious institutions, public transport, and shopping malls—has reduced attacks on these targets in several cases. Target hardening typically refers to strengthening the security of a building or site to protect it from attack. As we have seen, metal detectors have worked to make airlines a harder target for terrorist attacks. Similarly, concrete barriers installed in front of embassies and other potentially sensitive locations help to prevent the kidnapping and assassination of government officials. Of course, certain locations are easier to defend than others, and terrorists have launched attacks in a great number of varied locations. Target hardening might not, for example, be the most viable counterterrorism strategy in response to the November 2015 terrorist attacks in Paris, France. Installing barriers in front of restaurants and cafes throughout France is unfeasible, unappealing, and likely unnecessary. However, adding metal detectors or more security guards to protect public spaces such as theaters or dance clubs might be a more practical response, especially when combined with some of the other strategies highlighted below. And in the case of lone wolf terrorism, target hardening might be wholly ineffective, considering that these individuals tend to strike in familiar, local areas and to eschew the more typical, prominent urban targets (Becker 2014). These realities point to the necessary roles that local stakeholders play in providing security for their own communities.

Other policy implications also emerge from organizational approaches. Because groups are more likely to target civilians after losing a central leader or when they experience internal rifts, policies such as leadership decapitation may be counterproductive. Indeed, if leadership vacuums prompt younger generations of terrorists to turn to extravagant attacks against local populations to prove their worth, targeted killings of group leaders may lead to more indiscriminate violence. Similarly, policies that aim to split otherwise cohesive terrorist groups may foster competition among splinter groups, who may turn to targeting civilians as they seek to gain an edge over rival organizations. And because alliances among terror groups lead to tactical diversity and a larger menu of potential targets, disrupting connections across groups may be an important priority. Enhanced collaboration across the intelligence agencies of various states may help to identify and break up some of the transnational connections that help terrorist groups thrive. More generally, a nuanced understanding of the internal structure of various groups, as well as of transnational terrorist networks, should improve efforts to contain their capacity to do harm.

Importantly, the vast majority of studies that evaluate the effectiveness of terror attacks against civilians suggest that these strategies are often counterproductive for terror groups (Abrahms 2006; Cronin 2009). In fact, groups are more likely to gain concessions from the government when they attack military targets (Fortna 2015). As such, it is important that states remain resilient when faced with mass-casualty attacks against their populations. Avoiding overly repressive counterterrorism responses is particularly important, as these are likely to backfire and generate more support for the terror group that launched the attack.

Finally, while ideological approaches highlight important patterns that exist in the targeting decisions of different types of groups, many of the policy implications that follow are morally problematic. For example, the finding that religious groups are more likely to target civilians suggests that counterterrorism policies should focus on monitoring religious groups over others. However, placing individuals or groups who adhere to a specific set of beliefs under heightened surveillance is discriminatory, stigmatizing, and can backfire by creating additional grievances for these groups. Moreover, ideologies are difficult to observe and thus impossible to monitor without the use of highly invasive techniques. However, the finding that certain groups such as nationalist/separatist organizations are more likely than others to target military or police forces, or government officials, suggests that government policies against them should include a target hardening component.

TERRORISM AND WEAPONS OF MASS DESTRUCTION

A nuclear attack by a terror group could cause more than a million casualties and create political, economy, and psychological turmoil around the world. In the wake of the 9/11 attacks, US policymakers began to consider the implications of terrorism using weapons of mass destruction, and analysts reacted by recommending a variety of preventive measures in a flurry of reports, books, journal articles, and Congressional testimony. But how likely is this scenario to actually occur? In this special section, we address why so few groups have succeeded in staging attacks with weapons of mass destruction, including nuclear weapons.

Documents discovered from terror group caches over the last two decades largely confirm that many terrorists are striving to acquire and use nuclear weapons against the United States and other targets (Feinstein and Slaughter 2004). Groups such as Al Qaeda appeared to have detailed knowledge of nuclear weaponry, and intelligence suggests that some groups have made attempts to acquire nuclear material on the black market (ibid). For as long as they have been trying, however, no terrorist group has thus far achieved the unfathomable.

By and large, we can use the same arguments used to explain variation in terrorist target selection to explain why some groups decide to seek out or use weapon of mass destruction. For example, a terror group might use the mass destruction wreaked by a nuclear explosion as a costly signal to its targeted opponent that it means business. Or, a terrorist group might launch a large-scale chemical or biological attack to provoke its target into overreacting, baiting a government into responding with disproportionately repressive measures that increase popular support for the terrorist group. According to organizational approaches, the acquisition of nuclear weapons might lead to previously unimaginable prestige for a group, eliciting loyalty and respect from allies and rivals alike. Or it could lead to a chain reaction, whereby other groups turn to seeking out the technology in order to avoid being outbid or overshadowed by another group. Finally, a group's ideological underpinnings might incite it to seek out weapons that inflict the highest possible casualties, or to bring about a prophesied apocalypse. The use of nuclear weapons, for instance, might be particularly attractive to groups such as ISIS, which possesses an apocalyptic worldview. Of course, many of these approaches also help to explain why the use of weapons of mass destruction might be detrimental to a terror group's strategic objectives. The indiscriminate and hyper-violent nature of this hypothetical scenario might forever discredit and delegitimize the group in the eyes of potential supporters.

Let's discuss some key concepts relevant to the discussion of terrorism and **weapons of mass destruction**, or **WMD**. The definition of what constitutes a weapon of mass destruction has changed over time. The term was originally coined in reference to aerial bombing with chemical explosives, but since World War II, WMD has come to refer to large-scale weaponry that includes other technologies. A **nuclear weapon,** the most powerful WMD, is an explosive device that derives its destructive force from a nuclear reaction. A thermonuclear weapon weighing little more than 2,400 pounds can produce an explosive force comparable to the detonation of more than 1.2 million tons of TNT and destroy an entire city by blast, fire, and radiation. Other types of WMDs include radiological, chemical, and biological weapons; taken together, attacks using any of these weapons are commonly called CBRN attacks:

- Radiological weapon: Any weapon designed to spread radioactive material with the intent to kill and cause mass disruption. This includes any weapon or equipment other than a nuclear explosive device specifically designed to employ radioactive material by disseminating it to cause destruction, damage, or injury (US Department of Defense).
- Gun-type fission weapon: These are fission-based nuclear weapons whose design functions similarly to a gun. The method was applied in the early days of the US nuclear program. The "Little Boy" weapon detonated over Hiroshima is an example of a gun-type fission weapon. Currently, there are no known gun-type weapons in operation, as contemporary nuclear weapons are implosion-type weapons.
- Highly-enriched uranium (HEU): HEU is a critical component of both civilian nuclear power generation and military-grade nuclear weapons. The International Atomic Energy Agency attempts to monitor and control enriched uranium supplies to ensure nuclear power generation safety and curb nuclear weapons proliferation.
- Chemical weapon: Any weapon that uses chemicals formulated to inflict death or harm on human beings. Many countries, including the United States, stockpile chemical weapons. The most dangerous chemical weapons include nerve agents and vesicant (blister) agents. But chemical weapons can also be fairly basic. For instance, pepper spray is a chemical weapon.
- Biological weapon: Any weapon that uses biological toxins or infectious agents, such as bacteria, viruses, and fungi. The agents may be lethal or non-lethal, and can target a single individual, groups of people, or entire populations.

Why have so few terrorist groups sought to use weapons of mass destruction? And to what extent should the international community consider nuclear terrorism a serious threat? The United States has only experienced two CBRN attacks on its soil, and both attacks used biological weapons. The first was in 1984, when followers of **Bhagwan Shree Rajneesh** (or **Osho**) used salmonella bacteria to poison salad bars in ten restaurants in The Dalles, Oregon. The goal was to sicken the town's voting population so that their candidates would prevail in county elections. No one died in the attack, though more than forty

Continued

TERRORISM AND WEAPONS OF MASS DESTRUCTION
(Continued)

people were hospitalized. Then, one week after the 9/11 attacks in 2001, several news media outlets and the offices of two Democratic US senators received letters containing **anthrax** spores. Five people died as a result of the anthrax attacks. A scientist named Bruce Edwards Ivins, who worked at the US government's biodefense laboratories in Fort Derick, Maryland, was suspected of being behind the attacks. Ivins was never formally charged and committed suicide in 2008.

Global concern over the potential of a nuclear terrorist attack rose in the wake of the **Aum Shinriko attack on Toykyo's subway system in 1995**. In five coordinated attacks, the group released sarin on several lines subway lines during rush hour, killing twelve people and severely injuring 50 others. Nearly one thousand people also reported temporary vision problems as a result of the attack. Ten men carried out the attack—five released the gas, and another five served as getaway drivers (see Box 8.2 for a more detailed account of the attack).

In the attack's aftermath, the idea of more nuclear attacks by terrorists gained traction among a wide range of journalists and analysts, especially in the US. Some terrorism scholars contended even then that a great deal of reporting on the subject was careless and exaggerated, contributing to a sense of political paranoia (Stern 1999b). But after the 1995 Oklahoma City bombing, Al Qaeda's attack on the World Trade Center in 1993, Al Qaeda's attacks on the US embassies in Tanzania and Kenya in 1998, and the 9/11 attacks, even more analysts began to suspect that a nuclear terror attack was only a matter of time.

The debate over nuclear terrorism centers on two arguments: the first that considers CBRN terrorism to be a reality that the US should take seriously as part of its counterterrorism policy; and the second that dismisses the threat of nuclear terrorism as an exaggeration.

For instance, a few years after the Aum Shinrikyo attacks, Richard Falkenrath (1998) published an article in *Survival* arguing that a CBRN attack could have "devastating effects on the targeted society." He ranked the threat as among the most serious national security challenges faced by modern liberal democracies. Nuclear terrorism, he contended, was a real possibility. He caveated his argument by pointing to the low-probability, high-consequence nature of the threat, but emphasized the extent of harm and devastation wrought by just one successful attack. The probability of future acts of CBRN terrorism was low, but nevertheless rising.

Those who accuse policy-makers and academics of over-dramatizing the risks of CBRN base their arguments on what they consider to be a handful of important, if under-acknowledged realities (Bunn and Wier 2005). We review five of these briefly below, and also present the rebuttals of those that contend the risk of CBRN is underappreciated and should be addressed through robust preventive measures.

1. Terrorists are not especially interested in staging a nuclear attack. This line of thinking is in accordance with Brian Jenkins' (1975) conjecture

that "terrorists want a lot of people watching, but not a lot of people dead." The incineration of an entire city by nuclear attack is thus not something that terrorist groups strive to accomplish.

Critique. *While this conclusion is correct for the vast majority of terror groups, Al Qaeda's attacks against the US embassies in Tanzania and Kenya in 1998, and then on September 11, 2001 in the US, suggest that some terrorist groups might actually want a lot of people dead, in addition to people watching. In fact, Osama bin Laden and his global jihadist network made their desire for nuclear weapons for use against the West explicit, by both word and deed (Bunn and Wier 2005; Hoffman 2006, p. 272–281). See Box 8.1 for more details about Al Qaeda's CBRN aspirations.*

2. Even if terrorists wanted to stage a nuclear attack, the materials necessary to make a bomb are nearly impossible to procure. There is no significant risk of a government's nuclear weapon getting into the hands of a terrorist given states' significant efforts to maintain and upgrade their national nuclear security.

Critique. *Global stockpiles of potential nuclear bomb material are actually dangerously insecure. In fact, the International Atomic Energy Agency (IAEA) database of illicit trafficking incidents includes at least eighteen cases of stolen HEU or plutonium. In Russia specifically, tight budgets have prevented fully securing thousands of nuclear weapons and hundreds of tons of potential bomb-making material, and the fissile material that is or could become available from a Russian stockpile remains dangerously insecure (Pluta and Zimmerman 2006). In Pakistan, while the nuclear stockpile is heavily guarded, it continues to face continuous threats from armed groups in the country. Substantial smuggling networks are also shipping a wide variety of contraband back and forth across Russia's borders with Central Asian states (Bunn and Wier 2005).*

3. Even if terrorists wanted to stage a nuclear attack, the extremely complicated process of making a nuclear bomb would prevent them from doing so.

Critique. *This argument conflates the difficult of producing the nuclear material needed for a bomb with the difficulty of making the bomb once the material is in hand. The basic principles behind the construction of gun-type weapons are relatively simple and widely available in the open literature. A significant amount of nuclear technology has been leaked from Pakistan, including designs for uranium-enrichment centrifuges, specific bomb components, and nuclear weapon blueprints (Bunn and Wier 2005).*

4. If terrorists were to steal a nuclear bomb from a state with nuclear capabilities, the state's security precautions would prevent terrorists from actually detonating the device.

Critique. *Experts suggest that earlier Soviet-style weapons might not be equipped with modern versions of safeguards against unauthorized weapons use. Perhaps even more than benefitting from a stolen weapon, terror groups seeking to stage a nuclear attack might fare better with help of a knowledgeable*

Continued

TERRORISM AND WEAPONS OF MASS DESTRUCTION
(Continued)

insider. An insider might be willing to help steal a weapon and then provide help in setting it off. Even if a group were to steal a weapon that it did not know how to use, or was otherwise prevented from using, it could still potentially remove the fissile material and apply it to a different use (Bunn and Wier 2005).

5. The only plausible way for a terrorist to acquire a nuclear weapon is to be given one by a hostile state with nuclear capabilities. This requires preemptive counterterrorism doctrines, whereby the only solution to the possibility of a nuclear terror attack is to take on those hostile states.

Critique. *This argument is particularly concerning in its practical implications. The myth of state sponsorship to make a nuclear terror attack possible led many senior officials in the wake of the 9/11 attacks to place only modest priority on securing the world's stockpiles of nuclear weapons, favoring instead a preemptive invasion of Iraq on the basis of its WMD program (Zimmerman and Pluta 2006). Lieber and Press (2013) also find that concerns about these types of attacks are exaggerated if one considers the rate of attribution of terror attacks historically, and the small number of states that are actually considered state-sponsors of terrorism and have nuclear capabilities. In short, attributing a nuclear terror attack to a responsible party would be easier is often suggested, and that passing weapons to terrorists is unlikely to be in the best interest of any government because of the devastating military retaliation they would experience in the aftermath (Lieber and Press 2013, p. 84).*

What does this set of arguments and counter-arguments suggest for counterterrorism policy? Most scholars agree that the threat of nuclear terrorism reinforces the risks posed by nuclear proliferation. Nuclear nonproliferation should therefore remain a major goal for the international community. The dangers of states giving nuclear weapons to terrorist groups, however, may be largely exaggerated. Taking steps to prevent nuclear terrorism on these grounds is therefore likely to be a flawed approach that rests on a shaky foundation. US policymakers used these kinds of arguments to justify the US invasion of Iraq in 2003, and some continue to make the argument for preventively attacking Iran on the same grounds.

Given the ease with which terror groups might be able to access bomb-making materials, it arguably more important that major powers continue to lead efforts to remove or lock down bomb material from facilities around the world. This involves engaging potentially at-risk stockpiles in states such as Russia and Pakistan. Effective security measures must be put in place in nuclear states such as Israel, China, India, and Pakistan, where foreign experts are unlikely to obtain access to key facilities.

The implications for preventing a lone wolf CBRN terrorist attack are slightly different, as these individuals are unlikely to gain access to military-grade weapons. But people can make weapons using commonplace industrial chemicals, biological contaminants, and radioactive materials. The dual use of these materials makes controlling them particularly difficult. Some have suggested that the threat of lone wolf CBRN terrorism requires more intrusive counterterrorism measures, which of course poses significant risks to the protection of civil liberties (Ellis 2014).

In sum, though a small number of terror groups have expressed a desire to acquire nuclear weapons and stage a nuclear attack, it is extremely difficult for them to do so. They have had little observable success in achieving their goals, but that does not mean that they will stop trying. As such, concerted multilateral efforts aimed at reducing and securing nuclear stockpiles will likely continue.

BOX 8.1

AL QAEDA AND CBRN

Al Qaeda has made it clear that it seeks to use WMDs against the United States (Hoffman 2006, p. 272–281; Stone 2009). In the run-up to the 9/11 attacks, Al Qaeda had concentrated its efforts on acquiring nuclear weapons. Some studies suggest that bin Laden's quest for this capability began as long ago as the early- to mid-1990s, when an Al Qaeda agent attempted to purchase uranium from South Africa without success. Later, in 1998, Al Qaeda operatives were arrested in Germany while attempting to buy enriched uranium (Hoffman 2006, p. 273). Bin Laden would later declare that "acquiring [nuclear] weapons for the defense of Muslims is a religious duty" (Osama bin Laden, as quoted in Venzke and Ibrahim 2003). Other incidents that occurred in the aftermath of the 9/11 attacks suggest that the organization continued to pursue the acquisition of nuclear weapons.

In addition to nuclear weapons, the group has also sought to develop its capabilities in terms of chemical and biological weapons. Zawahiri organized the recruitment of a US-trained Malaysian microbiologist named Yazid Sufaat, a former California State University graduate in the biological sciences (Hoffman 2006, p. 274). Before 9/11, a separate team of Al Qaeda operatives engaged in a R&D effort to produce ricin and chemical warfare agents at one of the movement's camps in Afghanistan. The facility included labs and a school that trained a handpicked group of terrorists in the use of chemical and biological weapons.

As Bruce Hoffman (2006, p. 276) suggests, a common thread in all of these cases is a strong interest in and willingness to use nuclear weapons, even though it has rarely been met with the capability actually required to produce the weapon and put it to use. But technological advancements and the increasing ease with which information and material necessary to manufacture CBRN weapons can be accessed make CBRN terrorism a salient threat. It should be viewed for what it is—one of many threats currently facing the United States and many other states, but not likely the most likely or proximate threat, due to the myriad difficulties that surround the manufacture and use of such weapons.

AUM SHINKRIKYO'S CHEMICAL ATTACK ON THE TOKYO SUBWAY SYSTEM

In the group's most spectacular attack, the cult movement Aum Shinrikyo attacked passengers on the Tokyo subway using sarin gas on March 20, 1995. The group's leader, Shoko Asahara, had previously published a book in which he declared himself Japan's only fully enlightened master and outlined a doomsday prophecy in which he foresaw the advent of a Third World War (Snow 2003).

The group's first attack was recorded on June 27, 1994, when members released a cloud of sarin gas near the homes of judges in Matsumoto, Japan. The attack was claimed as retaliation against a lawsuit concerning a real-estate dispute in which the cult was involved. Hundreds of people were injured and eight were killed.

On March 20, 1995, five members of Aum Shinrikyo carried liquid sarin in plastic bags wrapped in newspaper onto the subway during rush hour. At prearranged stations, the attackers dropped their sarin packets and punctured them several times with umbrellas with sharpened tips. The perpetrators then exited the trains to meet their five getaway drivers. Left punctured on the floor of the trains, the sarin bags leaked gas into the trains and stations. Because sarin is one of the most volatile of nerve agents, it is one of the most effective and lethal chemical weapons. It quickly and easily evaporated from a liquid into a gas, easing its spread into the enclosed train care. People were exposed to the vapor without ever coming into contact with the liquid.

Investigators later discovered that Aum Shinrikyo had been developing and manufacturing its own supply of sarin gas for ten years prior to the subway attacks. Dummy companies operating on behalf of the cult had purchased large quantities of chemical raw materials in order to do so.

The subway attack was the most serious attack on Japanese soil since the US's bombing of Hiroshima and Nagasaki in 1945. It caused massive disruption and widespread fear in a society that had previously been perceived as virtually free of crime. In the wake of the attack, Aum Shinrikyo lost its status as a legal religious organization, and the Japanese government seized many of its assets.

The group's leader, Shoko Asahara, was sentenced to death in 2004, but lawyers called for a postponement of the ruling until results were obtained from a court-ordered psychiatric evaluation. In 2006, the court ruled that Ashara was indeed fit to stand trial, and the appeal against his death sentence was eventually rejected. The execution was again postponed in 2012.

SUMMARY

In this chapter, we introduced and evaluated how different approaches to studying terrorism explain variation in terrorist target selection. We reviewed different analytic explanations for why groups might choose discriminate, as opposed to indiscriminate targets, as well as why groups might target international, as opposed to domestic targets. We also discussed why groups might stage mass casualty attacks against civilians, as well as the practical implications of these explanations. In a special section, we introduced various concepts behind CBRN terrorism and the ongoing debate about the threat of nuclear terrorism. Finally, we presented case studies of groups that have used, or seek to use, WMDs in their attacks against their opponents.

Discussion Questions

1. Which approach do you think best explains variation in the target selection strategies of terrorist groups?
2. Which approach is least convincing in explaining terrorist target selection patterns?
3. After reading this chapter, how do you think the international community should respond to the targeting patterns of terrorist groups?
4. How would specific terrorist groups such as Al Qaeda or ISIS defend decisions to use of CBRN weapons? What potential benefits might they cite to justify these decisions? What risks might influence them to back away from such decisions?
5. How big of a risk does CBRN terrorism pose to the national security of the United States? Other states?

KEY TAKEAWAYS

- Terror groups vary in their target selection, choosing different locations, populations, and intensities of violence. Often the targeting varies by the ideology of the group, but there are also compelling strategic, organizational, and structural explanations for this variation.

- Weapons of mass destruction remain a concern. Chemical, biological, radiological, and nuclear terror attacks all remain possible given broad access to such materials in the contemporary context.

- Policies to minimize indiscriminate violence against civilians include target hardening, a defensive strategy that has produced some success. Moreover, governments should avoid splintering groups that might result in competitive rivalries. And targeted assassination of the leaders of terror group likely exacerbates, rather than reduces, the group's violence.

SUGGESTED FURTHER READINGS

Abrahms, Max, and Justin Conrad. 2017. "The Strategic Logic of Credit Claiming: A New Theory for Anonymous Terrorist Attacks." *Security Studies* 26 (2): 279–304. doi:10.1080.09636412.2017.1280304.

Asal, Victor, and R. Karl Rethemeyer. 2008a. "Dilettantes, Ideologues, and the Weak: Terrorists Who Don't Kill." *Conflict Management and Peace Science* 25 (3): 244–263. doi:10.1080/07388940802219000.

Asal, Victor and R. Karl Rethemeyer. 2008b. "The Nature of the Beast: Organizational Structures and the Lethality of Terrorist Attacks." *Journal of Politics* 70 (2): 437–449. doi:10.1017/s0022381608080419.

Asal, Victor H., R. Karl Rethemeyer, Ian Anderson, Allyson Stein, Jeffrey Rizzo, and Matthew Rozea. 2009 "The Softest Of Targets: A Study On Terrorist Target Selection." *Journal Of Applied Security Research* 4 (3): 258–278. doi:10.1080/19361610902929990.

Becker, Michael. 2014. "Explaining Lone Wolf Target Selection in the United States." *Studies in Conflict & Terrorism* 37 (11): 959–978. doi:10.1080/1057610x.2014.952261.

Brandt, Patrick, and Todd Sandler. 2010. "What Do Transnational Terrorists Target? Has It Changed? Are We Safer?" *Journal of Conflict Resolution.* 52 (2): 214–236. doi:10.1177/0022002709355437.

Bunn, Matthew, and Anthony Wier. 2005. "The Seven Myths of Nuclear Terrorism." *Current History* 104 (681): 153–161. Available online at: http://www.belfercenter.org/sites/default/files/files/publication/bunnwier.pdf. Last accessed 25-March-2016.

Crenshaw, Martha. 2007. "The Logic of Terrorism: Terrorist Behavior as a Produce of Strategic Choice." *Terrorism in Perspective* 24.

Drake, C. J. M. 1998. *Terrorists' Target Selection.* Basingstoke: Macmillan.

Goodwin, Jeff. 2006. "A Theory of Categorical Terrorism." *Social Forces* 84 (4): 2027–2046. doi:10.1353/sof.2006.0090.

Engene, Jan Oskar. 2004. *Terrorism in Western Europe: Explaining the Trends since 1950.* Cheltenham: Edward Elgar.

Findley, Michael G., and Joseph K. Young. 2012. "Terrorism and Civil War: A Spatial and Temporal Approach To A Conceptual Problem." *Perspectives on Politics* 10 (2): 285–305. doi:10.1017/s1537592712000679.

Fortna, Page Virginia. 2015. "Do Terrorists Win? Rebels' Use of Terrorism and Civil War Outcomes." *International Organization* 69 (03): 519–556. doi:10.1017/s0020818315000089.

Horowitz, Michael C. 2010. "Nonstate Actors and The Diffusion of Innovations: The Case of Suicide Terrorism." *International Organization* 64 (01): 33–64. doi:10.1017/s0020818309990233.

Horowitz, Michael, Evan Perkoski. and Philip P. K. Potter. 2016. "Tactical Diversity in Militant Violence." International Organization, *forthcoming.*

Kalyvas, Stathis N. 1999. "Wanton and Senseless? The Logic of Massacres in Algeria." *Rationality and Society* 11 (3): 243–285. doi:10.1177/104346399011003001.

Lieber, Keir A. and Daryl G. Press. 2013. "Why States Won't Give Nuclear Weapons To Terrorists." *International Security* 38 (1): 80–104. doi:10.1162/isec_a_00127.

Monaghan, Rachel. 2004. "'An Imperfect Peace: Paramilitary 'Punishments' in Northern Ireland." *Terrorism and Political Violence* 16 (3): 439–461. doi:10.1080/09546550490509775.

Neumayer, Eric and Thomas Plumper. 2010. "Foreign Terror on Americans." *Journal of Peace Research* 48 (1): 3–17. doi:10.1177/002234331039014

O'Neill, Bard. 2005. *Insurgency and Terrorism: From Revolution to Apocalypse, 2nd edition.* Washington, DC: Potomac Books.

Post, Jerrold. 2002. "Differentiating the Threats of Chemical and Biological Weapons: Motivations and Constraints." *Peace and Conflict* 8 (3): 87–200.

Pluta, Anna M. and Peter D. Zimmerman. 2006. "Nuclear Terrorism: A Disheartening Dissent." *Survival* 48 (2): 55–69. doi:10.1080/00396330600765583.

Sandler, Todd. 2013. "The Analytical Study of Terrorism: Taking Stock." *Journal of Peace Research* 51 (2): 257–271. doi:10.1177/0022343313491277.

Santifort, C., Todd Sandler, and P. T. Brandt. 2012. "Terrorist Attack And Target Diversity: Changepoints and Their Drivers." *Journal Of Peace Research* 50 (1): 75–90. doi:10.1177/0022343312445651.

Santifort, Charlinda, and Todd Sandler. 2012. "Terrorist Success In Hostage-Taking Missions: 1978–2010." *Public Choice* 156 (1–2): 125–137. doi:10.1007/s11127-012-0008-z.

Stern, Jessica. 1999a. *The Ultimate Terrorists*. Cambridge, MA: Harvard University Press.

Stern, Jessica. 1999b. "The Prospect of Domestic Bioterrorism." *Emerging Infectious Diseases* 5 (4): 517–522. doi:10.3201/eid0504.990410.

Wiktorowicz, Quitan, and John Kaltner. 2003. "Killing in the Name of Islam: Al-Qaeda's Justification for September 11." *Middle East Policy* 10 (2): 76–92. doi:10.1111/1475-4967.00107.

Wright, Austin L. 2013. "Terrorism, Ideology, and Target Selection." Working paper. Princeton University. Available online at: http://www.princeton.edu/politics/about/file-repository/public/Wright_on_Terrorism.pdf. Last accessed 25-March-2017.

CHAPTER 9

SUICIDE TERRORISM

Learning Objectives

After reading this chapter, readers should be able to:

- Describe and differentiate in their own words the various concepts that fall under the broader category of suicide terrorism, including martyrdom, suicide mission, and self-immolation.
- Explain and critique different analytic explanations for why terror groups use suicide attacks.
- Provide examples of terrorist organizations that use suicide terrorism, and compare and contrast them with groups that do not.
- Explain the different counterterrorism strategies suggested by the various explanations for suicide terror.

> "Terror is glamour—not only, but also. I am firmly convinced that there's something like a fascination with death among suicide bombers. Many are influenced by the misdirected image of a kind of magic that is inherent in these insane acts. The suicide bomber's imagination leads him to believe in a brilliant act of heroism, when in fact he is simply blowing himself up pointlessly and taking other peoples' lives."
> —SALMAN RUSHDIE, INTERVIEW WITH DER SPIEGEL, 2006

> "Sadly it turns out, if you're willing to die, you can kill a lot of people."
> —US PRESIDENT BARACK OBAMA, NOVEMBER 22, 2015

> "A large part of the problem is that young people are being born into the world and growing up without much hope. And so, they become murderers, they become suicide bombers."
> —ARTHUR HERTZBERG

"The reprisal against the suicide bomber does not bring
peace. There is a suicide bomber, a reprisal and then a
counter-reprisal. And it just goes on and on."
—DESMOND TUTU

THE PUZZLE

Why do some groups use suicide terror, whereas others eschew the technique? Why are some people willing to kill themselves while killing others?
The impressive wealth of publications that addresses the topic of suicide
terror reflects a growing interest in a mode of violence that necessitates the
death of its perpetrator to ensure its success (Moghadam 2008).

We define **suicide terrorism** in much the same way as we characterize
terrorism more broadly. Suicide terror is a tactic of violence against noncombatants in which the primary purpose of the attack is to affect a large
public audience to achieve a political goal. The primary target of the act is
not the direct victims, but an explicitly identified opponent—often a government—that the group is trying to influence. But compared with tactics like
airplane hijackings, or say the planting of explosive devices in public spaces,
the suicide terror attack is marked by the intentional self-destruction of the
perpetrator. This chapter surveys explanations of why individuals choose to
become suicide bombers, and why groups employ this specific tactic.

Why dedicate an entire chapter to the phenomenon of suicide terrorism? First, suicide terrorism has generated a significantly larger number of
casualties per attack, relative to other types of terrorist attacks (Horowitz
2015). Second, some have argued that suicide terrorism is the most politically destabilizing and psychologically devastating form of terrorism (Atran
2003)—a claim that warrants both attention and critique. Finally, suicide terrorism presents an important puzzle within the broader literature on terrorism insofar as its successful implementation must result in the death of
the perpetrator. Indeed, the use of a tactic that must result in an immediate
sacrifice of a violent organization's members is truly puzzling.

Regardless, suicide terrorism usually occurs in combination with other
methods, with similar targets and motives that characterize other terror tactics. As such, we do not make an argument for the study of suicide terrorism
as a *sui generis* phenomenon, but instead bring attention to the literature that
has considered it alongside other tactics and strategies of resistance available
to individuals and groups.

THE EVOLUTION OF SUICIDE TERROR

The self-killing of terrorists is a relatively contemporary phenomenon. Although
history is rife with incidents where people perished during the commission

of violent acts, their suicides were not necessarily intentional or anticipated as part of the attacks. For example, Narodnaya Volya member Ignacy Hryniew-iecki assassinated Tsar Alexander II in 1881 by detonating a bomb at the tsar's carriage feet, killing himself in the process. But this was only after the first bomb, thrown by fellow conspirator Nikolai Rysakov, disabled the tsar's car-riaige without killing him. All remaining Narodnaya Volya conspirators in-volved in the Tsar's assassination were executed several weeks later. Although not technically a suicide attack, this assassination may very well have qualified as a suicide mission—a mission that is likely to result in one's death.

Although they do not qualify as terrorism as scholars typically define it, suicide missions have featured in at least one other major twentieth century conflict. The term **kamikaze** was first adopted in World War II to refer to the Japanese suicide pilots who deliberately crashed their planes into enemy targets. The kamikaze movement evolved out of desperation when it became evident that Japan was going to lose the war against the United States. The technique caused significant damage to the US fleet. In the Battle of Okinawa of April 1945, some 200 kamikaze pilots rammed fully fueled fighter planes into more than three hundred US ships, killing five thousand Americans in the most costly naval battle in US history (Atran 2003). Unlike the suicide mission involved in Tsar Alexander's death, the manner of the kamikaze pilots' tactics ensured that their deaths would be weaponized—that their deaths would kill others.

The first major contemporary suicide terrorist attack occurred in the Middle East in December 1981, when the Iraqi Shia Islamist group al-Dawa carried out a suicide car bombing targeting the Iraqi embassy in Beirut. The attack resulted in the deaths of more than fifty people, including Iraq's ambassador to Lebanon. Shortly thereafter, suicide bombing became a strategically politi-cal weapon for groups such as Hizballah. The September 1982 assassination of pro-Israeli Lebanese President Bashir Gemayel and the 1983 truck bomb-ings of nearly 300 French and American servicemen in Lebanon are also early examples of contemporary suicide terror. The phenomenon returned to the spotlight a decade later in the context of the Israeli-Palestinian conflict, when attacks by Hizballah-trained members of Hamas and Islamic Jihad aimed to derail the Oslo Peace Accords throughout the 1990s (Atran 2003).

Since that time, the tactic has spread to a number of violent groups oper-ating worldwide. Militant organizations as diverse as the Vanguard of Arab Christians in Lebanon, the Liberation Tigers of Tamil Eelam (LTTE) in Sri Lanka, and the Kurdistan Workers Party (PKK) in Turkey and Iraq have all used suicide terror among their strategies of resistance. Al Qaeda's adoption of the tactic introduced a transnational dimension to the phenomenon and prompted a surge of interest among policymakers and academics alike, par-ticularly in the wake of the September 11, 2001 attacks on the United States.

As Figure 9.1 shows, the frequency of suicide attacks increased globally beginning in the mid-1990s and jumped significantly at the turn of the cen-tury. According to Figure 9.2, the intensity of suicide attacks has also risen, as evidenced by the increase in fatalities and number of wounded over the years. In 2015 alone, the Chicago Project on Security and Terrorism (CPOST) reported a total of six hundred suicide terror attacks that killed nearly six thousand people. The vast majority of the attacks occurred in Iraq (109), followed by Nigeria (96), Afghanistan (76), and Syria (59). Over half of the attacks could not be attributed to a known perpetrator. The Islamic State in Iraq and Syria (ISIS) and the Taliban in Afghanistan were responsible for the majority of attacks staged by a known perpetrator (CPOST 2016). The Global

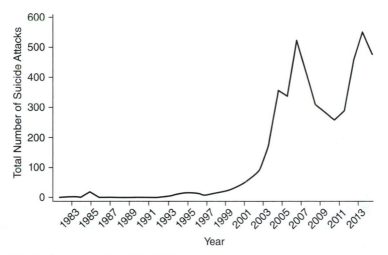

Figure 9.1   Suicide Attacks, 1982–2015

Source: Chicago Project on Security and Terrorism (CPOST) 2016

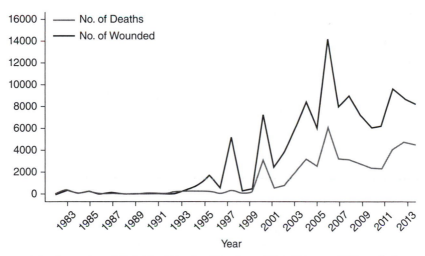

Figure 9.2   Intensity of Suicide Attacks: Number of Fatalities and Wounded, 1982–2015

Source: CPOST 2016

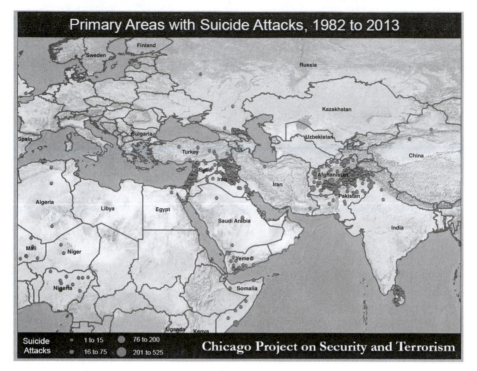

Figure 9.3   Geographic Distribution of Suicide Attacks, 1982–2013

Source: CPOST 2016

Terrorism Database reported a higher number of suicide attacks in 2015 (906 out of a total of 14,806 attacks for the year).

Because of the manner of the attack, popular narratives often characterize suicide terrorists as religious fanatics or crazed psychopaths who thrive in the midst of poverty and ignorance. Many associate suicide attacks with religious terror groups, whose ideologies might make the organization more likely to influence its members to give up their lives for their cause, compared with secular organizations. The academic literature and accompanying empirical evidence, however, show that psychological and ideological factors are insufficient in explaining why individuals and groups turn to suicide terrorism (Krueger 2008). The rest of this chapter surveys how the various analytic approaches explain the use (or non-use) of suicide tactics by terror groups. But first we introduce several concepts that are key to the broader discussion.

KEY CONCEPTS

Some recurring themes that appear in the literature on suicide terrorism surround the concepts of martyrdom; suicide missions; and self-immolation. The term **martyrdom** brings attention to subjective interpretations of the perpetrators of suicide terrorism (Crenshaw 2007). A preference for the term

THE CHICAGO PROJECT ON SECURITY AND
TERRORISM (CPOST)

Because of the rise of suicide bombing as a global phenomenon, many scholars have developed research programs to study this distinct method of terrorism. For example, CPOST is a research institute based at the University of Chicago that maintains a comprehensive database on suicide attacks worldwide. Compiled by a research team led by Robert Pape, the Suicide Attack Database comprises a list of global suicide attacks from 1982–2015. It currently includes a total of 4,933 attacks in more than forty countries. For each attack, the database contains information about the geographic location, target category, and weapons used, as well as information on the demographic and general biographical characteristics of the attackers.

CPOST defines a suicide attack as "an attack in which [a nonstate] attacker kills himself or herself in a deliberate attempt to kill others" (http://cpost. uchicago.edu/database/methodology/). This typically involves an individual detonating a suicide vest or explosives hidden in a vehicle driven by that individual. The data does not include failed suicide bombing attempts in which the device does not explode and the perpetrator is not killed. The database also excludes attacks in which an attacker expects to be killed as a result of the mission, but does not directly kill themselves.

DISCUSSION EXERCISE

- *Compare and contrast the number of suicide terror attacks reported in CPOST with the number of suicide attacks reported in the Global Terrorism Database (GTD). What are some potential explanations for the difference in total counts of suicide terror attacks?*

- *Compare and contrast the number of suicide terror attacks with the total number of terror attacks reported in the Global Terrorism Database (GTD) from 1970–2015. What proportion of terror attacks are suicide terror attacks? Does this proportion surprise you?*

- *How might researchers in the critical terrorism studies tradition (Chapter 7) interpret scholars' fascination with suicide bombing as a distinct tactic? Do you agree or disagree with their interpretation? Why or why not?*

"martyrdom" over "suicide attack" highlights the objectionable nature of the term "suicide" to those who often practice or condone such forms of violence. Many religious traditions categorize suicide as a sin and consider anyone accused of committing suicide as subject to suffering in the afterlife. The replacement of the term "suicide terror" or "suicide attack" with "martyrdom" destigmatizes the act, making it instead glorious and worthy of eternal bliss. Islamist extremists, for instance, sometimes rationalize martyrdom operations as praiseworthy embraces of death at the hands of the enemy, making such tactics legitimate and noble in battle.

Other scholars prefer to stick to the term **suicide missions**, as opposed to suicide terrorism per se (Gambetta 2005). The logic underlying the choice to refer to missions as opposed to attacks or bombings stems from the desire to separate individual acts from those decided by and executed with the support of an organization. The studies that comprise Gambetta's (2005) edited volume on understanding suicide missions thus focus explicitly on explaining organizations' rationale for using suicide attacks. They are less concerned with attempting to understand individual motivations for suicide terrorism specifically, or why people might become suicide bombers.

The term **self-immolation** typically refers to an act in which an individual intentionally kills herself on behalf of a collective cause. Unlike a suicide attack or suicide mission, however, an act of self-immolation is not intended to cause any harm to anyone else or to inflict material damage upon others (Biggs 2005). It is more akin to an act of symbolic protest in that it is intended to be public, either through the performance of the act in a public space, or the intentional leaving behind of a written letter addressed to political figures or to the general public. A prominent recent example of self-immolation is Mohamed Bouazizi's act of setting himself on fire in December 2010 in Tunisia, which set off the wave of popular protests that has come to be known as the Arab Spring. Most scholars do not consider acts of self-immolation as methods of terrorism because of their deliberate avoidance of harm to others. In fact, some argue that self-immolation, albeit a method of deliberate self-harm, does not qualify as a violent act for the same reason.

EXPLAINING SUICIDE TERROR

Strategic approaches start from the assumption that there is nothing irrational about sacrificing one's life for a cause, or in sending others to do so. Like other forms of terrorism, a suicide attack is a weapon of terror usually chosen by weaker parties against materially stronger opponents. Proponents of this approach therefore see the use of suicide bombers as a strong signal of resolve and credibility (Pape 2003). Others see it as a valuable recruitment tool. For instance, surveys conducted in the wake of the 9/11 suicide attacks on New York and Washington, DC showed that an overwhelming 95 percent of educated Saudis aged twenty-five to forty-one supported Al Qaeda and its use of suicide terrorism tactics (Atran 2003). The massive retaliation that is expected to ensue in the wake of a suicide attack is also likely to deepen a population's sense of victimization, bolstering support for the violent organization as a defender of the aggrieved—a clear implication of the provocation logic of terrorism. And there are tactical benefits to suicide terrorism as well; the bomber can carry the device directly to the site of the explosion, and no escape route is required.

Strategic approaches also emphasize how different counterterrorism policies—like target hardening—might create unintended substitution effects, including suicide terror. For example, many countries have installed large cement barricades in front of airport terminals to guard against truck-bombings. Although this means that truck-bombings may be less likely, it also means that groups that are committed to attacking airports may use people as delivery systems, concealing explosives under their clothing or in luggage that is difficult to detect. This was the case during the bombing of the Domodedovo International Airport in Moscow on January 24, 2011. Fortifications on the outside of the international arrivals hall did not prevent one or more suspected suicide bombers from entering the baggage claim area and detonating an improvised device, killing dozens and wounding hundreds.

Whether terror groups adopt suicide tactics to attack soft targets or military targets that remain out of the reach of conventional tactics, strategic approaches contend that groups employ suicide terror as a rational and effective means by which to further their goals. Suicide terrorism is cheap and reliable relative to other forms of attacks such as improvised explosive devices or intricate hijackings. In his work on the topic, Robert Pape (2005) contends that groups employing coordinated campaigns of suicide bombings achieve success more than 50 percent of the time. Suicide terrorism, according to his studies, has been particularly effective at forcing the withdrawal of foreign occupiers, particularly when those occupiers are democratic states. This early research originally suggested that suicide bombings were thus largely driven by foreign occupation, and that groups turned to this particular tactic to impose high costs on the occupier, signal their willingness to use brute force to fight to the death, and raise the media profile of their struggle (Pape 2003, 2005). Pape saw democracies as particularly susceptible to such tactics because of the sensitivity and responsiveness of democratic leaders to the opinions of their publics, as well as the existence of a free media—both of which are less assured in autocratic contexts.

A key critique of Pape's argument, however, is that he **selected on the dependent variable** to arrive at these findings. In his analysis, he focuses only on instances in which suicide terrorism occurred, thus failing to compare the success of this particular tactic to other forms of terrorism, such as hijackings or non-suicide bombings, or other methods of resistance more generally. Subsequent literature that expands the dependent variable to account for all forms of terrorist violence finds that foreign occupation is statistically more related to violent resistance as a whole, as opposed to suicide terrorism in particular (Horowitz 2010; Moghadam 2006; Piazza 2008). Indeed, suicide terrorism is but one in a menu of tactical choices available to terror organizations. In many cases—such as Saudi Arabia and Pakistan—suicide bombings take place within the country against domestic targets, therefore undermining the idea that groups only employ suicide terrorism against democratic occupiers. In addition, narrowing Pape's definition of success leads to the finding that suicide bombings are only effective in 24 percent of cases, as opposed to 50 percent (Moghadam 2006). Thus, there is no real evidence to suggest that suicide terrorism is more effective than other forms of terrorism—if effectiveness is measured by overall strategic success.

Of course, as with the strategic approach more generally, the claim that suicide terrorism is ineffective depends on how one measures success. Suicide attacks tend to be considerably more lethal than other tactics. In a 2016 study, Joseph Mroszczyk finds that the average suicide attack kills 9 people, compared with an average of 2 people per non-suicide terror incident (p. 8). On the other hand, Mroszczyk suggests that despite these average effects, remotely-detonated bombs, such as improvised explosive devices and roadside bombs, are actually more reliably lethal than suicide bombings. This is because remotely detonated bombs have the same (or greater) explosive power, but they are less subject to accidents, ambivalence, last-minute changes of heart, or other operational interference.

At the level of individuals, some have modeled the decision to become a suicide bomber as a type of intergenerational wealth transfer, whereby the bomber attempts to protect more wealth for future generations—particularly his or her own family members—by making sacrifices in the present (Azam 2005). Because many suicide bombers receive promises of payment to their families upon successful completion of their attacks, using suicide terrorism as a key repertoire attracts recognition, recruits, and power to a violent organization. The decision of an individual to become a suicide bomber is thus a rational one, assuming that the ultimate preference of the bomber is to maximize a collective good, rather than a personal one. Moreover, some suggest that promises of benefits, relief, or the amelioration of suffering in the afterlife may appeal to rational individuals more than the assurance of continued suffering on earth. This may be particularly true in contexts where deprivations and grievances are intense (we expand upon this idea in our discussion of the structural approach below; see also Chapter 6).

The individual-level strategic approach provides another puzzle, which is why groups or their sponsors would specifically seek out suicide bombers over other types of recruits for support. Why would suicide bombers be more valuable to an organization than participants who live to fight another day?

Recall that **organizational approaches** emphasize that terrorist organizations tend to behave in relation to the other political groups operating in their environments. Thus, they tend to see suicide terrorism as a function of competitive inter-group dynamics. A group's decision to use suicide terror may be a way to gain an edge over the competition. The tactic may be particularly attractive insofar as it enhances an organization's prestige and provides it with advantages when it comes to public image, recruiting, publicity, and funding (Bloom 2005). Suicide bombings thus not only help terrorist groups achieve their ultimate ends, but also more intermediary organizational goals necessary to their survival, such as attracting more recruits and money. Bloom (2005) uses the LTTE in Sri Lanka, the PKK in Turkey, and Palestinian terrorist organizations to demonstrate that **outbidding** can be a powerful determinant of suicide terrorism.

Other organizational theories point to somewhat different inter-group dynamics to explain the use of suicide bombing. The actions of Al Qaeda, for instance, may not be as easily explained through competition theories such as Bloom's (2005). Instead, a more convincing argument may be that the organization turned to suicide terrorism to become a role model for Islamist militant groups worldwide (Schweitzer and Ferber 2005). If interpreted along these lines, the use of suicide terrorism may be a marker of Al Qaeda's success in the world of global terrorism— sacrificing one's life has been made into the near-exclusive symbol of global jihad, intended to inspire imitation in affiliate groups. Suicide terrorism has not necessarily emerged out of local competition among terrorist organizations, but made inroads in strengthening transnational cooperation and coordination among violent groups. Organizational approaches also emphasize the social satisfaction derived from an intense commitment to a group preparing an individual for the ultimate sacrifice, promising blissful afterlife rewards, and guaranteeing care for one's family after the sacrifice is complete.

When it comes to suicide terrorism, in particular, some organizational theories frequently consider suicide bombings as a technological (or military) innovation. For example, Horowitz (2010) finds that younger terrorist organizations, or those that are less set in their ways, are more likely to adopt suicide bombing as a tactic against their opponent. Thinking about suicide terrorism as a particular case of **diffusion** in the arena of military tactics available to groups, he shows how the propensity for a violent group to adopt the tactic depends in part on its external linkages, and on the organizational capabilities of the group. Other theories highlight how direct or indirect connections between terrorist groups, as well as alliances, allow groups to learn from one another (Asal and Rethemeyer 2008; Horowitz and Potter 2014). The LTTE of Sri Lanka, for instance, is infamous for having pioneered the design of the **suicide vest**, an innovation that spread rapidly to other terrorist organizations throughout the world. It is also notable that the LTTE was a largely secular nationalist group, despite the fact that many people associate suicide bombings with jihadist-inspired terrorism.

In short, for proponents of the organizational approach, suicide terror is an effective way of demonstrating a group's determination and dedication to a cause, it sets those who use it apart from competitors, and it contributes to binding together the members of a terrorist group to its supporters.

That said, the organizational approach possesses several important shortcomings, not least of which is the contradictory expectations produced by the approach. Specifically, organizational approaches speculate that suicide terrorism can emerge from competition (Bloom 2005) or cooperation (Horowitz 2010) between groups. This makes it difficult to derive any specific practical recommendations for how to address it. Moreover, organizational approaches do not explain why suicide terrorism specifically increases public perceptions of the group's commitment to the cause compared with others types of tactics.

The fact that groups such as Hizballah were the first to employ suicide bombings as part of their tactical repertoire led many early scholars

BOX 9.2

SOCIAL NETWORK APPROACHES TO SUICIDE TERRORISM

A growing number of studies in conflict and terrorism orient themselves towards understanding how the internal network of a terrorist organization might affect outcomes such as target selection, robustness to detection, and the use of suicide bombing. These studies are based on social network theory and use **social network analysis** (SNA) to examine relationships that exist among actors within analytically specific boundaries. These patterns of relationships are then linked to the types of outcomes enumerated above. Specific research questions that draw on network logic to study terrorism include: are decentralized networks more capable and adaptive than decentralized ones? How does network structure reflect the trade-off between the need for coordination and the risk of detection by counterterrorism elements? Do terrorist networks characterized by highly connected hubs improve information flow across members (Zech and Gabbay 2016)?

In some ways, network approaches are complementary to socio-organizational approaches like the ones discussed earlier in this chapter. For instance, social networks appear to play a significant role in predicting which members of a violent organization become suicide bombers based on the position of individuals in an organization's internal network of members. Those located at the periphery of social networks (i.e., those who remain relatively disconnected from others) are more likely to become suicide attackers relative to highly connected individuals (Pedahzur and Perliger 2006). This finding ties well with others that show that the suicide bomber is a weapon in the service of an elite that prefers to assign individuals of minimal importance to the task. At the inter-group level, Horowitz (2010) shows that a large number of connections between groups helped speed the diffusion of suicide bombing as a tactic. Al Qaeda and its affiliate network have played a particularly prominent role in the spread of knowledge and expertise to partner groups. Hence, social networks may play a major role in determining which groups employ the tactic as well.

to believe that suicide terrorism could be largely attributed to religious organizations—in particular, Islamist fundamentalists. **Ideological approaches** explain suicide terrorism as a symbolic act meant to evoke specific moral or spiritual meanings or identities that make the tactic salient to the constituency and the target population. Proponents of this approach point to the lengths to which some terrorists go to justify their actions in religious terms, manipulating the writings of religious texts and finessing the meanings of key concepts such as suicide, martyrdom, and jihad to rationalize this activity. In the aftermath of the 9/11 attacks, analysts seized on the fact that the 19 attackers were members of Al Qaeda, implicating their adherence to **Salafist** interpretations of Islam (Gerges 2009).

As Horowitz (2015) highlights, one of the most robust findings in the suicide bombing literature is that the tactic is positively correlated to specific religious beliefs. Pape (2005) and Pape and Feldman (2010), for instance, find that religious differences between a group and its target make the use of suicide attacks more likely. They hypothesize that these differences enflame sectarian or nationalist sentiment and reduce barriers to increasingly radical tactics such as suicide terrorism. Others such as Bruce Hoffman (2004) and Assaf Moghadam (2009) point specifically to the theology of Salafi jihadists to explain why terrorist groups adopt suicide tactics.

In fact, studies show that the spread of suicide terrorism in recent years, particularly in the wake of the 9/11 attacks, may be a result of the rising global appeal of Salafi jihad. Al Qaeda's evolution to global terrorist actor has contributed to the spread of the tactic, suggesting that what had once been a relatively localized phenomenon has converged towards exhibiting a global influence (Moghadam 2009). Figure 9.4 shows the distribution of suicide terrorist attacks between 1982 and 2015 according to the religious identity of the perpetrators.

Quasi-ideological explanations of suicide terrorism combine religious ideology with insights from other fields. For instance, Braun and Genkin (2014) hypothesize that entrenched societal orientations toward **collectivism** lower the cost of adopting suicide tactics, because it makes recruiting suicide bombers easier and reduces popular backlash against self-sacrifice.

Some cultural explanations of suicide terrorism unpack religious devotion by pointing to the actual practices of potential supporters of the tactic. Ginges, Hansen, and Norenzayan (2009), for example, use survey methodology to demonstrate that religious devotion measured through attendance at religious services is a significant predictor of support for suicide terrorism.

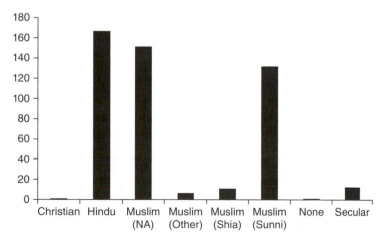

Figure 9.4   Religious Affiliation of Known Suicide Attackers, 1982–2015

Source: CPOST 2016

Regular attendance at a place of worship increased the likelihood of individuals to express willingness for martyrdom, and to demonstrate higher out-group hostility. Routine prayer, on the other hand, was not statistically related to support for suicide terrorism. These results hold across six different religions, intimating that the relationship is not unique to Islam (ibid.).

The problem with assigning causality to religion in explanations of suicide terrorism, however, is the fact that some of the tactic's most devoted practitioners were not motivated by religion. In fact, for quite some time, the Tamil Tigers (LTTE) of Sri Lanka were the single most prolific producers of suicide terrorism in the world. The LTTE was a Hindu group, but as an ideology, Hinduism does not have a system of potential religious rewards for martyrs. Instead, the LTTE's suicide missions were inspired more by cultish devotion to the group's leader, Velupillai Prabhakaran, than by any religion. Similarly, the Kurdish Worker's Party (PKK), which has deployed suicide bombers in its quest for Kurdish autonomy in the Middle East, is influenced not by Islam but by Marxist-Leninism. In their work on the use of suicide terrorism, Berman and Laitin (2008) argue that religious group's use of the tactic may actually be unrelated to theology itself. Instead, they argue that religious groups are more likely to adopt suicide bombing in response to intragroup dynamics (Berman 2009; Berman and Laitin 2008). Those that provide social services to their members have a universal claim on their cadre of fighters. The possibility that members may be required to sacrifice their lives as suicide bombers is used to weed out lukewarm supporters of the organization and to prevent the infiltration of potential informants or defectors. The use of suicide tactics—even by religious organizations—may thus result from efforts to ensure organizational survival.

Psychological explanations seek to understand why individuals become suicide bombers. Perhaps the best-known scholar of individual propensities towards suicide terrorism is the late psychologist Ariel Merari. His book *Driven to Death: Psychological and Social Aspects of Suicide Terrorism* (2010) contains rich evidence and insight into the phenomenon. In his interviews of 15 would-be suicide bombers in the Palestinian Territories, he finds that each individual was systematically different from members of a control group of convicted terrorists who did not use suicide bombing. In particular, more than half of the interviewed subjects were diagnosed with Avoidant-Dependent Personality Disorder, and almost half displayed suicidal tendencies. They did not, however, display psychopathic or impulsive tendencies. Other researchers have found that female suicide bombers in particular seem in part driven by **post-traumatic stress disorder**, hopelessness, and despair (Lester 2010).

One study aggregates the various motives for becoming a suicide bomber under the umbrella term "quest for personal significance" (Kruglanski et al. 2009). As we discuss in more detail in Chapter 4, this "quest" may explain a range of motivations for suicide terrorism in response to personal causes (trauma, humiliation); ideological motivation (liberation from foreign occupation, nationalism); and social pressures. Therefore, suicide terrorism may be representative of attempts at what scholars call "significance restoration, significance gain, and prevention of significance loss" (ibid. 331).

Some have criticized this integrative approach as absolving researchers from the responsibility of taking context into account. By lumping all motivations for suicide terrorism into a broad "quest for personal significance," the context in which the individual acts and chooses to become a suicide bomber falls out of the picture. Critics argue that such explanations are consistent with fundamental attribution error, whereby researchers underestimate or ignore the powerful impact of a situational context on the attitudes and motivations of these would-be perpetrators (Bloom 2009). In the case of Merari's study, for instance, the general plight of hopelessness of Palestinian youth may be due primarily to life under Israeli occupation rather than to pathological personality disorders (ibid.).

Another weakness of this approach is that the psychological correlates of suicide terrorism appear identical to those predicting individual engagement in violence more generally (Merari 2002). Particular socioeconomic or personality factors, such as social dysfunction or suicidal tendencies, make individuals vulnerable to recruitment in violent organizations that may or may not use suicide terror as a tactic. Ultimately, most psychological explanations emphasize the normality and absence of individual psychopathology that might differentiate suicide bombers from other types of militants. Because suicide bombers tend to come from many different types of communities and from different situations, making individual-level generalizations about suicide terrorism is particularly difficult (Pedahzur 2005).

In response to such criticisms, social-psychological explanations address the intersection of individual-level psychology and broader dynamics that occur at the societal level. Atran (2003), for instance, cites a study of 900 Palestinian Muslims that finds that exposure to violence is correlated with pride and social cohesion, more than it is to depression or antisocial behavior. Other studies show how pain and suffering alone is not sufficient to explain participation in suicide attacks. Instead, observers must analyze these strong feelings alongside an environment where there is no political outlet through which to express grievances and achieve change (Hassan 2001).

Therefore, many scholars turn to **structural approaches** to explain suicide terrorism, which focus on macro causes of the perpetrators' hardships. Recall the discussion above, where we alluded to certain circumstances that might lead a rational individual to prefer life after death to life on earth. At one point, for example, individual suicide bombers appeared to fall into a recognizable category: young, male, single, religious, and unemployed. Some studies argue that high levels of **gender differentiation, polygyny,** and limited marriage markets in Islamic societies might influence individual propensities to become suicide bombers (Thayer and Hudson 2010). For some men living in Islamic societies, becoming a suicide bomber or **shaheed** is the most effective response to life under patriarchal systems where gendered expectations and hierarchies are incredibly rigid and potential mates are scarce. In other words, there may be material and nonmaterial expected benefits derived from sacrificing one's own life in the killing of others (Rosendorff and Sandler 2010). We would therefore expect suicide attacks to be higher in places with high poverty, high unemployment rates, few options for social mobility, high gender differentiation, and little chance for political expression to change these systems.

Of course, like structural theories of terrorism more broadly, direct connections between poverty and suicide terrorism are difficult to establish. For instance, the nineteen suicide bombers that took part in the September 11 attacks on New York and Washington all had relatively middle-class backgrounds. The complexity of many suicide missions (such as the 9/11 attacks) suggests that individuals with high levels of education and socio-economic privilege, rather than those living in abject poverty, might make more valuable recruits. Consider the patterns depicted in Figures 9.5 and 9.6 below.

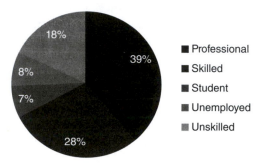

Figure 9.5   Occupations of Known Suicide Bombers, 1982–2015

Source: CPOST 2016

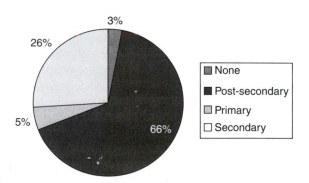

Figure 9.6   Education Levels of Known Suicide Bombers, 1982–2015

Source: CPOST 2016

Professionals with post-secondary educations carried out the majority of suicide attacks between 1982–2015.[1]

While poverty itself may not be an important variable in determining the likelihood of becoming a suicide bomber, related factors such as high unemployment might create incentives for groups to use the tactic (Bueno de Mesquita 2005). Benmelech and Berrebi (2007), for example, find that as societal poverty increases, the ability of militant organizations to recruit more qualified suicide bombers increases. These individuals are also more likely to succeed in their missions (Benmelech and Berrebi 2007).

Moreover, the gender differentiation argument fails to capture the complicated dynamic of women's participation in terrorism as suicide bombers—a phenomenon that has gained increasing attention in Chechnya, Somalia, Nigeria, and elsewhere (Bloom, Thayer, and Hudson 2010)—although in some places, like, Nigeria, observers suspect that Boko Haram kidnapped and coerced many women suicide bombers into their missions. We discuss women suicide bombers more in Chapter 12.

Another structural variable theorized to affect the likelihood of suicide terrorism is regime type. Recall from Chapter 6 the myriad established relationships between terrorism and democracy. With respect to suicide terrorism in particular, early theories suggested that democracies engaged in foreign military occupations were more likely to experience suicide attacks relative to other types of regimes (Pape 2003). As highlighted above, however, later studies based on country-year units of analysis failed to find a statistically significant relationship between suicide terror and democracy. Indeed, some findings even show that groups from nondemocracies are more likely to use suicide bombing (Piazza 2008) due to the relative ease of recruiting suicide bombers in more closed societies.

Other structural studies further disaggregate the relationship between regime type and terrorism, showing that, on its own regime type may be unrelated to the use of suicide tactics. Instead, the interaction between regime openness and the number of religious groups in a country is more powerful in explaining why groups use suicide terror. Wade and Reiter (2007) show that for states that are either fully or partially democratic, an increase in the number of religiously distinct groups may increase propensities for suicide terrorism. The relationship disappears for autocratic states. Nevertheless, the strongest macro-level predictors of suicide terrorism remains the size of a country, whether it is a Muslim majority state, and its past experience with terrorism. Within Muslim countries specifically, education level and income fail to act as stable predictors of support for suicide terrorism.

The primary weakness of the structural approach is its failure to account for the rarity of suicide bombings in places where it is the most likely. If macro indicators like poverty or country size are to blame for terrorism, then

---

[1] The figures include data for suicide attacks carried out by known perpetrators. The majority of attackers included in the CPOST data are unknown.

it is difficult to explain why so few perpetrators of suicide terrorism are from large, poor countries.

Critical approaches tend to see suicide terrorism as a socially constructed phenomenon, largely derived from immoral and unjustifiable policies of states. For instance, citing Pape (2003), Jackson et al. (2011) argue that foreign military interventions tend to precipitate suicide terrorism, leading them to conclude that suicide bombers emerge under desperate conditions of occupation as well as the West's humiliating and unrelenting need to characterize Muslims as sub-human. Critical terrorism scholars likewise point out that military interventions—such as those in Iraq and Afghanistan—have resulted in far more death and destruction than suicide bombers have caused. Such scholars point to the violence imposed by states as the primary problem, arguing that without such militaristic approaches to resolving conflicts, human beings would be much less likely to resort to such desperate tactics in the first place. Critical terrorism scholars would also point out that the fascination with suicide bombing, in particular, does a disservice to the study of conflict by further detaching the field from a frame of reference that accounts for the roots of conflict rather than the specific tactics of nonstate actors.

Of course, empirical terrorism scholars would reject this critique as a caricature of the field, arguing that people who attempt to study suicide terror from an empirical perspective do take into account the political, social, and historical contexts in which the phenomenon takes place. Indeed, they attempt to do so precisely to demystify suicide terrorism such that contemporary understandings of the phenomenon are not subject to baseless claims. Moreover, Pape's work is itself part of the empirical terrorism studies tradition (2003, 2005), and critical terrorism scholars happily cite it over other empirical studies because it provides evidence that confirms their own moral orientations.

PRACTICAL IMPLICATIONS

Structural explanations of suicide terrorism—in particular, the lack of a robust correlation between poverty, education, and suicide bombings—suggest that policies aimed at raising literacy rates are unlikely to be effective in curbing suicide terrorism. Indeed, such policies could be counterproductive if they increase access to terror group propaganda found on the Internet or in print.

The findings that suicide bombers are more likely to hail from nondemocratic countries suggests that suicide terrorism is affected by the political opportunities and avenues for political participation afforded to individuals. Though democracies have long produced more terrorism, they do appear to produce less *suicide* terrorism. This may have implications for democracy-promotion as a productive way to prevent suicide terrorism specifically. That said, promoting democracy through force—especially through military interventions—tends to produce more, not less, suicide terrorism (Pape 2003). Ending foreign occupations and reducing humiliation of certain populations may help, but not if such policies are seen as concessions in direct response to suicide terror attacks. Instead, this could effectively generate a demonstration effect that would embolden others to use the technique. The primary practical implication of the strategic approach, then, is to fortify vulnerable targets against suicide terror attacks.

Yet some experts argue that suicide terrorism is perhaps the most resilient tactic in the face of target hardening for several reasons (Atran 2003). First, suicide attackers have a wide range of options when it comes to choosing potentially easy-to-hit targets. A suicide bomber can walk into any number of potentially sensitive targets, ranging from sports stadiums, to nightclubs, to malls. It is virtually impossible to defend every conceivable target. Second, would-be suicide bombers are in relative abundance and require little supervision or direction to complete their mission. They are likely to maintain low profiles until their assigned attacks and remain unassuming in crowds. Finally, the relative simplicity and wide availability of materials used in making the components required for a suicide attack—such as a suicide vest—make it difficult to detect plots in advance.

If this view is correct, the only suitable defense is to prevent people from becoming suicide bombers in the first place. A direct counterterrorism response to psychological explanations of suicide terrorism would be to expose the suicidal motives that individual terrorists exhibit. This could decrease the appeal or credibility of the concept of martyrdom, which groups frequently use to justify and glorify acts of suicide terrorism. If suicide attackers are widely perceived as desperate, traumatized, and mentally ill people, the populations in whose name they claim to act may become less eager to glorify them. Efforts to capture would-be suicide bombers alive might further contribute to reducing suicide attacks. By definition, death as part of a struggle against a targeted opponent is a critical component of a suicide mission's success. If would-be bombers are captured alive before having the chance to complete their suicidal missions, their constituents may see them as having failed in their missions to become martyrs.

A more complete understanding of the various organizational structures and recruiting practices of terrorist organizations may be a particularly valuable component of any strategy. More interviews with captured or would-be suicide bombers can continue to expand knowledge of the individual-level grievances that drive people to volunteer for suicide terror.

Finally, consideration of causal relationships between specific policies and the use of suicide terrorism will help to identify points of contention between perpetrators and targets. For instance, a primary lesson from the literature warns against indiscriminate and highly repressive responses and policies that may further legitimize terror groups in the eyes of the broader population (Kydd and Walter 2006). Benmelech, Berrebi, and Klor (2015) also show that the use of selective house demolition practices by Israeli Defense Forces that targeted the homes of Palestinian suicide terrorists led to a decrease in the number of suicide attacks. Precautionary or preemptive demolitions that did not discriminate between suicide bombers' homes and the homes of Palestinian civilians, however, caused a significant increase in attacks.

Empirical findings on suicide bombing are diverse, with some of the most prominent hypotheses receiving only mixed support. For instance, whether and how religion is related to suicide bombing remains an open question. And it is unclear how exactly suicide tactics might differ from the other tactical choices available to terrorist groups. This is a particularly relevant topic for policymakers and counterterrorism officials as use of the tactic continues. For further discussion on counterterrorism instruments, see Chapter 13.

SUMMARY

In this chapter, we have reviewed how different analytic approaches can help to explain suicide terrorism. Existing scholarship addresses variation in the use of suicide terrorism over time and explains why individuals might volunteer to become suicide bombers. We concluded the chapter with a discussion of the practical implications of these approaches for reducing instances of suicide terrorism.

Discussion Questions

1. Pakistan has recently seen a rise in suicide bombing. Watch Sharmeen Obaid Chinoy's TED Talk from 2010, entitled "Inside a School for Suicide Bombers." After watching the video, which analytic perspective presented in this chapter do you think best explains the recent rise of suicide bombing in Pakistan?
2. What approach do you think best explains the spread of suicide terrorism globally?
3. Do you find individual-level or group-level theories more convincing to explain the use of suicide terrorism?
4. How do you think suicide terrorism differs conceptually from terrorism more generally? Does it make sense to study suicide terror as its own, separate tactic?
5. What are some of the most effective counterterrorism strategies directed specifically at curbing suicide attacks?

KEY TAKEAWAYS

- Contrary to widespread views that suicide bombers are irrational or suicidal, scholars have developed a wide variety of plausible explanations for why individuals and groups might use this tactic.
- One of the most prominent explanations for suicide terror comes from Robert Pape, who argues that the tactic has been particularly effective at driving out military occupations by democratic countries. However,

others have contested this view, suggesting that suicide terrorism is motivated by ideology, poverty and unemployment, or personal hardships and indignities.

- Suicide terrorism has become a far more prominent method of terrorism in the past thirty years, leading many observers to associate it with the rise of Salafi jihadi groups, in particular. However, it is notable that one of the largest proponents of the tactic has been the LTTE, a Hindu-Marxist group, suggesting that the method is certainly not exclusive to Salafi jihadi groups.

SUGGESTED FURTHER READINGS

Atran, Scott. 2003. "Genesis of Suicide Terrorism." *Science* 299 no. 5612: 1534-1539.

Atran, Scott, and Ara Norenzayan. 2004. "Why Minds Create Gods: Devotion, Deception, Death, And Arational Decision Making." *Behavioral and Brain Sciences* 27.06.

Atran, Scott. 2006. "The Moral Logic and Growth of Suicide Terrorism." *The Washington Quarterly* 29 (2): 127–147.

Benmelech, Efraim, and Claude Berrebi. 2007. "Human Capital and The Productivity Of Suicide Bombers." *Journal of Economic Perspectives* 21 (3): 223–238. doi:10.1257/jep.21.3.223.

Benmelech, Efraim, Claude Berrebi, and Esteban F. Klor. 2015. "Counter-Suicide-Terrorism: Evidence from House Demolitions." *The Journal of Politics* 77 (1): 27–43. doi:10.1086/678765.

Berman, Eli, and David D. Laitin. 2008. "Religion, Terrorism and Public Goods: Testing The Club Model." *Journal of Public Economics* 92 (10–11): 1942–1967. doi:10.1016/j.jpubeco.2008.03.007.

Berman, Eli. 2009. "Response to Adrian Guelke." *Critical Studies on Terrorism* 2 (2): 325–326. doi:10.1080/17539150903024831.

Bloom, Mia. 2009. "Chasing Butterflies and Rainbows: A Critique of Kruglanski et al.'s Fully Committed: Suicide Bombers' Motivation And The Quest For Personal Significance." *Political Psychology* 30 (3): 387–395. doi:10.1111/j.1467-9221.2009.00703.x.

Bloom, Mia, Bradley A. Thayer, and Valerie M. Hudson. 2010. "Life Sciences and Islamic Suicide Terrorism." *International Security* 35 (3): 185–192. doi:10.1162/isec_c_00027.

Braun, Robert, and M. Genkin. 2014. "Cultural Resonance and The Diffusion of Suicide Bombings: The Role Of Collectivism." *Journal of Conflict Resolution* 58 (7): 1258–1284. doi:10.1177/0022002713498707.

Crenshaw, Martha. 2007. "Explaining Suicide Terrorism: A Review Essay." *Security Studies* 16 (1): 133–162. doi:10.1080/09636410701304580.

Freedman, Lawrence D. 2005. "Making Sense of Suicide Missions." *Foreign Affairs* 84 (6): 141.

Freedman, Lawrence D., Robert Pape, and Mia Bloom. 2005. "Dying To Win: The Strategic Logic of Suicide Terrorism." *Foreign Affairs* 84 (5): 172. doi:10.2307/20031726.

Ginges, Jeremy, Ian Hansen, and Ara Norenzayan. 2009. "Religion and Support for Suicide Attacks." *Psychological Science* 20 (2): 224–230. doi:10.1111/j.1467-9280.2009.02270.x.

Hoffman, Bruce, and Gordon H. McCormick. 2004. "Terrorism, Signaling, And Suicide Attack." *Studies in Conflict & Terrorism* 27 (4): 243–281. doi:10.1080/10576100490466498.

Horowitz, Michael C. 2010. "Nonstate Actors and the Diffusion of Innovations: The Case of Suicide Terrorism." *International Organization* 64 (1): 33–64.doi:10.1017/s0020818309990233.

Horowitz, Michael C. and Philip. B. K. Potter. 2014. "Allying To Kill: Terrorist Intergroup Cooperation and the Consequences for Lethality." *Journal of Conflict Resolution* 58 (2): 199–225. doi:10.1177/0022002712468726.

Horowitz, Michael. 2015. "The Rise and Spread of Suicide Bombing". *Annual Review of Political Science* 18 (1): 69–84. doi:10.1146/annurev-polisci-062813-051049.

Kruglanski, Arie W., Xiaoyan Chen, Mark Dechesne, Shira Fishman, and Edward Orehek. 2009. "Fully Committed: Suicide Bombers' Motivation And The Quest For Personal Significance." *Political Psychology* 30 (3): 331–357. doi:10.1111/j.1467-9221.2009.00698.x.

Merari, Ariel. 2002. "Deterring Fear: Government Responses to Terrorist Attacks." *Harvard International Review* 23 (4): 26–31. Available online at: http://www.jstor.org/stable/42762757, last accessed 17-March-2017.

Merari, Ariel. 2010. *Driven to Death: Psychological and Social Aspects of Suicide Terrorism.* Oxford: Oxford University Press.

Moghadam, Assaf. 2003. "Palestinian Suicide Terrorism In The Second Intifada: Motivations and Organizational Aspects." *Studies in Conflict & Terrorism* 26 (2): 65–92. doi:10.1080/10576100390145215.

Moghadam, Assaf. 2006. "Suicide Terrorism, Occupation, and the Globalization of Martyrdom: A Critique of Dying to Win." *Studies in Conflict & Terrorism* 29 (8): 707–729. doi:10.1080/10576100600561907.

Moghadam, Assaf. 2008. *The Globalization of Martyrdom: Al Qaeda, Salafi Jihad, and the Diffusion of Suicide Attacks.* Baltimore: Johns Hopkins University Press.

Moghadam, Assaf. 2009. "Motives for Martyrdom: Al-Qaida, Salafi Jihad, And The Spread Of Suicide Attacks." *International Security* 33 (3): 46–78. doi:10.1162/isec.2009.33.3.46.

Pape, Robert A. 2003. "The Strategic Logic of Suicide Terrorism." *American Political Science Review* 97 (03). doi:10.1017/s000305540300073x.

Pape, Robert. 2005. *Dying to win: The Strategic Logic of Suicide Terrorism.* New York: Random House.

Pape, Robert A. 2008. "Methods and Findings in The Study of Suicide Terrorism." *American Political Science Review* 102 (02): 275–277. doi:10.1017/s000305540300073x.

Pape, Robert A., and James K. Feldman. 2010. *Cutting the fuse: The Explosion of Global Suicide Terrorism and How to Stop It.* Chicago Series on International and Dome. Chicago: University of Chicago Press.

Pedahzur, Ami. 2005. *Suicide Terrorism.* Cambridge, UK; Malden, MA: Polity.

Pedahzur, Ami., and Arie Perliger. 2006. "The Changing Nature of Suicide Attacks: A Social Network Perspective." *Social Forces* 84 (4): 1987–2008. doi:10.1353/sof.2006.0104.

Rosendorff, B. Peter, and Todd Sandler. 2010. "Suicide Terrorism and the Backlash Effect." *Defence and Peace Economics* 21 (5–6): 443–457. doi:10.1080/10242694.2010.491679.

Wade, Sara. J., and Dan Reiter. 2007. "Does Democracy Matter?: Regime Type And Suicide Terrorism." *Journal of Conflict Resolution* 51 (2): 329–348. doi:10.1177/0022002706298137.

CHAPTER 10

TERRORISM AND SOCIAL SERVICES

Learning Objectives

After reading this chapter, readers should be able to:

- Use logics from different analytical approaches to explain why some terror groups provide social services while others do not;
- Give examples of various types of social services that terror groups provide to surrounding populations;
- Provide examples of terrorist organizations that engage in the provision of social services;
- Describe the effects of social service provision on various outcomes of interest related to terrorism, such as relative levels of violence;
- Explain the implications of service provision by terrorist organizations from both practical and moral perspectives.

> "Even when we examine an organization whose members are dismissed as terrorists . . . an honest appraisal of its strategy must recognize the importance of service provision in generating popular support among its targeted population."
>
> —ZACHARIAH MAMPILLY (2011, P. 2)

> "We are linked to politics. Politics is number three. There is the human factor first, then religion, then politics. It's a hierarchy. You have politics and above it religion . . . Politics is in the service of religion and religion is in the service of humanity. That's the way it goes."
>
> —HIZBALLAH SOCIAL SERVICE PROVIDER,
> AS QUOTED IN FLANIGAN (2008, P. 505)

THE PUZZLE

Since its origins in the 1970s, the secessionist **Oromo Liberation Front (OLF)** has cultivated a powerful military force and developed education and healthcare services, built roads, and promoted agricultural development throughout OLF-controlled territory in Ethiopia. In doing so, the group has fostered strong ties to the civilian population and rarely uses direct violence against local civilians (Stewart and Liou 2017). **Boko Haram** (which operates primarily in Nigeria), on the other hand, has killed tens of thousands of civilians during its organizational lifetime. The group has perpetrated numerous atrocities, including a massacre of as many as two thousand civilians during a single attack in January 2015. Unlike the OLF, Boko Haram provides only limited services to local populations in Nigeria, choosing instead to rely primarily on violence to advance its goals of territorial expansion.

Why do some violent groups provide extensive public services to civilians under their control, while others do not? The performance of governmental functions by violent groups is common throughout history, as evidenced by groups such as **UNITA** in Angola, the **FARC** in Colombia, and **Hizballah** in Lebanon. Yet this practice contrasts with the dominant perception of the majority of armed groups, most frequently caricatured as little more than self-serving warlords. While this characterization is certainly valid for the leadership of many armed groups, such as the **Revolutionary United Front (RUF)** in Sierra Leone or **the Forces démocratiques de liberation du Rwanda (FDLR)** in the DRC, many groups control large territories for extended periods of time and establish government structures that allow them to provide basic **social services** and **governance** to local populations. Consider the various armed groups active in Syria today. Al Qaeda-affiliated groups entered the conflict during the summer of 2011, soon after the nonviolent movement against Assad's brutal rule had devolved into civil war. During this early phase, the largely moderate opposition had coalesced into a group called the Free Syrian Army (FSA), which remained fragmented and resorted to looting in many "free" areas. Elements of the more radical opposition, groups such as Jabhat al Nusra (JaN) and the Islamic State of Iraq and Syria (ISIS), entered these areas and provided starving civilians with food, water, medical supplies, care, and sometimes impromptu Islamic courts. Concurrent to the widely publicized atrocities these groups committed, they also helped local populations meet basic needs in areas that the international community found difficult or impossible to reach. These governance practices created a sense of order in these contexts, albeit ones that involved violent regulation and implicit or explicit coercion.

Such incidents are not unique to the ongoing conflict in Syria and Iraq. Indeed, the model of social service provision stems from the age-old strategy of guerrilla warfare: the practice of imposing costs on an adversary while avoiding direct confrontation (Arreguin-Toft 2001). Importantly, guerrilla warfare requires a supportive population in order to achieve victory in a struggle against the state. Local populations prove crucial in supplying fighters with intelligence, shelter, logistical support, and human resources. Indeed, insurgents tend to gain legitimacy when they serve the local population's interests and enjoy some degree of popular consent (Gross 2015, p. 6). At its core, the concept of service provision by militant organizations comes from Che Guevara's theory of guerrilla warfare, which highlights the necessity of a rebel group's helping a local population by providing clothing and food while also representing the aspirations of the local populace. Viewed through these lenses, the provision of public goods and services by armed actors begins to make more sense. Applying theories and findings gleaned from the literature on guerrilla warfare to terrorist organizations may help us to better understand why some of these groups engage in the provision of social services, and to what effect.

The Palestinian militant group Hamas provides significant social services to the populations living in the territories that it controls (particularly in the Gaza Strip). In fact, one of the reasons the group has been so difficult to counter is because it is so deeply immersed in the local Palestinian population. What this suggests is that the nonviolent activities of some terror groups—specifically the provision of public services to local populations—may be an important component of their broader strategies to build support and defeat their opponents.

The scholarly literature on civil war, as well as patterns of empirical evidence observed among militant organizations, strongly suggests that abusing local populations seldom results in armed groups achieving their ultimate goals. For ISIS in Syria and Iraq and Al Qaeda affiliates in places like Yemen, Somalia, and Mali, violence is only part of a broader strategy to establish a local caliphate or emirate. A significant element of this broader strategy consists of implementing a way of life in specific territories and earning trust and legitimacy among the local population. To do so, the group may provide teachers, medical services, and food to populations that have not received services from the state for decades. For many of these populations, a day of electricity or a policeman on duty goes a long way toward building or renewing trust in whatever authority is willing to provide order.

The provision of social services by terror groups in particular is an especially intriguing puzzle, seeing as terrorists are less likely to control large swaths of territory relative to groups most often characterized as insurgents (de la Calle and Sanchez-Cuenca 2012). In this chapter, we address the puzzle of why terrorist groups provide social services, and to what effect. First we review some definitional issues with respect to terrorism itself, as well as those associated with social service provision. We then move to addressing the specific puzzle of service provision: why do some terror groups engage in service provision while others do not? Why do groups offer some specific services over others? We evaluate the effect of social service provision on whether armed nonstate actors achieve their goals, and we conclude by discussing the practical and normative implications of such practices in reducing terror violence.

WHAT IS SOCIAL SERVICE PROVISION?

What do we mean when we refer to the provision of social services, or to the provision of public goods more generally? In their dataset of Terrorist and Insurgent Organization Social Services (TIOS), Heger and Jung (2015) record the service provision trends of 400 armed groups. They suggest that service provision in conflict zones can take many forms. While some groups provide welfare, food, medical services, education, or religious services, others focus on developing public syndicates, establishing a police presence, or providing an independent media. Heger and Jung classify services into seven major categories, each comprised of more specific subtypes:

- Education/youth/recreation services
- Health/emergency services
- Security/justice services
- Jobs/welfare/financial services
- Natural disaster relief services
- Public services
- Religious services

The Revolutionary Armed Forces (FARC) in Colombia, for instance, supplied medical services to local populations, whereas the LTTE in Sri Lanka maintained mail delivery and other services for Tamil civilians during times of war. The IRA provided transportation services within Republican neighborhoods in Northern Ireland, and Hamas's elaborate service sector in the Gaza Strip covers a range of charitable operations and non-profit community resources.

Many of the goods provided to the local populace by service-providing terror groups are public or club goods. A **public good** is a commodity or service provided to all members of a society, either by the government or a nonstate organization or individual. A defining characteristic of such a good is that its consumption by one individual in society does not actually reduce the amount available to another individual. Thus public goods are non-excludable and non-rival. Building a road for public use, for instance, is a public good.

Club goods, on the other hand, are excludable but non-rival, in that their benefits accrue only to members of the group providing the good, but their consumption does not reduce the usefulness of the goods to other club members. For example, building a road or tunnel for use by villagers who have sworn allegiance to an armed group (but only those villagers who have

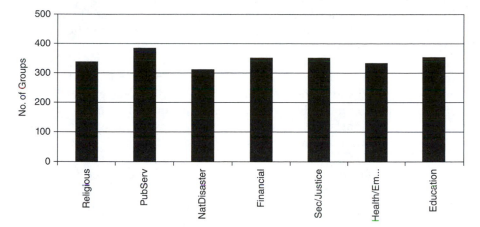

Figure 10.1 Terror and Insurgent Group Service Provision

Source: TIOS 2015

sworn allegiance) is an example of a club good. As we will see below, the concepts of public and club goods are used frequently in rational choice explanations of service provision by terror groups.

The TIOS data show that most of the 400 groups engage in some sort of service provision (see Figure 10.1). In fact, 144 groups (36 percent) provide as many as nine different types of services to local populations or to their members, while only five groups (1 percent) provide just one type of service. Public services are most prevalent, followed by financial and educational services. Security and justice services are also prevalent services offered by armed groups. Least common are the provision of services related to natural disasters and health care (Heger and Jung 2015, p. 10).

Heger and Jung also examine the relative service profiles of all groups to illustrate the variety of service provision patterns. Hizballah, for example, is among the top overall service providers. The group is heavily engaged in public services, disaster relief, and welfare. Second-tier groups include organizations such as the Irish Republic Army and the **Baloch Liberation Army** (Pakistan and Afghanistan), while the May 15 Organization for the Liberation of Palestine is among the lesser providers (ibid., p. 12).

TERROR, TERRITORIAL CONTROL, AND SERVICE PROVISION

In Chapter 1, we defined terrorism as the application of violence or threat of violence by a nonstate actor to sow fear in a broader audience to achieve a political goal. In the context of this chapter in particular, it is important to recognize that terrorism can often morph into or approach the limits of guerrilla warfare, typically characterized as irregular warfare in which a small group of combatants uses violent tactics to fight a larger, more technologically advanced military force.

In some scholarship, an important differentiation between terrorism and guerrilla warfare lies in the control of territory (de la Calle and Sánchez-Cuenca 2011, 2012) and in the targeting strategy. While some groups labeled as terror groups are incapable or disinterested in controlling territory, guerrilla warfare is a constant struggle over territorial control between an armed nonstate group and the state. Additionally, a key difference between guerrilla warfare and terrorism is the nature of their targets. Whereas guerrilla warfare constitutes hit-and-run assaults on military and police forces, terrorism tends to target noncombatants (see Chapter 1 for more discussion). As may be expected, then, the boundary between terrorism and guerrilla warfare is fuzzy and in many cases indistinguishable.[1]

Many groups that engage in guerrilla warfare also employ terror. And some of the armed groups that we consider in this chapter do control territory. Others do not, though they still provide public goods to the populations in whose midst they fight. Take, for example, the cases of the Provisional Irish Republic Army (IRA), Hamas in the Palestinian Territories, or the Tamil Tigers of Sri Lanka (LTTE)—all groups broadly considered terrorist organizations. While territorial control has been an important part of the strategies of the LTTE and Hamas, the IRA has been able to engage in service distribution without ever controlling territory. The political wings of these organizations have nevertheless provided social services and education to local populations; in many cases they have run businesses. Their military wings, on the other hand, have engaged in the violent attacks that governments and scholars have used to justify calling the groups terror groups. Some terror groups, on the other hand, have done little to engage in service provision toward the local population. For example, the Lord's Resistance Army in Uganda has brutalized civilians, but it has done nothing to improve life for people living within its range.

As will become evident over the course of this chapter, most explanations of service provision by terror and rebel groups are grounded in strategic and structural approaches to understanding specific political outcomes and processes. Certain structural factors may make territorial control easier to establish for armed groups. For instance, the absence of a strong and effective government presence may open doors for armed actors to engage in administering towns and taking on the role of a de facto government. Some explanations also fall under the rubric of organizational approaches, focusing on how service provision affects group recruitment strategies and the

---

[1] De la Calle and Sanchez Cuenca, for instance, contend that "if a rebel group that holds territory in the countryside decides to act in the capital city, it will be forced to operate there as any other underground group and therefore will use terrorist tactics" (2011, p. 453).

management of violence. A ready-made internal leadership infrastructure within the organization can enhance its capacity to govern. The ideological approach stresses that the group's claims may affect the likelihood that the group provides services. Fewer explanations are based on the psychological approaches reviewed in the first half of this text.

EXPLAINING VARIATION IN SERVICE PROVISION BY TERROR GROUPS

The most obvious—and perhaps most common—explanation for social service provision by terror groups emerges from the **strategic approach**. Rational choice theories acknowledge that the provision of social services by a militant organization does not necessarily mean that the group ceases to engage in violent activities. Indeed, since potential supporters of a group might benefit from successful attacks launched by the group, as well as from the services it provides, an organization balances the amount of resources and effort dedicated to one or the other (service provision or violence). Militant groups therefore face a trade-off when deciding between the level of investment into club goods like healthcare and education services to its supporters and the number and intensity of its violent attacks.

Viewed through the lens of rational choice theory, terror groups only invest in the provision of social services when they perceive some benefit from doing so. If the utility of providing a specific benefit becomes greater than the utility provided by other types of activities, such as heightened armed attacks, the group predictably provides social services. When a group perceives few benefits from providing such services, it tends towards heightened levels of violent attacks and away from social services. For instance, if a government begins to provide the social services needed by the supporters of a terror group, the group may switch tactics and begin to expend additional resources on armed attacks and military operations.

Thus, popular support for terror groups can be construed as a function of the level of social services provided, the capacity of the group to perpetuate further attacks, and the counterterrorism strategy of the government. Ly (2007) develops a model whereby the cost function of a terrorist organization assumes that a group's terror attacks and service provision affect and interact with one other. He organizes terror groups into three categories based on their relative balance of activity focused on service provision versus violence, differentiating between pure terrorist groups that invest in attacks but not service provision, hybrid organizations that invest both in attacks and charities, and groups that are directly active only in service provision, launching attacks solely on the basis of voluntary contributions of time and resources by its members. Ly places the following groups into the aforementioned categories based on their relative engagement in service provision and violence:

- Groups such as ETA in Spain or the Corsican Armata Corsa in France operate in developed democracies where access to public goods is high. Terrorist groups operating under such environments are unlikely to have much opportunity to add to the supply of public goods in society, and thus rely exclusively on violent actions to achieve their aims. Ly (2007) refers to these groups as pure terrorist organizations.

- Groups such as the LTTE in Sri Lanka, Hizballah in Lebanon, or Hamas in the Palestinian Territories fall under the hybrid category, whereby groups invest in both violent attacks and the provision of public goods. These three organizations can take advantage of the poor economic opportunities under which local populations live and accumulate popular support through engagement in both violent and nonviolent activities.

- The Muslim Brotherhood in Egypt is an example of the third, and most counterintuitive, type of group described by Ly (2007), which includes groups that focus almost exclusively on nonviolent strategies to achieve their goals. Despite sharing some of the same goals as violent organizations and a history of radicalization from within the group, these groups mobilize popular support at the grassroots level without promoting or engaging in violence. As Ly writes, the Muslim Brotherhood is committed to a "non-violent, reformist approach to Islamism" (ibid., p. 20) but is nonetheless officially listed as a terrorist organization in Russia, Syria, Egypt, Saudi Arabia, Bahrain, and the UAE.

As the strategic model suggests, the ability of both the government and the terror group to correctly distinguish supporters from non-supporters is critically important to understanding how the provision of social services might feed into the strategic goals of the organization. Should non-supporters benefit from the public goods provided by the militant group as easily as supporters, temptations to free ride would increase, and increases in popular support might become less certain. This incentive to provide services that improve the capacity of the group for differentiation may be why particular types of service provision, such as dispute adjudication and resolution services, are more common. These types of institutions are less capital-intensive than, say, providing education or health services to a population, but they provide terror groups with strategically important information about the communities in which they operate (Heger and Jung 2015).

The main critique of strategic approaches is that they are unable to explain why some groups do not engage in such nonviolent activities, or why groups differ in the extent to which they provide services. If social service provision presents groups with such critical strategic advantages, all groups should engage in service provision, and do so relatively equally. But as Heger and Jung's (2015) data show, this is not the case. Rates of service provision vary widely across groups in terms of frequency and type, suggesting that not all armed organizations have similarly extensive nonviolent wings dedicated to service provision.

Organizational approaches to understanding terrorism focus on the internal processes within groups to explain engagement in service provision. Because of an organization's struggle for survival in a competitive environment, social service provision may be a method of outbidding rival organizations for power and influence. Leaders offer varied incentives to group members to ensure organizational maintenance, some of which may stray from the group's overall goal. Most importantly, leaders seek to prevent defection or desertion by developing intense loyalties among group members. When it comes to understanding why armed groups engage in service provision, organizational approaches focus on how such activities might stabilize the internal structure of groups, attract new members into the organization, and deter defection (Heger 2010; Heger and Jung 2015).

Furthermore, Berman (2011) writes that radical religious organizations of all types rely on the provision of mutual aid to maintain a cohesive and particularly lethal cadre of fighters. Radical religious communities, whether Christian, ultra-Orthodox Jewish, or Muslim, require that members demonstrate their commitment to the group through costly or painful sacrifices. Hizballah, Hamas, and the Taliban, for instance, built loyalty by means of mutual aid, weeding out free riders and producing a reliable membership base.

Some have also linked the provision of social services by militant organizations to engagement in specific forms of violence—namely suicide bombing and other forms of highly lethal attacks against civilians (Heger, Jung, and Wong 2012, p. 749). This link rests primarily on the argument that these forms of violence are only possible when groups are internally strong, hierarchically organized, and have a significant degree of support from the population. Ultimately, because service-providing groups benefit from higher levels of organization, they are able to functionally differentiate themselves from competitors.

On the other hand, some argue that heightened organizational capacity and engagement in activities linked to service provision tend to produce more pacific outcomes. With clearly established lines of command and control, service-providing terror groups have been found to be more adept at negotiation as well as fighting. As a consequence, highly organized, service-providing militant groups are associated with shorter conflict durations, largely due to a smaller number of veto players or spoilers within their ranks (Cunningham 2006).

Together, organizational approaches to understanding social service provision by militant organizations point to the benefits of hierarchical organization. In most of these groups, leadership retains a high degree of operational command and control. This renders the organization increasingly immune to defections, and at the same time allows them to benefit from the support of a broad population base that is willing to tolerate or celebrate highly lethal attacks against targets.

Structural explanations suggest that when governments are absent, neglectful, or inefficient at providing their populations with public services—particularly economic opportunities or financial stability—terror groups can step in to become the principal suppliers of social services. Weak state capacity at the national level or in areas contested by armed groups opposing the state is an important precondition for the rise of militant group social service provision. In areas where states are unable to maintain a monopoly on the legitimate use of force, armed groups have the potential to further erode the legitimacy of the state by undermining its social contract with its citizens. For instance, in Afghanistan, the Taliban cut off the revenue streams for other armed groups by initially halting poppy production and reducing criminality. By securing trade routes, they restored commerce. The Muslim Brotherhood, which some states consider a terrorist group, has similarly provided health care, schooling, disaster relief, welfare, and community services to communities in Gaza and the West Bank. A group that uses its social welfare arm to undermine state legitimacy, obtain the loyalty of the populace, and supplant the state's social contract with its own poses a significant threat to the state (Grynkewich 2008). Ultimately, social welfare can create lasting infrastructures and loyalties not easily eroded when the state attempts to reassert control.

Consider the examples of ETA or the National Liberation Front of Corsica. Both of these groups exist in well-developed economies and functioning democracies, so they have limited opportunities to provide public goods where the state is absent or otherwise weak. Organizations such as Hamas and Hizballah, on the other hand, operate in a context of weak state capacity and the under-provision of social services by the state. These structural variables of state capacity and regime type more broadly may therefore be important in understanding when terrorist organizations might avail themselves of opportunities to engage in the provision of social services with an eye towards gaining popular support.

Socio-structural explanations for terrorist group and service provision further suggest that groups accrue three major benefits from providing social service to the local populace (Grynkewich 2008). First, the dissemination of public goods to desperate populations helps to highlight the inadequacy and sometimes the failure of the state, ultimately undermining its legitimacy in the eyes of local civilians. The creation of social welfare infrastructure by armed groups helps to underscore the state's failure to fulfill its side of the social contract, as discussed above.

Second, and as a result of the degradation of the state's legitimacy, violent organizations that have stepped in to provide social services are likely to see their own legitimacy increase among a target population. Over time, as non-state social welfare organizations offer alternatives to state-led governance, these violent organizations may accrue higher levels of loyalty than their government counterparts. Grynkewich points to the Muslim Brotherhood in the 1980s in Egypt as an example: "through its efforts to provide social services the Brotherhood built an Islamic version of the state's social contract, and succeeded in gaining a measure of social legitimacy" (2008, p. 354).

Consider this additional example. In July 2010, heavy monsoon rains led to devastating floods in Pakistan that affected nearly 20,000 Pakistanis, mostly by destroying property, livelihood, and infrastructure. Nearly 2,000 people died. Aid was slow in reaching affected populations, and the government's failure to respond to the crisis dismayed many local residents. During this time, militants belonging to the Pakistani Taliban, **Tehrik-i-Taliban (TTP)**, recognized that the catastrophe presented them with a unique and exploitable opportunity. The organization stepped in to provide extraordinary levels of aid to local populations, which helped them gain supporters. Their long-term engagement in regions devastated by the floods that had felt neglected by the government for decades provided local Taliban militants with measurable gains in local legitimacy and popular support (Kazim 2010).

The third benefit accrued to service-providing violent organizations is the influx of recruits, support, and sympathy from the population. In exchange for the public goods provided by social welfare organizations, the population provides a consistent stream of resources benefitting regime opponents. A gradual process of institutionalization may bring new forms of order to a previously contested and unstable environment.

One of the most important resources provided by nonstate armed groups in the face of weak government presence has been the provision of local justice and dispute arbitration. In the case of the Pakistani floods, heavy waters destroyed mud walls that had been used to demarcate property boundaries in rural areas. Many locals had little faith in the government's justice system to resolve problems of field demarcation, and local members of TTP stepped forward to arbitrate disputes effectively and efficiently (ibid.). The legitimacy of the fundamentalists grew strong as a direct result of state weakness, at a time when the national government failed to take care of basic sovereign duties. Local militant groups easily filled the vacuum.

In fact, the problem of weak local order and the Pakistani government's failure to grant its citizens recourse to courts and a justice system more broadly extends well beyond the 2010 floods. In addition to TTP, other militant groups such as **Jamaat-ud-Dawa (JuD)** and the emerging Islamic State (ISIS) have also stepped in deliver local governance as an alternative to the state. JuD has established a **Shariah** tribunal in the Lahore, a major city, revealing an underlying popular dissatisfaction with the official government's judicial system. Since corruption, bureaucracy, and political patronage have undermined the state's provision of justice, popular will has demanded community-based dispute resolution and justice provision through local and tribunal councils (Zaidi 2016).

Ultimately, structural explanations point strongly to the impact of state weakness, and in some cases state failure, to understand why some terror groups gravitate towards strategies of service provision. Armed groups provide goods and services when state institutions are either inadequate or nonexistent. By doing so, these groups gain power, legitimacy, and influence over the communities they serve. Indeed, by providing public goods and services to local populations, these groups expect acceptance of their authority in the areas where they are active. Territorial and political control are central motivators of organizational decision-making and behavior in this regard (Idler and Forest 2015), and the absence of the state provides a significant opening for militant groups. Importantly, the amount of power a social service provider is able to gain over the recipient of the services is a direct function of the recipient's ability to get aid from somewhere else. When the state is absent or considered inefficient, the potential for a nonstate actor to gain power via service provision is bolstered.

A key insight from this research program is that some forms of governance other than that provided exclusively by the state may result in higher levels of security for local populations, therefore providing real humanitarian benefits. Studying alternative forms of political order that depart from conventional state-centric models of authority constitutes an important avenue for future study, and may be particularly salient in the evolution of terrorism research.

Ideological approaches focus on understanding whether particular ideologies are more predisposed to service provision than others. Some posit that groups aiming to control territory and govern a population (e.g., nationalist-separatist groups) may be more prone to attempting to perform these state-like functions than groups that do not aspire to territorial control and governance (e.g., apocalyptic groups) (Heger and Jung 2015).

There is, however, mixed empirical support for this assertion. Some scholars argue instead that even radical ideological groups at times provide social services to people whom they would otherwise brutalize. Consider religious groups. Armed religious sects often become major suppliers of social services because of their organizational structures, rather than their theological beliefs per se. Religious militancy is most effective through a combination of strategies that work to raise the direct costs of violence, foster religious competition, improve social services, and encourage private enterprise (Iannacone and Berman 2006). From Egypt and Palestine to Afghanistan, Pakistan, and Indonesia, radical Islamist groups have enjoyed broad popular support not because of their doctrinal affiliations, but because they are major suppliers of aid and social services (ibid., 119). In Indonesia specifically, Muslims with reduced incomes in the wake of the 1997 currency crisis increased their participation in Islamic mutual insurance networks, as well as in Koran study groups (Chen 2003). And in Afghanistan, when the US stopped sending money to Islamist resistance fighters after the Soviet occupation ended there, militant groups stepped in to fill the income vacuum. They provided free education, room, and board to young boys and began training them to become members of the Taliban (Fritsch 2001). In short, such explanations of why terror groups engage in service provision are powerful rebuttals to ideological arguments that religion itself attracts individuals to joining violent groups, and those that suggest that groups that adhere to religious doctrines are ambivalent about providing social services compared with secular, nationalist groups.

Extant studies have not attempted to assess whether terror group ideologies are correlated with service provision, though new efforts to explore the relationship between the beliefs and actions of terror groups provide important avenues for future research. Information from the Big, Allied, and Dangerous (BAAD) dataset (Asal and Rethemeyer 2015), or from the currently under-development Terrorist Ideology Project (TIP), for instance, could be merged with extant data such as TIOS (Heger and Jung 2015) to ascertain whether certain types of terrorist organizations–such as nationalist-separatist groups–might be more likely to engage in service provision activities relative to other types of groups.

For example, a cursory review of the top service-providing armed groups included in the TIOS dataset suggests that nationalist-separatist groups are more likely than other types of groups to engage in service provision. Of the 78 groups included in the TIOS dataset that provided ten different types of services, 33 of these (42 percent) were nationalist-separatist organizations. By contrast, 17 religious groups and 17 leftist groups (22 percent each) and only nine ethnocentric/supremacist groups (12 percent) engaged in similarly high levels of service provision. Interestingly, no right-wing groups were among the top service providers among the global population of terrorist and insurgent groups included in TIOS.

Finally, **critical approaches** point to the provision of social services as an important indicator of the fact that terrorism is often a politicized, subjective, and arbitrary term meant to deliberately delegitimize such groups and their claims. Many groups labeled as terrorists—including Hamas and Hizballah—spend considerable time and resources providing basic social services that sovereign state authorities are either incapable or unwilling to provide to their constituents. The **Black Panther Party**, put under investigation by the FBI on suspicion of being a terrorist organization in 1969, likewise devoted far more time and energy to community organizing, mutual aid, and other civic activities than its militant image would imply. Critical terrorism scholars would argue that by designating such groups as terrorist groups, opposing governments can conveniently disregard all of the claims these groups make and undermine and thwart all of the legitimate, nonviolent activities they promote. The same can be said for the **Muslim Brotherhood,** which has for years relied explicitly on nonviolent popular mobilization to achieve its goal of Islamization.

For critical terrorism scholars, a crucial question is why states fail to provide public services in the first place. In the United States, for instance, critical terrorism scholars would likely point out that the Black Panther Party emerged to fill needs vacated by the state, which actively discriminated against black people by denying them equal access to education, health care, employment, housing, security, and voting rights. Because many so-called terror organizations provide far more benefit to their populations than do their governments—while governments often actively harm their populations—critical terrorism scholars consider the labeling of such groups as "terrorists" a distraction from and distortion of the much broader root causes of these conflicts.

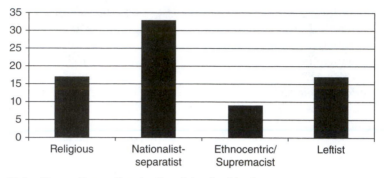

Figure 10.2 Terror Group Service Provision by Ideology

Source: TIOS 2015; BAAD; Terrorism Research & Analysis Consortium (TRAC)

Similar arguments can be made for those terror groups with political representation. In such cases, critical scholars might suggest that the line between who is considered a terrorist and who is labeled as a political party may not be so clear-cut. Take as an example **Aum Shinrikyo**, the Japanese apocalyptic group that dispersed sarin gas in the Tokyo subway system, killing a dozen people, in 1995. In addition to relying on terror tactics, the group engaged in the selection of political candidates to contest local elections in a way that was perfectly legal and compatible with the democratic process. Should the group be considered a religious organization, a terrorist organization, a political party, or potentially all three? We might also look to **Narodnaya Volya**, a group widely regarded as among the first modern terror organizations. While the group was responsible for the assassination of Tsar Alexander II in 1881 and a number of other terror attacks, its members also saw their organization as a political party (Naimark 1983, p. 41–68).

The line between political party and terrorist group becomes even less clear-cut under the auspices of authoritarianism, as Leonard Weinberg and Ami Pedahzur (2003) discuss in their book, *Political Parties and Terrorist Groups*. Indeed, such political environments might actually reverse the roles that we typically assign to political parties as opposed to terror groups. In autocracies, a single ruling party may act to stifle dissent and repress alternative forms of political participation, such as voting or protesting. It may even do so violently. In this case, it is the political party that works to crush its opponents and ultimately democracy. On the other hand, groups that conduct campaigns of terror in such settings may do so in the hopes of promoting or restoring democratic rule (Weinberg and Pedahzur 2003). Consider the example of the **Islamic Salvation Front (FIS)** in Algeria. In 1991, the FIS turned to violence only after the country's military nullified the results of national elections and banned the group out of fear that the FIS would emerge victorious.

Critical scholars would thus likely contend that attempting to understand why armed groups provide social services might make little sense, seeing as it unclear in the first place why the group—as opposed to the state—should be considered terroristic in nature.

PRACTICAL IMPLICATIONS

Much of the increase in attention granted to links between public service provision, charities, and terrorist organizations has come in response to the terror attacks in New York and Washington, DC in September 2001. Specifically, international efforts at curbing the ability of terrorist organizations to raise funds led to scrutiny of a number of charitable organizations purportedly linked to terror groups. Governments shut down many of these organizations as a result of counterterrorism efforts directed at terrorist financing, whose success has been variable (Enders and Sandler 2012, p. 197).

The US government, for instance, does not allow the allocation of federal funds to any governments or nonprofit organizations that cooperate with designated terror organizations (US Department of Treasury 2007). Given the complexity of some terror group-charitable organization relationships, however, such policies may end up doing more harm than good. In the case of Hizballah in Lebanon, for instance, the organization itself has become one of the most prominent providers of reconstruction and public works services in the country, and has frequently contracted with the Lebanese government itself in providing essential services (Flanigan 2008). Severely constricting the activity of Hizballah's nonviolent wing could disrupt the flow of services to the broader Lebanese population and contribute to further instability in the country.

The notion that the provision of social services by violent armed groups also helps increase the legitimacy of such organizations vis-à-vis the national government may also suggest that limiting groups' abilities to provide goods to surrounding communities in need may have unintended consequences (Flanigan 2008). In moral terms, when a power vacuum exists, the ability of these actors to improve the living conditions and security of civilian populations, if only marginally, may be the lesser of a number of evils. Recognizing the increased potential for negotiation that may exist when dealing with service-providing groups (Cunningham 2006), engaging them in dialogue towards the peaceful resolution of conflict may be a superior strategy to efforts that seek to cut off their funding or eradicate them via repressive or coercive tactics.

Finally, many of the insights provided in the literature suggest that the provision of basic social services by competent governments can add a critical, nonviolent component to any strategy to reduce violence. In the case of armed religious groups, for instance, approaches that focus on improving local governance are likely to undermine the violent potential of radical religious organizations without disrupting freedoms of religion, engaging in theological debates with radicals, or endangering civilians. If governments and other local actors are able to provide high-quality and widely accessible services to local populations, civilians may no longer feel forced to accept the authority of violent terror groups to meet their basic needs for survival.

A COMPARATIVE STUDY OF HIZBALLAH & THE TAMIL TIGERS (LTTE)

The means and mechanisms through which armed groups provide social services to local populations differ in important ways. According to some scholars, differences in the resource endowments and capacities of terror organizations play a direct role in shaping the structures through which they provide social services to the local population. Take Flanigan's (2008) comparison of Hizballah in Lebanon and the LTTE in Sri Lanka. The ways in which Hizballah and the LTTE use charitable service provision to garner popular support have resulted in the passive acceptance of the groups on the part of civil society, widespread favorable opinion, and broad participation from community members in Lebanon and Sri Lanka. While the former autonomously operates a sophisticated group of nongovernmental organization (NGO) service providers, the latter developed a highly elaborate system for controlling and channeling the resources of existing local and international NGO service providers. Figure 10.3 recreates Flanigan's schematics to give a clear picture of how armed groups might organize service provision (ibid.).

The groups employ starkly contrasting mechanisms when it came to the distribution of nonprofit services to communities in an effort to gain legitimacy. In terms of building local trust and political support, Hizballah proved more effective. The LTTE, in its efforts to build its legitimacy as a governing authority, devoted far greater resources and capacity to violence than it did to autonomous service provision. Ultimately, this strategy inhibited the group's ability to generate the high levels of political support that have allowed Hizballah to remain a dominant figure in Lebanese politics and society (Flanigan 2008).

Hizballah's overwhelming success in establishing itself as a legitimate actor supplanting the state derives from two main factors. First, the high levels of corruption that permeate the Lebanese government have created an important space for a militant group such as Hizballah to efficiently distribute a wide variety of social, economic, and political services to a desperate and frustrated population in an accessible way. Second, the organization's longstanding position in Lebanese society as a consistent provider of social services has made it a credible and reliable partner in the eyes of civilians, especially in the country's southern regions.

Service provision benefits the militant organization as much as it does those who received its services. Retaining its strong religious affiliation, Hizballah has used social services such as education, charity committees, and sport clubs to socialize and recruit new members. The material and social benefits offered by the militant group to its members have provided strong incentives to join and, at times, to engage in violence on behalf of the group. Thus Hizballah's engagement in service provision is not a purely altruistic component of its broader strategy, but a means of strengthening its organization through a continuous flow of new recruits.

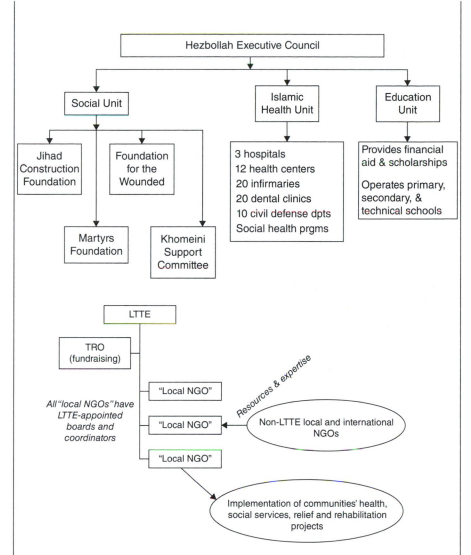

Figure 10.3 Hizballah and LTTE Structures of Service Provision

Source: Flanigan 2008

The provision of special benefits to fighters and their families was an important part of the LTTE's strategy in Sri Lanka as well. The families of child soldiers, for example, did not pay taxes to the military organization, and financial packages offered to soldiers and their family members made joining the group especially appealing to orphans, the poor, and the displaced (Manoharan 2003, as cited in Flanigan 2008).

The deliberate use of service provision to encourage and reward participation in violence was much more explicit for the LTTE than it has been for Hizballah. This variation stems largely from the resource and capacity differences between

Continued

293

ON GROUP ORGANIZATION & SERVICE PROVISION

A COMPARATIVE STUDY OF HIZBALLAH & THE TAMIL TIGERS (LTTE)
(Continued)

Hizballah and the LTTE. Hizballah's broad resource base and widespread legitimacy as a political and social actor made the group less dependent on violent forms of coercion. In contrast, by devoting the bulk of its attention to military operations, the LTTE diverted resources away from service provision, and instead become highly reliant on the limited resources of the Sri Lankan government and local NGO community. The group taxed NGOs that provided social services to the local population, and the activities of these organizations were steered towards meeting the strategic needs of the LTTE. According to local Tamils, NGOs working in LTTE areas had little autonomy, and the LTTE regularly undermined their work by imposing restrictions in the areas the group controlled (Flanigan 2008).

The cases of the LTTE and Hizballah show how service provision by terror or rebel organizations can garner popular support, albeit via different organizational structures and to varied effect. Importantly, the resources and capacities with which groups enter the realm of service provision shapes the extent to which they dedicate efforts towards social services versus violence. Groups that dedicate sufficient resources to social service provision over violence—and that enter the scene with preexisting resources in terms of social trust and credibility—can successfully supplant the state in providing public goods to desperate local populations. Groups that must continue to devote significant resources to fighting, however, are limited in terms of the level of popular support they are able to gain via nonviolent activities such as social service provision. These groups are often unable to gain the level of social trust and credibility necessary to supplant the state in terms of popular legitimacy.

PRACTICAL EXERCISE:

- *Imagine that you and your family live in an area controlled by one of the armed groups described in this case study. Discuss how you feel about the armed group, and how you feel about your government. You may consider such questions as: Who is helping you provide for your family? Who do you think has your best interest in mind? Why do you think this? In whose hands do you see your future as most secure?*

SUMMARY

In this chapter, we reviewed the literature on why terror groups provide social services to populations while also producing violence. We discussed diverse cases, such as Hizballah and the LTTE, and we discussed the humanitarian implications of government policies aimed at degrading groups that otherwise provide public goods to the population.

Discussion Questions

1. Consider the various terror groups cited as examples in this chapter. Which approach to studying terrorism do you think best explains why some groups turn to the provision of social services as part of their overall strategy?

2. Explain how the provision of social services impacts the strategic evolution of terror groups. Provide concrete examples.

3. Do you think that government strategies restricting the funding and activity of charity organizations linked to terror groups have been effective?

4. What could be an effective strategy for reducing violence when armed groups are actively providing social services to civilians?

KEY TAKEAWAYS

- Some terror groups provide social services. This is a puzzle for two reasons. First, why would organizations that seemingly thrive on sowing chaos and fear build hospitals, schools, and courts? Second, if such activities have strategic benefits, why do some terror groups invest heavily in providing social services whereas others do not?

- Terror groups provide many social services—like health care, education, community organizing, policing, financial assistance, religious services, dispute resolution, and political party organizing.

- Existing scholarship includes explanations from the strategic, organization, ideological, structural, and critical approaches. Each explanation has its own strengths and weaknesses.

- An implication of current research is that governments can often deter or reduce support to terror groups by effectively providing social services in areas where they have underperformed.

SUGGESTED FURTHER READINGS

Arreguín-Toft, Ivan. 2001. "How The Weak Win Wars: A Theory of Asymmetric Conflict." *International Security* 26 (1): 93–128. doi:10.1162/016228801753212868.

Berman, Eli and David D. Laitin. 2008. "Religion, Terrorism and Public Goods: Testing the Club Model." *Journal of Public Economics* 92 (10–11): 1942–1967. doi:10.1016/j.jpubeco.2008.03.007.

Cunningham, David E. 2006. "Veto players and Civil War Duration." *American Journal of Political Science* 50 (4): 875–892. doi:10.1111/j.1540-5907.2006.00221.x.

De La Calle, Luis, and Ignacio Sánchez-Cuenca. 2011. "The Quantity and Quality of Terrorism: The DTV Dataset." *Journal of Peace Research* 48 (1): 49–58. doi:10.1177/0022343310392890.

Enders, Walter, and Todd Sandler. 2012. *The Political Economy of Terrorism*. New York: Cambridge University Press.

Flanigan, Shawn Teresa. 2008. "Nonprofit Service Provision by Insurgent Organizations: The Cases of Hizballah and the Tamil Tigers." *Studies in Conflict and Terrorism* 31 (6): 499–519. doi:10.1080/10576100802065103.

Gross, Michael L. 2015. *The Ethics of Insurgency*. New York: Cambridge University Press.

Grynkewich, Alexus G. 2008. "Welfare as Warfare: How Violent Non-State Groups use Social Services to Attack the State." *Studies in Conflict and Terrorism* 31 (4): 350–370. doi:10.1080/10576100801931321.

Heger, Lindsay, et al. 2010. "In the Crosshairs: Explaining Violence Against Civilians." Doctoral Dissertation, University of California, San Diego. Available on Proquest Dissertations and Theses.

Heger, Lindsay, Danielle Jung, and Wendy H. Wong. 2012. "Organizing For Resistance: How Group Structure Impacts The Character Of Violence." *Terrorism And Political Violence* 24 (5): 743–768. doi:10.1080/09546553.2011.642908.

Heger, Lindsay L. and Danielle F. Jung. 2015. "Negotiating With Rebels: The Effect of Rebel Service Provision on Conflict Negotiations." *Journal of Conflict Resolution* (January 15, 2017): 1–27. doi:10.1177/0022002715603451.

Iannaccone, Laurence R., and Eli Berman. 2006. "Religious Extremism: The Good, The Bad, and The Deadly." *Public Choice* 128 (1–2): 109–129. doi:10.1007/s11127-006-9047-7.

Idler, Annette, and James J. F. Forest. 2015. "Behavioral Patterns Among (Violent) Non-State Actors: A Study of Complementary Governance." *Stability: International Journal of Security & Development* 4 (1): 1–19. doi:10.5334/sta.er.

Ly, Pierre-Emmanuel. 2007. "The Charitable Activities of Terrorist Organizations." *Public Choice* 131 (1–2): 177–195. doi:10.1007/s11127-006-9112-2.

Mampilly, Zachariah. 2011. *Rebel Rulers and Civilian Life During War*. Ithaca, N.Y.: Cornell University Press.

Stewart, Megan A. and Yu-Ming Liou. 2017. "Do Good Borders Make Good Rebels? Territorial Control And Civilian Casualties." *The Journal Of Politics* 79 (1): 284–301. doi:10.1086/688699.

Weinberg, Leonard and Ami Pedahzur. 2003. *Political Parties and Terrorist Groups*. Routledge Studies in Extremism and Democracy. New York: Routledge.

CHAPTER 11

STATE SPONSORSHIP OF TERROR

Learning Objectives

After reading this chapter, readers should be able to:

- Use logics from different analytical approaches to explain why some states sponsor terror groups while others do not;
- Describe the reasons why some groups may not want state sponsorship;
- Describe the spectrum of state sponsorship, which focuses on different levels of willingness and capacity of states to support terror groups;
- Describe and explain the different types of support states have provided to terror groups;
- Describe various historical incidents of state support to terror groups;
- Explain the implications of state sponsorship of terror from a practical perspective.

> "How can you have a war on terrorism when war itself is terrorism?"
> —HOWARD ZINN

> "Because the United States itself has a long record of supporting terrorists and using terrorist tactics, the slogans of today's war on terrorism merely makes the United States look hypocritical to the rest of the world."
> —LT. GENERAL WILLIAM ODOM, UNITED STATES ARMY, RET.

> "The US State Department report on Iranian involvement in terrorism needs to be a wake-up call for anyone who does not understand the magnitude of Iranian subversion and aggression both within and beyond the Middle East."
> —ISRAELI PRIME MINISTER BENJAMIN NETANYAHU, JUNE 21, 2015.

THE PUZZLE

When armed groups receive support from outside states, they tend to enjoy a number of strategic benefits—from longer duration to higher rates of success (Chenoweth and Stephan 2011; Salehyan, Gleditsch, and Cunningham 2011). Support from a state can provide a group access to the state's diplomatic, economic, military, and intelligence resources. This can translate into much more sophisticated weaponry, training, access to intelligence and information, safe havens, logistical materials (such as the provision of fraudulent identities through genuine passports), or protection from infiltration (Hoffman 2006, p. 259).

Yet governments' continual support for terror groups is puzzling for several reasons. First, states can often face direct and immediate reprisals for supporting terror groups. For instance, the United States retaliated for the 9/11 attacks through a full-scale multilateral invasion of Afghanistan, removing the Taliban regime that had hosted the leaders of the Al Qaeda network. The Reagan Administration likewise responded to a Libyan-backed attack on a Berlin nightclub that killed several American servicemen and wounded dozens more with air strikes on Tripoli and Benghazi in 1986. Iran's economy has been devastated by the international sanctions regime imposed in retaliation for its hostage-taking of American diplomats in 1979 and for the country's support of Hizballah and Hamas. Sudan paid a heavy price for providing sanctuary to Osama bin Laden's network from 1991–1996. In 1993, the United States designated Sudan as a State Sponsor of Terrorism, exposing the country to an exhaustive list of costly legal and economic sanctions. Moreover, even after the country expelled bin Laden in 1996 under pressure from the United States and Egypt, Sudan's erstwhile support of bin Laden and its suspected manufacture of **nerve agents** made it the target of US airstrikes in 1998, which destroyed the Al Shifa pharmaceutical factory, killed one worker, and injured eleven. It is clear that actively creating, financing, or hosting terror groups can be extremely costly for states (Carter 2012; Byman 2005, p. 50).

Second, terror groups often make for fickle and unreliable allies, suggesting that supporting terror groups does not always yield the intended results (Carter 2012). Terrorists can be notoriously untrustworthy, sometimes botching their missions, failing to deliver on their promises, or deriving their own internal agendas that clash with their sponsors' (Byman and Kreps 2010; Byman 2005, p. 51). In fact, no studies have convincingly demonstrated that sponsoring armed groups systematically yields long-term influence for the sponsor (Mazzetti 2014). At times, such support can elicit deadly backlash against the state sponsor. For instance, India's support of the **Liberation Tigers of Tamil Eelam (LTTE)** in Sri Lanka backfired significantly. Throughout the 1970s and 1980s, India offered material and political support to the LTTE in its struggle against the government of Sri Lanka. While the relationship initially served the interests of both parties, India's actions proved costly as each side's suspicions of the other grew stronger over time. The suspicion reached a peak when India began to work with the Sri Lankan government on a peace deal that fell short of the LTTE's goal of complete independence. The two sides eventually clashed militarily, and an LTTE suicide bomber killed Indian Prime Minister Rajiv Gandhi in 1991 (Byman and Kreps 2010, p. 2).

Third, state-sponsored terror groups can often engage in killings that diminish the reputations of their sponsors. As Weinstein (2006) points out in his study on the use and management of violence among rebel groups, external financing of armed groups can lead them to be more abusive toward local populations, given that they no longer need to turn to them for resources. As a result, many armed groups with external support are particularly brutal. The same principle applies to terror groups. Because many groups do not require the cooperation or approval of the local population, they do not necessarily have to restrain themselves in their uses of violence (Hoffman 2006, p. 261). Indeed, Hoffman argues that during the 1980s, those terror attacks perpetrated by state-sponsored terror groups were about eight times more lethal than others (ibid.). Although such lethal actions may affect the short-term interests of these state sponsors, they also run the risk of eliciting popular backlash that undermines the states' long-term interests.

The decision of armed groups to seek **state sponsorship** is also puzzling, given the possibility that such relationships might actually restrict the groups' strategic options and degrade their ability to achieve their stated goals. Sometimes states themselves can be fickle partners, expelling or eliminating terror groups that begin to threaten their interests. For instance, after the Six-Day War in 1967, during which Israel seized the West Bank from Jordan, the **Palestine Liberation Organization (PLO)** established a base in Jordan. The Hashemite Kingdom negotiated an agreement with the PLO allowing it to remain in the country provided the PLO did not threaten the country's leadership. During that time, the PLO and other Palestinian militant organizations continued to attack Israel from their bases in Jordan, sometimes clashing with Jordanian security forces as well. The PLO began to demonstrate more and more autonomy within the country, alongside the **Democratic Front for the Liberation of Palestine (DFLP)** and the **Popular Front for the Liberation of Palestine (PFLP)**, which meanwhile had been established there. The groups engaged in cross-border attacks that became increasingly threatening to Israel, and the PFLP conducted several failed assassination plots to overthrow the Hashemite monarchy within Jordan as well. Ostensibly to protect the monarchy from further attacks and to avoid potential war with Israel, in 1970 Jordan expelled the PLO, the PFLP, and the DFLP from its territory in a bloody episode commonly known as **Black September**. During this assault, thousands died (mostly Palestinians) and thousands more fled to Lebanon.

In another example, after decades of allowing the group to conduct operations from its territory, Iraq expelled the **Mujahedeen e Khalq** (MeK) group in 2009. It is widely believed that the Shia-dominated Iraqi government did this to demonstrate its displeasure at the United States' diplomatic overtures toward the group (Londoño and Jaffe 2009).

Finally, some studies point out that state sponsorship limits the ability of armed groups to act freely. In their study of external state sponsorship of rebel organizations, Salehyan et al. (2014) point out that some outside sponsors vary in the extent to which they tolerate human rights violations by the groups that they support. In particular, democracies with strong human rights lobbies tend to support less abusive groups, imposing specific conditions on the groups that they sponsor. The logic applies to terror groups as well. When terrorists receive resources from states, they lose some autonomy over their operations because states rarely provide support with no strings attached (ibid., p. 638). Pakistan, for instance, keeps a close eye on and strongly influences the activities and targeting decisions of a number of anti-Indian groups that it supports, such as Lashkar-e-Taiba (LeT) (Bajoria 2010). These dynamics may help to explain why not all terrorist groups seek state sponsorship.

Given all of these downsides and risks, why do states sponsor terror groups? In this chapter, we shift from explaining the behavior of terror groups to understanding why states might seek to sponsor them. We discuss various ways in which states have supported terror groups—intentionally or inadvertently—and the reasons why. We identify and evaluate the different arguments available to understand this choice. Before we apply the different analytic approaches to this puzzle, we first look at what state support means, what types of state support exist, and some examples of state-supported terror groups.

STATE SUPPORT DEFINED

As with the term terrorism itself (see Chapter 1), the phenomenon of state-sponsored terrorism lacks a well-established, consensus definition. The critical definitional element is the role played by a state in providing some form of support—advertently or inadvertently—to an entity that commits a transnational act of terror. Byman defines state sponsorship as "a government's international assistance to a terrorist group to help it use violence, bolster its political activities, or sustain the organization" (2005, p. 10). At times, states help to create terror organizations as their own agents; Iran's creation of Hizballah may fall into this category (see below). Other times, states may choose to back certain existing groups as a way to assert influence over them and encourage them to act in ways that are consistent with the state's goals. For instance, the governments of Iraq, Libya, and Syria all backed the Abu Nidal Organization (ANO), led by Palestinian Sabri al-Banna, at different times and to different degrees (Banks, de Nevers, and Walensteen 2011, p. 14).

While often associated with the behavior of different governments in the Middle East, state sponsorship of terrorism has occurred on every continent.

Western governments have sponsored terror groups throughout the world, from France turning a blind eye to ETA's cross-border operations against Spain to the United States funding and training the right-wing Contras in Nicaragua. Indeed, as with most discussion about terrorism more generally, state sponsorship is a subjective and contested topic. For instance, claiming that state support for state terrorism is just as morally problematic as state support for nonstate terrorism, different Arab governments routinely condemn the United States government for its unconditional support of Israel (Byman 2005, p. 7). In the eyes of many Arab governments, Israel's occupation of the West Bank and Gaza Strip—and its continued military operations against Palestinian civilians—represent a form of state terrorism that benefits from direct and active material support from the United States. The US, for its part, likewise condemns many Middle Eastern governments for directly supporting Palestinian and Lebanese terror groups in their commission of attacks against Israel and its civilians (ibid.).

In some cases, support may be more passive than active. For instance, states may not directly support terror groups, but they may choose not to clamp down on them either. Alternatively, states may wish to prevent terrorist groups from using their territory to commit attacks but find themselves unable to do so. Hence, there are many different gradations of support and opposition—from strong support to weak support to lukewarm or sympathetic support to passive support to antagonistic support to unwilling support (Byman 2005, p. 15). Byman suggests the following spectrum of state support and opposition among willing and unwilling hosts (Figure 11.1).

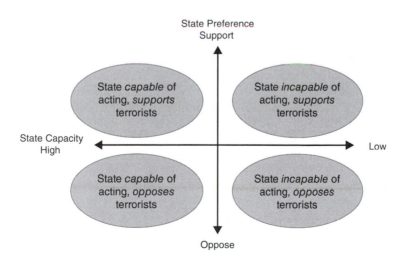

Figure 11.1 Byman's Spectrum of State Sponsorship

Source: Adapted from Byman 2005, p. 11

In Figure 11.1, states in the upper-left hand quadrant are the most aggressive supporters of terrorism. They are all high-capacity states that actively use terror groups as agents in conflict. For them, sponsoring these groups is a deliberate form of asymmetric or political warfare through which weak states can confront stronger states. For example, after the revolutionary overthrow of the Shah of Iran's US-backed dictatorship in 1979, the new regime under Ayatollah Khomenei created Hizballah as a way to project Iranian interests throughout the region. Moreover, Iran has given money to Hamas—despite Hamas's Sunni orientation—because of both parties' shared interest in weakening Israel. That said, if Iran became hostile to either Hizballah or Hamas, it could easily expel, withhold support from, or significantly damage the groups.

In contrast, the countries categorized on the lower-left hand quadrant are the high-capacity states that may oppose or remain neutral to terror groups, all while maintaining the ability to expel them or cut off their sources of support. For example, the PIRA enjoyed the sympathy and support of many Irish-Americans, yet the United States turned a blind eye to the smuggling of weapons and funds to the PIRA for many decades. Only in the mid-1990s— and more so after 9/11—did the United States government actively pursue legal instruments that allowed it to shut down networks of financial support between US citizens and the PIRA (Byman 2005, p. 222).

The upper-right hand quadrant in Figure 11.1 represents countries that support different terror groups but could also not expel them if they wanted to. The Taliban in Afghanistan is the prototypical example. After a ten-year occupation, the Soviet Union withdrew from Afghanistan in 1989, thanks in part to US efforts that armed and financed the **mujahedeen**, a group of jihadist warriors that fought the Soviets for a decade. Many of these mujahedeen factions eventually coalesced into the Taliban. The country was soon engulfed in a bloody civil war, which killed millions and devastated the country's infrastructure between 1992 and 1996. With few remnants of a functioning government left standing, the Taliban emerged as the dominant armed actor towards the war's end. Declaring victory, the group claimed sovereign authority over Afghanistan—a claim contested both inside and outside the country. Nevertheless, the Taliban began governing the country as a theocracy. In 1996, the leader of the group, **Mullah Muhammad Omar**, granted entry to Osama bin Laden and his network after Saudi Arabia and Sudan had expelled Al Qaeda. Although bin Laden swore allegiance to Omar's government, Al Qaeda operated as a somewhat autonomous entity within Afghanistan, stockpiling weapons, training new recruits, communicating with network members worldwide, and planning attacks. Moreover, the Taliban never fully defeated other armed groups operating in the country, such as the Northern Alliance and a number of other factions. After 9/11, when the United States issued a demand to Mullah Omar and the Taliban to turn over bin Laden for trial, Omar and his entourage refused to comply (Burns and Wren 2001). It is unclear whether they did so out of loyalty to bin Laden, whether they did so because they knew that they were incapable of expelling him, or some combination of both. Many observers speculate that by 2001, Al Qaeda had grown into a formidable force that Mullah Omar could not control or expel, even if the Taliban wanted to do so (Byman 2005, p. 202).

Finally, those states on the lower-right hand quadrant are those that oppose certain terror groups but are also incapable of controlling or expelling them even if they wanted to. For example, the Iraqi government has been opposed to Al Qaeda in Iraq (AQI) since the group's formation in 2005. After AQI's perceived military defeat in 2007, the Iraqi government began to consolidate power with the assistance of United States occupation forces. Former members of Al Qaeda in Iraq began to reformulate themselves into the so-called ISI (the Islamic State of Iraq), developing bases of support in Iraq's Sunni-dominated northwest. In 2012, after neighboring Syria devolved into civil war, the ISI began to launch attacks in Syria, capturing several cities and towns from rival rebel groups. And in 2014, the Islamic State of Iraq and Syria (ISIS) swept through Iraq in a lightening offensive that resulted in the capture of numerous large Iraqi cities, including Mosul, Ramadi, Fallujah, and Tikrit. In the face of these assaults, the Iraqi army abandoned their defensive positions and fled the fighting en masse. These events made it clear that the Iraqi government was incapable of expelling ISIS regardless of the government's enmity for the group.

Somalia is another example of a country that opposes a terror group but remains incapable of expelling it. In addition to attacks within Somalia, Al Shabab routinely crosses the border into Kenya, attacking civilian targets in retaliation for Kenyan armed forces' intervention in Somalia. Yet the Somali government has little capacity with which to contest the considerable military strength of the group. The Iraq and Somali cases demonstrate the possibility that state support of terror groups can often be inadvertent. Such forms of sponsorship may be more common among weak, failed, and collapsed states, which create permissive conditions for terrorism. As we saw in Chapter 6, claims to state authority are challenged among a number of groups in certain contexts. In these cases, terror groups can move about undetected and interrupted and ultimately become the beneficiaries of an authority vacuum.

The differentiation across Byman's spectrum of supporters relies on the ability to infer the intentions of the state in supporting the group. Yet the true intentions of a state supporter of terrorism may be difficult to ascertain (Byman 2005, p. 10). Bapat, et al. (2016) argue that states have incentives to misrepresent the degree to which they sponsor their groups so as to elicit foreign aid to help them fight terrorism. Consider Pakistan's complicated relationship with Al Qaeda. On the one hand, after 9/11 Pakistan emerged as a key partner in the United States' Global War on Terrorism. Pakistani President Pervez Musharraf routinely pledged support to US efforts to eradicate Al Qaeda in Afghanistan and Pakistan, resulting in military assistance and intelligence sharing. In doing so, Musharraf presented Pakistan as an unwilling host to Al Qaeda and its supporters. However, some critics argued that the Pakistani government actually harbored many Al Qaeda sympathizers—particularly within the powerful intelligence services—making the country more of a weak (albeit fragmented) supporter rather than an unwilling host (see e.g., Gregory 2007). In fact, countries like Pakistan may have incentives to deliberately misrepresent their relationships with different terror groups as a way to extract more funds from their counterterrorism allies. In short, while Pakistan may have pledged to crack down on Al Qaeda after 9/11, it is unclear whether the country actually used the funds it received from the US to attack the group (Boutton 2014).

Although Byman recognizes that states' intentions in supporting terror groups are often obscure, other scholars have also argued that states' capacity to expel or cut off support to terrorists is also difficult to determine. Understanding the limits and constraints of **weak states** may be particularly difficult to observe from the outside (Bapat, et al. 2016). Weak states are therefore exceedingly risky partners when it comes to counterterrorism cooperation.

TYPES OF STATE SUPPORT

Although there are numerous types of support by which states sponsor nonstate terrorism, scholars typically focus on six specific types of support: (1) sanctuary, (2) money, arms, and logistics; (3) training and operations; (4) help with organizing; (5) diplomatic backing; and (6) ideological direction (Byman 2005, p. 55).

First and most consequential is sanctuary. When terror groups have enjoyed safe havens in which to train, plan, and recruit without interruption, they have received an enormous advantage (Salehyan 2010). For instance, members of the Lord's Resistance Army (LRA), a primarily Ugandan group, have sanctuaries in neighboring Sudan (Salehyan 2007). States that protect terrorists by allowing them to remain on their own sovereign territory make

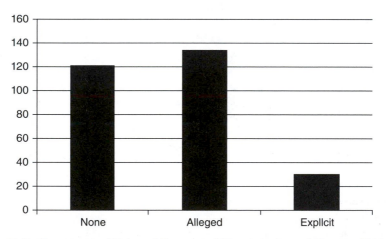

Figure 11.2   Frequency of External Support of Nonstate Armed Groups, 1946–2003

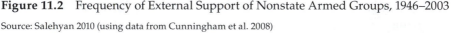

Source: Salehyan 2010 (using data from Cunningham et al. 2008)

it more costly for other states to attack the groups, since doing so would necessarily escalate into an interstate confrontation. When terror groups do not have to worry about protecting themselves from a foreign state's intervention, they can devote more time and resources to planning attacks and other operations. The tangible advantages that sanctuaries afford terrorist groups help to explain why some groups seek the support of states. During Algeria's war of independence against France, the Algerian Liberation Front (FLN) staged its main operating bases in Tunisia, where it could arm and train its forces that launched raids into Algeria. Since invading Tunisia was not a viable military strategy, France decided instead to construct a barrier running 200 miles along the Algeria-Tunisia border. From that point forward, the FLN's strength and operational capabilities declined significantly (Record 2006).

Second, money, arms, and logistical support (like safe passage or transportation through one's country) have been highly consequential forms of support. Money has helped terror groups pay recruits and support day-to-day operations (Shapiro 2013). Recruits to terror groups are of little use if the group does not have weapons for them to use. Funds have also allowed terror groups to purchase arms, establish more effective propaganda platforms, purchase encrypted communications technologies and transportation equipment, and pay specialists to assist with technical tasks such as bomb-making. Because funds are fungible resources, armed groups that receive money from a donor expend fewer resources on their own fundraising efforts. For instance, since its inception, Hizballah has received significant amounts of weapons and cash from Iran each year, allowing it to focus less attention and resources on its arms smuggling and money laundering operations. In 1996 alone, at least three 747s flew from Iran to Lebanon containing

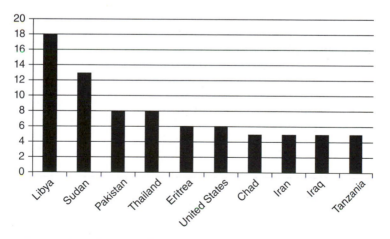

Figure 11.3 Number of Groups Supported by the Top Ten State Sponsors of Nonstate Armed Groups, 1946–2011

Source: Cunningham, et al. 2013.

shipments of weapons. Iran has reportedly contributed about $100 million to Hizballah in support of its political and humanitarian activities to solidify its position and influence in Lebanon (Hoffman 2006, p. 265).

Other types of logistical support—such as transport options or safe passage during the course of an operation—has also benefited terror groups. For example, on June 27, 1976, the PFLP and the Baader Meinhof Group jointly hijacked Air France Flight 139 en route from Tel Aviv to Paris via Athens. Idi Amin, Uganda's autocratic leader, was sympathetic to Palestinian self-determination, and he was reportedly eager to gain favor among pro-Palestinian Arab leaders more generally. He allowed the hijackers to land the plane in Entebbe, where they held 246 passengers and twelve crew members hostage for several days. During this time, Amin also supplied the hijackers with more weapons and personnel, but a largely successful raid by Israeli special forces interrupted the exchange. Dubbed "Operation Entebbe," Israeli forces freed most of the hostages and killed all of the hijackers. Three hostages, one Israeli commando, and dozens of Ugandan soldiers who were protecting the hijackers also died during the raid.

Third, states sometimes provide terror groups with training and operational support. For example, members of the Russian military reportedly provided paramilitary training for members of the Japanese Aum Shinrikyo cult. Similarly, the United States used military training camps, such as the School of the Americas, to train Central American paramilitaries in various combat and intelligence techniques, including methods of interrogation and torture. At times, states also support terror groups by providing them with direct information or intelligence about their opponents' movements.

Fourth, organizational assistance has helped terror groups or factions overcome some of the informational problems frequently encountered during the group's nascent period. For instance, volunteers may not know how to go about joining a group. Others may distrust self-styled leaders of the organization, or some groups may simply struggle with cooperation among different rival factions. States have coordinated various groups or provided them with incentives to join together. For instance, Byman cites Iran as having played an important role in unifying disparate Shia factions in Lebanon into the movement now known as Hizballah (2005, p. 63).

Fifth, states have provided terror groups with diplomatic backing. One of the most prominent examples of this is the support of the PLO by various Arab governments, who have criticized Israeli actions toward Palestinians and advocate for Palestinian statehood in various international forums (Byman 2005, p. 61). Similarly, Iran has accused the United States of supporting MeK, which Iran considers a terrorist group.

Finally, states have provided terror groups with ideological direction and inspiration. This was certainly true during the Cold War, when the Soviet Union provided intellectual and ideological fodder for terror groups representing Marxist/Leninist aims. And the Iranian Revolution is often considered a clear inspiration for Islamist groups worldwide (Byman 2005, p. 63–4).

TERROR GROUP FINANCING BY NONSTATE ACTORS

Not all transnational supporters of terror groups are states. In fact, sympathetic publics around the world sometimes provide cash, weapons, safe haven, training, and personnel to terror groups. For example, the LTTE received a great deal of money directly from Tamils living abroad—particularly in Canada, where a large Tamil community engaged in various fundraising efforts to support the LTTE. Similarly, some Islamic charities, such as CARE International, purportedly provided direct funds to Al Qaeda affiliates via a global financing network (Berger 2013). And some groups receive voluntary or coerced support directly from the populations they claim to represent. For example, some Irish Catholic civilians in Northern Ireland provided the PIRA with various forms of support—from hiding different PIRA operatives to giving them money. And in areas in which ISIS has driven out its competitors, the group has forcibly extracted taxes from the civilians left behind (Stern and Berger 2015).

Until 2001, there were few global regulations on financing that could allow governments to cooperate on tracking and seizing monies headed from people or groups to terror organizations. But after 9/11, several international organizations designed global legislation to crack down on financing by nonstate groups. This included the Terrorist Finance Tracking program (FATF), a collaboration between the US and the United Nations, which many people considered a success (see Giraldo and Trinkunas 2007).

UNDERSTANDING STATE SPONSORSHIP OF TERROR

Strategic approaches tend to explain state sponsorship of terrorism as a function of power maximization and cost effectiveness by states (Wardlaw 2001; Salehyan 2010). As Byman writes, "the terrorist group can serve the strategic interest of foreign states, gain their leaders' sympathy for ideological reasons, or play a role in bolstering leaders' domestic positions" (2005, p. 21). Yonah Alexander suggests that sponsoring terrorist organizations can be a "form of secret or undeclared warfare" for states for which "overt or declared warfare could be inconvenient and riskier" (2006, p. 6). Covertly creating or supporting a terror group is a way for states to achieve their goals while often providing them a degree of plausible deniability about their involvement in terror operations. This reduces the chances that more powerful states retaliate against them militarily or economically (Byman 2005, p. 22). Sponsoring terror groups may also be a productive means of weakening and destabilizing a hated neighbor (Byman 2005, p. 37). For example, although the majority of MeK members fled to France after repeated crackdowns against the group in 1980s Iran, some MeK exiles also fled to Iraq, where they continued through 2001 to plot assassinations and the overthrow of the Ayatollah's theocracy. Saddam Hussein's regime in Iraq provided the MeK with material support and sanctuary, while the MeK helped the regime suppress domestic opposition and provided internal security support.

Finally, strategic approaches to state-sponsored terrorism also suggest that some states may sponsor terror groups overtly as way to project power beyond their own borders (Byman 2005, p. 38). These arguments are somewhat akin to realist approaches to international relations more broadly, which search for the causes of conflict in the structure of the international system and in underlying balances of power. As an example of this logic, one can argue that Iran provides support to Hizballah as a proxy in its fight against a distant Israel, with the ultimate goal of shifting the regional balance of power in its favor. And states certainly use terror groups as agents in regime change campaigns, as the United States did in Central America during the 1980s. The United States' mission in supporting the Contras in Nicaragua was to force out the Sandinista government and replace it with a right-wing, pro-US regime. And certainly some states support terror groups as a way to shape the claims or ideologies of these groups (Byman 2005, p. 43). For example, the Iranian government has attempted to influence Hamas' hardline agenda by providing the group with funds.

The practical implications of the strategic approach would generally suggest that punishing states that sponsor terrorism is the most effective way to end the behavior. If state sponsorship of terrorism is the most cost-effective way for a state to pursue its goals, then a logical response would be to increase the costs associated with this behavior, such that no rational state would pursue this course of action.

Empirical evidence is mixed regarding the strategic approach to state sponsorship. If the approach were right, we would expect to see states sponsor terrorist organizations when they are relatively weak compared to other states, especially their rivals. Michael Findley, James Piazza, and Joseph Young evaluated the degree to which militarily weak states resort to supporting transnational terror as a way to wage asymmetric warfare against their more powerful opponents (2012). Using a quantitative research design, they found strong correlations between the power ratios between rival countries and the tendency for the weaker state to wage war through terrorism. Their analysis suggests that the adoption of transnational terror by a state is not random but rather is motivated by enmity against a particular rival state. This finding provides some support for the strategic approach.

However, if the strategic approach were right, we would also expect to see state sponsorship of terrorism result in states' desired outcomes—that is, the effective projection of power at a minimal cost. But several empirical findings cast doubt on these implications. First, as mentioned above, states often pay a considerable price for sponsoring terror groups abroad—including retaliatory military action, overwhelming economic sanctions, and diplomatic isolation (think back to the example of Afghanistan and the provision of sanctuary to Al Qaeda). Second, states rarely maintain indefinite control or influence over terror groups, suggesting that such groups are unreliable as agents of the state (Byman and Kreps 2010; Mazzetti 2014). These realities contest the implication that sponsoring terror groups is strategically effective or cost-effective. Finally, when states sponsor terrorist groups to wage proxy wars against other states, Salehyan (2010) suggests that they lose a degree of autonomy over their foreign policy. Since it is often very difficult to gather complete information on a particular group, states leave themselves open to the risk that the terror group that they sponsor will have its own agendas that may diverge from the state's foreign policy goals. Salehyan (2010) points to the example of Jordan, which supported and played host to a number of Palestinian groups during the 1960s. A number of these groups, such as the PLO, began to launch unauthorized strikes into Israel, prompting reprisals against Jordan. PLO forces started openly arming themselves in Jordan, setting up police checkpoints, and collecting taxes from the local population. After another group, the PFLP, began to hijack airplanes and land them in Jordan despite government objections, the Jordanian government broke ties with the groups in 1970, and expelled them from the country during the Black September episode described above (ibid.).

The **organizational approach** may also provide a useful framework for understanding how domestic politics within states might affect the propensity to sponsor terror groups. Supporting terror groups in other states might provide leaders with credibility among their own constituents that they are doing something to challenge and undermine rival states. For example, Iran's leadership can claim that the country openly defies its enemies by continually supporting the Shi'a group Hizballah and actively contains Israeli expansion by supporting various Palestinian militant groups. Thus by aiding kin abroad, domestic leaders can shore up support at home (Byman 2005, p. 47).

Moreover, the socio-organizational approach also suggests ways that passive sponsorship of terrorism can bolster a leader's position in domestic politics by extracting rents from foreign states that are interested in containing the threat. In the case of Pakistan, for example, the United States has provided billions of dollars in aid to help the country combat terrorism. Yet rather than using such funds to bolster security, political leaders in Pakistan can use such funds to purchase loyalty among political party elites or supporters, strengthening their own political power at home (Boutton 2014).

The organizational approach also questions the unitary nature of the state, suggesting instead that not all states are monolithic entities. Instead, there may be factions within a government that support or conspire with terror groups to conduct foreign attacks, whereas other parts of the government remain ignorant of or incapable of preventing such actions. Once again Pakistan provides a useful illustration. Whereas many people argue that the Pakistani government knowingly sponsors terror, a more accurate portrayal might be that some officials within the Pakistani intelligence services, the ISI, sympathize with or support Al Qaeda and its affiliates. Other officials in the Pakistani government may not actively support such groups and may be pursuing strategic goals that directly contradict those pursued by other elements within the government.

The policy implications of the organizational approach are not straightforward. However, if this approach is right, then foreign states should avoid providing aid to governments that knowingly harbor terrorists or their sympathizers, even when that aid is distributed to bolster the capacity of the state to defeat terrorists. This is because providing funds to such governments will often fail to result in effective action against terror groups, and often be disbursed as payouts to political elites.

If the organizational or domestic politics explanation were correct, then we would expect to see the *timing* of support to terror organizations correspond to domestic political strife—such as a political scandal among the country's leadership, a decline in popularity of the ruling party, or a specific public demand for action by the leadership—rather than international events alone. So far no study has systematically shown that this phenomenon does indeed play out.

Ideological approaches of state sponsorship focus on the ways in which particular cultures or belief systems—in particular, those that favor regional or global dominance—might affect the choice to sponsor terror abroad. For example, some have argued that Saudi Arabia has turned a blind eye to its citizens contributing funds to ISIS, seeing as the Saudi regime and ISIS share common ideological undertones centered on a fundamentalist and messianic version of Islam (Norton 2016). Byman also emphasizes that some states pursue state sponsorship as a way to achieve international notoriety and prestige (2005, p. 43). In other words, the idea of state sponsorship provides states with nonmaterial benefits, such as an identity of defiance, status, and respect from their rivals.

Practically speaking, if a country is ideologically committed to exporting terror, then military responses should be largely ineffective. Instead, practical responses based on ideological approaches focus on two key implications. First, states can and should identify those most likely to sponsor terror organizations and contain their ability to do so by isolating them physically and economically. This means imposing travel bans, financial freezes, and other measures that prevent the country from being able to export terrorism. Second, if the motivation is prestige rather than a specific ideology, then the international community should remove any possible prestige value from engaging in this type of behavior. Governments and international organizations should never reward state sponsorship of terrorism by giving in to the demands of the sponsors. Instead, states should remove the offending state from participating in global events, such as the Olympic Games, high-level economics meetings like the G7, or different international organizations and agreements, all of which contain prestige value.

If the ideological explanation were accurate, we would see evidence that states sponsor terrorists primarily to export specific political ideologies—such as political Islam—and therefore tend to bestow their sponsorship upon groups with similar ideological beliefs. Moreover, if Byman's (2005) ideational hypothesis is correct, we would see from official documents or statements that the primary motivating factor behind the choice to support such groups is to expand the country's status or prestige on the global scene.

There are several problems with this explanation. First is the lack of systematic empirical support. Using cross-national data, Findley, Piazza, and Young (2012) find no evidence to suggest that Muslim countries are more likely to sponsor terror organizations in the pursuit of their goals than others. Qualitative and anecdotal evidence also suggests that states sometimes support terror organizations that share dissimilar doctrinal commitments. Iran has supported Sunni Palestinian groups including Islamic Jihad, the PFLP, and the Al Aqsa Martyrs Brigade—despite Iran's Shia orientation (Hoffman 2006, p. 265). And Libya, Syria, and Iraq have supported the quasi-criminal ANO, suggesting that states are sometimes willing to support terror groups that are not necessarily strict adherents to their belief systems. Furthermore, no studies have yet systematically evaluated whether state sponsorship of terrorism is considered by its sponsors to generate more prestige, or whether this is a secondary (or irrelevant) concern.

Second, some suggest that ideological arguments tend to wrongly focus on a few select cases, which tend to be singled out as state sponsors of terrorism. This neglects a great number of states that engage in this behavior but do not adhere to a specific ideology. For instance, most studies of state-sponsored terrorism focus on non-Western, predominantly Muslim-majority states, often glossing over the fact that many Western democracies such as the United States have provided support to violent nonstate groups.

Third, there are compelling competing explanations for why states like Saudi Arabia fund terror groups like ISIS—in particular from the strategic and organizational approaches. From a strategic perspective, Saudi Arabia stands to gain regional power and influence by diminishing the power of its regional rivals—most importantly Iran. To support ISIS means to support a group that is actively chipping away at the territory of two important Iranian-backed regimes: Syria and Iraq. By supporting ISIS, Saudi Arabia can thwart Iran's efforts to preserve or expand its influence in these countries. From a domestic politics perspective, some have argued that Saudi Arabia's governing elites tend to turn a blind eye to the more radical Islamist elements within their country to prevent them from turning against the regime itself (Norton 2016). Because of these compelling alternative arguments, the ideological explanation does not hold much sway over other approaches to explaining state sponsorship of terrorism.

On its face, it may seem like the **psychological approach** is irrelevant for this particular puzzle, since such explanations tend to emphasize individual-level motivations. Because state sponsorship occurs at the level of the state (rather than at the level of the individual), the unit of analysis does not appear congruent with psychological explanations. However, if we were to consider state sponsorship of terrorism as a direct result of the decisions of a particular leader, rather than of a particular state, then one might imagine the utility and relevance of psychological approaches. For example, some have argued that Libya's Muammar Qaddafi was uniquely prone to supporting foreign terror organizations, in part because of his peculiar personality that featured signs of narcissistic vanity, clinical depression, and intense paranoia (Blundy and Lycett 1987, p. 21). Moreover, group-level psychological approaches may also be relevant. In particular, **groupthink** might play a role in the decision by certain governments to create or sponsor terror organizations. Whereas an individual might be less likely to take this risky action on his own, one might imagine that the decision to dispatch the Iranian Revolutionary Guards to join, train, arm, and finance Hizballah in Lebanon would become a plausible option when made in the context of a group of victorious revolutionary leaders, like the Ayatollah's inner council.

Practical responses based on individual-level psychological approaches are fairly simplistic: the primary implication is to remove the individual responsible for the choice to sponsor terror groups, either through arrest, interdiction, or assassination. Indeed, the United States attempted to assassinate Muammar Qaddafi in 1986 in response to the Berlin bombing through air strikes launched on his palace. Policy responses based on group-level psychological approaches are less obvious, since the theory suggests that groups of people can engage in high-risk behaviors regardless of the

Photo 11.1   Muammar al-Qaddafi at the 12th African Union Summit in Addis Ababa, 2009

circumstances—and they may be more likely to do so when they feel threatened. As a result, the implications are to instead offer groups assurances that they should not feel threatened—a practical implication that directly contradicts the hardline or isolating policy postures that most of the other analytical approaches examined here advocate.

If the individual-level psychological approach is correct, then we should expect to see the psychological traits of leaders who choose to sponsor terror groups to be different from leaders who do not. If group-level psychological approaches are correct, we should expect to see evidence that in private, individual leaders were doubtful that state sponsorship of terrorism was a wise choice whereas in a group, the same individuals were more willing to indulge higher-risk decisions such as sponsoring terror groups. The problem is that such records—for both individuals and groups—are often simply unavailable, particularly across cases. While anecdotal evidence may reveal some support for this idea, it is not clear that such evidence is systematic or present in all cases. Nor is it clear that primary documents allowing researchers to evaluate these hypotheses exist at all.

Structural explanations may also provide some useful insight as to why some states sponsor terror organizations while others do not. Most of these explanations seek to specify the conditions under which countries will receive the greatest benefit from sponsoring terror, relative to the risks. Many have found, for example, that weak states are the likeliest both to host terrorists inadvertently and to support them explicitly. By inadvertently harboring terrorists, weak states often elicit foreign aid from countries that are interested in containing such groups (Boutton 2014; Bapat 2010). For example, as mentioned above, since 9/11 the United States has provided billions of dollars in aid to Pakistan, which claimed to inadvertently and unwillingly host Al Qaeda and its affiliates in its northwest frontier. On the other hand, weak states are also the likeliest to sponsor terrorists to project power beyond their borders, because they are most averse to direct confrontations with militarily-superior adversaries yet also remain nominally capable of exercising control over such groups (Boutton 2014; Findley, Piazza, and Young 2012). For instance, Pakistan is clearly wary of provoking a direct war with its rival India, yet it maintains the ability to project or constrain transnational terror groups that might attack India from within Pakistani territory.

Another structural factor that should prevent states from using state-sponsored terrorism against one another is mutual democracy. When both states are democratic, scholars argue, they should be less likely to use covert violence like state-sponsored terrorism to resolve conflicts. If the United States and Canada have a dispute, they tend to rely on their own transparent institutions and various diplomatic mechanisms to reach an agreement. In contrast, if the United States and Iran have a dispute, they have far fewer transparent institutions and direct diplomatic channels through which to signal their intentions and make credible commitments to one another. Indeed, quantitative studies have shown that democratic dyads are much less likely than autocratic dyads or democratic-autocratic dyads to engage in state-sponsored terrorism against one another (Findley, Piazza, and Young 2012).

If structural explanations are correct, the practical implications are long-term. Ideally, the international community would combat state-sponsored terrorism by strengthening the capacity of weak states and promoting democracy worldwide.

One downside to these explanations is that many structural factors—such as state weakness or authoritarian regime type—are generally poor at explaining variation in state sponsorship across similar structural conditions. For example, why do some weak states like Colombia tend not to support terror organizations abroad, whereas others like Pakistan do? Moreover, such explanations fail to explain important exceptions where strong states have supported terror groups. For instance, the United States has supported terror groups in Nicaragua, Afghanistan, and elsewhere, even as it was the most materially powerful country in the international system. This reality calls into question the claim that state sponsorship of terror is largely a function of the relative weakness of the sponsor.

Second, structural explanations, which tend to focus on fairly static, unchanging characteristics of states, tend to be poor at explaining the timing of state sponsorship of terror groups. Such explanations have difficulty explaining why some states—which appear to have all of the hallmarks of a potential state sponsor of terrorism—might suddenly turn on such groups and expel them, much like Jordan expelled the PLO after several years of providing sanctuary to the group.

Third, the policy implications of such arguments generate a host of new dilemmas. One is whether states can actively promote democracy abroad without exacerbating state weakness or episodic violence. For example, one of the claimed goals of the US invasion of Iraq was to promote democracy in the country. But despite the introduction of elections, the United States provoked a period of civil war and chronic state fragility that have undermined the country's prospects for democratic consolidation. Although Saddam Hussein's autocratic rule (and occasional sponsorship of Palestinian militant groups) has ended, Iraq has become a base of terror operations for Al Qaeda in Iraq and ISIS in the past decade, meaning that the process of transition itself ushered in a period in which Iraq became a prototypical weak state that exported terror at a far greater level than before. Hence, the policy implications of structural approaches are not as straightforward as they might seem.

Finally, **critical explanations** question the entire category of state-sponsored terrorism as a distinct form of behavior. Recall from Chapter 7 that critical terrorism scholars believe that states themselves are just as capable as nonstate groups of committing acts of terror. Because these scholars describe terrorism as the practice of using violence to terrorize others, they argue that it does not matter whether states do this by supporting agents or doing it directly. As Howard Zinn implies in the opening quote of this chapter, there is no substantive difference between supporting a terror group and waging a war with a regular army that also rains terror upon the targeted population.

Critical terrorism scholars argue that efforts to categorize state-sponsored terrorism as a separate kind of violence is itself another way of legitimizing state terrorism and delegitimizing nonstate terrorism. Seeing terrorism as an entirely subjective phenomenon, critical terrorism scholars would agree with Brian Jenkins' quip that "Terrorism is what the bad guys do" (quoted in Byman 2005, p. 7). Critical terrorism scholars would likely note that the political uses of the term "state-sponsored terrorism" are more important than trying to explain it as an objective phenomenon (see, for example, Box 11.2). Instead, they would point to the many ways that status quo, Euro-centric powers tend to accuse particular kinds of states of supporting terrorism, while neglecting their own tendencies to commit or support acts of terror themselves. In fact, a common critique of the US use of drones to counter terrorism is that these aerial strikes cause as much damage and carnage as terror attacks and should not be separated from terrorism perpetrated by nonstate actors.

By singling out countries as state sponsors of terrorism, the United States and its allies can cause massive harm to their civilian populations. Sanctions in Iraq and Iran have devastated their economies and hurt ordinary people, while having no real effect on (or occasionally emboldening) the ability of these states to support terror groups abroad. By imposing this designation on their enemies, powerful countries use the pretext of terrorism to arbitrarily hurt and marginalize them. And when these powerful states resort to direct force—as the United States did when it invaded Iraq—they do so with impunity. Moreover, critical terrorism scholars would argue that studies that attempt to study state-sponsored terrorism from an empirical standpoint are, themselves, contributing to the problem. By treating state-sponsored terrorism as a distinct category and attempting to study it from a positivist, scientific perspective, empirical terrorism scholars may legitimize the status quo orientation while marginalizing those who challenge it.

The primary flaw of the critical terrorism studies approach is its tendency to overstate or neglect the contributions that empirical researchers have made to illuminating many of the normative challenges raised by critical terrorism scholars. In particular, empirical researchers have argued that state-sponsored terrorism is critical to study empirically precisely because of its politicized, contested nature. For example, by defining state-sponsored terrorism in a straightforward manner—as a government's intentional assistance to a group that has used terror (Byman 2005, p. 5)—scholars can identify the full range of states that have engaged in this behavior. Such analyses, including Byman's, include a full account of support for terrorists by the United States, France, and many other Western countries. In other words, by attempting to define and study the phenomenon by what it is (rather than who perpetrates it), research often arrives at similar conclusions. As such, critical terrorism studies overgeneralizes the degree to which empirical terrorism studies truly work against just causes.

BOX 11.2

WHY DOES THE US DESIGNATE SOME COUNTRIES AS STATE SPONSORS OF TERRORISM BUT NOT OTHERS?

The US State Department maintains an active list of State Sponsors of Terrorism. This designation involves heavy penalties for designated states. Because of the United States' powerful and central position in the international community, states on the list are subject to extreme economic, political, and diplomatic isolation.

To be added to the list, the US Secretary of State "must determine that the government of such country has repeatedly provided support for acts of international terrorism" (https://www.state.gov/j/ct/list/c14151.htm). The Secretary of State then makes a recommendation to the President that the state be added to the list, and the US Congress votes on whether or not to block the move.

But some suggest that the list actually has more to do with domestic politics and the foreign policy goals of the United States than it does with terrorism per se. For example, Republican presidents have made all of the changes to the list (either adding or removing states) except for two. President Bill Clinton was the only Democratic president to add a state to the list when he added Sudan in 1993. President Obama became the first Democratic president to remove a country when he de-listed Cuba in 2015. The fact that he did so near the end of his second term as President (and not earlier) might be explained by the fact that he did not have to worry about what the action might do to his popularity among Cuban Americans. And at the same time as Cuba was added to the list (1982), Iraq was removed, allowing US companies to sell arms to that country. Iran was prevailing in the Iraq-Iran war at the time, and then-US President Ronald Reagan was loath to see Iraq lose (Jett 2015).

As of 2017, only three countries remain on the list: Syria (designated December 29, 1979), Iran (designated January 19, 1984), and Sudan (designated August 12, 1993). However, prior to 2017, several other countries appeared on the list. These included Cuba, Iraq, Libya, and North Korea, for the following stated reasons:

Cuba (1982–2015)

The US added Cuba to the list in response to its inspiration of various left-wing revolutionary movements throughout Latin America, as well as its apparent role as a transit point for different leftist groups like FARC and ETA. Cuba was removed from the list in 2015 following negotiations to normalize diplomatic relations with the United States.

Iraq (1979–1982; 1991–2004)

The United States added Iraq to the list in 1979 in response to the country's alleged support for ANO and several other groups in the region. However, the United States removed Iraq from the list in 1982 so that it could sell weapons to Saddam Hussein's regime and provide material support to the country in the context of the Iran-Iraq War. The United States added Iraq to the list again in 1991 after Iraq invaded Kuwait, igniting the Gulf War. The United States removed Iraq from the list again in 2004, after the US invasion and overthrow of Saddam Hussein's regime.

Libya (1979–2006)

The US added Libya to the list after its alleged support for various militant organizations in the region. In 2006, the United States removed Libya from the list in return for the country's 2003 decision to abandon its nuclear program.

North Korea (1988–2008)

The United States added North Korea to the list following the bombing of Korean Air flight 858 from Baghdad to Seoul on November 29, 1987, which killed all 115 people on board. The country also allegedly harbored several leftist Japanese terrorists. The United States removed North Korea from the list in 2008 as a concession during negotiations related to the country's nuclear weapons program.

DISCUSSION QUESTIONS

- *Consider the various frameworks that we present in this chapter to explain why states might sponsor terrorism. Now use these approaches, as well as the preceding discussion of why states are added to and removed from the US list, to name some countries that might be missing.*

- *North Korea was removed from the US list of State Sponsors of Terrorism in 2008 because it agreed to verification procedures during negotiations over its nuclear program. However, in the years since, Korea has gone on to test its nuclear weapons, and disallowed any form of verification. What are some of the arguments for and against North Korea belonging on the list once again?*

PRACTICAL IMPLICATIONS

If states sponsor terrorist groups as a cost-saving measure to wage proxy wars against other states, or to pursue increased regional relevance or foreign regime change, the logical policy implication would be to implement measures that make sponsorship more costly for states. This might be accomplished through a variety of measures, ranging from the implementation of sanctions against the state sponsor to military retaliation. For example, when Palestinian groups that enjoyed sanctuary in Jordan in the 1960s began to launch cross-border attacks into Israel, they provoked harsh Israeli reprisals. Israeli forces invaded the Jordanian town of Karameh seeking to destroy Palestinian militant camps and punish Jordan for its support to the PLO. While the raids accomplished the goal of destroying the militant camps, global opinion heavily condemned what was construed as a disproportionate response on the part of Israel. The highly repressive response boosted popular sentiment in favor of Palestinian militant groups and elevated the Palestinian question on the international agenda.

Other states have also responded militarily to state-sponsored terrorism. One of the more prominent examples is the US invasion of Afghanistan in the wake of the 9/11 attacks by Al Qaeda. The aims were to deny Al Qaeda a safe haven in the country, and remove the Taliban from power as punishment for having provided protection to Osama bin Laden and other Al Qaeda operatives. While the US-led invasion of Afghanistan succeeded in dispersing the Taliban and Al Qaeda in its early phases, the lengthy war that continues to this day, and the current resurgence of the Taliban in many areas of Afghanistan call into question the response's overall effectiveness.

States have also used sanctions to punish other states that sponsor terrorism. Consider the case of Libya. As we discuss at other points in this chapter, Libya has a long history of sponsoring terror groups, and was first placed on the US State Sponsors of Terrorism list in 1979 (see Box 11.2). In 1986, the Reagan administration barred exports and imports of Libyan goods and services, and prohibited all forms of financial support to the Libyan government. When Libyan leader Muammar Qaddafi refused to extradite two intelligence agents suspected of planning the 1988 bombing of Pan Am flight 103, the UN imposed an arms and petroleum embargo on Libya and closed off travel to and from the country. According to the US Department of State, Libyan-sponsored terrorism fell sharply following the UN sanctions, and the two agents were extradited in 1999 (US Department of State 2000). Libya also expelled the radical Palestinian group Abu Nidal, and accepted a general responsibility for other acts of terrorism committed under its direction. But other efforts to curb state-sponsored terrorism through the implementation of sanctions have not been as successful. Sudan, for instance, has yet to comply with a number of UN Security Council Resolutions passed in 1996 that demand the extradition of individuals suspected of planning the assassination attempt of Egyptian president Hosni Mubarak in 1995. The same is true with North Korea. Though the country was included on the US's State Sponsors of Terrorism list from 1988–2008, and has publicly condemned various forms of terrorism, it continues to provide shelter to transnational terrorists (Hufbauer et al. 2001).

As we discuss at various points in this chapter, it is very difficult, if not impossible, for states to monitor the terror groups that they sponsor. Some scholars suggest that counterterrorism officials might successfully exploit this "information gap" (Byman and Kreps 2010). Disinformation campaigns led by counterterrorism intelligence agents, for example, might make states more hesitant to trust certain violent nonstate groups. Intelligence services can stress and make public the mistakes that terrorist groups make, discredit individual members of these organizations, or emphasize group goals that might diverge from those of their potential sponsor (ibid.). Making public classified information to embarrass states for sponsoring terror groups might be especially useful in decreasing the perceived advantages of sponsoring terrorist groups as a mechanism of plausible deniability. The Central Intelligence Agency has used similar strategies to destroy terror groups from the inside out, such as the ANO.

If other explanations are correct, such as those that emphasize the role of ideology to explain why states sponsor terrorism, then counterterrorism officials might find it useful to play up concerns over nationalism. Loyalty to a foreign government, for instance, might make a violent group less popular among local populations, particularly if that foreign government is not perceived as a legitimate voice of the people (Byman and Kreps 2010). In Lebanon, for instance, opponents of Hizballah stress the group's ties to Syria and Iran in order to discredit it.

Finally, Byman and Kreps (2010) suggest that curbing state sponsorship of terror organizations might have harmful unintended consequences for particular types of groups. Specifically, they argue that a state sponsor might control the ability of groups to acquire nuclear or other types of unconventional weapons. The acquisition and use of such destructive agents by violent nonstate groups is rarely, if ever, in the best interest of any state. By maintaining the allegiance of powerful terror groups, states can manage and contain the groups' capacity for developing the most destructive weapons. However, highly ideological states might be an exception; the Taliban, for instance, supported Al Qaeda even as the group experimented with chemical weapons and actively sought to develop its nuclear capabilities (Tenet 2007).

SUMMARY

In this chapter, we have discussed the different dimensions of state support for terror groups, while also exploring whether and how various social science approaches apply to the puzzle of state sponsorship. We also learned about several prototypical examples of state-sponsored terrorism, and we explored the politics of designating some countries as State Sponsors of Terrorism while leaving others off that list.

Discussion Questions

1. Why is sponsoring terror groups risky for states? How might the benefits accrued from sponsoring a terror group outweigh these potential risks?

2. If a state turns a blind eye to its own citizens sending money to support terror groups, does this constitute state sponsorship of terrorism? Why or why not?

3. One might assume that all terror groups would be equally interested in obtaining support from a more powerful state ally, which could provide the group with sanctuary, cash, weapons, intelligence and logistical

support, diplomatic cover, access to training, and political and/or ideological inspiration. Yet not all terror groups actually seek out support from states. Why is that?

4. Historically, the United States has designated some countries that do not currently sponsor terror organizations as State Sponsors of Terrorism (e.g., Cuba), yet many states that do sponsor terrorist groups are not designated as such. Why?

5. Why do some states support terror while others do not?

6. By providing aid to countries such as Pakistan, is the US a state sponsor of terrorism? Why or why not?

Key Takeaways

- Some terror groups receive sponsorship from states. Sponsorship can be direct or indirect, willing or unwilling. It can come in many forms, including financial support, sanctuary, training, ideological inspiration, or diplomatic cover. States that sponsor terror groups do so for a variety of reasons, which often parallel strategic, psychological, ideological, psychological, or structural arguments.

- Critical theorists tend to downplay the significance of this activity, arguing instead that most states that engage in violent activity also engage in state-directed terror and that the focus on support of violent nonstate actors is subjective and reinforces existing power structures. For example, the United States has routinely used the label "State Sponsors of Terrorism" to punish its rivals but has applied the term arbitrarily, inconsistently, and punitively.

- Regardless, state sponsorship of terror groups can be a double-edged sword for both the groups and their sponsors. This activity introduces principal-agent problems between the sponsors and the groups they support, which can ultimately weaken and undermine the relationships between them.

SUGGESTED FURTHER READINGS

Bapat, Navin A. 2007. "The Internationalization of Terrorist Campaigns." *Conflict Management and Peace Science* 24 (4): 265–280. doi:10.1080/07388940701643607.

Bapat, Navin A., Luis de la Calle, Kaisa H. Hinkkainen, and Elena V. McLean. 2016. "Economic Sanctions, Transnational Terrorism, and Incentives to Misrepresent." *Journal of Politics* 78 (1): 249–264. doi:10.1086/683257.

Boutton, Andrew. 2014. "US Foreign Aid, Interstate Rivalry, and Incentives for Counterterrorism Cooperation." *Journal of Peace Research* 51 (6): 741–754. doi:10.1177/0022343314543144.

Byman, Daniel. 2005. *Deadly Connections: States that Sponsor Terrorism*. New York: Cambridge University Press.

Byman, Daniel, and Sarah Kreps. 2010. "Agents of Destruction? Applying Principal-Agent Analysis to State Sponsorship of Terrorism." *International Studies Perspectives* 11 (1): 1–18. doi:10.1111/j.1528-3585.2009.00389.x.

Carter, David B. 2012. "A Blessing or a Curse? State Support for Terrorist Groups." *International Organization* 66 (1): 129–151. doi:10.1017/s0020818311000312.

Croissant, Aurel, and Daniel Barlow. 2007. "Following the Money Trail: Terrorist Financing and Government Responses in Southeast Asia." *Studies in Conflict and Terrorism* 30 (2): 131–156. doi:10.1080/10576100600959721.

Findley, Michael G., James A. Piazza, and Joseph K. Young. 2012. "Games Rivals Play: Terrorism in International Rivalries." *Journal of Politics* 71 (1): 235–248. doi:10.2139/ssrn.1676555.

O'Sullivan, Meghan. 2003. *Shrewd Sanctions: Statecraft and State Sponsors of Terrorism*. Washington, DC: Brookings Institution Press.

Salehyan, Idean. 2010. "The Delegation of War to Rebel Organizations." *Journal of Conflict Resolution* 54 (3): 493–515. doi:10.1177/0022002709357890.

Salehyan, Idean, Kristian Skrede Gleditsch, and David Cunningham. 2011. "Explaining External Support for Insurgent Groups." *International Organization* 65 (4): 709–744. doi:10.1017/s0020818311000233.

Shapiro, Jacob N. 2013. *The Terrorist's Dilemma*. Princeton: Princeton University Press.

Wardlaw, Grant. 2001. "Terror as an Instrument of Foreign Policy," in David Rapoport, ed., *Inside Terrorist Organizations*, revised edition. New York: Columbia University Press.

Weinstein, Jeremy M. 2006. *Inside Rebellion: The Politics of Rebel Organization*. New York: Cambridge University Press.

CHAPTER 12

GENDER AND TERRORISM

Learning Objectives

After reading this chapter, readers should be able to:

- Explain the differences between studies of terrorism that take gender into account, or depart from a gendered perspective to understanding violence, and those that do not;
- Explain how various approaches explain why women join terror organizations, become suicide bombers, or why organizations decide to recruit women into their ranks;
- Give examples of terror groups that have explicitly recruited women and their stated reasons for doing so;
- Explain the practical implications of women's involvement in terrorism.

> "Protest is when I say this does not please me. Resistance is when I ensure what does not please me occurs no more."
>
> —ULRIKE MEINHOF, LEADER OF THE ROTE ARMEE FRAKTION
> (RED ARMY FACTION) (MEINHOF 1968, P. 5)

> "I, the martyrdom-seeker Umm Suheib, have dedicated myself for the sake of Allah, and for the sake of redeeming my family, from which I have lost eight martyrs so far. I swear by Allah that I will turn my body parts into a fire that will burn the occupation soldiers, if they move towards my house."
>
> —UMM SUHEIB, HAMAS SUICIDE BOMBER, IN A DECEMBER 2008
> VIDEO, QUOTED IN RAJAN 2011, P. 91)

THE PUZZLE

In 1985, the Syrian Socialist National Party (SSNP) deployed a seventeen-year old girl to blow herself up near an Israeli military convoy in Lebanon. In May 1991, Dhanu, a woman of Sri Lankan origin, strapped an explosive device to her stomach to give the impression that she was pregnant, walked up to Indian Prime Minister Rajiv Gandhi during a public appearance, and blew herself up, killing herself, Gandhi and many others. A leader of the Red Army Faction, Ulrike Meinhof, formed one half of the eponymous Baader-Meinhof Group in West Germany in the 1970s. And in 1954, Lolita Lebron, a Puerto Rican nationalist, participated in an assault on the US Capitol that resulted in the wounding of five Congressmen.

These and many other cases have been puzzling to observers of terrorism and political violence because of one striking feature: deviating from the typical biographical profile of the terrorist in the popular imagination, the perpetrators were women. Contrary to this popular depiction, however, women have actively joined terror groups and participated in acts of terrorism throughout history. Among contemporary groups, the use of women suicide bombers has continued to grow, spreading to conflicts in Sri Lanka, Turkey, Chechnya, Iraq, and Nigeria.

Women have participated in acts of terrorism in a number of capacities: they have acted as attackers, kidnappers, hijackers, and support and logistics personnel. According to Mia Bloom, women account for nearly 15 percent of all suicide terror attacks (2011). Some estimates are even higher, suggesting that almost 30 percent of suicide attackers are women (ibid.). Alongside the growth in women's participation in terrorism over the years has come increased attention from both the media and academia (Sjoberg and Gentry 2011). Today, a number of studies address the particular role of women as agents of political violence, granting increased attention to sex and gender in theories of conflict.

WOMEN AND VIOLENCE

The idea of women's violence typically falls outside of **essentialist** understandings of what it means to be a woman. Social constructions associate femininity with notions of innocence, fragility, peace, and conciliation. The bulk of studies on war, terrorism, or other forms of political conflict have traditionally portrayed women as **victims**—not **perpetrators**—of violence.

Early studies of the role of women in violent organizations portrayed them as relatively voiceless. Such studies saw women as capable of combat only under the shadows of the men who controlled them, thus dispossessing women terrorists of any individual agency. In this vein, scholars interpreted women's terrorism as fundamentally different from men's (Gentry 2009). Studies argued that men recruited women into violent organizations to offer emotional and ideological support to male members, and valued women primarily for their potential to fill the stereotypical role of mother, wife, or caretaker. Alternatively, they might handle tasks short of fighting, like administration, but women remained theoretically distinct actors from their male counterparts who were assumed to engage in acts of violence (ibid.).

When women engage in violence directly, they turn these **stereotypes** on their heads. More recent work recognizes the explicitly violent roles that women play in conflict, and the literature points to various motivations as to why they choose to do so. Some studies point to engagement in terror as a response to emotional or physical harm (Galvin 1983). Others show that the pursuit of women's liberation influenced some women to become terrorists (Glynn 2013). Explicit in these later theories is attention to the particular role that gender plays in shaping various outcomes related to terrorism.

Although people frequently use the terms interchangeably, **gender** and **sex** are not the same thing. Whereas the term sex refers explicitly to one's biological maleness or femaleness, gender describes "the socially constituted behavioral expectations, stereotypes, and rules that construct masculinity and femininity" (Sjoberg and Gentry 2011, p. 6). Feminist scholars argue that the social differences between masculinity and femininity are not innate and reify interpretations of power based on gender.

Gender analysis often informs contemporary scholarship on terrorism. The literature on the topic studies women as **gendered** actors who navigate gendered relationships and live in a gendered world, thus seeking to identify and analyze the implications of approaching terrorism with a **gendered lens**. Studies that fall under this rubric investigate, among other things, how gender relations emerge within and shape the structure of a terror organization, or relations between these groups and their audiences. Proponents of gender analysis suggest that it is important to build our understanding of why women do or do not participate in terror, as well as how gender might impact the evolution of tactics used by terrorist groups (Sjoberg and Gentry 2011). Do men and women have different motivations to become terrorists, or join terrorist organizations? Do the logics of men and women suicide bombers differ? Why do groups recruit women into their organizations, and to what effect? The remainder of this chapter synthesizes the growing literature where scholars have addressed some of these questions.

BOX 12.1
PROFILE OF A PFLP HIJACKER: LEILA KHALED

Photo 12.1   Mural of Leila Khaled painted on the concrete barrier in Bethlehem that separates the West Bank and Israel

Leila Khaled is a member of the Popular Front for the Liberation of Palestine (PFLP), a Marxist-Leninist Palestinian nationalist movement. Born in Haifa to Palestinian parents in 1944, she fled to Lebanon in 1948 as part of the forced Palestinian national exodus, referred to by Palestinians as the Nakhba ("Catastrophe"). At the age of 15, she joined the pan-Arab Arab Nationalist Movement. The Palestinian branch of this movement became the PFLP in 1967. Khaled worked to convince the PFLP to train her as a guerrilla fighter, and eventually the group's leadership acquiesced. Of her time training in the Jordanian countryside with the group, Khaled says "I was so happy that for the first three days and nights, I could not sleep" (quoted in Irving 2012, p. 29). Her joy at becoming an armed guerrilla bucks common stereotypes of women's docility and passivity.

Khaled is best known for her role as part of the team that hijacked TWA flight 840 on its way from Rome to Tel Aviv in August 1969. The flight was eventually diverted to Damascus, and no one was injured despite the fact that the attackers blew up the nose of the aircraft once the plane had emptied. The following year, Khaled and Patrick Arguello, a Nicaraguan-American, attempted the hijack of El Al Flight 219 from Amsterdam to New York as part of a series of attacks planned by the PFLP. The attack was foiled when Israeli sky marshals killed Arguello and overpowered Khaled. UK security services arrested her after the plane was diverted to London but released her soon thereafter in exchange for the release of hostages from a different hijacking.

Khaled subsequently became involved in Palestinian electoral politics, and today she is a member of the Palestinian National Council. When interviewed about her motivations for joining the PFLP, she addressed her belief in the cause: "armed struggle is the means to achieve the goals of the people" (Khaled, as quoted in Gentry 2009). The broader social influence of Nasserism was also important in shaping her decision. At the time, most Palestinians were involved in some sort of political mobilization, with

Continued

BOX 12.1

PROFILE OF A PFLP HIJACKER: LEILA KHALED

(Continued)

teachers encouraging students to become engaged in fighting for Palestinian self-determination.

Overall, Khaled describes her experience in the PFLP as personally enriching. She is adamant in her belief of the worthiness and justice of Palestinian liberation, and in the possibility of achieving the ultimate goal. Importantly, she flatly denies that men have manipulated women who have fought and continue to fight, contradicting many studies suggesting that women's participation in armed struggle is primarily guided by men's strategic goals. Her participation has been voluntary from the beginning, she explained, and is an explicit articulation of her political commitments (see Irving 2012).

APPROACHES TO STUDYING GENDER AND TERRORISM

Most gendered theories apply a critical approach to understanding terrorism. Recall from Chapter 7 that **critical approaches** are primarily concerned with questioning the politics behind the production of knowledge and policy related to terrorism. In particular, critical theorists call into question the very use of the term terrorism, highlighting its pejorative connotations and the ways that power structures have used it to delegitimize disempowered opponents. In the case of gender analysis, many critical theorists focus on the **patriarchal** status quo as the main frame through which to view the power relations that motivate violent behavior by men or women.

Like other approaches that study the impact of gender on terrorism-related outcomes, critical feminist approaches acknowledge that women participate in terrorism, they are impacted by terrorism, they engage in the struggle against terrorism, and they are represented in discussions of the phenomenon. What sets critical, gendered approaches apart from ideological, strategic, or other approaches is an explicit focus on the gendered context terrorism, counterterrorism, and the study and representation of terrorism and terrorists. Critical theorists that focus on gender seek to transform the very ways that we associate with "being" or "knowing" terrorism (Peterson 1992).

For instance, a number of studies show that gender plays a key role in discussions of what a terrorist is. H.H.A. Cooper, for example, suggested in his work that contextualizing terrorist violence by a woman is difficult (1979). However, he writes that "women are playing a male game using thinly disguised and poorly adapted male roles," seeing terrorism as a "perversion of herself as a woman" (1979, p. 155). Thus, because of their transgressions of social convention, Cooper condemned and vilified the woman terrorist even more vehemently than he did male terrorists.

Consider popular portrayals of Leila Khaled, a member of the Popular Front for the Liberation of Palestine (PFLP), which often refer more to her femininity and attractiveness than to the personal and political reasons that may have led her to forming a strong commitment to Palestinian self-determination. Continual references to her beauty, Arab identity, and participation in political violence fed problematic constructions of Leila Khaled as an uncivilized non-Westerner (Gentry 2009). In reality, her violent actions did not come close to inflicting the level of damage wrought by figures such as Osama bin Laden or Abu Bakr al-Baghdadi. Yet because she both committed hijackings but also transgressed her socially-prescribed gender roles, Gentry argues, she has received special notice and condemnation (2009). To this point, the men with whom Leila Khaled participated in the hijacking of TWA Flight 840 in 1969 have received little to no attention.

In a critical review of the extant literature on women suicide bombers, Brunner (2007) shows how observers often frame women terrorists as representative of a truly novel and transgressive phenomenon, separate from similar forms of historical or contemporary political violence that occurred in Western contexts. Women's actions are frequently decontextualized, with scholarship preferring instead to focus on the individual as the primary focus of research. Popular portrayals of women often construct them as mistaken individuals acting under the heavy influence of their male leaders, or deceived into giving their lives to a cause to which they are not really committed. The imagery of strong women's leadership is lacking in most studies of women suicide bombers, which frame their roles in terrorism as a direct result of the inherent oppression of Arab or Muslim societies. Such portrayals of women militants, explains Brunner, are severely flawed thanks to their complicity with patriarchal ways of knowing (ibid.).

Other critical studies take a gendered approach to discerning how to define terrorism. Sjoberg (2009) argues that terrorism is often portrayed as the product of the fears and problems of a small, often masculine population. Do acts of violence perpetrated by women's groups then not count as terrorism, and can such groups never present themselves as potential threats given their gender? Ultimately, we can trace many biases that occur in definitions of what it means to be a terrorist, or what terrorism is, to the gender biases in what counts as security in global politics. For example, far more women are killed by their husbands or male family members than by terrorists; domestic violence is therefore a much greater threat to women's security around the world than terrorism. Moreover, gender-based violence among intimate partners is arguably intended to inculcate fear so as to coerce compliance or reinforce gender hierarchies within a relationship. But domestic violence rarely counts as terrorism, in part because the term derives from what men consider most personally threatening than from what women consider most personally threatening.

Some scholars also point to gender relationships and expectations as motivating violent attacks by men. In a study of white supremacist groups, Abby Ferber, for example, argues that perceived threats to masculinity often motivate spectacular acts of violence as a man attempts to reclaim his status when he cannot achieve financial or social power in other ways (1998). And, of course, one of the popular explanations for why jihadi men volunteer for suicide missions is the promise of an afterlife in which, having proven their masculinity, they are rewarded by seventy-two virgins (Thayer and Hudson 2010).

Feminists and critical theorists also suggest that terrorism is not limited to nonstate actors. If feminists are more apt to defining security broadly and are critical of the patriarchal and exclusionary study of security, then gender lenses might also perceive terrorism as the inculcation of fear to coerce on the part of state actors (Sjoberg 2009). In short, these approaches strongly suggest that we cannot define terrorism as a simple, unidirectional relationship in which nonstate groups terrorize states and civilians. Feminists suggest that adopting such an understanding on a broader scale might reduce gender biases in the study of terrorism.

Strategic approaches to understanding women's participation in violence suggest that the operational imperatives of groups often make women highly effective actors within their organizations (Cunningham 2003). According to this perspective, tactical necessity appears to help some terrorist organizations overcome gender barriers when it comes to using women in attacks. This need may be the direct result of a shortage of male recruits, which may result from factors such as labor migration, recruitment into other ongoing conflicts, or state repression. For example, in some contexts, women may more easily move through security checkpoints because of lower levels of suspicion or heavy cultural stigmas attached to searching women in modest dress. Women may have a greater ability to conceal weapons under clothing, in purses, or in baby strollers (Eager 2008, p. 108).

Along the same lines, women might have particular tactical advantages in environments where women can move around more freely than men. In conflict zones, women are less likely to arouse suspicion and be subjected to searches by security services. Young males are typical targets of arrest and interrogation, leaving women relatively unobstructed to plan and carry out attacks against an unassuming target. Hamas, for example, has publicized their decision to use women attackers at Israeli checkpoints due to the increasing operational difficulties of getting men to their targets. The traditional placement of women in public spaces such as markets or shopping centers also contributes to groups' strategic decisions to use them as attackers. Moreover, terrorists likely recognize the sensitivities involved in carrying out body searches of women, particularly Muslim women (Bloom 2005).

Providing some support for the strategic approach, empirical studies have shown that suicide attacks perpetrated by women bombers are more deadly than those committed by male bombers (O'Rourke 2009). Table 12.1 compares the average casualties inflicted by attacks of suicide bombers by gender.

O'Rourke (2009) shows that the superior tactical effectiveness of women's suicide bombings derives from the very norms that regulate women's behavior in societies where the attacks take place. The five cases she examines reveal that social prejudices against women lead to less suspicion against them; superior ability to conceal explosives; and less subjection to stringent security precautions.

That said, women remain rare among the total number of suicide bombers. From 1982–2015, women made up only 8.8 percent of the world's total suicide bombers (CPOST 2016). If the strategic perspective were right, we might expect to see far greater numbers of women suicide terrorists.

TABLE 12.1 Average Casualties Per Individual Attack By Group

	Lebanese	*PKK*	*LTTE*	*Chechen*	*Palestinian*	*Total*
Women	2.3	2.3	12.1	20.9	3.4	8.4
Men	3.3	1.4	10.4	13.3	4.0	5.3
% (Women: Men)	70%	164%	116%	157%	85%	158%

Source: O'Rourke 2009

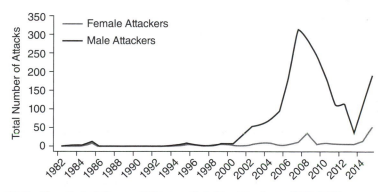

Figure 12.1 Trends in Men and Women Suicide Attackers, 1982–2015;
Source: CPOST 2016

Organizational approaches suggest that the use of women terrorists appears to be contagious between organizations. Broadly, women can yield three types of benefits to the organizations whose ranks they join (Dalton and Asal 2011). First, their caregiving skills and expertise fill important organizational needs, particularly when male labor becomes scarce due to casualties. Moreover, women often provide emotional and psychological solace as well as sex to their male counterparts. Second, gender norms that typically portray women as pacifists are quickly turned into a strategic advantage for those groups that decide to employ women as fighters and as weapons, as discussed above (Cunningham 2003). Third, terror groups have used women fighters to encourage more volunteers—in particular men—to take on the cause (Cock 1991).

Dalton and Asal (2011) further find that larger and older organizations are more likely to recruit and deploy women. This relationship is likely driven by the heightened ability of larger groups to engage in tactical innovation. Similar reasoning explains why the age of a terrorist organization might also be an important variable influencing its decision to recruit women. Organizational age may be reflective of a prolonged struggle, which over time may have far-reaching effects on motivation and capacity for both men and women to mobilize. The Algerian struggle against French occupation in the 1950s, which ultimately involved men and women as active members, is an example of this dynamic (Dalton and Asal 2011).

That said, it is not clear why some organizations seem to feature such high participation rates for women compared to others. For example, up to fifty percent of the Communist Party of Nepal's (CPN) cadres were women, compared with much smaller proportions in other groups (Guneretne and Weiss 2013, p. 329).

As you recall from Chapter 5, **ideological approaches** focus on particular belief systems that motivate, incite, and legitimize the use of violence by women. Remember that the ideologies of terrorism encompass a range of motivations from ethno-nationalist goals to leftist versus rightist tendencies to religious beliefs. An additional ideology that has worked to mobilize individuals, in particular women, towards violence and terrorism has been **feminism**. Some women may decide to join a terrorist group as part of a struggle for the liberation of women in their societies. For instance, the CPN subscribed to a feminist strand of Maoism, which promoted the full equality of women in Nepalese society. As we discuss throughout the chapter, women's roles are culturally limited in many societies. Indeed, some researchers have observed that the intent of some women suicide bombers is not just to fight on the part of their country, religion, or a specific leader, but in the name of their gender (Bloom 2005). In Algeria, while the mobilization of women in the 1950s resistance movement against French occupation largely responded to nationalist goals, women's increased participation in violence lessened women's marginalization from politics (Cunningham 2003).

BOX 12.2

CASE STUDY: THE WOMEN OF ISIS

A surge in the number of women joining ISIS in 2015 brought the phenomenon of women and terrorism into stark focus. Why would women voluntarily join a terror group that openly engaged in sex slavery? What does the involvement of women foreign fighters in ISIS tell us about radicalization? Are the mechanisms of radicalization the same for women as they are for men? In this case box, we explore some issues related to gender and the ISIS phenomenon.

Of the approximately four thousand westerners that have joined ISIS over the last several years, approximately 550 are women. Research on the women who have traveled to Iraq and Syria to become members of ISIS highlight that there is no broad profile that fits all of those who have joined, or who have been radicalized by Islamic State propaganda.

Far from being slaves to their sexual desires or victims of predatory men, the women who join ISIS appear do so to satisfy their own aspirations of jihad. Unlike the secular liberal democracies in which many of these women live, the Islamic State reflects their moral and political convictions. They do not seek freedom in the Western sense, but instead seek to live under a **caliphate**, which they believe it is their divine duty to support. Ultimately, their motivations for joining, and their susceptibility to radicalization more generally, are no different from those of men who join ISIS (Cottee 2016).

Accounts from the battlefield in Iraq and Syria suggest that ISIS has formed at least two all-women brigades. Members of the Umm Al-Arayn and Al-Khansaa brigades patrol the towns of Raqqa, Syria and Mosul, Iraq to ensure that women are fully covered when in public, and are accompanied by a man. They administer punishments to those who do not adhere to the strict behavior and dress codes dictated by ISIS. According to some accounts of the organization, members of the brigade are also charged with exposing men attempting to disguise themselves in women's clothing to avoid detection.

Of course, many women have joined ISIS to marry and have children. But in addition to being wives to their jihadi husbands, and to becoming mothers to a future generation of Islamic fighters, the women of ISIS play crucial roles in disseminating propaganda and recruiting other women through online platforms (Hoyle, Bradford, and Frenett 2015; Peresin and Cervone 2015; Saltman and Smith 2015).

Given the many reasons women join ISIS, there is a great need to establish a strong counternarrative to the organization's propaganda. Increasing the awareness of youth about extremist propaganda to allow for the development of a more genuine resilience might help to reduce the effectiveness of the group's online and offline recruitment efforts.

Ensuring that women are adequately represented in these counternarrative efforts is equally important. Most anti-extremism prevention programs are still far from adopting gender-neutral rhetoric and practices, much in the same way as counterterrorism policies face shortcomings due to the gendered assumptions of violence upon which they are based.

Women's participation in violence has altered gender relations in other contexts as well. In the Palestinian Territories, for example, participation in acts of terrorism has placed women in the public eye, often alongside men to whom they are unrelated. This is in stark contrast to local norms that otherwise dictate the distinct separation of the sexes and that confine women to the home, out of sight. Through violence, women in otherwise closed societies have convinced the public of their contributions to the struggle against an opponent regime, and also have emancipated themselves from restrictive gender roles. Nevertheless, empirical studies continue to provide little evidence that women's participation in terrorist groups has helped improve norms such as gender equality on a larger and more enduring scale.

Some studies have argued that women are better represented in left-wing groups, relative to their right-wing counterparts. One possible reason for this trend is that leftist ideologies—whose message revolves largely around political and social justice—resonates with women. A second reason is that ideas of social equality influence leadership structures within these groups. As a result, women may be overrepresented in leadership positions within left-wing groups. Women's participation in leftist organizations has been particularly prominent in Europe and Latin America, with the FARC in Colombia and the Shining Path in Peru attracting particularly high numbers (Cunningham 2003). Right-wing terrorist organizations, on the other hand, tend to have much more traditional, patriarchal beliefs. Unsurprisingly, they have recruited far fewer women, and their leadership structures reflect a virtual absence of women's representation (Handler 1990).

Some are dubious of ideological explanations for women's involvement in terror groups, since ideologies seem so malleable under different conditions. For example, despite the fact that women's involvement in Muslim society has been notoriously limited, extremist Islamist religious authorities have made numerous exceptions to traditions that would otherwise preclude women's involvement in terrorism. In 2003, for example, an Al Qaeda cell claimed to have set up squads of women suicide bombers to target the United States under orders from Osama bin Laden. In 2004, an Al Qaeda publication focused specifically on a call to women to participate in jihad. In the context of today's conflicts, groups such as Boko Haram and the Islamic State (ISIS) are turning more and more to the use of women suicide bombers in their attacks. ISIS's first recorded use of women suicide bombers came in Libya in February 2016, when seven women were arrested for plotting attacks, and more than three died while carrying out attacks.

In terms of **psychological approaches**, researchers have yet to establish consensus regarding personality traits that may be unique to women terrorists. In the majority of cases, the women who have joined terrorist organizations are not unbalanced sociopaths, nor are they prone to self-destructive tendencies. Indeed, many of the same psychological characteristics that apply to male suicide bombers apply to their female counterparts. Often, these women may feel a sense of alienation from their societies, or seek retribution for humiliation. However, some argue that trauma may indeed play a role in the decision to engage in terrorism—especially suicide terrorism. Women who have experienced the deaths of close family members or life partners at the hands of an opposing group may be more likely to join the ranks of a terrorist organization. Anecdotal evidence does suggest that many women suicide bombers have been raped or sexually abused either by representatives of the state or by insurgents, thereby contributing to a sense of humiliation and powerlessness (Bloom 2005). Bloom finds support for these claims among women who have acted as suicide bombers in diverse contexts including the separatist conflict in Chechnya, the Kurdistan Worker's Party's struggle for Kurdish autonomy in Turkey, and the Tamil insurgency in Sri Lanka.

A potentially important point of contrast between men's and women's participation in terrorism may lie in how observers have characterized their motivations. Psychological explanations of individual participation in violence, for instance, typically characterize men as being motivated by the search for power. When it comes to women, however, some scholars argue that their motivations are more frequently linked to a desire to achieve a greater social good. Galvin (1983) and Alison (2003), for example, suggest that women might be more attracted to the prospect of a higher quality of life, and increased opportunities for their children. Alternatively, women who are unable or unwilling to fulfill prescribed gender roles as childbearers or wives (due to personal choice, infertility, homosexuality, or the death of their husbands) may see high-risk militant action as an acceptable alternative (Bloom 2011). However, these interpretations of individual motivation tend to reinforce gender stereotypes and may be difficult to generalize across all individuals—regardless of gender—who participate in terrorism.

Finally, a handful of scholars have pointed to the unique psychological impact left by acts of violence carried out by women terrorists. In her work on the cultural representations of women and terrorism in Italy, Glynn (2013) demonstrates that Italian society has largely interpreted women's involvement in the political violence of the 1970s as signifying an intensification of violence. This is grounded in the fact that women who perpetrate violence disrupt established gender roles. Observers construe their participation in acts of violence as a "double wound"—violence committed by women is abnormal and therefore doubly traumatic for its victims and onlookers. In fact, women's involvement in the violence sharply influences Italians' collective memory of the 1970s violence (ibid.).

As with psychological approaches more generally, such explanations fall short in two key respects. First, it is difficult to explain why some women victims of trauma volunteer for terror missions while others do not. And second, such accounts neglect systematic analysis of the societal structures that make traumatic episodes like rape or domestic violence so widespread.

Studies that take a **structural approach** to understanding women's participation in terror organizations and their role as terrorists assume that women make decisions within the social, political, and economic constraints of their specific environments. In particular, some theories of women's participation in terrorism point to changes in political opportunity as an important driving factor. The loosening of societal restrictions over women in certain contexts, for instance, could explain the rise in women's participation in violent mobilization.

An interesting stream of research that falls under the structural approach shows how factors such as age, educational attainment, and economic status affect participation in terrorism. Most women suicide bombers, for example, are relatively young. Suicide bombers in Turkey were on average 21.5 years old, and the mean age of women bombers in Lebanon was twenty-three (Zedalis 2004). Other studies identified a positive association between education and economic status and the likelihood of becoming a suicide bomber. In their large-n cross-national study of women's participation in terrorism, Dalton and Asal (2011) find that women's educational attainment, social rights, and a country's level of economic development, together with organizational age and size, are all important determinants of women's participation in terrorism. A lack of employment or education opportunities may lessen the cost of joining a violent organization as much for women as it does for men. Consider the argument found in some studies that women's social rights are negatively related to women's participation in terrorism (Krueger and Maleckova 2002). This suggests that a more open society where men and women are treated as equals—and where women are strongly represented in the national workforce—may significantly weaken women's incentives to join violent organizations.

In her work on women militants in the LTTE, for example, Miranda Alison (2009) finds that women's decisions were influenced by a host of structural factors such as the disruption of education in the wake of the Sri Lankan standardization scheme. In 1971, the government of Sri Lanka introduced a system of standardization for admission into universities directed against Tamil minority students. The state required students of Tamil ethnicity to achieve higher marks on medical school entrance exams relative to their Sinhalese peers. Similar patterns of achievement were set in other fields of study, severely limiting the ability of Tamil youth to attend university. Displacement policies further disrupted the education of Tamil secondary school students, often preventing them from completing high school. Five women LTTE militants interviewed by Alison cited displacement and the inability to complete school as a principal reason for enlisting in the organization (Alison 2009).

In contrast, Cunningham (2003) demonstrates how the use of women by the Algerian resistance movement in the 1950s was largely a response to changing French counterterrorist tactics. More specifically, France's adaptation to resistance tactics prompted male FLN leaders to hesitantly transform their strategy and include women in the public struggles. When the conflict moved to public areas, unveiled Algerian women moved freely among crowds and were better able to exploit and evade their opponent. By the late 1950s, the veil reappeared in response to indiscriminate targeting of all Algerians as potential terrorism suspects. Its return facilitated the concealment of weapons and explosives, and was considered a technique of camouflage critical to successful guerrilla warfare (Decker 1990).

The use of women in the context of the Algerian resistance was at once a strategic response to French counterterrorism actions, and a response to changing societal standards. The structural explanation focuses primarily on the revolutionary features of Algerian resistance against external colonial control, which led to broad public mobilization that included women. The growing participation of women promised heightened equality, and was also a rejection of France's efforts at regulating the use of the veil in public (Decker 1990).

Much as the broader terrorism literature has addressed the relationship between foreign occupation and terrorism, so too have scholars attempted to explain the potential interaction between foreign occupation and women's involvement in terror. Most notably, Mia Bloom (2010) points to Al Qaeda's emphasis on the dangers to Muslim women by Western occupying forces—and to allegations that US soldiers raped and impregnated Iraqi detainees at Abu Ghraib—to motivate further Al Qaeda attacks against US interests. Al Qaeda's strategy shows how terrorist groups can use gendered conceptualizations of threat and accusations of sexual violence to mobilize people to join and act on behalf of a militant group. Gendered rhetoric might thus be an important mobilization strategy on the part of some groups. In many cases, acts of sexual abuse by occupying forces have directly increased the mobilization of women into conflicts. This has been the case in the context of the conflict in Iraq as well as the Israel-Palestinian conflict, where Palestinian militant groups frequently accuse Israeli soldiers of sexually abusing Palestinian women (Bloom 2010).

In the West, too, women's participation in terrorist organizations in the 1960s and 1970s corresponded to a period of momentous social change, evidenced by growing popular mobilization around issues of

BOX 12.3
WOMEN IN THE LTTE

Photo 12.2   Women of the LTTE

The LTTE's use of women in their political and military struggle against the Sri Lankan state stands out among nationalist struggles. When substantial numbers of women first joined the LTTE in the 1990s, they initially distributed propaganda materials, administered medical care, raised money, or gathered information and intelligence. Shortly thereafter, their roles grew to include participation in combat.

Explanations for why the organization chose to recruit women into its ranks are manifold. In her work on women's roles in the LTTE's nationalist struggle, Miranda Alison (2003) identifies three main reasons for the recruitment of women. First, the LTTE leadership saw women as filling the strategic need of additional fighters, owing in large part to an insufficient number of men. Second, the need to demonstrate that the organization was an all-encompassing social movement was important to the LTTE. The group's leadership was open and vocal about the LTTE's gender-liberal approach to women's participation, and encouraged women to actively pursue armed roles in the struggle. Finally, recruitment patterns were responsive to pressure from Tamil women themselves, who pushed for women's equal status in society. The organization thus represented itself not just as a nationalist movement, but also as a movement fighting for women's empowerment and the elimination of caste discrimination more broadly (Alison 2009).

Why did the women volunteer? Many of the reasons cited for women's participation in the LTTE are similar to those that would apply to men: a commitment to the Tamil nationalist cause. Personal suffering and Sinhalese oppression were other oft-cited motivations. Reduced educational opportunities were another reason that many Tamil joined the resistance. For women in particular, decisions to join were based on commitments to women's emancipation. Some were forcibly conscripted (Bloom 2005).

The leadership of the LTTE divided men and women into separate units and prevented them from fraternizing. Through experience fighting along cadres of women, however, men within the group came to accept and respect them. As comradeship grew from participating in battle together, gender distinctions began to transform (Alison 2009). The organization began to oppose domestic violence and punished offenders.

The inclusion of women into the ranks of the LTTE improved the status of Tamil women at large. Nonmilitant women began to behave unconventionally (Maunaguru 1995), changing their attire in ways that transgressed social prescriptions. The change from "brave mother" to "woman warrior" was a major categorical shift away from the expected roles for Tamil women in society.

The status of Tamil women and former women LTTE fighters in the post-conflict context is mixed. The LTTE's defeat in 2009 led to reprisals against former militants—men and women— and many remain in detention or in displaced persons camps. As with many people in such settings, they have been subjected to abuse, including sexual violence. There are some signs to suggest, however, that militant Tamil women and LTTE feminism remain influential in addressing gender relations. Tamil society has granted women more space, and a female Sri Lankan Tamil MP was elected to parliament in 2010.

divorce, abortion, education, and employment. In Italy, for instance, such gendered public discourse opened the door for violent leftist organizations to successfully target women as part of their recruitment efforts (Glynn 2013).

WOMEN TERRORISTS AS PROPAGANDA?

Some studies of women and terrorism claim that attacks carried out by women have higher **propaganda** value than those carried out by men (Stack-O'Connor 2007). The propaganda value of woman-perpetrated terror rose to the fore in the context of the Chechen separatist conflict in Russia at the time of the Dubrovka Theater seizure in Moscow in 2002. Prior to this particular attack, observers generally saw Chechen women as victims of the violent conflict. Once they became involved in actual attacks, however, women began to provide propaganda benefits to Russian counterinsurgency efforts and insurgent groups alike.

The use of women terrorists played into the hands of the Russian state by reinforcing the brutality experienced by Chechen women. Portrayed as "zombies" by the Russian media, the Russian government claimed that the leaders of the Chechen insurgency had forced or tricked women into conducting terror attacks. The image of the "zombie" effectively discredited the insurgency and attracted media attention favorable to the state. This has bolstered a highly gendered public perception of women perpetrators of violence within Russia: in a July 2003 public opinion poll of Russians, more than 80 percent of respondents believed that women terrorists were under the control of someone else (as cited in Stack-O'Connor 2007). The insurgency, on the other hand, has portrayed Chechen women terrorists as "black widows," or women who have lost their partners to the struggle against Russia. In this case, the group exploited the propaganda value of women terrorists by portraying them as victims of brutal Russian repression. Feminist scholars tend to critique both kinds of narratives, accusing them of removing the agency of the women involved and instrumentalizing the suffering of women for the political purposes of men.

The use of women terrorists as propaganda is not unique to the Chechen case. Indeed, the Israeli government has frequently drawn on the personal stories of Palestinian women to discredit them and the movements they represent (Stack-O'Connor 2007). And the LTTE in Sri Lanka held women-only press conferences with the media and published books about their women fighters, called Freedom Guerrillas (ibid.).

PRACTICAL IMPLICATIONS

Many terror groups recruit women or use them in specific attacks as a direct response to state counterterrorism policies. Arguments to this effect suggest that women might attack targets that are difficult for men to reach. Alternatively, terror organizations may turn to recruiting women if not enough men are available in the wake of repressive operations. In Russia at the turn of the twentieth century, for example, women's roles in revolutionary movements grew in response to rising scarcity in available men, who were drafted to fight in the Russo-Japanese War. In Israel, Stack-O'Connor argues that mass arrests of Palestinian men in an effort to reduce militancy among Palestinians influenced Palestinian nationalist groups' decisions to recruit more women into their ranks (2007). Attention to how specific counterterrorism operations might cause violent groups to shift their recruitment strategies to recruiting more women may help to anticipate future group behavior.

For decades, counterterrorism officials and analysts almost exclusively expected terrorists to be young and male. This generalization continues to characterize contemporary approaches to countering terrorism and has limited the reach of certain efforts at stemming radicalization, for example.

The involvement of women in acts of terrorism throughout time should reinforce the notion that terrorism is not a uniquely male activity. If the international community excludes women from programs aimed at countering violent extremism, armed groups may see an increased opportunity in recruiting them. On the other hand, the Russian response to the increase in women-perpetrated attacks has been to expand repressive operations in Chechnya to include women. This particularly repressive approach may backfire by creating more terror attacks overall, whether the perpetrators are men or women.

In contrast to the Russian approach, the Israeli Foreign Ministry has taken to publishing reports on women suicide bombers in an effort to counter the further recruitment of women into violence. These reports highlight descriptions of both successful and unsuccessful women bombers, illustrating the personal challenges of individuals who turned to terrorism. The most important outcome of this approach has been the move away from profiling individual terrorists, and towards profiling situations and placing more emphasis on the broad nature of security (Stack-O'Connor 2007). The adoption of gender-neutral counterterrorism policies may be one implication of this approach. Moreover, some suggest that the increasing emphasis on addressing personal trauma is a promising direction in countering violent extremism (CVE) programs—particularly as conflict-related trauma may be more common among women than men (Gavrandidou and Rosner 2003; Simmons and Granvold 2005; Solomon, Gelkopf, and Bleich 2005).

Finally, some states have attempted to discredit terror groups by increasing attention to groups' uses of women terrorists. Highlighting the discriminatory policies or sexual abuses that occur within certain violent organizations can help to erode their sources of public support—especially among women. For instance, in 2014, the Nigerian group Boko Haram began to use women and girls as forced wives and suicide bombers in attacks throughout the country. Arrested women bombers confessed to a Boko Haram plan that posted fifty women suicide bombers across Maiduguri ready to blow themselves up, with the intention of killing upwards of one hundred thousand people. The group had coerced many of these women and girls into the plan, having abducted them from villages around the country. This recent epidemic of suicide bombings by women likely draws on the kidnapping of over two hundred fifty schoolgirls in Chibok, Nigeria in April 2014. On some occasions, wives of Boko Haram fighters report that they have adjusted to their new lives and remain in the group voluntarily. Emphasizing that the acts of violence carried out by young Nigerian women and girls is often the direct result of brainwashing or sexual humiliation via rape could help to degrade the organization's popular support. However, it is also important to remember that not all women continue to participate in such activities by force; many do so by choice. Therefore, such approaches must take care to differentiate women who have been unwilling accomplices to terror from those who engage in terrorism willingly.

SUMMARY

In this chapter, we introduced and evaluated approaches to studying terrorism that take gender into account. We reviewed the various theories that explain why women choose to join a terrorist organization as well as why certain organizations might decide to recruit women into their ranks.

Discussion Questions

1. How do critical approaches differ from other approaches in understanding the role of women in terrorism?
2. What distinguishes terrorism by women from terrorism in general?
3. What approach do you think best explains why some women become terrorists, or why certain groups may choose to recruit women into their ranks?
4. What approach do you think best explains why women become suicide bombers, or why groups use women as suicide bombers?
5. After reading this chapter, what practical recommendations would you have for reducing violence by women? Against women?

KEY TAKEAWAYS

- Whereas some observers have found women's participation in terrorism puzzling, many scholars have argued that the study of terrorism has been dominated by assumptions that terrorism is a fundamentally masculine activity. In contrast to the standard profile of a terrorist as a young male, most terror groups involve women participants in varying degrees. Many terror groups involve women leaders or symbolic figures.
- There are strategic, organizational, ideological, psychological, and critical explanations for the involvement of women in terror groups. Among studies that engage in qualitative research of women terrorists, women articulate many different reasons for joining terror groups.

In contrast to some approaches that exclusively see women's involvement in terrorism as coerced and exploitative, many women identified in the literature volunteer freely to engage in armed action.

- Responses to terrorism that can account for the varying motivations for women's involvement in terror are likelier to succeed than those that essentialize the rationales for their participation and ignore gendered relationships.

SUGGESTED FURTHER READINGS

Alison, Miranda. 2003. "Cogs In The Wheel? Women In The Liberation Tigers Of Tamil Eelam." *Civil Wars* 6 (4): 37–54. doi:0.1080/136982140308402554

Alison, Miranda. 2009. *Women and Political Violence: Female Combatants in Ethno-National Conflict*. Contemporary Security Studies. Hoboken: Taylor & Francis.

Bloom, Mia. 2005. *Dying To Kill: The Allure of Suicide Terror*. New York: Columbia University Press.

Bloom, Mia. 2010. "Death Becomes Her: Women, Occupation, And Terrorist Mobilization." *PS: Political Science & Politics* 43 (03): 445–450. doi:10.1017/s1049096510000703.

Bloom, Mia. 2011. *Bombshell: Women and Terrorism*. Philadelphia: University of Pennsylvania Press.

Brunner, Claudia. 2007. "Occidentalism Meets The Female Suicide Bomber: A Critical Reflection On Recent Terrorism Debates; A Review Essay." *Signs: Journal Of Women In Culture And Society* 32 (4): 957–971. doi:10.1086/512490.

Cottee, Simon. 2016. "What ISIS Women Want." *Foreign Policy*. (May 17). Available online at: http://foreignpolicy.com/2016/05/17/what-isis-women-want-gendered-jihad/. Last accessed 20-March-2017.

Cunningham, Karla J. 2003. "Cross-Regional Trends in Female Terrorism." *Studies in Conflict and Terrorism* 26(3): 171–195. doi:10.1080/10576100390211419.

Dalton, Angela, and Victor Asal. 2011. "Is It Ideology Or Desperation: Why Do Organizations Deploy Women In Violent Terrorist Attacks?." *Studies In Conflict & Terrorism* 34 (10): 802–819. doi:10.1080/1057610x.2011.604833.

Galvin, Deborah M. 1983. "The Female Terrorist: A Socio-Psychological Perspective." *Behavioral Sciences & the Law* 1 (2): 19–32. doi:10.1002/bsl.2370010206.

Gentry, Caron E. 2009. "Targeting Terrorists: A License To Kill." *Journal Of Military Ethics* 8 (3): 260–262. doi:10.1080/15027570903230331.

Glynn, Ruth. 2013. *Women, Terrorism, and Trauma in Italian Culture*. New York: Palgrave Macmillan.

O'Rourke, Lindsey A. 2009. "What's Special About Female Suicide Terrorism?." *Security Studies* 18 (4): 681–718. doi:10.1080/09636410903369084.

Peresin, Anita, and Alberto Cervone. 2015. "The Western *Muhajirat* of ISIS." *Studies in Conflict and Terrorism,* 38 (7): 495–509. doi:10.1080/1057610X.2015.1025611.

Sjoberg, Laura. 2009. "Introduction to Security Studies: Feminist Contributions." *Security Studies* 18 (2): 183–213. doi:10.1080/09636410902900129.

Sjoberg, Laura, and Caron E. Gentry, eds. 2011. *Women, Gender, And Terrorism*. Athens: University of Georgia Press.

Stack-O'Connor, Alisa. 2007. "Picked Last: Women and Terrorism." *Joint Forces Quarterly* 44 (1): 95–100.

Zedalis, Debra D. 2004. *Female Suicide Bombers*. The Minerva Group, Inc.

PART III

COUNTERING TERRORISM

This final section addresses state responses to terrorism. In Chapter 13, we introduce a variety of counterterrorism acts and policies that states have used to address terrorism at home and abroad. We also ask which of these counterterrorism methods have been the most effective in reducing or containing terror while allowing the societies in which terrorism takes place to continue to abide by contemporary standards of human rights. Chapter 14 addresses the politics of counterterrorism, focusing on the key puzzle of why states seem to adopt and perpetuate counterterrorism policies that are quite counterproductive. And in Chapter 15, we conclude the book by outlining the various ways terror groups have ended.

CHAPTER 13

COUNTERTERRORISM INSTRUMENTS

Learning Objectives

After reading this chapter, readers should be able to:

- Explain what counterterrorism is, and provide examples of counterterrorism policies.

- Describe how scholars have attempted to measure the effectiveness of counterterrorism policies.

- Explain the difference between counterterrorism policies based on projections of hard power and those based on projections of soft power; provide examples of each.

- Explain why repressive approaches are often ineffective at reducing terrorism.

- Discern arguments emphasizing the effectiveness of counterterrorism from those emphasizing the morality (or immorality) of different counterterrorism actions. Identify areas where the two approaches overlap and areas where they are in tension with one another.

> "We will respond to [terrorism] and other threats the way we know best—by reaffirming the very ideals that distinguish us from those who wish us harm: freedom of speech; religious tolerance; the open exchange of ideas; and government that represents the will of the people."
> —FORMER US ATTORNEY GENERAL LORETTA LYNCH, KEYNOTE
> ADDRESS ON COUNTERTERRORISM AND INTERNATIONAL
> COOPERATION, LONDON, DECEMBER 9, 2015

> "Those who harbor terrorists, or who finance them, are going to pay a price. Every nation, in every region, now has a decision to make. Either you are with us, or you are with the terrorists."
>
> —FORMER US PRESIDENT GEORGE W. BUSH,
> ADDRESS TO JOINT SESSION OF US CONGRESS,
> SEPTEMBER 20, 2001

> ". . . only security will lead to peace. And in that sequence. Without the achievement of full security within the framework of which terror organizations will be dismantled, it will not be possible to achieve genuine peace, a peace for generations."
>
> —FORMER ISRAELI PRIME MINISTER ARIEL SHARON,
> ADDRESS AT 4TH HERZLIYA CONFERENCE, DECEMBER 18, 2003

THE PUZZLE

As you have likely noticed in previous chapters, states and other actors vary significantly in the types of actions and policies they adopt to address terrorism. How do the various **counterterrorism** policies indicated by different analytic approaches (Chapters 2–7) compare in terms of relative effectiveness? Are they all equally as effective in reducing terror, or are some approaches more successful than others?

The concept of counterterrorism is very broad, but in this chapter, we hone in on a specific question: Why do repressive counterterrorism approaches work in some cases but not others? Governments vary in the type and amount of coercive force, or repression, that they use to contain and combat terror. They also vary in the level of discrimination that they employ when targeting terror suspects for interdiction or reprisal. While some state actions target terror suspects specifically, others target entire populations believed to be supporters of the violent group.

We begin by defining what it means for a counterterrorism strategy to be successful—is success measured by a reduction in attacks, the demise of a group or campaign, or the containment of terrorism to a particular geographical region? Acknowledging differences in the definition and measurement of success across studies is important insofar as it allows us to compare and contrast findings in the literature. It also adds precision to debates about which counterterrorism strategies work and which ones are ethically defensible.

This chapter also makes a distinction between counterterrorism instruments that rely of the projection of **hard power** versus **soft power**, and provides examples of specific policy responses that fall under each category. By the end of the chapter, we hope readers will have a sense of how scholars and policymakers evaluate the relative effectiveness of a variety of counterterrorism instruments and apply these tools to specific scenarios.

WHAT IS COUNTERTERRORISM?

Broadly speaking, counterterrorism involves the practice, tactics, techniques, and strategies by which various arms of the state combat or prevent terrorism. Counterterrorism can involve the use of the military, law enforcement, intelligence agencies, political offices, community groups, and/or the private sector, either in unison as part of a coherent strategy, or in more piecemeal fashion as specific terrorist threats arise. However, it is often associated with a top-down, state-led approach to confronting terror.

The first-known counterterrorism unit, the **Irish Special Branch**, was established by Great Britain in the 1880s. The unit was formed in response to escalating violence carried out by the Irish Fenians, who sought to end British rule in Ireland. The role of the Irish Special Branch was to combat Irish Republican terror attacks through **infiltration** and **subversion**. It gradually expanded to protecting British national security against a wider variety of what were deemed terrorist threats, such as foreign subversion and organized crime (Masferrer and Walker 2013).

In the late twentieth century and especially following Al Qaeda's September 11 attacks on US targets, states around the world greatly expanded their counterterrorism forces. Today, many western governments consider counterterrorism a top national security priority. Most counterterrorism strategies involve increasing standard police operations and domestic intelligence gathering, focusing on activities such as intercepting communications between individuals and **tracking** the movements of individuals. New technology has also expanded the range of military and law enforcement operations to reach across borders, as we will see in the examples presented in this chapter.

Counterterrorism is sometimes a component of **counterinsurgency** operations, depending upon the context. This is similar to the notion that some insurgent groups use terrorism as part of their tactical repertoire during their struggle against the government, muddying any clear distinction between terrorism and insurgency. But despite tendencies in the media and elsewhere to conflate the terms, counterterrorism and counterinsurgency are different concepts, much as insurgency and terrorism are different concepts. At its most basic, insurgency is defined as an "organized, protected politico-military struggle designed to weaken the control and legitimacy of an established government, occupying power, or other political authority while increasing insurgent control" (Nagl et al. 2008, p. 1–2). Counterinsurgency, in turn, involves a range of military, political, economic, psychological, civic, and other actions aimed at protecting a population and restoring the legitimacy of the government. The major differences between counterterrorism and counterinsurgency lie in the scope of the state's goals and activities and the resources used to pursue them.

Take the example of Al Qaeda. In 2001, US counterterrorism efforts against the group focused strictly on preventing Al Qaeda from planning an attack from its safe havens in Afghanistan. The strategy required a great deal of intelligence, control of financial flows, and various defensive measures, but it did not involve a significant military footprint on the ground in Afghanistan, nor did it require the removal of the Taliban government from power. A counterinsurgency strategy, on the other hand, had as its central aim the permanent eradication of Al Qaeda and its allies from Afghanistan, the removal of the Taliban from power, and the establishment of a new Afghan government that would be relatively friendly to the United States and capable of exercising control over the population. This latter type of intervention involved a significant military commitment from many countries that contributed to the counterinsurgency campaign. Viewed from the perspective of US policymakers, both strategies sought to ensure the security of the American people, and the prevention of terror attacks against the west. However, they differed significantly in terms of scope, with one strategy requiring a significantly higher level of commitment and resources than the other.

Sometimes people erroneously use the terms counterterrorism and counterinsurgency interchangeably. With the US onset of the wars in Afghanistan and Iraq in 2001 and 2003, for example, American politicians' framing of each conflict within the so-called Global War on Terror led to significant increase in the use and conflation of the two terms. To illustrate, we created a Google Ngram of the terms "counterterrorism" and "counterinsurgency." Note the spike in the usage of "counterterrorism" around 2001, following the 9/11 attacks by Al Qaeda, as well as the enduring prevalence of both terms through 2008.

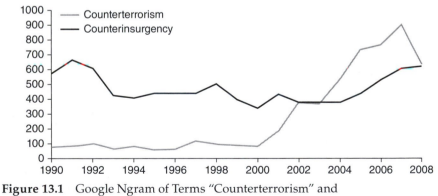

Figure 13.1   Google Ngram of Terms "Counterterrorism" and "Counterinsurgency"

Source: Google Ngram

US COUNTERTERRORISM AGENCIES

The US government divides the implementation of counterterrorism strategy among a handful of organizations, some which focus explicitly on domestic, or homegrown terrorism, and others on transnational threats. The **National Counterterrorism Center (NCTC)** was established in 2004 to serve as the primary organization within the US government for integrating and analyzing all intelligence pertaining to counterterrorism. The NCTC primarily addresses transnational terror.

Much like the NCTC, the aim of the **US Department of State's Bureau of Counterterrorism and Countering Violent Extremism** is to "counter terrorism abroad and to secure the United States against foreign terrorist threats." The agency helps to develop and implement counterterrorism strategies and operations, and oversees specific programs aimed at countering violent extremism, strengthening homeland security, and building the capacity of allies to deal with terrorism effectively (US Department of State 2016).

The US intelligence community—including the **Central Intelligence Agency**, the **Defense Intelligence Agency,** and the **National Security Agency**—has significant mandates in surveillance, the collection and processing of human intelligence, and, at times, the conducting of extrajudicial killings through drone strikes and other special operations. The United States Army also has a special unit, called **Delta Force**, whose specific responsibilities involve responding to terror attacks and extracting civilians from hostage situations.

The **Federal Bureau of Investigation (FBI)** as well as number of other domestic agencies such as the **Department of Justice** and the **Department of Homeland Security (DHS)** also comprise an important component of the United States's counterterrorism community. These agencies focus primarily on domestic actors and also play a role in disaster response. Many argue that a key to successful counterterrorism in the United States as well as abroad is the close collaboration and coordination of these various agencies with one another, as well as with the counterterrorism agencies of other states.

DEFINING SUCCESS

The Congressional Budget Office reported that the US government's budget for counterterrorism amounted to approximately $7 billion in 1998. By 2005 that number had increased to just over $88 billion (Lum et al. 2006). Given the increases in expenditures on antiterrorism strategies over the years, understanding whether particular programs have succeeded is quite important. What does it mean for a counterterrorism policy to be successful?

The first step in assessing effectiveness is determining what counts as a counterterrorism policy. Some strategies, programs, or approaches may be more clearly defined or delineated than others. Different strategies may target a wide variety of phenomena and potential outcomes, complicating evaluations of effectiveness. Some counterterrorism policies, for instance, focus on measures to prevent and alleviate early risk factors of individual radicalization. Others are designed to prevent terror attacks in a specific context, or address post-attack issues such as emergency response or post-traumatic stress disorder (Lum et al. 2006). If every government policy counts as counterterrorism, it becomes very difficult to evaluate what is actually working.

We can break down the literature on assessing counterterrorism effectiveness into four broad categories. The first and perhaps the most common approach focuses on whether a counterterrorism program worked to reduce terror attacks as well as damage and/or casualties caused by attacks. This question applies to programs or policies that seek to protect specific places from attack, such as airports or embassies. If the number of attacks against such targets decreases significantly after the implementation of a particular policy, then one can reasonably call that program successful. Alternatively, one might seek to understand whether a counterterrorism program that targets a specific group has been successful. If the number of attacks staged by a particular group declines in response to the counterterrorism strategy, it was likely effective in achieving its goals.

For example, consider Figure 13.2, which shows the rise and fall of extremist attacks in Canada, prior to and in response to the implementation of two categories of counterterrorism policies. The study evaluates the relative

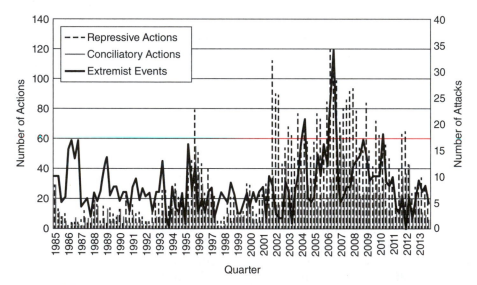

Figure 13.2 Government Actions against Violent Extremist Events in Canada

Source: Chenoweth & Dugan 2016, p. 320

effectiveness of repressive versus conciliatory counterterrorism instruments, and the primary outcome of interest is the number of extremist attacks between 1985 and 2013 (Chenoweth and Dugan 2016). As the figure shows, violent extremist events tended to peak during three periods—the late 1980s, the mid–1990s, and then 2004–2010. Interestingly, counterterrorism actions became much more common in Canada after 2001, when the country joined the US coalition in Afghanistan and subsequently implemented a number of stricter security measures at home toward many different extremist groups. At times, the Canadian government has also adopted a more conciliatory posture toward such groups, attempting to address legitimate political, economic, or social grievances while continuing to renounce violence as an acceptable means of addressing them. Figure 13.2 illustrates how this combination of conciliatory and repressive measures ultimately reduced the number of extremist attacks between 2010–2013.

A second set of studies explains how specific counterterrorism policies affect the likelihood of a terror group's demise. Do specific measures taken against a group lead to its downfall, or to a shift away from violent contention to achieve its goals? Many early studies that seek to explain differences in the survival rates of terror groups take individual, case-study approaches, though cross-national studies of terrorist group longevity are now more common.

For example, Martha Crenshaw, Erik Dahl, and Margaret Wilson recently identified 109 jihadist-linked plots to launch violent attacks in the United States from 1993 through 2016 (Crenshaw, et al. 2016). Of these plots, only 13 were successful; the majority of plots were either foiled (72 percent) or partially foiled (9 percent) (ibid.). Figure 13.3 shows the foiled plots by type of intervention. The use of surveillance or reliance on informants yielded the greatest number of successes in terms of foiled plots. But other types of

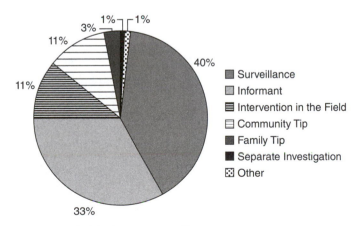

Figure 13.3   Plots Foiled by Intervention Type;

Source: START (Crenshaw et al. 2016)

counterterrorism instruments, such as relying on information provided by family or community members, have also played a significant role in reducing the number of attacks committed in the United States.

Because studies in this category often arrive at different findings, it is important to discuss some measurement issues that arise when researchers try to use group demise to judge counterterrorism policies. As an example, consider two studies on the relative effectiveness of leadership decapitation. To understand the effects of leadership decapitation on terrorism, Jordan (2009) evaluates whether a targeted group was inactive for two years following the incident of decapitation (in which case counterterrorism was successful), or whether the group resumed activities within two years (in which case the counterterrorism operation is coded as a failure). Her findings suggest that younger and smaller terrorist groups are more likely to desist from terrorism after the removal of a leader, while religious organizations in particular are more resilient to decapitation. She concludes that terror groups decline at a higher rate when their leaders are not targeted, highlighting that decapitation was only successful in 17 percent of the 298 cases she evaluates (Jordan 2009). According to her study, leadership decapitation has been ineffective in the fight against terrorist groups.

Price (2012), on the other hand, argues that Jordan's (2009) decision to work with a two-year time horizon is arbitrary, and thus cannot accurately evaluate the effects of a counterterrorism policy. In response, Price (2012) provides a longer-range analysis that examines the effect of leadership decapitation on the mortality rate of terrorist groups. He finds that groups whose leaders are killed have a significantly higher mortality rate than groups whose leaders stay alive longer, and religious groups are less resilient and easier to destroy than nationalist groups. Additionally, the earlier that decapitation occurs in a group's lifetime, the greater the effect the counterterrorism operation will have on the group's mortality rate. Importantly, Price also finds that any type of leadership turnover increases the rates at which terrorist groups die. This is an important finding, because it implies that states do not have to carry out targeted assassinations to defeat terror groups. Table 13.1 provides a brief overview of terror group mortality rates according to Price's (2012) data.

A third set of studies addresses whether specific instruments or policies are effective in **containing** terrorism. In this case, the objective is not

TABLE 13.1 Terrorist Mortality and Leadership Decapitation, 1970–2008

		GROUP ENDED	
		No	*Yes*
Group experienced decapitation	No	32	44
	Yes	38	93

Source: Price 2012, p. 33

necessarily to measure whether a policy leads to a decrease in attacks globally, but rather whether the state successfully restricted a group to a particular locality, type of attack, or technology. For instance, studies that address the containment of terrorism often address the issue of CBRN terrorism, arguing that while a nuclear terror attack is certainly a possibility, governments can significantly lower the risk of such an attack through the implementation of containment policies (Graham and Kokoshin 2002). By this standard, we can consider policies aimed at containing nuclear terrorism effective to date, seeing as no group has successfully staged a nuclear attack as of this writing.

Finally, a fourth category of studies assesses the normative impact of counterterrorism policies, focusing explicitly on the maintenance of core values in the face of threat. In other words, though a specific policy may be successful in thwarting or reducing terrorist attacks in a particular context, it may concurrently harm or damage the society in which the measures were implemented. Some policies, for instance, might violate international law or civil rights, challenge the values that underpin a society, or displace problems of violence to another geographical location (Lum et al. 2006).

COUNTERTERRORISM STRATEGIES, TOOLS, AND POLICIES

The range of counterterrorism instruments itself is wide. Consider the strategies, tactics, and tools that Lum et al. (2006) identify in their study on counterterrorism effectiveness (Table 13.2). The list is certainly extensive, and covers many different types of instruments that range from domestic and international political solutions, to military strategies, law enforcement responses, target hardening, and many more in between.

Lum, Kennedy, and Sherley (2006) break down counterterrorism strategies into six major categories: (1) metal detectors and security screening; (2) fortification of embassies; (3) increasing severity of punishment for terrorism;

TABLE 13.2 Examples of Counterterrorism Strategies, Tactics, and Programs

Airport screening	Emergency preparedness	Prison building
Anti-terrorism home products	Foreign aid	Psychological counseling
Arrests	Embassy fortification	Punishment/sentencing
Assassinations	Gas mask distribution	Religious interventions
Bilateral agreements	Hostage negotiation	Situational crime
Blast-resistant luggage	Investigation strategies	prevention
Building security	Legislation (e.g., Patriot Act)	UN conventions
CCTV	Medical antidotes	UN resolutions
Community/NGO initiatives	Media efforts	Vaccinations
Weapons detection devices	Metal detectors	War (counterinsurgency)
Diplomacy	Military intervention	
Educational programs	Multilateral agreements	

Source: Lum, Kennedy, and Sherley 2006

(4) UN resolutions; (5) military retaliation; and (6) changes in political governance. They assess the relative effectiveness of each of these different strategies in terms of reducing terror attacks. Let's consider how some of the various tactics or programs might benefit counterterrorism. Airport screenings and the installation of weapons detection devices such as metal detectors might reduce the ability of terrorists to carry out mass shootings or plant explosive devices in public spaces. Arrests and assassinations that target suspected terrorists might reduce the operational capacity of terror groups, depriving them of operatives and limiting their ability to stage attacks. Psychological counseling, education programs, and community initiatives help to identify individuals who may be at risk of radicalization or joining terror groups, and provide them with nonviolent alternatives or community/medical assistance to alleviate their grievances. Finally, bilateral or multilateral agreements between states, or the development of UN resolutions and membership in UN conventions, help to coordinate transnational cooperation around counterterrorism, whereby governments share intelligence on terror groups, agree to sanctioning individuals or organizations they believe help to finance terror groups, or disseminate lessons learned with respect to their counterterrorism successes and failures.

Lum et al. (2006) find that metal detectors were associated with a decrease in airplane hijackings, but an increase in other forms of terrorism, such as kidnapping. This is consistent with Enders and Sandler's findings (1993) discussed in Chapter 2. They also find that embassy fortification had no effect on terrorism—neither increasing nor decreasing terrorist attacks. Similarly, they find that increasing the severity of punishment for terrorist activity does not lead to a decrease in terrorism. Military retaliation was statistically associated with an increase in terrorism in the short term, and likely does not have any long-term impacts—a finding that is consistent with Dugan and Chenoweth's (2012) study on the effect of counterterrorism actions on terror attacks by Palestinian militant groups against Israel. With regard to international political context, Lum et al. (ibid.) find that UN resolutions against terrorism do not have a significant deterrent effect, although they do find that the effect of changes in domestic political governance is uncertain, suggesting that paying attention to the political context in which terrorism occurs is likely an important component of countering terrorism (Lum, et al. 2006). This finding lends support to the structural approach (Chapter 6) and the critical terrorism studies approach (Chapter 7), which focus on understanding how the perceived legitimacy or illegitimacy of political life can influence the use of violence.

The example of vaccines as a counterterrorism instrument is particularly intriguing. In 2011, the CIA employed a Pakistani doctor to conduct a fake vaccination campaign in an effort to track down Osama bin Laden. News of the scheme reinforced the local population's deepest suspicions of the United States, and of western-backed immunization campaigns more broadly. Polio vaccine workers became regular targets of violent attacks by Pakistani armed groups in the aftermath; gunmen killed as many as nine in December 2010 (Rubenstein 2013). The vaccination program was subsequently suspended, a major setback to public health in Pakistan. The incident brings to light the harmful unintended consequences of counterterrorism interventions and highlights the deep ethical concerns that surround many policies: although the vaccine drive may have contributed to finding bin Laden, it had serious negative implications for public health outcomes in a country suffering from high rates of polio.

One of the main takeaways from Lum et al.'s comprehensive study (2006) is that counterterrorism policies have had mixed success in addressing terrorism. The mixed record likely reflects the complexities that characterize terrorism itself. Because the effectiveness of different types of interventions appears to depend so heavily on contextual factors, evidence-based research is particularly important to improve understanding of which policies work as well as the strategic and ethical tradeoffs involved in adopting them.

DISTINCTIONS BETWEEN HARD AND SOFT POWER

A number of studies suggest that punitive counterterrorism measures are not statistically associated with decreases in terrorism (see e.g., Dugan and Chenoweth 2012). Studies also seem to suggest that military retaliation may not be the best response to terrorism, given that it may actually lead to increases in terror especially in the short term. To better understand this repression-terrorism nexus, let's take a look at how policies that use **hard power** differ from those that rely on **soft power**.

Hard power counterterrorism instruments are characterized as those that deploy **tangible** sources of power—such as the military or police forces—to attack, punish, and deter purported terrorists (and sometimes their constituents). Such direct approaches to counterterrorism typically employ **enemy-centric doctrines** consisting primarily of tactics such as **drone strikes,** military interventions, military occupations, Special Forces operations, and/or increased policing and intelligence operations (Rineheart 2010). Typically, the main goal of hard power counterterrorism strategies is to isolate or destroy terror groups.

Soft power instruments, on the other hand, are considered a more indirect approach to countering terrorism. These tools consist of **population-centric methods** that might include capacity-building initiatives, efforts at stemming financial flows to terror groups, programs focused on economic development, and countering radicalization. Rather than focusing on an explicit enemy, most soft power instruments hone in on the underlying causes that allow terrorism to thrive. They may also include political solutions, such as negotiation with terror groups, or changing the political context in such a way that draws popular support away from extremist groups and deters radicalization.

Examples of Hard Power Instruments: Indiscriminate Repression. The underlying purpose of hard power counterterrorism policies is to impose real costs on groups and individuals that engage in terrorism, and offer real benefits to those that abstain or shift away from violence. Key to hard power counterterrorism instruments is the element of **coercion** and the imposition of punishment, calibrated in such a way that terrorism is no longer an appealing option (Dugan and Chenoweth 2012). These types of repressive actions typically arouse anger in the targeted population, regardless of the actions' legality or legitimacy (Chenoweth and Dugan 2016). When states raise the cost of engaging in terrorism to a sufficiently high level, engaging in terrorism becomes increasingly costly, up to a point where the decision to use violence is no longer utility maximizing. Ultimately, these basic insights derive from the strategic approach and inform **deterrence theory**, which posits that fear of punishment or retribution controls the behavior of individuals or groups.

Deterrence involves two types of repressive policies: those that are **discriminate**, and those that are **indiscriminate** in their targeting. More specifically, deterrence is indiscriminate when it targets individuals who have not yet broken any laws. It is discriminate when it targets known perpetrators of terrorism (Dugan and Chenoweth 2012). Consider the example of Israel's policy of house demolitions in response to suicide terror attacks during the Second Intifada. House demolitions that explicitly targeted the homes of known Palestinian terror operatives were considered discriminate. In contrast, house demolitions justified solely according to the location of the house, but not by the identity or actions of the home's owner, were considered indiscriminate (Benmelech, Berrebi, and Klor 2010).

Studies suggest that the distinction between discriminate and indiscriminate counterterrorism operations is at the root of much of the variation that we see in the relative effectiveness of repressive policies. In their article, for instance, Benmelech, Berrebi, and Klor (2010) find that house demolitions that explicitly targeted the homes of known suicide bombers were more effective at reducing terror attacks than those that indiscriminately targeted the homes of Palestinians. Dugan and Chenoweth (2012) also find more generally that repressive actions by the Israeli government directed towards Palestinians are unlikely to deter Palestinian terrorism, and may instead precipitate higher levels violence. Populations often view indiscriminate repression as illegitimate, and its use can cause counterterrorism policies to **backfire**.

Cross-national studies of repressive counterterrorism policies also support the hypothesis that indiscriminate abuses by states tend to aggravate political grievances that perpetuate terrorism. Walsh and Piazza (2010) find that counterterrorism policies that violate a particular category of human rights—**physical integrity rights**—increase terrorism by alienating the government from members of the population, inciting conflict among a broader scope of constituents, and reducing international willingness to help the government in its fight against terrorism.[1] Greater respect for physical integrity rights consistently reduces the number of both domestic and transnational terrorist attacks globally (Walsh and Piazza 2010).

---

[1] Physical integrity rights are those that protect individuals from extrajudicial murder, disappearance, torture, or political imprisonment by the authorities.

BOX 13.2

MASS SURVEILLANCE AS COUNTERTERRORISM IN THE UNITED STATES

The driving force behind many indiscriminate counterterrorism policies is the precautionary principle—that a lack of knowledge does not justify inaction. This assumption suggests that the best counterterrorism policy is preemptive so that terrorists do not have the chance to plan and act. Mass surveillance programs deployed by the US government, such as the Terrorist Surveillance Program implemented by the National Security Agency (NSA), are examples of far-reaching, preemptive counterterrorism instruments. The objective of the Terrorist Surveillance Program was to intercept Al Qaeda communications overseas where at least one party is not a US person. Technical glitches in the software, however, resulted in the interception of purely domestic communications and ignited controversy over the NSA's use of surveillance without warrants (Risen and Lichtblau 2005).

Revelations about the breadth and depth of government surveillance have spurred numerous critiques surrounding the right of individuals to privacy. Another critique of many of the mass surveillance and national registration programs in place in countries including the United States is that they serve only to prevent foreign groups from inserting operatives into the United States. This neglects the fact that US nationals already in the United States have staged the vast majority of recent attacks conducted on US soil. As a result, such policies might not only raise serious normative concerns, but they may also be wholly ineffective at reducing the terror threat. Furthermore, most of the homegrown terrorists who have acted in the United States were law-abiding citizens prior to staging their attacks. Mass surveillance programs did little to identify them as potential risks prior to their actual attacks.

In the post-9/11 period, terrorism scholars have also attempted to assess the effectiveness of counterterrorism strategies of **mass surveillance** of individuals and their movements. While attempts to pass such sweeping security measures were largely considered illegitimate or indefensible in the 1990s, a result of the Global War on Terrorism has been the surveillance of the US population as well as compulsory fingerprinting of visitors to the United States, immigrants, and asylum seekers. Federal databases contain the personal information of many individuals, with personal details available to law enforcement and intelligence agencies (Maras 2010). These policies are largely indiscriminate in their targeting; critics argue that they erode many of the civil liberties Americans have previously enjoyed. Critics of such programs of mass surveillance speak to the normative costs of counterterrorism policies, arguing that the US government must not neglect its moral commitments to protect its citizens' rights to privacy and freedom of conscience in favor of preventing terror attacks.

Military interventions are also considered a type of indiscriminate counterterrorism operation. For countries such as the United States, the decision to stage the Global War on Terror was part of a strategy of preemptive force against "terrorism of global reach" (Sheehan 2009). The basic assumption behind engagements in places such as Afghanistan, Iraq, Yemen, and elsewhere was that the United States had to kill or apprehend terrorists and cut off the flow of their resources to prevent them from mounting attacks. But whether the Global War on Terror has actually led to a reduction in attacks is highly questionable.

Consider the trend in Al Qaeda attacks from 1990–2011 in Figure 13.4. While attacks remained at relatively low levels before 2001, they jumped to unprecedented highs in the years following US actions in Afghanistan in 2001, and to even higher levels following the United States invasion of Iraq in 2003. This strongly suggests that the use of military force to counter Al Qaeda in response to the 9/11 attacks may have significantly backfired.

Indeed, Sheehan (2009) finds that military intervention, and the GWOT in particular, did not reduce terrorist attacks around the globe. Instead, the onset of the GWOT was associated with a 74 percent increase in terror incidents over and above the period preceding the GWOT. Similarly, the release of photos of the abuse of Iraqi prisoners of war at the US military prison in Abu Ghraib in 2004 was associated with a 110 percent rise in attacks (Sheehan 2009, p. 752–753). These results strongly suggest that the invasion of Iraq, as well as revelations of US abuses of detainees in Abu Ghraib, incited additional acts of terror. When indiscriminate repression disintegrates into what Sheehan calls "barbarism," military interventions can have an **escalatory**

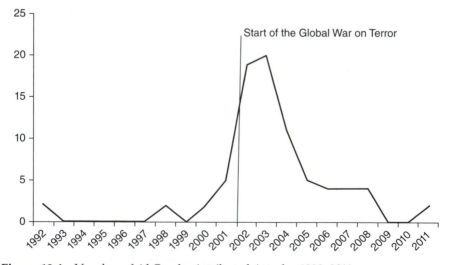

Figure 13.4 Number of Al Qaeda–Attributed Attacks, 1990–2011

Source: GTD

effect on attacks. This is largely in line with findings that suggest that abuses of physical integrity rights are highly ineffective as counterterrorism policy. *Examples of Hard Power Instruments: Discriminate Repression.* Let's consider how discriminate targeting might have different effects on terrorism. A relatively common form of discriminate repression that relies on hard power tactics is the **targeted assassination** of group leaders, or the practice of **leadership decapitation** that we discussed earlier in this chapter. Some studies contend that decapitation strikes are not effective as a coercive tool in interstate war broadly speaking (Pape 1996). The effect is the same when the tactic is applied to terrorist groups; they rarely collapse after their top leaders have been captured or killed (Pape 2003).

To date, few scholars have conducted a systematic analysis of the outcome of targeted assassination strategies, making any general assessment of the tactic's effectiveness difficult. And as we have already seen in this chapter, the way that scholars measure the dependent variable in question—in this case the effectiveness of the counterterrorism operation—greatly influences any assessment. Let's consider some individual cases. Decapitation may have influenced the demise of several groups, including the Shining Path in Peru and the PKK in Turkey. In the former, the capture of Abimeal Guzman in 1992 severely impeded the group's bid for power. The capture of Abdullah Ocalan in Turkey in 1999 similarly precipitated the PKK's steep decline. Similarly, analysts attribute the end of the Liberation Tigers of Tamil Eelam (LTTE) to the death of their leader Velupillai Prabhakaran, who was shot by Sri Lankan forces on May 18, 2009. The Sri Lankan government formally declared an end to the twenty-five-year civil war the following day.

These two examples stand in sharp contrast to the Al Qaeda case. The killing of Osama bin Laden in Pakistan in 2011 may have done little to curb the group's operations, and instead increased popular support for Al Qaeda, as well as the commitment of hard-core members of Al Qaeda. Many analysts suspected in the wake of the assassination that the group would attempt to stage a large attack on the West to prove its resilience. While no such attack occurred, it is difficult to directly attribute the lack of such an attack to bin Laden's death, given the multitude of other confounding factors that could have affected the group's ability or willingness to attack. For instance, the Syrian civil war, which began in 2011, and the rise of ISIS in the years after, have both likely shifted the attention and commitment of Al Qaeda operatives, distracting them from attacking the West.

The effectiveness of leadership decapitation tactics may also hinge strongly on the **organizational structure** of the targeted groups. Johnson's (2012) analysis of leadership decapitation, for instance, focuses primarily on insurgent groups, which may influence his finding that targeted assassinations of group leaders are in fact effective counterterrorism or counterinsurgency strategies. Because insurgent groups are frequently characterized by their hierarchical structure, they may be particularly vulnerable to decapitation.

BOX 13.3

THE DEATH OF OSAMA BIN LADEN

Early in the morning of May 2, 2011, a team consisting of US Navy SEALS and other US Special Forces raided a compound in Abbottabad, Pakistan after receiving intelligence that Osama bin Laden, the founder and leader of Al Qaeda, had holed up inside. During the operation, officially named Neptune Spear, Navy Seal team members found and shot bin Laden before he had time to react. His body was reportedly buried at sea within twenty-four hours of his death.

The successful operation against Osama bin Laden was the product of a decades long manhunt that began well before the 9/11 attacks. In June 1995, almost two years after the February 1993 bombing of the World Trade Center, then President Bill Clinton issued a Presidential Decision Directive labeling terrorism a national security issue. This was a departure from previous administrations, which had always addressed terrorism as a law enforcement matter. In early 1996, the CIA formed a special unit dedicated to gathering intelligence on Osama bin Laden, whom US officials linked to the 1993 bombings in New York. He was living in Sudan at the time, but was later expelled after the US failed to reach an agreement with the government of Saudi Arabia regarding a Sudanese offer to turn him over (Legum 2011).

A secret grand jury investigation against bin Laden began in New York in August 1996, and he was eventually indicted in June 1998. Following bin Laden-linked attacks against the US embassies in Tanzania and Kenya two months later, President Clinton ordered a missile attack against a chemical weapons factory associated with bin Laden in Sudan. Clinton also ordered attacks against bin Laden's suspected training camps in Afghanistan, but neither operation led to his capture or death (Legum 2011).

In 1998, the CIA began secret efforts with Pakistani intelligence to capture bin Laden in Afghanistan, training and equipping as many as 60 commandos from Pakistan's intelligence services. These efforts ended with the overthrow of then-Pakistani Prime Minister Nawaz Sharif in 1999. After his election in 2000, George W. Bush in 2000 significantly curtailed the search for Bin Laden (Legum 2011).

After Al Qaeda's successful attacks in the US in 2001, US intelligence agencies redoubled on their efforts to identify and pursue leads about bin Laden and his inner circle, with a particular interest in his couriers. Bin Laden was known to have stopped using phones as early as 1998, following the missile strikes against his bases in Afghanistan. As a result, he relied on couriers to communicate with others, but continued to conceal his whereabouts from the vast majority of Al Qaeda members. Some of the information about his couriers came from suspected Al Qaeda operatives imprisoned at the US military prison in Guantanamo Bay, Cuba, and appeared to focus especially on one individual whom bin Laden trusted more than others. US officials reported that they were eventually able to identify this person in 2007, learning that he went by the pseudonym Abu Ahmed al-Kuwaiti (MacAskill 2011).

In 2010, the CIA identified the approximate location of al-Kuwaiti's residence, eventually narrowing it down to a compound in Abbottabad not 35 miles from Islamabad. Various aspects of the compound aroused the suspicion of intelligence agencies. It was surrounded by twelve to eighteen foot high walls, which were topped with barbed wires. There were few entrances to the interior, and access was severely restricted. It was valued at US$1 million, yet had no phone or internet connections. In addition, the fact that al-Kuwaiti had no known source of income, yet was able to afford such accommodations, further raised suspicions.

The United States dedicated significant resources to identifying whether bin Laden was actually in that compound. While the most commonly employed techniques included the use of advanced surveillance techniques and the deployment of a stealth drone, US officials also tried less conventional approaches. For example, the CIA recruited Pakistani health workers to try to obtain DNA samples from individuals inside the compound under the guise of a vaccination program. It is unclear whether they ever succeeding in extracting the DNA (Whitlock and Gellman 2013).

Despite continued efforts to identify bin Laden with confidence, US officials never confirmed that bin Laden was actually inside the compound. When President Obama ordered the raid to proceed in May 2011, US intelligence officials told him that the odds that bin Laden was there were only 40 percent. Somewhat controversially, US officials did not share their intelligence on the Abbottabad compound with any other country, including Pakistan. The final operation's success was the product of extensive cooperation among the US government's numerous intelligence agencies and armed forces. A fleet of satellites operated by the National Reconnaissance Office guided the May 2 raid that eventually resulted in bin Laden's death. The National Security Agency (NSA) penetrated communications channels used by Al Qaeda operatives, and the CIA pinpointed the specific locations of mobile phones, eventually linking one to the Abbottabad compound. Navy Seals carried out the raid, and shortly thereafter, a forensic intelligence laboratory run by the Defense Intelligence Agency matched the DNA taken from bin Laden's body, confirming his identity.

Of course, the exact details of the campaign to capture or kill bin Laden vary widely, as do accounts of exactly what happened on May 2, 2011 in the Abbottabad compound. Nevertheless, the events related to bin Laden's death show how the United States employed virtually every tool in its substantial surveillance capability to locate and kill bin Laden.

More **networked** groups, on the other hand, may be more resilient in the face of discriminate leadership targeting. In fact, a group whose structure is organized into a more decentralized, "small world" network that features multiple leaders and clusters of local activists is likely to remain more immune to police pressures or infiltration by counterterrorism agents more broadly, relative to hierarchical groups (Kenney, Coulthart, and Wright 2016). In both the "war on drugs" as well as the "war on terrorism," government attempts to destroy the largest, most powerful illicit networks have been largely unsuccessful because of how these groups are organized (Kenney, et al. 2006). The removal of one or two highly placed and highly connected individuals is unlikely to disrupt the organization's operations.

An important part of the debate around targeted assassination as a counterterrorism instrument concerns the use of **unmanned aerial vehicles (UAVs)**, more commonly known as **drones.** Since 2001, drones implemented a majority of the targeted assassinations that comprise a part of the US's counterterrorism strategy. Governments often use this technology to target individuals far away from any battlefield where US troops are engaged, in places such as Pakistan, Yemen, or Somalia.

In July 2016, the Obama administration in the United States released statistics on drone strikes conducted by US forces outside of active war zones such as Afghanistan and Iraq. According to the report issued by the Office of the Director of National Intelligence (ODNI), the United States launched 473 strikes between January 2009 and December 2015, killing between 2,372 and 2,581 combatants and between 64 and 116 noncombatants (Zenko 2016a). But other estimates provided by other sources such as the New America Foundation, *Long War Journal,* and the Bureau of Investigative Journalism were much higher. These nongovernmental research organizations reported that the Obama administration has actually been responsible for 528 strikes that killed 4,189 persons, including as many as 474 civilians (Zenko 2016b). The discrepancy between what is reported by official US government and nongovernmental sources highlights yet another challenge for attempts to measure the effectiveness of drone strikes.

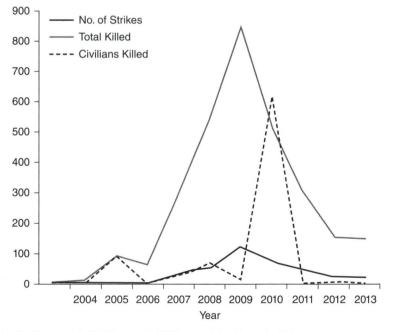

Figure 13.5 Reported US Targeted Killings & Fatalities in Pakistan

Source: New America Foundation 2016

Absent clarifying information on who is considered a noncombatant versus a combatant, statistics on drone strikes remain somewhat misleading.

But do drones help or hurt US counterterrorism strategy? Some scholars and analysts say that drones work against the strategic aims of the United States when it comes to reducing terror attacks. For instance, Audrey Kurth Cronin (2013) argues that drones may help to protect US lives at home, but they are working to create sworn enemies abroad. Furthermore, these strikes have done little to defeat Al Qaeda, one of the main goals of US counterterrorism strategy. She argues that the elimination of one or two highly placed Al Qaeda operatives does little to disrupt the far-reaching global network on which the organization relies to recruit individual members, plan, and stage attacks. Finally, the legal and moral framework that surrounds these strikes is shaky at best; many view it as a violation of the national sovereignty of states and of the physical integrity rights of individuals. As a result, drone strikes may work to drive local populations into the arms of extremist groups (ibid.).

Others, however, defend drones as an effective tool of counterterrorism, arguing that strikes have killed key terrorist leaders, denied terrorists sanctuaries, and protected the US from attacks at a relatively low cost in blood and treasure (Byman 2013). Proponents suggest that drones provide significant advantages over conventional airstrikes because of their accuracy and precision. Furthermore, UAV attacks kill fewer civilians per strike, thus leading some to claim that they help US counterterrorism efforts by evading the so-called provocation trap, hypothesized to severely undermine counterterrorism and support the long-term goals of terrorist groups (see Kydd and Walter 2006).

However, what little evidence does exist to support the effectiveness or ineffectiveness of drone strikes as a counterterrorism strategy is far from systematic. It is not clear whether the use of UAV technology has actually degraded the operational capabilities of groups such as Al Qaeda, or contributed to the deaths of enough civilians to create sizable public backlash against the United States. While the use of drones may be a politically and militarily attractive way to combat terrorism in some cases, one should not view this particular strategy as panacea to terrorism. In short, the verdict is still out as far as the effectiveness of drones is concerned. As is the case for all of the tactics and strategies that we review in this chapter, they are likely to be most effective when used as part of a more nuanced and multi-pronged strategy to fight specific groups.

Examples of Soft Power Instruments: Economic Influence. As opposed to counterterrorism policies based on the projection of hard power, soft power policies focus less on imposing perceived costs on terrorist behavior and more on heightening the perceived benefits of abstaining from terrorism. Soft power instruments may be punitive but are non-coercive in nature; they include measures such as rewards or conciliation for abstention from terrorism. They take a persuasive approach to countering terrorism, and typically involve the use of political concessions, economic rewards or sanctions, or cultural influence.

A counterterrorism strategy embraced by a number of states around the globe has been to limit the flow of funds traveling to terrorist organizations. International organizations such as the UN and the Group of Seven (G7) have sought to establish specific counterterror finance standards for governments, banking systems, and private companies. Terror finance began to take center stage as part of the global effort to address terrorism in the aftermath of 9/11. Many of the laws were inspired by experiences in combatting money laundering; freezing an organization's resources should significantly affect a group's ability to operate. But such policies involve important tradeoffs. Excessive regulations can create severe backlogs for intelligence agencies and also impose large costs on the financial industry. Perhaps more importantly, financial regulations tied to counterterrorism often hinders much-needed resources in the form of remittances from reaching developing countries, and can infringe on individual rights and liberties.

Targeting **passive state sponsorship** of terrorism is another policy used to limit terrorist financing. Spain and the UK have achieved major successes by using these types of methods, particularly insofar as they have done so through diplomatic channels. Crackdowns on US-based funding for the IRA and on French support for ETA operatives in southern France inflicted serious damage on both groups. In 1987, the United Kingdom managed to end Libya's funding of the IRA by having two infiltrators betray a major shipment of arms from Tripoli (Jonsson and Cornell 2007).

Examples of Soft Power Instruments: Cultural & Social Influence. Over the last five years, many Western states have turned to the implementation of early prevention programs falling under the banner of **Countering Violent Extremism (CVE)** to complement traditional hard power counterterrorism instruments. These broad-brush approaches encapsulate a range of non-coercive tools and programs developed by community organizations and government partners focused explicitly on **counter-radicalization**.

Analysts have defined CVE in myriad ways. The key to CVE is the principle of non-coercion. In practice, this means that CVE can include a host of potentially unlimited activities for governments and others to pursue to prevent radicalization. Initiatives might be based on messaging strategy, through speeches, television, programs, and social media. Alternatively, they might focus on engagement and outreach, such as town hall meetings, roundtable discussions, and the formation of advisory councils. CVE programs might also include capacity-building programs, such as youth and women's empowerment initiatives, community development; or education and training, for example of community leaders, public employees, and law enforcement. Broadly speaking, CVE-related initiatives center themselves on increasing community cohesion and trust by fostering interaction and network overlap across a range of communities, government, police, and social service providers; dissuading individuals from using violence by supporting nonviolent forms of expression and political participation; and reintegrating groups and individuals that have become involved in violent extremism by facilitating disengagement from violent networks.

The purpose of such programs is thus not just to counter the influence of violent extremism in specific communities deemed as vulnerable, but also to locate individuals who benefit from local credibility and exhibit a willingness to partner with others in their community. CVE is as much of a network- and trust-building initiative as it is a strategy of countering violence.

Efforts to evaluate the impact of CVE measures across countries remain in their early stages. To date, there remains an absence of metrics by which to assess effectiveness. This is largely due to the fact that CVE is so broadly defined and can include so many different types of initiatives. CVE has emerged very quickly—largely in response to political pressures to jettison the Global War on Terror as the United States' primary approach to combating terrorism. Notably, resources allocated to CVE programs are still modest relative to those dedicated to more conventional counterterrorism instruments, such as military intervention or law enforcement.

Although CVE has received increasing attention in the US following the Boston marathon attacks and the rise of ISIS, it is by no means a new concept. In fact, for the last decade, governments throughout the world have invested significant resources into designing CVE strategies, and the experience of a number of European countries are likely to provide valuable lessons for further implementation of CVE initiatives around the world. Perhaps most importantly, lawmakers in Europe have increasingly rejected large and expensive preventive programs, preferring instead to focus on pointed, individual interventions that are proving to be more cost-effective and easier to evaluate (Vidino and Hughes 2015).

Because radicalization is not a straightforward or easily observable process, European deradicalization programs seek to tailor interventions to specific situations. While this may complicate efforts to scale up programs to the national level, and requires investing time to identify and recruit competent, local leaders, the context- and case-specific approach has helped to avoid further alienating Muslim communities in particular. Indeed, Muslim communities decried earlier macro-level approaches to CVE as opening doors to mass surveillance, or as singling out Muslims (Vidino and Hughes 2015). In 2010, the United Kingdom's House of Commons called a British CVE program's exclusive focus on Muslims "unhelpful. . ., stigmatizing, [and] potentially alienating" (quoted in Patel and German 2015). Engaging a wider array of local partners with roots in specific communities is likely a more promising counter-radicalization strategy than relying on national-level actors who are disconnected from local communities.

Finally, European countries have found that the language that surrounds the implementation of CVE programs is also critical to disrupting radicalization. A number of governments, for example, have adopted the language of "safeguarding" communities (Vidino and Hughes 2015). When radicalization is presented as a problem similar to gang recruitment or drug addiction, it is clear that community leaders and teachers have a larger role to play in curbing its spread.

Examples of Soft Power Instruments: Political Influence. A final set of soft power counterterrorism instruments includes policies based on conciliation, and those based on altering the political context to make terrorism appear less appealing as a strategy of contention. These are two separate strategies, so let's consider each one in turn.

Peter Neumann (2007) suggests that governments can win the legitimacy battle with terror groups in part by approaching constituents of the violent group with a conciliatory tone and set of actions. Conciliation (as opposed to punishment) is based on the principle that raising the benefits of abstaining from terrorism should reduce the marginal utility of engaging in terrorism. In their article on the use of repressive versus conciliatory actions by the Israeli government to combat Palestinian terrorism, Dugan and Chenoweth (2012) explain conciliatory rhetoric and action as the act of making material concessions to terrorist groups, or taking action that signals an intention to cooperate or negotiate with the terrorist group (2012, p. 608).

Much like punishing actions based on military force or law enforcement can be discriminatory or indiscriminate, so too can conciliatory counterterror-ism policies vary in their targeting practices. Some **deradicalization** programs, for instance, work explicitly with known offenders, or with the families of de-tained terrorists (Dugan and Chenoweth 2012). The Italian government offered leniency to members of the Red Brigades when they provided information that led to the arrest of other members (Crenshaw 2001; Cronin 2006). Other poli-cies, however, are indiscriminate and focus on entire populations in an effort to induce a large-scale shift in popular opinion away from violent extremism.

In the case of Israel, Dugan and Chenoweth find that conciliatory actions by the government were associated with a decrease in terrorist attacks by Palestinian groups (2012). Indiscriminate conciliatory actions also seemed to have a dampening effect on terror attacks, while repression did not decrease attacks by Palestinian militant groups in any model.

Importantly, the success of conciliatory approaches is based on a relationship of trust between the state and the affected population itself. One-off concilia-tory measures or expressed intentions are unlikely to reduce attacks, in large part because a state with a long history of repressive actions may lack credibil-ity. If they are to succeed, conciliatory measures should therefore be a sustained component of a state's counterterrorism strategy. A reversion to repressive tac-tics could easily dismantle any progress achieved on the basis of conciliation.

Of course, many critics are skeptical of this approach, arguing that nego-tiating with terrorists—or giving in to the demands of different groups as a result of terrorist violence by a few—necessarily emboldens more terrorism. Some critics are also uncomfortable with the **moral hazard** of conciliation in the face of terrorism—that rewarding bad behavior penalizes those who have followed the rules. Finally, as we discussed in the context of CVE, indis-criminate soft power approaches that fail to recognize the diversity inherent in large populations of individuals, such as Muslims, run the risk of further stigmatizing entire groups of people.

The last approach that we consider focuses on shifting the political context in which terrorism occurs. For example, in a study of interactions between the government of Spain and ETA, Gil-Alana and Barros (2010) find that anti-terrorist policies were generally ineffective at stopping attacks unless the government implemented proactive political policies. These included the Spanish government's signing of a political pact by all political parties with representation in the Basque parliament, with the exception of Herri Batasuna (HB), the radical nationalist party closest to ETA. The marginalization of HB had a significant impact on weakening the popularity of radicals among the Basque population and also on curbing the flow of financial resources to ETA. This case reinforces the notion that policies based on repression and deterrence are unlikely to reduce terrorism lest they contain policies that also alter or resolve the underlying political conflict at hand.

WHEN IS REPRESSION AN EFFECTIVE COUNTERTERRORISM POLICY?

Returning to the puzzle that motivates this chapter, a review of the counterterrorism literature strongly suggests that indiscriminate repressive policies are generally ineffective at countering terrorism. Such strategies often backfire, creating more popular support for terror groups and heightening the perceived illegitimacy of the state. Intervention strategies based on the use of military force are particularly ineffective, as is evident from the United States's experience with Al Qaeda, and Israel's strategy against Palestinian terrorism. Other types of indiscriminate, repressive policies such as mass surveillance programs may also be highly problematic, particularly when it comes to the protection of civil liberties.

The use of discriminate repression such as targeted assassination may reduce terror attacks or significantly weaken terror groups in some cases. Like many other counterterrorism instruments, the success of tactics such as leadership decapitation is highly context-dependent. Whereas targeted assassinations may be effective at degrading the capacity of hierarchically organized groups, they are unlikely to reduce the effectiveness of networked groups. Careful evaluation of the group in question, and an understanding of its organizational structure, may be critical in assessing whether this particular tool will bring added value to a counterterrorism strategy.

Finally, soft power policies seem to hold significant promise when it comes to countering terrorism. Conciliatory approaches carry less potential for engendering the harmful unintended consequences wrought by indiscriminate policies based on hard power. In fact, they may be particularly useful in conveying to the populations from which extremist groups emerge that conventional forms of political participation have more benefits than terrorism. However, these policies are politically risky (see Chapter 14), and they are often difficult to implement because mutual trust is key to their success.

DISCUSSION EXERCISE: COUNTERTERRORISM SCENARIOS

Consider the following plot, which draws on a real-world example of a foiled terror attack (see Jenkins and Trella 2012).

A group of three men plant explosive devices in garbage cans in the 34th Street station of New York city's subway system, which is part of the Herald Square subway station complex and one of the busiest transportation hubs in the city. The Manhattan Mall sits above the station and runs the risk of collapsing if the blast is powerful enough. The bombs are set to detonate at 8:30am, during New York city's rush hour. One of the men is a US citizen, while the other two are immigrants from Tunisia and Jordan. The men cite anti-Arab sentiment in the United States as motivation for their attack in a video recorded prior to the explosions, and also reference their anger towards US actions in the Middle East—in particular the invasion of Iraq, the Abu Ghraib prison abuses, and American support for Israel.

SCENARIO 1: Imagine that you are an advisor to the New York Police Department's (NYPD) Counterterrorism Bureau. The attack has not yet taken place. Discuss the counterterrorism tactics and strategies that you would recommend to pre-empt the implementation of attacks similar to the one described above. Which tactics or instruments might best contribute to the early detection of this plot while also preserving basic rights and liberties? Consider both short and long term strategies, as well as the potential unintended consequences of your recommendations.

SCENARIO 2: Imagine that you work in the US State Department's Bureau of Counterterrorism and Countering Violence Extremism. The attack has just occurred, causing two hundred fifty casualties and many more wounded. What do you recommend as effective counterterrorism responses from the US government? Again, consider both short and long term actions, as well as the potential consequences of the response both in the United States and around the world.

Regardless, any successful approach to reducing and preventing terror attacks requires a keen understanding of the political context under which a group chooses to turn to terrorism in the first place.

SUMMARY

In this chapter, we reviewed the myriad policies, programs, and instruments that states have used to counter terrorism. We discussed what it means for a counterterrorism policy to be successful and presented several examples of how to measure effectiveness from the literature. The main focus of the chapter consisted of presenting the differences between counterterrorism policies based on hard versus soft power, and the effect of these diverse strategies on countering terrorism. Throughout the chapter, we drew on various empirical examples of how states have successfully or unsuccessfully applied counterterrorism policies to a number of different groups.

Discussion Questions

1. How can we gauge whether a counterterrorism policy has been successful or unsuccessful?

2. What are the major differences between counterterrorism policies based on projections of hard power versus those based on projections of soft power?

3. What are the potential shortcomings of counterterrorism policies based on repression or deterrence?

4. Provide examples of successful counterterrorism policies that have been applied to a particular group.

5. Provide examples of cases in which counterterrorism policies have backfired.

There are two logics to evaluating counterterrorism—one that focuses on the efficacy of different actions, and the other that focuses on their morality. At times, these perspectives overlap, but at other times, they seem to be in tension with one another. In the United States, the tension between these perspectives is often reflected in the debate about whether it is appropriate to sacrifice civil liberties in the name of security in countering terrorism. Do you think it is acceptable to use an effective counterterrorism strategy that is immoral? Or should morality trump efficacy when it comes to counterterrorism? Why do you feel this way?

KEY TAKEAWAYS

- There are many different ways to categorize counterterrorism policies—as repressive or conciliatory; as criminal justice, military, intelligence, or economic; as defensive, offensive, or preventive; and as involving hard or soft power. Most counterterrorism instruments are not used in isolation, but rather are used in combination with other measures.

- Scholars and analysts often attempt to measure the success of counterterrorism by focusing on two outcomes: a reduction in attacks, and the demise of terror groups. A third indicator of success is whether a country maintains its basic values, principles, and identity as it addresses potential terror attacks.

- In using different types of counterterrorism policies – especially repressive ones—there is always a risk of eliciting backfire. In this scenario, repressive counterterrorism further escalates underlying grievances of various constituencies, thereby enabling and emboldening a terror group to commit worse acts of violence. Backfire can even cause a more limited conflict between a government and terror group to escalate into a full-blown war.

SUGGESTED FURTHER READINGS

Benmelech, Efraim, Claude Berrebi, and Esteban Klor. 2010. "Counter-suicide-terrorism: Evidence from house demolitions." NBER Working Paper No. 16493.

Byman, Daniel. 2006. "Do Targeted Killings Work?" *Foreign Affairs* 85 (2): 95. doi:10.2307/20031914.

Byman, Daniel. 2013. "Why Drones Work: The Case for Washington's Weapon of Choice." *Foreign Affairs* 92 (4): 32–43.

Cronin, Audrey K. 2013. "Why Drones Fail: When Tactics Drive Strategy." *Foreign Affairs*, Vol. 92: 44.

Dugan, Laura and Erica Chenoweth. 2012. "Moving Beyond Deterrence: The Effectiveness of Raising the Benefits of Abstaining from Terrorism in Israel." *American Sociological Review*, 77 (3): 597–624. doi:10.1177/0003122412450573.

Gil-Alana, L. A. and C. P. Barros. 2010. "A Note on The Effectiveness Of National Anti-Terrorist Policies: Evidence From ETA." *Conflict Management and Peace Science* 27 (1): 28–46. doi:10.1177/0738894209352130.

Graham, Allison and Andrei Kokoshin. 2002. "The New Containment: An Alliance against Nuclear Terrorism." *The National Interest* 69: 35–43.

Johnston, Patrick B. 2012. "Does Decapitation Work? Assessing The Effectiveness Of Leadership Targeting In Counterinsurgency Campaigns." *International Security* 36 (4): 47–79. doi:10.1162/isec_a_00076.

Jonsson, Michael and Svante Cornell. 2007. "Countering terrorist financing: Lessons from Europe." *Georgetown Journal of International Affairs*, 8 (1): 69–78.

Kenney, Michael, Stephen Coulthart, and Dominick Wright. 2016. "Structure and performance in a violence extremist network: The small-world solution." *Journal of Conflict Resolution*, March. doi: 10.1177/0022002716631104

Lum, Cynthia, Leslie Kennedy, and Alison Shirley. 2006. "Are Counter-Terrorism Strategies Effective? The Results of the Campbell Systematic Review on Counter-Terrorism Evaluation Research." *Journal of Experimental Criminology* 2 (4): 489–516.

Maras, Marie-Helen. 2010. "How To Catch A Terrorist: Is Mass Surveillance The Answer?" *Journal of Applied Security Research* 5 (1): 20–41. doi:10.1080/19361610903411790.

Masferrer, Aniceto and Clive Walker (2013). *Counterterrorism, Human Rights and The Rule of Law: Crossing Legal Boundaries in Defence of the State.* Cheltenham, UK: Edward Elgar Publishing.

Neumann, Peter. 2007. "Negotiating With Terrorists." *Foreign Affairs*, 86: 128–138.

Pape, Robert A. 1996. *Bombing to Win: Air Power and Coercion in War.* Ithaca, NY: Cornell University Press.

Pape, Robert A. 2003. "The Strategic Logic of Suicide Terrorism." *Am. Pol. Sci. Rev.* 97 (03). doi:10.1017/s000305540300073x.

Rineheart, Jason. 2010. "Counterterrorism and counterinsurgency." *Perspectives on Terrorism*, 4(5): 31–47.

Sheehan, Ivan Sascha. 2009. "Has The Global War On Terror Changed The Terrorist Threat? A Time-Series Intervention Analysis." *Studies in Conflict and Terrorism* 32 (8): 743–761. doi:10.1080/10576100903039270.

Walsh, James I. and James A. Piazza. 2010. "Why Respecting Physical Integrity Rights Reduces Terrorism." *Comparative Political Studies* 43 (5): 551–577. doi:10.1177/0010414009356176.

CHAPTER 14

THE POLITICS
OF COUNTERTERRORISM

Learning Objectives

After reading this chapter, readers should be able to:

- Provide some historical examples of cases where counterterrorism policies have been counterproductive;
- Explain how different analytic perspectives can shed light on the decision to adopt various counterterrorism policies.
- Explain the strengths and weaknesses of the different analytic approaches in explaining the choice to use certain counterterrorism policies.

> "To know them means to eliminate them. Consequently,
> the military aspect is secondary to the police method."
> —JEAN MARTIN AS COLONEL MATHIEU IN THE FILM
> "BATTLE OF ALGIERS"

THE PUZZLE

As we saw in Chapter 13, there is wide variation in the application and outcomes of counterterrorism policies. Sometimes states opt for highly militarized, repressive approaches to counterterrorism, and other times they negotiate with terrorists (Neumann 2007). At times, states pass legislation granting extraordinary powers to their security and intelligence agencies, as the United States did with its creation of the **PATRIOT Act** in 2001. Other times states call for restraint and even forgiveness of the perpetrators, as did Norwegian Prime Minister Jens Stoltenberg following the simultaneous attacks perpetrated by **Anders Brevik** in 2011 (Orange 2012).

Of course, one could argue that states adopt different counterterrorism strategies because they face different threats. Certainly, Al Qaeda and individuals like Anders Brevik differ significantly insofar as the nature and scope of the danger they pose. But states also vary drastically in terms of counterterrorism strategies when they respond to the same threats. Consider the wildly different approaches that European states and the US have taken to counter Al Qaeda in the wake of 9/11 and more recently ISIS.

Strategies to address terrorism also vary widely within countries, as is evident through the different counterterrorism postures of the Clinton, Bush, Obama, and Trump administrations in the United States. For instance, the Obama administration and then-president-elect Donald Trump reacted very differently to the December 2016 terror attack on a Christmas market in Germany. Keep in mind that at the time that these statements were made, the identity of the attacker was still unknown. The Obama administration's official statement read as follows:

> "The United States condemns in the strongest terms what appears to have been a terrorist attack on a Christmas market in Berlin, Germany . . . We stand together with Berlin in the fight against all those who target our way of life and threaten our societies." (The Obama White House Archives 2016, available at https://obamawhitehouse.archives.gov/the-press-office/2016/12/19/statement-nsc-spokesperson-ned-price-attack-berlin-germany).

Donald Trump's statement read as follows:

> "Innocent civilians were murdered in the streets as they prepared to celebrate the Christmas holiday. ISIS and other Islamic terrorists continuously slaughter Christians in their communities and places of worship as part of their global jihad . . . These terrorists and their regional and worldwide networks must be eradicated from the face of the earth, a mission we will carry out with all freedom-loving partners" (Morton 2016).

The very different reactions from Obama and Trump suggest entirely different orientations to countering terrorism. Obama's statements suggest that he viewed the fight against terrorism as one that pitted countries of all religious and ideological types against one common enemy. Trump's reaction construed the attack as one that pitted Christians against Muslims. Obama's statement thus implied that defeating terrorism requires cooperation across states, while Trump's rhetoric identified the attack as an act of Islamic extremism, effectively calling for all-out war between Christians and Muslims.

The wide disparities that we observe in counterterrorism policies across states, as well as within states at different points in time, thus raises an important puzzle: what explains the variation in the ways in which states combat terrorism? Are some states predisposed to more repressive approaches than others? Do only some kinds of states negotiate with terrorists? Why do states alternately select repressive or conciliatory counterterrorism measures?

These questions are all the more puzzling when we consider the empirical record of the success and failures of counterterrorism policies, as we did in Chapter 13. Repressive postures—particularly those employing indiscriminate repression—are extremely costly and are often counterproductive in that they exacerbate the frequency and/or lethality of violence by terrorists. Discriminate repression against the terror groups themselves combined with conciliatory postures toward the general population can often reduce terrorist incidents (Dugan and Chenoweth 2012; Cronin 2009). Yet when countries face protracted conflicts with terror groups, many of them nevertheless rely on counterterrorism methods that exacerbate the conflict. For example, to respond to the 9/11 attacks, rather than conducting limited strikes against Osama bin Laden and his Al Qaeda network in Afghanistan, the United States and its allies invaded Afghanistan and used the pretext of 9/11 to invade and occupy Iraq—a decision that even the United States' CIA chief admitted has likely created more terrorism than it prevented (Brennan 2016). Other countries, such as Germany, France, Italy, and Spain, have paid ransoms to ISIS to free hostages captured in Syria and Iraq—a practice some say encourages more hostage-takings (Gander 2014).

It may be that states are unaware of the counterproductivity of certain counterterrorism actions, choosing what they think to be the best alternatives in an uncertain environment. But if states were behaving as rational, unitary actors, then they would also learn from their mistakes over time. And we know that some states persist in using ineffective policies long after they have become counterproductive. In the Government Actions in Terror Environments (GATE) Dataset, which counts the number of repressive and conciliatory counterterrorism actions in Israel, the United States, Canada, Turkey, Algeria, Egypt, and Lebanon, Dugan and Chenoweth (2016) find that most counterterrorism actions by these states are indiscriminately repressive, despite ample historical evidence demonstrating the strategic ineffectiveness of indiscriminate repression. Data collected on 30 western democracies by Epifanio (2011) shows that such countries routinely pass restrictions on immigration, privacy, and other civil liberties in the face of terrorist threats.

EXPLAINING COUNTERTERRORISM POLICIES

Strategic explanations see the state as a unitary actor and focus primarily on the process by which states ascertain that a threat exists, derive policy alternatives considered to be proportional to the threat, and make decisions about which counterterrorism alternatives would maximize return on the state's preferences. Strategic approaches imply a deliberate, calculated process by which rational states intend to produce counterterrorism policies that match the threats they face and provide plausible solutions to confronting them. Because of **bounded rationality**, states may not always select the most effective policies at the outset of the conflict. However, the strategic approach suggests that states would nevertheless devise methods by which they would process information as it becomes available, consistently re-evaluating whether their counterterrorism strategy is increasing or decreasing terrorism. Moreover, they might quickly abandon policies that appeared to be counterproductive, opting for more appropriate policies.

Some scholars have identified cases where the strategic approach seems to predict the behavior of states fairly well. For instance, Jaeger and Paserman (2008) have shown that Israeli counterterrorism resulting in Palestinian fatalities tends to be predicted by the number of Israeli fatalities that occurred in the previous fourteen days. This suggests that Israeli counterterrorism actions are directly correlated to incidents of lethal violence by Palestinian militants. Repressive counterterrorism increases immediately in response to increases in Palestinian terror attacks.

Yet other studies cast doubt upon the strategic approach as a useful one for explaining variation in states' counterterrorism policies. For instance, Munroe (2009) critiques the strategic framework to understanding counterterrorism, arguing that "Strategic choice is often heavily circumscribed by the effects of crisis," when government is strongly influenced by disorganized processes informed by a foggy understanding of current events (2009, p. 288). Moreover, Schurrman (2013) suggests that governments do not reach decisions on counterterrorism policies through a deliberate, organized conversation, but rather through sloppy, improvisational processes. He argues that such policies "may have less to do with either side's clever planning than with unforeseen consequences and blunders" (2013, p. 158).

In his research on counterterrorism doctrine in Britain and France, Frank Foley (2015) similarly casts doubt on the implication that states choose counterterrorism policies based solely on the threats they face. Such an approach, he argues, fails to explain why France has adopted draconian counterterrorism policies against Islamist extremism that abandon privacy protections in the name of intelligence and harsh police operations, whereas Britain has adopted a more restrained, criminal justice approach (ibid.). Relying on interviews of counterterrorism officials in both countries, Foley (2015) suggests that threat perception is not the most important determinant of a country's counterterrorism approach. This is consistent with research by Schuurman (2013), who argues that choices to escalate British counterterrorism actions have not directly corresponded to the intensity of terrorist attacks in that country.

As described in Chapter 2, the strategic approach generally assumes that states are unitary actors. But if one relaxes the assumption and instead focuses on the relationship between national leaders and their domestic political environment, then strategic arguments tend to better approximate reality. For instance, Ethan Bueno de Mesquita (2007) suggests that while terrorism is not nearly as grave a threat as many governments tend to project, those governments are primarily interested in pursuing their own political survival. Their constituents react to terrorism with fear and look to the government to restore security. Although many governments recognize that they cannot provide security 100 percent of the time, they can establish policies and defensive measures meant to reassure the public. For example, placing large concrete planters in front of airport terminals is a way to demonstrate that the government is doing something to prevent large vehicles full of explosives from crashing into the terminal. And, placing metal detectors in airports is another way to demonstrate defensive activity despite the fact that these instruments do not prevent all weapons from making it onto airplanes (Bradner and Marsh 2015). Bueno de Mesquita (2007) acknowledges that these visible counterterrorism actions have limited effectiveness in stopping all terrorist attacks, since committed terrorists can simply circumvent these measures and develop new tactics. He suggests that covert policies—those hidden from both the public and terrorists—are likely to be more effective in thwarting attacks, infiltrating terror groups, and arresting would-be terrorists. However, he writes that governments have few incentives to invest in covert actions that the public cannot observe and reward at the polls. Rather than eliminating all terrorist attacks, states are more interested in providing visible counterterrorism policies that demonstrate to the public that the state is taking action. If we accept Bueno de Mesquita's explanation, then there is a clear strategic explanation as to why governments adopt counterproductive counterterrorism policies—to sway the public so they will continue to support the government.

Furthermore, in more general studies on self-assessment of counterterrorism, scholars have found that few states have robust practices by which to evaluate the progress of their counterterrorism policies, even in the short-term (Munroe 2009; see also Freilich 2012). Still others puzzle over the fact that states tend to select counterterrorism policies that are so obviously counterproductive (Chenoweth and Dugan 2012). For instance, the Turkish government routinely resorts to overwhelming, indiscriminate violence against the Kurdish population in retaliation for terror attacks by Kurdish groups, and has done so for decades. Yet terror attacks by such groups has not diminished as a result.

What's more, governments must be aware that one of the key logics of terrorism involves provocation—the deliberate provoking of an overreaction by a state (see Chapter 2). Given that terror groups often seek overreactions through their violence, it is puzzling that states seem to oblige them so often.

Socio-organizational explanations focus more on the internal, institutional dynamics of counterterrorism within states. In this context, arguments focus on the ways in which counterterrorism policies are the product of institutional legacies within the government—how security is structured within the state (i.e. whether militaries or police have more power) and which agencies successfully outbid the others to maintain their status, positions, and access to resources—as well as domestic political events. This approach also focuses on the ways in which internal dynamics within counterterrorism agencies affect the different choices they recommend and implement (Allison and Zelikow 1999). Thus, a state's counterterrorism policy may be a function of the constellation of and friction between institutions that are primarily responsible for counterterrorism in the country.

In France, for example, counterterrorism has often been the domain of the military, intelligence services, and police, whereas in Britain counterterrorism has been primarily the responsibility of the national police force (Foley 2015). This variation across institutions helps to explain why France has adopted such an aggressive, militarized approach to counterterrorism, whereas Britain has adopted a more legalistic, criminal justice approach.

The Canadian government's response to rising Front de Libération du Québec (FLQ) violence in 1970 is illustrative of these arguments. During the so-called October Crisis, the Canadian government's decision to impose a state of emergency and militarize its response to the FLQ was based on unclear and ambiguous information as well as bureaucratic processes and constraints. Reviewing Cabinet records from discussions on the crisis, Munroe (2009) writes that the government did not make its decision to escalate to extraordinary powers on the basis of strategic calculation. Instead, escalation was "the least preferred" but "most workable" option, considered among many others by Cabinet officials, who faced tremendous uncertainty as to the capacity of the FLQ to launch a full insurrection (2009, p. 294). The author cites then-Prime Minister Pierre Trudeau as saying " 'the government did not have a clear statement even from its own police force as to how many people were involved in the hard core of the FLQ'" and that 'it should not be forgotten that one only got to know after the fact whether what one was facing was insurrection or not'" (Munroe 2009, p. 294). In fact, because of an idiosyncratic parliamentary procedure that prevented the government from introducing more comprehensive (and potentially self-limiting) legislation on the evening of the crisis, Munroe argues that the Act was the result of standard operating procedures ("bureaucratic machinery") that involved the Montreal Police, the Sûreté du Québec, and the RCMP Security Service" (2009, p. 298).

Following Allison and Zelikow (1999), Munroe further suggests that the Canadian government's move to orchestrate mass detentions of individuals can be explained by the fact that the Cabinet delegated handling of the crisis to organizations whose "specialized capacities" for crisis management involved police work. As a result, "detentions became a solution to the deteriorating public order situation largely because arresting people is what police forces have highly specialized capacities for, and because the situation was being treated as a police matter" (Munroe 2009, p. 298).

Sometimes observers point to specific interagency rivalries to explain certain suboptimal counterterrorism outcomes. For example, an article by Richard Schultz (2004) asks why the United States did not send Special Operations Forces after Osama bin Laden before 9/11, despite the fact that his network had conducted attacks against the United States since 1993. In interviews with key US officials tasked with counterterrorism policy, Schultz uncovered important interagency rivalries that undermined the collective counterterrorism effort. Richard Clarke, head of the National Security Council's Counterterrorism and Security Group, was considered a civilian hardliner due to his support of aggressive counterterrorism measures. In fact, Clarke spent nearly a decade pushing for more offensive operations against bin Laden and Al Qaeda under the Clinton administration. However, he would often soften his calls for these offensive operations because of pushback from Pentagon officials, who were reticent to advocate for such policies. His colleague Michael Sheehan recalls that when Clarke began to advocate for more forceful policies, "The establishment 'systematically starts to undermine you. They would say 'He's a rogue, he's uncooperative, he's out of control, he's stupid, he makes bad choices.' It's very damaging. . . . You get to the point where you don't even raise issues like that. If someone did, like me or Clarke, we were labeled cowboys, way outside our area of competence' " (Schultz 2004, p. 31; see also Kassop (2013)).

The socio-organizational approach also focuses on habits and practices— or **organizational routines**—that may predispose a country to a certain set of typical behaviors. For example, Schuurman (2013) argues that following the British Army's deployment to Northern Ireland in 1970, the army's own military history strongly influenced the way it approached the conflict. He writes: "the British political establishment believed that the Army's colonial experiences had provided it with the necessary skills to restore order to Northern Ireland on its own accord, thereby failing to recognize that this was a domestic operation and that, unlike for example in Malaya, the Army could not count on an effective local police force" (2013, p. 156). Having reviewed the British Army's orders, Schuurman suggests that the British government expressed no real political goals, failed to formulate a clear policy, and neglected to define the Army's role in the policy, instead leaving the soldiers on the ground to "come up with their own answers to the deteriorating security situation" (ibid.). As a result, the British Army made severe errors in its policing of the Northern Irish conflict, conducting home raids, imposing highly unpopular curfews, implementing aggressive crowd control measures during protests, interning suspects without trial, adopting harsh interrogation techniques, and escalating direct violence against Northern Irish Catholics to culminate in Bloody Sunday in 1972 (Schuurman 2013, p. 157). As a result of these actions, the PIRA gained considerable support among the Catholic population, while the popularity of British forces declined dramatically.

Turning to a non-western example, Omelicheva (2010) looks to Russia's imperialist tradition to explain the Russian government's history of forceful, excessive, and uncoordinated responses to terrorism. The tradition, rooted in the Tsarist era and enduring through the Soviet regime, was rekindled more recently by the fear of disintegration and Russia's reduced prestige globally. In response to unrest in Chechnya, the Yeltsin administration adopted the federal law "On Combating Terrorism," which has since provided legal justification for Russian actions that fall under the rubric of counterterrorism. This has included the use of military battalions in support of scorched earth operations in Chechnya, and the use of indiscriminate and overwhelming force in the name of fighting terrorism. Russia's actions in Chechnya have been marked by frequent abductions, summary executions, and torture. Omelicheva (2010) characterizes Russia's contemporary approach to counterterrorism as indicative of an age-old understanding of the terror threat, inherited from the Tsarist era and passed on through subsequent regimes: "since . . . the late 19th century, terrorism in Russia has been regarded as an assault against the state, personified by the Tsar, the Communist Party, or the central government and leadership of the modern state." In Russia, as in many other countries, protection of the state has involved the use of sophisticated and highly repressive authoritarianism.

Of course, while historical tradition, organizational routines, and bureaucratic inertia may all impede governments from implementing the most optimal measures to defeat terrorist groups, this does not mean that counterterrorism strategy is always static. Returning to the British example, it is important to note that for 30 years, the British government "tried everything within its control to eliminate terrorism in Northern Ireland" (O'Connor and Rumann 2003, p. 1750). While nearly all variations of emergency power, including a thirty-year military occupation of the territory and massive detentions, trials, and abusive searches failed to quell the violence, dialogue, cooperation, and respect for civil liberties eventually lead to peace in 2005. To explain the passage of counterterrorism laws that often promote backlash—like the repressive emergency laws enacted by the British in the immediate aftermath of IRA violence—O'Connor and Rumann (2003) point to the collective passion that naturally follows terror attacks. In the context of uncertain and overly heated environments, "we dramatically increase the risk that our laws will be based upon false assumptions and incomplete understandings." The implementation of counterterrorism policies that succeed in reducing levels of violence—such as mechanisms for increased social justice among all groups in a society—are often the product of a lengthy process of inter-communal dialogue. For instance, violence also dropped significantly in Northern Ireland from 1973–1974, following the negotiation of a new constitution based on power-sharing principles between Catholic Republics and Protestant Loyalists (ibid., 1703).

Finally, if the organizational explanation is the most accurate one, we would expect to see the timing of different counterterrorism actions correspond not to patterns of terrorism per se, but rather to domestic political events, such as elections. Chenoweth and Dugan (2012) identified support for this argument in the Israeli case. For example, they found that as the Israeli government approaches election times, it is far less likely to adopt conciliatory policies toward Palestinians and more likely to maintain (or increase) repression. Others have shown support for the notion that public opinion generally favors draconian responses to terrorism, suggesting that politicians who adopt these postures are rewarded at the polls (Berrebi and Klor 2008). Cycles of terrorist violence might also have an impact on the electoral choices of voters, which may in turn prompt shifts in counterterrorism policies when certain parties or politicians are voted out of office. For example, Kibris (2011) finds that violence by the Kurdistan Worker's Party (PKK) in Turkey led voters to favor right-wing parties, who were less conciliatory toward the terrorist group relative to their left-wing predecessors.

The socio-organizational/domestic politics approach has several weaknesses as well. In particular, it is unclear why governments would *ever* adopt conciliatory policies toward terrorism, given the unpopularity of such approaches. Yet we occasionally see governments negotiating with terrorists or making concessions at times, despite potentially negative outcomes for themselves on election day (Thomas 2014; Neumann 2007).

Psychological explanations may be relevant at the individual or group level. First, at the individual level, it may be that certain decision-makers are more inclined to selecting certain types of counterterrorism policies. For example, Israeli Prime Minister Yitzak Rabin was more willing to pursue negotiations with the Palestine Liberation Organization during the Oslo Peace Process than his successor Benjamin Netanyahu. As the comparison of Barack Obama and Donald Trump suggests, responses to terrorism also vary dramatically across the administrations of various US presidents. Can these divergences in policy preferences be explained by the varying personality traits among these different leaders?

Ultimately, it is very difficult to know. A recent study provides some insight into how the risk aversion tendencies of individual leaders might shape counterterrorism policy. Using content analysis of speeches made by each president on the use of drones versus conventional airstrikes, Macdonald and Schneider (2017) find that President Obama's aversion to risk led him to rely more on drones during his tenure, as opposed to conventional airstrikes. This includes decisions to use unmanned aerial vehicles (UAVs) in the context of counterterrorism campaigns in active and inactive warzones such as Afghanistan and Pakistan, respectively. President George W. Bush, on the other hand, was more risk-acceptant and thus more willing to use conventional, manned aircraft to carry out strikes in those same locations. The propensity of individuals to accept different degrees of risk is a function of their personality traits, and in some cases genetic characteristics (Kowert and Hermann 1997; Rosier et al. 2009). Macdonald and Schneider (2017) conclude that differences in the risk orientations of these particular US leaders ultimately affected their approach to counterterrorism policy.

When it comes to explaining variation in counterterrorism policies, the psychological approach may be especially relevant at the group level. Here one could focus on **groupthink** as a source of counterproductive counterterrorism actions, since this process highlights the inability of groups to adjust to new information, or to accurately assess their own influence on a situation. **Motivated bias**—or the tendency to see what one wants to see—can be a primary driver of poor policy decisions. A classic example is the United States' invasion of Iraq in 2003, which Mearsheimer and Walt (2007) argue was a function of a relatively small group of neoconservatives, who were confident about the United States' offensive military power, observed the US's apparent success in invading Afghanistan, and interpreted 9/11-like attacks as existential threats to American security. In evaluating intelligence about Iraq's capabilities, this group of pundits saw Iraq's weapons programs as both a threat and an opportunity to attack a country about which many neoconservatives had long-held suspicions.

Of course, psychological explanations are often difficult to untangle from ideological arguments, which aim to identify different belief systems. If Mearsheimer and Walt (2007) are correct, then why did neoconservatives interpret terrorism as an existential threat in the first place?

COUNTERTERRORISM WITHOUT STRATEGY? ISRAELI COUNTERTERRORISM DOCTRINE

Strategic approaches to counterterrorism in Israel would suggest that counterterrorism tactics directly correspond to threats of terrorism or terrorist attacks. In other words, Israeli counterterrorism doctrine should be motivated mostly by security threats. Scholars and analysts within Israel cast doubt on this depiction of Israeli counterterrorism policy. In a provocative book, Chuck Freilich, a former Israeli National Security Advisor, argued that Israel has no real counterterrorism strategy, nor does it have active governmental organs charged with the responsibility of devising and evaluating progress on such a strategy (2012). Instead, the country's security posture is characterized by an organizational culture of improvisation, flexibility, and adaptation. Although this flexibility and adaptive approach has some advantages in a dynamic region often dominated by turmoil, Freilich argues that such a posture also undermines the country's security. This is because the country, when attacked, tends to rely on organizational routines and habits rather than devising a response that will achieve both tactical and strategic progress toward enhancing Israeli security (2012). Although Israeli government officials often say that they have no specific strategy for dealing with terrorism, they definitely have a routine set of procedures by which they typically respond to terror attacks. When Hamas fires rockets from the Gaza Strip, for example, the Israeli military immediately retaliates via air or drone strikes, raids, restricting Palestinian movements, or conducting arrests (Jaeger and Paserman 2008). Such actions do not emerge from an overall sense that they will accelerate an end to the overall conflict between Israelis and Palestinians; instead, Israeli officials say that these strikes are "just what we do" in response to attacks by Hamas, PIJ, and other militant Palestinian organizations. Moreover, there is a tendency to assess impacts of counterterrorism actions immediately rather than over the long term. In other words, Israeli counterterrorism officials tend to judge immediately (within minutes) whether their counterterrorism tactic was successful or not; however, there is no national-level process for determining whether and how such tactical events yield longer-term improvements to Israeli security.

DISCUSSION QUESTIONS

- *Which analytic approach best characterizes the argument Freilich makes above?*
- *What are the strengths and weaknesses of this analytic approach?*
- *Is this analytic approach applicable to other countries of which you are aware? Which countries?*

Ideological explanations focus on the particular ideas, norms, or cultures that dominate states' interpretations of threats as well as their responses. For example, Katzenstein (2003) argues that Germany and Japan see terrorism and counterterrorism very differently from the United States (and one another) in large part due to the different norms in each country about what constitutes a threat as well as what constitutes an appropriate response. He argues that whereas the United States interpreted the 9/11 attacks as an act of war, Germany interpreted the attacks as a crime, and Japan interpreted the attacks as a political crisis. These interpretations reflect differences in the historical practices of each country when faced with domestic terrorism, as well as differences in the ways each country conceives of "self and other" (733). As Katzenstein argues:

> Although Japan had lived for two decades with a domestic cycle of terrorism culminating in the world's first-ever terrorist attack with weapons of mass destruction, the government responded with considerable caution after September 11. Germany's multilateral and activist stance after September 11 was different. It evoked memories of Germany's counterterrorist campaign in the 1970s and 1980s when Germany viewed terrorism as a crime against the state and pursued its defenses energetically both at home and abroad (2003, p. 733).

Beliefs about the source and nature of a threat and the appropriateness of different counterterrorism policies can be strong determinants of (or constraints on) the choice to use forceful counterterrorism policies. For instance, Perliger (2012) argues that terror attacks themselves do not produce counterterrorism policies, but rather the **symbolic power** inherent in some attacks provokes governments to take action. It is not the attacks per se that matter, but rather the subjective perceptions of these attacks that influence narratives about which counterterrorism policy is most appropriate as a response. Perliger suggests that "escalation in the state response will not result just from an increase in the level of violence, but also from an increase in the symbolic power of the violence" (2012, p. 507). He argues that the symbolic power of a terrorist attack is determined by the ideological tendency of the group, whether the group strikes prominent interests, the targets attacked, the level of public exposure to the attack, and the attack's exceptional nature (2012, p. 507–9). Beliefs and narratives about each of these elements inform the degree to which governments interpret attacks as existential threats requiring significant departures from ordinary police practice. For instance, in contrast to the 1993 World Trade Center bombings, the 9/11 attacks had far greater symbolic power, resulting in an exceptional subjective response by the United States. Counterterrorism policies may thus be a direct response to the messaging tactics used by terror groups. The more powerfully terrorists attempt to convey their message, specifically in terms of casualties caused by an attack, or via the selection of a particular target, the more powerful we can expect the counterterrorism response to be.

Another set of ideological arguments focuses on the ways in which people divide their social worlds into "virtuous ingroups and nefarious outgroups"—what scholars call **ethnocentrism** (Kam and Kinder 2008). People with strong ethnocentric beliefs tend to support more forceful policies against terror groups (and the communities from which they emerge).

In a survey of Americans, Kam and Kinder indeed find that Americans who subscribe to ethnocentric beliefs are far more likely to endorse the United States' **Global War on Terrorism** than those that were more cosmopolitan in their beliefs (2008, p. 320). However, this relationship was most prominent after the 9/11 attacks, providing further evidence for the notion that the symbolic power of extraordinary events strongly influences popular beliefs about the nature of the threat (and its appropriate response) (Kam and Kinder 2008, p. 320; Perliger 2012).

Another ideology relevant to counterterrorism policy is **authoritarianism**. In this context, we do not mean dictatorship, but rather a set of beliefs in the nature of authority and socio-political relationships. People who subscribe to authoritarianism tend to "submit to established authority, to support violence against targets sanctioned by established authority, and to adhere rigidly to traditional social conventions" (Kam and Kinder 2008, p. 326–7; see also Adorno et al. 1950; Altemeyer 1981, 1996; Feldman and Stenner 1997; Stenner 2005). Kam and Kinder found that Americans who reflected a significant propensity for authoritarianism—measured by attitudes toward obedience and control during child-rearing—tended to also support extraordinary measures in counterterrorism including policies related to the Global War on Terrorism (2007, p. 327).

Moreover, some have argued that the particular political beliefs of government officials—in particular whether they are more **hawkish** or **dovish** in their worldviews—may have a powerful effect on the range of options such politicians are willing to consider (Koch and Cranmer 2007). Specifically, hawkish politicians may be more likely to adopt repressive policies, whereas dovish politicians may be more likely to adopt more conciliatory ones. It is no accident that Jens Stoltenberg, Norway's Prime Minister and the head of the country's left-leaning Labour Party, showed such contrition towards Anders Breivik in 2011.

That said, studies that attempt to evaluate the general effect of ideology on different counterterrorism choices yield mixed results. For example, in their study of thirty democracies, Neumayer, Plumper, and Epifanio (2014) find that right- and left-wing governments are equally likely to enact counterterrorism policies based on their peer states' adoption of such policies. In other words, similarities in geography and threat perception may be more important determinants of counterterrorism policies—a finding that points to the potential power of structural explanations for counter terrorism.

Structural explanations focus on the domestic or international circumstances in which a state operates as the main determinants of counterterrorism policy. At the domestic level, studies suggest that democracies are particularly constrained when it comes to responding to terrorism with repression. This is largely due to constraints on an executive's power driven by checks and balances, and because democracies are more accountable to their populations than are authoritarian governments (Blankenship 2016). Yet Perliger (2012) argues that strong democracies are more likely than weak democracies to remain resilient to terror attacks in terms of their institutional commitments to civil liberties. He posits that in general, strong democracies try to avoid deploying their military forces within their borders, opting instead for legal restrictions on terrorism. In weak democracies, on the other hand, governments are more likely to deploy their militaries domestically and to circumvent constitutional limits on executive authority (2012, p. 503).

Related studies point to the role of state capacity in shaping counterterrorism policy. For instance, Brian Blankenship finds that states with limited bureaucratic capacities are more likely to crack down harshly on terror groups. A weak capability to control, monitor, and collect intelligence on their own populations curtails the ability of these governments to respond with more selective forms of punishment (Blankenship 2016). On the other hand, when states have robust intelligence agencies, a strong judiciary, and compliant and effective law enforcement, they can implement more fine-grained counterterrorism operations and avoid large-scale repression of their own population. For instance, the Peruvian government heavily repressed its population in the 1980s and 1990s and put the military in charge of its counterterrorism efforts in the wake of Sendero Luminoso (Shining Path) violence. Spain, on the other hand, did not wage a campaign of indiscriminate violence in the 1970s and 1980s in its efforts to defeat Euskadi Ta Askatasun (ETA) (ibid.). An abundance of bureaucratic capacity allowed the Spanish government to base its counterterrorism efforts on a more judicious approach that sought to address grievances and provided amnesty to ETA defectors (Holmes 2001).

Regime type also plays a role in determining the propensity for states to rely on a particular type of counterterrorism instrument: torture. Conrad et al. (2014), for instance, find that governments are more likely to engage in acts of torture in response to acts of transnational terrorism and as the level of democracy increases. Since protection against foreign enemies typically falls under the purview of a country's military, heightened torture is associated with military efforts to curb terrorism. The institutional autonomy that militaries enjoy, especially in democracies, makes democratic states more likely to use torture as a counterterrorism tool after a transnational terror attack rather than a domestic attack. Moreover, democratic regimes are more prone to use torture in response to an act of foreign, as opposed to domestic, terrorism because the public is more likely to approve of torturing foreigners than members of their own population. Military intervention in response to domestic threats is much more common in autocracies than democracies (ibid.).

At the international level, the United States, as the dominant hegemon in the international system, should be able to dictate the rules by which states confront global terrorism. It should be able to do this through institutional coordination, by modeling the types of policy changes that its allies should implement at home and abroad, and by leading in military engagements or economic sanctions abroad. That said, Katzenstein (2003) suggests that the United States has not yet been able to compel its allies to agree on counterterrorism activities, instead noting the considerable variation in national responses to terrorism based both on historical institutional practices and interpretations of the threat.

Neumayer, Plumper, and Epifanio (2014) explain variation in counterterrorism policies as a function of threat perception and geography. They argue that states might be more prone to adopting a certain set of counterterrorism policies if they belong to a "peer group" of like-minded states in the same geographic location (Neumayer, Plumper, and Epifanio 2014). European states with a low perception of threat tend to adopt fewer counterterrorism policies. These include Austria, Denmark, Finland, Greece, Ireland, New Zealand, Norway, Portugal, Sweden, and Switzerland. They find that Australia, Canada, France, Germany, Italy, Netherlands, and Spain have experienced an intermediate level of threat and have adopted a similar regimen of mid-level counterterrorism policies that include moderate restrictions. The United States and the UK, on the other hand, tend to orient themselves toward a common set of counterterrorism policies because of their similar geographic orientations and threat perceptions, which is how the authors designate them as peers (Neumayer, Plumper, and Epifanio 2014, p. 212). Hence, it is both the threat perception and the geo-political orientations of the countries that affect the counterterrorism policies they choose.

That said, structural explanations have a difficult time accounting for the variation in counterterrorism policies promoted by the various branches of government within a state. If this explanation were correct, then the derivation of counterterrorism policies should be fairly uniform within states. Yet as we saw with the organizational approach, different agencies within the same country often promote different counterterrorism alternatives. For instance, within the United States the CIA advocates for a specific type of counterterrorism approach—one that involves enhancing human intelligence and conducting targeted assassinations—compared with the National Security Agency (NSA), which advocates for surveillance and interdiction. Structural explanations also fail to account for the ways in which these different agencies' priorities shape the types of counterterrorism policies a state considers, as well as the ways in which the status of these agencies within a country's institutional hierarchy affects the policies that the state ultimately implements.

Finally, **critical explanations** tend to see counterterrorism as a function of politics alone. Instead of seeing counterterrorism as the natural outgrowth of legitimate threats, critical terrorism scholars see counterterrorism policies as an active manipulation of the population by the state to consolidate power and maintain the status quo. Moreover, critical terrorism scholars see counterterrorism policies as largely **performative** (de Graaf and de Graaf 2010), meaning that much like terrorism, counterterrorism is a form of political theater wherein states seek to maintain their authority and legitimacy in the eyes of a terrorized population.

Critical terrorism scholars advance a cynical view of counterterrorism policies, seeing the designation of certain counterterrorism policies as arbitrary and objectively meaningless compared with other forms of coercive state action. CTS scholars tend to see most restrictive counterterrorism policies as benefiting only the state rather than keeping the population secure. Moreover, by casting its policies as counterterrorism policies, governments delegitimize the intended targets of these policies. For instance, by targeting Islamic groups with counterterrorism policies, Western governments have effectively delegitimized political Islam as an inherently terroristic belief system (Jackson 2007).

The main flaw of the critical terrorism studies approach is its tendency to exaggerate the degree to which counterterrorism is a subjective invention of the state based on largely overhyped threats. In fact, terror may be an observable phenomenon—whether it occurs by the hand of states or nonstate actors—and as such, countering it is a natural policy concern for governments charged with providing security for their populations. Moreover, critical terrorism studies tends to see itself as the sole research program concerned with the moral consequences of counterterrorism, whereas many different empirical terrorism studies researchers have likewise concerned themselves with such questions (see, for example, Crenshaw 2010).

SUMMARY

In this chapter, we have discussed and evaluated numerous arguments regarding why countries choose the counterterrorism policies they do. We have reviewed some of the existing empirical evidence addressing this question and have applied the different analytic techniques to the case of Israeli counterterrorism specifically.

Discussion Questions

1. Why did the United States invade Afghanistan in 2001? Why did it invade Iraq in 2003? Discuss at least three different competing explanations for each.

2. How would we know if a state were developing and pursuing a counterterrorism strategy rationally? What kinds of behaviors and processes would the country display?

3. What are some examples of counterproductive counterterrorism policies? Why do states seem to adopt them so often?

4. Revisiting the film *The Battle of Algiers*, which of the explanations discussed here best characterizes the depiction of why the French government responded to terror attacks in Algeria in the way that it did?

5. Why did the Obama Administration not engage in a full-scale military intervention to defeat ISIS?

KEY TAKEAWAYS

- Many governments seem to adopt counterterrorism policies that produce counterproductive results. There are strategic, organizational, psychological, ideational, structural, and critical explanations for this puzzle.

- Ironically, democracies are often more susceptible to counterproductive counterterrorism. The reelection motive incentivizes immediate and visible counterterror actions that are therefore often ineffective in preventing terror attacks in the long term.

SUGGESTED FURTHER READINGS

Allison, Graham and Philip Zelikow. 1999. *Essence of Decision: Explaining the Cuban Missile Crisis, 2nd edition.* New York: Longman.

Azam, Jean-Paul, and Alexandra Delacroix. 2006. "Aid and the Delegated Fight Against Terrorism." *Review of Development Economics* 10 (2): 330–344. doi:10.1111/j.1467-9361.2006.00321.x.

Bueno de Mesquita, Ethan. 2007. "Politics And The Suboptimal Provision Of Counterterror." *International Organization* 61 (1): 9–36. doi:10.1017/s0020818307070087.

Bueno de Mesquita, Ethan, and Eric Dickson. 2007. "The Propaganda of the Deed: Terrorism, Counterterrorism, and Mobilization." *American Journal of Political Science* 51 (2): 364–381. doi:10.1111/j.1540-5907.2007.00256.x.

Byman, Daniel. 2006. "Friends Like These: Counterinsurgency and the War on Terrorism." *International Security* 31 (2): 79–115. doi:10.1162/isec.2006.31.2.79.

Byman, Daniel. 2006. "Remaking Alliances in the War on Terrorism." *Journal of Strategic Studies* 29 (5): 767–811. doi:10.1080/01402390600900887.

Chowdhury, Arjun and Ronald Krebs. 2009. "Making and Mobilizing Moderates: Rhetorical Strategy, Political Networks, and Counterterrorism." *Security Studies* 18 (3): 371–399. doi:10.1080/09636410903132961.

Crenshaw, Martha, ed. 2010. *The Consequences of Counterterrorism.* New York: Russell Sage.

de Graaf, Beatrice and Bob de Graaf. 2010. "Bringing Politics Back in: The Introduction of the 'Performative Power' of Counterterrorism." *Critical Studies on Terrorism* 3 (2): 261–275. doi:10.1080/17539153.2010.491337.

Dugan, Laura, and Erica Chenoweth. 2012. "Moving Beyond Deterrence: The Effectiveness of Raising the Benefits of Abstaining from Terrorism in Israel." *American Sociological Review* 77 (3): 597–624. doi:10.1177/0003122412450573.

Epifanio, Mariaelisa. 2011. "Legislative Response to International Terrorism." *Journal of Peace Research* 48 (3): 399– 411. doi:10.1177/0022343311399130.

Eppright, Charles T. 1997. " 'Counterterrorism' and Conventional Military Force: The Relationship Between Political Effect and Utility." *Studies in Conflict and Terrorism* 20: 333–344. doi:10.1080/10576109708436045.

Foley, Frank. 2015. *Countering Terrorism in Britain and France: Norms, Institutions, and the Shadow of the Past.* New York: Cambridge University Press.

Freilich, Chuck. 2012. *Zion's Dilemmas: How Israel Makes National Security Policy.* Ithaca: Cornell University Press.

Kam, Cindy, and Donald R. Kinder. 2008. "Terror and Ethnocentrism: Foundations of American Support for the War on Terrorism." *The Journal of Politics* 69 (2): 320–338. doi:10.1111/j.1468-2508.2007.00534.x.

Kassop, Nancy. 2013. "Rivals for Influence on Counterterrorism Policy: White House Political Staff Versus Executive Branch Legal Advisors." *Presidential Studies Quarterly* 43 (2): 252–273. doi:10.1111/psq.12023.

Katzenstein, Peter J. 2003. "Same War—Different Views: Germany, Japan, and Counterterrorism." *International Organization* 57 (4): 731–760. doi:10.1017/s0020818303574033.

Kruglanski, Arie W, Martha Crenshaw, Jerrold M. Post, and Jeff Victoroff. 2007. "What Should This Fight Be Called? Metaphors of Counterterrorism and Their Implications." *Psychological Science in the Public Interest* 8 (3): 97–133. doi:10.1111/j.1539-6053.2008.00035.x.

Lyall, Jason. 2010. "Do Democracies Make Inferior Counterinsurgents? Reassessing Democracy's Impact on War Duration and Outcome." *International Organization* 64 (1): 167–192. doi:10.1017/s0020818309990208.

Messmer, William B., and Carlos L. Yordan. 2011. "A Partnership to Counter International Terrorism: The UN Security Council and the UN Member States." *Studies in Conflict and Terrorism* 34 (11): 843–861. doi:10.1080/1057610x.2011.611932.

Munroe, H. D. 2009. "The October Crisis Revisited: Counterterrorism as Strategic Choice, Political Result, and Organizational Practice." *Terrorism and Political Violence* 21 (2): 288–305. doi:10.1080/09546550902765623.

Neumayer, Eric, Thomas Plumper, and Mariaelisa Epifanio. 2014. "The 'Peer-Effect' in Counterterrorist Policies." *International Organization* 68 (1): 211–234. doi:10.1017/s0020818313000362

Nohrstedt, Daniel, and Dan Hansen. 2010. "Converging Under Pressure? Counterterrorism Policy Developments in the European Union Member States." *Public Administration* 88 (1): 190–210. doi:10.1111/j.1467-9299.2009.01795.x.

Omelicheva, Mariya Y. 2010. "Russia's Counterterrorism Policy: Variations On An Imperial Theme." *Perspectives on Terrorism* (November) 3 (1).

Perliger, Arie. 2012. "How Democracies Respond to Terrorism: Regime Characteristics, Symbolic Power and Counterterrorism." *Security Studies* 21 (3): 490–528. doi:10.1080/09636412.2012.706505.

Piazza, James A., and James Igoe Walsh. 2009. "Transnational Terror and Human Rights." *International Studies Quarterly* 53 (1): 125–148. doi:10.1111/j.1468-2478.2008.01526.x.

Porter, Andrew L. and Annegret Bendiek. 2012. "Counterterrorism Cooperation in the Transatlantic Security Community." *European Security* 21 (4): 497–517. doi:10.1080/09662839.2012.688811.

Sandler, Todd M. 2003. "Collective Action and Transnational Terrorism." *World Economy* 26 (6): 779–802. doi: 10.1111/1467-9701.00548

Sandler, Todd. 2010. "Terrorism Shocks: Domestic verses Transnational Responses". *Studies in Conflict and Terrorism* 33 (10): 893–910. doi:10.1080/1057610x.2010.508485.

Schultz, Richard H. 2004. "Showstoppers: *Nine Reasons Why We Never Sent Our Special Operations Forces After Al Qaeda Before 9/11." The Weekly Standard* 9 (January 26). Available online at: http://www.weeklystandard.com/showstoppers/article/4846. Last accessed 25-March-2017.

Schuurman, Bart. 2013. "Defeated by Popular Demand: Public Support and Counterterrorism in Three Western Democracies, 1963–1998". *Studies in Conflict & Terrorism* 36 (2): 152–175. doi:10.1080/1057610x.2013.747072.

Sheehan, Ivan Sascha. 2009. "Has the Global War on Terror Changed the Terrorist Threat? A Time-Series Intervention Analysis". *Studies in Conflict and Terrorism* 32 (8): 743–761. doi:10.1080/10576100903039270.

Walter, Barbara F. 2006. "Building Reputation: Why Governments Fight Some Separatists but Not Others". *American Journal of Political Science* 50 (2): 313–330. doi:10.1111/j.1540-5907.2006.00186.x.

CHAPTER 15

How Terror Groups End

Learning Objectives

After reading this chapter, readers should be able to:

- Explain what scholars mean by the end of terrorism.
- Use the analytic approaches explain variation in the longevity of groups, or why individuals choose to leave terrorist groups.
- Describe the link between patterns of terrorist group survival and different counterterrorism strategies.

> "All wars end."
>
> —JOHN MASEFIELD

THE PUZZLE

David Rapoport (1992) claims that the majority of terrorist groups barely survive for one year. Among those that survive past the one-year mark, almost half cease to exist within one decade. Audrey Cronin finds that the modal terror group lasts between five and nine years (2006, p. 213). Whereas some groups such as Direct Action in France or the Red Brigades in Italy lasted for only one decade, more or less, other groups such as ETA in Spain, the IRA in Ireland, or Hizballah in Lebanon have existed for several decades. And the Ku Klux Klan (KKK)—perhaps the longest-lasting group in the world today—has been active since 1866.

The puzzle we address in this final chapter concerns the variation that exists in the longevity of terrorist groups: Why do some groups last only a few weeks, whereas others survive for decades? In addition, we address variation in the persistence of individual participation in terrorism: Why do some people choose to leave the violent organizations whose ranks they have joined, where as others remain?

Studies addressing the end of terrorism are far fewer in number than those that address its underlying causes. In an early study, Ross and Gurr (1989) explain that insofar as the decline of terrorism was addressed at all, it was generally assumed to follow from the success or failure of groups in achieving their goals. The relative rates of success or failure were in turn linked to the political capabilities of groups in terms of resources and popular support. Broadly speaking, terror groups faded away in one of two ways: as a result of preemptive or deterrence-based counterterrorism policies; or as a result of group burnout or societal backlash. These two mechanisms reduced or eliminated the coercive capabilities of groups, leading to their eventual demise.

More recently, scholars have made advances in understanding why some terror organizations last longer than others, increasing the typology of reasons for decline well beyond Ross and Gurr's (1989) original preemption-deterrence-burnout-backlash model. Group attributes such as the number of members, for instance, seem to play an important role, as do differences in group motivation, or ideology. Some studies focus on intergroup relationships or shifts in political opportunity structures to explain the demise of groups or the disengagement of individuals from terrorist organizations.

In this chapter, we review how the various approaches to studying terrorism explain variation in group longevity, and include illustrative cases throughout to demonstrate the plausibility of the mechanisms identified in the literature. We begin by addressing how existing scholarship defines the end of a terrorist group, and survey some general trends related to terrorist group longevity.

WHAT QUALIFIES AS "THE END" OF A TERRORIST GROUP?

Scholars vary in the way they operationalize the end of a terrorist group. Jones and Libicki (2008, p. 5), for instance, define it as "the earliest evidence that the group no longer exists or that the group no longer uses terrorism to achieve its goals . . . Regardless of reason, the group does not commit further terrorist attacks under its name." Studies of this nature use terror attacks as the dependent variable and model the probability that a terrorist group that perpetrated a successful attack in a given time period survives to perpetrate another attack in a later period (Blomberg, Engel, and Sawyer 2010).

A second way of operationalizing a terrorist group's end might be to record its removal from state terrorism lists, such as the US State Department's list of Designated Foreign Terrorist Organizations. But as we have discussed earlier, given the high level of subjectivity that enters into the decision to designate a group as a terror organization, this latter research design would best explain the motivation and reasoning behind the de-listing of particular groups by a state actor, as opposed to understanding why the group itself ends.

Other approaches to understanding the decline of violent groups focus more on the mechanisms through which terrorist organizations might cease to exist, shifting the unit of analysis from the group itself to the **terrorist campaign**. In her book *How Terrorism Ends*, Audrey Kurth Cronin takes a thematic approach to understanding the decline and eventual end of terrorist campaigns, a view that she argues enables the reader to transcend piecemeal studies of individual terrorist campaigns (2012). The patterns of terrorism decline that she identifies on the basis of historical analysis are as follows: (1) capture or killing of the group's leader (**decapitation**); (2) entry of the group into a legitimate political process (**negotiation**); (3) achievement of the group's aims (success); implosion or loss of the group's public support (failure); (5) defeat and elimination by brute force (**repression**); and (6) transition from terrorism into other forms of violence (**reorientation**) (Cronin 2009, p. 22–23). These mechanisms of decline reflect factors that are both internal and external to the terrorist campaign. A seventh mechanism Cronin identified in an earlier article is the failure of a terrorist group to pass on its cause to the next generation (Cronin 2006). Examples of such groups include the Red Brigades in Italy, the Weather Underground in the US, and the Second of June Movement in Germany. In most cases of **cross-generational failure**, the nature of the group's ideology appears to play a particularly important role. Left-wing/anarchist groups in various countries in the 1970s, for instance, were notorious for their inability to articulate a clear vision of their goals that successors from younger generations could inherit. Right-wing groups that are adherents to fascist or racist ideologies may also have more trouble passing on their cause to future generations (Chermak, Freilich, and Suttmoeller 2013). This latter category of groups, however, might also be harder to track given their tendency to operate according to a common modus operandi (Crenshaw 1999). This includes so-called leaderless resistance, which involves highly decentralized networks of small cells functioning independently (Cronin 2006).

Table 15.1 provides examples of how various terrorist groups have declined, elaborating on Cronin's typology (2006, 2009).

Some groups appear to end, but then they return on the scene later. For instance, Cronin identifies the **Kurdish Workers Party (PKK)** as an example of a terror group that has ended, primarily through the mechanism of decapitation (2009). She argues that the arrest, imprisonment, and disavowal of the group's leader, **Abdullah Öcalan**, ultimately led to the demise of the group. That said, according to the GTD, the PKK has perpetrated hundreds of attacks in Turkey since 2010.

This example points to the possibility that some of these mechanisms of group demise may be more temporary than others. For instance, leadership decapitation might undermine a group in the short-term without addressing the underlying grievances and power structures that yielded violence in the first place.

Moreover, it may be the case that some of these mechanisms work in tandem with one another within the same conflict. For instance, the Real IRA ultimately failed because of leadership decapitation, while the PIRA more

TABLE 15.1 How Terrorist Groups End

Mechanism	Notable Examples
Decapitation (capture/killing of leader)	Shining Path (Peru) Aum Shinrikyo (Japan) Real IRA (Northern Ireland)
Negotiation	Provisional IRA (Northern Ireland) PLO (Palestinian Territories) Moro Islamic Liberation Front (Philippines) FARC (Colombia)
Success	Irgun (Israel) African National Congress (South Africa)
Failure	Real IRA (Northern Ireland) ETA (Spain) Shining Path (Peru)
Cross-Generational Failure	Weather Underground (US) Red Brigades (Italy) Second of June Movement (Germany)
Repression	Shining Path (Peru) People's Will (Russia) LTTE (Sri Lanka)
Reorientation	*Towards criminality:* Abu Sayyaf (Philippines) *Towards full insurgency:* Khmer Rouge (Cambodia) Communist Party of Nepal—Maoists Armed Islamic Group (GIA) (Algeria)

Source: Cronin 2006; 2009

broadly ended after the Good Friday Accords. These mechanisms may also work sequentially. For example, negotiations with the IRA followed failed attempts at repression. Likewise, numerous failed attempts at negotiation with the LTTE precipitated a massive counterinsurgency campaign by the Sri Lankan government, which ultimately destroyed the group.

WHY TERROR GROUPS END

In a comprehensive report examining 648 terrorist groups active from 1968–2008, Jones and Libicki (2008) find that most groups end because they joined the political process, or as a result of police and intelligence efforts to arrest or kill key members. Outright military force has rarely led to the demise of terrorist organizations, while very few terror groups achieved outright victory.

The report also points to the influence of several factors such as ideology and organizational dynamics on terrorist group longevity. First, religious

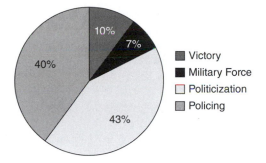

Figure 15.1 How Terror Groups End

Source: Adapted from Jones and Libicki 2008, p. 19, based on the Terrorism Knowledge Base (TKB)
(full report available at http://www.rand.org/pubs/monographs/MG741-1.html)

terrorist groups take longer to fade out than other types of groups. Whereas 62 percent of all groups have ended since 1968, only 32 percent of all religious groups have renounced terrorism. Second, larger terrorist groups on average last longer than smaller groups. And third, groups with limited political goals, like territorial autonomy or representation in parliament, are more likely to end as a result of a political solution, relative to groups with broader aims (like territorial secession or the toppling of a government). Hence groups that seek policy change are more likely to end due to negotiation than are groups whose aim is to set off a social revolution.

Of course, most theories of terrorism's decline are connected to the broader body of hypotheses that explain its origin. As such, many of the explanations for variation in the longevity of groups that we present in this chapter directly mirror the explanations for terrorism that we discussed in the first half of this book.

Think back, for instance, to how **strategic approaches** explain why groups turn to terrorism. Studies that adopt this approach assume that terrorist organizations are rational actors, and that they use violence because they view it as being of higher marginal utility relative to other modes of political contestation, such as participation in the political system or nonviolent resistance. An observable implication of strategic approaches should thus be that when a group has met its strategic objectives, it should cease using terrorism. Alternatively, when a group receives public recognition for both itself and the cause it espouses, the continuation of terrorist activity might work to alienate hard-earned support. A group that acts according to principles of utility maximization may thus cease to use violent tactics once certain intermediary goals are achieved (Crenshaw 1999).

Two such examples of successful terrorist groups that ceased to exist after achieving their objectives are the Irgun in Israel and the African National Congress (ANC) in South Africa. We discussed Irgun in detail in Chapter 2, so let's focus on the ANC here. The ANC emerged in 1912 in response to systemic oppression against black South Africans at the hands of a newly formed white government. The organization turned to armed struggle and terror tactics in the 1960s, and its leader Nelson Mandela was imprisoned from 1964 to 1990. The last ANC attack occurred in 1989, and the organization became a legal political party in 1990. Alongside widespread mass protests, boycotts, and sanctions, the ANC ultimately achieved its objectives of ending legal apartheid (Cronin 2006, p. 24). Mandela was eventually elected as South Africa's first black president in 1994.

The suggestion that terrorist groups end when they succeed in achieving their goals has important implications for counterterrorism. First among these is the concern that allowing violent groups to win on their terms may set a dangerous precedent. Fully conceding to groups who show little regard for democratic processes and who have victimized civilians is likely to lead to furthering the perception that violence is a legitimate and effective means of achieving one's goals (see Neumann 2007).

This leads to the second implication, which suggests that if terror groups are rational actors, they may be more amenable to reaching negotiated solutions with their opponents. Indeed, negotiations may bring a group closer to achieving its stated objectives, and reduce the incentives of engaging in violence in order to do so. Groups such as the PIRA in Ireland, the PLO in Palestine, and the LTTE in Sri Lanka have all transitioned away from terrorism at times following the formal opening of a political process with their targeted opponent.

For negotiations to be possible, the group itself must have negotiable aims. Groups that seek territorial autonomy, for instance, may be perceived as having more negotiable goals than groups that follow a religious, left-wing, or right-wing ideology. Negotiations, however, are rarely a panacea. The negotiation process itself may lead to other outcomes associated with enduring terrorism, such as group fractionalization, splintering, and spoiling behavior. Negotiations that isolate the more hardline elements of terror groups may thus be effective at reducing or eliminating violence from certain elements of an organization, but lead others to refocus their efforts on increasing their use of violence. In fact, splinter organizations are often much more violent than their parent organizations, suggesting that negotiated settlements with certain groups may simply displace the use of violence from one group to another (Christia 2012; Cunningham, Bakke, and Seymour 2012; Perkoski 2016).

Strategic approaches aimed at understanding **individual desistance** from terrorism offer unique contributions. Studies departing from rational actor assumptions argue that while the decisions of many individuals to either remain in or disengage from terrorist groups may be influenced by broad shifts in a certain socio-political context, they are ultimately decisions made on the basis of utility considerations. In the case of ETA, for instance, Reinares (2011) argues that militants made decisions to leave the organization on the basis of opportunity assessments. A militant may have left the organization or changed his individual behavior, but without rejecting the doctrine of violence to which she adhered when she joined. In such cases, the decision to abandon the ranks of a terrorist group often followed questions about the viability of the terrorist organization and the utility of violence in a particular context (Reinares 2011). The relative utility of violence for an individual can depend as much on idiosyncratic, personal reasons as it may on shifting socio-political contexts.

As is clear from the discussion thus far, the scenario of a terrorist group's decline involves a process much more complex than the simple pursuit or achievement of a negotiated settlement. For the most part, studies that focus on the strategic choices made by governments and groups have only focused on single case studies, preventing a broad understanding of the broader dynamics that explain the decline of terrorism among many groups. Indeed, a host of factors such as organizational dynamics, group ideology, and broad structural factors shape the ability of groups to endure. To better understand some of these complex dynamics, let's consider how other approaches have explained variation in the longevity of terror groups.

Structural approaches hone in on the operating conditions and environmental contexts that facilitate or impede the operations of terrorist groups and their survival. An ongoing debate surrounds the effect of regime type (Brooks 2009). The institutional recourse that democratic societies offer to aggrieved individuals should lessen the incentives of turning to violence, as people have formal mechanisms for resolving issues that may arise between themselves and the state. As such, terrorist organizations should be more short-lived in democracies. While studies have found that democracies play host to a larger number of terrorist groups than autocracies (Weinberg and Eubank 1994; Chenoweth 2010), this does not always translate to more attacks. This strongly suggests that the way that we measure terrorism—whether by counting the number of groups present in a society, or by counting the number of attacks staged by groups in a society—may significantly affect the results of particular studies. Moreover, some groups seem to maintain recognition as terror groups long after they have stopped using terror as a tactic. Take the Zapatista National Liberation Army (EZLN) in Mexico, for example. Although this group has not claimed an act of violence since its initial foray into revolutionary action in the mid-1990s (according to the GTD), many observers still refer to it as a terrorist group. In this example, we can see how the subjective use of the term terrorism serves power rather than objective reality (see also Chapter 7).

Furthermore, the ways in which we measure the key independent variable of interest— democracy in this case—has important implications. Different aspects of democracy might encourage or discourage terrorist acts and the survival of groups. The notion that major transnational terror organizations consider engagement with free societies a key component of their strategies severely undermines the notion that democratization will mitigate the risk of terrorist activity by prompting the demise of particular groups (Blomberg et al. 2010).

The dynamics that link democracy to terrorist group endurance may be particular to specific cases. In a study addressing the factors that motivated the members of ETA in Spain to abandon or remain in terrorist groups, for instance, Alonso (2011) finds that the socialization of young Basques in the 1960s and 1970s in an undemocratic context enabled radicalization and eventually membership in violent groups. Following the end of the Franco regime and the emergence of new democratic political institutions, however, many individuals left ETA. Importantly, the implementation of decentralization and increased autonomy for the Basque region contributed to an erosion of support for violence in the Basque country (Alonso 2011, p. 698). The transition from dictatorship to democracy was thus influential in encouraging a split within the terrorist organization—one that isolated radicals from elements of the group that were more amenable to finding a negotiated settlement on the question of Basque autonomy.

In a large-n study of the factors explaining survival patterns across terrorist groups globally, Young and Dugan (2014) find that for the 2,223 terror organizations listed in the GTD, the average lifetime of a group is 3.33 years, although over half of the groups stopped operating within their first year (Young and Dugan 2014, p. 12). This study shows that state capabilities are important in influencing the survival of groups. Of note, increases in measures of economic development, operationalized as GDP per capita, significantly shorten the life span of a terrorist group. This finding could have two separate implications. First, high measures of GDP likely indicate high state capacity in areas such as policing and intelligence, which reduce the ability of clandestine violent groups to operate effectively in such societies. Second, high per capita GDP is suggestive of the high **opportunity costs** involved in engaging in violence when other economic opportunities are also present.

While the study does not find a significant direct relationship between democracy and group survival, the authors do find that several other structural factors might be important in explaining variation in terrorist group longevity (Young and Dugan 2014). Specifically, every additional year that a regime has been in place leads to an average decrease in the risk of a group ending by 0.4 percent. In other words, an increase in the age of a regime is correlated with an increase in the survival of terrorist groups in that particular society. Additionally, groups that operate in Asia and the Americas are more likely to die out by the following year than their counterparts in the Middle East (Young and Dugan 2014). This is true in spite of the fact that many groups in India—such as the **United Liberation Front of Assam** and **Babbar Khalsa**— have been active for decades. Other studies drawing on the ITERATE database corroborate these findings. Blomberg, Gaibulloev, and Sandler (2011), for instance, find that organizations operating in sub-Saharan Africa are more likely to survive than those active in North America.

Finally, some studies have pointed to the role that **globalization** plays in shaping terror group longevity. This perspective suggests that as a more interdependent global context enables groups to diversify their resourcing, financing, and bases of recruitment, they are also more likely to achieve longer lifespans, even in the absence of physical safe havens (Vittori 2009).

A second set of factors that explain variation in the longevity of terrorist groups draw on assumptions from the **organizational approach**, focusing in particular on how inter-group dynamics affect the ability of groups to survive. Competition between groups, for instance, poses a significant challenge to survival. A competitive environment in which many other groups are active makes it difficult for groups to recruit members and attract important resources such as financing or popular support. As we have reviewed in earlier chapters, competitive environments may induce dynamics such as **outbidding**, as groups seek to distinguish themselves from competitors (Bloom 2005). On average, this logic suggests that when there is a limited number of groups, violent organizations should last longer. Heavy inter-group competition is more likely to lead to a group failing out of a contentious environment.

This hypothesis finds support in several studies of terror group longevity. Cronin (2009), for instance, argues that groups may decline because they lose in a competition for members and support from the population. The competitive environment ultimately leads to shorter terrorist group lifespans. For instance, the highly competitive contentious environment that characterizes the Israeli-Palestinian conflict is a powerful example of these dynamics. During the Second Intifada, Hamas and other more violent organizations successfully attracted a large number of supporters, effectively threatening the survival of the PFLP as an organization (Young and Dugan 2014). A study of the survival rates of terrorist groups globally finds that an increase in the number of groups operating in one country significantly increases the chances of group demise. The modal number of groups that use terrorism in a country year is eleven. In a country in which fifteen groups operate, Young and Dugan estimate the expected decrease in survival rate of any of the groups is as high as 12 percent (2014, p. 15).

That said, the effect of competition on group survival is contested. In fact, recent studies contend that violent rivalries might actually increase group longevity. Since civilians are ultimately forced to choose between groups, these groups are themselves forced to innovate, spoil negotiations, and prolong the conflict in search of a more favorable outcome (Phillips 2015). Factors such as **tactical innovation** that are prompted by the competitive environment may work to make certain groups more durable. Phillips (2015) uses the FARC in Colombia to illustrate these dynamics. Attacks from self-defense groups in the 1980s did little to weaken the FARC, which seems to have drawn inspiration from emerging violent rivalries. For example, paramilitary attacks against the organization inspired many peasants to join its ranks. When the FARC increased attacks against paramilitaries, the latter groups turned to hiring Israeli mercenaries to train their members in new techniques such as C-4 letter bombs, taking over houses, and shooting from moving vehicles (Phillips 2015, p. 66). This same study finds a statistically significant positive relationship between violent inter-group rivalries and group survival (Phillips 2015).

A key distinction between the Phillips (2015) and Young and Dugan (2014) findings may be the operationalization of inter-group dynamics. While the former focuses on dyadic rivalry between two terrorist groups, the latter is more attentive to the broader competitive context measured by the number of active groups. The particular nature of the inter-group relationship may therefore best explain whether competitive environments lead to longer or shorter terror group lifespans.

A number of studies highlight the importance of factors such as organizational age, size, and strength in explaining group longevity. Phillips (2015), for instance, finds that a group's size in terms of members is negatively correlated to its termination. Larger organizations benefit from the collective expertise of members, and are able to more easily engage in tactical innovation, which also contributes to survivability (Jones and Libicki 2008; Horowitz 2010). With respect to age, Blomberg et al. (2010) find that a majority of attacks staged between 1968 and 2007 were committed by organizations that were active only once. Most organizations can thus be considered what the authors refer to as "one-hit wonders," while the rest are characterized as "recidivists." Among organizations that do remain active beyond their first attack, a small group of usual suspects seems to monopolize transnational terrorism in particular. Whereas the number of active transnational terrorist groups reached a peak of 578 in 1991, the number dropped to an all-time low of 52 in 2001, rising only to 89 by 2007 (Blomberg et al. 2010, p. 307). In short, the older an organization becomes, the lower the likelihood of its continued survival.

The amount of resources available to groups may also affect their propensity to survive. Groups that bring in the most and highest quality resources—including personnel, financing, and expertise—are likely to survive the longest. Those that find a state sponsor that allows them a certain degree of autonomy are also more likely to survive relative to other groups (Vittori 2009). Additionally, the formation of alliances across terrorist organization might be a particularly effective way of bolstering individual resources. While cooperation with others makes groups more vulnerable to detection, the pooling of resources and coordination of attacks leads to heightened longevity, on average (Phillips 2015). Collaboration may thus be an important pathway towards increased resilience in the face of government efforts aimed at a group's elimination.

Dynamics internal to groups may be particularly important in explaining longevity. Factors such as group leadership and organizational structure may also be important. Asal, Brown, and Dalton (2012), for instance, find that organizations with factional or competing leadership are more likely to break apart relative to groups with more coherent leadership structures. Similarly, decentralization and networked forms of organization may make groups more susceptible to demise, relative to groups with strong hierarchical structures. Leaders with decentralized authority have reduced abilities to police and control their members, increasing the propensity for diverse opinions to take hold (Shapiro 2013). Reinares (2011) similarly finds that individuals left ETA after personal disagreements with other group members, and

Dalgaard-Nielsen (2013) shows how doubts related to group and leadership issues can prompt exit from both left-wing and right-wing violent groups. Leaders perceived to be self-seeking, manipulative, cowardly, or outright incompetent appear frequently in the narratives of ex-militants from a wide variety of contexts (Dalgaard-Nielsen 2013).

How do **ideological approaches** to terrorism understand and explain variation in group longevity? One of the best-known studies of terror group survival suggests that religious groups are the most likely to survive, relative to rightist or leftist terrorist organizations, or those that espouse ethno-nationalist goals (Jones and Libicki 2008). Because of their ready-made constituencies, religious groups may not need to constantly replenish their legitimacy among would-be followers. Others scholars suggest that groups with nationalist goals appear to be most-represented among long-lasting terrorist groups, due to the innate support that they receive from their constituencies and the potential for territorial sanctuary (Crenshaw 1991; Cronin 2006).

On average, studies seem to suggest that leftist groups may be particularly short-lived due to their inability to recruit a mass following, and an inability to pass on their influence and message across generations (Cronin 2006). The aims of leftist groups may be more ambiguous in nature, relative to ethno-nationalist groups whose more clearly articulated goals reflect territorial ambitions. Like left-wing groups, right-wing groups are also expected to have a shorter existence due to the need to recruit and proselytize potential recruits, rather than having a natural constituency at their disposal (Vittori 2009). Overt recruitment might also make these groups more vulnerable to counterterrorism operations and infiltration by unreliable outsiders (Hoffman 2006, p. 242–243).

Figure 15.2 provides a summary of these trends. According to the data on terrorist groups included in the Terrorism Knowledge Base (TKB) maintained by the Memorial Institution for the Prevention of Terrorism (MIPT) and used by Vittori (2009), no right-wing group has survived past the 10-year threshold.[1] This claim is controversial, however, since many people consider the KKK a right-wing terror group; it has survived for well over a century.

These summary statistics seem to indicate that groups with nationalist, religious, and leftist ideologies may not exhibit significant variation in terms of expected longevity. More specifically, they share similar average lifespans of about 3 years, and a 30–44 percent chance of surviving beyond the first year. Among nationalist and leftist groups, almost one-third live to reach their 10th year, while as many as 80 percent of religious organizations achieve the same goal. Some scholars suggest that this discrepancy may be

---

[1] In her study of terrorist group longevity, Vittori (2009) selected 100 cases at random from the TKB database. The beginning of a terrorist group was coded as its first known attack. The end date was assumed as that of the group's last known attack, even if it had declared a cease-fire or otherwise claimed to have renounced violence.

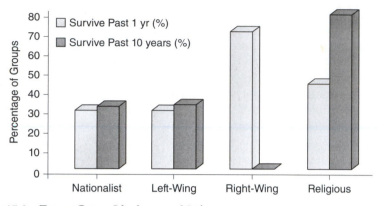

Figure 15.2   Terror Group Ideology and Lifespan

Source: Vittori 2009; TKB[1]

due to the fact that very few religious terror groups existed prior to 2000, and those that did exist still survive today (Vittori 2009, p. 462). Hizballah is an example of such a group.

Right-wing groups present an interesting puzzle in that, on average, they are short-lived relative to other groups. Some authors argue that such groups may face heightened difficulties when recruiting members to their cause, and also experience challenges in carrying on their cause across generations. Both of these dynamics may also make them particularly vulnerable to counterterrorism efforts aimed at provoking their demise (Chermak, Freilich, and Suttmoeller 2013). Moreover, right-wing governments tend to sponsor many right-wing groups, at least in their initial phases. This is particularly true of right-wing groups in Latin America. As formal state structures took over the activities carried out by right-wing paramilitaries, or governments evolved away from strategies of promoting political violence, many of these groups died off (Vittori 2009, p. 462). The Colombian context provides a particularly salient example of these dynamics.

We could ask the inverse question of religious terrorist groups—why do they appear to last so much longer than groups with non-religious ideologies? Jones and Libicki (2008) find that religious terrorist groups take longer to fade away, and they also rarely achieve their objectives. Of all the religious groups that have ceased to exist since 1968, none have done so by achieving their stated objectives. This suggests that the probability of Al Qaeda achieving its goal of overthrowing multiple regimes in the Middle East and the West is close to zero, although the group is likely to persist regardless.

Terrorism scholars suggest that religious groups may endure so long because of the staying power of sacred or spiritual motivations (Rapoport 1984). Because the deity is perceived as being directly involved in the determination of the ends and means of a religious organization, constituents' attachment to the group is unlikely to waver in response to repression, however indiscriminate or brutal. Religion can also play a major role in ethnic identification, which explains why political groups such as the IRA or the FLN in Algeria stressed their Catholic and Muslim underpinnings, respectively. Thus the nature of the popular support that religious terrorist organizations accrue may be similar to that built up by ethno-nationalist organizations, who also appeal strongly to ethnic identity.

Of the religious terror organizations that do end, most seem to splinter off into smaller groups. According to Jones and Libicki's (2008) analysis, none of these splinters achieved their aims. Most fell to policing activities, while a smaller proportion fell as a result of military operations aimed at their eradication. A small minority abandoned violence in favor of joining the political process (Jones and Libicki 2008, p. 37).

At the level of the individual, some studies explain desistance from terrorism as a result of a loss of faith in the militant ideology. In a study of individual recidivism from ETA, Reinares (2011) points out that the great majority of individuals who walked away from the organization did so of their own volition. Most of them did so while serving jail sentences, usually after a long period of internment. The direct prompt for renouncing violence was rarely the result of a normative rejection of violence, but rather a reflection of shifting opportunity assessments. In the minds of the individual extremists who decided to abandon the organization, the utility of violence had simply dropped to a point where remaining in ETA's ranks no longer made sense. In many instances, the idealized notions that individual recruits held prior to joining were discarded when political, social, or personal conditions changed (Reinares 2011).

Psychological approaches may also shed light into the process by which individuals desist from terrorism. In a study of individual members of right-wing and left-wing groups, Dalgaard-Nielsen (2013) finds that extremists often exit violent groups after having caused death or harm to a presumed enemy. She identifies three broad clusters of issues that appear to cast doubt on the benefits of violent political contention and prompt exit: (1) ideological doubt; (2) doubt related to internal group dynamics, such as leadership effectiveness; and (3) doubt related to personal and practical issues (2013). Doubt in a narrative about a world divided into "us" and "them"—alongside persistent calls for engagement in brutal acts of violence—can be a powerful motivation for leaving a group. In some cases the doubt was linked to a reinforced notion that violence was not leading to the attainment of political or ideological goals, but instead backfiring against the group. Increased contact with the outside world can also make some of the taken for granted truths of the militant narrative and ideology appear less plausible. Leveraging these forms of doubt is an important element of successful counterterrorism strategies aimed at encouraging individuals to desist from terrorism.

As the example above suggests, psychological approaches are particularly salient when it comes to explaining why individuals voluntarily—as opposed to forcibly—disengage from terrorism. Most studies that adopt this approach are based fully or partially on primary sources such as interviews with former extremists, which are likely to offer a unique window into what induces a person to reject extremism or to leave it behind.

Recall our discussion of **cognitive theory** from Chapter 4. A key takeaway from this chapter was that people display cognitive conservatism and strive for consistency in what they do, feel, and say. The sense of urgency applied to cognitive consistency is a significant barrier to persuasion and attitude change, but it does not imply that changing the attitudes or feelings of an extremist is categorically impossible. Dalgaard-Nielsen (2013) suggests that **cognitive therapy** can alter extremist attitudes, behavior, or emotions. The method is based on the premise that criminals tend to exhibit particular traits such as self-justification, displacement of blame, lack of empathy towards victims, etc. Therapy is directed towards training offenders in conflict resolution and anger management to promote a different set of behaviors, which might provide pathways to influencing their attitudes and beliefs away from violence (Dalgaard-Nielsen 2013, p. 110). While this type of therapy has not been tested on terrorist convicts, it could provide inroads towards enhancing policies aimed at promoting an exit from extremism.

In short, generalizing on the reasons why individuals decide to exit terror groups may be difficult. To a large extent, this is a direct reflection of the fact that the reasons for joining a violent group vary so much across individuals (see Chapters 4 and 5). If the reasons for joining are difficult to generalize, then reasons for leaving the organization are likely just as complex.

We end by considering how **critical approaches** contribute to understanding the end of terrorism, which is a bit trickier than for other approaches. Recall from Chapter 7 that the foundation of CTS lies in critiquing the empirical basis of terrorism studies. Scholars of this tradition question the very application of the terms "terrorist" and "terrorism," and claim that everything that we purport to know about terrorism is ultimately empirically flawed and morally misplaced.

Since one of CTS's main critiques of empirically-based terrorism analysis surrounds the field's generally state-centric orientation, studies based on this approach may exhibit a tendency to focus on explaining variation in the longevity of what they perceive to be state-perpetuated terrorism. Recall the discussion of the US atomic bombings of Hiroshima and Nagasaki from Chapter 7. A reorientation of state policies surrounding the use of nuclear weapons, for instance, might be an explanation for what critical scholars conceptualize as the end of terrorism.

CTS is also strongly critical of any state-led counterterrorism policies, which they conceive as serving to perpetuate Western-centric understandings of what constitutes terrorism. The "end" of a terrorist group might thus not be a direct result of counterterrorism efforts such as policing or military intervention, but rather reflect changes in what states perceive as terrorism in the first place. As is clear from this discussion, questioning the overarching definition of terrorism, and what it means to be a terrorist organization, makes it difficult to focus on what constitutes the end of a group, or a campaign, or even individual desistance from terrorism

BOX 15.1

THE LIFESPANS OF THE TEN LONGEST-ENDURING TERROR GROUPS

Cronin identifies 19 terror groups active during the twentieth century that endured longer than four decades (200, p. 221). Consider the following ten examples from her list:

Group	Location	Start Year	End Year	Total Lifespan in Years
Ku Klux Klan (KKK)	US	1866	Ongoing	152
Irish Republican Army	Northern Ireland	1922	Ongoing	96
Islami Chhatra Shibir	Bangladesh	1941	Ongoing	77
Syrian Social Nationalist Party	Syria	1931	1989	58
Kurdish Democratic Party	Turkey	1946	1993	47
Khmer Rouge	Cambodia	1951	1998	47
Basque Fatherland and Freedom (ETA)	Spain	1959	Ongoing	59
Karen National Union (KNU)	Burma/ Myanmar	1959	Ongoing	59
Popular Movement for the Liberation of Angola	Angola	1956	2002	46
Revolutionary Armed Forces of Colombia (FARC)	Colombia	1964	Ongoing	54

DISCUSSION EXERCISE

(1) *What, if anything, do you find surprising about the groups on the list?*

(2) *Write a brief profile on one or more of these groups. Why do you think each group persisted so long? Which of the analytic approaches best characterizes your assessment?*

PRACTICAL IMPLICATIONS

Wide variation in the findings highlighted in this chapter suggest that no single factor explains the decline of terrorism, or why some groups might last longer than others. The impact of structural factors such as regime type or level of development varies according to particular measures of the independent variables, as well as across datasets. Findings from this approach are therefore difficult to generalize. Similarly, there is little variation in longevity across some groups with diverse ideologies, suggesting that ideology is likely insufficient in explaining why certain groups last longer than others. The most robust findings seem to come from studies based on the organizational approach. Larger groups that are resource-rich appear to last longer than smaller groups that lack resources. When these variables interact with factors such as religious or ethno-nationalist ideologies, we may be coming closer to understanding why some groups have higher survival rates than others. What are the practical implications of these findings?

First, empirical evidence strongly suggests that the defeat of a terror group requires a range of policy instruments, including police and intelligence work, political negotiation, and various economic instruments such as sanctions. But as we saw in Chapter 13, some counterterrorism instruments are more effective than others. How to prioritize each of these approaches depends on the specific context, on key organizational attributes of the group itself, and on what moral principles the parties to the conflict value the most. In this chapter we can see that some groups are naturally inclined to persist longer than others—particularly when the groups are religious, possess maximalist claims, or maintain a steady flow of resources.

Setting aside the standard repertoire of counterterrorism instruments, however, it is also notable that the vast majority of terrorist organizations do not survive past their first attacks. Because most groups act autonomously (Vittori 2009), local law enforcement may be particularly well placed to detect potential attacks before they occur. Training, equipping, and empowering local officials and police forces, rather than national militaries, should thus be an important priority of national counterterrorism strategies. The local and more nuanced knowledge of agencies embedded within cities, towns, and local networks, can enhance understandings of specific environments. Some scholars call for military force against large, well-armed, and well-organized insurgent groups that also use terrorist violence (Jones and Libicki 2008). As we saw in Chapter 13, however, this type of force is usually too blunt an instrument to use effectively against conventional terror groups—both because it may backfire and also because it raises troubling ethical and normative concerns.

Another important counterterrorism strategy is to work closely with allies in the hope of containing terrorists. While globalization may make resources more easily available to groups seeking to stage attacks, increased interdependence at the global level also provides significant advantages to states in the way of enhanced intelligence and information sharing. Making the right choice naturally depends on the precise definition of success, or what the end of terrorism actually means (Byman 2007).

This chapter has offered some suggestions as to what types of groups might be more amenable to negotiated solutions with their targeted opponent. The clear delineation of goals, such as increased territorial autonomy, may signal opportunities for negotiation or an openness towards shifting away from the use of violence and towards engagement with the political process. Attention to the specific goals of terrorist groups may thus help to assess which types of counterterrorism strategies may be appropriate in the first place.

At the level of the individual, programs aimed at countering violent extremism and promoting desistance from terrorism should seek to understand the motivations of individuals, and provide resources that lead to alternative ways of airing grievances. Dalgaard-Nielsen (2013) points specifically to the use of cognitive therapy to change the behaviors and ultimately the attitudes of individuals engaged in violent political activity.

As Audrey Cronin asserts in her study on the end of terrorism, "terrorism, like war, never ends" (Cronin 2006, p. 48). Terror groups, however, do end. They die out, they cease to use terrorism, and individuals decide to leave terrorist organizations. There is no panacea that will end the use of terror as a tactic. But nuanced, limited, and proportional strategies aimed at containing groups committed to violence can be effective at reducing overall levels of harm.

SUMMARY

In this chapter, we reviewed how the various approaches to studying terrorism explain variation in the longevity of terrorist groups. We discussed how scholars conceptualize the end of terrorism, and we reviewed different explanations that address the end of terror campaigns as well as individual desistance from terrorism. The chapter provided examples of groups that have ended in diverse ways, and concluded with a discussion of what these patterns mean for the design and implementation of practical strategies to reduce and prevent terror.

Discussion Questions

1. How can one know when a terror group has ended?

2. What approach do you think provides the most analytic purchase to understanding variation in the longevity of terrorist groups?

3. Based on what the various approaches suggest regarding the survival of terrorist groups, what do you think are some of the more effective strategies that can be used to defeat ISIS?

4. What are the biggest mistakes in the application of counterterrorism policy aimed at bringing about the end of Al Qaeda?

5. Select two historical terror groups discussed in this book. Compare and contrast their emergence and demise. What does your comparison tell you about the most effective or ineffective ways to confront terror?

KEY TAKEAWAYS

- Scholars typically argue that a terror group ends when there is no sign of further violence emanating from the group. Most terror groups are surprisingly short-lived, ending in less than ten years.

- Most groups die out on their own, although many also end by reconstituting themselves into other organizational forms. Some groups end through repression.

- On average, the longest-enduring terror groups are those that are religious, maximalist, and well-resourced with recruits, weapons, and funds. However, the longer a group endures, the higher the risk that the group will expire.

- Given the fact that many terror groups die out on their own, extraordinary counterterrorism measures may often be unnecessary or inappropriate relative to the actual level of violence a group is likely to produce. Proportionality is a guiding principle, in both strategic and moral terms.

SUGGESTED FURTHER READINGS

Alonso, Rogelio. 2011. "Why Do Terrorists Stop? Analyzing Why ETA Members Abandon or Continue with Terrorism." *Studies in Conflict & Terrorism* 34 (9): 696–716. doi:10.1080/1057610x.2011.594944.

Asal, Victor, Mitchell Brown, and Angela Dalton. 2012. "Why split? Organizational Splits Among Ethnopolitical Organizations in the Middle East." *Journal of Conflict Resolution,* 56 (1): 94–117. doi:10.1177/0022002711429680.

Blomberg, S. Brock, Rozlyn C. Engle, and Reid Sawyer. 2010. "On the duration and sustainability of transnational terrorist organizations." *Journal of Conflict Resolution* 54 (2): 303–330. doi:10.1177/0022002709355431.

Crenshaw, Martha. 1991. "How Terrorism Declines." *Terrorism and Political Violence* 3 (1): 69–87.

Crenshaw, Martha. 1999. *How Terrorism Ends.* United States Institute of Peace (USIP).

Cronin, Audrey K. 2006. "How Al Qaida Ends: The Decline and Demise of Terrorist Groups." *International Security* 31 (1): 7–48. doi:10.1162/isec.2006.31.1.7.

Cronin, Audrey K. 2009. *How Terrorism Ends: Understanding the Decline and Demise of Terrorist Campaigns.* Princeton, NJ: Princeton University Press.

Dalgaard-Nielsen, Anja. 2013. "Promoting Exit from Violent Extremism: Themes and Approaches." *Studies in Conflict & Terrorism* 36 (2): 99–115. doi:10.1080/10576 10x.2013.747073.

Jones, Seth G., and Martin Libicki. 2008. *How Terrorist Groups End: Lessons for Countering al Qa'ida.* Santa Monica, CA: RAND Corporation. Available online at: http://www.rand.org/pubs/monographs/MG741-1.html. Last accessed 25-March-2017.

Phillips, Brian J. 2015. "Enemies with benefits? Violent rivalry and terrorist group longevity." *Journal of Peace Research* 52 (1): 62–75. doi:10.1177/0022343314550538.

Reinares, Fernando. 2011. "Exit from Terrorism: A Qualitative Empirical Study on Disengagement and Deradicalization Among Members of ETA." *Terrorism and Political Violence* 23 (5): 780–803. doi:10.1080/09546553.2011.613307.

Ross, Jeffrey I., and Ted Robert Gurr. 1989. "Why Terrorism Subsides." *Comparative Politics* 21 (4): 405–426. doi:10.2307/422005.

Suttmoeller, Michael, Steven Chermak, and Joshua D. Freilich. 2015. "The Influence of External and Internal Correlates on the Organizational Death of Domestic Far-Right Extremist Groups." *Studies in Conflict & Terrorism* 38 (9): 734–758. doi:10.108 0/1057610x.2015.1038106.

Vittori, Jodi. 2009. "All Struggles Must End: The Longevity of Terrorist Groups." *Contemporary Security Policy* 30 (3): 444–466. doi:10.1080/13523260903326602.

Young, Joseph K., and Laura Dugan. 2014. "Survival of the Fittest: Why Terrorist Groups Endure." *Perspectives on Terrorism* 8 (2): 1–23.

GLOSSARY

1983 Bombing of the Marine Corps Barracks An attack conducted by two suicide bombers against US and French armed forces at the US Marine compound in Beirut, Lebanon during the Lebanese Civil War on October 23, 1983, which killed 241 US service personnel and fifty-eight French soldiers. Although the bombings were traced to Hezbollah, involvement from both the Iranian and Syrian governments was also suspected. The attacks led to the withdrawal of US troops and the entire international peacekeeping force from Lebanon in February 1982. The multi-national peacekeeping force consisting of the United States, France, and Italy had been stationed in Lebanon since 1982 as part of a cease-fire agreement signed by the Palestinian Liberation Organization (PLO) and Israel. This incident was the deadliest attack against US Marines since the battle over Iwo Jima in 1945.

A

Abdullah Öcalan Leader of the Kurdish Workers Party (PKK).

Abdullah Yusuf Azzam A Palestinian scholar and militant known as the "Father of Jihad" and the founding leader of Al Qaeda. He fought against Soviet Russia as part of the mujahadeen in Afghanistan and was a mentor to Osama bin Laden. Together they raised funds and trained and supported militias in their quest for global Jihad. Azzam rejected attacking civilians, emphasizing that such actions could turn them against the movement. He was killed by a roadside bomb in 1989.

Abu Nidal Organization (ANO) A breakaway faction from the Palestine Liberation Organization (PLO) founded in 1974 that was headed by Sabri al-Banna (aka Abu Nidal). It advocated the elimination of Israel and conducted many terrorist attacks starting in the mid-1970s, including incidents involving hotels, embassies, airports, both in the Middle East and internationally. Many hundreds of people were killed in at least twenty countries. The group is currently considered inactive by the US State Department.

Abu Sayyef Group (ASG) An extremist Islamist group located in the southwestern Philippines. It began in the early 1990s with the goal of creating an independent Islamic state in western Mindanao and the Sulu Archipelago. Its terrorist tactics included kidnappings for ransom, extortion, bombings, robbery, and beheadings. Its first attacks began in the mid-1990s and continued into the mid-2000s. Its targets included maritime vessels among other soft targets, usually hitting Filipinos, along with military personnel, foreign workers and tourists. Due to their increasing interest in financial returns rather than religious or ideological goals, the Philippine government has not considered the ASG a viable partner for peace negotiations.

Accidental Guerilla Syndrome   A process coined by David Kilcullen that explains how military intervention can motivate retaliatory terrorism. When militaries occupy countries in response to terrorism, they tend to anger the local population, motivating them to begin to join in armed struggle against the occupier. Often this activity takes the form of guerilla warfare, where local recruits attack military forces in the occupied territory.

African National Congress   Originally a civil society organization founded in 1912 in South Africa with the mission of ending apartheid via nonviolent protest, but was banned by the government in 1960. Following the ban, the ANC formed the Umkhonto we Sizwe (Spear of the Nation), a radical branch that used guerrilla tactics and sabotage to further the ANC's original mission. The ANC was reinstated as a political party in 1990, and its leader Nelson Mandela was elected president of South Africa in 1994 after apartheid was removed in 1992. As of 2017, the ANC remains South Africa's governing political party.

Afrikaner Resistance Movement   A Neo-Nazi extremist group formed in 1973 in South Africa, whose membership base consists of ultra-right wing Afrikaners. The group opposed the removal of apartheid in 1992, and in 1993 its members attacked the World Trade Centre in Gauteng, where pro-democracy negotiations were being held. The attacks caused significant damage to the building but did not result in any deaths.

Al-Aqsa Martyrs Brigade or Battalion (AAMB)   A Palestinian nationalist group that formed in 2000 at the start of the Second Intifada with the goal of expelling Israeli forces and civilians from the Palestinian territories, and establishing a free Palestinian state loyal to Fatah. It has launched more than two hundred attacks in the Middle East, at times allying with other groups such as Islamic Jihad. The group declared open war on Israel in early 2015, and as of 2017 remains active.

Al-Gama'a Al-Islamiyaa (Islamic Group, IG)   An Islamist organization that formed out of a group of Egyptian students in the early 1970s to oppose Israel and advocate for Arab nationalism. The group was outlawed in Egypt in 1981, and played a role in the assassination of Egyptian leader Anwar El Sadat the same year. The group was implicated in a number of attacks against political figures and civilians in Egypt from the early 1990s to the early 2000s, but renounced violence in 2003 and formed a political party that won seats in the 2011-2012 parliamentary elections in Egypt.

Al-Jihad or Egyptian Islamic Jihad (EIJ)   An Egyptian Islamist terror group that formed in 1979 after the Muslim Brotherhood (its parent organization) renounced violence. The group is best known for its involvement in the assassination of Egyptian President Anwar El Sadat in the wake of a peace deal with Israel. The EIJ found safe haven in Afghanistan during the country's war against Soviet occupiers, eventually fully merging with Al Qaeda 2001. EIJ's leader since 1991, Aymenn al-Zawahiri, likely played a major role in organizing the September 11 terrorist attacks against the United States in 2001, and as of 2017 serves as Al Qaeda's leader.

Alliances   Cooperative arrangements between groups that they perceive as mutually beneficial to both. Alliances between terrorist groups often help them learn from one another in a variety of ways and bolster their individual resources. This type of cooperation can increase a terrorist group's longevity and resilience, particularly in the face of a government whose aim is a group's, elimination.

Al Qaeda (AQ)   Meaning "The Base," Al Qaeda is a global terrorist organization originally founded by Osama Bin Laden in the late 1980s. The group has its origins in the Afghan insurgency against Soviet occupying forces, but dispersed in 1989 to focus its attention on attacking what it considered corrupt Islamic regimes in the Middle East and North Africa (the "near enemy"), and subsequently Western regimes (the "far enemy"). The group has since merged with a number of militant Islamic organizations throughout the world, and is responsible for staging hundreds of attacks that have killed thousands globally (most notably the 9/11 terrorist attacks in the United States).

Al Qaeda in Iraq   The local Al Qaeda affiliate in Iraq. It emerged in response to the 2003 US invasion of Iraq, and also opposed the country's Shiite-dominated government. The group's first leader Abu Musab al-Zarqawi pledged allegiance to Osama Bin Laden in 2004, and launched some of the most destructive terror attacks in Iraq, targeting foreign and Iraqi security forces, government officials, and civilians. The organization lost most of its strength when US forces killed Zarqawi in 2006, and also as a result of its brutal treatment of civilians. The group reinvented itself as the Islamic State (ISIS) beginning in 2011, taking advantage of regional instability to regroup.

Al Qaeda in the Arabian Peninsula   An Al Qaeda's affiliate in the Arabian Peninsula, mostly active in Yemen, though it has claimed responsibility for several acts of international terrorism. The group's most prominent member was Anwar al-Awlaki, an American killed by a US drone strike in September 2011. Since the Houthi ascent to power in Yemen in early 2015, AQAP has prioritized fighting against Houthi expansion, and regularly attacks Yemeni government and military targets.

Al-Shabab   A Salafist jihadist fundamentalist group based in Somalia, which describes itself as engaged in the struggle against the enemies of Islam, as well as the Government of Somalia and African Union forces in the country. Al Shabaab pledged allegiance to Al Qaeda in 2012, and in 2014 experts believed that its membership hovered between seven thousand to nine thousand fighters. The Somali government and foreign forces captured Mogadishu, the capital city, from Al Shabaab in 2011, and the group has mainly retreated to rural areas but still remains active as of 2017.

Anarchism   A philosophy that advocates for the removal of all forms of government, with a reorganization of society on the basis of voluntary, cooperative, nonviolent self-organization.

Anarchist   An individual who subscribes to anarchist philosophy.

Anders Breivik   A far-right lone wolf who killed seventy-seven people and injured hundreds more in a violent rampage on July 22, 2011 in the capital of Norway.

Involved were two back to back attacks, including a car bombing at a government building in central Oslo that killed eight and injured hundreds more, and a second assault at a youth summer camp that killed sixty-eight people and, again, injuring over a hundred more. Before his attacks he sent a manifesto over the Internet attempting to explain his reasons for his actions.

Animal Liberation Front (ALF)   An international eco-terrorist group that formed in 1976 to uphold animal rights, abolish widespread, institutionalized animal exploitation, and end animal abuse generally. The group is active in forty countries, and has used tactics as diverse as booby-trapped mail, bombings, vandalism, and property destruction to achieve its goals. The group has links to People for the Ethical Treatment of Animals (PETA) and other organizations, and operates as a network of small, isolated groups that are rarely in contact with one another.

Ansar Al-Islam (AL or AAI)   A Sunni militant group founded in 2001 and active in Iraq and Syria. The group formed as a result of a merger between two Kurdish extremist factions, and seeks to expel western interests from Iraq in order to form an independent state based on Sharia law. The group has staged a number of attacks against foreign and Iraqi security forces and government officials, and has also staged attacks against civilians in Syria.

Anthrax   Spores of a bacteria spread by contact via breathing (inhaling), eating and contact (absorption) and open skin, thereby causing a potentially deadly infection. The spores have been used as an agent of biological warfare, particularly in the United States in 2001, after the September 11 attacks. Letters containing these spores were mailed to members of the media at several newspapers, and several US senators (Tom Daschle and Patrick Leahy), killing a few people (Robert Stevens at The Sun) and infecting more than twenty.

Antonio Gramsci   An Italian Marxist theorist and politician (1891-1937) whose theories on cultural hegemony have informed a critical discussion explaining how the ruling classes use various symbolic, linguistic, artistic, educational, and cultural institutions to sustain rules and norms that allow the state to consolidate power.

April 19th Movement   The second largest guerrilla movement in Colombia after the FARC, with membership reaching fifteen hundred to two thousand fighters by 1985. The group, which espoused a leftist-nationalist ideology, formed in the wake of fraudulent elections in Colombia on April 19, 1970, and remained active until 1990. It waged a revolutionary struggle against the government, until giving up its weapons to become a political party in the late 1980s (the Alianza Democratica M-19).

Armed Islamic Group of Algeria (GIA)   An Islamist group that fought in the Algerian civil war from 1993-2002. It formed in 1992 following a military coup and unlike other armed groups that fought the government, the GIA explicitly sought to overthrow the ruling regime. The GIA orchestrated a series of civilian massacres from 1992-1998, also launched attacks in France in pursuit of its goal of overthrowing the Algerian government. The GIA split in 2004, and any remaining members who were not offered or did not accept amnesty offered by the government went on to join the Salafist Group for Preaching and Combat (GSPC).

Army of God   A group formed in 1982 as a single-issue terrorist group that acted on an anti-abortion platform motivated by Christian beliefs. The group has used kidnapping, murder, and attempted murder to achieve its aims of eliminating abortion and killing individuals who perform abortions. Its members are devoted to the writings and teachings of Eric Rudolph, the man behind the 1996 bombing at the Atlanta Olympic Games and murders of abortion doctors.

Aryan Nations   A white supremacist religious group founded in the 1970s, believed to be the first nationwide terrorist network to emerge in the United States (Rand Corporation). There are three main Aryan Nation factions, each based in different parts of the country. One of the organization's goals is to instigate a race war, which led several members to commit murders in the 1980s. The group has approximately two hundred active members.

Asymmetric Warfare   A method whereby a militarily weak state resorts to supporting transnational terror as a way to wage warfare against a more powerful opponent.

Assassins, The   A cohort of Nizari Ismailis (a sect of Shia Islam) that formed in the late eleventh century and existed until the fifteenth century. The group targeted political and religious rivals with the aim of establishing a Nizari Islami state within Persia. The Mongol Empire eventually eradicated the group.

Attribution Error   The inferences that people draw about the causes of their own behavior or the behavior of others.

Attrition   One of the five strategies of terrorism, which also include intimidation, provocation, spoiling, and outbidding.

Aum Shinrikyo   A Japanese apocalyptic cult that carried out a series of five coordinated attacks using chemical weapons on Tokyo's subway system on March 20, 1995, killing twelve people and severely injuring fifty others. The group's leader, Shoko Asahara, published a book in which he declared himself Japan's only fully enlightened master, and outlined a doomsday prophecy that foreshadowed the Third World War. In addition to relying on terrorist tactics, the group also engaged in the selection of political candidates to contest local elections.

Aum Shinrikyo Attack on Tokyo's Subway System (1995)   A chemical weapons attack perpetrated on March 20, 1995 in Tokyo, Japan, wherein ten men of the Japanese cult, Aum Shinrikyo, released sarin on several subway lines during rush hour in a series of five coordinated attacks, killing twelve people and severely injuring fifty others. Nearly one thousand people also reported temporary vision problems as a result of the attack. This act of terrorism instigated wide concern among journalists and analysts over the potential of a nuclear terrorist attack in the future.

Authoritarianism   A condition of government where power is concentrated and centralized. It can also refer to a set of beliefs in the rigid nature of authority and socio-political relationships.

B

Baader-Meinhof Gang   A far-left group in West Germany active during the 1970s *(See also Red Army Faction/Rote Armee Fraktion).*

Backfire   A plan or an action that rebounds negatively on the originator, thereby creating the opposite effect as originally intended. In counterterrorism, some government strategies that are particularly repressive may further escalate underlying grievances and empower a terror group to commit even worse acts of violence.

Backlash   A strong and immediate negative reaction to a government response that ultimately undermines the government's long term goals or interests.

Baloch Liberation Army   Militant groups located in Afghanistan and Pakistan fighting mainly for regional autonomy.

Barbarism   Where in some instances of military intervention disintegrate into acts of barbarism by military staff creating even more acts of terrorism against the United States (referring specifically to the Abu Ghraib military prison abuses in Iraq in 2004).

Bargaining   Among social scientists, supports what is known as the strategic approach, and which generally assumes that political outcomes are the result of rational decisions by two or more actors, each seeking to "bargain" in order to achieve their own ends.

Basque Fatherland and Liberty (ETA)   A separatist organization established in the mid 1950s, mainly located in northern Spain and southwestern France. Their general goal is one of achieving independence for the Greater Basque country. Their terrorist efforts, involving bombings and abductions, have involved over sixteen hundred attacks, nearly nine hundred deaths and thousands of citizens injured. Ceasefires have been attempted over the years but all have failed.

Bhagwan Shree Rajneesh (or Osho)   His followers were the first group to organize a CBRN attack on US soil by using salmonella bacteria to poison salad bars in ten restaurants in Dallas, Oregon, which ultimately left forty people hospitalized. The goal was to sicken the town's voting population so that their candidates would prevail in county elections.

Black Panther Party   The group was put under investigation by the FBI on suspicion of being a terrorist organization in 1969. However, it devoted more time and energy to community organizing, mutual aid, and other civic activities than its militant image would imply. The group was founded in 1966 with the original purpose of policing African American neighborhoods to protect individuals from police violence.

Black September   An episode in the history between Palestine and Jordan where the PLO established a base in Jordan after the six-day war wherein Israel seized the West Bank from Jordan. The arrangement worked to ensure that the PLO did not threaten Jordan's leadership; however it subsequently deteriorated as the

PLO continued attacks against Israel, which occasionally created clashes with the Jordanian army and other Palestinian groups (DFLP and PFLP) that challenged the existing Hashemite monarchy. Jordan expelled the PLO and other groups to avoid further attacks in a bloody episode called "Black September," which killed thousands and caused many Palestinians to flee to Lebanon.

Blowback A retaliatory action or revenge activity in response to a provocation. In international relations, it can be the side effect of a government action or operation that had the (intended or unintended) consequence of creating an intense negative response in return.

Boko Haram (BH) An Islamist extremist group primarily based in Nigeria that seeks to overthrow the Nigerian government and replace it with a regime based on Sharia Law. The group provides limited services to Nigerian local populations, but chooses to rely primarily on violence to advance its goals of territorial expansion—especially by conducting attacks in Nigeria as well as in Chad, Niger, and Cameroon. The group is notoriously known for the kidnapping of 276 schoolgirls in 2014 and its violent attacks causing thousands of civilian deaths throughout its existence. The group killed as many as two thousand civilians during a single attack in January 2015. Boko Haram also pledged allegiance to the Islamic State in Iraq and Syria (ISIS) in 2015. The US StateDepartment officially designated Boko Haram as a terrorist organization in 2013.

Boston Tea Party On December 16, 1773, Sam Adams and the Sons of Liberty boarded three ships in Boston Harbor and tossed 345 chests of British tea overboard in protest of the tea tax. This symbolic gesture was a catalyst toward further protests and eventually, the war of independence.

Bounded Rationality The observation that human beings cannot make pure rational choice decisions because of imperfect information and cognitive and emotional barriers to emotionless reasoning. Proponents of bounded rationality emphasize that despite our human limitations, the attempt to make self-interested choices and to find the least costly alternatives for pursuing self-interest is a generalizable pattern among human behavior.

Brigatte Rosse (Red Brigades, BR) A group that subscribed to the Marxist ideology calling for the armed overthrow of the bourgeoisie by the proletariat. The Red Brigades saw the Italian Communist Party's success in the elections as a betrayal of the Marxist imperative to confront and dismantle existing institutions rather than cooperating with them. In 1978, they abducted and murdered the Italian Prime Minister, Aldo Moro, and left his body in an alley near the Communist party's headquarters.

C

Caliphate Technically, a caliphate is the territory ruled by a "caliph", or the head of a community, territorial jurisdiction, or state. The caliph's role is one of a religious and political leader who rules and oversees the affairs of the people in accordance with Islamic rules, laws and principles. The first caliphate was established after the death of Muhammad, founder of Islam, and continued for several centuries.

The last caliphate was held by the Ottomans and ended in the early 1920s. Recently, the leader of the Islamic State, Abu Bakr al-Baghdadi, has claimed the creation of a caliphate in Iraq and Syria in 2014, as part of his goal to take over these territories.

Cambodian Freedom Fighters (CFF) a paramilitary group located generally around the Northeastern Cambodia near the Thai border. It was established in 1989 by Chhun Poipt with the aim of overthrowing the government of Cambodia. Some of the faults of the current regime include corruption, mismanagement and the perpetuation of inequality. It is a US-based group led by Chun Yasith, but with ties to Cambodian-Americans based in Thailand. They conducted attacks during the 1990's and early 2000s, including an attack on government installations that killed eight and wounded dozens. They also planned but were unsuccessful in blowing up a fuel depot outside of Phnom Penh with antitank weapons; its members were caught and arrested. In 2008, the founder of the CFF was tried and convicted in the United States for masterminding a 2000 coup attempt.

CBRN An acronym designating chemical, biological, radiological, and nuclear weapons.

Central Intelligence Agency (CIA) The US's civilian intelligence agency responsible for collecting, analyzing, and disseminating foreign intelligence.

Christian Patriot Movement This radical group emphasizes conspiratorial, anti-government, white supremacist, anti-Semitic, and racist views, believing generally that the federal government has abandoned its ties to liberty, Christianity and fundamental rights. The Oklahoma bombing perpetrator, Timothy McVeigh, claimed a loose affiliation with the group; however, there is no proof that their ideology was the reason or the motivation for his actions.

Christian Identity A far-right, fundamentalist Christian extremist movement that advances the belief that Anglo-Saxon, Nordic, and Germanic peoples are the true descendants of the Biblical Israelites, Jews are descendants of Satan, and the white race is supreme. They claim the righteous must wage war to hasten the end-times described in the Book of Revelation.

Childhood Trauma In the study of terrorist behavior, childhood trauma has been advanced as a theory for whether certain psychological conditions may be involved in why a person may, or may not, become a terrorist. However, because it is difficult, if not impossible, to study this in an empirical way with randomized, controlled experiments, researchers typically do not study these conditions in order to evaluate the differences between terrorists and non-terrorists.

Club Goods Commodities or services characterized as excludable but non-rival, meaning that their benefits accrue only to members of the group providing the good, but their consumption does not reduce the usefulness of the goods to their club members.

Coercion The use of force.

Coercive Effectiveness The ability to coerce an opponent into making concessions.

Cognitive Distortion   A concept closely linked with social cognition theory referring to exaggerated or irrational thought patterns that perpetuate false beliefs, such as the tendency to suppress or ignore information that contradicts one's prior beliefs.

Cognitive Theory   The cognitive theory approach holds that a person's acquired knowledge relates to how they have observed the behavior of others within their social interactions, experiences, or other external influences. When people witness certain types of behavior and the consequences of that behavior, they remember the sequence of events and use the information to guide and shape their own future behaviors.

Cognitive Therapy   Therapy intended to promote a different set of behaviors, which might provide pathways to influencing attitudes and beliefs away from an existing behavior.

Collective Punishment   A form of punishment whereby a suspected perpetrator's entire family, workplace, neighborhood, or ethnic group is targeted with retaliatory action.

Collectivism   Where a group's interests has priority over the individual's interests. This is particularly influential in the study of terrorism where cultural, ethnic, or religious identity may affect terrorism choices.

Communist Party of India–Maoist (CPI-M)   A group founded in 2004 following a merger of the Maoist Communist Centre of India (MCC) and the Communist Party of India (Marxist-Leninist). The objective of the group (also called Naxalite) in India was to overthrow those in power and establish a new socialist state and further the cause of revolution in India. The group is part of the broader Naxalite-Maoist insurgency in India.

Communist Party of Nepal (Maoist)/United People's Front   This group was founded in 1994 as a result of a split within the communist party of Nepal. The group engaged in a guerilla war that lasted four years and killed multiple thousands. Their purpose was to defeat the forces of the central government and end the Nepalese monarchy. After a United Nations brokered peace treaty ended the insurgency, the group eventually was able to engage in the political process, winning seats in Parliament, and the Nepalese monarchy was dissolved. Many of the fighters were incorporated into the army of the new republic. *(See also United People's Front of Nepal)*

Communist Party of Philippines/New People's Army (CPP/NPA)   The CPP was formed in 1968 as a Marxist/Leninist movement seeking to overthrow the government and replace it with a state led by the working class. They also sought to remove US colonial influence. Its armed group, the NPA, was founded in 1969. The group, referred to as CPP-NPA, was listed as a terrorist orgnization by the US in 2002, but the Philippine government de-listed it in 2011. The groupo engaged in a number of student demonstrations, protests and rallies through the 70s and 80s, mainly in opposition to Ferdinand Marco's regime. The group is still active.

Conciliatory Actions   A willingness to appease, dismiss, or end an existing disagreement demonstrated through some affirmative action or behavior.

Constitutive Constructivist A type of constructivist that is interested in identifying where ideas and identities come from, and how such ideas and identities motivate human behavior.

Constructivist A school of thought in international relations that speculates that particular beliefs, ideas, and identities are the most important factors in explaining how individuals, groups, and states behave.

Containment The ability to restrict a terrorist group to a particular locality, type of attack, or technology.

Context as Permissive When the underlying environment and circumstances create the means, reasons, or motivation for terrorists to seek political change and perceive terrorism as a viable option.

Continuity Irish Republican Army (CIRA) An armed Irish separatist group resulting from a split in the Provisional IRA in 1986. The group was essentially inactive until the Provisional ceasefire of 1994, when it conducted its first attack in the Irish town of Enniskillen. In 2004, the United States declared the CIRA a Foreign Terrorist Organization.

Contras, The A series of US-supported death squads in Central America that relied on terror against civilian populations to intimidate and overthrow the government. They ultimately expelled the socialist Sandinista government in Nicaragua.

Cosa Nostra A euphemism for the Italian mafia.

Cost-Benefit Calculation A process involving the analysis of the strengths and weaknesses of alternative actions or decisions.

Costly Signaling When people engage in altruistic acts—those that involve sacrifice—to convey or communicate a signal about themselves, for example, to demonstrate their status, resources, money, time, and/or influence.

Countering Violent Extremism (CVE) A term referring to early prevention programs implemented by Western states, meant to complement traditional hard power counterterrorism instruments. These programs are characterized by broad-brushed approaches consisting of a range of non-coercive tools and programs developed by community organizations and government partners that are focused on both countering radicalization and fostering network and trust-building mechanisms.

Counterinsurgency A range of military, political, economic, psychological, civic, and other actions or policies aimed at protecting a population and restoring the legitimacy of the government, typically in response to an insurgency aimed at the existing regime.

Counter-radicalization An anticipatory risk-reduction program or policy aimed at deterring those possibly disaffected individuals from conditions which may propel or radicalize them into becoming terrorists.

Counterterrorism A range of policies adopted in response to, and to counter, future acts of terrorism. Counterterrorism can involve the use of the military, law enforcement, intelligence agencies, political offices, community groups, and/or private sector, either in unison as part of a coherent strategy, or in more piecemeal fashion as specific terrorist threats arise. Counterterrorism can also be a component of or be confounded with counterinsurgency operations, depending on context. Today, many Western governments make counterterrorism a top national security priority where most counterterrorism strategies involve increasing standard police operations and domestic intelligence gathering.

Critical Explanations Explanations that view terrorism and counterterrorism as functions of politics alone. Instead of seeing counterterrorism as the natural outgrowth of legitimate threats, critical terrorism scholars see counterterrorism policies as an active manipulation of the population by the state as an effort to consolidate power and maintain the status quo.

Critical Race Theory An application of critical theory to race; a new set of lenses through which to look at the relationship between race, racism, and power.

Critical Terrorism Studies A theory that rejects the notion that the phenomenon of terrorism exists as such. In the view of critical studies scholars, terror is used as a tactic by a variety of state and non-state actors, and thus we should not be studying terrorism as a phenomenon. According to critical terrorism studies, the use of the term is problematic given that terrorism occurs in the context of wider political struggles in which the use of other contentious tactics is also prominent. Critical terrorism scholars see counterterrorism policies as a form of political theater wherein states seek to replenish their authority and legitimacy in the eyes of a terrorized population.

Cross-Generational Failure The failure of a terrorist group to pass on its cause and vision of its goals to the next generation.

Cultural Hegemony A concept derived by Antonio Gramsci depicting how the ruling classes use various symbolic, linguistic, artistic, educational, and cultural institutions to sustain rules and norms that allow the state to consolidate power.

D

Death to Kidnappers A paramilitary organization active in Colombia during the 1980s that frequently targeted communist insurgents from the April 19th Movement or the FARC, as well as their supporters, to protect the economic interests of drug cartels and Colombian politicians.

Decapitation The capture or killing of a group's leader.

Decentralization The delegation or diffusion of power, people, or things from central to local.

Defense Intelligence Agency (DIA) The US's military intelligence and combat support agency within the Department of Defense.

Delta Force A special unit in the US Army whose specific responsibilities involve responding to terrorist attacks and extracting civilians from hostage situations.

Democracy A system of government relying on rule by the people. Indicators of democracy include representative government by freely-elected officials, political participation through voting, free political competition among political parties or organized groups, separation of powers between executive, legislative, and judicial power, and respect for various civil liberties.

Demonstration Effect A process where groups emulate and adopt methods seen to succeed elsewhere.

Democratic Front for the Liberation of Palestine (DFLP) A splinter organization from the PLO in 1969. Among other actions, it advocated disruption of the Hashemite regime in Jordan, and was subsequently expelled from Jordan. Its focus is replacing Israel with a Palestinian state for both Arabs and Jews. Its terrorist activities have been limited to actions against Israel and within the occupied territories. It has not operated internationally. Its methods have included use of bombs, rocks, grenades, and kidnapping hostages to be bargained for the return of Palestinians.

Department of Homeland Security (DHS) US federal government agency founded by President George W. Bush in 2002 in reaction to the September 11th attacks tasked with protecting the nation by preventing terrorism and enhancing security, securing and managing US borders, enforcing and administering US immigration laws, safeguarding and securing cyberspace, and ensuring the country's resilience to disasters.

Department of Justice (DOJ) The United States' executive department responsible for administering the Federal Bureau of Investigation (FBI), running the federal prison system, reviewing actions of law enforcement, and enforcing civil rights legislation and all federal laws.

Dependent Variable The outcome of interest. It depends upon, or responds to, the independent variable.

Deradicalization A method, or methods, used to suspend or reduce radical or extreme positions or views.

Determinism A theory arguing that people are so strongly conditioned by their environments that their actions are more or less predetermined, automatic, and inevitable.

Deterrence The practice of preventing an action through both offensive and defensive postures that impose a fear of punishment or retribution on the opponent.

Deterrence Theory A theory which posits that fear of punishment or retribution controls the behavior of individuals or groups.

Diffusion Spread, dispersal, or scattering.

Discriminate Focus on single target.

Displaced Responsibility A condition where people conceive of their actions as springing from the dogma of authorities, rather than from their own volition.

Domestic Terrorism   Refers to terrorist incidents that start and end within a sovereign country.

Dovish (*see also Hawkish*)   Peaceful, docile, passive, placid or non-aggressive, as opposed to aggressive, focused, demanding or insistent.

Drones   A common term used to refer to Unmanned Aerial Vehicles (UAVs).

Dyadic   The interaction between two things.

Dynamic System   A system with ever-changing social relationships that are interdependent with one another.

E

Earth First!   A single-issue, radical environmental advocacy group founded in the United States in 1980. Their terrorist tactic of choice is civil disobedience against various companies, including those involved in logging (1985) and livestock companies (1989) and a ski resort in Colorado (1991).

Earth Liberation Front (ELF)   Also referred to as the "Elves," this group formed in the United Kingdom in 1992. Members employ sabotage, guerrilla warfare, and domestic terrorism to stop the exploitation of the environment. They conducted an attack involving vandalism in Eugene, Oregon in 1995. In 1998, the ELF claimed responsibility for an arson that burned down five buildings and four chairlifts at the Vail Mountain Ski Resort in Vail, Colorado.

Eastern Turkistan Islamic Movement (ETIM)   A Muslim separatist organization founded in 1989 by militant Uighurs belonging to a Turkic-speaking ethnic majority in a province in China. Between 1990 and 2001 it is claimed that the group committed more than two hundred acts of terrorism, causing at least 162 deaths and more than 440 injuries.

Economic Grievances   A possible underlying monetary or financial cause (or contribution) for individual or group terrorist activity.

Egyptian Islamic Jihad   An Egyptian movement from 1970's. Its original goal was reform in Egypt and rejection of its secular government. It engaged in a series of assassination attempts and eventually the successful killing of Anwar Sadat in 1981. It eventually joined with Osama bin Laden and the Al Qaeda network in the 1980s and proceeded with additional terrorist acts after that. It opposed western influence in the Muslim world and rejected secularism and America's support for Israel. It has been active worldwide on the terrorism stage and has played key parts in both attacks on the World Trade Center in the United States.

Ejército de Liberación Nacional (ELN)   A leftist group active in Colombia since 1964.

Emancipation   The constant respect for human rights, social, economic, and political justice and equality, and an end to discrimination and violence in all forms.

Empirical Terrorism Studies   an approach to the study of terrorism that aspires to find objective, observable patterns of behavior.

Enabling Factors Preconditional factors that provide opportunities for terrorism to occur and situations that can be construed as direct motivations for actors and groups to engage in terrorism.

Enemy-Centric Doctrines An approach used in counterterrorism strategies to isolate or destroy terrorist groups by employing tactics such as drone strikes, military interventions, military occupations, Special Forces operations, and/or increased policing and intelligence operations.

Epistemological The study of knowledge to understand the origins, methods and validation practices involved in developing consensus, knowledge, and belief.

Ernesto "Che" Guevara Che Guevara constructed the concept of service provision by militant organizations derived from his theory of guerilla warfare, which highlights the necessity of a rebel group's duty to help the local population by providing clothing and food while also representing the aspirations of the local populace.

Escalatory Effect An increased or heightened consequence to an action.

Essentialism The practice of assigning fixed attributes to an identity group. For instance, gender essentialism is the tendency to assume that all women possess certain attributes associated with femininity (e.g., the notion that women are innately more peaceful than men).

Ethnocentrism A set of ideological arguments that focuses on the ways in which people divide their social worlds into "virtuous ingroups and nefarious outgroups" (Kam and Kinder 2008).

Euskadi Ta Askatasuna (Basque Fatherland and Freedom, ETA) A militant, Basque nationalist and separatist organization in northern Spain and southwestern France established in 1959 with the goal of gaining independence for the Greater Basque Country.

Expected Utility An anticipated result based on a specific objective.

External Linkages Connections between groups.

F

Faction A splinter, fragment, or diminutive entity typically operating under the umbrella of a larger organization or group.

Failed State Also referred to as a "weak state". Typically a failed state occurs when the state is unable to control its territory, citizens and institutions, thereby fostering a vacuum of power from which other groups may seize an opportunity to exert their will or become opportunistic.

Far Left Outside of the politically left mainstream so as to be considered on the "extreme" left.

Far Right Outside of the politically right mainstream so as to be considered on the "extreme" right.

Fascism A nationalistic ideology characterized by the rejection of liberal democracy, communism and anarchism as valid doctrines. Instead, it calls for a typically right-wing militarized citizenry ruled by a powerful authoritarian leader.

Federal Bureau of Investigation (FBI) The federal agency within the United States responsible for investigating and interdicting threats posed by domestic actors.

Feminism An ideology that has worked to mobilize individuals, in particular women, towards violence and terrorism. Basically some women may decide to join a terrorist group as part of a struggle for the liberation of women in their societies.

First of October Antifascist Resistance Group (GRAPO) An armed Maoist group founded in 1975 with the aim of creating a Spanish Republican state based on Mao's model of the People's Republic of China. They murdered Spanish policemen in 1975 and gained notoriety in 1975 and 1976 with several abductions.

Forces Démocratique de Liberation du Rwanda (FDLR) A group formed in 2000 by Rwandan Hutus associated with the 1994 genocide, including members of the former Rwandan government and army, in the Democratic Republic of Congo (DRC).

Formal Models An explanatory descriptor capable of analysis and testing using logical methods or rules.

Fragmentation The fracturing or breaking up of a group into parts.

Free Aceh Movement (GAM) A separatist Islamic group formed in the 1970s in the Indonesian archipelago seeking an independent state from Indonesia. The insurgent movement has continued for many decades.

Front De Liberation Nationale (FLN) The FLN emerged in 1954 in French-occupied Algeria and became the face of the Algerian struggle for independence. The war continued until 1962 when the French signed a cease fire agreement with the FLN, in Evian-les-Bains. Thereafter the FLN became involved in the political process and has performed well in subsequent elections.

Fundamentalist Ideologies A literalist interpretation of an idea, doctrine or dogma that typically defines itself in terms of distinctions, polarizations and otherness.

G

Game A political interaction between two or more actors where each actor—whether terror group, government, or some other actor—brings to bear its own best guess regarding how it can achieve its political goals.

Gangs/Drug Cartels Organized groups of criminals / an organized group of criminals involved in supplying drugs and the trafficking of drugs.

Gender Analysis An analytical process aimed at understanding how gender matters in shaping relationships. With regard to the topic of terrorism, gender analysis seeks to identify and analyze the implications of approaching terrorism with a gendered lens. For instance, proponents of gender analysis suggest that gender is important to build our understanding of why women participate in terror, and why certain dynamics might occur within organizations.

Gender Differentiation The extent to which gender affects the assignment and expectations of social, political, and inter-personal roles in a society.

Gender Lens A point of view that focuses on how gender might impact relationships, behaviors, and systems.

Gender vs. Sex Whereas gender describes "the socially constituted behavioral expectations, stereotypes, and rules that construct masculinity and femininity," (Sjoberg and Gentry 2011: 6), sex refers explicitly to one's biological maleness or femaleness. These are terms that people frequently used interchangeably but do not mean the same thing.

Globalization An array of trends highlighting the increasing movement of people and goods, technological progress, secularization, democratization, consumerism, or the growth of market capitalism.

Global North A term often used synonymously with rich, developed countries of the world.

Global South A term often used synonymously with poor countries of the world.

Global Terrorism Database (GTD) A database collected by researchers at the University of Maryland. The database includes open-source reports of domestic, transnational, and international terrorist incidents worldwide from 1970 through 2015. It releases annual updates, and the data are available at https://www.start. umd.edu/gtd/about/.

Global War on Terrorism (GWOT) The international campaign against terrorism launched by President George W. Bush in response to the Al Qaeda terrorist attacks on September 11, 2001. The GWOT consisted largely of military operations (particularly in Iraq and Afghanistan) and new security legislation in order to combat terrorism at home and abroad.

Governance The practice of governing by governments of other organized groups or actors.

GRAPO (*See First October Antifascist Resistance Group*)

Group Psychology A set of psychological approaches focusing on the behavior and dynamics of groups. In the context of terrorism, these approaches take group-level dynamics into consideration to explain terrorist behavior or counterterrorism.

Groupe Islamiste Armé (GIA) (*See Armed Islamic Group of Algeria*)

Groupe Salafiste pour la Prédication et le Combat (GSPC) A Salafist jihadist faction formed during the Algerian Civil War in 1998 by Hassan Hattab as a splinter group of the Groupe Islamiste Armé (GIA). *(See also Salafist Group for Call and Combat)*

Groupthink A psychological phenomenon that occurs within a group of people in which the desire for conformity in the group results in a somewhat irrational and at times dysfunctional decision-making outcome (Janis 1972). Members of the group attempt to minimize conflict and reach a consensus decision without critical evaluation of alternatives, and thus actively suppress dissenting viewpoints and isolate themselves from external influence. In the context of counterterrorism, groupthink may be a source of counterproductive counter-terrorism actions for governments since the process highlights their inability to adjust to new information, or accurately assess their own influence on the situation.

Gush Emunim An apocalyptic, Jewish ultra-nationalist group that plotted to blow up the Dome of the Rock in Jerusalem to provoke a massive confrontation between Israel and Muslim-majority countries.

H

Haganah A Zionist faction operating in the British Mandate of Palestine.

Hamas (*see Islamic Resistance Movement*)

Hardening Targets The process of strengthening the physical security of a building or site in order to deter or mitigate a potential attack or threat.

Hard Power Tangible means of power. This typically refers to the use of military and/or economic means to coercively influence the behavior of other state or non-state actors. Hard power counterterrorism instruments are those that deploy tangible sources of power such as the military or police forces to attack, punish, and deter purported terrorists (and sometimes their constituents) to the point that terrorism is no longer appealing.

Harmony Program An archive housed at the Combating Terrorism Center at West Point, which publishes documents recovered from Al Qaeda and other jihadi groups during US military operations.

Hawkish (*see also Dovish*) Aggressive, focused, demanding or insistent, as opposed to peaceful, docile, passive, placid or non-aggressive.

High-Casualty Attacks (*see Mass Casualties*)

Hijacking of Air Malta 830 On June 9, 1997, two Turkish men hijacked Air Malta 830 and demanded that the pilot divert the plane from Istanbul to Germany. The two men claimed that their goal was to secure the release of Mehmet Ali Agca, who was in prison for his attempted assassination of Pope John Paul II in 1981. The incident resulted in no casualties, and the hijackers received four- and five-year prison terms.

Hizballah (Party of God)   A Lebanese Shi'a Islamist militant organization arising in the early 1980's. The group has an anti-Zionist and anti-imperialist stance and receives support from Iran. It is often credited with a well-known attack on the US Marine Corps barracks in Beirut in 1983. More generally, the group engaged in a long-enduring fight against Israeli occupation of southern Lebanon, which ultimately resulted in Israel's withdrawal from Lebanon in 2000. Since 2005, the group has been active in Lebanese parliament after performing well in elections there. In 2006 the group kidnapped two Israeli soldiers sparking another war with Israel. In 2008, they seized parts of Beirut and in July 2011, the UN indicted four members for the assassination of Prime Minister Rafiq al-Hairiri, killed by a car bomb in Beirut in 2006. In 2012, the group detonated a bomb on a bus in Bulgaria, killing five Israeli tourists. Since 2012 they have supported Bashar al-Assad in the Syrian Civil War. The EU designated Hizballah's military wing as a terrorist organization in 2013.

I

Ideological Approach   The analytic approach that assumes that the dominant beliefs of an actor supply that actor with an initial motive for action, and provide a lens through which to interpret events and the actions of others.

Imperfect Information   The situation or process in which actors do not have access to complete or accurate information, raising the level of uncertainty.

Improvised Explosive Devices (IEDs)   Easy-to-assemble devices consisting of commonly available materials such as flammable gas or liquids used to create explosives.

Indiscriminate   A policy that does not differentiate between the intended targets, sympathizers, or bystanders.

Indira Gandhi   Former Prime Minister of India (1966-1977, 1980-1984). She presided over Operation Blue Star, a controversial raid on the Golden Temple in Armitsar, Punjab in 1984, which resulted in the deaths of many militants and civilians. Several of her Sikh bodyguards assassinated her in retaliation for Operation Blue Star on October 31, 1984.

Individual Desistance   When an individual voluntarily exits a group or ceases to practice a certain behavior.

Individual Psychological Approaches   A set of psychological approaches that focus on the individual level of analysis, meaning that they attempt to differentiate the personal traits of people who use terrorism from those who do not.

Infiltration   The practice of entering a group or community undetected, usually in an attempt to conduct surveillance, disrupt the group or community, or subvert the group or community's goals.

Innate vs. Acquired   Refers to an ongoing controversy within psychological approaches regarding whether people are born with their traits or whether they develop traits as a result of their environments.

Innovation   The creation of new tactics, methods, technologies, or ideas.

Instrumental   Purposive, strategic, and/or rational process aimed at producing a certain intended outcome.

Insurgency   An organized, protected politico-military struggle designed to weaken the control and legitimacy of an established government, occupying power, or other political authority while increasing insurgent control (see Nagl et al. 2008: 1-2).

Inter-Group Violence   Where organized groups violently attack one another's constituencies.

Intra-Group Violence   Where organized groups escalate violence within and against their own constituencies to compete with other groups operating within their own constituencies (*see also Outbidding*).

Internecine Violence   Violence that occurs within the same nation, population, or group.

Intimidation   In the context of terrorism, a strategy aimed at controlling a population through fear.

Irgun   A Zionist nationalist group operating in British Mandate Palestine between 1931 and 1948. They claimed the killing of a British Police Officer and head of the Jewish Department in the Palestinian police, as well as two famous bombing attacks against the King David Hotel in Jerusalem in 1946 and the Deir Yassin massacre in 1948.

Irish National Liberation Army (INLA)   A group founded in 1974 as a republican socialist paramilitary organization seeking to break away from the United Kingdom and set up an independent socialist republic. Its first attack was in 1975 followed by a bombing in 1982. In 2009 the group announced that it was renouncing violence and seeking to pursue its aims through more peaceful political methods.

Irish Republican Army (IRA)   The Irish Republican Army was established in 1919, but became an armed wing of the political movement Sin Fein in 1969. Its goal is an independent Irish republic, separate from British rule. In their efforts to remove British forces from the North and the re-unification of Ireland, they conducted numerous attacks, including bombings, assassinations, kidnappings and robberies, until a cease-fire in 1997 where they agreed to disarm as part of the 1998 Belfast Agreement. This led to the fracturing into radical splinter groups, such as the Continuity IRA (CIRA) and Real IRA (RIRA) in the mid-1990s. As of 2015, elements of the IRA continue, but it is no longer engaged in terrorism or paramilitary activity.

Irish Special Branch   The first-known counterterrorism unit established by Great Britain in the 1880s in response to escalating violence carried out by the Irish Fenians, who sought to end British rule in Ireland.

Islamic Movement of Uzbekistan (IMU) The IMU, initially named Adolat ("justice") was founded in Uzbekistan in 1991. Its goal was the implementation of a Shari'a Islamic state. Its campaign against the Uzbek government came to an end around 2001, and group members disbursed into smaller cells located in Afghanistan and Pakistan, where they continue to operate with suicide bombings, attacks against the Haqqani network and other targets directed closer to their bases, rather than against their original goal, Uzbekistan. A new faction emerged in 2016 wherein they announced their pro-Taliban, pro Al Qaeda stance. The IMU remains active today.

Islamic Salvation Front (FIS) One of the two prominent warring Islamist insurgency movements that fought the Algerian government during the civil war in the 1990s. The FIS began as an Algerian Islamist political party founded in 1989 with a core objective of establishing an Islamic state ruled by Shariah Law. In 1992, the FIS turned to violence after the National Liberation Army nullified the results of the national elections to prevent a FIS electoral victory and banned the group.

Islamic State in Iraq and Syria (ISIS) An offshoot of Al Qaeda in Iraq that developed into its own full-blown insurgency in 2014, when it expelled Iraqi military forces out of much of Western Iraq, captured the important city of Mosul, and established bases of control within Syria (including the city of Raqqa). Once it established territorial control, the group proclaimed itself a caliphate called the Islamic State. Like Al Qaeda, the group follows a neo-Wahhabi, Sunni fundamentalist religious doctrine and has inspired and/or directed terror attacks in many countries around the world. However, the group controlled far more territory and attracted far more active members than Al Qaeda, with many people traveling to Iraq and Syria to participate in a strict Islamic society. The group is known for its hyper-brutal acts of violence, including crucifixions, public executions, mass rape, and immolation of its perceived enemies. It is also known for its exploitation of modern technology, including social media platforms, to spread its message and attract followers. The group engages in various forms of illicit behavior, including the sale of contraband (antiquities), the seizing and sale of oil, slavery, and sex trade.

Islamic Resistance Movement Colloquially known as Hamas, the Islamic Resistance Movement is a Palestinian Sunni Islamist group founded in 1987 and has routinely used violence against Israel since. In 2006, Hamas won the majority of parliamentary seats in election in the Gaza Strip, becoming the ruling government in 2007. As a result of its status as the legitimately elected government of Palestinians in Gaza, many major powers including Russia, Turkey, China, Iran, and most Arab countries, do not consider Hamas a terrorist organization, although the United States, the European Union, Israel, Japan, Canada, Jordan, and Egypt continue to do so.

Islamism The view that Islamic law should govern political and public life.

J

Jamaat-u-Dawa (JuD) The JuD is a group operating in Pakistan. It has recently been called a "front organization" for the Lashkar-e-Tayyba (LeT), a group fighting at the Pakistan-India border. The LeT was accused of the 2008 Mumbai attacks that killed nearly two hundred. The US State Department named the JuD a terrorist organization in 2014, after designating the LeT a terrorist organization back in 2001. The JuD claimed to be an organization focused on a peaceful mission of preaching Islam and engaging in charitable community activities; but this is disputed by the media based on recent activities. The group remains active today.

Jamiat-ul-Mujahedin (JUM)   The JUM was founded in 1990 with Sheikh Abdul Basit as a small pro-Pakistan organization located in Indian-controlled Kashmir, fighting against the Indian military and political targets. Its followers are mainly Kashmiris, and is operated primarily as a military organization with a commander and vice-commander. The group remains active today.

Japanese Red Army   This group formed in 1970 after splitting from the Japanese Communist League. Its overall plan was to overthrow the Japanese government and monarchy and pursue a global revolution. During the 1970s the group conducted a massacre in 1972 at Lod Airport in Israel, conducted an airline hijacking and an unsuccessful takeover of the embassy in Kuala Lumpur. The group, led by Fusako Shigenobu, renounced revolutionary violence in 2001, after her arrest, when she stated her commitment to pursue the group's goals through political means.

Jarnail Singh Bhindranwale   A Sikh fundamentalist who advocated the expansion of rights for Sikhs. This was notable in his endorsement of the Anandpur Resolution in the early 1980s. The resolution was largely construed as a secessionist document by Indira Gandhi's Congress Party-led government, precipitating a direct conflict with the Indian government. After seizing and occupying the Golden Mosque in Amristrar, Punjab, Bhindranwale died during the subsequent assault known as Operation Blue Star in 1984.

Jemaah Islamiya (JI)   The JI is a jihadist organization founded in the early 1990s, with cells widely diffused throughout Indonesia. It seeks to establish a caliphate in Southeast Asia. It conducted its first attacks in the late 1990s, including bombings of western interests between 2002 and 2005 that killed more than two hundred people. JI's co-founder, Abu Bakar Bashir, pledged loyalty to ISIS in 2014. The group has links to the 2001 World Trade Center bombing as well as to Al Qaeda and the Abu Sayyaf groups.

Jihad   An Arabic term referring to an internal struggle within oneself or a quest or struggle in the world.

K

Kach Movement   An ultra-nationalist Jewish group.

Kaczynski, Ted (*See Unabomber*)

Kahane Chai (*see also Kach*)   An Israeli militant group seeking to expel Arabs from the Biblical territory of Israel through violent means. The group has used terrorism as methods to expand Jewish rule across the West Bank and to expel Palestinians. The group is one of several that follows the nationalist teachings of the late Rabbi Meir Kahane, a US-born extremist. The group's attacks have included opening fire on civilians in the Ibrahimi Mosque in Hebron, killing twenty-nine people and wounding dozens. Kanaists have shot, stabbed and thrown grenades at Palestinians in Jerusalem. There are no reported attacks since 1994, although there have been minor attacks since 2000 according to State Department reports.

Kahanism   Doctrine that suggests that Arabs were enemies of the Jews and Israel, that Israel should be a Jewish theocracy, that all Jews should be educated enough about the Torah to qualify as rabbis, and that Jews should settle and occupy their historical homelands of Judea and Samaria (what Palestinians refer to as the West Bank).

Kamikaze   A Japanese term adopted during World War II in reference to suicide missions wherein Japanese pilots deliberately crashed their planes into enemy targets.   It is widely believed that the kamikaze movement evolved out of desperation when it became evident that Japan was going to lose the war against the United States, which led to the kamikaze pilots to weaponize their deaths to ensure that they would kill as many Americans as possible. Two hundred pilots engaged in suicide attacks during the Battle of Okinawa in April 1945, killing about five thousand American soldiers.

Kosovo Liberation Army   An ethnic Albanian Kosovar militant group that used terrorist tactics at times to pursue its goal of secession from Serbia. The group is now represented in the government of the Republic of Kosovo.

Ku Klux Klan (KKK)   A white-supremacist extremist group active in the United States since 1866. The group uses biblical references to formulate a racist ideology and carry out far-right terror. The group has used distortions of Christianity to justify killings in the United States and is currently among the longest active terror groups in the world.

Kurdish Workers' Party (PKK, Kadek)/Kongra-Gel (KGK)   founded in 1978, this militant organization based in Turkey sought the creation of a Kurdish state. Since 2010, the PKK has perpetrated hundreds of attacks in Turkey, according to the GTD. In 2015 it declared a willingness to accept a ceasefire agreement under US supervision; however, in 2016 it called for a revolutionary overthrow of the Turkish government and an end of capitalism, culminating with a failed coup attempt. The conflict between the Turkish government and Kurdish nationalists has cost more than forty thousand lives, thousands of destroyed villages, and thousands of internally displaced Kurds.

Kumpulan Mujahidin Malaysia (KMM)   commencing activities in 1999, this terrorist organization supported an Islamic state in southern Thailand, Indonesia and the southern Philippines. Local reports claim that the KMM was disbanded in 2014.

L

Lashkar-e-Taiba (LeT)   established in 1987 in Pakistan, the group is allied with Al Qaeda and is one of the larger and most active South Asian terrorist organizations. It claimed responsibility for a 2001 attack at the Indian Parliament and an attack in Mumbai that left 164 dead. It has been declared a terrorist organization by both the British and American governments.

Lashkar-i-Jhangvi (LiJ) created in 1996, this Sunni jihadist group has claimed responsibility for the 1997 killing of four US oil workers in Karachi, Pakistan, as well as a bus bombing resulting in fifteen deaths. The United States designated the LiJ a terrorist group in 2003.

Leadership Decapitation a counterterrorism or counterinsurgency tactic that aims to eliminate a group's leadership by arresting or assassinating them.

Leaderless Resistance refers to decentralized group structures, where members of a resistance autonomously organize without a central leadership or figurehead guiding them.

Least-Preferred Outcome an outcome producing the lowest level of satisfaction.

Liberation Tigers of Tamil Eelam (LTTE) Commonly known as the "Tamil Tigers," this is a separatist organization founded in 1972 by Velupillai Prabhakaran, with the goal of an independent homeland for the country's minority in Northern Sri Lanka. Since 1980 it has been the dominant Tamil militant group in the county. A large conflict ensued between the LTTE and the government, leaving more than seventy thousand dead. In its path of terrorism, LTTE members carried out assassinations of several Indian officials. It had use of an effective military, suicide unit and was known for using children and women in combat. The LTTE is reputed for having received overseas financial support. Reportedly, the LTTE disbanded due to military defeat in 2009 but may be in the process of reactivation.

Lone Wolves People who engage in terror activities individually, without belonging to or acting on behalf an organized group.

Lord's Resistance Army (LRA) a group founded in 1987 by Joseph Kony in Uganda aimed at overthrowing the Ugandan government and restoring (Kony's) Christian values. The group is credited with massacres, torture, rape and mutilations aimed at the local Acholi communities as well as the abduction of thousands of children to use as sex slaves and child soldiers. The United States listed the LRA on the terrorist list in 2001. The group still appears to be active.

Loyalist Volunteer Force (LVF) the LVF is a Protestant paramilitary separatist group in Northern Ireland, formed in 1996 when it splintered from the Ulster Volunteer Force (UVF). Its stated goal has been combatting Irish republicanism and preventing a political settlement with Irish nationalists. Its targets are primarily Catholic civilians. The LVF is a proscribed organization in the United Kingdom and designated as a terrorist organization by the United States and the Republic of Ireland.

M

Ma'alim fi al-Tariq ("Milestones") A basis for Qutbism; it is a text by Sayyid Qutb that argues the global Muslim community has been suppressed and replaced by a corrupt and evil system of secular values, ideas, and rules. To overcome, sharia law must be revived and imposed by an Islamic vanguard to impose a complete moral, political, social, and legal system.

Maoism A far-left theory of revolution that emphasizes the permanence in political, social, and economic revolution and stresses the primacy of peasants, small-scale, state-owned industry, and agricultural collectivization.

Maoist Communist Center of India (MCCI) a group founded in India in 1979 after an uprising in Bengal which was brutally suppressed by the then government. Its goals were revolution and the abolition of class hierarchies. As with some other terror organization, it provided services to the community in the form of support for hospitals, schools, water supply, and creation of a parallel court system.

Martyrdom a concept that refers to death as a glorious act worthy of eternal bliss. For instance, some jihadi groups rationalize suicide terrorism as martyrdom operations that are praiseworthy embraces of death at the hands of the enemy, making such tactics legitimate in battle instead of sinful.

Marxism A far-left theory of revolution based on the writings of Karl Marx and Georg Wilhelm Friedrich Hegel. The theory argues the only way for the system to correct itself is for the working class (the proletariat) to revolt against the capitalist class (the bourgeoisie), recapture the means of production, and distribute wealth equally across classes. The ideology became the basis for many Communist parties, social movements seeking economic justice, and revolutionary movements.

Mass Casualties casualties that overwhelm the capabilities of first responders.

Mass Surveillance the in-depth monitoring of a substantial proportion of the population.

Meir Kahane an American-Israeli rabbi who promulgated an ultra-nationalist Jewish ideology and founded both the ultra-right Jewish Defense League and the political party Kach ("Thus").

Militarism an attitude or culture where the government or population values a strong military and favors the use of the military above other alternatives in the pursuit and defense of national interests.

Moral Disengagement the psychological process of disengaging from the moral barriers to conducting inhumane acts. The process typically involves the development of a new moral justification, the displacement of responsibility, the distortion of consequences, the attribution of blame to victims, and dehumanization of victims.

Moral Hazard the lack of incentives to avoid or protect against risky activity because one does not bear the consequences of the activity.

Motivated Bias the tendency to see what one wants to see. Motivated Bias can be a primary driver of government's poor policy decisions.

Movement for the Emancipation of the Niger Delta (MEND) A loose group consisting of many factions operating in Nigeria's Niger Delta Region since late-2005. Its goal, mainly pursed through violent acts against oil infrastructure and kidnappings for ransom of oil workers, is primarily for control of the oil resources in the region. Thus, their actions have primarily been focused on the disruption of the global oil supply as leverage for financial resources and media attention on their economic neglect. The group remains active at the present time, though not in a united structure.

Mujahideen   A loose network of jihadist warriors that ultimately consolidated themselves as the Taliban in Afghanistan. The group fought against Soviet military intervention from 1979 to 1989, expelling the Soviet Union from Afghanistan with the help of US efforts that armed and financed them as part of a decade-long operation called Operation Cyclone conducted by the US Central Intelligence Agency. At the end of the Afghan civil war in 1996, the Taliban overran Afghanistan and declared itself the ruling government of the country. In the same year, the leader of the group, Mullah Muhammad Omar, granted entry to Osama bin Laden, which opened the door to the presence of Al Qaeda in Afghanistan. From 2001 to 2014, the United States led an offensive war in Afghanistan aimed at attacking Al Qaeda in response to the September 11th terrorist attacks, which in part involved removing the Taliban from power.

Mujahedin-E Khalq Organization (MeK or MKO)   A group founded in 1965 in opposition to the Shah's regime in Iran. The United States listed it as a terrorist organization due to killings of US personnel in Iran in the 1970s. The group helped overthrow the Shah in 1979, but was forced into exile in the early 1980s. It moved operations to Iraq in the mid-1980s, but Iraq expelled the group in 2009.

Mullah Muhammad Omar   the first leader of the Taliban in Afghanistan. He granted entry to Osama bin Laden and his network in 1996 after Saudi Arabia and Sudan had expelled Al Qaeda. He lived on the run from the 2001 United States and coalition invasion of Afghanistan until his death in 2013.

Muslim Brotherhood   a Sunni religious network founded in Egypt in 1928. The group emerged as an opposition group opposing the growing secular Arab nationalism in the Egyptian government at that time. Despite the group's rejection of violent resistance, the Brotherhood's opponents in the governments of Egypt, Saudi Arabia, Bahrain, the U.A.E., and other states continue to designate it as a terrorist organization.

N

Narco-Terrorism   Refers to terrorism associated with the trade of illicit drugs. For example, the campaign of violence led by Pablo Escobar and his drug cartel in Colombia in the 1980s and early 1990s is likely the most well known example of narco-terrorism. Escobar and his associates targeted members of the Colombian government and security forces with bombings, assassinations, and other violence to hinder their ability to control his dealings with drugs.

Nationalism   An ideology centered around a shared identification with one's nation. Groups who seek territorial autonomy or full independence, such as the PFLP in Palestine, or ETA in Spain, typically appeal to a broad community's sense that it should have the right to govern itself.

National Consortium for the Study of Terrorism and Responses to Terrorism (START) A consortium established in 2005 at the University of Maryland as a US Department of Homeland Security Center of Excellence. The consortium conducts research and educational activities to incorporate insights from the social and behavioral sciences to better understand terrorism. For instance, the Global Terrorism Database is housed at START.

National Counterterrorism Center (NCTC) The NCTC is a US government entity established in 2004 to integrate and analyze intelligence pertaining to counterterrorism.

National Liberation Army (ELN) A group founded in Colombia by Fabio and Manuel Vasquez in 1964. Its goal was democracy for Colombia. The ELN engaged in kidnappings and assassinations, among other tactics, often for building up revenue. While the ELN was overshadowed by the government's negotiations with FARC in the 2000s, the ELN responded violently by killing police offers and blowing up oil pipelines. In 2014 the Colombian government restarted talks with the ELN.

National Liberation Front of Algeria (the FLN) *(See Front De Liberation Nationale (FLN))*

National Security Agency (NSA) A US government intelligence agency responsible for cryptology, signals intelligence, cyber defense, and network operations.

National Union for the Total Independence of Angola (UNITA) A guerrilla movement founded in 1966 by Jonas Savimbi in Angola that was initially leftist when it fought alongside the Marxist Movement for the Liberation of Angola (MPLA) against the Portuguese colonial rule. After the Portuguese withdrawal in 1975, the group became strongly anti-Communist and pro-Western during the civil war against the MPLA. The crisis in Angola developed into a Cold War battleground where the United States and South Africa supported the FNLA and UNITA while the Soviet Union and its allies provided assistance to the MPLA. The assassination of Savimbi in 2002 eventually led to negotiations between UNITA and the MPLA, resulting in a peace agreement.

Naxalite-Maoist A Maoist-inspired far-left, radical communist insurgency active throughout the West Bengal and rural areas of central and eastern India whose objective started as the redistribution the land to working peasants and evolved to include the overthrow of the Indian government through a "people's war."

Necessary but Insufficient Implies a logical relationship between statements. Saying that one statement (he is a male sibling) is a necessary and sufficient condition of another statement (he is a brother) means that the first statement is true if and only if the second statement is true. Statements can also be necessary but not sufficient. For instance, "my car has gas" is a necessary but insufficient in relation to the statement "my car starts." To start, a car also needs a charged battery, electricity for the spark plugs, etc.

Negative Externality A cost incurred by a third party from the actions of another. For example, air pollution caused by the burning of fossil fuels is commonly used as an example of a widespread negative externality. It contributes to climate change, causing damage to our atmosphere, natural environment, and public health.

Negotiation   A process of bargaining, often associated with the entry of a group into a legitimate political process.

Neo-Fascism   The contemporary equivalent of the far-right fascism emerging after World War I in Germany, Spain, and Italy.

Neo-Imperialism   Colonial expansion by European countries, the United States, and the Japanese Empire during the late nineteenth to early twentieth centuries. During this time, countries pursued overseas territorial conquests, especially in Africa and parts of Asia. Most of the colonies established during this time period gained independence after World War II.

Neoliberal Economic Policies   Neoliberalism refers to policies that reflect laissez-faire approaches to economics, such as privatization, deregulation, free trade, and reduced government expenditures in favor of leadership from the private sector. These market-based ideas and policies were a direct response to a post-war Keynesian consensus, which lasted until 1980.

Neo-Wahabism   An extremist Sunni ideology that advocates for a strict and historical version of Islam that calls its followers to adhere to seventh century Islamic practices, doctrines, and ideals.

Nerve Agents   Highly toxic chemicals that poison the nervous system by disrupting the mechanisms in the body by which nerves send signals to organs. Common nerve agents include sarin, soman, tabun, and VX. For instance, Aum Shinrikyo's terrorist attack in 1995 claimed a dozen lives by releasing the nerve agent sarin on the Tokyo subway system, which raised concerns about the future use of nerve agents by terrorist groups in attacks on civilian populations.

Networked   Describes groups whose structure is organized into a more decentralized, "small world" network that features multiple leaders and clusters of local activists.

New terrorism   Beginning in the late 1990s, and especially after the 9/11 Al Qaeda attacks in the United States, policymakers, journalists, and scholars suggested that the world was entering an era marked by a new variant of terrorism, which was unlike terrorism of the past. Proponents of "new terrorism" argued that terrorism could now be defined as a "war against the West" driven in large part by Islamic extremists. Many analysts, particularly those from the academic community, challenge this view.

Nihilism   A view that rejects all moral and religious principles, and advocates the belief that life itself is essentially meaningless.

Normative   pertaining to morality, ethics, or core values.

Nuclear Weapon   An explosive device that derives its destructive force from a nuclear reaction. It is the most powerful kind of weapon of mass destruction (WMD).

O

One-Hit Wonders   A colloquial term for terror groups that conduct a single attack.

Operation Blue Star   An Indian military operation that took place in June 1984, in which the Prime Minister ordered the army to clear separatist rebels from a holy shrine in Amritsar. The confrontation ended in a bloody gun fight, and the deaths of more than one thousand people. The incident remains highly controversial, as many believe that the Indian government responded with indiscriminate violence. Prime Minister Indira Gandhi was assassinated four months after the operation, in a purported act of revenge for Operation Blue Star.

Opportunity Costs   Potential gain that is relinquished as a result of taking one action over another.

Order, The   Also known as the Silent Brotherhood, a white supremacist group active in the United States between 1983-1984. The group's overarching goal was to foment a revolution against the government, which members criticized for being under the control of Jews. The Order received media attention for its role in the killing of Alan Berg, a liberal radio talk show host based in Denver, Colorado.

Ordered Preferences   A set of preferences that are ordered by preferred outcome, next-preferred outcome, and least-preferred outcome and ranked from high to low in terms of their level of satisfaction they produce.

Organizational Approach   An approach that looks to a group's surrounding environment, or to dynamics that occur internally within the organization, to explain its behavior.

Organizational Model (*See Organizational Approach*)

Organizational Routines   A concept that refers to static, repetitive, and interdependent habits and practices. In the context of counterterrorism, organizational routines may predispose countries to a certain set of typical behaviors and thus, impede governments from implementing the most optimal measures to defeat terrorist groups.

Organizational Structure   How activities or groups are structured. For example, a group's organizational structure can be hierarchical or more loosely organized into a network of small groups or nodes.

Oromo Liberation Front (OLF)   A secessionist organization established in the 1970s in Ethiopia seeking self-determination for the Oromo people.

Oslo Accords   A series of agreements between the Israeli government and the Palestinian Liberation Organization in 199, which established the Palestinian Authority's territorial and political autonomy from Israel.

Outbidding   The practice of offering a higher price for something than another person. In terrorism, outbidding refers to a process that takes hold when groups, or individuals within a group, attempt to gain relevance over their competitors. *(See also Intra-Group Violence)*

Overgeneralization   The tendency to draw (more to here) more general conclusions about something than is warranted by available evidence.

P

Pakistani Taliban *(see Tehrik-I-Taliban (TTP))*

Palestinian Islamic Jihad (PIJ)   The PIJ was founded in 1981 with the purpose and goal of destroying the state of Israel. In its place they seek a sovereign Islamic Palestinian state. The group was identified as a terrorist organization by the United States among at least a half dozen other countries, although Iran continues to be a large financial supporter. The violent wings are active in the Gaza Strip and West Bank with suicide bombings, firing rockets into Israel, and violent actions against Israeli civilians. The PIJ remains active into the present day.

Palestine Liberation Organization (PLO)   The PLO was established in 1964 as an organization supporting Palestinian nationalism, considering itself the legitimate representative of the Palestinian people. Its goal was the liberation of Palestine through armed struggle and the destruction of Zionism in the Middle East. It split into various groups over time (PFLP, DFLP and PFLP-GC) but were all generally under the PLO and Yasser Arafat. The PLO engaged in numerous terrorist campaigns, causing hundreds of casualties, both Israeli and Palestinian. Their tactics did not yield the results they sought so they changed focus towards more diplomatic channels, particularly after the United Nations gave recognition to the PLO as the representative of the Palestinian people. In 1988 Arafat recognized the right of Israel to exist and renounced PLO terrorism. While talks continue to this day some groups still engage in campaigns of violence.

Parsimonious   Exhibiting frugal or stingy qualities. An explanation that is parsimonious uses assumptions, steps, or conditions sparingly.

Passive State Sponsorship   Unknowing or unwilling support. For example, a state may be a passive supporter of terrorism if it turns a blind eye to a nonstate armed group planning a terror attack from within its borders, but does not actively promote this activity either.

Patriarchal   Relating to or characteristic of system ruled and controlled by men.

PATRIOT Act   A US Congressional Act signed into law in 2001 in response to the 9/11 terrorist attacks, to help government agencies detect and thwart acts of terrorism.

Performative   Relating to drama or expression.

Permissive Factors   attributes that allow a certain condition to take hold and persist or multiply (**see also** *Precipitants*).

Perpetrators   Individuals or agents who carry out harmful or illegal activities.

Personal Significance Having meaning to an individual; having a positive meaning or contribution in life.

People's Will Movement (Narodnaya Volya) A Russian populist network that was highly active from the late 19th century through the early 20th century. The group was widely regarded as among the first modern terror organizations. While the group was responsible for the assassination of Tsar Alexander II in 1881 along with a number of other terrorist acts, its members also saw their organization as a political party.

Physical Integrity Rights Rights that protect all individuals from torture, extrajudicial killing, political imprisonment, and disappearance (see the CIRI Human Rights Data Project, http://www.humanrightsdata.com/).

Political Grievances A wrong or hardship, either actual or perceived, that leads to complaint, and that are political in nature.

Popular Front for the Liberation of Palestine (PFLP) A Marxist-Leninist Palestinian nationalist movement founded in 1967 by George Habash after the occupation of the West Bank by Israel. The group was responsible for armed aircraft hijackings in the late 60's and early 70's, as well as a 2014 massacre at a Jerusalem synagogue.

Population-Centric Methods Methods of counterterrorism or counterinsurgency that use soft power tactics such as capacity building, economic development, or political solutions, among others, to curb political violence.

Populism A philosophy that speculates that ordinary people are consistently abused by a corrupt circle of establishment elites, and that by working together, the masses can overthrow these elites and create a fairer society.

Positivist An epistemological approach that asserts truth as objective, knowable, value-free, and scientifically justified.

Post-Colonial Ideology A nationalist-separatist movement that rose in the twentieth century that believed in the right of people to self-determination and use of armed struggle to confront colonial or imperial powers.

Post-Colonial Theories Approaches that examine the consequences of colonialism and economic exploitation on native peoples and their lands.

Post-Positivist An epistemological approach that asserts that knowledge is not value-free, but instead for someone or some purpose, and thus fallible and error-prone.

Post-Traumatic Stress Disorder A disorder that develops after experiencing intensely shocking, frightening, or dangerous events.

Precautionary Principle The principle that, in the absence of scientific consensus, a proposed action or policy that risks causing public harm must be proven unharmful by those taking or proposing the action.

Precipitants   The direct causes of a particular action or event.

Precipitant Conditions   Circumstances that lead to a particular action or event.

Preconditions   Conditions that must be met before a specific action or event can take place.

Preferences as Given   An actor or actor category's preferences are exogenous to a theory, i.e., they are not explained but rather taken for granted in the development of a particular theory.

Preferred Outcome   A result with the highest level of satisfaction.

Process Goals   Organizational tasks or intermediate goals needed to achieve an ultimate strategic outcome.

Profiling   A practice wherein authorities attempt to monitor and detect certain attributes, habits, and behaviors to single out people for early interdiction.

Pro-Government Militias   Non-state armed groups that are organized by states to perform acts of political violence on behalf of states.

Propaganda   Biased or misleading information used to advance a particular political cause or opinion.

Propaganda of the Deed   A concept debated and popularized by various anarchist groups in France and Italy the mid-late nineteenth century, wherein clandestine groups could contest entrenched authority by acts of violence rather than by narrative or criticism alone. These debates inspired some other groups to use violence as a way to dislodge ruling elites from power.

Proto-State   A quasi-state or political entity that does not fully represent an autonomous state in the *de jure* sense.

Provisional Irish Republican Army (PIRA)   Founded in 1969, the PIRA was a paramilitary organization seeking an independent republic encompassing all of Ireland. It engaged in bomb attacks in the 1970s, but in 2005 the group renounced violence and sought its aims through diplomatic means.

Provocation   Action or words meant to instigate a specific response. Often a strategy where the aim of the violence is to provoke the government to overreact.

Psychological Barrier   Belief that influences how a person sees herself, as well as her ability, potential, and self-worth, such as denial, perceived lack of knowledge or social support, etc.

Psychological Impact   The effects that actions or states of being have on the way that individuals think or act.

Psychological Traits   The distinguishing qualities, attributes, and habitual behavioral patterns that describe a person's nature.

Public Good A commodity or service that is provided to all members of society, either by the government or non-state organization or individual. A defining characteristic of such a good is that it is non-excludable and non-rival, meaning that its consumption by one individual in society does not actually reduce the amount available to another individual.

Q

Quasi-Ideological A quasi-ideological approach assumes that the dominant beliefs of an actor interact with other factors—such as structural, psychological, organizational, or other factors— to explain that actor's behavior.

Quebec Liberation Front (FLQ) The FLQ was founded in 1963 as a separatist military group in Canada whose goal was the creation of a sovereign Quebec state. Its activities included bombing the Montreal Stock Exchange in 1969.

Quest for Significance A variant of social identity theory that suggests that the quest for meaning, such as achieving happiness or social status, drives human behavior.

Qutbism An Islamist ideology originating from the works of Sayyid Qutb, a key figure in of Muslim Brotherhood.

R

Racial-ethnic supremacist extremism A far-right ideology that sees specific race and ethnic identities as superior to others, and creates racial or ethnic hierarchy within society.

Racial Supremacy A worldview that a particular race is superior to all others.

Radicalization The adoption of radical or extremist views on political or social issues.

Rashtriya Swayamsevak Sangh (RSS) A fundamentalist, Hindu extremist group that fights for a pure "Hindustan."

Rational Choice a theory suggesting that rational actors make a reasonably calculated assessment at the outset based on projections that their chosen method will be the most productive way to arrive at their set objectives vis-á-vis their opponents' choices. *(See also Strategic Approach)*

Rationalist Model A model of behavior that is based on a rational choice approach. *(See also Rational Choice)*

Rationality A process by which different actors individuals or groups with set objectives examine available alternatives for achieving their objectives. The quality of thinking or acting in accordance with reason or logic.

Real IRA (RIRA) An Irish republican separatist organization founded 1997. It is a splinter group from the Provisional IRA. This group saw itself as the successor to the Irish Republican Army. It aimed its terrorist tactics against British security forces with bombings intended to harm particularly economic interests. Its Omagh bombing in 1998 left twenty-nine dead, and its Massereene barracks shooting killed several British soldiers.

Recidivism   The tendency of an individual convicted of committing a crime to return to committing crime.

Red Army Faction (RAF)/Baader-Meinhof Gang   A German quasi-Marxist group established 1970 who utilized parts of Marxism to justify its goal of overthrowing the West German government and undermining American military and economic hegemony. It conducted attacks in 1970 and 1975 when the West German embassy in Stockholm was taken hostage. The group dissolved in 1998. *(See also Baader-Meinhof Gang)*

Red Brigades (RB)   An Italian Marxist group in the 1970s that sought to overthrow the government, end Italy's membership in NATO, and create a new Italian state through revolutionary armed struggle. In 1978 the group abducted and murdered former Italian Prime Minister Aldo Moro. *(See also Brigatte Rosse)*

Regime Type   The set of institutions through which a state governs, such as democracy, or dictatorship, and their variations.

Regulative Constructivist   A type of constructivist that is interested in how ideas and norms shape and constrain human behavior.

Reign of Terror   A period of extreme violence during the French Revolution, lasting form 1793-1794, that resulted in more than sixteen thousand deaths as Robespierre sought to purge enemies of the Revolution, and protect France from outside invaders.

Reintegration   The process of integrating an individual back into society.

Relational   An approach that considers human behavior as the result of relationships or ties between individuals.

Religion   A belief in or worship of a supernatural power, usually in the form of a God or number of gods.

Religious Terrorist Groups   Extremist groups that espouse a commitment to religion, and who recruit individuals to their cause and justify their actions on the basis of that religion.

Reorientation: The process of changing the focus or direction of something, such as a policy or particular form of behavior.

Repression   The act or process of subduing someone or something through the use of brute force.

Reputational Effects   The effect that a particular action or set of actions will have on an individual's or group's reputation.

Retribution   Punishment inflicted as vengeance.

Retrospective Bias   Also known as hindsight bias, the process of seeing an event being analyzed as having been predictable before it occurred, despite there being no objective basis for doing so at the time.

Revolutionary Armed Forces of Colombia (FARC)   a terrorist organization formed in 1964 as a Marxist-Leninist guerilla movement opposed to the Columbian state and seeking to reorganize society along socialist lines to carry out a redistribution of land and wealth. After decades of war and nearly two hundred thousand killed, in 2016 the disputing sides signed the Colombian peace accord. Under the deal, thousands of guerillas agreed to demobilize. The process is ongoing.

Revolutionary Organization 17 November (17N)   A group formed in 1975 by far-leftists seeking to overthrow the Greek government, as well as being anti-United States and anti-NATO. They sought removal of US bases from Greece. They conducted assassinations, bombings, and robberies. The group apparently disbanded in 2002.

Revolutionary United Front (RUF)   Originally a rebel group led by Foday Sankoh in Sierra Leone that overthrew the government and led the country into a long civil war from 1991 to 2002. United Nations peacekeeping efforts disabled the group in 2002. The group was notorious for its use of violence and crimes against humanity, carrying out violent attacks on civilians, recruiting children into its ranks, and raping and maiming its victims.

Reward   Something given to recognize one's service, achievement, or effort.

Right-wing groups   Organizations that adopt right-wing ideologies, and that believe that certain social orders or hierarchies based on race, religion, or ethnicity are natural and desirable.

Root Causes   The underlying or initiating causes of an event or series of events.

Rote Armee Fraktion *(see Red Army Faction, RAF)*

S

Saffron Terror   A colloquial term that refers to Hindu terrorism, originating from Hindu nationalists' symbolic use of the yellowish color of saffron.

Salafist(s)   Adherents to the Salafi movement, an ultra-conservative reform branch of Sunni Islam that originated in Arabia during the first half of the eighteenth century.

Salafi Jihadi   An Islamist militant who sees the military movement to which he or she belongs as rooted in Islam and as posing an existential threat to the West.

Salafist Group for Call and Combat (GSPC)   The GSPC was established in 1995 as an Islamist militant organization aiming to overthrow the secular Algerian government and replace it with an Islamic state. The group has killed thousands of Algerian civilians, including targeting women and children. In 2006 the group allied with Al Qaeda and renamed itself Al Qaeda in the Islamic Magreb or AQIM. *(See also GSPC)*

Sayyid Qutb   An Egyptian, Western-educated ideologue aligned with the Egyptian Muslim Brotherhood in the 1950s and 60s whose perception of the west and its effects on Islam led him to author Ma'alim fi al-Tariq and form the basis of Qutbism.

Second- and Third-Generation Groups   Groups that have survived past one generation of existence, meaning that their membership spans several generation.

Sectarian and Extremist Right-Wing Groups   Groups that have a particular set of interests, and that engage in various forms of bigotry or discrimination as a result of their beliefs that their group is superior to all others in society.

Select on the Dependent Variable   The tendency to restrict a set of observations to cases where the outcome variable is observed, and excluding those cases where the outcome is not observed.

Selection Bias   The selection of phenomena or data for study that is not based on randomization, resulting in an obtained sample that is not representative of the full population of cases.

Selective Violence   Violence that discriminate (i.e., non-random) in its selection of victims.

Self-Determination   The process through which a state determines its independence or statehood, and forms its own government.

Self-Immolation   The act of burning oneself to death, often as a sacrifice for a specific cause.

Sendero Luminoso (Shining Path)   A group that formed in Peru in 1970 as a Marxist-Leninist military group opposed to the Peruvian state. The group, led by its founder, Abimael Guzman, sought to restore an ideology such as that of China under Mao Zedong. Their terror tactics included car bombings, assassinations, among other terror methods. Over a twenty-year period this led to the deaths of over seventy thousand people by Sendero Luminoso or Shining Path adherents.

Sex   Biological maleness or femaleness, distinguished on the basis of reproductive organs.

Shaheed   A Muslim martyr.

Shariah   Islamic canonical law based on the teachings of the Qu'ran and the traditions of Prophet Mohammed, which is applied in different ways depending on its interpretation (i.e., traditionalist versus reformist interpretations).

Sicarii   An extremist offshoot of the Jewish Zealots movement to expel Roman occupation from Judea operating from about 63–73 AD.

Social Desirability Bias   The tendency to present oneself in a way the interviewer wants to hear, rather than presenting oneself the way one actually is.

Social Grievances   A real or perceived wrong that becomes a cause for complaint, and is social in nature.

Socialism   An economic and political theory of organization, and the policies or practices that follow, founded on the premise that the means of production, distribution, and exchange should belong to and be managed by the entire community.

Social Movement Organization   Formal organizations that share goals within a broader social movement, and typically execute tasks required for a social movement to survive and succeed in achieving its objectives.

Social Network   A configuration of ties, or relationships, that link together various types of actors, such as groups, governments, companies, individuals, etc.

Social Network Analysis   The mapping and measurement of relationships between different actors belonging to one or more networks, where the nodes are the people or groups included in the network, and the links between them denotes the flow of information across the network.

Social Perspectives   Points of view that rest on the assumption that individuals' or groups' social environments are critical to understanding human behavior.

Social Services   Services provided by entities such as the government that benefit a community, such as education, medical care, housing, courts, etc.

Sociopath   An individual with a personality disorder that manifests itself in powerful anti-social attitudes and behavior, and a lack of conscience.

Soft Power   A concept used in international relations that refers to non-coercive methods used to change the behavior of an actor such as a state. Soft power tactics are based on the principles of attraction or cooptation, rather than coercion.

Soft Targets   A person, space, or facility that is relatively unprotected and vulnerable to various forms of attack.

Sovereign Citizen Movement   A active US-based, far-right group whose adherents hold complex anti-government beliefs, such as the need to obey only the laws of one's choosing and the right to not pay taxes.

Sovereignty   Supreme power or authority over a territory and its population.

Splinter   A fragment or piece of a larger object or entity.

Splinter Groups   Factions that emerge from a larger group.

Spoiling   To diminish, destroy, or disrupt negotiations, settlements, or peace processes.

State-Centric (or State Centrism)   An approach in international relations that considers states as the main actors in the international arena, and the drivers of decision-making processes.

State-Sponsored Terrorism   Terror groups that are actively or passively supported by a state.

Stereotypes   Widely held but grossly oversimplified characterizations of particular people or things.

Strategic Interactions In game theory, the various material or non-material exchanges that occur between individuals.

Structural Violence Commonly attributed to the work of John Galtung, the term refers to forms of violence whereby particular social structures or institutions cause harm by preventing people to meet basic needs.

Suboptimal Outcome An outcome that is below the most preferred outcome, or of substandard quality.

Substitution Effect The process of replacing a newly-costly strategy or tactic with a less costly one. With regard to terrorism, the best-known example of the substitution effect is when airline hijackings—a common tactic among internationalized terrorist groups in the 1960s and 1970s—dropped significantly as airports installed metal detectors worldwide.

Subversion The act of undermining authority in the context of an established system.

Suicidal Tendencies The propensity of individuals to have suicidal thoughts or to attempt suicide.

Suicide Missions Tasks or operations likely to lead to the death of those involved.

Suicide Terrorism Acts of terrorism that involve attacks in which the attacker expects death as part of the process.

Suicide Vest Usually a belt or vest packed with explosives and attached to a detonator, worn by attackers and used in suicide bombings.

Sunni One of the two main branches of Islam, which differs from the other main branch, Shia, on account of its acceptance of the first three caliphs.

Symbolic Power First introduced by the sociologist Pierre Bourdieu, this concept refers to the tacit, social domination that occurs as a result of everyday social habits, and more recently to actions that carry discriminatory or harmful meaning, such as gender dominance or racism.

T

Tactical Innovation The transition to a new tactic.

Tactical Repertoire A stock of tactics that an individual or group habitually employs.

Taliban In 1996, the Taliban overran Afghanistan and declared itself the government of the country—a declaration that Pakistan, Saudi Arabia, and the United Arab Emirates recognized while the rest of the world did not. *(See also Mujahideen)*

Targeted Assassination A form of killing based on the assumption that the specific target is guilty of some crime or wrong doing.

Targeting Decisions The decisions of individuals or groups to select specific persons, objects, or places for attack.

Tehrik-I-Taliban (TTP) an alliance of radical militant networks belonging to the Pakistani spin-off of the Taliban formed in 2007 to unify opposition against the Pakistani military. TTP's objectives are the expulsion of Islamabad's influence in the Federally Administered Tribal Areas and neighboring Khyber Pakhtunkhwa Province in Pakistan, the implementation of a strict interpretation of Sharia Law throughout Pakistan and the establishment of an Islamic caliphate, and the expulsion of Coalition groups from Afghanistan. The organization has provided a significant amount of aid to local populations, especially during the devastating floods in July 2010, which helped them garner local support. *(See also Pakistani Taliban)*

Terror-Crime Nexus The connection and intersection between terrorism and criminal activities.

Terrorist Campaign A series of operations and attacks launched by a terrorist group in service of a particular goal.

Thugs, The A cult-like group operating throughout India from the thirteenth through the nineteenth centuries and considered by many to be the deadliest terrorist group of all time.

Troubles, The The ethno-nationalist conflict that took place from the 1960s to the late 1990s in Northern Ireland, which pitted unionists (loyalists) against nationalist (republicans) in the struggle for Irish independence from the United Kingdom.

Timothy McVeigh The perpetrator of the terrorist attack on the Oklahoma City federal building in April 1995.

Tracking Following the trail of individuals' movements to determine their current location or the various points they were located at previously.

Transitive A relationship is transitive if it holds across successive levels or members in a sequence (for example, if A is greater than B, and B is greater than C, then A is greater than C).

Transnational Targets Targets that are located across an international border.

Transnational Terrorism Terrorist activity that involves perpetrators and targets from different sovereign countries.

Tunisian Combatant Group (TCG) An extremist Islamist group formed in 2000 by Seifallah ben Hassine and Tarek Maaroufi. The group advocated for a more radical fundamentalist Islam, and was believed to be actively affiliated with Al Qaeda in Afghanistan and North Africa. The United States declared it a terrorist organization in 2002 due to these affiliations.

Tupac Amaru Revolutionary Movement (MRTA) A Peruvian revolutionary movement founded in 1983 which sought to overthrow the Peruvian government and substitute it with a Marxist regime, effectively ridding itself of all imperialist elements. Its terrorist tactics included assassinations, hostage-taking, kidnappings and other crimes. Peru's counterterrorist program diminished the group's ability to carry out attacks over time and there were claims of infighting and clashes with rival groups along with the imprisonment of several of the groups senior leaders. The State Department de-listed the group as a terrorist organization in 2001.

Tupamaros-West Berlin (TW) a precursor to the Rote Armee Fraktion in West Berlin. The group launched a highly publicized attack in 1969 to demonstrate the West German left's solidarity with Palestinians. The TW attempted to bomb the Jewish Community Center in West Berlin on the anniversary of Kristallnacht, an attack on Jewish business, institutions, and individuals in 1938, to symbolize a parallel between Israeli oppression of Palestinians and Nazi persecution of the Jews. Though the bomb never exploded, but the group was responsible for a spate of other attacks in the late 1960s conducted under various pseudonyms.

Turkish Hizballah A Sunni Islamist militant organization formed in the early 1980s which sought to replace Turkey's secular regime with an Islamic state and strict Sharia law— essentially an independent Kurdistan. Its terrorist tactics during the mid 1990s forward included torture, murder of various officials, including journalists and businessmen and suicide bombings. It has not conducted a terrorist campaign since the early 2000s.

Turner Diaries, The A novel by William Pierce that showcases a protagonist who successfully wages a revolution, overthrows the US government, and exterminates all non-white, Jewish, and gay people.

U

Ulster Defense Association/Ulster Freedom Fighters (UDA/UFF) A Northern Irish separatist paramilitary group formed in 1971 as an umbrella group for a variety of loyalist groups in Belfast that emerged in response to the outbreak of the Troubles. At its height it claimed over ten thousand members seeking their unionist cause and independence for Northern Ireland. Its terrorist tactics included sectarian assassinations, torture-killings, and bombings, regularly targeting Roman Catholics and prominent republicans. The group often claimed responsibility for its sectarian murders under a pseudonym, "The Ulster Freedom Fighters (UFF)." Notorious UFF attacks included the deadly shooting of five Catholics at a Belfast bookmarkers shop in 1992 and the Greysteel massacre in 1993. The British Government banned the group in 1992. In 1994, the UDA joined with other loyalist paramilitary organizations in declaring a cease-fire, although sporadic violence continued until the UDA announced an end to its armed campaigns in 2007.

Umkhonto we Sizwe (MK) The armed wing of the African National Congress (ANC) that was jointly formed by leading members of the banned ANC and the South African Community Party (SACP) in 1961. Called "Spear of the Nation" in Zulu, MK emerged after a series of repressive acts by the South African apartheid government—including the 1960 Sharpeville Massacre and the banning of black liberation organizations—which ultimately convinced ANC and SACP members that is was necessary for them to shift from using methods of nonviolent resistance to those of political violence to combat the regime.

Uncertain Information Environment   A lack of information and inability to anticipate unforeseen factors in order to obtain a complete assessment for each interested outcome before making a choice.

Underlying Causes   Structural variables—such as democracy, state capacity, welfare provision, economic factors, demographics—that can be identified within the political, social, cultural, and economic structures of societies to identify the dominant macro-level processes that give people the grievances and opportunities to engage in different behaviors.

Unabomber, The   An American anarchist and domestic terrorist infamously known as the "Unabomber" for mailing a series of homemade bombs to universities and airlines between 1978 and 1995, killing three people and injuring twenty-four more. *(See also Kaczynski, Ted).*

UNITA *(See National Union for the Total Independence of Angola)*

Unitary Actor   A single actor with uniform preferences.

United Liberation Front of Assam   An ethnic secessionist group founded in 1979 by Arabinda Rajkhowa and Paresh Baruah in the northeastern Indian state of Assam with the purpose of forming a separate country of Assam under socialist government rule. The group adopted violent tactics primarily aimed at government officials and security force personnel in Assam. UFLA enjoyed widespread support in upper Assam in its early years, but lost popularity after it expanded its target selection to public installations and civilians. ULFA's kidnapping, killings and extortion led the Indian Government to ban the group and start a military offensive against it in 1990, which forced it to go underground. As of 2005, the group maintains considerable strength and is a potent threat to peace initiatives in the state of Assam.

United People's Front of Nepal *(See Communist Party of Nepal (Maoist)/United People's Front, CPN-M)*

United Self-Defense Forces / Group of Colombia (AUC)   A right-wing Colombian group formed in 1997 to defend primarily drug-traffickers and landowners and having links to the army. Its terrorist tactics involved massacres and assassination, mainly against left-wing activists who rose against them. The group was named a terrorist organization by the United States but it essentially disbanded in 2006.

Unité Radicale   A neo-fascist, neo-Nazi group created in 1998 in France espousing racial supremacy, xenophobia, nationalism, and militarism through a secular dimension. After one of its members, Maxime Brunerie, attempted to assassinate French President Jacques Chirac during the Bastille Day parade, the group was dissolved by the French Government in 2002.

Unmanned Aerial Vehicle (UAV)   Commonly known as a drone, a UAV is an aircraft that can be navigated remotely without a human pilot onboard via a remote controller or an onboard computer. It is sometimes used in counterterrorism tactics such as targeted assassination *(see also Drones).*

US Department of State's Bureau of Counterterrorism and Countering Violent Extremism A bureau within the US State Department that helps to develop and implement counterterrorism strategies and operations.

V

Victims Persons who have suffered harm, including physical or mental injury, emotional suffering, economic loss, or substantial impairment of their fundamental rights.

Violence The act of physically harming another.

Violent Rivalries Enduring, antagonistic, and violent relationships.

W

Weak States Countries that lack the capacity to fulfill critical government responsibilities.

Weapon of Mass Destruction (WMD) Weaponry involving toxic or poisonous chemicals, biological agents, radiation, radioactivity, or fissile material.

Weather Underground (Weathermen) A radical left-wing organization that emerged in 1969 from a group called the Students for a Democratic Society (SDS) with aims to overthrow the US government, as claimed in the group's 1974 manifesto called *Prairie Fire*. By 1975, the organization claimed credit for twenty-five bombings—including the US State Department's headquarters, the US Capitol, the Pentagon, the California Attorney General's office, and a New York City police station. The group disbanded in 1977.

X

Xenophobia An extreme dislike, hatred and/or fear of foreigners, their customs, religion or generally people who are culturally different from oneself.

Y

Yasser Arafat The head of the Palestine Liberation Organization (PLO) (1969-2004), who condoned or ordered numerous armed attacks against Israeli targets beginning in 1970. Arafat was also the first president of the Palestinian Authority (PA) (1996-2004), and former leader of Fatah, the largest of the constituent PLO groups. He was awarded the Nobel Peace Prize in 1994 for his role in the Oslo Accords, which established the PA's territorial and political autonomy of Israel.

Z

Zapatista National Revolutionary Army (EZLN) A Mexican revolutionary militia that began in the mid-1990s, generally opposed to globalization and imperialism. "Zapatistas" referred most broadly to groups, including indigenous persons, seeking democracy and land reform. Their signature rebellion coincided with the signing of NAFTA in 1994, which they saw as thwarting their independence and depriving them of their land, communities, resources, and livelihood.

Zero-Sum Game An all-or-nothing conflict.

REFERENCES

Chapter 1   Analyzing Terrorism

Arafat, Yasser. 1974. "Speech by Yasser Arafat at the United Nations General Assembly, New York." Le Monde *Diplomatique*. November 13, last accessed January 11, 2017 at http://mondediplo.com/focus/mideast/arafat74-en.

Asal, Victor, Luis De La Calle, Michael Findley, and Joseph Young. 2012. "Killing Civilians or Holding Territory? How to Think About Terrorism." *International Studies Review* 14 (3): 475–497. doi:10.1111/j.1468-2486.2011.01127.x.

Ballina, Santiago. 2011. "The Crime-Terror Continuum Revisited: A Model for the Study of Hybrid Criminal Organizations." *Journal of Policing, Intelligence and Counter-Terrorism* 6 (2): 121–136. doi:10.1080/18335330.2011.605200.

Berrebi, Claude, and Esteban F. Klor. 2008. "Are Voters Sensitive to Terrorism? Direct Evidence from The Israeli Electorate." *The American Political Science Review* 102 (3): 279–301. doi:10.2139/ssrn.1003908.

Bush, George W. 2010. *Decision Points*. 1st ed. New York: Crown Publishers.

Claridge, David. 1996. "State Terrorism? Applying a Definitional Model." *Terrorism and Political Violence* 8 (3): 47–63. doi:10.1080/09546559608427363.

Crenshaw, Martha. 2003. "'New' versus 'Old' Terrorism." *Palestine-Israel Journal of Politics, Economics, and Culture* 10 (1): 48–53.

De la Calle, Luis, and Ignacio Sánchez-Cuenca. 2011. "The Quantity and Quality of Terrorism: The DTV Dataset." *Journal of Peace Research* 48 (1): 49–58. doi:10.1177/0022343310392890.

Donahue, Thomas J. 2013. "Terrorism, Moral Conceptions, and Moral Innocence." *The Philosophical Forum* 44 (4): 413–435. doi:10.1111/phil.12021.

Cronin, Audrey Kurth. 2009. *How Terrorism Ends: Understanding the Decline and Demise of Terrorist Campaigns*. Princeton: Princeton University Press.

Dash, Mike. 2005. *Thug: The True Story of India's Murderous Cult*. London: Granta Books

Douglas, Roger. 2010. "Must Terrorists Act for A Cause? The Motivational Requirement in Definitions of Terrorism in The United Kingdom, Canada, New Zealand and Australia." *Commonwealth Law Bulletin* 36 (2): 295–312. doi:10.1080/0 3050718.2010.481400.

English, Richard. 2009. "The Future of Terrorism Studies." *Critical Studies on Terrorism* 2 (2): 377–382. doi:10.1080/17539150903025119.

Foster, Dennis M. 2017. "Inter Arma Silent Leges? Democracy, Domestic Terrorism, and Diversion." *Journal of Conflict Resolution* 0 (0): 1–30. doi:10.1177/0022002715613842. –

Gage, Beverly. 2009. *The Day Wall Street Exploded. A Story of America in its First Age of Terror*. 1st ed. Oxford: Oxford University Press.

Ganor, Boaz. 2002. "Defining Terrorism: Is One Man's Terrorist Another Man's Freedom Fighter?" *Police Practice and Research* 3 (4): 287–304. doi:10.1080/1561426 022000032060.

Harmon, Christopher C. 1992. "Terrorism: A Matter for Moral Judgement." *Terrorism and Political Violence* 4 (1): 1–21. doi:10.1080/09546559208427135.

Hitler, Adolf. 1939. *Mein Kampf* (Complete and Unabridged). New York: Reynal and Hitchcock.

Hoffman, Bruce. 2006. *Inside Terrorism*. 1st ed. New York: Columbia University Press.

Human Security Research Group. 2012. *Human Security Report 2012 |: Sexual Violence, Education, and War: Beyond the Mainstream Narrative*. Vancouver: Simon Fraser University. http://hsrgroup.org/docs/Publications/HSR2012/2012HumanSecurityReport-FullText-LowRes.pdf

Jackson, Richard. 2007. "Constructing Enemies: 'Islamic Terrorism' in Political and Academic Discourse." *Government and Opposition* 42 (3): 394–426. doi:10.1111/j.1477-7053.2007.00229.x.

Jackson, Richard, Marie Breen Smyth, and Jeroen Gunning. 2011. *Terrorism: A Critical Introduction*. London: Palgrave Macmillan Ltd.

Jagger, Alison M. 2005. "What Is Terrorism, Why Is It Wrong, And Could It Ever Be Morally Permissible?" *Journal of Social Philosophy* 36 (2): 202–217. doi:10.1111/j.1467-9833.2005.00267.x.

LaFree, Gary, and Laura Dugan. 2007. "Introducing the Global Terrorism Database." *Terrorism and Political Violence* 19 (2): 181–204. doi:10.1080/09546550701246817.

Londoño, Ernesto. 2013. "Study: Iraq, Afghan War Costs to Top $4 Trillion." *The Washington Post*, March 28, last accessed January 11, 2017 at https://www.washingtonpost.com/world/national-security/study-iraq-afghan-war-costs-to-top-4-trillion/2013/03/28/b82a5dce-97ed-11e2-814b-063623d80a60_story.html?utm_term=.ebeb226ca190.

Makarenko, Tamara. 2004. "The Crime-Terror Continuum: Tracing the Interplay Between Transnational Organised Crime and Terrorism." *Global Crime* 6 (1): 129–145. doi:10.1080/1744057042000297025.

Meisels, Tamar, and Ted Honderich. 2010. "Can Terrorism Ever Be Justified?." In *Debating Terrorism and Counterterrorism: Conflicting Perspectives on Causes, Contexts, and Responses*, edited by Stuart Gottlieb, Washington, DC: CQ Press.

Merari, Ariel. 1993. "Terrorism As A Strategy of Insurgency." *Terrorism and Political Violence* 5 (4): 213–251. doi:10.1080/09546559308427227.

Mueller, John. 2006. "Is There Still A Terrorist Threat?: The Myth of the Omnipresent Enemy." *Foreign Affairs* 85 (5): 2–8. doi:10.2307/20032065.

Mueller, John. 2006. *Overblown: How Politicians and the Terrorism Industry Inflate National Security Threats, and Why We Believe Them*, 1st ed. New York: Free Press.

Obama, Barack H. 2014. "Remarks by the President at the United States Military Academy Commencement Ceremony." The White House Office of the Press Secretary. May 28, last accessed January 11, 2017 at https://www.whitehouse.gov/the-press-office/2014/05/28/remarks-president-united-states-military-academy-commencement-ceremony.

Orr, Allan. 2012. "Terrorism: A Philosophical Discourse." *Journal of Applied Security Research* 7 (1): 93–106. doi:10.1080/19361610.2011.604022.

Pat-Horenczyk, Ruth. 2005. "Post-Traumatic Distress in Israeli Adolescents Exposed to Ongoing Terrorism." *Journal of Aggression, Maltreatment, and Trauma* 9 (3–4): 335–347. doi:10.1300/j146v09n03_04.

Pew Global Attitudes and Trends. 2007. "Spring 2007 Survey Data." last accessed January 11, 2017 at http://www.pewglobal.org/2007/05/28/spring-2007-survey-data/.

Rapaport, David. 1984. "Fear and Trembling: Terrorism in Three Religious Traditions." *American Political Science Review* 78 (3): 658–677. doi:10.2307/1961835.

Rapin, Ami-Jacques. 2011. "What Is Terrorism?." *Behavioral Sciences of Terrorism and Political Aggression* 3 (3): 161–175. doi:10.1080/19434472.2010.512155.

Sandler, Todd. 2011. "New Frontiers of Terrorism Research: An Introduction." *Journal of Peace Research* 48 (3): 279–286. doi:10.1177/0022343311399131.

Schmid, Alex P., ed. 2011. *The Routledge Handbook of Terrorism Research*. 1st ed. New York: Routledge.

Shughart, William F. 2006. "An Analytical History of Terrorism, 1945–2000." *Public Choice* 128 (1/2): 7–39. doi:10.1007/s11127-006-9043-y.

US Department of Homeland Security. 2002. "President George W. Bush's Proposal to Create the Department of Homeland Security." June. Last accessed January 12, 2017 at: https://www.dhs.gov/sites/default/files/publications/book_0.pdf.

Weinberg, Leonard, Ami Pedahzur, and Sivan Hirsch-Hoefler. 2004. "The Challenges of Conceptualizing Terrorism." *Terrorism and Political Violence* 16 (4): 777–794. doi:10.1080/095465590899768.

Wilkinson, Paul. 1981. "Can A State Be 'Terrorist'?." *International Affairs (Royal Institute of International Affairs 1944-)* 57 (3): 467–472. doi:10.2307/2619580.

Zulaika, Joseba, and William A. Douglass. 1996. *Terror and Taboo: The Follies, Fables, and Faces of Terrorism*. 1st ed. New York: Routledge.

Chapter 2   The Strategic Approach

Abrahms, Max. 2004. "Are Terrorists Really Rational? The Palestinian Example." *Orbis* 48 (3): 533–549.

Abrahms, Max. 2006. "Why Terrorism Does Not Work." *International Security* 31 (2): 42–78. doi:10.1162/isec.2006.31.2.42.

Abrahms, Max. 2008. "What Terrorists Really Want: Terrorist Motives and Counterterrorism Strategy." *International Security* 32 (4): 78–105. doi:10.1162/isec.2008.32.4.78.

Abrahms, Max. 2012. "The Political Effectiveness of Terrorism Revisited." *Comparative Political Studies* 45 (3): 366–393. doi:10.1177/0010414011433104.

Abrahms, Max. 2013. "The Credibility Paradox: Violence as a Double-Edged Sword in International Politics." *International Studies Quarterly* 57 (4): 660–671. doi:10.1111/isqu.12098.

Abrahms, Max, and Justin Conrad. 2017. "The Strategic Logic of Credit Claiming: A New Theory For Anonymous Terrorist Attacks." *Security Studies* 26 (2): 279–304. doi:10.1080/09636412.2017.1280304.

Ashworth, Scott, Joshua D. Clinton, Adam Meirowitz, and Kristopher W. Ramsay. 2008. "Design, Inference, and the Strategic Logic of Suicide Terrorism." *American Political Science Review* 102 (2): 269–273. doi:10.1017/s0003055408080167.

Bapat, Navin, and Rebecca Best. 2014. "The Rise of Extremism in Terrorist Movements: Negotiation and the Internal Commitment Problem." Paper presented at the 2014 Annual Meeting of the Peace Science Society International, Philadelphia, Pennsylvania, October 10 – 11.

Benmelech, Efraim, Claude Berrebi, and Esteban F. Klor. 2010. *Counter-Suicide-Terrorism: Evidence from House Demolitions*. (No. W16493). National Bureau of Economic Research, http://www.nber.org/papers/w16493.

Benson, David C. 2014. "Why the Internet Is Not Increasing Terrorism." *Security Studies* 23 (2): 293–328. doi:10.1080/09636412.2014.905353.

Berrebi, Claude, and Esteban F. Klor. 2008. "Are Voters Sensitive to Terrorism? Direct Evidence from the Israeli Electorate." *The American Political Science Review* 102 (3): 279–301. doi:10.2139/ssrn.1003908.

Bueno De Mesquita, Ethan. 2005. "Conciliation, Counterterrorism, and Patterns of Terrorist Violence." *International Organization* 59 (1): 145–176. doi:10.1017/s0020818305050022.

Bueno De Mesquita, Ethan, and Eric S. Dickson. 2007. "The Propaganda of the Deed: Terrorism, Counterterrorism, and Mobilization." *American Journal of Political Science* 51 (2): 364–381. doi:10.1111/j.1540-5907.2007.00256.x

Caplan, Bryan. 2006. "Terrorism: The Relevance of the Rational Choice Model." *Public Choice* 128 (1/2): 91–107. doi:10.1007/s11127-006-9046-8.

Chenoweth, Erica, and Maria J. Stephan. 2011. *Why Civil Resistance Works: The Strategic Logic of Nonviolent Conflict*. New York: Columbia University Press.

Clauset, Aaron, Lindsay Heger, Maxwell Young, and Kristian. S. Gleditsch. 2010. "The Strategic Calculus of Terrorism: Substitution and Competition in The Israel—Palestine Conflict." *Cooperation and Conflict* 45 (1): 6–33. doi:10.1177/0010836709347113.

CNN. 2004. "Bin Laden: Goal is to Bankrupt U.S.: Al Jazeera Releases Full Transcript of al Qaeda Leader's Tape." Monday, November 1, 2004. Last accessed January 17, 2017 at http://www.cnn.com/2004/WORLD/meast/11/01/binladen.tape/index.html

Crenshaw, Martha. 2001. "Theories of Terrorism: Instrumental and Organizational Approaches." in David Rapaport, ed., *Inside Terrorist Organizations*, revised edition. London: Frank Cass Publishers.

Dershowitz, Alan. 2002. *Why Terrorism Works: Understanding the Threat, Responding to the Challenge*. New Haven: Yale University Press.

Enders, Walter, and Todd Sandler. 1993. "The Effectiveness of Anti-Terrorism Policies: A Vector-Autoregression-Intervention Analysis." *American Political Science Review* 87 (4): 829–844. doi:10.2307/2938817.

Enders, Walter, and Todd Sandler. 2006. *The Political Economy of Terrorism*. New York, NY: Cambridge University Press.

English, Richard. 2016. *Does Terrorism Work? A History*. 1st ed. Oxford: Oxford University Press.

Feinstein, Jonathan S., and Edward H. Kaplan. 2010. "Analysis of a Strategic Terror Organization." *The Journal of Conflict Resolution* 54 (2): 281–302. doi:10.1177/0022002709355438

Flanigan, Shawn Teresa. 2008. "Nonprofit Service Provision by Insurgent Organizations: The Cases of Hizballah and the Tamil Tigers." *Studies in Conflict & Terrorism* 31 (6): 499–519. doi:10.1080/10576100802065103.

Fromkin, David. 1975. "The Strategy of Terrorism." *Foreign Affairs* 53 (4): 683–698. doi:10.2307/20039540.

Greenhill, Kelly M., and Solomon Major. 2007. "The Perils of Profiling: Civil War Spoilers and the Collapse of Intrastate Peace Accords." *International Security* 31 (3): 7–40. doi:10.1162/isec.2007.31.3.7.

Jackson, Richard, Lee Jarvis, Jeroen Gunning, and Marie Breen-Smyth. 2011. *Terrorism: A Critical Introduction*. London: Palgrave Macmillan Ltd.

Krause, Peter. 2013. "The Political Effectiveness of Non-State Violence: A Two-Level Framework to Transform a Deceptive Debate." *Security Studies* 22 (2): 259–294. doi:10.1080/09636412.2013.786914.

Kydd, Andrew H., and Barbara F. Walter. 2006. "The Strategies of Terrorism." *International Security* 31 (1): 49–80. doi:10.1162/isec.2006.31.1.49

Lake, David A. 2002. "Rational Extremism: Understanding Terrorism in the Twenty-First Century." *Dialogue IO* 1 (01): 15–28.

Min, Eric. 2013. "Taking Responsibility: When and Why Terrorists Claim Attacks" (Paper presented at the Annual Meeting of the American Political Science Association, Chicago, IL, August 29 – 31, 2013).

Moghadam, Assaf. 2003. "Palestinian Suicide Terrorism in the Second Intifada: Motivations and Organizational Aspects." *Studies in Conflict and Terrorism* 26 (2): 65–92. doi:10.1080/10576100390145215

Neumann, Peter R., and Michael LR Smith. 2005. "Strategic Terrorism: The Framework and Its Fallacies." *The Journal of Strategic Studies* 28 (4): 571–595. doi:10.1080/01402390500300923.

Pape, Robert A. 2005. *Dying to Win: The Strategic Logic of Suicide Terrorism.* 1st ed. New York: Random House.

Pearlman, Wendy. 2009. "Spoiling Inside and Out: Internal Political Contestation and The Middle East Peace Process." *International Security* 33 (3): 79–109. doi:10.1162/isec.2009.33.3.79.

Peffley, Mark, Marc L. Hutchison, and Michal Shamir. 2015. "The Impact of Persistent Terrorism on Political Tolerance: Israel, 1980 to 2011." *American Political Science Review* 109 (4): 817–832.

Pinker, Steven. 2011. *The Better Angels of Our Nature: Why Violence Has Declined.* New York: Viking.

Shapiro, Jacob N. 2013. *The Terrorist's Dilemma: Managing Violent Covert Organizations.* Princeton: Princeton University Press.

Simon, Herbert. 1982. *Models of Bounded Rationality: Economic Analysis and Public Policy, Vol. 1.* Cambridge, MA: MIT Press.

Stern, Jessica. 2003. *Terror in the Name of God: Why Religious Militants Kill.* New York: Ecco.

Stern, Jessica, and John M. Berger. 2015. *ISIS: The State of Terror.* New York: Ecco.

Thatcher, Margaret. 1985. "Speech to American Bar Association." *Margaret Thatcher Foundation* July 15, 1985. Last accessed January 19, 2017 at http://www.margaretthatcher.org/document/106096

Thomas, Jakana. 2014. "Rewarding Bad Behavior: How Governments Respond to Terrorism in Civil War." *American Journal of Political Science* 58 (4): 804–818. doi:10.1111/ajps.12113.

Wood, Reed M., and Jacob D. Kathman. 2014. "Too Much of a Bad Thing? Civilian Victimization and Bargaining in Civil War." *British Journal of Political Science* 44 (3): 685–706. doi:10.1017/S000712341300001x.COMPLETE MS.docx

Woodworth, Paddy. 2001. "Why Do They Kill: The Basque Conflict in Spain?." *World Policy Journal* 18 (1): 1–12. doi:10.1215/07402775-2001-2002.

Chapter 3 The Organizational Approach

Abrahms, Max. 2008. "What Terrorists Really Want: Terrorist Motives and Counterterrorism Strategy." *International Security* 32 (4): 78–105. doi:10.1162/isec.2008.32.4.78.

Abrahms, Max and Justin Conrad. 2017. "The Strategic Logic of Credit Claiming: A New Theory on Anonymous Terrorist Attacks." *Security Studies* 26 (2): 279–304. doi:10.1080/09636412.2017.1280304.

Abrahms, Max, and Philip BK Potter. 2015. "Explaining Terrorism: Leadership Deficits and Militant Group Tactics." *International Organization* 69 (2): 311–342. doi:10.1017/s0020818314000411.

Asal, Victor, and R. Karl Rethemeyer. 2008. "The Nature of the Beast: Organizational Structures and The Lethality of Terrorist Attacks." *The Journal of Politics* 70 (2): 437–449. doi:10.1017/s0022381608080419.

Barrell, Howard. 2014. Personal correspondence with Erica Chenoweth, June.

Biberman, Yelena, and Farhan Zahid. 2016. "Why Terrorists Target Children: Outbidding, Desperation, and Extremism in the Peshawar and Beslan School Massacres." *Terrorism and Political Violence* 1–16. doi:10.1080/09546553.2015.1135425.

Bloom, Mia M. 2004. "Palestinian Suicide Bombing: Public Support, Market Share, and Outbidding." *Political Science Quarterly* 119 (1): 61–88. doi:10.2307/20202305.

Bloom, Mia M. 2005. *Dying to Kill: The Allure of Suicide Terror*. New York: Columbia University Press.

Byman, Daniel. 2014. "Buddies or Burdens? Understanding the Al Qaeda Relationship with its Affiliate Organizations." *Security Studies* 23 (3): 431–470. Doi:10.1080/0963 6412.2014.935228.

Chenoweth, Erica, Nicholas Miller, Elizabeth McClellan, Hillel Frisch, Paul Staniland, and Max Abrahms. 2009. "What Makes Terrorists Tick." *International Security* 33 (4): 180–202. doi:10.1162/isec.2009.33.4.180.

Chenoweth, Erica. 2010. "Democratic Competition and Terrorist Activity." *The Journal of Politics* 72 (1): 16–30. doi:10.1017/s0022381609990442.

Crenshaw, Martha. 2001. "The Causes of Terrorism: Instrumental and Organizational Approaches," in David Rapaport, ed., *Inside Terrorist Organizations*, revised edition. London: Routledge.

Christia, Fotini. 2012. *Alliance Formation in Civil Wars*. New York: Cambridge University Press.

Cronin, Audrey Kurth. 2009. *How Terrorism Ends: Understanding the Decline and Demise of Terrorist Campaigns*. Princeton, NJ: Princeton University Press.

Della Porta, Donatella. 1995. "Left-Wing Terrorism in Italy," in Martha Crenshaw, ed., *Terrorism in Context*. University Park, PA: Pennsylvania State University Press.

Dugan, Laura, and Gary LaFree. 2007. "Introducing the Global Terrorism Database." *Terrorism and Political Violence* 19 (2): 181–200. doi:10.1080/09546550701246817.

Findley, Michael G., and Joseph K. Young. 2012. "More Combatant Groups, More Terror?: Empirical Tests of an Outbidding Logic." *Terrorism and Political Violence* 24 (5): 706–721. doi:10.1080/09546553.2011.639415.

Findley, Michael G., and Joseph K. Young. 2015. "Terrorism, Spoiling, and the Resolution of Civil Wars." *The Journal of Politics* 77 (4): 1115–1128. doi:10.1086/682400.

Flanigan, Shawn Teresa. 2008. "Nonprofit Service Provision by Insurgent Organizations: The Cases of Hizballah and The Tamil Tigers." *Studies in Conflict & Terrorism* 31 (6): 499–519. doi:10.1080/10576100802065103.

Heger, Lindsay, Danielle Jung, and Wendy H. Wong. 2012. "Organizing for Resistance: How Group Structure Impacts the Character of Violence." *Terrorism and Political Violence* 24 (5): 743–768. doi:10.1080/09546553.2011.642908.

Hoffman, Aaron M. 2010. "Voice and Silence: Why Groups Take Credit for Acts of Terror." *Journal of Peace Research* 47 (5): 615–626. doi:10.1177/0022343310376439.

Horowitz, Michael C. 2010. "Nonstate Actors and the Diffusion of Innovations: The Case of Suicide Terrorism." *International Organization* 64 (1): 33–64. doi:10.1017/s0020818309990233.

Horowitz, Michael C., Evan J. Perkoski, and Philip BK. Potter. 2017. "Tactical Diversity in Militant Violence." Last Accessed August 4, 2017 online at SSRN: https://ssrn.com/abstract=2605952 or http://dx.doi.org/10.2139/ssrn.2605952

Horowitz, Michael C., and Philip BK. Potter. 2014. "Allying to Kill: Terrorist Intergroup Cooperation and the Consequences for Lethality." *Journal of Conflict Resolution*, 58 (2): 199–225. doi:10.1177/0022002712468726

Jones, David Martin, Ann Lane, and Paul Schulte. 2010. *Terrorism, Security and the Power of Informal Networks*. Cheltenham: Edward Elgar Publishing.

Kennedy, Jonathan, and Gabriel Weimann. 2011. "The Strength of Weak Terrorist Ties." *Terrorism and Political Violence* 23 (2): 201–212. doi:10.1080/09546553.2010.521087.

Kilberg, Joshua. 2012. "A Basic Model Explaining Terrorist Group Organizational Structure." *Studies in Conflict & Terrorism* 35 (11): 810–830. doi:10.1080/1057610x.2012.720240.

McCormick, Gordon H. 2003. "Terrorist Decision Making." *Annual Review of Political Science* 6 (1): 473–507. doi:10.1146/annurev.polisci.6.121901.085601.

Mironova, Vera, Loubna Mrie, and Sam Whitt. 2014. "Fight or Flight in Civil War? Evidence from Rebel-Controlled Syra." Available online at: https://papers.ssrn.com/sol3/papers.cfm?abstract_id=2478682. Last accessed August 4, 2017.

Mishal, Shaul, and Maoz Rosenthal. 2005. "Al Qaeda as a Dune Organization: Toward a Typology of Islamic Terrorist Organizations." *Studies in Conflict & Terrorism* 28 (4): 275–293. doi:10.1080/10576100590950165.

Moghadam, Assaf. 2013. "How Al Qaeda Innovates." *Security Studies* 22 (3): 466–497. doi:10.1080/09636412.2013.816123.

Moore, Will H., Ryan Bakker, and Daniel W Hill. 2011. "How Much Terror? Dissidents, Governments, Institutions and the Cross-National Study of Terror Attacks." (December 28) *SSRN Electronic Journal*. Available online at https://www.researchgate.net/publication/228215542_How_Much_Terror_Dissidents_Governments_Institutions_and_the_Cross-National_Study_of_Terror_Attacks. Last accessed August 4, 2017. doi:10.2139/ssrn.1977262.

Morrison, John F. 2013. *The Origins and Rise of Dissident Irish Republicanism: The Role and Impact of Organizational Splits*. New York: Bloomsbury Academic.

Oots, Kent L. 1986. *A Political Organization Approach to Transnational Terrorism*. Westport, CT: Greenwood Press.

Pearlman, Wendy. 2009. "Spoiling Inside and Out: Internal Political Contestation and The Middle East Peace Process." *International Security* 33 (3): 79–109. doi:10.1162/isec.2009.33.3.79.

Perkoski, Evan. 2015. "Organizational Fragmentation and the Trajectory of Militant Splinter Groups" (January 1, 2015). *Dissertations available from ProQuest*. Paper AAI10003874.http://repository.upenn.edu/dissertations/AAI10003874.

Sageman, Marc. 2004. *Understanding Terror Networks*. Philadelphia: University of Pennsylvania Press.

Sánchez-Cuenca, Ignacio, and Paloma Aguilar. 2009. "Terrorist Violence and Popular Mobilization: The Case of the Spanish Transition to Democracy." *Politics & Society* 37 (3): 428–453. doi:10.1177/0032329209338927.

Shapiro, Jacob N. 2013. *The Terrorist's Dilemma: Managing Violent Covert Organizations*. Princeton: Princeton University Press.

Smith, Allison G. 2008. "The Implicit Motives of Terrorist Groups: How The Needs for Affiliation and Power Translate into Death and Destruction." *Political Psychology* 29 (1): 55–75. doi:10.1111/j.1467-9221.2007.00612.x.

Stern, Jessica. 2003. *Terror in the Name of God*. 1st ed. New York: Ecco.

Stern, Jessica, and J. M. Berger. 2015. *ISIS: The State of Terror*. New York: Harper Collins.

Tarrow, Sidney. 1989. *Democracy and Disorder: Protest and Politics in Italy, 1965–1975*. Oxford: Oxford University Press.

Turner, Mark. 2003. "The Management of Violence in a Conflict Organization: The Case of the Abu Sayyaf." *Public Organization Review* 3 (4): 387–401. doi:10.1023/b:porj.0000004816.29771.0f.

Zelin, Aaron Y. 2014. "The War Between Al Qaeda and ISIS for Supremacy of the Global Jihadist Movement." *The Washington Institute for Near East Policy* 20 (1): 1–11.

Zirakzadeh, Cyrus Ernesto. 2002. "From Revolutionary Dreams to Organizational Fragmentation: Disputes over Violence within ETA and Sendero Luminoso." *Terrorism and Political Violence* 14 (4): 66–92. doi:10.1080/714005641.

Chapter 4 The Psychological Approach

Abrahms, Max. 2013. "The Credibility Paradox: Violence as a Double-Edged Sword In International Politics." *International Studies Quarterly* 57 (4): 660–671. doi:10.1111/isqu.12098.

American Psychological Association (APA). 2009. Annual Report. Available online at: www.apa.org/pubs/info/reports/2009-annual.pdf. Last accessed August 4, 2017.

Bandura, Albert. 1999. "Social Cognitive Theory of Personality" in *Handbook of Personality: Theory and Research*, Lawrence A. Pervin and Oliver P. John, eds. New York: Guilford, pp. 154–196.

Begin, Menachem. 1977. *The Revolt*. New York: Nash Pub. Co.

Bloom, Mia. 2005. "Mother, Daughter, Sister, Bomber." *Bulletin of the Atomic Scientists* 61 (6): 54–62. doi:10.2968/061006015.

Cottee, Simon, and Keith Hayward. 2011. "Terrorist (E)Motives: The Existential Attractions of Terrorism," *Studies in Conflict & Terrorism* 34 (12): 963–986. doi:10.1080/1057610x.2011.621116.

Crenshaw, Martha. 1981. "The Causes of Terrorism." *Comparative Politics* 13 (4): 379–399. doi:10.2307/421717.

Crenshaw, Martha. 1986. "The Psychology of Political Terrorism." *Political Psychology* 21 (2): 379–413.

Crenshaw, Martha. 1988. "The Subjective Reality of the Terrorist: Ideological and Psychological Factors in Terrorism," in *Current Perspectives on International Terrorism*, eds. Robert O. Slater and Michael Stohl. London: Palgrave MacMillan Press.

Crozier, Brian. 1960. *The Rebels: A Study of Post-War Insurrections*. Boston, MA: Beacon Press.

Daddis, Gregory A. (Major). 2004. "Understanding Fear's Effect on Unit Effectiveness." *Military Review* (July-August): 22–27. Available online at: http://www.au.af.mil/au/awc/awcgate/milreview/daddis.pdf. Last accessed 4-August-2017.

DeAngelis, Tori. 2009. "Understanding Terrorism," *Monitor on Psychology*, American Psychological Association 40 (10): 60. Available online at: http://www.apa.org/monitor/2009/11/terrorism.aspx. Last accessed 4-August-2017.

Della Porta, Donatella. 1995. *Social Movements, Political Violence, and the State: A Comparative Analysis of Italy and Germany*. New York: Cambridge University Press.

Fanon, Frantz, Jean-Paul Sartre, and Constance Farrington. 1965. *The Wretched of the Earth*. New York: Grove Press, Inc.

Freedman, Lawrence D., Robert Pape, and Mia Bloom. 2005. "Dying to Win: The Strategic Logic of Suicide Terrorism". *Foreign Affairs* 84 (5): 172. doi:10.2307/20031726.

Frankl, Viktor E. 2000. *Man's Search for Ultimate Meaning*, revised edition. New York: Basic Books.

Grossman, David. 1995. *On Killing: The Psychological Cost of Learning to Kill in War and Society*. Boston: 1st ed. Little, Brown, and Company.

Hassan, Riaz. 2014. *Life as a Weapon: The Global Rise of Suicide Bombings*. New York: Routledge.

Horgan, John. 2008. "From Profiles to Pathways and Roots to Routes: Perspectives from Psychology on Radicalization into Terrorism." *The Annals of the American Academy of Political and Social Science* 618 (1): 80–94. doi:10.1177/0002716208317539.

James, Patrick A., and Daniela Pisoiu. 2016. "Mental Illness and Terrorism." (August 10). Available online at: http://smallwarsjournal.com/jrnl/art/mental-illness-and-terrorism. Last accessed 4-August-2017.

Janis, Irving L. 1972. *Victims of Groupthink; A Psychological Study of Foreign-Policy Decisions and Fiascoes*. Boston: Houghton, Mifflin.

Jensen, Michael, Patrick James, and Herbert Tinsley. 2015. "Profiles of Individual Radicalization in the United States: Preliminary Findings." *National Consortium for the Study of Terrorism and Responses to Terrorism*. College, Park, MD: START. January. Available online at http://www.start.umd.edu/publication/profiles-individual-radicalization-united-states-preliminary-findings. Last accessed 4-August-2017.

Kohut, Heinz. 1972. "Thoughts on Narcissism and Narcissistic Rage." *Psychoanalytic Study of the Child* 27 (1): 360–400. Available online at:http://chicagoanalysis.org/system/files/readings/Kohut,%20H.%20%5B1972%5D%20-%20Thoughts%20on%20Narcissism%20and%20Narcissistic%20Rage.pdf. Last accessed 4 -August-2017.

Kohut, Heinz. 1978. *The Search for the Self: Selected Writings of Heinz Kohut, 1950–1978*. New York: International Universities Press.

Knutson, Jeanne N. 1981. "Social and Psychodynamic Pressures Toward a Negative Identity The case of an American Revolutionary Terrorist." *Behavioral and Quantitative Perspectives on Terrorism* 105–150.

Knutson, Jeanne N. 1984. "Toward a United States Policy on Terrorism." *Political Psychology* 5 (2): 287–294. doi:10.2307/3791191.

Kramer, Martin S. 1998. "The Moral Logic of Hizballah," in Walter Reich, ed. *Origins of Terrorism: Psychologies, Ideologies, Theologies, States of Mind.*. Washington, DC: Woodrow Wilson Center Press.

Kruglanski, Arie W. and Edward Orehek. 2011. "The Role of the Quest for Personal Significance in Motivating Terrorism," in J. Forgas, A. Kruglanski, and K. Williams eds., *The Psychology of Social Conflict and Aggression*, New York: Psychology Press, pp. 153–166.

Lankford, Adam. 2011. "Could Suicide Terrorists Actually Be Suicidal?." *Studies in Conflict & Terrorism* 34 (4): 337–366. doi:10.1080/1057610x.2011.551721.

Lankford, Adam. 2014. "Précis of The Myth of Martyrdom: What Really Drives Suicide Bombers, Rampage Shooters, and Other Self-Destructive Killers." *Behavioral and Brain Sciences* 37 (4): 351–362. doi:10.1017/s0140525x13001581.

Mayer, Jean-Francois. 2001. "Cults, Violence and Religious Terrorism: An International Perspective." *Studies in Conflict and Terrorism* 24 (5): 361–376. doi:10.1080/10576100 1750434222.

McCauley, Clark, and Sophia Moskalenko. 2008. "Mechanisms of Political Radicalization: Pathways Toward Terrorism." *Terrorism and Political Violence* 20 (3): 415–433. doi:10.1080/09546550802073367.

McVeigh, Karen. 2014. "Peer pressure lures more Britons to Syria than ISIS Videos, Study finds." *The Guardian*, November 6. Available online at: https://www.theguardian.com/world/2014/nov/06/isis-recruitment-peer-pressure-friendships-more-decisive-social-media-luring-jihadis. Last accessed 4-August-2017.

Merari, Ariel, I., et al. 1990. "Personality Characteristics of 'Self Martyrs'/'Suicide Bombers' and Organizers of Suicide Attacks." *Terrorism and Political Violence* 22 (1): 87–101. doi:10.1080/09546550903409312.

Merari, Ariel. 2010. *Driven to Death: Psychological and Social Aspects of Suicide Terrorism.* Oxford: Oxford University Press.

Milgram, Stanley. 1965. "Liberating Effects of Group Pressure." *Journal of Personality and Social Psychology* 1 (2): 127–134. doi:10.1037/h0021650.

Milgram, Stanley. 1974. *Obedience to Authority: An Experimental View.* London: Tavistock Publications.

Mynatt, Clifford and Steven J. Herman. 1975. "Responsibility Attribution in Groups and Individuals: A Direct Test of the Diffusion of Responsibility Hypothesis." *Journal of Personality and Social Psychology* 32 (6): 1111–1118. doi:10.1037/0022-3514.32.6.1111.

Nordheimer, Jon. 1983. "5 Killed in London as Bomb Explodes Outside Harrods." *The New York Times* (December 18). Available online at: http://www.nytimes.com/1983/12/18/world/5-killed-in-london-as-bomb-explodes-outside-harrods.html. Last accessed 4-August-2017.

Paulhus, Delroy. L. 1991. "Measurement and Control of Response Biases," in Robinson, J.P. et al., eds. *Measures of Personality and Social Psychological Attitudes.* San Diego, CA: Academic Press, Inc.

Post, Jerrold. 1998. "Terrorist Psycho-Logic: Terrorist Behavior as a Product of Psychological Forces," in Walter Reich, ed. *Origins of Terrorism: Psychologies, Ideologies, Theologies, States of Mind.* Woodrow Wilson Center Press.

Post, Jerrold. 2005. "The New Face of Terrorism: Socio-Cultural Foundations of Contemporary Terrorism." *Behavioral Sciences and the Law* 23 (4): 451–465. doi:10.1002/bsl.658.

Post, Jerrold M. 2010. "When Hatred is Bred in the Bone': The Social Psychology of Terrorism." *Annals of the New York Academy of Sciences* 1208 (1): 15–23. doi:10.1111/j.1749-6632.2010.05694.x.

Post, Jerrold, Ehud Sprinzak, and Laurita Denny. 2003. "The Terrorists in Their Own Words: Interviews with 35 Incarcerated Middle Eastern Terrorists." *Terrorism and Political Violence* 15 (1): 171–184. doi:10.1080/09546550312331293007.

Quantum Communications. 2015. *Understanding Jihadists in Their Own Words.* The White Papers (March, Issue No. 2).

Raines, Howell. 1987. "Bombing in Ulster Kills 11 in Crowd; I.R.A. Is Suspected." (November 9). Available online at: http://www.nytimes.com/1987/11/09/world/bombing-in-ulster-kills-11-in-crowd-ira-is-suspected.html. Last accessed 4-August-2017.

Reich, Walter. 1998. *Origins of Terrorism.* Washington, DC: Woodrow Wilson Center Press.

Richardson, Louise. 2006. *What Terrorists Want: Understanding the Enemy, Containing the Threat.* New York: Random House, Inc.

Robins, Robert. S. and Jerrold M. Post. 1997. *Political Paranoia: The Psychopolitics of Hatred.* New Haven, CT: Yale University Press.

Roese, Neal J. and Kathleen D. Vohs. 2012. "Hindsight Bias." *Perspectives on Psychological Science* 7 (5): 411–426. doi:10.1177/1745691612454303

Sack, Kevin. 2017. "Trial Documents Show Dylann Roof Had Mental Disorders." *The New York Times,* (February 2). Available online at: https://www.nytimes.com /2017/02/02/us/dylann-roof-charleston-killing-mental.html?_r=0. Last accessed 4-August-2017.

Sageman, Marc. 2004. *Understanding Terror Networks.* Philadelphia, PA: University of Pennsylvania Press.

Samuel, Henry and Tom Morgan. 2016. "Who Is the Nice Terror Attack Suspect? Everything We Know So Far about Mohamed Lahouaiej Bouhlel." *The Telegraph.* (July 18). Available online at: http://www.telegraph.co.uk/news/2016/07 /15/who-is-the-nice-terror-attacker-everything-we-know-so-far/. Last accessed 4-August-2017.

Sanchez, Ref and Peter Foster. 2015. "'You Rape Our Women, and You're Taking Over Our Country,' Charleston Church Gunman Told Black Victims." *The Telegraph* (18 June). Available online at: http://www.telegraph.co.uk/news/worldnews/northamerica/ usa/11684957/You-rape-our-women-and-are-taking-over-our-country-Charleston-church-gunman-told-black-victims.html. Last accessed 4-August-2017.

Schwartz, Seth J., and Curtis S. Dunkel, and Alan S. Waterman. 2009. "Terrorism, an Identity Theory Perspective." *Studies in Conflict & Terrorism* 32 (6): 537:559. doi:10. 1080/10576100902888453.

Sedgwick, Mark. 2004. "Al-Qaeda and the Nature of Religious Terrorism." *Terrorism and Political Violence* 16 (4): 795–814. doi:10.1080/09546550590906098.

Sedgwick, Mark. 2010. "The Concept of Radicalization as a Source of Confusion." *Terrorism and Political Violence* 22 (4): 479–494. doi:10.1080/09546553.2010.491009.

Seligman, Martin E.P. 2002. *Authentic Happiness: Using the New Positive Psychology to Realize your Potential for Lasting Fulfillment.* New York: Free Press.

Sharkey, Noel. 2012. "Killing Made Easy: From Joysticks to Politics," in Lin, P., K. Abney, G.A. Bekey, eds. *Robot Ethics: The Ethical and Social Implications of Robotics.* Cambridge, MA: The MIT Press.

Speckhard, Anne, and Khapta Akhmedova. 2006. "Black Widows: The Chechen Female Suicide Terrorists," in Yoram Schweitzer, ed. *Female Suicide Terrorists.* Jaffe Center Publication, Tel Aviv, Israel.

Staff Writer. 1987. "IRA 'Regrets' Bombing, Blames British for Civilian Toll." *San Francisco Chronicle,* November 10, p. 19.

Stout, C. E. 2002. *The Psychology of Terrorism: Programs and Practices in Response and Prevention, Vol. IV.* Westport: Praeger.

Stritzke, Werner G.K., S. Lewandowsky, D. Denemark, J. Clare, F. Morgan. 2009. *Terrorism and Torture: An Interdisciplinary Perspective.* New York: Cambridge University Press.

Tajfel, Henri. 1974. "Social Identity and Intergroup Behaviour." *International Social Science Council* 13 (2): 65–93. doi:10.1177/053901847401300204.

Torres, Manuel R., Javier Jordan, and Nicola Horsburgh. 2006. "Analysis and Evolution of the Global Jihadist Movement Propaganda." *Terrorism and Political Violence* 18 (3): 399–421. doi:10.1080/09546550600751990.

Tsintsadze-Maass, Eteri, and Richard W. Maas. 2014. "Groupthink and Terrorist Radicalization." *Terrorism and Political Violence* 26 (5): 735–758. http://dx.doi.org/1 0.1080/09546553.2013.805094.

Schwartz, Seth J, Curtis S. Dunkel and Alan S. Waterman. 2009. "Terrorism: An Identity Theory Perspective." *Studies in Conflict & Terrorism* 32 (6): 537–559. doi:10.1080/10576100902888453.

Wasmund, Klaus. 1986. "The Political Socialization of West German Terrorists," in P.H. Merkel, ed., *Political Violence and Terror: Motifs and Motivations*. Berkeley, CA: University of California Press, pp. 191–228.

Weine, Stevan., B.H. Ellis, Haddad, R., A.B. Miller, R. Lowenhaupt, and C. Polutnik. 2015. *Lessons Learned from Mental Health and Education: Identifying Best Practices for Addressing Violent Extremism*. Final Report. College Park, MD: Office of University Programs, Science and Technology Directorate. US Department of Homeland Security.

Wright, Lawrence. 2006. *The Looming Tower: Al Qaeda and the Road to 9/11*. New York: Vintage Books.

Victoroff, Jeff. 2005. "The Mind of the Terrorist: A Review and Critique of Psychological Approaches." *Journal of Conflict Resolution* 49 (1): 3–42. doi:10.1177/0022002704272040.

Chapter 5 The Ideological Approach

Abrahms, Max. 2013. "The Credibility Paradox: Violence as a Double-Edged Sword In International Politics." *International Studies Quarterly* 57 (4): 660–671. doi:10.1111/isqu.12098.

Ackerman, Spencer. 2014. "'Apocalyptic' ISIS Beyond Anything We've Seen, Say US Defence Chiefs." *The Guardian* (August 22). Available online at: https://www.theguardian.com/world/2014/aug/21/isis-us-military-iraq-strikes-threat-apocalyptic. Last accessed 4-August-2017.

Asal, Victor and R. Karl Rethemeyer. 2008. "Dilettantes, Ideologues, and the Weak: Terrorists Who Don't Kill." *Conflict Management & Peace Science*. 25 (3): 244–263. doi:10.1080/07388940802219000.

Ayers. Bill. 2008. *Fugitive Days: Memoirs of an Anti-War Activist*. Boston: Beacon Press.

Berberoglu, Berch. 2009. *The National Question: Nationalism, Ethnic Conflict, and Self-Determination in the Twentieth Century*. Philadelphia: Temple University Press.

Berman, Eli and David D. Laitin. 2008. "Religion, Terrorism and Public Goods: Testing The Club Model." *Journal of Public Economics* 92 (10–11): 1942–1967. doi:10.1016/j.jpubeco.2008.03.007.

Berntzen, Lars Erik, and Sveinung Sandberg. 2014. "The Collective Nature of Lone Wolf Terrorism: Anders Behring Breivik and the Anti-Islamic Social Movement." *Terrorism and Political Violence*, 26 (5): 759–779. doi:10.1080/09546553.2013.767245.

Bush, George W. 2006. *Speaking at the American Legion National Convention, Salt Lake City, Utah*. (August 31). Available online at: http://www.deseretnews.com/article/645197682/Text-of-President-Bushs-speech-to-the-American-Legion-National-Convention.html. Last accessed 4-August-2017.

Byman, Daniel. 1998. "The Logic of Ethnic Terrorism." *Studies in Conflict and Terrorism*. 21 (2): 149–169. doi:10.1080/10576109808436060.

Byman, Daniel. 2016. "ISIS Goes Global: Fight the Islamic State by Targeting its Affiliates." *Foreign Affairs*. (March/April). Available online at: https://www.foreignaffairs.com/articles/middle-east/isis-goes-global. Last accessed 4-August-2017.

Cavanaugh, William T. 2009. *The Myth of Religious Violence: Secular Ideology and the Roots of Modern Conflict*. New York: Oxford University Press.

Childs, Steven. 2011. "From Identity to Militancy: The Shi'A of Hezbollah." *Comparative Strategy* 30 (4): 363–372. doi:10.1080/01495933.2011.605026.

Cockburn, Patrick. 2015. *The Rise of the Islamic State: ISIS and the New Sunni Revolution.* London: Verso Books.

Conrad, Justin and Daniel Milton. 2013. "Unpacking the Connection Between Terror and Islam." *Studies in Conflict & Terrorism* 36 (4): 315–336. doi:10.1080/10576 10x.2013.763600.

Dees, Morris and James Corcoran. 1996. *Gathering Storm: America's Militia Threat.* New York: HarperCollins Publishers.

Dohrn, Bernardine, William Ayers, and Jeff Jones. 2006. *Sing A Battle Song: The Revolutionary Poetry, Statements, and Communiqués of the Weather Underground 1970–1974.* New York: Seven Stories Press.

Fausset, Richard. 2015. "For Robert Dear, Religion and Rage Before Planned Parenthood Attack." *New York Times* (December 1). Available online at: https://www.nytimes.com/2015/12/02/us/robert-dear-planned-parenthood-shooting.html?_r=2. Last accessed 4-August-2017.

Gambetta, Diego, and Steffen Hertog. 2009. "Why Are There So Many Engineers Among Islamic Radicals?." *European Journal of Sociology/Archives* 50 (2): 201–230. doi:10.1017/s0003975609990129.

Gregg, Heather S. 2010. "Fighting The Jihad of The Pen: Countering Revolutionary Islam's Ideology." *Terrorism and Political Violence* 22 (2): 292–314. doi:10.1080/09546551003597584.

Gregg, Heather S. 2014. "Defining and Distinguishing Secular and Religious Terrorism." *Perspectives on Terrorism* 8 (2): 36–51.

Hoffman, Bruce. 2006. *Inside Terrorism,* 2nd ed. New York: Columbia University Press.

Jacobs, Ron. 1997. *The Way the Wind Blew.* London: Verso.

Jones, David Martin, and M. L. R. Smith. 2010. "Beyond Belief: Islamist Strategic Thinking and International Relations Theory." *Terrorism and Political Violence* 22 (2): 242–266. doi:10.1080/09546550903472286.

Juergensmeyer, Mark. 2003. *Terror in the Mind of God: The Global Rise of Religious Violence,* 2nd ed. Berkeley: University of California Press.

Kalyvas, Stathis. 1999. "Wanton and Senseless? The Logic of Massacres in Algeria". *Rationality and Society* 11 (3): 243–285. doi:10.1177/104346399011003001.

Kaufman, Stuart J. 2009. "Narratives and Symbols in Violent Mobilization: The Palestinian-Israeli Case." *Security Studies* 18 (3): 400–434. doi:10.1080/09636410903132938.

Kellen, Konrad. 1998. "Ideology and Rebellion: Terrorism in West Germany," in Walter Reich, ed. *Origins of Terrorism: Psychologies, Ideologies, Theologies, States of Mind.,* Ch. 3. Washington, DC: Woodrow Wilson Center Press.

Laqueur, Walter. 2004. *Voices of Terror.* UK: Reed Press.

Levitt, Matthew. 2006. *Hamas.* New Haven: Yale University Press.

Masters, Daniel. 2008. "The Origin of Terrorist Threats: Religious, Separatist, Or Something Else?" *Terrorism and Political Violence* 20 (3): 396–414. doi:10.1080/09546550802073359.

McCants, William F. 2015. *The ISIS Apocalypse: The History, Strategy, and Doomsday Vision of the Islamic State.* New York: St. Martin's Press.

McVeigh, Timothy. 2010. *Manifesto.* Available online at: http://www.truthinourtime.com/2010/02/19/timothy-mcveighs-manifesto/. Last accessed 4-August-2017.

Merkl, Peter H, and Leonard Weinberg. 2003. *Right-Wing Extremism in The Twenty-First Century.* London: Frank Cass.

Nixon, Ron. 2016. "Homeland Security Looked Past Antigovernment Movement, Ex-Analyst Says." *New York Times* (January 8). Accessible at https://www.nytimes.com/2016/01/09/us/politics/homeland-security-looked-past-militia-movement-ex-analyst-says.html?_r=0, last accessed 4-August-2017.

Pantucci, Raffaello. 2011. "A Typology of Lone Wolves: Preliminary Analysis of Lone Islamist Terrorists". *The International Centre of Radicalization and Political Violence (ICSR): Developments in Radicalisation and Political Violence.* (March). Available online at http://icsr.info/wp-content/uploads/2012/10/1302002992ICSRPaper_ATypologyofLoneWolves_Pantucci.pdf. Last accessed 4-August-2017.

Pedahzur, Ami. 2001. "Struggling with the Challenges Of Right-Wing Extremism And Terrorism Within Democratic Boundaries: A Comparative Analysis." *Studies in Conflict & Terrorism* 24 (5): 339–359. doi:10.1080/105761001750434213.

Piazza, James A. 2009. "Is Islamist Terrorism More Dangerous?: An Empirical Study Of Group Ideology, Organization, And Goal Structure." *Terrorism and Political Violence* 21 (1): 62–88. doi:10.1080/09546550802544698.

Pratt, Douglas. 2010. "Religion and Terrorism: Christian Fundamentalism and Extremism." *Terrorism and Political Violence* 22 (3): 438–456. doi:10.1080/09546551003689399.

Ranstorp, Magnus. 1996. "Terrorism in the Name of Religion." *Journal of International Affairs,* Vol. 50 (1): 41–63.

Rapoport, David C. 1984. "Fear and Trembling: Terrorism in Three Religious Traditions." *The American Political Science Review* 78 (3): 658–677. doi:10.2307/1961835.

Ron, James. 2001. "Ideology in Context: Explaining Sendero Luminoso's Tactical Escalation." *Journal of Peace Research* 38 (5): 569–592. doi:10.1177/0022343301038005002.

Rudolph, Eric. Available online at: http://www.armyofgod.com/EricRudolphHomepage.html. Last accessed 4-August 2017.

Rushdie, Salman. 2002. *Step Across This Line: Collected Non-Fiction 1992–2002.* New York: Random House.

Sànchez-Cuenca, Ignacio. 2007. "The Dynamics of Nationalist Terrorism: ETA and the IRA." *Terrorism and Political Violence* 19 (3): 289–306. doi:10.1080/09546550701246981.

Sedgwick, Mark. 2004. "Al-Qaeda and the Nature of Religious Terrorism." *Terrorism and Political Violence* 16 (4): 795–814. doi:10.1080/09546550590906098.

Sedgwick, Mark. 2010. "The Concept of Radicalization as a Source of Confusion." *Terrorism and Political Violence* 22 (4): 479–494. doi:10.1080/09546553.2010.491009.

Schbley, Ayla H. 1990. "Religious Terrorists: What They Aren't Going to Tell Us." *Terrorism* 13 (3): 237–241. doi:10.1080/10576109008435834.

Snow, David A, and Scott Byrd. 2007. "Ideology, Framing Processes, and Islamic Terrorist Movements." *Mobilization; An International Quarterly* 12 (2): 119–136.

Spaaij, Ramon, FJ, and Ebooks Corporation. 2012. *Understanding Lone Wolf Terrorism and Global Patterns, Motivations and Prevention.* SpringerBriefs in Criminology. Dorderecht; New York: Springer.

Stern, Jessica. 2003. *Terror in The Name of God: Why Religious Militants Kill.* New York: Ecco.

Stern, Jessica and J. M Berger. 2015. *ISIS: The State of Terror.* New York: Ecco.

Warrick, Joby. 2015. *Black Flags: The Rise of ISIS.* New York: Doubleday.

Weiss, Michael and Hassan Hassan. 2015. *ISIS: Inside the Army of Terror.* New York: Regan Arts.

Wood, Graeme. 2015. "What ISIS really wants." *The Atlantic* (March). Available online at: https://www.theatlantic.com/magazine/archive/2015/03/what-isis-really-wants/384980/. Last accessed 4-August-2017.

Woodworth, Paddy. 2001. "Why Do They Kill: The Basque Conflict in Spain?" *World Policy Journal* 18 (1): 1–12. doi:10.1215/07402775-2001-2002.

Chapter 6   Structural Approaches

Ahmed, Saladdin.   2015. "Islamic State: More popular than you think." openDemocracy, June 17. Available online at https://www.opendemocracy.net/arab-awakening/saladdin-ahmed/aljazeera-poll-81-percent-support-for-islamic-state. Last accessed 4-August-2017.

Atzili, Boaz. 2010. "State Weakness and 'Vacuum of Power' in Lebanon." *Studies in Conflict & Terrorism* 33 (8): 757–782. doi: 10.1080/1057610X.2010.494172.

Azam, Jean-Paul, and Véronique Thelen. 2010. "Foreign Aid Versus Military Intervention in the War on Terror." *Journal of Conflict Resolution* 54 (2): 237–261. doi:10.1177/0022002709356051.

Bakke, Kristin M. 2014. "Help Wanted?: The Mixed Record of Foreign Fighters in Domestic Insurgencies." *International Security* 38 (4): 150–187. doi:10.1162/isec_a_00156.

Benson, David C. 2014. "Why the Internet is Not Increasing Terrorism." *Security Studies* 23 (2): 293–328. doi:10.1080/09636412.2014.905353.

Berkman, Alexander. 1922. "Russian Revolution and the Communist Party." Available online at http://theanarchistlibrary.org/library/alexander-berkman-russian-revolution-and-the-communist-party. Last accessed 4-August-2017.

Blanford, Nicholas. 2011. *Warriors of God: Inside Hezbollah's Thirty-Year Struggle Against Israel*. New York: Random House.

Bradshaw, York W. 1987. "Urbanization and Underdevelopment: A Global Study of Modernization, Urban Bias, and Economic Dependency." *American Sociological Review* 52 (2): 224–239. doi:10.2307/2095451.

Braithwaite, Alex, and David Sobek. 2005. "Victim of Success: American Dominance and Terrorism." *Conflict Management and Peace Science* 22 (2): 135–148.

Brandt, Patrick T. and Todd Sandler. 2010. "What Do Transnational Terrorists Target? Has it Changed? Are We Safer?." *Journal of Conflict Resolution* 54 (2): 214–236. doi:10.1177/0022002709355437.

Bunn, Matthew, and Anthony Wier. 2005. "The Seven Myths of Nuclear Terrorism." *Current History* 104 (681): 153–161.

Burgoon, Brian. 2006. "On Welfare and Terror: Social Welfare Policies and Political-Economic Roots of Terrorism." *Journal of Conflict Resolution* 50 (2): 176–203. doi:10.1177/0022002705284829.

Byman, Daniel. 2005. *Deadly Connections: States that Sponsor Terrorism*. New York: Cambridge University Press.

Chenoweth, Erica. 2010a. "Democratic Competition and Terrorist Activity." *The Journal of Politics* 72 (1): 16–30. doi:10.1017/s0022381609990442.

Chenoweth, Erica. 2010b. "Democratic Pieces: Democratization and the Origins of Terrorism," in William R. Thompson and Rafael Reuveny, eds., *Coping with Contemporary Terrorism: Origins, Escalation, Counter-Strategies, and Responses* (SUNY Press, 2010).

Chenoweth, Erica, and Joseph Young. 2017. "Resilient Republics: Terrorism's Negligible Effect on Democracy," with Joseph K. Young. Unpublished Manuscript, University of Denver.

Chenoweth, Erica. 2012. "Is Terrorism Still a Democratic Phenomenon?" *Uluslararasi Iliskiler- International Relations* 8 (32): 85–100.

Choi, Seung-Whan. 2010 "Fighting terrorism through the rule of law?" *Journal of Conflict Resolution* 54 (6): 940–966. doi:10.1177/0022002710371666.

Crenshaw, Martha. 1981. "The Causes of Terrorism." *Comparative Politics* 13 (4): 379–399. doi:10.2307/421717.

Cronin, Audrey Kurth. 2006. "How Al-Qaida Ends: The Decline and Demise of Terrorist Groups." *International Security* 31 (1): 7–48. doi:10.1162/isec.2006.31.1.7.

Cronin, Audrey Kurth. 2013. "Why Drones Fail: When Tactics Drive Strategy." *Foreign Affairs* 92 (4): 44-V.

Davenport, Christian. 2007. "State Repression and Political Order." *Annual Review of Political Science* 10 (1): 1–23. doi:10.1146/annurev.polisci.10.101405.143216.

De la Calle, Luis, and Ignacio Sánchez-Cuenca. 2011. "What We Talk About When We Talk About Terrorism." *Politics & Society* 39 (3): 451–472. doi:10.1177/0032329211415506.

Della Porta, Donatella. 1988. "Recruitment Processes in Clandestine Political Organizations: Italian Left-Wing Terrorism." *International Social Movement Research* 1: 155–169.

Denning, Dorothy E. 2001. "Is Cyber Terror Next?" Social Science Research Council Essay Forum (November 1). Accessible at http://essays.ssrc.org/10yearsafter911/is-cyber-terror-next/. Last accessed 4-August-2017.

Directorate of National Intelligence (DNI). 2006. Declassified Key Judgments of the National Intelligence Estimate "Trends in Global Terrorism: Implications for the United States"), April. Available online at: http://www.dni.gov.

Dreher, Axel, and Martin Gassebner. 2008. "Does Political Proximity to the U.S. Cause Terror?" *Economics Letters* 99 (1): 27–29. doi:10.1016/j.econlet.2007.05.020.

Dugan, Laura, and Erica Chenoweth. 2012. "Moving Beyond Deterrence: The Effectiveness of Raising the Expected Utility of Abstaining from Terrorism in Israel." *American Sociological Review* 77 (4): 597–624. doi:10.1177/0003122412450573.

Findley, Michael G., James A. Piazza, and Joseph K. Young. 2012. "Games Rivals Play: Terrorism in International Rivalries." *The Journal of Politics* 74 (1): 235–248. doi:10.2139/ssrn.1676555.

Gassebner, Martin, and Simon Luechinger. 2011. "Lock, Stock, and Barrel: A Comprehensive Assessment of the Determinants of Terror." *Public Choice* 149 (3–4): 235–261. doi:10.1007/s11127-011-9873-0.

Hoffman, Bruce. 2006. *Inside Terrorism*. 2nd ed. New York: Columbia University Press.

Hübschle, Annette. 2011. "From Theory to Practice: Exploring the Organized Crime-Terror Nexus in Sub-Saharan Africa." *Perspectives on Terrorism* 5 (3–4).

Huntington, Samuel P. 1993. "The Clash of Civilizations?" *Foreign Affairs* 72 (3): 22–49. doi:10.2307/20045621.

Idler, Annette, and James J.F. Forest. 2015. "Behavioral Patterns Among (violent) Non-State Actors: A Study of Complementary Governance". *Stability: International Journal of Security and Development,* 4 (1): 1–19.

Johnson, Chalmers. 2000. *Blowback: The Costs and Consequences of American Empire.* New York: Holt.

Johnston, Patrick B. 2012. "Does Decapitation Work? Assessing the Effectiveness of Leadership Targeting in Counterinsurgency Campaigns." *International Security* 36 (4): 47–79. doi:10.1162/isec_a_00076.

Johnston, Patrick B., and Anoop K. Sarbahi. 2016. "The Impact of US Drone Strikes on Terorrism in Pakistan." *International Studies Quarterly* 60 (2): 203–219. doi:10.1093/isq/sqv004.

Jones, Seth G. and Patrick B. Johnston. 2013. "The Future of Insurgency." *Studies in Conflict & Terrorism* 36 (1): 1–25. doi.org/10.1080/1057610X.2013.739077

Kilcullen, David. 2009. *The Accidental Guerrilla.* New York: Oxford University Press.

Krieger, Tim, and Daniel Meierrieks. 2011. "What Causes Terrorism?" *Public Choice* 147 (1/2): 3–27. doi:10.1007/sl1127-010-9601-1

Li, Quan and Drew Schaub. 2004. "Economic Globalization and Transnational Terrorism: A Pooled Time-Series Analysis." *Journal of Conflict Resolution* 48 (2): 230–258. doi:10.1177/0022002703262869.

Li, Quan. 2005. "Does Democracy Promote or Reduce Transnational Terrorist Incidents?" *Journal of Conflict Resolution* 49 (2): 278–297. doi:10.1177/0022002704272830.

Lichbach, Michael I. 1989. "An Evaluation of 'Does Economic Inequality Breed Political Conflict?' Studies'" *World Politics* 41 (4): 431–470. doi:10.2307/2010526.

Malet, David. 2013. *Foreign Fighters: Transnational Identity in Civic Conflicts.* Oxford: Oxford University Press.

Mansfield, Edward D, and Jack Snyder. 1995. "Democratization and the Danger of War." *International Security* 20 (1): 5–38. doi:10.2307/2539213.

Mares, Miroslav. 2011. "Terrorism-Free Zone in East Central Europe? Strategic Environment, Risk Tendencies, and Causes of Limited Terrorist Activities in the Visegrad Group Countries." *Terrorism and Political Violence* 23 (2): 233–253. doi:10.1080/09546553.2010.529389.

Massey, Douglas S. 1996. "The Age of Extremes: Concentrated Affluence and Poverty in the Twenty-First Century." *Demography* 33 (4): 395–412. doi:10.2307/2061773.

Mousseau, Michael. 2002/2003. "Market Civilization and Its Clash with Terror." *International Security* 27 (3): 5–29. doi:10.1162/01622880260553615.

Mousseau, Michael. 2006. *Market Civilization and its Clash with Terror.* Cambridge: MIT Press

Mousseau, Michael. 2011. "Urban Poverty and Support for Islamist Terror: Survey Results of Muslims in Fourteen Countries." *Journal of Peace Research* 48 (1): 35–47. doi:10.1177/0022343310391724.

Newman, Edward. 2006. "Exploring the 'Root Causes' of Terrorism." *Studies in Conflict & Terrorism* 29 (8): 749–772. doi:10.1080/10576100600704069.

Pape, Robert. 2003. "The Strategic Logic of Suicide Terrorism." *American Political Science Review* 97 (3): 343–361. doi:10.1017/s000305540300073x.

Pape, Robert. 2005. *Dying to win: The strategic logic of suicide terrorism.* New York: Random House.

Parkinson, Sarah Elizabeth. 2013. "Organizing Rebellion: Rethinking High-Risk Mobilization and Social Networks in War." *American Political Science Review* 107 (3): 418–432. doi:10.1017/s0003055413000208.

Piazza, James A. 2006. "Rooted in poverty? Terrorism, Poor Economic Development, and Social Cleavages." *Terrorism and Political Violence* 18 (1): 159–177. doi:10.1080/095465590944578.

Piazza, James A. 2008. "Incubators of Terror: Do Failed and Failing States Promote Transnational Terrorism?" *International Studies Quarterly* 52 (3): 469–488. doi:10.1111/j.1468-2478.2008.00511.x.

Piazza, James A. 2008 "Do Democracy and Free Markets Protect Us From Terrorism?" *International Politics* 45 (1): 72–91. doi:10.1057/palgrave.ip.8800220.

Piazza, James A. and Karin von Hippel. 2013. "Does Poverty Serve as a Root Cause of Terrorism?" in Stuart Gottlieb, ed, *Debating Terrorism and Counterterrorism: Conflicting Perspectives on Causes, Contexts and Responses*, CQ Press.

Rich, Ben and Dara Conduit. 2015. "The Impact of Jihadist Foreign Fighters on Indigenous Secular-Nationalist Causes: Contrasting Chechnya and Syria." *Studies in Conflict & Terrorism* 38 (2) 113–131. doi.org/10.1080/1057610X.2014.979605

Robison, Kristopher K., Edward M. Crenshaw, and J. Craig Jenkins. 2006. "Ideologies of Violence: The Social Origins of Islamist and Leftist Transnational Terrorism." *Social Forces* 84 (4): 2009–2026. doi:10.1353/sof.2006.0106.

Rollins, John, and Clay Wilson. 2007. "Terrorist Capabilities for Cyberattack: Overview and Policy Issues," in Linden, Edward V., ed. *Focus on Terrorism, Vol. 9*, New York: Nova Science Publishers, Inc.

Ross, Jeffrey Ian. 1993. "The Structural Causes of Oppositional Political Terrorism: Towards a Causal Model." *Journal of Peace Research* 30 (3): 317–329. doi:10.1177/002 2343393030003006.

Routledge, Paul. 1994. "Backstreets, Barricades and Blackouts: Urban Terrains of Resistance in Nepal." *Environment and Planning D: Society and Space* 12 (5): 559–578. doi:10.1068/d120559.

Sánchez-Cuenca, Ignacio, and Luis de la Calle. 2009. "Domestic Terrorism: The Hidden Side of Political Violence." *Annual Review of Political Science* 12 (1): 31–49. doi:10.1146/annurev.polisci.12.031607.094133.

Sandler, Todd. 1995. "On the Relationship Between Democracy and Terrorism." *Terrorism and Political Violence.* 7 (4): 1–9. doi:10.1080/09546559508427315.

Sobek, David, and Alex Braithwaite. 2005. "Victim of Success: American Dominance and Terrorism." *Conflict Management and Peace Science* 22 (2): 135–148. doi:10.1080/07388940590948565.

Stern, Jessica, and J. M. Berger. 2015. *ISIS: The State of Terror.* New York: Harper Collins.

Swanson, Ana. 2015. "How the Islamic State Makes its Money." *The Washington Post,* November 18. Available online at https://www.washingtonpost.com/news/wonk/wp/2015/11/18/how-isis-makes-its-money/. Last accessed 4-August-2017.

Urdal, Henrik. 2006. "A Clash of Generations? Youth Bulges and Political Violence." *International Studies Quarterly* 50 (3): 607–629. doi:10.1111/j.1468-2478.2006.00416.x.

Volgy, Thomas J., Lawrence E. Imwalle, and Jeff J. Corntassel. 1997. "Structural Determinants of International Terrorism: The Effects of Hegemony and Polarity on Terrorist Activity." *International Interactions* 23 (2): 207–231. doi:10.1080/03050629708434907.

Walsh, James I., and James A. Piazza. 2010. "Why Respecting Physical Integrity Rights Reduces Terrorism." *Comparative Political Studies* 43 (5): 551–577. doi:10.1177/0010414009356176.

Yeginsu, Ceylan. 2014. "ISIS Draws a Steady Stream of Recruits from Turkey." *The New York Times,* September 15. Available at http://www.nytimes.com/2014/09/16/world/europe/turkey-is-a-steady-source-of-isis-recruits.html?_r=0. Last accessed 4-August-2017.

Yunus, Muhammad. 2006. "Nobel Lecture." Oslo, Norway (December 10). Available at https://www.nobelprize.org/nobel_prizes/peace/laureates/2006/yunus-lecture-en.html. Last accessed 4-August-2017.

Chapter 7 Critical Approaches

Bell, Derrick, A., Jr. 1980. "Brown v. Board of Education and the Interest-Convergence Dilemma." *Harvard Law Review* 93 (3): 518–533. doi:10.2307/1340546.

Blakeley, Ruth. 2007. "Bringing the State Back into Terrorism Studies." *European Political Science* 6 (3): 228–235. doi:10.1057/palgrave.eps.2210139.

Barsamian, David. 2001. "The United States Is Leading a Terrorist State: An Interview With Noam Chomsky." *Monthly Review* (1 November). Available online at http://monthlyreview.org/2001/11/01/the-united-states-is-a-leading-terrorist-state/. Last accessed 4-August-2017.

Bloom, Mia M. 2005. *Dying to Kill: The Allure of Suicide Terror.* New York: Columbia University Press.

Caprioli, Mary. 2000. "Gendered Conflict." *Journal of Peace Research* 37 (1): 53–68. doi:10.1177/0022343300037001003.

Chomsky, Noam, John Junkerman, and Takei Masakazu. 2011. *Power and Terror: Conflict, Hegemony, and the Rule of Force.* London: Routledge.

Chomsky, Noam, and Andre Vitchek. 2013. *On Western Terrorism: From Hiroshima to Drone Warfare.* London: Pluto Press.

Cox, Robert W. 1981. "Social Forces, States and World Orders: Beyond International Relations theory." *Millennium: Journal of International Studies* 10 (2): 126–155. doi:10.1177/03058298810100020501.

Donahue, Thomas J. 2013. "Terrorism, Moral Conceptions, and Moral Innocence." *The Philosophical Form* 44 (4): 413–435. doi:10.1111/phil.12021.

Egerton, Frazer. 2009. "A Case for a Critical Approach to Terrorism." *European Political Science* 8 (1): 57–67. doi:10.1057/eps.2008.47.

Erlenbusch, Verena. 2014. "How (Not) to Study Terrorism." *Critical Review of International Social and Political Philosophy* 17 (4): 470–491. doi.org/10.1080/13698230.2013.767040

English, Richard. 2009. "The Future of Terrorism Studies." *Critical Studies on Terrorism* 2 (2): 377–382. doi:10.1080/17539150903025119.

Fanon, Frantz. 1963. *The Wretched of the Earth.* New York: Grove Press.

Galtung, Johan. 1969. "Violence, Peace and Peace Research." *Journal of Peace Research* 6 (3): 167–191. doi:10.1177/002234336900600301.

George, Alexander. 1991. "The Discipline of Terrorology." In: A. George, ed. *Western State Terrorism.* London: Frank Cass: pp. 76–101.

Gramsci, Antonio. 1971. *Selections from the Prison Notebooks.* New York: International Publishers.

Gunning, Jeroen. 2007. "Babies and Bathwaters: Reflecting On The Pitfalls Of Critical Terrorism Studies." *European Political Science* 6 (3): 236–243. doi:10.1057/palgrave.eps.2210144.

Gunning, Jeroen. 2007. "A Case for Critical Terrorism Studies?" *Government and Opposition,* 42 (3): 363–393. doi:10.1111/j.1477-7053.2007.00228.x

Herman, Edward S, and Gerry O'Sullivan. 1989. *The "Terrorism" Industry: The Experts and Institutions that Shape our View of Terror.* New York: Pantheon Books.

Herring, Eric. 2008. "Critical Terrorism Studies: An Activist Scholar Perspective." *Critical Studies On Terrorism* 1 (2): 197–212. doi:10.1080/17539150802187507.

Horgan, John, and Michael J. Boyle. 2008. "A Case Against 'Critical Terrorism Studies'." *Critical Studies on Terrorism* 1 (1): 51–64. doi:10.1080/17539150701848225.

Hudson, Valerie, Bonnie Spallif-Banvill, Mary Caprioli, and Chad F. Emmett. 2012. *Sex and World Peace*. New York: Columbia University Press.

Jackson, Richard. 2005. *Writing The War On Terrorism: Language, Politics and Counter-terrorism*. Manchester: Manchester University Press.

Jackson, Richard. 2007. "The Core Commitments of Critical Terrorism Studies." *European Political Science* 6 (3): 244–251. doi:10.1057/palgrave.eps.2210141.

Jackson, Richard. 2007. "Constructing Enemies: 'Islamic Terrorism' in Political and Academic Discourse." *Government and Opposition* 42 (3): 394–426. doi:10.1111/j.1477-7053.2007.00229.x.

Jackson, Richard, Marie Breen Smyth, and Jeroen Gunning, eds. 2009. *Critical Terrorism Studies: A New Research Agenda*. Hoboken: Taylor and Francis.

Jackson, Richard. 2009. "The Study of Political Terror After 11 September 2001: Problems, Challenges and Future Developments." *Political Studies Review* 7 (2): 171–184. doi:10.1111/j.1478-9299.2009.00177.x.

Jackson, Richard, Lee Jarvis, Jeroen Gunning, and Marie Breen Smyth. 2011. *Terrorism: A Critical Introduction*. London: Palgrave Macmillan.

Jaggar, Alison M. 2005. "What Is Terrorism, Why Is It Wrong, and Could It Ever Be Morally Permissible?" *Journal of Social Philosophy* 36 (2): 202–217. doi:10.1111/j.1467-9833.2005.00267.x.

Jarvis, Lee. 2009. "The Spaces and Faces of Critical Terrorism Studies." *Security Dialogue* 40 (1): 5–27. doi:10.1177/0967010608100845.

Jackson, Richard. 2007. "The Core Commitments of Critical Terrorism Studies." *European Political Science* 6 (3): 244–251. doi:10.1057/palgrave.eps.2210141.

Mueller, John. 2006. *Overblown: How Politicians and the Terrorism Industry Inflate National Security Threats and Why We Believe Them*. New York, Simon and Schuster.

Pape, Robert. 2005. *Dying to Win*. New York: Random House.

Sjoberg, Laura, and Caron E. Gentry. 2008. "Profiling Terror: Gender, Strategic Logic, and Emotion in the Study of Suicide Terrorism." *Österreichische Zeitschrift für Politikwissenschaft* 37 (2): 181–196.

Smyth, Marie Breen. 2007. "A Critical Research Agenda for the Study of Political Terror." *European Political Science* 6 (3): 260–267. doi:10.1057/palgrave.eps.2210138.

Spaaij, Ramon. 2012. *Understanding Lone Wolf Terrorism: Global Patterns, Motivations, and Prevention*. New York: Springer.

Stump, Jacob L., and Priya Dixit. 2013. *Critical Terrorism Studies: An Introduction to Research Methods*. Hoboken: Taylor and Francis.

Tickner, Ann. 2001. *Gendering World Politics: Issues and Approaches in the Post-Cold War Era*. New York: Columbia University Press.

Vitalis, Robert. 2015. *White World Order, Black Power Politics: The Birth of American International Relations.*. Ithaca: Cornell University Press.

Weinberg, Leonard, and William Eubank. 2008. "Problems with the Critical Studies Approach to The Study of Terrorism." *Critical Studies on Terrorism* 1 (2): 185–195. doi:10.1080/17539150802184595.

Wilkinson, Paul. 1981. "Can a State Be a 'Terrorist?'" *International Affairs* 57 (3): 467–472. doi:10.2307/2619580.

Chapter 8   Terrorist Target Selection

Abrahms, Max. 2006. "Why Terrorism Does Not Work." *International Security.* 31 (2): 42–78. doi:10.1162/isec.2006.31.2.42.

Abrahms, Max. 2012. "The Political Effectiveness Of Terrorism Revisited." *Comparative Political Studies* 45 (3): 366–393. doi:10.1177/0010414011433104.

Abrahms, Max, and Philip B.K. Potter. 2015. "Explaining Terrorism: Leadership Deficits and Militant Group Tactics." *International Organization* 69 (2): 311–342. doi:10.1017/s0020818314000411.

Akimoto, Haruo. 2006. "The Aum Cult Leader Asahara's Mental Deviation And Its Social Relations." *Psychiatry and Clinical Neurosciences* 60 (1): 3–8. doi:10.1111/j.1440-1819.2006.01454.x.

Asal, Victor, and R. Karl Rethemeyer. 2008a. "Dilettantes, Ideologues, and the Weak: Terrorists Who Don't Kill." *Conflict Management and Peace Science* 25 (3): 244–263. doi:10.1080/07388940802219000.

Asal, Victor, and R. Karl Rethemeyer. 2008b. "The Nature of the Beast: Organizational Structures and the Lethality of Terrorist Attacks." *The Journal of Politics* 70 (2): 437–449. doi:10.1017/s0022381608080419.

Asal, Victor H., R. Karl Rethemeyer, Ian Anderson, Allyson Stein, Jeffrey Rizzo, and Matthew Rozea. 2009. "The Softest Of Targets: A Study On Terrorist Target Selection." *Journal Of Applied Security Research* 4 (3): 258–278. doi:10.1080/19361610902929990.

Asal, Victor and Justin V. Hastings. 2015. "When Terrorism Goes to Sea: Terrorist Organizations and The Move to Maritime Targets." *Terrorism and Political Violence* 27 (4): 722–740. doi:10.1080/09546553.2013.855636.

Becker, Michael. 2014. "Explaining Lone Wolf Target Selection in the United States." *Studies in Conflict & Terrorism* 37 (11): 959–978. doi:10.1080/1057610x.2014.952261.

Biberman,Yelena, and Farhan Zahid. 2016. "Why Terrorists Target Children: Outbidding, Desperation, and Extremism in the Peshawar and Beslan School Massacres." *Terrorism and Political Violence*, pp. 1–16. doi:10.1080/09546553.2015.1135425.

Brandt, Patrick, and Todd Sandler. 2010. "What Do Transnational Terrorists Target? Has It Changed? Are We Safer?" *Journal of Conflict Resolution.* 54 (2): 214–236. doi:10.1177/0022002709355437.

Bunn, Matthew, and Anthony Wier. 2005. "The Seven Myths of Nuclear Terrorism." *Current History* 104 (681): 153–161. Available online at: http://www.belfercenter.org/sites/default/files/files/publication/bunnwier.pdf. Last accessed 4-August-2017.

Crenshaw, Martha. 2001. "Why America? The Globalization of Civil War." *Current History* 100 (650): 425–432.

Crenshaw, Martha. 2007. "The Logic of Terrorism: Terrorist Behavior as a Product of Strategic Choice." in *Terrorism in Perspective*, Sue Mahan and Pamela L. Griset, eds. pp. 24–32.

Cronin, Audrey Kurth. 2009. *How Terrorism Ends: Understanding the Decline and Demise of Terrorist Campaigns.* Princeton, NJ: Princeton University Press.

Downes, Stephen M. 2007. "Life after Evolutionary Psychology." *Metascience* 16 (1): 1–24. doi:10.1007/s11016-006-9063-8.

Drake, Charles. J. M. 1998. *Terrorists' Target Selection.* London: Macmillan.

Goodwin, Jeff. 2006. "A Theory of Categorical Terrorism." *Social Forces* 84 (4): 2027–2046. doi:10.1353/sof.2006.0090.

Enders, Walter, and Todd Sandler. 1993. "The Effectiveness of Anti-Terrorism Policies: A Vector-Autoregression-Intervention Analysis." *American Political Science Review* 87 (4): 829–844.

Engene, Jan Oskar. 2004. *Terrorism in Western Europe: Explaining the Trends since 1950.* Cheltenham: Edward Elgar Publishing

Feinstein, Lee, and Anne-Marie Slaughter. 2004. "A Duty To Prevent." *Foreign Affairs* 83 (1): 136–150. doi:10.2307/20033835.

Findley, Michael G., and Joseph K. Young. 2012. "Terrorism and Civil War: A Spatial and Temporal Approach To A Conceptual Problem". *Perspectives on Politics* 10 (2): 285–305. doi:10.1017/s1537592712000679.

Findley, Michael G., Alex Braithwaite, and Joseph K. Young. 2015. "The Local Geography of Transnational Terrorism." *International Studies Association Annual Meeting, New Orleans, Lousiana* (March 17).

Fortna, Page Virginia. 2015. "Do Terrorists Win? Rebels' Use of Terrorism and Civil War Outcomes." *International Organization* 69 (3): 519–556. doi:10.1017/s0020818315000089.

Hinkkainen, Kaisa, and Steve Pickering. 2017. "Strategic Risk of Terrorist Targets in Urban vs. Rural Locations." Unpublished manuscript. Working Paper available online at: http://www.michael-findley.com/uploads/2/0/4/5/20455799/kaisasteve_v1.pdf. Last accessed 4-August-2017.

Hoffman, Bruce. 1999. "Terrorism Trends and Prospects." In *Countering the New Terrorism*, in Ian O. Lesser, Bruce Hoffman, John Arquilla, David Ronfeldt, and Michele Zanini, eds. San Monica, CA: RAND.

Hoffman, Bruce. 2006. *Inside Terrorism*. New York: Columbia University Press.

Horowitz, Michael C. 2010. "Nonstate Actors and The Diffusion of Innovations: The Case of Suicide Terrorism." *International Organization* 64 (1): 33–64. doi:10.1017/s0020818309990233.

Horowitz, Michael, Evan Perkoski. and Philip P. K. Potter. 2015. "Tactical Diversity in Militant Violence." International Organization, *forthcoming*. Last revised 10-January-2017, available online at: https://papers.ssrn.com/sol3/papers.cfm?abstract_id=2605952. Last accessed 4-August-2017.

Human Rights Watch. 2002. "We Are Not The Enemy: Hate Crimes Against Arabs, Muslims, and Those Perceived To Be Arab or Muslim After September 11." (November 14, No. 6). *Human Rights Watch*. Available online at: https://www.hrw.org/reports/2002/usahate/. Last accessed 4-August-2017.

Johnson, Chalmers. 2000. *Blowback: The Costs and Consequences of American Empire.* New York: MacMillan.

Jenkins, Brian Michael. 1975. *International Terrorism*. Los Angeles, Calif.: Crescent Publications.

Jones, Seth G., and Martin Libicki. 2008. *How Terrorist Groups End: Lessons for Countering Al Qa'ida.* Santa Monica, CA: RAND Corporation.

Juergensmeyer, Mark. 2003. *Terror in the Mind of God: The Global Rise of Religious Violence.* Berkeley, CA: University of California Press.

Kalyvas, Stathis N. 1999. "Wanton and Senseless? The Logic of Massacres in Algeria." *Rationality and Society* 11 (3): 243–285. doi:10.1177/104346399011003001.

Kepel, Gilles, Jean-Pierre Milelli, and Pascale Ghazaleh. 2009. *Al Qaeda In Its Own Words.* 1st ed. Cambridge: The Belknap Press of Harvard University Press.

Kydd, Andrew H., and Barbara F. Walter. 2006. "The Strategies of Terrorism." *International Security.* 31 (1): 49–80.

Lieber, Keir A. and Daryl G. Press. 2013. "Why States Won't Give Nuclear Weapons To Terrorists." *International Security* 38 (1): 80–104. doi:10.1162/isec_a_00127.

Llera, Francisco J., José M. Mata, and Cynthia L. Irvin. 1993. "ETA: From Secret Army To Social Movement—The Post-Franco Schism Of The Basque Nationalist Movement." *Terrorism And Political Violence* 5 (3): 106–134. doi:10.1080/09546559308427222.

Moghadam, Assaf. 2015. "The Interplay Between Terrorism, Insurgency, and Civil War in the Middle East." Real Institute Elcano. Available online at: http://www.realinstitutoelcano.org/wps/portal/rielcano_en/contenido?WCM_GLOBAL_CONTEXT=/elcano/elcano_in/zonas_in/ari4-2015-moghadam-interplay-between-terrorism-insurgency-and-civil-war-middle-east. Last accessed 4-August-2017.

Monaghan, Rachel. 2004. "An Imperfect Peace: Paramilitary 'Punishments' in Northern Ireland." *Terrorism and Political Violence* 16 (3): 439–461. doi:10.1080/09546550490509775.

Nemeth, Stephen Charles, Brian Lai, and Sara McLaughlin Mitchell. 2010. *A Rationalist Explanation Of Terrorist Targeting.* [Iowa City, Iowa]: University of Iowa.

Nemeth, Stephen C., Jacob A. Mauslein, and Craig Stapley. 2014. "The Primacy of the Local: Identifying Terrorist Hot Spots Using Geographic Information Systems." *The Journal of Politics* 76 (2): 304–317. doi:10.1017/s0022381613001333.

Neumayer, Eric, and Thomas Plümper. 2011. "Foreign Terror on Americans." *Journal of Peace Research* 48 (1): 3–17. doi:10.1177/0022343310390147.

O'Neill, Bard. 2005. *Insurgency and Terrorism: From Revolution to Apocalypse,* 2nd *ed.* Washington, DC: Potomac Books.

Post, Jerrold. 2002a. "Differentiating the Threats of Chemical and Biological Weapons: Motivations and Constraints." *Peace and Conflict: Journal of Peace Psychology* 8 (3): 187–200.

Post, Jerrold. 2002b. "Differentiating the Threats of Chemical and Biological Weapons: Motivations and Constraints." *Peace and Conflict* 8 (3): 87–200. Pluta, Anna M. and Peter D. Zimmerman. 2006. "Nuclear Terrorism: A Disheartening Dissent." *Survival* 48 (2): 55–69. doi:10.1080/00396330600765583.

Ross, Michael. 2004. "How Do Natural Resources Influence Civil War? Evidence from Thirteen Cases." *International Organization* 58 (1): 35–67. doi:10.1017/s002081830458102x.

Sánchez-Cuenca, Ignacio, and Luis de la Calle. 2009. "Domestic Terrorism: The Hidden Side Of Political Violence." *Annual Review of Political Science* 12 (1): 31–49. doi:10.1146/annurev.polisci.12.031607.094133.

Sandler, Todd. 2014. "The Analytical Study of Terrorism: Taking Stock," *Journal of Peace Research* 51 (2): 257–271. doi:10.1177/0022343313491277.

Santifort, Charlinda., Todd Sandler, and Patrick T. Brandt. 2012. "Terrorist Attack And Target Diversity: Changepoints and Their Drivers." *Journal Of Peace Research* 50 (1): 75–90. doi:10.1177/0022343312445651.

Santifort, Charlinda, and Todd Sandler. 2012. "Terrorist Success In Hostage-Taking Missions: 1978–2010." *Public Choice* 156 (1–2): 125–137. doi:10.1007/s11127-012-0008-z.

Stern, Jessica. 1999a. *The Ultimate Terrorists.* Cambridge, MA: Harvard University Press.

Stern, Jessica. 1999b. "The Prospect of Domestic Bioterrorism". *Emerging Infectious Diseases* 5 (4): 517–522. doi:10.3201/eid0504.990410.

Stone, John. 2009. "Al Qaeda, Deterrence, and Weapons of Mass Destruction." *Studies in Conflict & Terrorism* 32 (9): 763–775. doi:10.1080/10576100903109693.

Wiktorowicz, Quitan, and John Kaltner. 2003. "Killing in the Name of Islam: Al-Qaeda's Justification for September 11." *Middle East Policy* 10 (2): 76–92. doi:10.1111/1475-4967.00107.

Wilkinson, Paul. 2014. *Terrorism Versus Democracy: The Liberal State Response*. Hoboken: Taylor and Francis.

Wright, Austin L. 2013. "Terrorism, Ideology, and Target Selection." Working paper. Princeton University. Available online at: https://www.princeton.edu/politics/about/file-repository/public/Wright_on_Terrorism.pdf. Last accessed 4-August-2017.

Chapter 9   Suicide Terrorism

Asal, Victor and R. Karl Rethemeyer. 2008. "The Nature of the Beast: Organizational Structures and the Lethality of Terrorist Attacks." *Journal of Politics* 70 (2): 437–449. doi: 10.1017/S0022381608080419.

Atran, Scott. 2003. "Genesis of Suicide Terrorism." *Science* 299 no. 5612: 1534–1539.

Atran, Scott, and Ara Norenzayan. 2004. "Why Minds Create Gods: Devotion, Deception, Death, and Arational Decision Making" *Behavioral and Brain Sciences* 27 (6): 754–770. doi:10.1017/s0120525x04470174.

Atran, Scott. 2006. "The Moral Logic and Growth of Suicide Terrorism." *The Washington Quarterly* 29 (2): 127–147. doi:10.1162/wash.2006.29.2.127.

Azam, Jean-Paul. 2005. "Suicide-Bombing as Inter-Generational Investment." *Public Choice* 122 (1–2): 177–98. doi.10.1007/s11127-005-5795-z.

Benmelech, Efraim, and Claude Berrebi. 2007. "Human Capital and The Productivity Of Suicide Bombers" *Journal of Economic Perspectives* 21 (3): 223–238. doi:10.1257/jep.21.3.223.

Benmelech, Efraim, Claude Berrebi, and Esteban F. Klor. 2015. "Counter-Suicide-Terrorism: Evidence from House Demolitions." *The Journal of Politics* 77 (1): 27–43. doi:10.1086/678765.

Berman, Eli, and David D. Laitin. 2008. "Religion, Terrorism and Public Goods: Testing The Club Model." *Journal of Public Economics* 92 (10–11): 1942–1967. doi:10.1016/j.jpubeco.2008.03.007.

Berman, Eli. 2009. "Response to Adrian Guelke." *Critical Studies on Terrorism* 2 (2): 325–326. doi:10.1080/17539150903024831.

Biggs, Michael. 2005. "Dying Without Killing: Self-Immolation 1963–2002," in Diego Gambetta, ed. *Making Sense of Suicide Missions, Chapter 5*. New York: Oxford University Press. pp. 173–208.

Bloom, Mia. 2005. *Dying To Kill: The Allure of Suicide Terror.* New York: Columbia University Press.

Bloom, Mia. 2005. "Mother, Daughter, Sister, Bomber." *Bulletin of the Atomic Scientists* 61 (6): 54–62. doi:10.2968/061006015.

Bloom, Mia. 2009. "Chasing Butterflies and Rainbows: A Critique of Kruglanski et al.'s Fully Committed: Suicide Bombers' Motivation And The Quest For Personal Significance." *Political Psychology* 30 (3): 387–395.doi:10.1111/j.1467-9221.2009.00703.x.

Bloom, Mia, Bradley A. Thayer, and Valerie M. Hudson. 2010. "Life Sciences and Islamic Suicide Terrorism." *International Security* 35 (3): 185–192. doi:10.1162/isec_c_00027.

Braun, Robert, and Michael Genkin. 2014. "Cultural Resonance and The Diffusion of Suicide Bombings: The Role Of Collectivism." *Journal of Conflict Resolution* 58 (7): 1258–1284.doi:10.1177/0022002713498707.

Crenshaw, Martha. 2007. "Explaining Suicide Terrorism: A Review Essay." *Security Studies* 16 (1): 133–162. doi:10.1080/09636410701304580.

De Mesquita, Ethan Bueno. 2005. "Conciliation, Counterterrorism, and Patterns of Terrorist Violence." *International Organization* 59 (1). doi:10.1017/s0020818305050022.

Freedman, Lawrence D. 2005. "Making Sense of Suicide Missions." *Foreign Affairs* 84 (6): 141. Available online at: https://www.foreignaffairs.com/reviews/capsule-review/2005-11-01/making-sense-suicide-missions. Last accessed 4-August-2017.

Freedman, Lawrence D., Robert Pape, and Mia Bloom. 2005. "Dying To Win: The Strategic Logic of Suicide Terrorism." *Foreign Affairs* 84 (5): 172. doi:10.2307/20031726.

Gambetta, Diego. 2005. *Making Sense of Suicide Missions.* Oxford University Press.

Gerges, Fawaz, A. 2009. *The Far Enemy: Why Jihad Went Global.* Cambridge: Cambridge University Press.

Ginges, Jeremy, Ian Hansen, and Ara Norenzayan. 2009. "Religion and Support for Suicide Attacks." *Psychological Science* 20 (2): 224–230.doi:10.1111/j.1467-9280.2009.02270.x. Available online at: https://www.ncbi.nlm.nih.gov/pubmed/19170938. Last accessed 4-August-2017

Hassan, Nasra. 2001."An Arsenal of Believers: Talking to the 'Human Bombs'" *The New Yorker* Nov. 19), available online at: http://www.newyorker.com/magazine/2001/11/19/an-arsenal-of-believers, last accessed 4-August-2017.

Hoffman, Bruce, and Gordon H. McCormick. 2004. "Terrorism, Signaling, And Suicide Attack." *Studies in Conflict & Terrorism* 27 (4): 243–281. doi:10.1080/10576100490466498.

Horowitz, Michael C. 2010. "Nonstate Actors and the Diffusion of Innovations: The Case of Suicide Terrorism." *International Organization* 64 (1): 33–64.doi:10.1017/s0020818309990233.

Horowitz, Michael C. and Philip. B. K. Potter. 2014. "Allying To Kill: Terrorist Intergroup Cooperation and the Consequences for Lethality." *Journal of Conflict Resolution* 58 (2): 199–225. doi:10.1177/0022002712468726.

Horowitz, Michael. 2015. "The Rise and Spread of Suicide Bombing." *Annual Review of Political Science* 18 (1): 69–84. doi:10.1146/annurev-polisci-062813-051049.

Jackson, Richard, Lee Jarvis, Jeroen Gunning, and Marie Breen Smyth. 2011. *Terrorism: A Critical Introduction.* London: Palgrave Macmillan.

Krueger, Alan B. 2008. *What Makes a Terrorist: Economics and the Roots of Terrorism?* Princeton: Princeton University Press.

Kruglanski, Arie W., Xiaoyan Chen, Mark Dechesne, Shira Fishman, and Edward Orehek. 2009. "Fully Committed: Suicide Bombers' Motivation And The Quest For Personal Significance." *Political Psychology* 30 (3): 331–357. doi:10.1111/j.1467-9221.2009.00698.x.

Kydd, Andrew H., and Barbara F. Walter. 2006. "The Strategies of Terrorism." *International Security* 31 (1): 49–80. doi:10.1162/isec.2006.31.1.49

Lester, David. 2010. "Are Suicide Bombers Heroes?." *Psychological Reports* 106 (2): 499–500. doi:10.2466/pr0.106.2.499-500.

Merari, Ariel. 2002. "Deterring Fear: Government Responses to Terrorist Attacks." *Harvard International Review* 23 (4): 26–31. Available online at: http://www.jstor.org/stable/42762757, last accessed 4-August-2017.

Merari, Ariel. 2010. *Driven to Death: Psychological and Social Aspects of Suicide Terrorism.* Oxford: Oxford University Press.

Moghadam, Assaf. 2003. "Palestinian Suicide Terrorism In The Second Intifada: Motivations and Organizational Aspects." *Studies in Conflict & Terrorism* 26 (2): 65–92. doi:10.1080/10576100390145215.

Moghadam, Assaf. 2006. "Suicide Terrorism, Occupation, and the Globalization of Martyrdom: A Critique of Dying to Win." *Studies in Conflict & Terrorism* 29 (8): 707–729. doi:10.1080/10576100600561907.

Moghadam, Assaf. 2008. *The Globalization of Martyrdom: Al Qaeda, Salafi Jihad, and the Diffusion of Suicide Attacks*. Baltimore: Johns Hopkins University Press.

Moghadam, Assaf. 2009. "Motives for Martyrdom: Al-Qaida, Salafi Jihad, and the Spread Of Suicide Attacks." *International Security* 33 (3): 46–78. doi:10.1162/isec.2009.33.3.46.

Mroszczyk, Joseph. 2016. "To Die or To Kill? An Analysis of Suicide Attack Lethality." *Terrorism and Political Violence* 1–21. doi: 10.1080/09546553.2016.1228632.

Parkinson, John, and Alexander Malin. 2015. "President Obama: Overcoming Fear 'Most Powerful Tool' to Fight ISIS." *ABC News*. (Nov. 22). Available online at: http://abcnews.go.com/Politics/president-obama-destroying-isis/story?id=35349029. Last accessed 4-August-2017.

Pape, Robert A. 2003. "The Strategic Logic of Suicide Terrorism." *American Political Science Review* 97 (3). doi:10.1017/s000305540300073x.

Pape, Robert. 2005. *Dying to win: The Strategic Logic of Suicide Terrorism*. New York: Random House.

Pape, Robert A. 2008. "Methods and Findings in The Study of Suicide Terrorism." *American Political Science Review* 102 (2): 275–277. doi:10.1017/s000305540300073x.

Pape, Robert A., and James K. Feldman. 2010. *Cutting the fuse: The Explosion of Global Suicide Terrorism and How to Stop It*. Chicago Series on International and Dome. Chicago: University of Chicago Press.

Piazza, James. A. 2008. "A Supply-Side View of Suicide Terrorism: A Cross-National Study." *The Journal of Politics* 70 (1): 28–39. doi:10.1017/s0022381607080024.

Pedahzur, Ami. 2005. *Suicide Terrorism*. Cambridge, UK; Malden, MA: Polity.

Pedahzur, Ami., and Arie Perliger. 2006. "The Changing Nature of Suicide Attacks: A Social Network Perspective." *Social Forces* 84 (4): 1987–2008. doi:10.1353/sof.2006.0104.

Rosendorff, B. Peter, and Todd Sandler. 2010. "Suicide Terrorism and the Backlash Effect." *Defence and Peace Economics* 21 (5–6): 443–457. doi:10.1080/10242694.2010.491679.

Rushdie, Salman. 2006. "Terror is Glamour." *Der Spiegel Online*. (August 28). Available online at: http://www.spiegel.de/international/spiegel-interview-with-salman-rushdie-terror-is-glamour-a-433969.html. Last accessed 4-August-2017.

Schweitzer, Yoram, and Sari Goldstein Ferber. 2005. *Al-Qaeda and The Internalization of Suicide Terrorism*. Tel Aviv University, Jaffee Center for Strategic Studies. Available online at: http://www-personal.umich.edu/~satran/Ford%2006/Wk%203-B%20Suicide%20Terrorism%20Schweitzer.pdf. Last accessed 4-August-2017.

Shear, Michael D. 2015. "Obama Orders Inquiry into Intelligence on ISIS." *The New York Times*, November 22. Available online at: https://www.nytimes.com/2015/11/23/world/asia/obama-says-he-expects-truth-in-intelligence-reports.html, Last accessed 4-August-2017.

Wade, Sara. J., and Dan Reiter. 2007. "Does Democracy Matter?: Regime Type And Suicide Terrorism." *Journal of Conflict Resolution* 51 (2): 329–348. doi:10.1177/0022002706298137.

Zech, Steven T., and Michael Gabbay. 2016. "Social Network Analysis In The Study Of Terrorism And Insurgency: From Organization To Politics." *International Studies Review* 18 (2): 214–243. doi:10.1093/isr/viv011.

Chapter 10   Terrorism and Social Services
Arreguín-Toft, Ivan. 2001. "How The Weak Win Wars: A Theory of Asymmetric Conflict." *International Security* 26 (1): 93–128. doi:10.1162/016228801753212868.

Asal, Victor H. and R. Karl Rethemeyer. 2015. "Big Allied and Dangerous (BAAD) Dataset Version 2." Available online at: http://start.umd.edu/baad/database. Last accessed 4-August-2017.

Berman, Eli and David D. Laitin. 2008. "Religion, Terrorism and Public Goods: Testing the Club Model" *Journal of Public Economics* 92 (10–11): 1942–1967. doi:10.1016/j.jpubeco.2008.03.007.

Berman, Eli. 2011. *Radical, Religious, and Violent: The New Economics of Terrorism.* Boston: MIT Press.

Chen, Daniel L. 2003. "Economic Distress and Religious Intensity: Evidence from Islamic Resurgence During the Indonesian Financial Crisis." American Economic Review. (Oct. 21).

Cunningham, David E. 2006. "Veto players and Civil War Duration." *American Journal of Political Science* 50 (4): 875–892. doi:10.1111/j.1540-5907.2006.00221.x.

De La Calle, Luis, and Ignacio Sánchez-Cuenca. 2011. "The Quantity and Quality Of Terrorism: The DTV Dataset." *Journal of Peace Research* 48 (1): 49–58. doi:10.1177/0022343310392890.

De la Calle, Luis, and Ignacio Sánchez-Cuenca. 2012. "Rebels Without a Territory: An Analysis of Nonterritorial Conflicts in the World, 1970–1997." *Journal of Conflict Resolution* 56 (4): 580–603. doi: 10.1177/0022002711431800.

Enders, Walter, and Todd Sandler. 2012. *The Political Economy of Terrorism.* New York: Cambridge University Press.

Flanigan, Shawn Teresa. 2008. "Nonprofit Service Provision by Insurgent Organizations: "The Cases of Hizballah and the Tamil Tigers." *Studies in Conflict and Terrorism* 31 (6): 499–519. doi:10.1080/10576100802065103.

Fritsch, Peter. 2001. "Lesson Plan: Religious Schools in Pakistan Fill Void—And Spawn Warriors." (Oct. 2). *The Wall Street Journal*, A1, A24.

Gross, Michael L. 2015. *The Ethics of Insurgency.* New York: Cambridge University Press.

Grynkewich, Alexus G. 2008. "Welfare as Warfare: How Violent Non-State Groups use Social Services to Attack the State." *Studies in Conflict and Terrorism* 31 (4): 350–370. doi:10.1080/10576100801931321.

Heger, Lindsay. 2010. "In the Crosshairs: Explaining Violence Against Civilians," Doctoral Dissertation, University of California, San Diego. Available on Proquest Dissertations and Theses.

Heger, Lindsay, Danielle Jung, and Wendy H. Wong. 2012. "Organizing For Resistance: How Group Structure Impacts The Character Of Violence." *Terrorism And Political Violence* 24 (5): 743–768. doi:10.1080/09546553.2011.642908.

Heger, Lindsay L. and Danielle F. Jung. 2015. "Negotiating With Rebels: The Effect of Rebel Service Provision on Conflict Negotiations." *Journal of Conflict Resolution* (January 15, 2017): 1–27. doi:10.1177/0022002715603451.

Iannaccone, Laurence R., and Eli Berman. 2006. "Religious Extremism: The Good, The Bad, and The Deadly." *Public Choice* 128 (1–2): 109–129. doi:10.1007/s11127-006-9047-7.

Idler, Annette, and James J. F. Forest. 2015. "Behavioral Patterns Among (Violent) Non-State Actors: A Study of Complementary Governance." *Stability: International Journal of Security and Development* 4 (1): 1–19. doi:10.5334/sta.er.

Kazim, Hasnain. 2010. "Race to provide aid emerges between West and extremists." Spiegel online, (August 16). Available online at http://www.spiegel.de/

international/world/taliban-courts-pakistan-flood-victims-race-to-provide-aid-emerges-between-west-and-extremists-a-712060.html. Last accessed 4-August-2017.

Ly, Pierre-Emmanuel. 2007. "The Charitable Activities of Terrorist Organizations." *Public Choice* 131 (1–2): 177–195. doi:10.1007/s11127-006-9112-2.

Mampilly, Zachariah. 2011. *Rebel Rulers and Civilian Life During War.* Ithaca, N.Y.: Cornell University Press.

Naimark, Norman M. 1983. *Terrorists and Social Democrats.* Cambridge, MA: Harvard University Press.

Stewart, Megan A. and Yu-Ming Liou. 2017. "Do Good Borders Make Good Rebels? Territorial Control And Civilian Casualties." *The Journal Of Politics* 79 (1): 284–301. doi:10.1086/688699.

Thornton, Thomas Perry. 1964. "Terror as a Weapon of Political Agitation." in Harry Eckstein, ed, *Internal War: Problems and Approaches.* New York: Free Press of Glencoe.

Weinberg, Leonard and Ami Pedahzur. 2003. *Political Parties and Terrorist Groups.* Routledge Studies in Extremism and Democracy. New York: Routledge.

Zaidi, Syed Manzar Abbas. 2016. "Reconstituting Local Order in Pakistan: Emergent ISIS and Locally Constituted Shariah Courts in Pakistan." Brookings Local Orders Paper Series, Paper 4, October. Available online at: https://www.brookings.edu/wp-content/uploads/2016/10/fp_20161129_pakistan_local_orders_web.pdf. Last accessed 4-August-2017.

Chapter 11   State Sponsorship of Terrorism

Alexander, Yonah, ed. 2006. *Counterterrorism Strategies: Successes and Failures of Six Nations.* Dulles, VA: Potomac Books.

Banks, William C., Renee de Nevers, and Mitchel B. Wallerstein. 2008. *Combating Terrorism: Strategies and Approaches.* Washington, DC: CQ Press.

Bajoria, Jayshree. 2010. *Backgrounder: Lashkar-e-Taiba.* New York: Council on Foreign Relations. Available online at: http://www.cfr.org/pakistan/lashkar-e-taiba-army-pure-aka-lashkar-e-tayyiba-lashkar-e-toiba-lashkar--taiba/p17882#p2). Last accessed 25-March-2017.

Banks, William C., Renee de Nevers, and Mitchel B. Wallerstein. 2008. *Combating Terrorism: Strategies and Approaches.* Washington, DC: CQ Press.

Bapat, Navin A. 2007. "The Internationalization of Terrorist Campaigns." *Conflict Management and Peace Science* 24 (4): 265–280. doi:10.1080/07388940701643607.

Bapat, Navin A., Luis de la Calle, Kaisa H. Hinkkainen, and Elena V. McLean. 2016. "Economic Sanctions, Transnational Terrorism, and Incentives to Misrepresent." *Journal of Politics* 78 (1): 249–264. doi:10.1086/683257.

Berger, J. M. 2013. "Boston's Jihadist Past." *Foreign Policy* (22 April). Available online at: http://foreignpolicy.com/2013/04/22/bostons-jihadist-past/. Last accessed 25-March-2017.

Blundy, David, and Andrew Lycett. 1987. *Qaddafi and the Libyan Revolution.* Boston: Little Brown.

Boutton, Andrew. 2014. "US Foreign Aid, Interstate Rivalry, and Incentives for Counterterrorism Cooperation." *Journal of Peace Research* 51 (6): 741–754. doi:10.1177/0022343314543144.

Boutton, Andrew and David B. Carter. 2014. "Fair-Weather Allies? Terrorism and the Allocation of US Foreign Aid." *Journal of Conflict Resolution* 58 (7): 1144–1173. doi:10.1177/0022002713492649.

Burns, John F., and Christopher S. Wren. 2001. "Without Evidence, the Taliban Refuses to Turn Over Bin Laden." *New York Times* (September 21).

Byman, Daniel, Peter Chalk, Bruce Hoffman, William Rosenau, and David Branna. 2001. *Trends in Outside Support for Insurgent Movements* (Washington, DC: RAND, 2001). Available online at: http://www.rand.org/content/dam/rand/pubs/monograph_reports/2007/MR1405.pdf. Last accessed 25-March-2017.

Byman, Daniel. 2005. *Deadly Connections: States that Sponsor Terrorism*. New York: Cambridge University Press.

Byman, Daniel. 2008. "Rogue Operators." *The National Interest* 96 (July/August). Available online at: http://nationalinterest.org/article/rogue-operators-2493. Last accessed 25-March-2017.

Byman, Daniel, and Sarah Kreps. 2010. "Agents of Destruction? Applying Principal-Agent Analysis to State Sponsorship of Terrorism." *International Studies Perspectives* 11 (1): 1–18. doi:10.1111/j.1528-3585.2009.00389.x.

Carter, David B. 2012. "A Blessing or a Curse? State Support for Terrorist Groups." *International Organization* 66 (1): 129–151. doi:10.1017/s0020818311000312.

Croissant, Aurel, and Daniel Barlow. 2007. "Following the Money Trail: Terrorist Financing and Government Responses in Southeast Asia." *Studies in Conflict and Terrorism* 30 (2): 131–156. doi:10.1080/10576100600959721.

Cunningham, David, Kristian Skrede Gleditsch, and Idean Salehyan. 2008. *Expanded Uppsala Non-State Actor Dataset*. Available online at: http://privatewww.essex.ac.uk/~ksg/eacd.html. Last accessed 25-March-2017.

Cunningham, David E.; Kristian Skrede Gleditsch, & Idean Salehyan. 2009. "It Takes Two: A Dyadic Analysis of Civil War Duration and Outcome." *Journal of Conflict Resolution* 53 (4): 570–597. doi:10.1177/0022002709336458.

Cunningham, David, Kristian Skrede Gleditsch, and Idean Salehyan. 2013. "Non-State Actors in Civil Wars: A New Dataset." *Conflict Management and Peace Science* 30 (5): 516–531. doi:10.1177/0738894213499673.

Findley, Michael G., James A. Piazza, and Joseph K. Young. 2012. "Games Rivals Play: Terrorism in International Rivalries." *Journal of Politics* 71 (1): 235–248. doi:10.2139/ssrn.1676555.

Giraldo, Jeanne K., and Harold A. Trinkunas, eds. 2007. *Terrorism Financing and State Responses*. Palo Alto: Stanford University Press.

Gregory, Shaun. 2007. "The ISI and the War on Terrorism." *Studies in Conflict and Terrorism* 30 (12): 1013–1031. doi:10.1080/10576100701670862.

Jett, Dennis. 2015. "Why The State Sponsors of Terrorism List Has So Little To Do With Terrorism." *The Huffington Post*. (June 29). Available online at http://www.huffingtonpost.com/dennis-jett/state-sponsors-of-terrorism-list_b_7658880.html). Last accessed 25-March-2017.

Hufbauer, Gary Clyde, Jeffrey J. Scott, and Barbara Oegg. 2011. *Using Sanctions to Fight Terrorism*. Policy Brief 01–11 (November). Washington, DC: Peterson Institute for International Economics. Available online at: https://piie.com/publications/policy-briefs/using-sanctions-fight-terrorism. Last accessed 25-March-2017.

Kreps, Sara, and Daniel Byman. 2010. "Agents of Destruction? Applying Principal-Agent Analysis to State Sponsorship of Terrorism." *International Studies Perspectives* 11 (1): 1–18. doi:10.1111/j.1528-3585.2009.00389.x.

Londoño, Ernesto, and Greg Jaffe. 2009. "Iraqi Security Forces Clash for Second Day with Iranian Opposition Group." *The Washington Post* (July 29).

Mazzetti, Mark. 2014. "CIA Study of Covert Aid Fueled Skepticism about Helping Syrian Rebels." *New York Times* (October 14). Available online at: https://www.nytimes.com/2014/10/15/us/politics/cia-study-says-arming-rebels-seldom-works.html?_r=0. Last accessed 25-March-2017.

Norton, Ben. 2016. "Saudi Arabia Funds and Exports Islamic Extremism: The Truth Behind the Toxic U.S. Relationship with the Theocratic Monarchy." Salon.com (January 6). Available online at: http://www.salon.com/2016/01/06/saudi_arabia_funds_and_exports_islamic_extremism_the_truth_behind_the_toxic_u_s_relationship_with_the_theocratic_nation/. Last accessed 25-March-2017.

Odom, General William. 2007. "American Hegemony: How to Use it, How to Lose it." *Proceedings of the American Philosophical Society.* 151 (4): 410. Available online at: http://www.middlebury.edu/media/view/214721/original/OdomPaper.pdf. Last accessed 25-March-2017.

O'Sullivan, Meghan. 2003. *Shrewd Sanctions: Statecraft and State Sponsors of Terrorism.* Washington, DC: Brookings Institution Press.

Prime Minister's Office. 2015. "PM Netanyahu's Remarks at the State of Weekly Cabinet Meeting." (June 21). Available online at: http://www.pmo.gov.il/English/MediaCenter/Spokesman/Pages/spokestart210615.aspx. Last accessed 24-March-2017.

Record, Jeffrey. 2006. "External Assistance: Enabler of Insurgent Success?" *Parameters* 36 (3): 36–49. Available online at: http://ssi.armywarcollege.edu/pubs/parameters/articles/06autumn/record.pdf. Last accessed 25-March-2017.

Salehyan, Idean. 2007. "Transnational Rebels: Neighboring States as Sanctuary For Rebel Groups." *World Politics* 59 (2): 217–242. doi:10.1353/wp.2007.0024.

Salehyan, Idean. 2010. "The Delegation of War to Rebel Organizations." *Journal of Conflict Resolution* 54 (3): 493–515. doi:10.1177/0022002709357890.

Salehyan, Idean, Kristian Skrede Gleditsch, and David Cunningham. 2011. "Explaining External Support for Insurgent Groups." *International Organization* 65 (4): 709–744. doi:10.1017/s0020818311000233.

Salehyan, Idean, David Siroki, and Reed M. Wood. 2014. "External Rebel Sponsorship and Civilian Abuse: A Principal-Agent Analysis of Wartime Atrocities." *International Organization* 68 (3): 633–661. doi:10.1017/s002081831400006x.

Siqueira, Kevin, and Todd Sandler. 2006. "Terrorists versus the Government: Strategic Interaction, Support, and Sponsorship." *Journal of Conflict Resolution* 50 (6): 878–898.doi:10.1177/0022002706293469.

Shapiro, Jacob N. 2013. *The Terrorist's Dilemma.* Princeton: Princeton University Press.

Stern, Jessica and J. M Berger. 2015. *ISIS: The State of Terror.* New York: Ecco.

United States Department of State, Office of the Coordinator for Counterterrorism. 2000. *Patterns of Global Terrorism 2000.* Washington, DC: Department of State. Available online at https://www.state.gov/j/ct/rls/crt/2000/. Last accessed 25-March-2017.

Wardlaw, Grant. 2001. "Terror as an Instrument of Foreign Policy." in David Rapoport, ed., *Inside Terrorist Organizations,* revised ed. New York: Columbia University Press.

Weinstein, Jeremy M. 2006. *Inside Rebellion: The Politics of Rebel Organization.* New York: Cambridge University Press.

Zinn, Howard. 2011. *Howard Zinn on War.* 2nd ed. Seven Stories Press.

Chapter 12   Gender & Terrorism

Alison, Miranda. 2003. "Cogs In The Wheel? Women in the Liberation Tigers Of Tamil Eelam." *Civil Wars* 6 (4): 37–54. doi:0.1080/136982140308402554.

Alison, Miranda.   2009. *Women and Political Violence: Female Combatants in Ethno-National Conflict*. Contemporary Security Studies. Hoboken: Taylor & Francis.

Bloom, Mia. 2005. *Dying To Kill: The Allure of Suicide Terror*. New York: Columbia University Press.

Bloom, Mia. 2010. "Death Becomes Her: Women, Occupation, and Terrorist Mobilization." *PS: Political Science & Politics* 43 (03): 445–450. doi:10.1017/s1049096510000703.

Bloom, Mia. 2011. *Bombshell: Women and Terrorism*. Philadelphia: University of Pennsylvania Press.

Brunner, Claudia. 2007. "Occidentalism Meets The Female Suicide Bomber: A Critical Reflection On Recent Terrorism Debates; A Review Essay." *Signs: Journal Of Women In Culture And Society* 32 (4): 957–971. doi:10.1086/512490.

Cooper, H. H. A. 1979. "Woman as Terrorist," in F. Adler and R. J. Simon, eds. *The Criminology of Deviant Women*. New York: Houghton Mifflin.

Cottee, Simon.   2016. "What ISIS Women Want." *Foreign Policy*. (May 17). Available online at: http://foreignpolicy.com/2016/05/17/what-isis-women-want-gendered-jihad. Last accessed 20-March-2017.

Cunningham, Karla J. 2003. "Cross-Regional Trends in Female Terrorism." *Studies in Conflict and Terrorism* 26(3): 171–195. doi:10.1080/10576100390211419.

Dalton, Angela, and Victor Asal. 2011. "Is It Ideology Or Desperation: Why Do Organizations Deploy Women In Violent Terrorist Attacks?." *Studies in Conflict and Terrorism* 34 (10): 802–819. doi:10.1080/1057610x.2011.604833.

Decker, Jeffrey L. 1990–1991. "Terrorism (Un)Veiled: Frantz Fanon and the Women of Algiers." *Cultural Critique* 17 (Winter): 177–195. doi:10.2307/1354144.

Eager, Patricia Whaley. 2008. *From Freedom Fighters to Terrorists: Women and Political Violence*. London: Routledge

Ferber, Abby L. 1998. *White Man Falling: Race, Gender and White Supremacy*. Boulder: Rowman & Littlefield.

Galvin, Deborah M. 1983. "The Female Terrorist: A Socio-Psychological Perspective." *Behavioral Sciences & the Law* 1 (2): 19–32. doi:10.1002/bsl.2370010206.

Gavrandidou, Maria, and Rita Rosner. 2003. "The Weaker Sex? Gender and Post-Traumatic Stress Disorder." *Depression and anxiety* 17 (3): 130–139. doi:10.1002/da.10103.

Gentry, Caron E. 2009. "Targeting Terrorists: A License To Kill." *Journal Of Military Ethics* 8 (3): 260–262. doi:10.1080/15027570903230331.

Glynn, Ruth. 2013. *Women, Terrorism, and Trauma in Italian Culture*. New York: Palgrave Macmillan.

Guneretne, Arjun and Anita M. Weiss, eds. 2013. *Pathways to Power: The Domestic Politics of South Asia*. New York: Rowman & Littlefield.

Hoyle, Carolyn, Alexandra Bradford, and Ross Frenett. 2015. "Becoming Mulan? Female Western Migrants to ISIS."   Institute for Strategic Dialogue. Available online at: http://www.isdglobal.org/wp-content/uploads/2016/02/ISDJ2969_Becoming_Mulan_01.15_WEB.pdf. Last accessed 5-August-2017.

Irving, Sarah. 2012. *Leila Khaled: Icon of Palestinian Liberation*. London: Pluto Press.

Krueger, Alan B, and Jitka Malečková. 2003. "Education, Poverty and Terrorism: Is There a Causal Connection?." *Journal of Economic Perspectives* 17 (4): 119–144: doi:089533003772034925

Meinhof, Ulrike. 1968. Vom Protest zum Widerstand" ["From Protest to Resistance]." *konkret*, no. 5 (May 1968).

O'Rourke, Lindsey A. 2009. "What's Special About Female Suicide Terrorism?." *Security Studies* 18 (4): 681–718. doi:10.1080/09636410903369084.

Peresin, Anita, and Alberto Cervone. 2015. "The Western *Muhajirat* of ISIS." *Studies in Conflict and Terrorism* 38 (7): 495–509. doi:10.1080/1057610X.2015.1025611.

Rajan, V. G. Julie. 2011. *Women Suicide Bombers: Narratives of Violence*. London: Routledge.

Saltman, Erin Marie, and Melanie Smith. 2015. " 'Till Martyrdom Do Us Part:' Gender and the ISIS Phenomenon." Institute for Strategic Dialogue.

Simmons, Catherine A, and Donald K. Granvold. 2005. "A Cognitive Model to Explain Gender Differences in Rate of PTSD Diagnosis." *Brief Treatment and* Crisis *Intervention* 5 (3): 290–99. doi: doi:10.1093/brief-treatment/mhi021.

Sjoberg, Laura. 2009. "Introduction to Security Studies: Feminist Contributions." *Security Studies* 18 (2): 183–213. doi:10.1080/09636410902900129.

Sjoberg, Laura, and Caron E. Gentry, eds. 2011. *Women, Gender, And Terrorism*. Athens: University of Georgia Press.

Solomon, Zahava, Marc Gelkopf, and Avraham Bleich. 2005. "Is Terror Gender-Blind? Gender Differences in Reaction to Terror Events." *Social Psychiatry and Psychiatric, Epidemiology* 40 (12): 947–954. 10.1007/s00127-005-0973-3.

Stack-O'Connor, Alisa. 2007. "Picked Last: Women and Terrorism." *Joint Force Quarterly* 44 (1): 95–100.

Thayer, Bradley A, and Valerie M. Hudson. 2010. Sex and the Shaheed: Insights from the Life Sciences on Islamic Suicide Terrorism. *International Security* 34 (4): 37–62. doi:10.1162/isec.2010.34.4.37.

Zedalis, Debra D. 2004. *Female Suicide Bombers*. The Minerva Group, Inc.

Chapter 13   Counterterrorism Instruments

Allison, Graham, and Andrei Kokoshin. 2002. "The New Containment: An Alliance Against Nuclear Terrorism." *The National Interest* 69: 35–43.

Benmelech, Efraim, Claude Berrebi, and Esteban Klor. 2010. "Counter-Suicide-Terrorism: Evidence from House Demolitions." NBER Working Paper No. 16493. Available online at: http://www.nber.org/papers/w16493. Last accessed 5-August-2017.

Byman, Daniel. 2006. "Do Targeted Killings Work?." *Foreign Affairs* (March/April) 85 (2): 95–111. doi:10.2307/20031914.

Byman, Daniel. 2013. "Why Drones Work: The Case for Washington's Weapon of Choice." *Foreign Affairs*. (July/August) 92 (4): 32–43.

Chenoweth, Erica, and Laura Dugan. 2016. "The Canadian Way of Counterterrorism: Introducing the GATE-Canada Data Set." *Canadian Foreign Policy Journal* 22 (3): 316–330. doi:10.1080/11926422.2016.1144210.

Crenshaw, Martha. 2001. "Theories of Terrorism: Instrumental and Organizational Approaches," in David Rapaport, ed., *Inside Terrorist Organizations* 2nd ed. London: Routledge.

Crenshaw, Martha, Erik Dahl, and Margaret Wilson. 2016. "Jihadist plots in the United States Jan. 1993-Feb. 2016: Interim findings Infographic." College Park, MD: START. Available online at: http://www.start.umd.edu/pubs/START_ FailedFoiled_JihadistPlotsInterimFindings_Infographic_Jan2017.pdf. Last accessed 5-August-2017.

Cronin, Audrey Kurth. 2006. "How Al Qaida Ends: The Decline and Demise of Terrorist Groups." *International Security* 31 (1): 7–48. doi:10.1162/isec.2006.31.1.7.

Cronin, Audrey Kurth. 2013. "Why Drones Fail: When Tactics Drive Strategy." *Foreign Affairs* 92 (4): 44–54.

Dugan, Laura, and Erica Chenoweth. 2012. "Moving Beyond Deterrence: The Effectiveness of Raising the Benefits of Abstaining from Terrorism in Israel." *American Sociological Review*, 77 (3): 597–624. doi:10.1177/0003122412450573.

Enders, Walter, and Todd Sandler. 1993. "The Effectiveness of Anti-Terrorism Policies: A Vector-Autoregression Intervention Analysis." *American Political Science Review* 87 (4): 829–844. doi:10.2307/2938817.

Gil-Alana, L. A. and C. P. Barros. 2010. "A Note on The Effectiveness of National Anti-Terrorist Policies: Evidence From ETA." *Conflict Management And Peace Science* 27 (1): 28–46. doi:10.1177/0738894209352130.

Jenkins, Brian Michael, and Joseph Trella. 2012. *Carnage Interrupted: An Analysis of Fifteen Terrorist Plots against Public Surface Transportation*. No. CA-MTI-12-2979. San Jose, CA: Mineta Transportation Institute. Available online at: http://transweb. sjsu.edu/PDFs/research/2979-analysis-of-terrorist-plots-against-public-surface-transportation.pdf. Last accessed 5-August-2017.

Johnston, Patrick B. 2012. "Does Decapitation Work? Assessing The Effectiveness Of Leadership Targeting In Counterinsurgency Campaigns". *International Security* 36 (4): 47–79. doi:10.1162/isec_a_00076.

Jonsson, Michael, and Svante Cornell. 2007. "Countering Terrorist Financing: Lessons from Europe." *Georgetown Journal of International Affairs* 8 (1): 69–78.

Jordan, Jenna. 2009. "When Heads Roll: Assessing the Effectiveness of Leadership Decapitation." *Security Studies* 18 (4): 719–755. doi:10.1080/09636410903369068.

Kenney, Michael, Stephen Coulthart, and Dominick Wright. 2016. "Structure and Performance in a Violent Extremist Network: The Small-World Solution." *Journal of Conflict Resolution*, March. doi:10.1177/0022002716631104

Kydd, Andrew H., and Barbara F. Walter. 2006. "The Strategies of Terrorism." *International Security* 31 (1): 49–80. doi:10.1162/isec.2006.31.1.49

Legum, Judd. 2011. "Timeline: The Hunt for Osama Bin Laden." *ThinkProgress*, (May 10). Available online at: https://thinkprogress.org/timeline-the-hunt-for-osama-bin-laden-648fc9347926#.780if0jmi. Last accessed 5-August-2017.

Lum, Cynthia, Leslie W. Kennedy, and Alison Sherley. 2006. "Are Counter-Terrorism Strategies Effective? The Results of the Campbell Systematic Review on Counter-Terrorism Evaluation Research." *Journal of Experimental Criminology* 2 (4): 489–516. doi:10.1007/s11292-006-9020-y.

MacAskill, Ewen. 2011. "Osama Bin Laden: It Took Years to Find Him But Just Minutes to Kill Him." *The Guardian*. (May 2). Available online at: https://www. thegurdian.com/world/2011/may/02/how-osama-bin-laden-found. Last accessed 5-August-2017.

Maras, Marie-Helen. 2010. "How to Catch A Terrorist: Is Mass Surveillance The Answer?" *Journal of Applied Security Research* 5 (1): 20–41. doi:10.1080/19361610903411790.

Masferrer, Aniceto, and Clive Walker. 2013. *Counter-Terrorism, Human Rights and The Rule of Law: Crossing Legal Boundaries in Defence of the State.* Cheltenham, UK: Edward Elgar Publishing.

Nagl, John A., James.F. Amos, Sarah Sewall, and David H. Petraeus. 2008. *The US Army/Marine Corps Counterinsurgency Field Manual.* Chicago: University of Chicago Press.

Neumann, Peter R. 2007. "Negotiating With Terrorists." *Foreign Affairs* 86: 128–138.

Pape, Robert A. 1996. *Bombing to Win: Air Power and Coercion in War.* Ithaca, NY: Cornell University Press.

Pape, Robert A. 2003. "The Strategic Logic of Suicide Terrorism." *American Political Science Review* 97 (3). doi:10.1017/s000305540300073x.

Patel, Faiza, and Michael German. 2015. "Fact Sheet: Countering violent extremism: Myths and Fact." New York University School of Law: Brennan Center for Justice. Available online at: https://www.brennancenter.org/sites /default/files/analysis/102915%20Final%20CVE%20Fact%20Sheet.pdf. Last accessed 5-August-2017.

Price, Bryan C. 2012. "Targeting Top Terrorists: How Leadership Decapitation Contributes to Counterterrorism". *International Security* 36 (4): 9–46. doi:10.1162/ isec_a_00075.

Rineheart, Jason. 2010. "Counterterrorism and Counterinsurgency." *Perspectives on Terrorism,* 4 (5): 31–47.

Risen, James, and Eric Lichtblau. 2005. "Spying Program Snared U.S. Calls." *The New York Times* (December 21). Available online at: http://www.nytimes.com /2005/12/21/politics/spying-program-snared-us-calls.html?_r=0. Last accessed 5-August-2017.

Rubenstein, Leonard S. 2013. "Unhealthy Practice: Medical Work in Conflict Zones is Compromised." *Foreign Affairs* (April 24). Available online at:https://www. foreignaffairs.com/articles/nigeria/2013-04-24/unhealthy-practice, last accessed 5-August-2017.

Sheehan, Ivan Sascha. 2009. "Has The Global War On Terror Changed The Terrorist Threat? A Time-Series Intervention Analysis." *Studies in Conflict and Terrorism* 32 (8): 743–761. doi:10.1080/10576100903039270.

Vidino, Lorenzo, and Seamus Hughes. 2015. "Countering Violent Extremism in America." The George Washington University: Center for Cyber & Homeland Security. Available online at https://cchs.gwu.edu/sites/cchs.gwu.edu/files/ downloads/CVE%20in%20America%20.pdf. Last accessed 5-August-2017.

Walsh, James I., and James A. Piazza. 2010. "Why Respecting Physical Integrity Rights Reduces Terrorism." *Comparative Political Studies* 43 (5): 551–577. doi:10.1177/0010414009356176.

Whitlock, Craig, and Barton Gellman. 2013. "To Hunt Osama Bin Laden, Satellites Watched Over Abbottabad, Pakistan and Navy SEALs." *The Washington Post* (August 29). Available online at:https://www.washingtonpost.com/world/ national-security/to-hunt-osama-bin-laden-satellites-watched-over-abbottabad-pakistan-and-navy-seals/2013/08/29/8d32c1d6-10d5-11e3-b4cb-fd7ce041d814_ story.html?utm_term=.6fa44c44dbaa. Last accessed 5-August-2017.

Zenko, Micah. 2016a. "Do Not Believe the U.S. Government's Official Numbers on Drone Strike Civilian Causalities." *Foreign Policy.* (July 5). Available online at:http:// foreignpolicy.com/2016/07/05/do-not-believe-the-u-s-governments-official-numbers-on-drone-strike-civilian-casualties/. Last accessed 5-August-2017.

Zenko, Micah. 2016b. "Questioning Obama's Drone Deaths Data." *Council on Foreign Relations*, (July 1). Available online at: http://blogs.cfr.org/zenko/2016/07/01/questioning-obamas-drone-deaths-data/. Last accessed 5-August-2017.

Chapter 14   The Politics of Counterterrorism

Adorno, Theodor W., Else Frenkel-Brunswik, Daniel J. Levinson, and R. Nevitt Sanford. 1950. *The Authoritarian Personality*. New York: Harper and Row.

Allison, Graham, and Philip Zelikow. 1999. *Essence of Decision: Explaining the Cuban Missile Crisis,* 2nd ed. New York: Longman.

Altemeyer, Bob. 1981. *Right-Wing Authoritarianism*. Winnipeg: University of Manitoba Press.

Altemeyer, Bob. 1996. *The Authoritarian Specter*. Cambridge: Harvard University Press.

Azam, Jean-Paul, and Alexandra Delacroix. 2006. "Aid and the Delegated Fight Against Terrorism." *Review of Development Economics* 10 (2): 330–344. doi:10.1111/j.1467-9361.2006.00321.x.

Berrebi, Claude, and Esteban F. Klor. 2008. "Are Voters Sensitive to Terrorism? Direct Evidence from The Israeli Electorate." *The American Political Science Review* 102 (3): 279–301. doi:10.2139/ssrn.1003908.

Blankenship, Brian. 2016. "When Do States Take The Bait? State Capacity and The Provocation Logic of Terrorism." *Journal of Conflict Resolution* 002200271664565: 1–29. doi:10.1177/0022002716645656.

Bradner, Eric and Rene Marsh. 2015. "Acting TSA Director Resigned After Screeners Failed Tests to Detect Explosives, Weapons." *CNN* (June 2). Available online at: http://www.cnn.com/2015/06/01/politics/tsa-failed-undercover-airport-screening-tests/. Last accessed 5-August-2017.

Brennan, John. 2016. "Statement by Director Brennan as Prepared for Delivery Before the Senate Select Committee on Intelligence." Available online at https://www.cia.gov/news-information/speeches-testimony/2016-speeches-testimony/statement-by-director-brennan-as-prepared-for-delivery-before-ssci.html. Last accessed 5-August-2017.

Bueno de Mesquita, Ethan. 2007. "Politics And The Suboptimal Provision Of Counterterror." *International Organization* 61 (1): 9–36. doi:10.1017/s0020818307070087.

Bueno de Mesquita, Ethan, and Eric S. Dickson. 2007. "The Propaganda of the Deed: Terrorism, Counterterrorism, and Mobilization." *American Journal of Political Science* 51 (2): 364–381. doi:10.1111/j.1540-5907.2007.00256.x.

Byman, Daniel. 2006. "Friends Like These: Counterinsurgency and the War on Terrorism." *International Security* 31 (2): 79–115. doi:10.1162/isec.2006.31.2.79.

Byman, Daniel. 2006. "Remaking Alliances in the War on Terrorism." *Journal of Strategic Studies* 29 (5): 767–811. doi:10.1080/01402390600900887.

Chenoweth, Erica, and Laura Dugan. 2012. "The Electoral Determinants of Counterterrorism." Unpublished paper, University of Denver.

Chowdhury, Arjun and Ronald Krebs. 2009. "Making and Mobilizing Moderates: Rhetorical Strategy, Political Networks, and Counterterrorism." *Security Studies* 18 (3): 371–399. doi:10.1080/09636410903132961.

Conrad, Courtenay R., Justin Conrad, James Igoe Walsh, and James A. Piazza. 2014. "Who tortures the Terrorists? Transnational Terrorism and Military Torture." *Foreign Policy Analysis* 9: 1–26. doi:10.1111/fpa.12066.

Crenshaw, Martha, ed. 2010. *The Consequences of Counterterrorism*. New York: Russell Sage Foundation.

Cronin, Audrey Kurth. 2009. *How Terrorism Ends: Understanding the Decline and Demise of Terrorist Campaigns*. Princeton: Princeton University Press.

de Graaf, Beatrice and Bob de Graaf. 2010. "Bringing Politics Back in: The Introduction of the 'Performative Power' of Counterterrorism." *Critical Studies on Terrorism* 3 (2): 261–275. doi:10.1080/17539153.2010.491337.

Dugan, Laura, and Erica Chenoweth. 2012. "Moving Beyond Deterrence: The Effectiveness of Raising the Benefits of Abstaining from Terrorism in Israel." *American Sociological Review* 77 (3): 597–624. doi:10.1177/0003122412450573.

Dugan, Laura and Erica Chenoweth. 2016. "Introducing Government Actions in Terror Environments Dataset." Unpublished manuscript, University of Maryland.

Epifanio, Mariaelisa. 2011. "Legislative Response to International Terrorism." *Journal of Peace Research* 48 (3): 399– 411. doi:10.1177/0022343311399130.

Eppright, Charles T. 1997. " 'Counterterrorism' and Conventional Military Force: The Relationship Between Political Effect and Utility." *Studies in Conflict and Terrorism* 20 (4): 333–344. doi:10.1080/10576109708436045.

Feldman, Stanley, and Karen Stenner. 1997. "Perceived Threat and Authoritarianism." *Political Psychology* 18 (4): 741–770. doi:10.1111/0162-895x.00077.

Foley, Frank. 2015. *Countering Terrorism in Britain and France: Institutions, Norms and the Shadow of the Past*. New York: Cambridge University Press.

Freilich, Charles D. 2012. *Zion's Dilemmas: How Israel Makes National Security Policy*. Ithaca: Cornell University Press.

Gander, Kashmira. 2014. "ISIS Hostage Threat: Which Countries Pay Ransoms to Release Their Citizens?" *The Independent* (September 3). Available online at: http://www.independent.co.uk/news/world/politics/isis-hostage-threat-which-countries-pay-ransoms-to-release-their-citizens-9710129.html. Last accessed 5-August-2017.

Holmes, Jennifer S. 2001. *Terrorism and Democratic Stability*. Manchester, UK: Manchester University Press.

Jackson, Richard. 2007. "Constructing Enemies: 'Islamic Terrorism' in Political and Academic Discourse." *Government and Opposition* 42 (3): 394–426. doi:10.1111/j.1477-7053.2007.00229.x.

Jaeger, David A., and M. Daniele Paserman. 2008. "The Cycle of Violence? An Empirical Analysis of Fatalities in the Palestinian-Israeli Conflict." *American Economic Review* 98 (4): 1591–1604. doi:10.1257/aer.98.4.1591.

Kam, Cindy, and Donald R. Kinder. 2008. "Terror and Ethnocentrism: Foundations of American Support for the War on Terrorism." *The Journal of Politics* 69 (2): 320–338. doi:10.1111/j.1468-2508.2007.00534.x.

Kassop, Nancy. 2013. "Rivals for Influence on Counterterrorism Policy: White House Political Staff Versus Executive Branch Legal Advisors." *Presidential Studies Quarterly* 43 (2): 252–273. doi:10.1111/psq.12023.

Katzenstein, Peter J. 2003. "Same War—Different Views: Germany, Japan, and Counterterrorism." *International Organization* 57 (4): 731–760. doi:10.1017/s00208183 03574033.

Kibris, Arzu. 2011. "Funerals and Elections: The Effects of Terrorism on Voting Behavior in Turkey." *Journal of Conflict Resolution* 55 (2): 220–247. doi:10.1177/0022002710383664.

Koch, Michael T, and Skyler Cranmer. 2007. "Testing the 'Dick Cheney' Hypothesis: Do Governments of the Left Attract More Terrorism Than Governments of the Right?." *Conflict Management and Peace Science* 24 (4): 311–326. doi:10.1080/07388940701643672.

Kowert, Paul A., and Margaret G. Hermann. 1997. "Who Takes Risks? Daring and Caution in Foreign Policy Making." *Journal of Conflict Resolution* 41 (5): 611–637. doi:10.1177/0022002797041005001.

Kruglanski, Arie W, Martha Crenshaw, Jerrold M. Post, and Jeff Victoroff. 2007. "What Should This Fight Be Called? Metaphors of Counterterrorism and Their Implications." *Psychological Science in the Public Interest* 8 (3): 97–133. doi:10.1111/j.1539-6053.2008.00035.x.

Lyall, Jason. 2010. "Do Democracies Make Inferior Counterinsurgents? Reassessing Democracy's Impact on War Outcomes and Duration." *International Organization* 64 (1): 167–192. doi:10.1017/s0020818309990208.

Macdonald, Julia, and Jacqueline Schneider. 2017. "Presidential Risk Orientation and Force Employment Decisions: The Case of Unmanned Weaponry." *Journal of Conflict Resolution* 61 (3): 511–536. doi:10.1177/0022002715590874.

Mearsheimer, John J., and Stephen M. Walt. 2007. *The Israel Lobby and US Foreign Policy.* New York: Farrar, Straus and Giroux.

Messmer, William B., and Carlos L. Yordan. 2011. "A Partnership to Counter International Terrorism: The UN Security Council and the UN Member States." *Studies in Conflict and Terrorism* 34 (11): 843–861. doi:10.1080/1057610x.2011.611932.

Morton, Victor. 2016. "Donald Trump: Germany, Turkey, Switzerland Attacks a Wake-Up Call on Terrorism." *The Washington Times* (December 19). Available online at: http://www.washingtontimes.com/news/2016/dec/19/donald-trump-germany-turkey-switzerland-attacks-wa/. Last accessed 5-August-2017.

Munroe, H. D. 2009. "The October Crisis Revisited: Counterterrorism as Strategic Choice, Political Result, and Organizational Practice.". *Terrorism and Political Violence* 21 (2): 288–305. doi:10.1080/09546550902765623.

Neumann, Peter R. 2007. "Negotiating with Terrorists." *Foreign Affairs* (January/February) 86: 128–138.

Neumayer, Eric, Thomas Plumper, and Mariaelisa Epifanio. 2014. "The 'Peer-Effect' in Counterterrorist Policies." *International Organization* 68 (1): 211–234. doi:10.1017/s0020818313000362

Nohrstedt, Daniel, and Dan Hansen. 2010. "Converging Under Pressure? Counterterrorism Policy Developments in the European Union Member States." *Public Administration* 88 (1): 190–210. doi:10.1111/j.1467-9299.2009.01795.x.

Omelicheva, Mariya Y. 2010. "Russia's Counterterrorism Policy: Variations on an Imperial Theme." *Perspectives on Terrorism* (November) Vol. 3 (1),

Orange, Richard. 2012. " 'Answer Hatred with Love': How Norway Tried to Cope with the Horror of Anders Breivik." *The Guardian* (April 14). Available online at: https://www.theguardian.com/world/2012/apr/15/anders-breivik-norway-copes-horror. Last accessed 5-August-2017.

O'Connor, Michael, and Celia M. Rumann. 2003. "Into the Fire: How to Avoid Getting Burned by the Same Mistakes Made Fighting Terrorism in Northern Ireland." *Cardozo Law Review* 24 (4): 1657–1751.

Perliger, Arie. 2012. "How Democracies Respond to Terrorism: Regime Characteristics, Symbolic Power and Counterterrorism." *Security Studies* 21 (3): 490–528. doi:10.1080/09636412.2012.706505.

Piazza, James A., and James Igoe Walsh. 2009. "Transnational Terror and Human Rights." *International Studies Quarterly* 53 (1): 125–148. doi:10.1111/j.1468-2478.2008.01526.x.

Porter, Andrew L. and Annegret Bendiek. 2012. "Counterterrorism Cooperation in the Transatlantic Security Community." *European Security* 21 (4): 497–517. doi:10.10 80/09662839.2012.688811.

Rosier, J.P., B. de Martino, G.C.Y. Tan, D. Kumaran, B. Seymour, N.W. Wood, and R.J. Dolan. 2009. "A Genetically Mediated Bias in Decision Making Driven by Failure of Amygdala Control." *The Journal of Neuroscience* 29 (18): 5985–5991. doi:10.1523/jneurosci.0407-09.2009.

Sandler, Todd M. 2003. "Collective Action and Transnational Terrorism." *The World Economy* 26 (6): 779–802. doi: 10.1111/1467-9701.00548

Sandler, Todd. 2010. "Terrorism Shocks: Domestic versus Transnational Responses." *Studies in Conflict and Terrorism* 33 (10): 893–910. doi:10.1080/1057610x.2010.508485.

Schultz, Richard H. 2004. "Showstoppers: Nine Reasons Why We Never Sent Our Special Operations Forces After Al Qaeda Before 9/11." *The Weekly Standard* 9 (January 26). Available online at: http://www.weeklystandard.com/showstoppers/article/4846. Last accessed 5-August-2017.

Schuurman, Bart. 2013. "Defeated by Popular Demand: Public Support and Counterterrorism in Three Western Democracies, 1963–1998." *Studies in Conflict & Terrorism* 36 (2): 152–175. doi:10.1080/1057610x.2013.747072.

Sheehan, Ivan Sascha. 2009. "Has the Global War on Terror Changed the Terrorist Threat? A Time-Series Intervention Analysis." *Studies in Conflict and Terrorism* 32 (8): 743–761. doi:10.1080/10576100903039270.

Stenner, Karen. 2005. *The Authoritarian Dynamic.* Cambridge: Cambridge University Press.

Thomas, Jakana. 2014. "Rewarding Bad Behavior: How Governments Respond to Terrorism in Civil War." *American Journal of Political Science* 58 (4): 804–818. doi:10.1111/ajps.12113

Walter, Barbara F. 2006. "Building Reputation: Why Governments Fight Some Separatists but Not Others." *American Journal of Political Science* 50 (2): 313–330. doi:10.1111/j.1540-5907.2006.00186.x.

Chapter 15 How Terror Groups End

Alonso, Rogelio. 2011. "Why Do Terrorists Stop? Analyzing Why ETA Members Abandon or Continue with Terrorism." *Studies in Conflict & Terrorism* 34 (9): 696–716. doi:10.1080/1057610x.2011.594944.

Asal, Victor, Mitchell Brown, and Angela Dalton. 2012. "Why split? Organizational Splits Among Ethnopolitical Organizations in the Middle East." *Journal of Conflict Resolution,* 56 (1): 94–117. doi:10.1177/0022002711429680.

Blomberg, S. Brock, Rozlyn C. Engel, and Reid Sawyer. 2010. "On the Duration and Sustainability of Transnational Terrorist Organizations." *Journal of Conflict Resolution* 54 (2): 303–330. doi:10.1177/0022002709355431.

Blomberg, S. Brock, Gaibulloev Khusrav and Todd Sandler. 2011. "Terrorist Group Survival: Ideology, Tactics, and Base of Operations." *Public Choice* 149 (3/4): 441–463. doi:10.1007/s11127-011-9837-4.

Bloom, Mia. 2005. *Dying to Kill: The Allure of Suicide Terror.* New York: Columbia University Press.

Brooks, Risa. 2009. "Researching Democracy and Terrorism: How Political Access Affects Militant Activity." *Security Studies* 18 (4): 756–788. doi:10.1080/09636410903369027.

Byman, Daniel. 2007. "US Counter-terrorism Options: A Taxonomy." *Survival* 49 (3): 121–150. doi:10.1080/00396330701564711.

Chenoweth, Erica. 2010. "Democratic Competition and Terrorist Activity." *Journal of Politics* 72 (1): 16–30. doi:10.1017/s0022381609990442.

Crenshaw, Martha. 1991. "How Terrorism Declines." *Terrorism and Political Violence* 3 (1): 69–87. doi:10.1080/09546559108427093.

Crenshaw, Martha. 1999. *How Terrorism Ends*. United States Institute of Peace (USIP).

Chermak, Steven, Joshua Freilich and Michael Suttmoeller. 2013. "The Organizational Dynamics of Far-Right Hate Groups in the United States: Comparing Violent to Non-Violent Organizations." *Studies in Conflict & Terrorism* 36 (3): 193–218. doi:10.1080/1057610x.2013.755912.

Christia, Fotini. 2012. *Alliance Formation in Civil Wars*. Cambridge: Cambridge University Press.

Cronin, Audrey Kurth. 2006. "How Al Qaida Ends: The Decline and Demise of Terrorist Groups." *International Security* 31 (1): 7–48. doi:10.1162/isec.2006.31.1.7.

Cronin, Audrey Kurth. 2009. *How Terrorism Ends: Understanding the Decline and Demise of Terrorist Campaigns*. Princeton, NJ: Princeton University Press.

Cunningham, Kathleen G., Kristin Bakke and Lee JM Seymour. 2012. "Shirts Today, Skins Tomorrow Dual Contests and the Effects of Fragmentation in Self-Determination Disputes." *Journal of Conflict Resolution* 56 (1): 67–93. doi:10.1177/0022002711429697.

Dalgaard-Nielsen, Anja. 2013. "Promoting Exit from Violent Extremism: Themes and Approaches." *Studies in Conflict and Terrorism* 36 (2): 99–115. doi:10.1080/1057610x.2013.747073.

Eubank, William Lee, and Leonard Weinberg. 1994. "Does Democracy Encourage Terrorism?" *Terrorism and Political Violence* 6 (4): 417–435. doi:10.1080/09546559408427271.

Hoffman, Bruce. 2006. *Inside Terrorism*, 2nd ed. New York: Columbia University Press, 2006.

Horowitz, Michael C. 2010. "Nonstate Actors and the Diffusion of Innovations: The Case of Suicide Terrorism"." *International Organization* 64 (1): 33–64. doi:10.1017/s0020818309990233.

Jones, Seth G., and Martin C. Libicki. 2008. *How Terrorist Groups End: Lessons for Countering al Qa'ida*. Santa Monica, CA: RAND Corporation. Available online at: http://www.rand.org/pubs/monographs/MG741-1.html. Last accessed 5-August-2017.

Neumann, Peter R. 2007. "Negotiating with Terrorists." *Foreign Affairs* (January/February) 86: 128–138.

Perkoski, Evan. 2016. "The Survival of Militant Splinter Groups." Harvard University.

Phillips, Brian J. 2015. "Enemies with benefits? Violent Rivalry and Terrorist Group Longevity." *Journal of Peace Research* 52 (1): 62–75. doi:10.1177/0022343314550538.

Rapoport, David. 1984. "Fear and Trembling: Terrorism in Three Religious Traditions." *American Political Science Review* 78 (3): 658–677. doi:10.2307/1961835.

Rapoport, David. 1992. "Terrorism," in Mary Hawkenworth Kogan ed., *Encyclopedia of Government and Politics*. Vol. 2. London: Routledge. pp. 1049–1081.

Reinares, Fernando. 2011. "Exit from Terrorism: A Qualitative Empirical Study on Disengagement and Deradicalization Among Members of ETA." *Terrorism and Political Violence* 23 (5): 780–803. doi:10.1080/09546553.2011.613307.

Rose, Adam Z., and S. Brock Blomberg. 2010. "Total Economic Consequences of Terrorist Attacks: Insights from 9/11." *Peace Economics, Peace Science and Public Policy* 16 (1). doi:10.2202/1554–8597.1189.

Ross, Jeffrey Ian, and Ted Robert Gurr. 1989. "Why Terrorism Subsides: A Comparative Study of Canada and the United States." *Comparative Politics* 21 (4): 405–426. doi:10.2307/422005.

Shapiro, Jacob N. 2013. *The Terrorist's Dilemma.* Princeton, NJ: Princeton University Press.

Suttmoeller, Michael, Steven Chermak, and Joshua D. Freilich. 2015. "The Influence of External and Internal Correlates on the Organizational Death of Domestic Far-Right Extremist Groups." *Studies in Conflict & Terrorism* 38 (9): 734–758. doi:10.1080/1057610x.2015.1038106.

Vittori, Jodi. 2009. "All Struggles Must End: The Longevity of Terrorist Groups." *Contemporary Security Policy* 30 (3): 444–466. doi:10.1080/13523260903326602.

Young, Joseph K., and Laura Dugan. 2014. "Survival of the Fittest: Why Terrorist Groups Endure." *Perspectives on Terrorism* 8 (2): 1–23.

INDEX

Boxes, figures, and tables are indicated by "b," "f," and "t" following the page numbers. Arabic surnames starting with "al-" or "el-" are alphabetized by the subsequent part of the name.